PASCAL

PASCAL

JAMES L. RICHARDS

Bemidji State University

ACADEMIC PRESS, INC.
(Harcourt Brace Jovanovich, Publishers)
Orlando   San Diego   San Francisco   New York   London
Toronto   Montreal   Sydney   Tokyo   São Paulo

Academic Press, Inc.
Orlando, Florida 32887

United Kingdom Edition published by
Academic Press, Inc. (London) Ltd.
24/28 Oval Road, London NW1 7DX

ISBN: 0-12-587520-7
Library of Congress Catalog Card Number: 81-66761

Printed in the United States of America

CONTENTS

CHAPTER ELEVEN
Dynamic Variables and Data Structures 401

PREFACE

This book provides an introduction to computer programming and to the programming language called Pascal. No prior experience either programming or using computers is required. Some knowledge of basic algebra is necessary to understand several of the examples presented in the book and is helpful in learning the rules which govern the formation and use of mathematical expressions in the Pascal language. Readers who have completed a course in college algebra or have taken 1½–2 years of high school algebra should have little difficulty with the mathematical examples and concepts that are used.

Books on computer programming tend to emphasize the development of programs to solve real-world problems or the valid structures of instructions in a specific programming language. In an introductory programming course, a problem-solving approach is usually more attractive to students than one which centers on the constructs of a particular programming language, and yet the end product of a student's programming efforts must be a correct program written in some programming language. Thus, a parallel approach that incorporates programming methodology and the grammar of a programming language is most appropriate. In this book, I have tried to give a balanced presentation of programming methodology and the Pascal language.

In order to design and implement efficient and effective computer programs, a logical development strategy and an equally logical programming language are necessary. Pascal is the language presented in this book because it facilitates teaching good programming practices and because it is also being used widely for applications in business, industry, and education. Furthermore, versions of Pascal are available for nearly every popular large-scale computer and microcomputer.

Chapter One gives some background material on computer systems, programming methods, and programming languages. Students who have previous programming experience should be able to proceed through this chapter very rapidly. Some discussion of the differences between batch and time-sharing computer systems and their control languages is presented, but the instructor will have to supply students with the specific control language instructions they will need to use.

Chapters Two and Three cover basic elements of the Pascal language such as representations for numbers and other types of data, mathematical and nonmathematical operations on data, and the fundamental composition of a Pascal program. Many short and simple programs appear as examples in these two chapters, mostly to show how various types of data can be represented and used in a program. All four of the Pascal standard scalar data types (CHAR, INTEGER, REAL, and BOOLEAN) and simple expressions involving operations on such data are presented in Chapter Two. Expressions that involve several operations are discussed in Chapter Three.

Chapter Four is devoted entirely to Pascal instructions that are used for data input and output. The principles that govern the way that Pascal handles data input from an external source and displays the results of processing under program control are explained and illustrated using many examples and diagrams. While these principles are fundamentally the same for all versions of Pascal, some of the specifics concerning input and output (particularly, input) given in this chapter and illustrated in the examples are not exactly the same for all versions of Pascal. Your instructor or local computer center can provide the specific information you need to know about input and output for the version of Pascal available on your computer system.

Chapters Five and Six cover all of the Pascal instructions that control the sequencing of data processing. In Chapter Five, only those instructions that govern the selection of alternative processing activities are discussed (IF and CASE statements). Instructions that are used to control repetitive processing activities are presented in Chapter Six (WHILE, REPEAT, and FOR statements). The GOTO statement, which can be used to control either selection or repetition, is introduced at the end of Chapter Six (Section 6.4). Since Pascal provides a wealth of control structures that are far more attractive in style than any that use GOTO statements, Section 6.4 is included more for completeness than anything else and may be skipped without loss of continuity.

Chapter Seven provides an introduction to data and data structures that can be defined in a program. Only one type of structured data (the array) is discussed in Chapter Seven, but it is the structured data type that most readers having previous programming experience will recognize. After a slight detour to discuss subprograms (functions and procedures) and their role in the modular design of a program, additional structured data types are introduced in Chapter Nine (sets and records), Chapter Ten (files), and Chapter Eleven (dynamic data structures).

The material in Chapters One through Nine can easily be covered in a one-quarter, 4-credit course or a one-semester, 3-credit course. In fact, I have been able to include selected sections of Chapters Ten and Eleven in one quarter. A thorough discussion of files and dynamic data structures is usually reserved for an advanced programming course that concentrates on data structures. However, the rather elementary presentation of files, pointers, and dynamic variables in Chapters Ten and Eleven should be included in the course, if time permits, since it can ease the transition to a follow-up course on data structures.

To date, there is no universally accepted standard for Pascal. However, work toward an international standardization of Pascal has been in progress for several years. The International Standards Organization (ISO) is considering a proposed standard that was originally developed as Working Draft/3 by the British Standards Working Group DPS/13/14. To the best of my knowledge, the features of Pascal presented in this book are consistent with the proposed standard.

There are many people to whom I will always be indebted for their help, advice, and encouragement during the preparation of this book. First and foremost, I would like to thank my family for their understanding and encouragement. I am also very grateful to my colleague Professor Tom Richard at Bemidji State University, who reviewed several versions of my manuscript and helped me class-test materials, and to Brent Cochran, Ron Elshaug, Jane Franz, Jim Herring, and Carol Mack, who devoted many hours to checking the examples, programs, and exercises that appear in this book. Finally, I would like to express my sincere appreciation to all the referees who reviewed the manuscript and made many helpful suggestions.

JAMES L. RICHARDS
Bemidji, Minnesota
August 1981

PASCAL

ONE/AN INTRODUCTION TO COMPUTER SYSTEMS AND PROGRAMMING

Modern computers are powerful machines that are used to collect, analyze, and process enormous amounts of information rapidly and with a high degree of accuracy. The physical form of this information is referred to as **data.** A computer processes data by executing a sequence of precise instructions called a **program.** Computer programs are designed and constructed by people known as **programmers** to perform data processing tasks that will solve real world problems. Programming a computer is not really difficult, but it is meticulous work because every computer understands only a limited set of very exact instructions.

This book is about computer programming. All programmers need to know some fundamental terminology and facts about computers and programming. These basics are presented in this chapter. Much of the information in the following sections is not very detailed, since it is meant to provide only an overview of computers and programming. As you read and study the material in this chapter, try to develop some understanding of how computers, programs, and people interact to accomplish data processing tasks. Pay particular attention to the terminology that is introduced, because much of it will be used frequently in the remainder of the text. This chapter will not answer all the questions you may have about how computers operate and how they are programmed, but it will give you some basic knowledge that will help you develop programming skills.

1.1 FUNCTIONAL UNITS OF A COMPUTER

The physical machinery of which a computer is constructed is referred to as **hardware.** Each hardware device consists of electronic circuits and wires assembled to give that device certain data processing capabilities. The general organization of the hardware components for a typical computer is depicted in Figure 1–1. Basically, a computer has four functional units: a **central processing unit (CPU),** an **input unit,** an **output unit,** and a **memory.** The arrows in Figure 1–1 represent the flow of data between the various units.

THE CENTRAL PROCESSING UNIT

The central processing unit consists of circuitry that monitors and controls all the other hardware devices that are part of the computer. Actually, the CPU is composed of two units: the **control unit** and the **arithmetic and logic unit.** The control

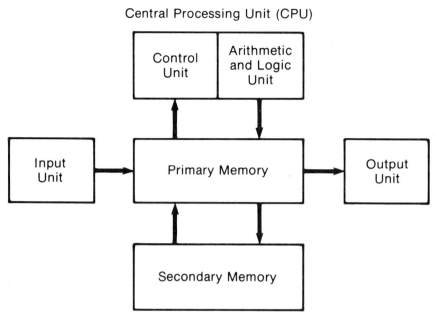

Figure 1–1
The functional units of a typical computer.

unit can access instructions from programs stored in memory, interpret those instructions, and then activate appropriate units of the computer to execute them. Other activities of the control unit include generating control and timing signals for the input and output units, entering and accessing data stored in memory, and routing data between memory and the arithmetic and logic unit.

The arithmetic and logic unit is a servant of the control unit. It can perform such simple arithmetic operations as addition and subtraction and it can perform certain logical operations such as comparing two numbers. The control unit provides the arithmetic and logic unit with appropriate data and then activates that unit to perform the desired operation.

MEMORY

As depicted in Figure 1–1, a computer has two types of memory: **primary memory** and **secondary memory.** Primary memory is sometimes called **internal memory** because it usually occupies the same physical enclosure as the central processing unit. A computer's primary memory consists of individually accessible storage cells, which we shall call **memory locations.** Each memory location can store exactly one data value, such as a number. A small computer may have only a few thousand of these memory locations, whereas large computers often have more than a million storage cells in their primary memory. Every memory location has a unique identification number, which serves as its **memory address.** We can think of an individual memory location as a box with a numbered lid whose contents are always visible through one end, as depicted in Figure 1–2. The central processing unit can access any memory location by using its memory address. Once the CPU has found a particular memory location, it can simply observe the con-

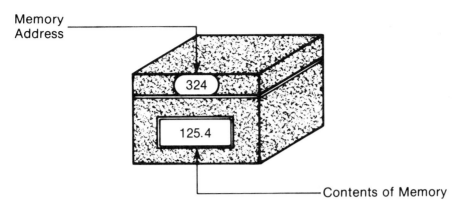

Memory Address

324

125.4

Contents of Memory

Figure 1–2
*A memory location simulated as a box with a window at one
end through which its contents are visible.*

tents of that storage cell or it can store some value there. In the latter case, the
new value replaces any value that is already in the memory location. The "old
value" is destroyed because a memory location has the capacity to store only one
value at a time.

The CPU accesses storage locations in primary memory very rapidly compared
to those in secondary memory. Primary memory is normally used to store only
information currently being processed by the CPU because the number of memory
locations in primary memory is always limited. Secondary memory (also known
as **mass storage**) provides more permanent data storage. Magnetic tapes and disks
are common forms of secondary memory. Magnetic tape is a plastic ribbon coated
with magnetic material on which information can be recorded in much the same
way that a voice or music is recorded on sound tapes. A magnetic disk is a thin
circular disk made of metal or plastic; it, too, is coated with magnetic material
that serves as a recording medium. The amount of secondary memory is essentially unlimited, since tapes and disks can be removed from recording devices
when they are filled with information and can be replaced by new tapes or disks.

INPUT AND OUTPUT UNITS

Input and output units link a computer with the outside world. Data and programs enter a computer's primary memory via some input device, and processed
information is displayed on some output device. There are many types of input
devices, and each one can "read" information represented in some physical form.
Programs and data prepared on punched cards or paper tape, mark-sense cards,
magnetic tape, or magnetic disks may be fed into an appropriate input device.
Some input devices have typewriter-like keyboards that can be used to enter information. An output device is used to copy information from the computer's
memory onto some recording medium. There are output devices that will print on
paper, punch cards, or paper tape; record on magnetic tape or disks; or display
information on a television screen. Although every computer normally uses at
least one input device and one output device, it is not uncommon for the input
and output units to have available several devices for input and output.

1.1
EXERCISES

1. What is a computer program?

2. To what does the term "hardware" refer with respect to computers?

3. Name the four functional units of a computer and briefly describe the function of each unit.

4. Why does a computer need both a primary memory and a secondary memory?

5. What does the phrase "memory address" mean?

1.2
COMPUTER PROGRAMS AND PROGRAMMING

The actual writing of a computer program is called **coding.** A program is simply a sequence of instructions for a computer that has been coded in a specific **programming language.** There are many programming languages and each one is a formal system of symbols, including rules for forming expressions, that can be used by a human being to communicate with a computer. Meaningful expressions are formed according to rigid **syntax rules** (or **grammar**) utilizing a well-defined vocabulary. Every program instruction must conform precisely to the syntax rules for the language in which the program is written. The rules are very rigid because a computer cannot "think" like a human being; it merely follows precise directions given in a program, and so those directions must be unambiguous. As with any language, the grammar for a programming language tells how to form "sentences" that are properly structured. There are rules of **semantics,** which tell when a syntactically correct instruction is also meaningful. Consider the following two English sentences.

Put the meat into the refrigerator.
Put the refrigerator into the meat.

Both sentences are syntactically correct according to the grammar of the English language, but the second sentence is semantically incorrect.

MACHINE-LEVEL LANGUAGES

The central processing unit can only execute instructions that are coded in **machine language.** In machine language, instructions and data are stored in the computer's memory as numbers composed solely of 1's and 0's. This is known as **binary coding** and the digits 0 and 1 are referred to as **bits** (short for **b**inary dig**its**). The number of bits that can be stored in a memory location is fixed for each computer. Suppose that our computer has memory locations that store 16-bit numbers. If we could look at the memory location whose addess is 327, we might see

327 | 0001010000001100 |

The contents of memory location 327 could represent a machine language instruction. If so, the control unit of the CPU can decode the instruction by examining groups of consecutive bits. For instance, the first six bits could be an operation code and the remaining ten bits could specify the source of data needed for the designated operation, as illustrated below.

$$\boxed{000101} \quad \boxed{0000001100}$$

Operation   Data Source
Code

A machine language program consists of a sequence of binary coded instructions that the control unit is able to decode and execute.

In order to execute a program, the CPU uses special storage locations called **registers.** These registers are not part of primary memory. The computer executes the instructions in a program one at a time by repeating the same sequence of activities over and over again. That sequence of activities is called the **instruction execution cycle.** Two registers play central roles in the execution of an instruction: the program counter (register PC) and the instruction register (register IR). Here is a typical instruction execution cycle.

1. Fetch the instruction whose memory address is in register PC and copy it into register IR.
2. Increment the contents of register PC by 1 so that the memory address of the next instruction will be available at the start of the next cycle.
3. Decode the contents of register IR and fetch the data needed to perform the specified operation.
4. Execute the instruction.

When execution of the program is initiated, the program counter must contain the address of the first instruction. After that, each instruction execution cycle establishes the memory address for the instruction to be executed during the next cycle.

The CPU also has registers that it can use as "scratch pads" for numerical calculations. A register of this type is called an accumulator, and so we will refer to it as register AC. Some typical machine operations and the corresponding codes are given in the table below. The operations and codes listed in this table are for a hypothetical computer.

Operation Code		
Binary	Decimal	Operation
000000	0	Halt the execution of the program.
000101	5	Store the value of the data source in register AC.
010000	16	Load a copy of the value in register AC into the memory location whose address is the data source.
101011	43	Add the value of the data source to the contents register AC.

The table shows the operation codes in both binary and decimal form, the latter being the usual way to represent a whole number. Consider the following machine language program, which is stored in memory locations 327 through 330. The operation codes and data sources are also shown in decimal form so that we can follow the execution of the program.

Memory Address	Memory Contents	Operation Code	Data Source
327	0001010000001100	5	12
328	1010110000110011	43	51
329	0100000101000110	16	326
330	0000000000000000	0	0

When this program is executed, the numbers 12 and 51 will be added and the sum will be stored in memory location 326. Initially, the program counter will contain the memory address of the first instruction (327). A summary of the effects of each instruction is shown below. This summary traces the changes made to the contents of registers IR, PC, and AC. The contents of registers PC and AC would be in binary form inside the computer, but they are shown in decimal form here so that we can follow the progress of the program more easily.

	Instruction Register IR	Register PC	Register AC
		327	
Store the value 12 in the accumulator (register AC).	0001010000001100	328	12
Add the value 51 to the contents of register AC.	1010110000110011	329	63
Load memory location 326 with a copy of the contents of AC.	0100000101000110	330	63
Halt the program.	0000000000000000	331	63

At the end of the program, both register AC and memory location 326 (not shown in this table) will contain the value 63 (decimal).

Coding machine language instructions is difficult because it is necessary to remember specific combinations of 1's and 0's or to be constantly looking them up in some reference manual. Even one bit that is misplaced can totally change the meaning of an instruction. It is very easy to make errors when coding a machine language program and very difficult to locate the errors so that they can be corrected. In short, machine language programming is so complicated and time consuming that it is rarely used.

As an alternative to machine language coding, programs can be written by using abbreviations instead of binary codes to represent machine-level instructions. A language of this type is known as an **assembly language.** An assembly language program is written at the same level of detail as a machine language program, but the instructions are written in a form that makes them easier for humans to read. Consider the following sequence of hypothetical assembly language instructions.

```
SUM        CON  0
PROG       LDAC 12
           ADD  51
           STAC SUM
           HALT PROG
           END
```

As we know, a computer can only execute a program that is written in machine language. An assembly language program must be translated into machine language before it can be executed. This task is performed by another program, called an **assembler,** that resides in the computer's memory. The assembler treats an assembly language program as data and produces an equivalent version of that program in machine language. When we say that an assembly language program is executed, we mean that the assembled machine language version of that program is executed.

In the assembly language program shown above, the symbolic names LDAC, ADD, STAC, and HALT represent machine-level operations. The assembler bears the burden of constructing machine language instructions in which the corresponding binary operation codes appear. Relative to the operation codes we discussed earlier, these symbolic operation codes may have the meanings shown in the following table.

Operation Code

Symbolic	Binary	Operation
HALT	000000	Halt the execution of the program.
STAC	000101	Store the value of the data source in register AC.
LDAC	010000	Load a copy of the value in register AC into the memory location whose address is the data source.
ADD	101011	Add the value of the data source to the contents of register AC.

The data sources appear after the symbolic operation codes in the assembly language program. SUM and PROG are symbolic names for memory addresses. SUM represents a memory location whose initial value is the CONstant 0. PROG is the symbolic name for the address of the first instruction in the program. When the program is assembled, the memory address corresponding to PROG is recorded so that the address of the first machine language instruction can be placed in the program counter when execution of the program is initiated. The word END marks the physical end of the assembly language program so that the assembler knows when to stop creating machine language instructions. If PROG has been associated with the memory address 327, the assembler language program and its corresponding machine language version will be as shown below.

Assembly Language Program			Machine Language Version	
			Memory Address	Memory Contents
SUM	CON	0	326	0000000000000000
PROG	LDAC	12	327	0001010000001100
	ADD	51	328	1010110000110011
	STAC	SUM	329	0100000101000110
	HALT	PROG	330	0000000000000000
	END			

The machine language program assembled here is identical to the one discussed earlier. Thus the purpose of the assembly language program is to add the numbers 12 and 51 and store the result in the memory location immediately preceding the one that contains the first program instruction (memory location 326, whose symbolic name is SUM).

Although an assembly language program looks different from a machine language program, programming in assembly language is still dominated by machine-oriented concepts. One of the major drawbacks to programming in machine language or assembly language is that there is no one machine language for all computers. In fact, machine languages (and hence assembly languages) vary considerably from computer to computer.

HIGH-LEVEL LANGUAGES

A computer's machine language is, unfortunately, far removed from languages that people use to communicate with other people. For this reason, modern computers are equipped with "built-in" programs called **systems programs** that enable them to communicate with people in a more human-like fashion. An assembler is a systems program that allows a programmer to create a machine-level program using symbols that are more descriptive of machine operations than binary code. The assembler's job is to translate a grammatically correct assembly language program into machine language. A systems program that takes a program written in one language and produces a version of that program in a different language is known as a **language processor.** There are three types of language processors: **assemblers, compilers,** and **interpreters.** Programs written in an assembly language specify operations at the machine level and so they must be coded with the hardware capabilities of the computer in mind. Other symbolic languages have been developed to take care of specific hardware requirements automatically so that the programmer can concentrate more on procedures and problem solving and less on the work of the computer. These so-called **high-level languages** allow program instructions to appear in an English-like form or with mathematical formulas. Compilers and interpreters are language processors used to produce translations of programs written in high-level languages.

While machine and assembly languages are tied to particular computers, high-level languages are not. Compilers and interpreters for a high-level language can be implemented as systems programs on a wide range of computers. This versatility makes possible the coding of "portable" programs; that is, a program coded in a high-level language can be translated and executed by many different computers. There are hundreds of high-level languages in existence, but only a few of

Language	General Description
ALGOL	(ALGOrithmic Language) a numerically oriented language that is widely used in Europe
APL	(A Programming Language) features many commonly used mathematical operations that facilitate scientific computing
BASIC	(Beginner's All-Purpose Symbolic Instruction Code) an easy-to-learn general-purpose language that is commonly used to teach programming at an introductory level
COBOL	(COmmon Business-Oriented Language) the most widely used language for business data processing
FORTRAN	(FORmula TRANslation) a numerically oriented language that is very widely used for scientific programming
Pascal	(named in honor of Blaise Pascal, a noted seventeenth-century French mathematician) a general-purpose language of recent vintage that is particularly suitable for teaching programming concepts
PL/1	(Programming Language 1) a very complex and powerful general-purpose language that combines some of the better features of ALGOL, COBOL, and FORTRAN

Figure 1–3
Some common high-level programming languages.

them are used extensively. Some of these languages are described in Figure 1–3. One instruction coded in a high-level language may translate into a sequence of machine language instructions. For instance, the Pascal instruction

$$\text{SUM} := 12 + 51$$

means "Add the numbers 12 and 51 and then store the result in a memory location whose symbolic name is SUM." If we use the assembly language instructions presented in the preceding section, the corresponding arithmetic and storage of the result is accomplished by the program segment

```
LDAC 12
ADD  51
STAC SUM
```

Each assembly instruction in this program segment corresponds to a machine language instruction. The single Pascal instruction does not specify how the hardware of a computer should be used to generate and store the sum of 12 and 51. It can be translated into machine language instructions that are appropriate for whatever computer is being used. Thus a Pascal programmer can specify what tasks are to be performed without being concerned with the intricate details of how the computer will perform those tasks.

A compiler is a program that can translate a **source program** coded in some high-level language into an **object program** coded in some other language. The object program generated by a compiler might be a machine language program or it might be a program coded in assembly language or some other intermediate language that requires further translation. An interpreter is much more than a translator. It is a program that can decode instructions and cause their immediate execution. The combination of an interpreter and a computer makes it seem that the computer is able to understand the language of the source program and can therefore execute that program directly. Some programs are compiled first and then the object program produced by the compilation is used as the source program for an interpreter.

When a program is to be coded in Pascal or any other high-level language, the coder need only be concerned with constructing appropriate instructions that meet the grammar requirements imposed by the language processor that generates the first translation. Throughout the remainder of this book, we will assume that the initial translation of a Pascal program is generated by a compiler. A computer equipped with a Pascal compiler represents an **implementation of Pascal.** Each implementation of Pascal can impose restrictions or allow variations that affect the way in which an instruction can be coded or used in a program. All **implementation-dependent** features of Pascal that are described in this book will be appropriately noted.

THE PASCAL LANGUAGE

Pascal was developed by Niklaus Wirth at the Eidgenössische Technische Hochschule (ETH) in Zurich, Switzerland during the late 1960s. The first Pascal compiler became operational in 1970, and the initial report on the language was published a year later. A revised report and reference manual appeared in 1974.† The reference manual, which describes Wirth's Standard Pascal, has continued to serve as the basic guide for Pascal implementors and users.

The development of a programming language is usually motivated by specific needs, along with the conviction that existing languages do not satisfactorily meet those needs. Pascal grew out of Niklaus Wirth's disenchantment with the major languages used to teach programming concepts. He felt that these languages lacked the order and discipline needed to support the logical construction of a computer program. In his 1974 report, Wirth listed the following two aims as the primary motivation for the development of Pascal:

1. To make available a language suitable for teaching programming as a systematic discipline based on certain fundamental concepts clearly and naturally reflected by the language.
2. To develop implementations of this language that are both reliable and efficient on presently available computers.

The Pascal language bears some similarity to FORTRAN and BASIC and it more closely resembles PL/1, but the basis for the development of Pascal was ALGOL (more specifically, a version of ALGOL known as ALGOL 60). In recent years it has gained wide acceptance both as a vehicle for teaching good programming concepts and as a general-purpose programming language.

†K. Jensen and N. Wirth, "Pascal User Manual and Report," Springer-Verlag, Heidelberg, 1974.

Most of the Pascal language described in this book follows Wirth's description of Standard Pascal included with the 1974 report. Exceptions and extensions are noted in the text. At this writing, work toward a national and international standardization of Pascal is in progress. Such a standardization would define a common base for modern implementations of Pascal, as has been done for other popular programming languages (notably FORTRAN). This is at best a difficult task because existing versions of Pascal vary widely in the language features they support. Early versions of Pascal, such as Pascal 6000, which is implemented on Control Data Corporation's Cyber and 6000 Series computers, were developed for use on large-scale computers and updated versions are still in use today. The recent trend toward the use of microcomputers, particularly in education and business, has encouraged the development for small computers of Pascal compilers that support language extensions that take advantage of various special hardware capabilities of those machines. One of the more popular microcomputer versions of Pascal was developed at the University of California at San Diego; it is called UCSD Pascal. The UCSD Pascal compiler produces an object program in a universal pseudocode, known as P-code, that can be executed by any computer that has a P-code interpreter. Thus, it can be implemented on a wide variety of different small computers.

1.2 EXERCISES

1. What is a programming language?

2. What is an instruction execution cycle?

3. Differentiate between machine language and assembly language?

4. What is an assembler?

5. What is a language processor? Name the three types of language processors.

6. What is a high-level language?

7. What makes a program portable?

8. How does a source program differ from an object program?

9. Differentiate between the purpose of a compiler and the purpose of an interpreter.

10. What do we mean by an implementation of Pascal?

11. What motivated the development of the Pascal language?

1.3 PROBLEM-SOLVING METHODOLOGY IN PROGRAMMING

A program coded in Pascal or any programming language is a list of formal instructions that the computer should execute in order to solve a problem, but programming involves much more than simply coding instructions in a particular language. In the broadest sense, the term "programming" refers to all the steps taken to develop a sound and appropriate sequence of instructions for a computer. The program development process consists of four basic steps:

1. **Define the problem.** Develop a full understanding of all the tasks that must be performed to solve the problem and be aware of the data needed to perform those tasks.
2. **Design a program.** Construct a clear and precise outline that gives a step-by-step procedure that can be followed to perform the required tasks.
3. **Detail (code) the program.** Use a programming language to write a program according to the design developed at Step 2.
4. **Debug and test the program.** To "debug a program" means to rid a program of errors. The testing and debugging are necessary to make sure that the program produces the intended results every time it is executed.

Since the first two steps of the program development process determine what the problem is and how it can be solved, they constitute the **problem-solving phase** of programming. Coding, debugging, and testing a program occur during the **implementation phase** of programming.

Although both the problem-solving and implementation phases of programming are important, the former has added significance, since how well a program is designed directly influences the ease with which it can be implemented. Beginning with Chapter Two, we will study elements of the Pascal language and how they are used to write a program. In this section, we will concentrate on the process of describing a model for a program, which is known as an **algorithm.** In general terms, an algorithm is a list of step-by-step instructions that clearly, accurately, and completely describes a procedure for performing some task or tasks. The purpose of the problem-solving phase of programming is to construct an algorithm that can readily be implemented by using some programming language (in our case, Pascal).

ALGORITHMIC DESIGN

The first step toward formulating an algorithm for solving a problem is to understand the nature of the problem. Although the initial statement of a problem may be expressed in very broad terms, it should be complete in the sense that the major facets of the problem are recognized. Consider the case of a person whose problem is to get to work on time in the morning. It is necessary for that person to awaken at a reasonable hour, get ready for work, and then drive to work. The starting point for the formulation of an algorithm to describe a process whereby the person will get to work on time is expressible in the following outline form:

1. Get up in the morning.
2. Get ready for work.
3. Drive to work.

This outline provides a step-by-step summary of the major activities involved in getting to work on time. As such, it provides an "overview" of the fundamental components of the problem and the sequence of activities that will lead to a solution.

Our objective in formulating an algorithm will be to start with a general description of the algorithm and then make **stepwise refinements** to the outline until sufficient details have been added to establish a clear, precise, and complete procedure for solving the problem. This is known as a **top-down approach** to problem solving. The foremost benefit to be derived from the top-down development of an algorithm is that after every refinement step, a more detailed description of the entire algorithm is available. This allows us gradually to insert details that add clarity and precision to the algorithm from the perspective of the total solution. Furthermore, we will be able to check the refinements made at each step to make sure that they contribute to the overall solution and thereby be convinced that we are closer to the final algorithm.

We return now to the problem of getting to work on time. Each of the steps listed in our initial outline needs some refinement. We will not try to add every conceivable detail to the outline at once; rather, we will try to expand the outline so that at each step the activity is more fully developed. Consider the following expansion of the initial outline.

1. Get up in the morning.
    1.1 Get out of bed at 6:30 A.M.
    1.2 Make the bed.
    1.3 Start a pot of coffee brewing.
2. Get ready for work.
    2.1 Eat breakfast.
    2.2 Get cleaned up.
    2.3 Dress for work.
3. Drive to work.
    3.1 Pick up Sam at his house.
    3.2 Take interstate highway 212 west to work.

This second outline provides a much more thorough description of the morning's activities than the first. Note that this new outline builds upon the activity structure established in the initial outline; it does not reflect any reconstruction in the initial design.

At this point, it is worthwhile for us to consider how much detail must be added to an outline before a final version is constructed. Indeed, the assumption is that this process of stepwise refinement will eventually result in some precise and complete description of an algorithm. How do we know when we have reached our goal? To answer this question, we must know how the algorithm will be implemented and who will be responsible for the implementation. If we are developing an algorithm to serve as the model for a computer program, then the final form of the algorithm should constitute a list of instructions that can easily be coded in some computer language by some person or persons. In the case of our algorithm for getting to work on time, the final outline should be in a form that a person can follow with ease in order to get to work on time, having carried out all the early morning responsibilities. The overriding concern in developing an algorithm is for the people who will implement the algorithm and their ability to derive proper meanings from it so that the problem that motivated the entire problem-solving process is accurately and completely solved. Thus, the acceptance of some description of an algorithm as final must be made very judiciously.

Some people may find that the refinements made to the initial outline in our example are not sufficient for the second outline to be regarded as final. The person for whom the outline is intended may need further clarification of the activities implied by "get cleaned up" or "pick Sam up at his house." That person might ask, "Should I take a shower?" or "Where is Sam's house?" Here is a third outline, which refines the second outline a bit further.

1. Get up in the morning.
   1.1 Get out of bed at 6:30 A.M.
   1.2 Make the bed.
   1.3 Start a pot of coffee brewing.
2. Get ready for work.
   2.1 Eat breakfast.
   2.2 Get cleaned up.
      2.2.1 Take a shower.
      2.2.2 Shave.
      2.2.3 Brush your teeth.
   2.3 Dress for work.
      2.3.1 Shine your shoes.
      2.3.2 Put on business attire.
      2.3.3 Comb your hair.
3. Drive to work.
   3.1 Pick up Sam at his house.
      3.1.1 Take 25th Street east to Central Avenue.
      3.1.2 Turn south and proceed to 4724 Central Avenue.
   3.2 Take interstate highway 212 west to work.
      3.2.1 Continue south on Central to I-212.
      3.2.2 Head westbound on I-212.
      3.2.3 Drive 16 miles to the Weston exit.
      3.2.4 Exit northbound 3 miles to the office.

This new outline is considerably more detailed than the second one, but it still may not be as thorough as necessary. For instance, a person reading the outline might wonder what "business attire" implies. The use of that phrase without further qualification would be appropriate only if it is clearly understood that business attire consists of a white shirt, blue suit, and dark tie and stockings or some other accepted standard of dress. We will not proceed with any further refinements of our outline merely for the sake of showing how an outline can be expanded, since we have already done this twice. Remember that the responsibility of the designer is to make suitable refinements until implementation of the algorithm becomes the natural next step.

DESCRIBING ALGORITHMS FOR PROGRAMS

Since the reason for designing an algorithm during the problem-solving phase of programming is to have that algorithm serve as a model for the logical structure of a program to be coded during the implementation phase, it is extremely important that the initial statement of the algorithm and all the refinements reflect careful planning and organization. These considerations and others have fostered a movement toward **structured programming.** Writers of textbooks and articles on programming do not all define structured programming the same way, but there is general consensus that the end product of structured programming (a **structured program**) is constructed in a logical and stylish manner that makes it easy to read, debug, and modify. The following three rules are offered as guides toward the development of a structured program:

1. **Envision a logical structure for the program.** That structure should reflect a natural procedure for solving the problem facing the programmer.
2. **Use a systematic process of stepwise refinement to design a suitable algorithm.** The algorithm should be developed by using a top-down approach in which the refinement steps gradually and systematically introduce pertinent details.
3. **When developing an algorithm, use notation that facilitates stepwise refinement.**

Suppose we want to design a program that will accomplish the following tasks:

Calculate the interest earned after one year on an investment of $425.00 that earns 5.75% annual interest. The interest and all data used to compute the interest should be printed by the program.

The initial outline of the algorithm to be used to solve our problem should recognize the major components of the algorithm, although the descriptions of those components can be rather general. For instance,

1. Establish the data to be used for the interest computations.
2. Calculate the interest.
3. Print the results.

Here we are using a narrative form to describe the algorithm, as we did in the preceding subsection. A stepwise refinement of this outline produces the following description of the algorithm:

1. Establish the data to be used for the interest computations.
   1.1 Set the principal amount invested at $425.00.
   1.2 Set the rate of interest at 0.0575.
2. Calculate the interest.
   2.1 The interest earned is the rate of interest multiplied by the principal amount invested.
3. Print the results.
   3.1 Print the principal amount invested and the rate of interest.
   3.2 Print the amount of earned interest.

In a narrative description of an algorithm, there is no need to number the activities if it is understood that they must occur sequentially. Thus, the initial description of an algorithm to solve our problem may appear in the form

Start
Establish the data to be used for the interest
     computations

Calculate the interest
Print the results
Stop

The activities specified in this initial outline may simply be replaced by more specific activities in the next refinement step:

Start
Set the principal amount invested at 425.00
Set the interest rate at 0.0575
Calculate the interest as the rate of interest multiplied by the principal amount invested
Print the principal amount invested and the rate of interest
Print the the amount of interest earned
Stop

So far the algorithm has been described in forms that are totally independent of the language that will be used to code the program. Symbolic names will be used in the actual program to identify memory locations used to store data that the program processes and generates. To ease the transition from an outline for a program to the eventual program, it is convenient to capitalize such names. There are other symbolic names that have significant meanings in a Pascal program, and they too can be introduced into the outline. For instance,

BEGIN
Set the PRINCIPAL amount invested at 425.00
Set the interest RATE at 0.0575
Calculate the INTEREST as RATE * PRINCIPAL
WRITE the PRINCIPAL and the interest RATE
WRITE the amount of INTEREST earned
END

In Pascal, an asterisk (*) is used to symbolize multiplication, and the words BEGIN, WRITE, and END are symbolic names that have a standard purpose known to the compiler. When the description of an algorithm utilizes both the English language and symbols from a specific programming language, the result is known as **pseudocode.** Pseudocoding merely makes an outline for a program resemble the program that will eventually be coded. Here is a Pascal program that has been coded based on the pseudocode description provided above.

```
PROGRAM SIMPLEINTEREST (OUTPUT);
VAR
     PRINCIPAL, RATE, INTEREST : REAL;
BEGIN
PRINCIPAL := 425.00;
RATE := 0.0575;
INTEREST := RATE * PRINCIPAL;
WRITELN(PRINCIPAL, RATE);
WRITELN(INTEREST)
END.
```

Note the similarities between the actual program instructions (shown after the program BEGINs) and the pseudocoded instructions in the outline.

In order to introduce pseudocode into the design of an algorithm in the right way, the designer must be familiar with the programming language that will be used to implement the algorithm. The program presented above contains several features of the Pascal language that have not yet been explained. This first glimpse at a Pascal program was provided merely to demonstrate how the description of an algorithm may begin to look like an actual program during the later stages of the problem-solving phase.

A **flowchart** is another form in which the algorithm for a program can be described. In a flowchart, the description of each activity is enclosed by a geometric figure to form a **node,** and the nodes are connected by directed lines, called **flow lines,** that indicate the sequencing of the activities. Consider the following flowchart, which provides a simple description of an algorithm for calculating annual interest.

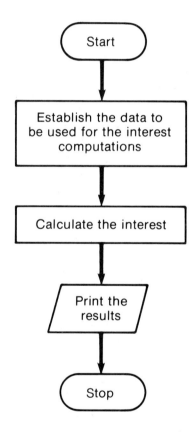

The geometric shapes used at each node of a flowchart are significant. In this book, ovals are used to denote the beginning and end of processing activities, parallelograms denote input or output activities, and rectangles are used for most other processing activities. A few additional flowchart shapes will be introduced in later chapters. (See Appendix D for a complete list of the flowchart symbols used in this book.)

Like a first outline, the initial flowchart for an algorithm can be quite general. Refinements to a flowchart are made by replacing existing nodes with flowchart segments that provide more explicit details. For instance, the first activity node in the flowchart shown above can be replaced by the following flowchart segment:

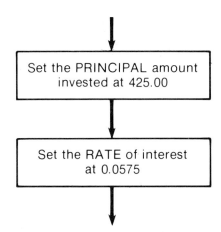

Actual symbolic names, such as **PRINCIPAL** and **RATE**, can be gradually introduced into the flowchart. The activity specified at a node can be further clarified by attaching an **annotation block** to the node by means of a dashed line. Annotation blocks are not flowchart nodes. They are employed merely to help the reader of a flowchart understand the activities specified at the nodes to which they are attached. In this more detailed flowchart of the interest calculation algorithm two annotation blocks are used:

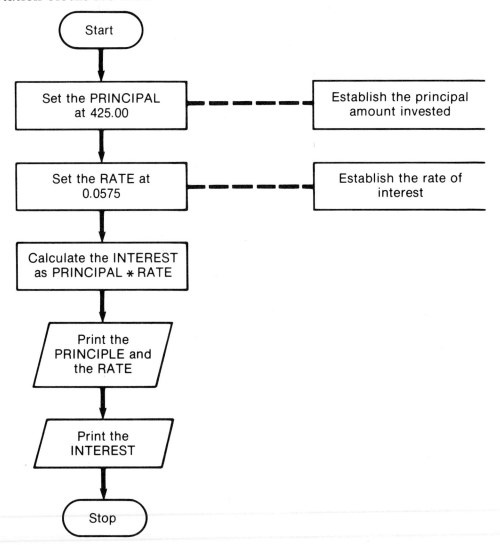

The purpose of a pseudocode outline and a flowchart is the same: to provide an orderly and logical description of an algorithm. All the algorithms presented from here on will be described by means of pseudocode outlines. However, some flow-chart segments will be employed in later chapters to describe the effects of various Pascal instructions.

1.3 EXERCISES

1. Describe the four basic steps in the program development process.

2. How does the problem-solving phase of program development differ from the implementation phase?

3. What is an algorithm?

4. What is a top-down approach to problem solving and what advantages does it offer?

5. Why is structured programming important?

6. What is pseudocode?

7. What is a flowchart?

8. Much research and planning are required to write a good term paper. Use a top-down approach with stepwise refinement to develop an algorithm that de-scribes a thorough procedure to follow when writing a paper.

9. Suppose that a square whose side length is 5.8 centimeters is inscribed in a circle and a smaller circle is inscribed in the square, as depicted below. The circles and the square share a common center.

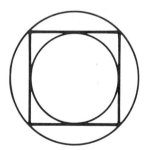

Develop an algorithm for finding the area of the doughnut-shaped region be-tween the concentric circles.

1.4
COMPUTER SYSTEMS

Computer hardware combined with language processors and other systems programs constitutes a **computer system.** The systems programs available in a computer system are designed to facilitate the efficient use of the hardware. A package of systems programs that will control the overall operation of the hardware is supplied by the manufacturer. That collection of programs is called an **operating system.** A computer user gives instructions to the operating system and then the operating system causes the central processing unit to perform the desired tasks. Some important tasks that the operating system controls are the following:

1. Access to the computer system.
2. Storage allocation for programs and data.
3. Input and output operations.
4. Access to language processors.
5. Scheduling of programs for execution.
6. Keeping track of memory utilization, time used by the CPU to execute a program, and other accounting information.

Computer users communicate with the operating system by issuing **system commands.** The exact form and function of each command is determined by the **control language** that the operating system will recognize.

A person learning to program a computer for the first time must learn some of the operating system's control language as well as the language used to write the programs. An operating system is tailored to suit a particular type of computer. Therefore, each operating system has its own control language. This section contains a brief introduction to two types of operating systems that are commonly available on computers used to teach programming. For specific information about the control language for the operating system used on your computer, consult your instructor or local computer center.

USING A COMPUTER WITH A BATCH OPERATING SYSTEM

A computer that has a **batch operating system** (or simply a **batch system**) receives jobs in batches and processes them one by one in order of their entry into the system or according to some priority scheme. The common procedure used to prepare and submit a job for batch processing is illustrated in Figure 1–4. First, a machine called a **keypunch** is used by a person to punch appropriate job control instructions (system commands), programs, and data on cards. Those cards must then be arranged in the proper sequence to form a **job deck.** A batch of job decks can be placed one behind the other in the input hopper of a **card reader.** The card reader must be manually activated, whereupon it will read the punched information on each card and transmit it to the computer's memory. Each job waits in the computer's memory until its turn for execution. When a job is finally processed by the computer, the output it produces may be printed on paper by a **line printer.**

A card reader and a line printer are referred to as **on-line** devices because they are attached directly to the computer system. A keypunch, on the other hand, is

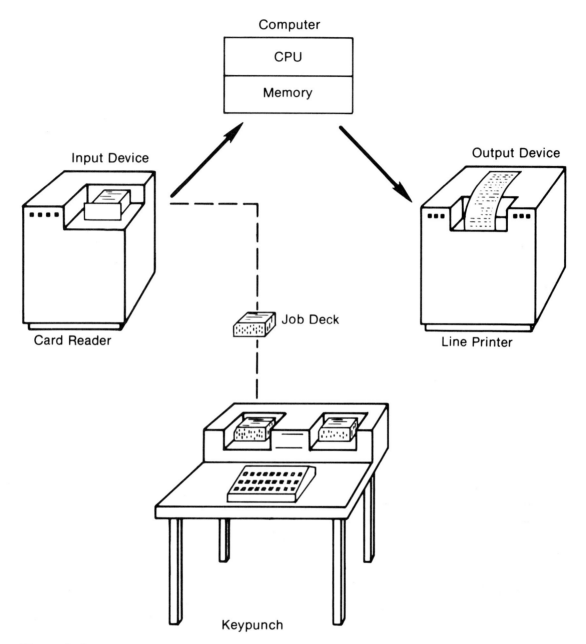

Figure 1–4
A typical batch processing system.

an **off-line** device. This means that a job prepared on cards does not enter the computer system until the job deck is read by a card reader. Figure 1–5 shows a typical 80-column punched card. A keypunch has a keyboard similar to a type-writer. When a character key is pressed, an image of the character is printed at the top of the card and one or more rectangular holes are punched in a column directly below that character. All punches produced on a card appear in 12 rows, the bottom 10 of which are numbered from 0 through 9. Every combination of punches produced by striking a key on the keypunch uniquely represents a character. When a card is read by a card reader, the character represented by each column of punches is transmitted to the computer's memory. The printing at the

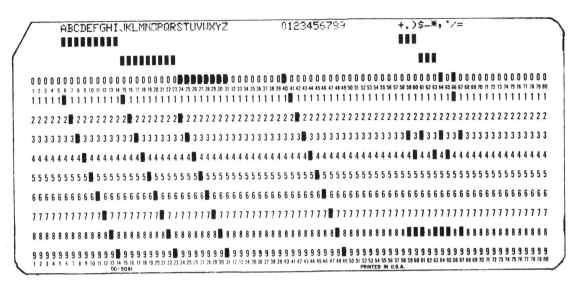

Figure 1–5
An 80-column punched card.

top of a card tells people who look at the card what characters have been punched. If the person punching a card accidentally presses the wrong key and produces an unwanted character, a new card will have to be punched because the holes representing a character cannot be repaired.

To **run** (compile and execute) a program on a batch system, the program and its data may be punched on cards and a job deck may be assembled by arranging the program cards, data cards, and various job control cards in an appropriate order. Figure 1–6 depicts the structure of a typical job deck used for a batch run of a Pascal program. The exact number of control cards required and the system commands on those cards are determined by the control language for the batch operating system in use. In general, at least one control card must appear in each of the positions indicated in Figure 1–6.

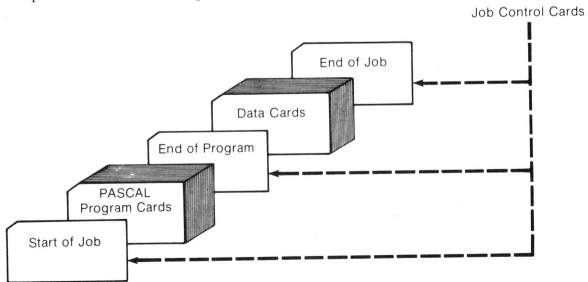

Figure 1–6
General structure of the job deck for a batch run of a Pascal program.

The card reader attached to a computer system may or may not be located in a place that is open to everyone who wants to use the system. Some computer centers allow individual users to operate the card reader, whereas others do not. Computer centers at educational institutions usually collect job decks submitted by students and send them through the card reader in batches. Once a job has entered the computer system, it will have to wait its turn to be processed. When the job is finally run, a compilation listing of the program instructions and output data generated by the execution of the program will be produced on the line printer. The paper containing the printed output from the run of a job is known as a **printout.** Computer center personnel periodically remove printouts from the line printer and take them to a distribution area where users of the computer system can pick them up. A common practice is to have students submit job decks at a distribution window and then return some time later to get the job deck and the printout produced by a run of the job.

The time difference between submission of a job and its completion is referred to as **turnaround time.** One of the major disadvantages of batch systems is that the turnaround times can vary from a few minutes to several hours or more, depending on the efficiency of the computer center staff and the number and complexity of jobs in the system. Batch processing is geared toward making efficient use of the computer hardware. Therefore, users generally experience long turnaround times when there are many jobs waiting in the system. At educational institutions this is often the case during the last few weeks of a school term, when many projects are due. To minimize the inconvenience of long turnaround times, it is important that students carefully check their job decks to make sure that the proper information has been punched on every card. Time spent checking a job deck before it is submitted for processing is well worth the effort.

USING A COMPUTER WITH A TIME-SHARING OPERATING SYSTEM

A computer that has a **time-sharing operating system** (or simply a **time-sharing system**) allows many users to have access to the computer at the same time. Each user communicates with the system by using an on-line **terminal** that serves as both an input device and an output device, as depicted in Figure 1–7. A terminal has a keyboard, which is used to send information and commands to the computer, and a printer or television monitor, which receives and displays output from the computer. All users on the system "share" the computer, but the operating system processes job requests so quickly that every user is given the illusion that he or she alone is using the computer.

Each person using a terminal attached to a time-sharing system carries on a "dialogue" with the operating system. When a user types a line containing a system command or some other information and then presses the "Return" key (the "Enter" or "New Line" key on some terminals), the operating system analyzes that line and takes the appropriate action. Some input lines typed by a user will cause the computer system to respond with printed output and others will not. When a computer system and its users "talk" to each other in this fashion, the system is said to be operating in **interactive mode.** A computer system need not have a time-sharing operating system in order to operate in interactive mode. For instance, **microcomputers** are small computers that typically operate in interactive mode

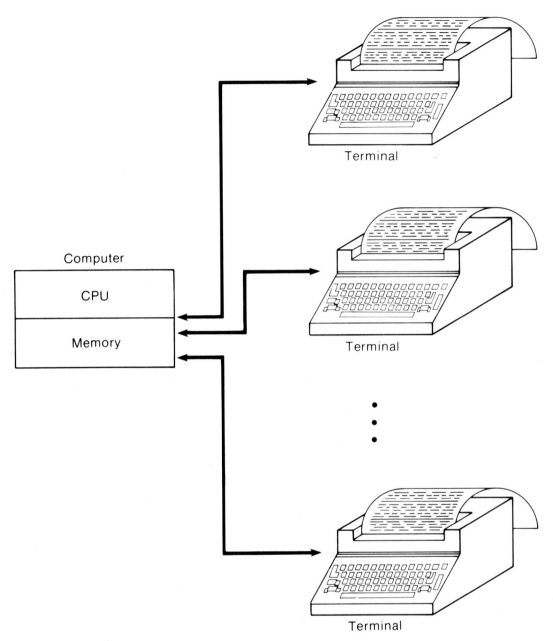

Figure 1–7
A typical time-sharing system.

while allowing only one user at a time. In fact, the central processing unit and memory may be housed in the same physical enclosure as the keyboard and the output device (usually a television monitor). In contrast to a microcomputer, the computer for a large time-sharing system may be hundreds of miles away from some of its terminals. Such terminals are connected to the system by cables or telephone lines.

The printed output from a sample session at a terminal connected to a time-sharing system is shown in Figure 1–8. Information typed by the user has been underlined to distinguish it from the computer's responses. Also, the symbol ® (which will not appear in the actual output) marks every place where the user

```
SYSTEM ON AT 1405.27 (02/11/81)
USER NUMBER: USR025 ®
PASSWORD: CPTR ®
TERMINAL #27
READY.

NEW,MYPROG ®
READY.
PASCAL ®
READY.
100 PROGRAM RECTANGLESIZE (INPUT, OUTPUT); ®
110 VAR ®
120     LENGTH, WIDTH, PERIMETER : INTEGER; ®
130 BEGIN ®
140 WRITELN('THIS PROGRAM WILL COMPUTE THE PERIMETER OF A'); ®
150 WRITELN('RECTANGLE USING A LENGTH AND WIDTH YOU SUPPLY.'); ®
160 WRITELN('WHAT IS THE LENGTH'); ®
170 READ(LENGTH); ®
180 WRITELN('WHAT IS THE WIDTH'); ®
190 READ(WIDTH); ®
200 PERIMETER := 2 * (LENGTH + WIDTH); ®
210 WRITELN('THE PERIMETER OF THE RECTANGLE IS', PERIMETER) ®
220 END. ®
RUN ®

PASCAL PROGRAM MYPROG
1409.37    02/11/81

THIS PROGRAM WILL COMPUTE THE PERIMETER OF A
RECTANGLE USING A LENGTH AND WIDTH YOU SUPPLY.
WHAT IS THE LENGTH
?54 ®
WHAT IS THE WIDTH
?32 ®
THE PERIMETER OF THE RECTANGLE IS        172

RUN COMPLETE.

SAVE,MYPROG ®
READY.

BYE ®

SYSTEM OFF AT 1411.19 (02/11/81)
TIME USED:  0.449 UNITS
```

Figure 1–8

A sample terminal session.

pressed the Return key. When a terminal becomes actively connected to the computer, the operating system may request from the person sitting at the terminal information that will identify that person as a valid user of the system. In our sample terminal session, the user is asked to supply a user number and a password. After the user has been validated, the computer system indicates that it is READY for a command. The purpose of this terminal session is to create a NEW program named MYPROG, have the computer RUN (compile and execute) the program, and then SAVE the program in a **library** (a part of the computer's secondary memory) so that it can be used again at some later time. The system commands "NEW,MYPROG" and "PASCAL" tell the operating system to provide an empty "workspace" in memory for lines of a Pascal program whose reference name will be MYPROG. When the computer signifies that it is READY to receive the program, each line of the program is typed, beginning with a line number. When the Return key is pressed at the end of each line, the line is inserted into the workspace. The operating system makes sure that the lines of the program are kept in sequence according to the line numbers. Thus, a user may insert the lines in any order and they will always be kept in the workspace in line number order (low to high).

After the entire program has been entered into the workspace, the system command RUN is issued to have the computer compile and execute the program. As the program is executed, it prints out some information as directed by WRITELN instructions in the program and also solicits some data from the user. When the two READ instructions (at lines 170 and 190) are executed, the computer causes a question mark to be printed at the terminal as a "prompt" to the user that the program needs some data before it can continue. (Some computers may use a different prompting symbol or merely wait without issuing a prompt.) This illustrates a major difference between a program that is run on a batch system (a **batch program**) and a program that is run on a system operating in interactive mode (an **interactive program**). All data required by a batch program must be specified on data cards in the job deck because the user is not allowed to interact with the program while it is being executed. An interactive program solicits data from the user as it is needed.

The running of a program does not affect the contents of the workspace. That is, the program is still available in the workspace, so that the user can run it again, make changes to it, and so on. In our example, the system command "SAVE,MYPROG" was issued after the program run was complete. That command placed a copy of the program into a user library. If the program had not been saved in the library, it would not be available after the terminal session ended. The system command "BYE" signaled the operating system that the terminal should be disconnected from the computer. When that happens, the contents of the workspace is permanently lost.

Every operating system recognizes its own set of system commands. While the commands shown in Figure 1–7 may not be completely acceptable for your computer system, they do represent the types of commands that are part of a control language. If a system command is improperly formed, the operating system will reject it. Suppose LIST is a system command that causes the computer to print out all the lines of a program that is currently in the workspace. Consider the following output, produced after the program MYPROG has been entered into the workspace.

```
LUST ®
ILLEGAL COMMAND.

LIST ®

PASCAL PROGRAM MYPROG
1410.22    02/11/81

100 PROGRAM RECTANGLESIZE (INPUT, OUTPUT);
110 VAR
120     LENGTH, WIDTH, PERIMETER : INTEGER;
130 BEGIN
140 WRITELN('THIS PROGRAM WILL COMPUTE THE PERIMETER OF A');
150 WRITELN('RECTANGLE USING A LENGTH AND WIDTH YOU SUPPLY.');
160 WRITELN('WHAT IS THE LENGTH');
170 READ(LENGTH);
180 WRITELN('WHAT IS THE WIDTH');
190 READ(WIDTH);
200 PERIMETER := 2 * (LENGTH + WIDTH);
210 WRITELN('THE PERIMETER OF THE RECTANGLE IS', PERIMETER)
220 END.

READY.
```

The command "LUST" typed by the user has no meaning to the operating system and so it is cited as an "ILLEGAL COMMAND." When the correct command, "LIST," is entered, the computer produces a printed copy of the entire program that is currently in the workspace. All operating systems recognize some command that is the equivalent of LIST in order to provide the user with a "picture" of the contents of the workspace on demand. Other commonly available system commands will clear the workspace of its contents, destroy a program that has been saved in a library, copy a program from a library into the workspace, and print the names of all programs stored in a library.

Note that system commands do not have line numbers. A system command is executed immediately after it is entered; it is not copied into the workspace. Only lines that begin with line numbers go into the workspace. Valid line numbers usually range from 1 through some maximum, like 9999 or 99999. The lines of a program need not be numbered consecutively. Line numbers are used simply to sequence the lines of a program. The best policy is to avoid numbering program lines consecutively, so that new lines can be inserted between existing lines when necessary. If a new line is entered that has the same line number as a line already in the workspace, the new line will replace the old line. To delete a line from the workspace without replacing it, just type its line number and then press the Return key.

A time-sharing system caters to the convenience of its users more than does a batch system. Terminal users get more immediate feedback from the computer system than those who submit job decks for batch runs. For programmers this speeds up the process of implementing a program. Because time-sharing systems are concerned with providing fast and convenient service to users, they do not utilize the computer hardware quite as efficiently as batch systems. Programs that require more than a few minutes of the central processing unit's time or those that generate hundreds of pages of output should be run on a batch system. Time-sharing systems generally impose much more severe time limit restrictions on program runs than batch systems, since they may be serving many users simultaneously.

1.4 EXERCISES

1. What is a computer system?

2. What is an operating system?

3. Why is a control language important?

4. Briefly describe how a batch system operates.

5. What is the difference between an off-line device and an on-line device? Name one on-line device and one off-line device.

6. What does the phrase "run a program" mean?

7. What is turnaround time?

8. Briefly describe how a time-sharing system operates.

9. Do the terms "interactive" and "time-sharing" mean the same thing? Explain.

10. How do batch programs and interactive programs differ?

11. Name some advantages and disadvantages of a batch system.

12. Name some advantages and disadvantages of a time-sharing system.

TWO/A FIRST LOOK AT PASCAL

A Pascal program consists of a **program heading** followed by a collection of program instructions called the **main block.** The main block is divided into the **declaration section** and the **executable section,** as depicted in Figure 2–1. Pascal instructions that a compiler must translate into machine language instructions (or some intermediate form that requires interpretation of further translation) are known as **statements,** and they must appear between the words BEGIN and END in the executable section. The declaration section consists of definitions and declarations that establish meanings for words and symbols used in the executable section. There are five parts to the declaration section, and they must appear in the order shown in Figure 2–1. Any or all of these parts may be absent when they are not needed.

A program must have at least one statement in the executable section. The period after the END of the executable section and the semicolons shown in Figure 2–1 are required. Basically, semicolons are used to mark the end of a program part or to separate consecutive definitions, declarations, or statements. This will be explained in more detail when the precise structures of the parts of the declaration section and statements within the executable section are presented.

In this chapter, only two kinds of statements will be introduced. We will also study forms for constant definitions and variable declarations. The other parts of

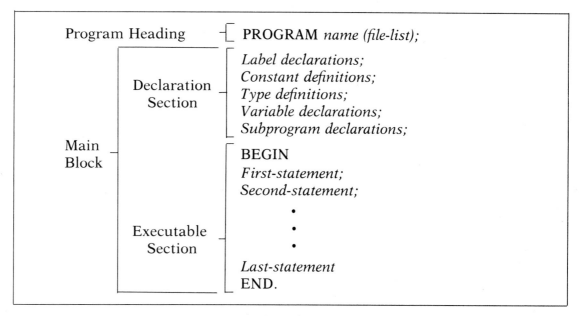

Figure 2–1
An overview of a Pascal program.

the declaration section will be considered in later chapters of this book (label declarations in Chapter Six, type definitions in Chapter Seven, and subprograms in Chapter Eight).

2.1 BASIC ELEMENTS OF A PASCAL PROGRAM

In this section we will consider the vocabulary of Pascal and forms in which certain kinds of data may be represented. As noted earlier, a Pascal program may have an empty declaration section. The example programs in this section do not require definitions or declarations. Thus, they are all of the form shown below:

```
PROGRAM name (OUTPUT);
BEGIN
First-statement;
Second-statement;
                .
                .
                .
Last-statement
END.
```

Portions of this general form that appear in italics must be replaced by suitable Pascal-coded information. The portion of the program heading designated *file-list* in Figure 2–1 has been replaced by the word OUTPUT, since OUTPUT is the only file we will use for the time being. A file is simply a source of data or a destination to which data may be transferred. Some standard device such as a line printer or terminal is used as the destination for printed information generated by a run of a program and this information constitutes the OUTPUT file. In most versions of Pascal, it is mandatory that the word OUTPUT appear in the program heading. Versions of Pascal that do not require the presence of OUTPUT in the *file-list* will not forbid its appearance there. Therefore, it is recommended that OUTPUT be specified in the program heading so that the heading will be acceptable to all versions of Pascal.

CHARACTER SETS

The characters that can be used to form words, numbers, and expressions in a Pascal program are limited to those that will be recognized by the computer system. Unfortunately, there is not one fixed set of characters that every computer will recognize. All existing character sets include the uppercase letters, digits, and the blank space character, as well as some collection of special characters such as the period, comma, semicolon, asterisk, and parentheses.

The American Standard Code for Information Interchange (ASCII) character set is the American version of a standard character set established by the International Standards Organization (ISO). ASCII (pronounced "askee") has been formally approved by the American National Standards Institute (ANSI) and is widely accepted as the standard for the computer industry. Most modern termi-

Letters

A B C D E F G H I J K L M N O P Q R S T U V W X Y Z

Digits

0 1 2 3 4 5 6 7 8 9

Special Characters

■ + − * / = ( ) [ ] < > ↑ ' " ! ? ; : , . @ # $ & % _ \

Note: The symbol "■" is used in this book to represent a single blank space character. Some computer terminals use a circumflex (ˆ) instead of an up-arrow (↑).

Figure 2–2
A typical 64-character ASCII subset.

nals and microcomputers use the full ASCII character set or some subset of it. However, there are other character sets still in use. The most notable of these is the Extended Binary Coded Decimal Interchange Code (EBCDIC), used primarily on IBM computer systems.

The full ASCII character set consists of 128 characters: 95 printable characters (including both lowercase and uppercase letters), and 33 nonprintable characters used for device control. Several official subsets of the ASCII character set are in common use today. Figure 2–2 lists a typical 64-character ASCII subset that is sufficient for writing Pascal programs. The full ASCII and EBCDIC character sets are given in Appendix A. Throughout this book only the 64 characters shown in Figure 2–2 will be used in the example programs.

When a program is handwritten, certain characters tend to look alike. For example, the digit 2 may look very much like the letter Z. This is also true for the letter "oh" and the digit zero. Programmers often "slash" one or the other of two characters that are similar in handwritten programs in order to avoid confusion. For instance, the symbol Ø may be used to represent a zero and the letter Z may be written as Ƶ. Some method of distinguishing similar characters should be employed in handwritten programs to prevent errors when the program is punched on cards or entered at a terminal. The only character represented by an alternate symbol in this book is the blank space character. Sometimes it is important to know the exact number of blank spaces present in a portion of a line. This would be difficult to determine unless the presence of each blank space were somehow marked. When it is important to emphasize the presence of a certain number of blank spaces in the examples given in this book, each one will be marked by the symbol "■." This method of identifying blank spaces is by no means standard or even widely used, but it serves our purpose.

SYMBOLIC NAMES

We have seen that words like PROGRAM, OUTPUT, BEGIN, and END are used in Pascal programs. Every Pascal word is classed as either a keyword (also known as a **reserved word**) or an **identifier.** All keywords have fixed meanings and those meanings cannot be changed. They serve as basic building blocks for program instructions and expressions. PROGRAM, BEGIN, and END are keywords. The keyword PROGRAM signals the beginning of the program heading and BEGIN and END mark the beginning and end of a sequence of statements, respectively. Other keywords and their meanings are presented in later chapters. For ease of reference, a list of the Pascal keywords appears in Appendix B.

An identifier is a word whose meaning can be established in the declaration section of a program. There are certain **standard identifiers** that have predefined meanings in Pascal. For instance, the word OUTPUT is a standard identifier that serves as the symbolic name for a file. It is possible to change the meaning of a standard identifier by redefining it in the declaration section of a program. If a standard identifier has been defined in a program, the meaning it would otherwise have no longer applies to that program. A list of the Pascal standard identifiers and their predefined meanings is in Appendix B.

All identifiers whose meanings are established in the declaration section of a program are referred to as **user-defined identifiers.** Each user-defined identifier must consist entirely of letters and digits, and the first character must be a letter. The following are examples of valid user-defined identifiers:

R
EX3PAGE29
NUMBER
A22CHARACTERIDENTIFIER
THETOTAL

Some invalid user-defined identifiers and the reasons why they are illegal are given below.

Invalid Identifier	Reason
2FORTHEMONEY	A digit cannot appear as the first character in an identifier.
CASH ON HAND	Blank spaces are not allowed within an identifier.
OVER&UNDER	An identifier cannot contain any special characters (such as "&").

A user-defined identifier can contain any number of letters and digits. However, the original version of standard Pascal determines the uniqueness of identifiers by examining only the first eight characters. In this case the user-defined identifiers AMOUNTINPOUNDS and AMOUNTINDOLLARS are considered identical, even though they do not look the same, because their first eight characters match. Some versions of Pascal determine the uniqueness of identifiers by examining more than the first eight characters, but none of them uses less. The *name* that must appear after the keyword PROGRAM in a program heading is a user-defined identifier. It serves as the name of the program. For instance,

PROGRAM FINDTHESUM (OUTPUT);

is a valid program heading. On the other hand,

PROGRAM FIND THE SUM (OUTPUT);

is an invalid program heading. (Why?) Some other meanings that can be given to user-defined identifiers are described in Section 2.2.

NUMBERS: INTEGER AND REAL DATA

A whole number represented by a sequence of digits that may or may not be prefixed with a plus (+) or minus (−) sign is called an **integer.** The collection of all integers within some predefined limits constitutes the data type known as INTEGER. An unsigned integer is considered the same as that integer with a leading plus sign (i.e., 325 and +325 represent the same integer). Thus, every negative integer must begin with a minus sign. Zeros at the beginning of an integer or immediately following the sign (if one is present) are insignificant. The integer −0026 is equivalent to −26 and the integer 01052 is equivalent to 1052 or +1052. The simplest way to represent the integer zero is 0, although any sequence of zero digits is acceptable. No commas or other nondigit characters are allowed within an integer. For instance, a number that could be written as 17,408 in mathematics must appear as 17408 or +17408 in Pascal.

The magnitude of an INTEGER constant (its absolute value ignoring the sign) is limited by the computer's ability to store such numbers. Most microcomputers require that integers not exceed 32767 (or $2^{15} - 1$). Large-scale computers can store integers of much greater magnitude. For example, IBM 360/370 computers permit the use of integers not exceeding 2147483647 (or $2^{31} - 1$) in magnitude, while the limit for Univac 1100 Series computers is 34359738367 (or $2^{35} - 1$). Any attempt to store an integer whose magnitude exceeds the fixed limit will result in an error known as an **overflow.**

A program will print an INTEGER constant that is listed in a WRITELN (pronounced "write line") statement. For instance, the statement

```
WRITELN(37)
```

will print the number 37 alone on one line. When an integer is printed, a certain **field** of consecutive character positions on a line is used, with the number occupying the rightmost positions in the field and blank spaces filling the remainder of the field. The number of character positions in a field is known as a **field width.** Every version of Pascal employs some standard field width for printing integers. A common field width used when printing integers is ten. In such a case the WRITELN statement shown above would produce a line of output that looks like this:

    ❘ ■■■■■■■■37

(The vertical line symbolizes the left edge of the paper on a terminal or line printer or the left edge of the screen on a television monitor.) A complete program whose sole purpose is to print the integer 37 is shown below.

```
PROGRAM PRINT37 (OUTPUT);
BEGIN
WRITELN(37)
END.
```

Every WRITELN statement in a program generates one line of output. Consider the following program:

```
PROGRAM PRINTINTEGERS (OUTPUT);
BEGIN
WRITELN(-108);
WRITELN(0);
WRITELN(+2752);
WRITELN(2752)
END.
```

The program PRINTINTEGERS will generate four lines of output with one integer appearing in the first ten character positions of each line (a standard field width of ten is assumed). Since the statements are executed in sequence from first to last, the output will look like this:

```
■■■■■■-108
■■■■■■■■■0
■■■■■■2752
■■■■■■2752
```

Note that a plus sign is not printed in front of positive integers. Also note the presence of semicolons in the program PRINTINTEGERS to separate consecutive WRITELN statements. A semicolon must always appear between two consecutive statements. No semicolon appears after the last WRITELN statement because the next line contains the keyword END, which is not a statement.

There is another Pascal data type, known as REAL, which consists of a much broader range of numbers than the INTEGER data type. Real numbers may have fractional parts. For instance, 1435.4 and −27.375 are valid REAL constants. These numbers are shown in **decimal notation,** which means that they have a whole number part followed by a decimal point (period character) and a fractional part. **The decimal point and at least one digit on each side of the decimal point are required when a real number is represented in decimal notation in Pascal.** As with INTEGER constants, a leading plus sign is optional for positive real numbers, but every negative real number must begin with a minus sign. The real number zero is represented by 0.0 in decimal notation. Here are some examples of valid and invalid REAL constants written in decimal notation.

Real Numbers in Decimal Notation	Valid REAL Constant?	Reason for Being Invalid
39.0	Yes	
5,204.62	No	No nondigit characters except one decimal point and a sign are allowed in a REAL number.
7.	No	At least one digit must appear to the right of the decimal point (e.g., 7.0).
−0.125	Yes	
.9	No	At least one digit must appear to the left of the decimal point (e.g., 0.9).
+6352.07	Yes	

A REAL number may also be expressed in **exponential notation** (or **scientific notation**). In exponential notation a number is expressed as some base value, called a **mantissa,** multiplied by ten raised to some integer power. The mantissa is listed first, followed immediately by the letter E and an integer, known as the **exponent,** that gives the appropriate power of ten. For example, 54.286E2 means 54.286 (the mantissa) multiplied by 10^2, which is equivalent to 5428.6 in decimal notation. Similarly, 54.286E−3 means 54.286 multiplied by 10^{-3}, which is equivalent to 0.054286 in decimal notation. If the exponent is positive, the decimal point in the mantissa properly belongs to the right of its given position, the number of places indicated by the exponent. If the exponent is negative, the proper position of the decimal point is to the left of its given position in the mantissa, the number of places specified by the absolute value of the exponent. Since the exponent for a number written in scientific notation causes the decimal point to "float" to its proper position, this notation is said to represent a real number in **floating point form.**

An exponential form of a real number may contain two signs: a leading sign for the number and a sign after the letter E for the exponent (both of which are assumed to be "+" if they are not present). The mantissa may appear either in decimal notation or as an integer. In the latter case, there is an implied decimal point after the last digit in the mantissa. For example, 164E1 is equivalent to 164.0E1, which in decimal notation is 1640.0. There are many ways to represent a real number by means of exponential notation. For instance, 123.456 is represented in exponential form as 0.123456E+3, 123.456E0, and 12345600E−05, to name just a few. Scientific notation is particularly useful for representing numbers that are either very large or very small in magnitude and contain relatively few nonzero significant digits. For example, 63800000000000000.0 can be written as 6.38E16 or 63.8E15 or 638.0E14. Similarly, −0.0000000000000000000000000025 is equivalent to −2.5E−27 or −0.25E−26 or −25E−28 in exponential notation.

When a REAL constant appears in a WRITELN statement, it will be printed in exponential form in a field of some standard size. Suppose the default field width used for printing real numbers is 16. The leftmost character in the field will always be a blank space and the rightmost portion of the field will contain the letter E followed by a signed exponent. Each version of Pascal will normally print a two-digit or three-digit exponent, depending on the limits imposed on the magnitude of REAL constants. Consider the following program:

```
PROGRAM PRINTREALS (OUTPUT);
BEGIN
WRITELN(372.4);
WRITELN(-0.000058);
WRITELN(20.36E-7);
WRITELN(-9.0)
END.
```

Assuming that real numbers are printed by using a standard field width of 16 with two-digit exponents, the output produced by the program PRINTREALS will look like this:

```
■■3.72400000E+02
■-5.80000000E-05
■■2.03600000E-06
■-9.00000000E+00
```

Note that a WRITELN statement always causes the decimal point to appear immediately after the leftmost nonzero digit in the mantissa, and the exponent tells how to float the decimal point to get the equivalent form of the number in decimal notation.

All INTEGER constants within a certain magnitude can be stored accurately in a computer's memory. We noted earlier that Univac 1100 Series computers can accurately store integers in the range -34359738367 to 34359738367, inclusive. The range for REAL constants is usually measured in terms of powers of ten. For instance, Univac 1100 Series computers can store real numbers in the approximate range from -10^{38} to 10^{38}. Since 34359738367 is smaller than 10^{11} and 10^{38} is equal to 10^{11} multiplied by 10^{27}, real numbers that are approximately 10^{27} times larger in magnitude than the largest possible INTEGER constant can be stored by Univac 1100 Series computers.

Not all real numbers in the range from -10^{38} to 10^{38} can be accurately stored in the memory of a Univac computer. For instance, numbers that are "very close" to zero (roughly in the range from -10^{-39} to 10^{-39}) will be stored as zeros. Thus, all the positive REAL constants lie in the approximate range from 10^{-39} to 10^{38} and all the negative REAL constants lie in the approximate range from -10^{38} to -10^{-39}. Within these limits on Univac 1100 computer systems, up to nine significant digits of precision for real numbers is possible. This means that a number like 47604.82697305, which has 13 significant digits, cannot be stored accurately in one memory location in a Univac 1100 Series computer. The value actually stored in memory will be some approximation, such as 47404.8269 or 42604.8270. Other computers will have similar constraints on the range and precision for REAL constants.

CHAR AND CHARACTER STRING DATA

The construct 'P' represents a data constant whose type is known as CHAR (short for "character") in Pascal. A CHAR constant is formed by enclosing a single character in apostrophes (single quotes). Hence, there are as many CHAR constants as there are characters in the available character set. When a CHAR constant is listed in a WRITELN statement, its value (the character between the apostrophes) is printed in a field of width one. Consider the following program:

```
PROGRAM VERTICALPASCAL (OUTPUT);
BEGIN
WRITELN('P');
WRITELN('A');
WRITELN('S');
WRITELN('C');
WRITELN('A');
WRITELN('L')
END.
```

The output produced by the program VERTICALPASCAL will look like this:

```
P
A
S
C
A
L
```

It is possible to list two or more constants in the same WRITELN statement so that their values will be printed on one line. This kind of WRITELN statement has the form

WRITELN(*constant, constant, . . . , constant*)

where the constants must be separated by commas. The order in which the constants are listed determines the order in which their values will be printed, and those values will appear in consecutive fields on the same line. A WRITELN statement containing several CHAR constants appears in the following program:

```
PROGRAM HORIZONTALPASCAL (OUTPUT);
BEGIN
WRITELN('P','A','S','C','A','L')
END.
```

The output produced by the program HORIZONTALPASCAL looks like this:

```
PASCAL                              .
```

Note that the apostrophes that must be used when representing a CHAR constant are never printed when a CHAR constant is listed in a WRITELN statement. Their purpose is merely to identify CHAR data constants in a program.

The form of representation for a CHAR constant is a special case of the representation for a more complex data type known as a **character string.** A character string constant (usually referred to simply as a string) is represented by enclosing any number of characters in apostrophes. For instance, 'PASCAL' is a string whose length is six because there are six characters between the apostrophes. The CHAR constants are represented as strings of length one. When a string constant is listed in a WRITELN statement, the value of the string (the sequence of characters between the enclosing apostrophes) is printed in a field whose width is equal to the length of the string. The program PRINTPASCAL shown below will produce the same output as the program HORIZONTALPASCAL:

```
PROGRAM PRINTPASCAL (OUTPUT);
BEGIN
WRITELN('PASCAL')
END.
```

Since apostrophes are used to mark the beginning and end of a string, it is not possible to use a single apostrophe to represent itself as a character in a string.

Instead, every apostrophe that is a character in a string must be represented by two consecutive apostrophes. Consider the following program:

```
PROGRAM APOSTROPHETEST (OUTPUT);
BEGIN
WRITELN('DON''T');
WRITELN('D','O','N','''','T');
WRITELN('DON','T')
END.
```

The output produced by this program will look like this:

```
DON'T
DON'T
DONT
```

In the first WRITELN statement, the string 'DON''T' has length four, since the two apostrophes between the letters N and T represent just one apostrophe in the string. Although the string '''' looks like it has length two, the innermost pair of apostrophes really represents only one apostrophe. Thus, '''' is the CHAR representation of an apostrophe character. The third WRITELN statement in the program APOSTROPHETEST contains the two strings 'DON' and 'T'.

Strings may contain blank spaces, and every blank space counts as a character. For instance, '■' is a string of length one containing one blank space (the CHAR representation of the blank space character), while '■■' is a string of length two containing two blank spaces. Remember that we are using each little black square to mark the presence of a blank space character. The computer does not print a black square for a blank space; it leaves one character position blank for every blank space in a string. This is demonstrated in the following program:

```
PROGRAM BLANKTEST (OUTPUT);
BEGIN
WRITELN('RED WHITE BLUE');
WRITELN(' RED  WHITE   BLUE');
WRITELN('  RED', ' WHITE ', 'BLUE');
WRITELN('RED WH', 'ITE', ' BLUE')
END.
```

The output generated by the program BLANKTEST looks like this:

```
RED■WHITE■BLUE
■RED■■WHITE■■■BLUE
■■RED■WHITE■BLUE
RED■WHITE■BLUE
```

INTEGER, REAL, and CHAR data may appear with character strings in a WRITELN list. The size of the field in which each value is printed is based on the data type of that value. Consider the following program:

```
PROGRAM PRINTMIXEDDATA (OUTPUT);
BEGIN
WRITELN(5,' SHIRTS @ $',12.00,' EACH');
WRITELN(5,' SHIRTS @ $',12,' EACH');
WRITELN('5 SHIRTS @ $12.00 EACH');
WRITELN('5',' SHIRTS @ $','12.00',' EACH')
END.
```

If we assume that integers are printed in 10-character fields and real numbers are printed in 16-character fields with a two-digit exponent, here is what the output generated by the program PRINTMIXEDDATA looks like:

```
■■■■■■■■■5■SHIRTS■@■$■■1.20000000E+01■EACH
■■■■■■■■■5■SHIRTS■@■$■■■■■■■■■■12■EACH
5■SHIRTS■@■$12.00■EACH
5■SHIRTS■@■$12.00■EACH
```

Note the distinction between the CHAR constant '5' and the INTEGER constant 5 and between the string '12.00' and the REAL constant 12.00. Digits appearing in a character string are treated as individual characters, not as numbers. In Chapter Four we will see that it is possible to change the sizes of the fields in which data values are printed to make the output more readable. We can also cause real numbers to be printed in decimal notation rather than exponential notation.

2.1 EXERCISES

1. Find out which character set your computer system uses.

2. How do keywords differ from standard identifiers?

3. How do standard identifiers differ from user-defined identifiers?

4. Give the rules for forming user-defined identifiers.

5. Tell which of the following symbolic names are valid user-defined identifiers and which are not.

a. MILESPERHOUR	b. P14309	c. AVERAGE DISTANCE
d. Z	e. 4THCHARACTER	f. UPPER-LIMIT
g. H2SO4	h. PROGRAM	i. $795
j. METERS/SEC/SEC	k. XXXXX	l. TRUCK#5

6. Find out how your version of Pascal determines the uniqueness of identifiers and then give at least three examples of identifiers that look different but are actually equivalent.

7. Tell whether each of the following is a valid INTEGER constant, REAL constant, or neither.

a. +273   b. 1478.   c. −0.045E3
d. 23,504   e. .35E+5   f. −1
g. +999.99   h. 6.2−3   i. 1E1
j. −72308   k. −625.E+9   l. E−2

8. Write each of the following real numbers in decimal notation.

   a. 27.4096E2   b. −0.782E+4   c. 295E−5
   d. 89.63E0   e. 19044.8E−4   f. −2E+3
   g. 2.695E21   h. 378.25E−11   i. −7E15

9. Identify the errors (if any) in each of the following WRITELN statements.

   a. WRITELN('A'   'B')   b. WRITELN(APRIL 22, 1981')
   c. WRITELN(' ' '■' ' ')   d. WRITELN('37 + 25 =', 62)
   e. WRITELN('SAY IT ISN'T SO')   f. WRITELN(1,1.0,1E0, '1')

10. The program XYDESIGN shown below is supposed to produce the following output:

```
X■X■Y
X■Y■X
Y■X■X
```

Will it generate the desired output? If not, explain why.

```
PROGRAM XYDESIGN (OUTPUT);
BEGIN
WRITELN('X■', 'Y■', 'X');
WRITELN('X', '■X■', 'Y');
WRITELN('Y■X', '■Y')
END.
```

11. Write a program that will print your mailing address in the following form:

```
JENNIFER J. JONES
496 W. CEDAR STREET.
HOMETOWN, IOWA  42599
```

12. Write programs that will print each of the following designs.

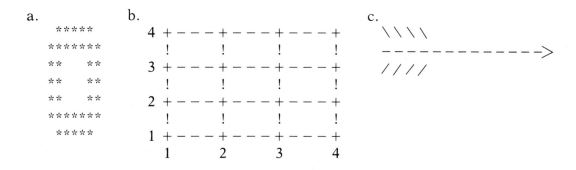

2.2
PROGRAMS USING DECLARED IDENTIFIERS

One more kind of statement is introduced in this section, along with constant definitions and variable declarations. The constant definitions must precede the variable declarations in the declaration section of a program, as illustrated below.

PROGRAM *name* (OUTPUT);
CONST
        constant-definitions;
VAR
        variable-declarations;
BEGIN
first-statement;
second-statement;
        •

        •

        •

last-statement
END.

CONST and VAR are keywords that mark the beginning of the constant definitions and the beginning of the variable declarations, respectively.

CONSTANT IDENTIFIERS

The purpose of a constant definition is to attach a symbolic name, known as a **constant identifer,** to a data constant. A constant definition must take the form

identifier = constant

where *identifier* is a valid user-defined identifier and *constant* is some data constant such as an integer, real number, or character string. For example,

SPEEDLIMIT = 55

is a valid constant definition that associates the identifier SPEEDLIMIT with the integer 55. We say that 55 is the **value of the constant identifier** SPEEDLIMIT because SPEEDLIMIT represents the integer 55. For instance, the statement

WRITELN(SPEEDLIMIT)

will cause the integer 55 to be printed. A constant identifier always serves as a stand-in for its defined value.

If there are two or more constant definitions in a program, semicolons must be used to separate them, as depicted in Figure 2–3. The semicolon after the last constant definition is required at the end of the constant definition part of a program. Here is a program in which four constant identifiers are defined.

```
                            CONST
                                   identifier = constant;
                                   identifier = constant;
                                             •
                                             •
                                             •
                                   identifier = constant;
```

Figure 2–3
General structure of the constant definition part of a Pascal program.

```
         PROGRAM CHECKCONST (OUTPUT);
         CONST
               LIMIT = 52;
               PI = 3.14159;
               PHRASE = 'END OF DATA';
               DOLLARSIGN = '$';
         BEGIN
         WRITELN('LIMIT REPRESENTS:', LIMIT);
         WRITELN('PI REPRESENTS:', PI);
         WRITELN('PHRASE REPRESENTS: ', PHRASE);
         WRITELN('DOLLARSIGN REPRESENTS: ', DOLLARSIGN)
         END.
```

The output produced by the program CHECKCONST looks like this:

```
         LIMIT REPRESENTS:          52
         PI REPRESENTS:   3.14159000E+00
         PHRASE REPRESENTS: END OF DATA
         DOLLARSIGN REPRESENTS: $
```

The program CHECKCONST merely demonstrates how constant identifiers are defined and what happens when they are listed in WRITELN statements. It is not necessary that an identifier be defined for every constant used in a program, but there are certain advantages to representing constants by constant identifiers. Consider the case of the identifier PI defined in the program CHECKCONST. The number 3.14159 is an approximation to a mathematical constant known as pi. Thus, the identifier PI is a suitable descriptive symbol for that mathematical constant. An approximation to pi may be used many times in a program, and each time its presence can be indicated by PI. Since 3.14159 is only an approximate value for pi, it may at times be necessary to use a more accurate approximation. If the constant specified in the definition of PI is changed, then every occurrence of PI in the program represents the new value. It is easier to change every instruction that contains a constant identifier for the number 3.14159 than to change every instruction that contains the number itself.

Every version of Pascal recognizes the standard identifier MAXINT as a constant identifier for the largest INTEGER constant. However, the value of MAXINT is not the same for every implementation of Pascal. This is because the largest integer that can be stored in one memory location varies from computer to computer. Some common values for MAXINT are listed in the following table:

Value of MAXINT	Applicable to
32767 (or $2^{15} - 1$)	Most small computer systems
2147483647 (or $2^{31} - 1$)	IBM 360/370 computer systems
34359738367 (or $2^{35} - 1$)	Univac 1100 Series computers
281474976710655 (or $2^{48} - 1$)	Control Data 6000 and Cyber computers

VARIABLES AND THE ASSIGNMENT STATEMENT

A **variable** is a symbolic name (identifier) for a memory location whose contents may be established or changed during the execution of the program. The value stored in a memory location identified as a variable is referred to as the **value of the variable.** Every variable must be associated with one data type, which fixes the type of value that variable may have. The purpose of a variable declaration is to establish the data type for one or more variables. Every variable declaration takes the form

list-of-variables : *data-type*;

where *list-of-variables* can consist of one identifier or several identifiers separated by commas and *data-type* specifies the kind of values to which all the variables in the list are restricted. For the present, the *data-type* specified in a variable declaration must be INTEGER, REAL, or CHAR. For instance,

DAYS : INTEGER;

is a valid variable declaration that identifies DAYS as a variable of INTEGER type. This means that DAYS is the name for a memory location that is permitted to store only an integer. The variable declaration

AMOUNT, TOTAL : REAL;

establishes AMOUNT and TOTAL as variables whose values must be real numbers.

Every variable used in a Pascal program must be declared, and all variable declarations must appear in the variable declaration part of the declaration section, which starts with the keyword VAR. For instance, a program whose only variables are the INTEGER variable DAYS and the REAL variables AMOUNT and TOTAL could have a variable declaration part that looks like this:

```
VAR
     DAYS : INTEGER;
     AMOUNT, TOTAL : REAL;
```

The variable declaration part of a program consists of a sequence of variable declarations separated by semicolons, as illustrated in Figure 2–4. There must be a semicolon after the last variable declaration to mark the end of the variable declaration part. The order in which the variables are listed in a declaration and the order of the declarations is not significant. For example,

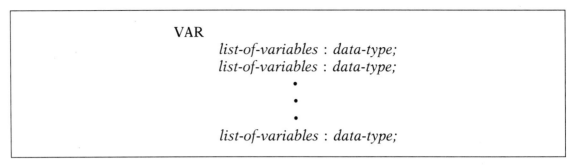

VAR

    list-of-variables : data-type;
    list-of-variables : data-type;

        •
        •
        •

    list-of-variables : data-type;

Figure 2–4
*General structure of the variable declaration part of a Pascal
program.*

```
VAR

    TOTAL, AMOUNT : REAL;
    DAYS : INTEGER;
```

has the same effect as the variable declaration part presented previously. In fact,
TOTAL and AMOUNT can be declared separately, as in

```
VAR

    TOTAL : REAL;
    AMOUNT : REAL;
    DAYS : INTEGER;
```

or even

```
VAR

    AMOUNT : REAL;
    DAYS : INTEGER;
    TOTAL : REAL;
```

However, a program is normally more readable if the declarations for variables of
the same type are grouped together.

A variable declaration **does not** assign any values to variables; it merely establishes identifers listed in the declaration as variables and "binds" them to a certain data type. Values for variables are established by statements in the program
during its execution. An "undefined variable" is one that has not yet been assigned
a value. In this sense all declared variables exist when a program begins execution, but they are undefined (have no values). Throughout this book, variables are
depicted by rectangular boxes that are labeled with the appropriate identifiers. If
the value of a variable is known, it will appear inside the box. When a variable
has not been assigned a value, the inside of the box is shaded. The variables
AMOUNT, TOTAL, and DAYS declared above are initially depicted like this:

    AMOUNT   TOTAL   DAYS

The size of a box used to represent a variable in this book is not significant. Enclosing a value in a box labeled with an identifier that denotes a variable is a way
of illustrating the value of that variable.

A variable may be assigned a value by an **assignment statement.** The simplest form of an assignment statement is

variable := *constant*

where *variable* is a declared variable and *constant* is a value of the type to which the *variable* is bound. The symbol ":=" (a colon followed immediately by an equals sign) is known as the **assignment operator.** When an assignment statement is executed, the value indicated to the right of the assignment operator is stored in the memory location represented by the specified *variable*. If DAYS is an INTEGER variable, then the statement

DAYS := 7

assigns the value 7 to the variable DAYS, as illustrated below.

```
┌─────────────────────┐
│          7          │
└─────────────────────┘
```

DAYS

The value of a variable may be printed by listing the variable in a WRITELN statement. Consider the following program:

```
PROGRAM ASSIGNMENTTEST (OUTPUT);
CONST
        PI = 3.1416;
VAR
        DAYS : INTEGER;
        X, Y : REAL;
        CH : CHAR;
BEGIN
DAYS := 7;
WRITELN('DAYS =', DAYS);
X := 652.5;
Y := PI;
WRITELN('X =', X, '   Y =', Y);
CH := '*';
WRITELN(CH)
END.
```

Note that the constant identifier PI represents the value 3.1416 in the third assignment statement. Here is what the output generated by the program ASSIGNMENTTEST looks like:

```
DAYS =                 7
X =   6.52500000E+02   Y =   3.14160000E+00
*
```

The value of a variable is always the last value assigned to that variable. When a variable that already has a value appears to the left of the assignment operator, the new value assigned to the variable replaces the old one. This is illustrated in the following program:

```
PROGRAM REPLACEMENTTEST (OUTPUT);
VAR
     NUMBER : INTEGER;
BEGIN
NUMBER := 25;
WRITELN(NUMBER);
NUMBER := 408;
WRITELN(NUMBER);
NUMBER := 1524;
NUMBER := 17;
WRITELN(NUMBER)
END.
```

The output produced by the program REPLACEMENTTEST is

```
        25
       408
        17
```

Each WRITELN statement in this program prints the "current" value of the variable NUMBER. Although 1524 is the third value assigned to NUMBER, it is not printed because the value of NUMBER has been changed to 17 by the time the next WRITELN statement is executed.

Variables can appear on both sides of the assignment operator:

$$variable\text{-}1 := variable\text{-}2$$

The effect of an assignment statement of this type is that *variable-1* is assigned the value of *variable-2*. No change occurs in the value of *variable-2*. Consider the program DUPLICATE given below:

```
PROGRAM DUPLICATE (OUTPUT);
VAR
     AGE, IQ : INTEGER;
BEGIN
AGE := 23;
IQ := 132;
WRITELN('       AGE', '         IQ');
WRITELN(AGE, IQ);
IQ := AGE;
WRITELN(AGE, IQ)
END.
```

WRITELN statements have been placed in this program to show the effect of the last assignment statement. Here is what the output looks like:

```
        AGE        IQ
         23       132
         23        23
```

There are two important differences between constant identifiers and variables. First, the values of all constant identifiers have been defined by the time program execution begins, and none of the variables have values. The second difference is that the value of a constant identifier cannot be changed during the execution of a program. A variable may have many different values during program execution. Suppose LENGTH is a constant identifier that has an integer value and DISTANCE is an INTEGER variable. The assignment statement

DISTANCE := LENGTH

is valid and causes the variable DISTANCE to be assigned the value of LENGTH. But the statement

LENGTH := DISTANCE

is illegal because only a variable may appear to the left of an assignment operator. The above statement is also invalid if LENGTH is an INTEGER variable and DISTANCE is a REAL variable, since a real number (the value of DISTANCE) cannot be assigned to an INTEGER variable. The value indicated to the right of the assignment operator must be of the same type as the variable to which the assignment is made with one exception. An integer value may be assigned to a REAL variable. This assertion requires further explanation. Consider the following statement:

DEPTH := 184

If DEPTH is an INTEGER variable, then the value of DEPTH will be 184 after the assignment. If DEPTH is a REAL variable, then the value of DEPTH must be a real number. The assignment of an integer value to a REAL variable causes automatic conversion of that value to REAL form. Thus, the value of DEPTH immediately after the assignment is as illustrated below:

184.0

DEPTH

2.2 EXERCISES

1. What is a constant identifer and what is a constant definition?

2. Examine the following constant definition part and tell which of the definitions are illegal and why they are invalid.

```
CONST
       BASE = 173.5;
       RATIO = 1/3;
       1STCHARACTER = '$';
       COUNT = 999;
       14.95 = CHARGE;
       VOWELS = AEIOU;
       LAMBDA = 504.63E+12;
       END = 7;
```

3. Write a constant definition part that defines the identifiers ROOT, ASTERISK, and MESSAGE to be synonymous with the constants −8.8, '*', and 'INVALID DATA', respectively.

4. Write and run a program that will print the value of MAXINT for your computer.

5. What is a variable and what is meant by the "value" of a variable?

6. What purpose does the variable declaration part of a program serve?

7. How do variables and constant identifiers differ?

8. Find the errors (if any) in each of the following variable declaration parts.

   a.
```
VAR
      RATEOFINTEREST = REAL;
```

   b.
```
VAR
      RED, WHITE : INTEGER;
      K1, K2, K3 : REAL;
```

   c.
```
VAR
      A, DIFFERENCE : REAL;
      NUMBER : 100;
      LETTER, DIGIT, SPACE : CHAR;
```

   d.
```
VAR
      'A', 'B', 'C' : CHAR;
      P, Q , REAL;
      ALPHA : CHAR;
```

9. Write a variable declaration part that declares the two INTEGER variables MULTIPLIER and ERROR, the CHAR variable SIGNAL, and the REAL variables LENGTH, WIDTH, and HEIGHT.

10. Consider the following definitions and declarations:

```
CONST
      PAGES = 235;
      ZEE = 'Z';
      GAMMA = 0.0045;
      WORD = 'HAPPINESS';
VAR
      MX7, MX9 : INTEGER;
      TARGET, RANGE : REAL;
      SYMBOL : CHAR;
```

Suppose the variables listed above currently have the following values:

MX7	MX9	TARGET	RANGE	SYMBOL
	42	19.2		'3'

Examine each of the following assignment statements and tell which of them (if any) are invalid. If an assignment statement is valid, assume that the variables have the values shown above prior to the assignment and show what the assignment statement does.

a. MX7 := 924   b. RANGE := GAMMA   c. MX9 := ZEE
d. SYMBOL := WORD   e. TARGET := MX9   f. MX9 := PAGES
g. RANGE := TARGET   h. MX7 := GAMMA   i. GAMMA := TARGET
j. SYMBOL := 'T'   k. TARGET := 23E+3   l. MX9 := MX9

11. Show the output produced by the following program:

```
PROGRAM SWAP (OUTPUT);
CONST
        X = 162;
        Y = 48;
VAR
        A, B, C : INTEGER;
BEGIN
A := X;
B := Y;
WRITELN(A, B);
C := A;
A := B;
B := C;
WRITELN(A, B)
END.
```

2.3
ARITHMETIC IN PASCAL

An expression that indicates one arithmetic operation, such as 25 + 132, is referred to as a **simple arithmetic expression.** In a simple arithmetic expression, two numbers called **operands** are separated by a symbol known as an **arithmetic operator.** The numbers 25 and 132 are the operands in the simple arithmetic expression 25 + 132 and "+" is an arithmetic operator that denotes addition. When the operation indicated in a simple arithmetic expression is performed, the result is a number that is called the **value of the expression.** For instance, the value of the expression 25 + 132 is 157.

Arithmetic expressions may appear in many different Pascal statements. A WRITELN statement may take the form

WRITELN(*arithmetic-expression*)

and an assignment statement may have the form

variable := *arithmetic-expression*

When statements of these types are executed, evaluation of the arithmetic expression occurs first. Thus, the statement

```
WRITELN(25 + 132)
```

causes the value of the expression 25 + 132 (namely, 157) to be printed, and the statement

$$X := 25 + 132$$

assigns the value of the expression 25 + 132 to the variable X (assuming that X is an INTEGER variable). The arithmetic operations available in Pascal and the operators used to denote those operations are presented in the following subsection.

INTEGER ARITHMETIC

When both operands in a simple arithmetic expression are integers, the expression is called an **INTEGER expression.** The value of an INTEGER expression is always of the type INTEGER. There are five **INTEGER operations** in Pascal, each one symbolized by a distinct operator, as shown in Figure 2–5. An INTEGER expression is valid when its value is within the range of allowable INTEGER values. For example, the expression 25000 + 12050 is not valid when the largest integer allowed is 32767. In this case an attempt to evaluate the expression 25000 + 12050 will result in an overflow, which should cause an error message to be printed and may even terminate the run of the program. When a program continues to be executed despite an overflow, the value produced by the operation that caused the overflow will be incorrect.

The symbols used as operators for addition and subtraction (+ and −) are the same symbols used as signs on numbers. In particular, a minus sign in front of an integer symbolizes an operation called **negation,** which requires only one operand. For example, − 5 means "the negative of 5." The expression 12 + − 5 is illegal in Pascal because the next nonblank character after an arithmetic operator cannot be another arithmetic operator. To produce the sum of 12 and − 5 we can use either 12 + (− 5) or − 5 + 12. Either of the operands in a simple arithmetic expression or the entire expression may be enclosed in parentheses. In the expres-

Operation	Operator	Effect of the Operation
Addition	+	*integer1* + *integer2* yields the sum of *integer1* and *integer2*
Subtraction	−	*integer1* − *integer2* means *integer2* subtracted from *integer1*
Multiplication	*	*integer1* * *integer2* produces *integer1* multiplied by *integer2*
Division	DIV	*integer1* DIV *integer2* gives the integer quotient when *integer1* is divided by *integer2* (the remainder is ignored)
Modulus	MOD	*integer1* MOD *integer2* yields the integer remainder when *integer1* is divided by *integer2*

Figure 2–5
The INTEGER operations and their operators.

sion 12 + (−5), the parentheses are required to avoid having two consecutive arithmetic operators. Although (−5) + 12 and (−5 + 12) are valid expressions, none of the parentheses in these expressions are really needed and they are therefore redundant.

An asterisk (*) must be used to symbolize multiplication in an arithmetic expression. For example, 12 * 7 means "12 multiplied by 7" and its value is 84. Similarly, the expressions 6 * (−25) and −25 * 6 both yield the value −150. In mathematics the product of 6 and −25 may be expressed as 6(−25) or (−25)6, but such expressions are not permitted in Pascal. Every multiplication must be explicitly indicated by the presence of an asterisk. Suppose we want to write a program that will compute and print the perimeter and area of a rectangle whose dimensions are known constants (say, 9 and 16). The following pseudocode describes an algorithm for those tasks:

Constants: WIDTH = 9 and LENGTH = 16
BEGIN
Calculate the SUM of the LENGTH and WIDTH
Compute the PERIMETER as 2 * SUM
Compute the AREA as LENGTH * WIDTH
Print the LENGTH, WIDTH, PERIMETER, and AREA
END

SUM, PERIMETER, and AREA will be INTEGER variables in our program, while WIDTH and LENGTH will identify the constants 9 and 16, respectively. A program written by using the pseudocode shown above as a model is given below:

```
PROGRAM RECTANGLE (OUTPUT);
CONST
        WIDTH = 9;
        LENGTH = 16;
VAR
        SUM, PERIMETER, AREA : INTEGER;
BEGIN
SUM := LENGTH + WIDTH;
PERIMETER := 2 * SUM;
AREA := LENGTH * WIDTH;
WRITELN('RECTANGLE WIDTH:', WIDTH);
WRITELN('RECTANGLE LENGTH:', LENGTH);
WRITELN('PERIMETER =', PERIMETER);
WRITELN('    AREA =', AREA)
END.
```

The program RECTANGLE produces the following output:

```
RECTANGLE WIDTH:          9
RECTANGLE LENGTH:         16
PERIMETER =         50
     AREA =        144
```

It is not necessary that the perimeter and area of a rectangle be assigned to the variables PERIMETER and AREA as in the program RECTANGLE. Expressions for the perimeter and the area may appear in WRITELN statements. Consider the following program:

```
PROGRAM PERIMETERANDAREA (OUTPUT);
CONST
        WIDTH = 9;
        LENGTH = 16;
VAR
        SUM : INTEGER;
BEGIN
WRITELN('RECTANGLE WIDTH:', WIDTH);
WRITELN('RECTANGLE LENGTH:', LENGTH);
SUM := LENGTH + WIDTH;
WRITELN('PERIMETER =', 2 * SUM);
WRITELN('     AREA =', LENGTH * WIDTH)
END.
```

The programs RECTANGLE and PERIMETERANDAREA produce identical output. When the WRITELN statements containing the expressions 2 * SUM and LENGTH * WIDTH are executed, these expressions are evaluated and the values are printed. The variable SUM is used in both programs to store the result of an intermediate calculation that is needed when the perimeter is computed.

Since the DIVision of two integers must produce an INTEGER result, the remainder is always ignored. For instance, the expressions 13 DIV 4, 25 DIV 40, and 36 DIV (−7) yield the integer quotients 3, 0, and −5, respectively. Zero DIVided by any nonzero integer always produces an integer zero as the quotient. An attempt to DIVide an integer by zero is an execution error that will terminate the program. The MOD operation complements DIVision by yielding the integer remainder resulting from the DIVision of two integers. For example, the value of 52 DIV 8 is 6 and the value of 52 MOD 8 is 4 (the remainder left when 52 is DIVided by 8). The following rule expresses the precise relationship between the DIV and MOD operations applied to the same operands:

If the value of *integer1* DIV *integer2* is *quotient* and the value of *integer1* MOD *integer2* is *remainder*, then

$$integer1 = integer2 * quotient + remainder$$

where the multiplication is performed first.

Here is a program that demonstrates the relationship between the DIV and MOD operations in a few specific instances:

```
PROGRAM DIVANDMODTEST (OUTPUT);
BEGIN
WRITELN('17 DIV 3 =', 17 DIV 3, ' WITH REMAINDER =', 17 MOD 3);
WRITELN('17 DIV (-3) =', 17 DIV (-3), ' WITH REMAINDER =',
     17 MOD (-3));
WRITELN('-17 DIV 3 =', -17 DIV 3, ' WITH REMAINDER =', -17 MOD 3);
WRITELN('-17 DIV (-3) =', -17 DIV (-3), ' WITH REMAINDER =',
     -17 MOD (-3))
END.
```

The output produced by DIVANDMODTEST is as follows:

```
17 DIV 3 =        5 WITH REMAINDER =         2
17 DIV (-3) =    -5 WITH REMAINDER =         2
-17 DIV 3 =      -5 WITH REMAINDER =        -2
-17 DIV (-3) =    5 WITH REMAINDER =        -2
```

Note that the value of *integer1* MOD *integer2* is negative if and only if *integer1* is negative. Furthermore, *integer1* MOD *integer2* yields the value (remainder) zero if and only if *integer1* is evenly DIVisible by *integer2*.

REAL ARITHMETIC

There are four arithmetic operations that can be applied to REAL operands to produce a REAL result: addition, subtraction, multiplication, and division. The symbols for the four REAL arithmetic operators are shown in Figure 2–6. Note that the operators for addition, subtraction, and multiplication of real numbers are represented by the same symbols used to denote the corresponding INTEGER operations. A simple arithmetic expression that has REAL operands always produces a REAL result. The operators DIV and MOD cannot appear with REAL operands. If even one of the operands for a DIV or MOD operation is REAL, the compiler will generate an error message. Every REAL operation produces a real number that is accurate within the range and precision limits for REAL data imposed by the computer system.

An arithmetic expression that contains only REAL operands is called a **REAL expression.** Any REAL constant used in an arithmetic expression can appear in either decimal or exponential notation. For instance, the following four expressions all mean "12.5 divided by 4.0":

$$12.5 / 4.0$$
$$0.125E2 / 4.0$$
$$12.5 / 40E-1$$
$$1.25E+01 / 40.0E-01$$

Operation	Operator	Effect of the Operation
Addition	+	*real1* + *real2* yields the sum of *real1* and *real2*
Subtraction	−	*real1* − *real2* means *real2* subtracted from *real1*
Multiplication	*	*real1* * *real2* produces *real1* multiplied by *real2*
Division	/	*real1* / *real2* yields the REAL quotient resulting from dividing *real1* by *real2*

Figure 2–6
The REAL operations and their operators.

The value of each of these expressions is the real number 3.125. Note that the + and − characters appearing in 40E−1, 1.25E+01, and 40.0E−01 are not used as arithmetic operators. REAL expressions, like INTEGER expressions, cannot contain adjacent arithmetic operators. For example, the multiplication of 2.3 and −6.25 may be represented as 2.3 * (−6.25) or −6.25 * 2.3, but not as 2.3 * −6.25.

Here is a pseudocode description of an algorithm for finding the area and circumference of a circle whose radius is 2.5:

```
Constants: PI = 3.14 and RADIUS = 2.5
BEGIN
Calculate PITIMESRADIUS as PI * RADIUS
Calculate RADIUSSQUARED as RADIUS * RADIUS
Print the RADIUS
Print the circumference computed as 2.0 * PITIMESRADIUS
Print the area computed as PI * RADIUSSQUARED
END
```

PITIMESRADIUS and RADIUSSQUARED represent REAL variables. A program written with this pseudocode as a model is shown below:

```
PROGRAM CIRCLE (OUTPUT);
CONST
        PI = 3.14;
        RADIUS = 2.5;
VAR
        PITIMESRADIUS, RADIUSSQUARED : REAL;
BEGIN
PITIMESRADIUS := PI * RADIUS;
RADIUSSQUARED := RADIUS * RADIUS;
WRITELN('RADIUS OF THE CIRCLE:', RADIUS);
WRITELN('CIRCUMFERENCE =', 2.0 * PITIMESRADIUS);
WRITELN('         AREA =', PI * RADIUSSQUARED)
END.
```

The program CIRCLE produce the following output:

```
RADIUS OF THE CIRCLE:  2.50000000E+00
CIRCUMFERENCE =   1.57000000E+01
         AREA =   1.96250000E+01
```

To compute the circumference and area of a circle whose radius is not 2.5, we need only change the constant definition of RADIUS and run the program again.

MIXED-MODE ARITHMETIC OPERATIONS

By definition an INTEGER expression contains only INTEGER data and a REAL expression contains only REAL data. However, it is possible for both REAL and INTEGER data to appear in an arithmetic expression. When this happens the expression is referred to as a **mixed-mode arithmetic expression.** For example, 100 / 4.0 is a simple mixed-mode expression that specifies that the integer 100 should be divided by the real number 4.0. Is the value of this expression the integer 25 or the real number 25.0? If either operand in a simple arithmetic expression is REAL, then only a REAL operation may be specified and the result is always a real number. Thus, the answer to our question is that the value of 100 / 4.0 is 25.0.

Remember that DIV and MOD are strictly INTEGER operators. Thus, expressions like 27 MOD 5.0, 27 DIV 5.0, 27.0 DIV 5, and 27.0 DIV 5.0 are illegal. A mixture of INTEGER and REAL operands may appear in simple arithmetic expressions where the operators +, −, *, and / are used. In the case of addition (+), subtraction (−), and multiplication (*), the result of the operation is a real number if one or both of the operands are REAL. Since / always symbolizes REAL division, the value of an expression of the form

operand1 / operand2

is always REAL. Thus 7 / 2, 7 / 2.0, and 7.0 / 2.0 all yield the value 3.5.

It is best to avoid the use of mixed-mode arithmetic expressions. Aside from the fact that it is very easy to inadvertently create an illegal mixed-mode expression, the use of such an expression may appear valid when it is not. Consider the following statement:

$$X := 7 / 2$$

Is this statement valid or not? If X is a REAL variable, the answer is yes, the assignment statement is valid because the value to be assigned to X is a real number. But if X is an INTEGER variable, that assignment statement is illegal, since a real number (3.5) cannot be assigned to an INTEGER variable.

2.3 EXERCISES

1. Tell whether each of the following simple arithmetic expressions is an INTEGER expression, a REAL expression, or a mixed-mode expression and find its value:

   a. −205 + 7921
   b. 12.0 * 5.0
   c. 5 * (−9)
   d. 140 MOD 60
   e. 1.5 − 1
   f. 14 / 5
   g. 7.2 / 3
   h. 23 DIV 6
   i. 71 MOD (−6)

2. Determine whether each of the following arithmetic expressions is valid or invalid. If an expression is invalid, explain why. Find the values of all the valid expressions.

   a. 9 MOD 15
   b. (15) (7)
   c. 3.5 − (−2)
   d. 1.5 + −3.2
   e. (−12.5 * 4.0)
   f. (−3)E+4
   g. 6.0 DIV 5
   h. −36 MOD 8
   i. 1E1 / 2E0

3. Suppose A is an INTEGER variable whose value is 16 when the assignment statement

$$A := A + 1$$

is executed. What effect will this assignment statement have on the value of A? In general, what effect will an assignment statement of the form

variable := variable + constant

have on the value of *variable?*

2.4
PROGRAM STYLE AND DEBUGGING

In all the example programs presented so far, the program heading, constant definitions, variable declarations, and statements all appear on separate lines. This is not a requirement of the Pascal language. Consider the following simple program, which is designed to print the sum of 25 and 38:

```
PROGRAM SUMOF25AND38 (OUTPUT);
BEGIN
WRITELN('25 + 38 =', 25 + 38)
END.
```

It is possible to write this entire program on one line (or card):

```
PROGRAM SUMOF25AND38(OUTPUT); BEGIN WRITELN('25 + 38 =',25+38) END.
```

The number of lines on which a program appears is not significant provided that the instructions are properly separated from one another. In the example above, the keyword BEGIN is a "word delimiter" that separates the program heading from the first (and only) statement in the executable section of the program.

Blank spaces can be used freely in a program provided that they do not appear within identifiers, keywords, or numbers. Only blank spaces that appear within character strings are significant. For instance, the program SUMOF25AND38 could be written in the form

```
PROGRAM     SUMOF25AND38         (  OUTPUT);
                      BEGIN
WRITELN   (   '25 + 38 ='   ,      25   + 38        )   END .
```

Although this program looks different from the two versions of SUMOF25AND38 shown above, it is not. All the extra blank spaces appearing in this version of SUMOF25AND38 do not affect the meaning of the program. In all three cases, the output produced when the program is executed is

```
| 25 + 38 =          63
```

Blank spaces should not appear haphazardly in a program because such spacing can make the program very difficult to read. The appearance of a program can be greatly enhanced by well-placed blank spaces just as easily.

Pascal instructions need not end on the line on which they begin. It is permissible to continue an instruction over two or more consecutive lines provided that no identifier, keyword, number, or character string is split between successive lines. Here is another valid form for the program SUMOF25AND38:

```
PROGRAM SUMOF25AND38
     ( OUTPUT );
BEGIN
          WRITELN ( '25 + 38 =',
                    25 + 38      )
END.
```

The basic rule to follow in order to continue an instruction properly is this: move to the next line only if a blank space could appear as the very next character on the current line without affecting the validity or meaning of the instruction. Normally, an instruction is continued over two or more lines when it is too long to fit on one line or when the continuation enhances the readability of the program.

Since people read programs, the style in which a program is written is very important. The ability of a person to read a program should not be hampered by the appearance of the program. You yourself may have to read a program that you wrote weeks earlier, and there is no worse feeling than finding out that you are not able to decipher what you wrote. You should develop an organized and disciplined programming style right from the start because the habits you fall into now, whether good or bad, will influence your style of programming in the future.

COMMENTS IN PROGRAMS

Programming languages permit the use of **comments** in a program to provide the readers of programs with useful information. Comments are not program instructions; that is, they do not contain information that affects the execution of the program. Therefore, all comments in a program are ignored by the compiler. Since the compiler must be able to recognize the difference between a comment and a program instruction, some standard method for representing comments must be employed. The two forms in which comments may be represented in Pascal are shown in Figure 2–7. When braces ("{" and "}") are available in the character set, they are used to mark the beginning and end of a comment. Otherwise, the character pairs "(*" and "*)" may be used in place of braces. Since braces are not available in all character sets, the latter method for denoting comments is used in this book.

A *comment* can consist of any sequence of characters (including blank spaces) that does not contain an asterisk followed by a right parenthesis, since that character pair is used to mark the end of a comment. Here is a valid comment:

$$\text{(*   THIS IS A SHORT COMMENT   *)}$$

A comment may start and end on the same line or it may extend over several lines, as in the following example:

```
(* THIS IS A MUCH LONGER COMMENT AND SO IT HAS BEEN
   EXTENDED OVER 3 LINES.
                        THE COMMENT ENDS HERE. *)
```

When the compiler encounters a "(*", it treats all characters up to the next "*)" as part of a comment and ignores them.

{ comment }

or

(* comment *)

Figure 2–7
The two forms for Pascal comments.

Consider the following version of the program RECTANGLE (Program 2.14):

```
00100   PROGRAM RECTANGLE (OUTPUT);
00110   (*********************************************************
00120   *                                                         *
00130   *   A PROGRAM TO COMPUTE AND PRINT THE PERIMETER AND AREA OF   *
00140   *   A RECTANGLE WHOSE LENGTH AND WIDTH ARE FIXED CONSTANTS     *
00150   *                                                         *
00160   *********************************************************)
00170   CONST                           (*-------- [CONSTANTS] ---------*)
00180         WIDTH = 9;                (* WIDTH OF THE RECTANGLE       *)
00190         LENGTH = 16;              (* LENGTH OF THE RECTANGLE      *)
00200                                   (*----------------------------*)
00210   VAR                             (*---- [INTEGER VARIABLES] ----*)
00220         SUM,                      (* SUM OF THE LENGTH AND WIDTH*)
00230         PERIMETER,                (* PERIMETER OF THE RECTANGLE *)
00240         AREA : INTEGER;           (* AREA OF THE RECTANGLE      *)
00250                                   (*----------------------------*)
00260   (*********************************************************)
00270   BEGIN (* PROGRAM RECTANGLE *)
00280   SUM := LENGTH + WIDTH;
00290   PERIMETER := 2 * SUM;
00300   AREA := LENGTH * WIDTH;
00310   WRITELN('RECTANGLE WIDTH:', WIDTH);
00320   WRITELN('RECTANGLE LENGTH:', LENGTH);
00330   WRITELN('PERIMETER =', PERIMETER);
00340   WRITELN('     AREA =', AREA)
00350   END (* OF PROGRAM RECTANGLE *).
```

There is no real difference between this version of the program RECTANGLE and the one presented earlier, in the sense that they both contain the same instructions. Comments have been inserted into the program to provide information that clarifies the content and purpose of the program.

The documented version of the program RECTANGLE exhibits a coding style that is used throughout this book in example programs. Here are some highlights of that style:

1. A brief description of the purpose of the program is placed after the program heading.
2. The purpose for every constant identifier and variable is explained in a short comment. To avoid overcrowding, every constant definition appears on a separate line and every variable in a variable declaration is placed on a separate line, with the *data-type* appearing on the same line as the last variable in a declaration.
3. Asterisks, dashes, and other characters are used in comments to form borders around related information.
4. A comment of the form

(* PROGRAM name *)

is placed where the executable section of a program BEGINs and a comment of the form

(* OF PROGRAM *name* *)

is used after the END of that section.

The author believes that the style in which the programs in this book are written is good, but not necessarily better than many other coding styles that could have been used. What is important is that the program instructions and comments appear in a readable form. Other style suggestions appear in later chapters.

PROGRAM ERRORS

When a program is translated prior to its execution, the compiler notes misuses of the language (improper punctuation, illegal instruction forms, misspellings, etc.) and displays a list of error messages on the standard output device. Violations of language rules are called **syntax errors.** A program that has been carefully designed and written should not contain any syntax errors, but it is conceivable that some inadvertent errors will appear in the program the first time it is punched on cards or entered at a terminal. Even one syntax error is enough to prevent a program from being executed because the compiler is unable to make a complete translation of the program.

Every version of Pascal has its own collection of syntax error messages. Some compilers will print every line that contains one or more errors with appropriate messages following each line. Other compilers will print each line containing one or more syntax errors and mark the approximate position of each error with reference numbers for standard error messages. After all the "bad" lines have been printed, the error messages that apply to one or more of these lines are listed in order of their reference numbers. Shown below is another version of the program RECTANGLE, but this time line numbers have been included so that the program is ready to be entered at a terminal. Some syntax errors exist in this program. Can you find them?

```
00100   PROGRAM RECTANGLE (OUTPUT);
00110   (**********************************************************
00120   *                                                        *
00130   *    A PROGRAM TO COMPUTE AND PRINT THE PERIMETER AND AREA OF  *
00140   *    A RECTANGLE WHOSE LENGTH AND WIDTH ARE FIXED CONSTANTS    *
00150   *                                                        *
00160   **********************************************************)
00170   CONST                              (*-------- [CONSTANTS] ---------*)
00180         WIDTH = 9;                   (* WIDTH OF THE RECTANGLE      *)
00190         LENGTH = 16;                 (* LENGTH OF THE RECTANGLE     *)
00200                                      (*-----------------------------*)
00210   VAR                                (*---- [INTEGER VARIABLES] ----*)
00220         SUM,                         (* SUM OF THE LENGTH AND WIDTH*)
00230         PERIMETER,                   (* PERIMETER OF THE RECTANGLE *)
00240         AREA : INTEGER;              (* AREA OF THE RECTANGLE      *)
00250                                      (*-----------------------------*)
00260   (**********************************************************)
00270   BEGIN (* PROGRAM RECTANGLE *)
00280   SUM := LENGTH + WIDTH;
00290   PERIMETER := 2.0 * SUM;
00300   AREA := LENGTH * WIDTH
```

```
00310    WRITELN('RECTANGLE WIDTH:', WIDTH);
00320    WRITELN('RECTANGLE LENGTH:   , LENGTH);
00330    WRITELN('PERIMETER =', PERIMETER);
00340    WRITELN('     AREA =', AREA)
00350    END (* OF PROGRAM RECTANGLE *).
```

This program was run on a Control Data Cyber 73 computer, and the Pascal 6000 compiler produced the following syntax error report:

```
00290    PERIMETER := 2.0 * SUM;
*****              '104
00310    WRITELN('RECTANGLE WIDTH:', WIDTH);
*****              '6,103,104'59
00320    WRITELN('RECTANGLE LENGTH:  , LENGTH);
*****                                         '202
00330    WRITELN('PERIMETER =', PERIMETER);
*****              '6                      '104
***** INCOMPLETE PROGRAM.
COMPILER ERROR MESSAGE(S).

   6:   UNEXPECTED SYMBOL.
  59:   ERROR IN VARIABLE.
 103:   IDENTIFIER IS NOT OF APPROPRIATE CLASS.
 104:   IDENTIFIER NOT DECLARED.
 202:   STRING CONSTANT MUST BE CONTAINED ON A SINGLE LINE.
ERROR(S) IN PASCAL PROGRAM.
```

Here is an analysis of this error report:

At line 290: Note that the comment that begins on line 220 does not end until the "*)" that appears at the end of line 230. Thus, PERIMETER appears within the comment and has been ignored by the compiler. A right parenthesis should have appeared immediately after the asterisk at the end of line 220 so that PERIMETER will be declared as an INTEGER variable. Note that the compiler did not object to the constant 2.0 that appears on line 290 because it did not recognize PERIMETER as an INTEGER variable. However, 2.0 must be replaced by the integer 2.

At line 310: There is no error in the statement at line 310. The reason for this error message is that no semicolon appears between the statements at lines 300 and 310.

At line 320: The start of a character string is marked by the apostrophe that appears in the WRITELN statement, but there is no apostrophe marking the end of the string. An apostrophe should appear after the colon.

At line 330: Error #6 is a carryover from the error at line 320. However, PERIMETER is referenced as an identifier at line 330 and it has not been declared, as far as the compiler is concerned. That error will be eliminated when PERIMETER is properly declared.

"INCOMPLETE PROGRAM." : In the case of our program, this message means that no period appears after the end

of the executable section. A period should
be inserted after the END in line 330 (but
not within the comment that is on that
line).

A compiler finds errors resulting from language violations. It is not the job of the compiler to anticipate errors that may occur during the execution of a program **(execution errors)**. However, certain logical errors may be so flagrant that the compiler will flag them as syntax errors before they have a chance to become execution errors. Consider the following program:

```
00100    PROGRAM DISASTER (OUTPUT);
00110    CONST
00120            A = 15;
00130            B = 0;
00140    VAR
00150            C : INTEGER;
00160    BEGIN (* PROGRAM DISASTER *)
00170    C := A DIV B;
00180    WRITELN(C)
00190    END (* OF PROGRAM DISASTER *).
```

Here is the error report on the program DISASTER that was generated by a Pascal 6000 compiler:

```
00170   C := A DIV B;
*****
COMPILER ERROR MESSAGE(S).

 300:  DIVISION BY ZERO.
ERROR(S) IN PASCAL PROGRAM.
```

Since B is a constant identifier whose value is zero, the DIVision specified at line 170 is impossible. The reason that the compiler is able to note this error is that the value of the divisor is an established constant. Now consider the following modified version of the program DISASTER:

```
00100    PROGRAM DISASTER (OUTPUT);
00110    CONST
00120            A = 15;
00130            B1 = 6;
00140    VAR
00150            B, C : INTEGER;
00160    BEGIN (* PROGRAM DISASTER *)
00170    B := B1 - 6;
00180    C := A DIV B;
00190    WRITELN(C)
00200    END (* OF PROGRAM DISASTER *).
```

This program will survive compilation and then reach execution, but the run will be aborted when an attempted division by zero (line 180) occurs. No error message is generated by the compiler during the translation of the program because the variable B has no value until the program is executed. Here is a sample error report that is printed when execution of the program is halted:

```
PROGRAM TERMINATED AT LINE 180 IN PROGRAM DISASTER.
DIVISION BY ZERO.

                    --- DISASTER ---
      B =           0                        C =      UNDEF

AT LINE 180 IN PROGRAM DISASTER.
```

The error report includes a listing of the values of the program variables at the time the attempted division by zero occurred.

It is generally much more difficult to locate the causes of execution errors than of syntax errors. Furthermore, execution errors are symptomatic of faulty program design, which may not be easy to correct. That is, the modifications that must be made to the program in order to eliminate the roots of an execution error may not fit nicely into the structure of the program. It is always better to spend time carefully planning and designing a program before it is written than to have to locate and repair execution errors. Programmers, particularly inexperienced programmers, tend to treat the symptoms of execution errors and to overlook their roots. This is a serious mistake and another reason why the design phase of program development is so important.

2.5 PROGRAMMING PROBLEMS

Each of the following problems requires that a program be written. Capitalized words in the problems are suggested constant identifiers and variables. Three sets of test data are included for every problem. Test your program with each set of data. This will require that you run the program three times, changing the data in the program prior to each run. Also, run the program with several sets of your own data.

1. Write a program that will convert POUNDS to GRAMS. (One ounce is equivalent to 28.3495 grams and there are 16 ounces in a pound.)

Test Data	POUNDS
Set #1	25.2
Set #2	0.35
Set #3	250.0

2. Write a program that will convert SECONDS to MINUTES and SECONDS. For instance, 252 seconds should be changed to 4 minutes and 12 seconds.

Test Data	SECONDS
Set #1	252
Set #2	8621
Set #3	31046

3. A temperature measured in degrees Fahrenheit (F) can be converted into an equivalent temperature on the Celsius (C) scale by subtracting 32 from the Fahrenheit temperature and then multiplying the result by five-ninths. The mathematical formula for the conversion is

$$C = \frac{5}{9}(F - 32)$$

Write a program that will find the Celsius equivalent of a Fahrenheit temperature.

Test Data	F
Set #1	62
Set #2	212
Set #3	−40

4. The straight-line method for computing the yearly depreciation of the value of an item is given by the following formula:

$$DEPRECIATION = \frac{purchase\ PRICE - SALVAGE\ value}{YEARS\ in\ service}$$

Write a program to compute the yearly DEPRECIATION for an item whose purchase PRICE, SALVAGE value, and expected YEARS in service are known.

Test Data	PRICE	SALVAGE	YEARS
Set #1	250.00	35.00	8
Set #2	2425.00	470.00	6
Set #3	1162.00	625.00	5

5. The approximate state gasoline tax paid by an automobile owner over a certain period of time can be computed by using the formula

$$GASTAX = \frac{MILES}{MILEAGE}(TAXPERGALLON)$$

where MILES represents the total number of miles driven during the period, MILEAGE is the average number of miles the automobile can be driven per gallon of gasoline, and TAXPERGALLON is the rate at which gasoline is taxed by the state in cents per gallon (e.g., 6 cents is 0.06 dollar). Write a program that will calculate the approximate state gasoline tax paid during a period for which the values of MILES, MILEAGE, and TAXPERGALLON are known.

Test Data	MILES	MILEAGE	TAXPERGALLON
Set #1	425.0	18.0	0.04
Set #2	916.0	22.4	0.03
Set #3	3506.0	15.5	0.05

6. A tax on property is usually based on a certain percentage of the property's market value. That is, the MARKET value is multiplied by some fraction

(RATE) to yield a BASE amount on which the tax is computed. The TAX is a fixed number of dollars (TAXPER1000) per thousand dollars of the BASE amount:

$$\text{TAX} = \frac{\text{BASE}}{1000.0} \text{(TAXPER1000)}$$

Write a program to compute the property tax when the MARKET value, RATE to determine the BASE, and TAXPER1000 are known.

Test Data	MARKET	RATE	TAXPER1000
Set #1	5000.00	0.6	25.00
Set #2	12450.00	0.8	17.50
Set #3	46800.00	0.75	22.25

7. Each person on a bowling team bowls three games and the sum of the SCOREs for the three games is that person's SERIES. Write a program to compute the SERIES for a bowler whose SCOREs are known; also, have the program find the AVERAGE of the SCOREs (the SERIES DIVided by 3).

Test Data	SCORE1	SCORE2	SCORE3
Set #1	145	172	151
Set #2	187	135	173
Set #3	179	215	234

8. The acceleration of a moving body is the change in the velocity of the body with respect to time:

$$\text{ACCELERATION} = \frac{\text{VELOC2} - \text{VELOC1}}{\text{TIME}}$$

Both velocities (VELOC1 and VELOC2) must be measured in the same units (say, meters per second) and TIME must be measured in units consistent with the velocities (seconds). A negative ACCELERATION, which occurs when the velocity at the start of the TIME period (VELOC1) is greater than the velocity at the end of the TIME period (VELOC2), means that the moving body is slowing down. Write a program to compute the ACCELERATION of a moving body over a known TIME period for which the starting and ending velocities have been measured.

Test Data	TIME	VELOC1	VELOC2
Set #1	2.0	25.0	55.0
Set #2	18.4	124.0	563.0
Set #3	9.2	365.0	140.0

THREE/PASCAL EXPRESSIONS

In Chapter Two, arithmetic operators and simple INTEGER, REAL, and mixed-mode arithmetic expressions were introduced. Only one operator appears in a simple arithmetic expression. We will see in this chapter that general arithmetic expressions may contain many operators. For instance,

$$38 + 100 + 64$$

is a valid INTEGER expression whose value is 202. The order in which the two additions specified in this expression are performed does not affect the value of the expression. However, in the evaluation of the expression

$$38 + 100 \text{ DIV } 64$$

the order in which the operators are applied is significant. If the addition is performed first, the value of the expression is 2. But if the DIVision precedes the addition, the value of the expression is 39. This ambiguity is avoided in programming languages by having priorities for the operators. In Pascal, DIVision has a higher priority than addition. Thus, the value of 38 + 100 DIV 64 must be 39.

3.1
ARITHMETIC EXPRESSIONS

When an arithmetic expression containing two or more operators is evaluated, the operations are performed one at a time in sequence. In this book, diagrams like the one shown below are used to trace the operation-by-operation evaluation of an expression:

$$
\begin{array}{c}
38 + \underline{100 \text{ DIV } 64} \\
\downarrow \\
\underline{38 + \qquad 1} \\
\downarrow \\
39
\end{array}
$$

At each stage of a trace, the next operator to be applied and its operands are underlined and the value produced by the operation is indicated by an arrow.

OPERATOR PRECEDENCE

There are two distinct levels of priority for the arithmetic operators in Pascal. Thus, each arithmetic operator has either a "high" priority or a "low" priority. The operators at the two priority levels are shown in Figure 3–1. The basic evaluation procedure for an arithmetic expression consists of two left-to-right passes through the expression. During the first pass, only high priority operators (if any) are ap-

Priority Level	Operators
High	* / DIV MOD
Low	+ −

Figure 3–1
Priority levels for the arithmetic operators.

plied as they are encountered. During the second pass, the low priority operators (if any) are applied as they are encountered. Here is an example:

$$
\begin{array}{ll}
125 + \underline{40\ MOD\ 6} * 5 - 70 & \left.\begin{array}{l}\\\\\end{array}\right] \text{first pass}\\
125 + \quad\quad 4 \quad * 5 - 70 &\\
125 + \quad\quad\quad\quad 20 \ - 70 & \left.\begin{array}{l}\\\\\end{array}\right] \text{second pass}\\
\underline{145} \quad\quad\quad\quad\quad - 70 &\\
\quad\quad\quad\quad 75 &
\end{array}
$$

The MOD operation is performed first because it is the leftmost high priority operation specified in the expression. Then the remaining high priority operation (a multiplication) is performed, and this concludes the first pass. Only low priority operations remain after the first pass and they are performed from left to right during the second pass.

The expression in the example presented above is an INTEGER expression because all the operands are integers and only INTEGER operations are performed. The value of an INTEGER expression is always an integer. A REAL expression contains only REAL operands and REAL operators. Thus, the value of a REAL expression is a real number. For instance,

$$
\begin{array}{l}
\underline{4.5\ /\ 9.0} + 1.5 * 6.2\\
0.5 \quad + \underline{1.5 * 6.2}\\
\underline{0.5 \quad + \quad 9.3}\\
\quad\quad 9.8
\end{array}
$$

An arithmetic expression may contain both INTEGER and REAL operands and operators, provided that evaluation of the expression is possible. Consider the following mixed-mode expression:

$$24\ DIV\ 6 * 5.0$$

Since DIVision and multiplication have the same priority, the DIVision must be performed first, as illustrated in the following trace:

$$
\begin{array}{c}
\underline{24\ \text{DIV}\ 6}\ *\ 5.0 \\
\downarrow \\
\underline{4\qquad *\ 5.0} \\
\downarrow \\
20.0
\end{array}
$$

The multiplication is performed as a REAL operation because one of the operands (5.0) is a real number. Thus, the value of the expression is a real number. Now consider the following expression:

$$5.0 * 24\ \text{DIV}\ 6$$

An attempt to trace the evaluation of this expression produces the results shown below:

$$
\begin{array}{c}
\underline{5.0\ *\ 24}\ \text{DIV}\ 6 \\
\downarrow \\
\underline{120.0\quad\text{DIV}\ 6} \\
\downarrow \\
\text{error}
\end{array}
$$

Since DIVision is strictly an INTEGER operation, the expression cannot be evaluated and it is therefore invalid. The Pascal compiler will discover an illegal mixed-mode expression and print an appropriate error message. Whenever possible, the use of mixed-mode expressions should be avoided in order to minimize the chance for program errors.

Only constants appear in the expressions we have examined so far, but that is not usually the case. An arithmetic expression may contain both constant identifiers and variables as well as constants. When an expression is evaluated, the values of the constant identifiers and the variables are used as operands for the indicated operators. Suppose TEN is a constant identifer whose value is 10, and PARTS, FACTOR, and BASE are INTEGER variables whose current values are depicted below:

7	5	19
PARTS	FACTOR	BASE

The INTEGER expression PARTS * FACTOR − 18 MOD FACTOR * TEN + BASE has the value 24, as the following trace reveals:

$$
\begin{array}{l}
\underline{\text{PARTS}\ *\ \text{FACTOR}}\ -\ 18\ \text{MOD}\ \text{FACTOR}\ *\ \text{TEN}\ +\ \text{BASE} \\
\qquad\downarrow \\
\quad 35 \qquad\qquad -\ \underline{18\ \text{MOD}\ \text{FACTOR}}\ *\ \text{TEN}\ +\ \text{BASE} \\
\qquad\qquad\qquad\qquad\qquad\downarrow \\
\quad 35 \qquad\qquad -\quad\underline{3\qquad\qquad *\ \text{TEN}}\ +\ \text{BASE} \\
\qquad\qquad\qquad\qquad\qquad\qquad\downarrow \\
\quad \underline{35 \qquad\qquad -\qquad\qquad 30}\ +\ \text{BASE} \\
\qquad\quad\downarrow \\
\qquad\quad\underline{5 \qquad\qquad\qquad\qquad\qquad +\ \text{BASE}} \\
\qquad\qquad\qquad\qquad\qquad\qquad\downarrow \\
\qquad\qquad\qquad\qquad 24
\end{array}
$$

The program PAVINGCOST presented next computes the cost of concrete for a sidewalk around a rectangular region. It is assumed that the cost of concrete per square foot (uniform thickness) is known. The number of square feet of concrete needed for the sidewalk can be calculated by subtracting the area of the region enclosed by the sidewalk from the area of the rectangular region bounded by the outer edge of the sidewalk (see the diagram below). Suppose the region bounded by the sidewalk is 25 feet wide and 60 feet long and the width of the sidewalk is 4 feet. Each square foot of concrete will cost $12.00. Here is a pseudocode description of the algorithm on which the program PAVINGCOST is based:

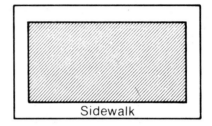

Sidewalk

Constants: WIDTH = 25.0, LENGTH = 60.0, WALKWIDTH = 4.0, and CONCRETECOST = 12.0
BEGIN
Compute the OUTERWIDTH of the region plus the sidewalk as WIDTH + 2.0 * WALKWIDTH
Compute the OUTERLENGTH of the region plus the sidewalk as LENGTH + 2.0 * WALKWIDTH
Calculate the square footage of CONCRETE needed for the sidewalk as OUTERLENGTH * OUTERWIDTH − LENGTH * WIDTH
Calculate the COST of the sidewalk as CONCRETECOST * CONCRETE
Print WIDTH, LENGTH, WALKWIDTH, CONCRETECOST, CONCRETE, and COST
END

The WIDTH, LENGTH, and WALKWIDTH are given real number values to avoid mixed-mode arithmetic and because the dimensions of the rectangular region and the width of the sidewalk may not be whole numbers in every case for which we might want to use the program.

```
PROGRAM PAVINGCOST (OUTPUT);
(***************************************************************************
*                                                                         *
*   THIS PROGRAM WILL COMPUTE THE COST OF PAVING A CONCRETE                *
*   SIDEWALK AROUND A RECTANGULAR REGION                                   *
*                                                                         *
***************************************************************************)
CONST                                   (*----------[CONSTANTS]----------*)
        WIDTH = 25.0;                   (* WIDTH OF THE RECTANGULAR      *)
                                        (* REGION (FT)                   *)
        LENGTH = 60.0;                  (* LENGTH OF THE RECTANGULAR     *)
                                        (* REGION (FT)                   *)
        WALKWIDTH = 4.0;                (* WIDTH OF THE SIDEWALK (FT)    *)
        UNITCOST = 4.20;                (* COST OF THE CONCRETE ($/FT)   *)
                                        (*-------------------------------*)
```

```
VAR                                     (*-------[REAL VARIABLES]--------*)
        OUTERWIDTH,                     (* WIDTH OF THE REGION PLUS THE  *)
                                        (* SIDEWALK (FT)                 *)
        OUTERLENGTH,                    (* LENGTH OF THE REGION PLUS THE *)
                                        (* SIDEWALK (FT)                 *)
        CONCRETE,                       (* SQUARE FEET OF CONCRETE       *)
                                        (* NEEDED                        *)
        COST : REAL;                    (* COST OF THE SIDEWALK          *)
                                        (*-------------------------------*)
(***********************************************************************)
BEGIN (* PROGRAM PAVINGCOST *)
OUTERWIDTH := WIDTH + 2.0 * WALKWIDTH;
OUTERLENGTH := LENGTH + 2.0 * WALKWIDTH;
CONCRETE := OUTERLENGTH * OUTERWIDTH - LENGTH * WIDTH;
COST := UNITCOST * CONCRETE;
WRITELN('WIDTH OF RECTANGULAR REGION: ', WIDTH, ' FEET');
WRITELN('LENGTH OF RECTANGULAR REGION:', LENGTH, ' FEET');
WRITELN('WIDTH OF THE SIDEWALK:       ', WALKWIDTH, ' FEET');
WRITELN('AMOUNT OF CONCRETE NEEDED:   ', CONCRETE, ' SQUARE FEET');
WRITELN;
WRITELN('CONCRETE COST PER SQUARE FOOT: $', UNITCOST);
WRITELN('TOTAL COST OF CONCRETE:        $', COST)
END (* OF PROGRAM PAVINGCOST *).
```

Note the use of a WRITELN statement without a list of items. That statement will generate a blank line of output. Here is the output produced by the program PAVINGCOST:

```
WIDTH OF RECTANGULAR REGION:    2.50000000E+01 FEET
LENGTH OF RECTANGULAR REGION:   6.00000000E+01 FEET
WIDTH OF THE SIDEWALK:          4.00000000E+00 FEET
AMOUNT OF CONCRETE NEEDED:      2.24400000E+03 SQUARE FEET

CONCRETE COST PER SQUARE FOOT: $   4.20000000E+00
TOTAL COST OF THE CONCRETE:    $   9.42480000E+03
```

We see from the output that the cost of putting a 4-foot-wide sidewalk around a 25- by 60-foot rectangular region is $9424.80 for the concrete alone at $4.20 per square foot.

SUBEXPRESSIONS

Since DIVision takes precedence over addition, the expression 38 + 100 DIV 64 has the value 39. It is possible to force the addition of 38 and 100 before the DIVision by 64. All we need to do is enclose 38 + 100 in parentheses:

$$\underline{(38 + 100)} \text{ DIV } 64$$
$$\downarrow$$
$$\underline{138 \qquad \text{DIV } 64}$$
$$\downarrow$$
$$2$$

An expression that is enclosed in parentheses within another expression is known as a **subexpression.** Thus in our example the parentheses dictate that the subexpression 38 + 100 must be evaluated first. If a subexpression does not itself contain any subexpressions, it is evaluated via the normal two-pass procedure. Consider the following example:

$$
\begin{array}{c}
(125 + \underline{40\ \text{MOD}\ 6}) * 5 - 70 \\
\downarrow \\
\underline{(125 + \quad 4 \quad)} * 5 - 70 \\
\downarrow \\
\underline{129 \qquad\qquad * 5} - 70 \\
\downarrow \\
\underline{645\ -\ 70} \\
\downarrow \\
575
\end{array}
$$

The subexpression 125 + 40 MOD 6 must be fully evaluated before the multiplication by 5 can occur.

An expression may contain several subexpressions. For instance, the expression 7 + (125 + 40) MOD (6 * 5 − 70 DIV 8) contains two subexpressions: 125 + 40 and 6 * 5 − 70 DIV 8. Both of these subexpressions must be evaluated before the MOD operation is performed. Although it would make no difference which of the two subexpressions in our example were evaluated first, the usual procedure is to evaluate subexpressions from left to right. Here is the evaluation trace for the entire expression:

$$
\begin{array}{l}
7 + \underline{(125\ +\ 40)}\ \text{MOD}\ (6 * 5 - 70\ \text{DIV}\ 8) \\
\qquad\quad \downarrow \\
7 + \quad 165 \quad \text{MOD}\ (\underline{6 * 5}\ -\ 70\ \text{DIV}\ 8) \\
\qquad\qquad\qquad\qquad \downarrow \\
7 + \quad 165 \quad \text{MOD}\ (30 \quad - \underline{70\ \text{DIV}\ 8}) \\
\qquad\qquad\qquad\qquad\qquad\qquad \downarrow \\
7 + \quad 165 \quad \text{MOD}\ \underline{(30 \quad - \quad 8 \quad)} \\
\qquad\qquad\qquad\qquad\qquad \downarrow \\
7 + \quad \underline{165 \quad \text{MOD} \quad 22} \\
\qquad\qquad\qquad \downarrow \\
\underline{7 + \qquad\qquad 11} \\
\quad \downarrow \\
18
\end{array}
$$

The placement of parentheses in mixed-mode expressions is sometimes crucial. For instance, the expression 2.5 * 12 DIV 5 + 8.2 is illegal because the multiplication must precede the DIVision and the value of 2.5 * 12 is the real number 30.0. One way to make the expression legal is to enclose 12 DIV 5 in parentheses:

$$
\begin{array}{c}
2.5 * \underline{(12\ \text{DIV}\ 5)} + 8.2 \\
\downarrow \\
\underline{2.5 * \quad 2} \qquad + 8.2 \\
\downarrow \\
\underline{5.0 \qquad\qquad + 8.2} \\
\downarrow \\
13.2
\end{array}
$$

If the subexpression 12 DIV 5 + 8.2 is enclosed in parentheses, the expression is legal and yields a different value:

$$2.5 \ * \ (\underline{12 \text{ DIV } 5} + 8.2)$$
$$\downarrow$$
$$2.5 \ * \ (\quad 2 \quad + 8.2)$$
$$\downarrow$$
$$2.5 \ * \quad \underline{\quad 10.2}$$
$$\downarrow$$
$$25.5$$

A subexpression may contain subexpressions. Consider the following example:

$$200 \text{ DIV } ((50 \text{ MOD } 17) + (9 \ * \ 5 - 1) - 30)$$

The divisor for the DIVision is the value of the subexpression enclosed in the outer pair of parentheses: (50 MOD 17) + (9 * 5 − 1) − 30. This subexpression contains the subexpressions 50 MOD 17 and 9 * 5 − 1. The evaluation of the overall expression is determined by the "nesting" levels of the subexpressions. There are two levels of nesting present in our example, as indicated in the diagram below:

$$200 \text{ DIV } ((50 \text{ MOD } 17) + (9 \ * \ 5 - 1) - 30)$$

```
           |  level 2  |     |  level 2  |
           |_____level 1_____|
```

Before the level 1 subexpression can be evaluated, both level 2 subexpressions must be evaluated. Here is the full trace of the evaluation for our example:

$$200 \text{ DIV } ((\underline{50 \text{ MOD } 17}) + (9 \ * \ 5 - 1) - 30)$$
$$\downarrow$$
$$200 \text{ DIV } (\quad 16 \quad + (\underline{9 \ * \ 5} - 1) - 30)$$
$$\downarrow$$
$$200 \text{ DIV } (\quad 16 \quad + (\underline{\ 45 \quad - 1}) - 30)$$
$$\downarrow$$
$$200 \text{ DIV } (\quad \underline{16 \quad + \quad 44} \quad - 30)$$
$$\downarrow$$
$$200 \text{ DIV } (\quad \underline{60 \quad\quad\quad\quad - 30})$$
$$\downarrow$$
$$\underline{200 \text{ DIV } \quad\quad\quad\quad\quad 30}$$
$$\downarrow$$
$$6$$

Level 2 subexpressions can contain subexpressions, which are said to be at level 3; level 3 subexpressions may contain level 4 subexpressions; and so on. In an expression that contains nested subexpressions, the subexpressions at the deepest level are evaluated first. Thus, a subexpression is not completely evaluated until every subexpression it contains has been evaluated. The two-pass procedure for evaluating an expression by using operator priorities applies only to expressions or subexpressions that contain no subexpressions and those whose subexpressions have already been evaluated.

When an expression has many levels of nested subexpressions, it can look very complicated. Complicated expressions detract from the readability of a program.

Consider the following assignment statement:

```
T := (A - (B + C) * ((D - E) / F)) / G
```

Note that the arithmetic expression in this assignment statement has three levels of nested subexpressions. Now consider the following sequence of assignment statements:

```
X := B + C;
Y := (D - E) / F;
T := (A - X * Y) / G
```

Both the original assignment statement and the sequence of assignment statements shown above will give T the same value. The price of using simpler expressions to ultimately produce the same value as one complex expression is the need to use additional variables to store intermediate results (variables X and Y in our example).

The first three statements in the program PAVINGCOST (Program 3.1) are

```
OUTERWIDTH := WIDTH + 2.0 * WALKWIDTH;
OUTERLENGTH := LENGTH + 2.0 * WALKWIDTH;
CONCRETE := OUTERLENGTH * OUTERWIDTH - LENGTH * WIDTH
```

OUTERWIDTH and OUTERLENGTH are not used anywhere else in the executable section of the program. These two variables are not needed if the expression whose value is assigned to CONCRETE contains subexpressions in place of them:

```
CONCRETE := (WIDTH + 2.0 * WALKWIDTH) * (LENGTH + 2.0 * WALKWIDTH)
            - LENGTH * WIDTH
```

This expression is somewhat complex, even though there are no subexpressions beyond the first level. The use of OUTERWIDTH and OUTERLENGTH does contribute to the readability of the program in the sense that the names of these variables support the meanings of the values of the expressions WIDTH + 2.0 * WALKWIDTH and LENGTH + 2.0 * WALKWIDTH. As a compromise, we could compute the values of these two expressions and then assign the product of the values to a variable:

```
OUTERAREA := (WIDTH + 2.0 * WALKWIDTH) * (LENGTH + 2.0 * WALKWIDTH)
```

The value of CONCRETE would then be determined by using the assignment statement

```
CONCRETE := OUTERAREA - LENGTH * WIDTH
```

A few words need to be said about the presence of parentheses in expressions. A properly formed expression will contain no unmatched parentheses; that is, there will be exactly the same number of left (opening) parentheses as there are right (closing) parentheses in the expression. For instance, the following expression is valid:

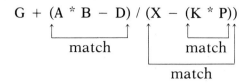

If any one of the parentheses is deleted from this expression, the result is illegal because there will be one unmatched parenthesis in the expression. For example, deleting the right parenthesis after the P leaves the left parenthesis in front of the X unmatched, as illustrated below:

$$G + (A * B - D) / (X - (K * P)$$

Parentheses used in an expression are redundant when their presence in the expression is unnecessary. Consider the following expression:

$$(A * B) / C$$

The multiplication in this expression will occur first even if the parentheses are deleted. Thus, the parentheses are redundant. Now consider a slightly more complicated expression:

$$(A * B) / (C * D)$$

The parentheses around A * B are again redundant, but the parentheses enclosing C * D are not. Suppose A, B, C, and D are REAL variables whose values are 4.0, 3.0, 2.0, and 5.0, respectively. The value of A * B / (C * D) is 1.2, as demonstrated below:

$$A * B / (C * D)$$
$$A * B / \ 10.0$$
$$12.0 \ / \ 10.0$$
$$1.2$$

However, the value of A * B / C * D is 30.0:

$$A * B / C * D$$
$$12.0 \ / C * D$$
$$6.0 \ * D$$
$$30.0$$

Enclosing A * B in parentheses will force this subexpression to be evaluated first in A * B / (C * D) and A * B / C * D, but this will not affect the values of these expressions no matter what values the variables have.

Redundant parentheses in an expression are not illegal, and in some cases they may help a reader to understand the meaning of an expression. For example, the cost of gasoline for an automobile trip can be calculated by using the formula

$$\text{GASCOST} = \left(\frac{\text{MILES}}{\text{MPG}}\right) \text{GASPRICE}$$

when the number of MILES traveled, the fuel efficiency of the automobile in miles per gallon (MPG), and the average price paid for a gallon of gasoline (GASPRICE) are known. The Pascal statement

```
GASCOST := (MILES / MPG) * GASPRICE
```

assigns the computed cost for gasoline to the variable GASPRICE. Although the parentheses enclosing the subexpression MILES / MPG can be omitted because they are redundant, they do serve a purpose. The value of the subexpression is the number of gallons of gasoline used during the trip.

STANDARD FUNCTIONS

Certain operations on data are available in Pascal through the use of mechanisms known as **standard functions.** Each standard function has a name, and that name can be used in a program to "call" the function. The form of a call to a standard function is

function-name (argument)

where *function-name* is a standard identifier for a function (see Appendix B) and the *argument* is a constant, variable, or expression whose value is of the type required by the function. A function uses the value of the argument supplied when it is called to produce another value, referred to as the **value of the function** or the **value returned by the function.** For example, the standard function named SQRT may be called to produce the square root of the number 4.0 by SQRT(4.0). In this case, the value of the function is 2.0, since 2.0 * 2.0 has the value 4.0. (It is also true that $(-2.0) * (-2.0)$ yields the value 4.0, but the SQRT function always returns the nonnegative square root of a nonnegative number.) **A call to a function is not a Pascal statement.** The call itself is an expression and the value of that expression is the value returned by the function. Thus, function calls may appear wherever expressions are allowed, even within other expressions. For instance, the statement

```
A := SQRT(4.0)
```

causes the value of SQRT(4.0) to be computed and then this value (2.0) is assigned to the variable A (assumed to be a REAL variable). A call to a function may appear in a WRITELN statement such as

```
WRITELN('THE SQUARE ROOT OF 4.0 IS', SQRT(4.0))
```

This statement will produce the following output:

```
THE SQUARE ROOT OF 4.0 IS  2.00000000E+00
```

A list of standard Pascal functions is given in Appendix C. Some of the functions that return numeric (INTEGER or REAL) values are described in Figure 3–2. Note that a call to the ABS or SQR functions produces a value of the same type as the value of the argument specified in the call. Thus, ABS(− 5.0) returns the real number 5.0 and ABS(− 5) returns the integer 5. Similarly, SQR(4.0) has the value 16.0, while SQR(4) has the value 16. Although the SQRT function accepts either an INTEGER or a REAL argument, it always returns a REAL result. For example, SQRT(4) and SQRT(4.0) both return the real number 2.0. ROUND and TRUNC are referred to as **transfer functions** because they accept an argument of one type (REAL) and return a value of another type (INTEGER). For instance, the value of ROUND(17.64) is 18 and the value of TRUNC(17.64) is 17. The ROUND function rounds a real number in the usual way. That is, the value of the argument is rounded up to the next whole number if its fractional part equals or exceeds 0.5; otherwise, ROUND returns the same value as TRUNC.

Function Call	Argument Type	Type of Result	Value of the Function
ABS*(argument)*	INTEGER or REAL	Same as the type of the argument	The absolute value of the argument
ROUND*(argument)*	REAL	INTEGER	The value of the argument rounded to the nearest whole number (an integer)
SQR*(argument)*	INTEGER or REAL	Same as the type of the argument	The square of the value of the argument
SQRT*(argument)*	INTEGER or REAL	REAL	The square root of the value of the argument (the value of the argument must be positive or zero)
TRUNC*(argument)*	REAL	INTEGER	The value of the argument truncated to a whole number

Figure 3–2
Some standard functions that return INTEGER or REAL values.

If the argument in a call to a function is an expression, the value of the expression is computed first. This is illustrated in the following example:

$$\text{SQRT}(72.0 - \underline{32.0 * 0.25})$$
$$\downarrow$$
$$\text{SQRT}(72.0 - \quad 8.0 \quad)$$
$$\downarrow$$
$$\text{SQRT}(\quad 64.0 \quad)$$
$$\downarrow$$
$$8.0$$

When the argument in a function call is an expression that contains subexpressions, each subexpression must be enclosed in a distinct pair of parentheses and the entire argument must be enclosed in parentheses. Consider the following function call:

$$\text{ROUND}(28.0 \,/\, (12.2 - 7.2)$$

This call is not valid because it does not include a unique right parenthesis for every left parenthesis. If the argument is supposed to be the expression 28.0 / (12.2 − 7.2), then ROUND is correctly called by

$$\text{ROUND}(28.0 \,/\, (12.2 - 7.2))$$

The parentheses enclosing the argument in a function call must be distinct from any parentheses within the argument.

A function call can appear anywhere in an arithmetic expression where an operand is allowed, provided that the value returned by the function does not make the expression illegal. Consider the following expression:

$$5 * \text{ABS}(15 - 22) - 9$$

The value of the argument in the call to the function ABS is evaluated first and then the remainder of the expression is evaluated:

$$5 * \text{ABS}(\underline{15 - 22}) - 9$$
$$\downarrow$$
$$5 * \underline{\text{ABS}(-7)} - 9$$
$$\downarrow$$
$$\underline{5 * \quad 7} \quad\quad - 9$$
$$\downarrow$$
$$\underline{35 \quad\quad\quad\quad - 9}$$
$$\downarrow$$
$$26$$

An expression serving as the argument for a function call may contain a call to a function. For instance, the argument for the call to the function TRUNC in the expression

$$\text{TRUNC}(\text{SQR}(2.5) + 8.3) \text{ DIV } 4$$

is the expression SQR(2.5) + 8.3. Thus, the square of 2.5 must be added to 8.3 before TRUNCation occurs:

$$\text{TRUNC(\underline{SQR(2.5)} + 8.3) DIV 4}$$
$$\downarrow$$
$$\text{TRUNC(\underline{6.25} + 8.3) DIV 4}$$
$$\downarrow$$
$$\text{TRUNC(\underline{14.55}) DIV 4}$$
$$\downarrow$$
$$\underline{14 \qquad\qquad\qquad\qquad \text{DIV 4}}$$
$$\downarrow$$
$$3$$

The simpler expression TRUNC(SQR(2.5)) has the value 6, since the value of the argument for TRUNC is 6.25. In this case, the square of 2.5 serves as the argument for a call to the function TRUNC. If the function TRUNC is called to produce the value of the argument for a call to the function SQR, then the TRUNCation occurs first. This is the case for the expression SQR(TRUNC(2.5)), the value of which is 4.

Suppose that we want to write a program that will compute the distance in miles between two towns known simply as Town A and Town B, where Town B is north and west of Town A. This can be accomplished by marking a path due west of Town A and a path due south of Town B so that the distances between the intersection of these paths and the towns can be measured (see the diagram below). The paths necessarily intersect at a 90° angle at the point labeled C in the diagram. If a and b are the distances (in miles) from point C to Towns A and B, respectively, the relationship between the distance from Town A to Town B (d in the diagram) and the distances a and b is given by the formula $d^2 = a^2 + b^2$. Thus, d is the square root of the sum of the squares of a and b:

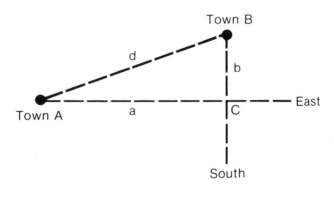

$$d = \sqrt{a^2 + b^2}$$

(This is an application of the Pythagorean theorem from plane geometry.) If the distances a and b are represented by constant identifiers A and B in our program, the sum of the squares of these distances could be assigned to the REAL variable SUMOFSQUARES using the statement

$$\text{SUMOFSQUARES := SQR(A) + SQR(B)}$$

Although the squares of A and B are computed by the SQR function in this statement, the same results can be achieved by using the statement

$$SUMOFSQUARES := A * A + B * B$$

Once the SUMOFSQUARES has been calculated, the distance between the towns can be calculated and assigned to the REAL variable DISTANCE:

$$DISTANCE := SQRT (SUMOFSQUARES)$$

The variable SUMOFSQUARES is not really needed, since the DISTANCE can be computed by using a single expression:

$$DISTANCE := SQRT(SQR(A) + SQR(B))$$

In the program TOWNDISTANCE given below, the distances from Towns A and B to the point C are set at 13.5 miles and 6.2 miles, respectively.

```
PROGRAM TOWNDISTANCE (OUTPUT);
(**************************************************************
*                                                            *
*    THIS PROGRAM WILL COMPUTE THE DISTANCE IN MILES BETWEEN TWO   *
*    TOWNS WHEN ONE OF THE TOWNS IS NORTH AND WEST OF THE OTHER ONE. *
*    IT IS ASSUMED THAT TOWN B IS NORTH AND WEST OF TOWN A AND THAT  *
*    THE DISTANCES FROM THE TWO TOWNS TO A POINT C, WHICH IS LOCATED *
*    DUE WEST OF TOWN A AND DUE SOUTH OF TOWN B, ARE KNOWN.   *
*                                                            *
***************************************************************)
CONST                          (*---------- [CONSTANTS]----------*)
      A = 13.5;                (* DISTANCE FROM TOWN A TO THE    *)
                               (* POINT C (IN MILES)             *)
      B = 6.2;                 (* DISTANCE FROM TOWN B TO THE    *)
                               (* POINT C (IN MILES)             *)
                               (*------------------------------- *)
VAR                            (*------- [REAL VARIABLES]--------*)
      DISTANCE : REAL;         (* DISTANCE FROM TOWN A TO        *)
                               (* TOWN B (IN MILES)              *)
                               (*------------------------------- *)
(**************************************************************)
BEGIN (* PROGRAM TOWNDISTANCE *)
WRITELN('THE STRAIGHT LINE PATHS FROM TOWNS A AND B INTERSECT AT A ',
        'POINT C.');
WRITELN;
WRITELN('DISTANCE (IN MILES) FROM TOWN A TO POINT C:', A);
WRITELN('DISTANCE (IN MILES) FROM TOWN B TO POINT C:', B);
WRITELN;
DISTANCE := SQRT(SQR(A) + SQR(B));
WRITELN('TOWNS A AND B ARE APPROXIMATELY', DISTANCE, ' MILES ',
        'APART.')
END (* OF PROGRAM TOWNDISTANCE *).
```

The variable DISTANCE could be eliminated from the program TOWNDISTANCE, since the expression used to compute the distance between the towns can appear in place of DISTANCE in the last WRITELN statement. If this change is made, the assignment statement should be deleted. With or without the use of the variable DISTANCE, the program produces the following output:

> THE STRAIGHT LINE PATHS FROM TOWNS A AND B INTERSECT AT POINT C.
>
> DISTANCE (IN MILES) FROM TOWN A TO POINT C: 1.35000000E+01
> DISTANCE (IN MILES) FROM TOWN B TO POINT C: 6.20000000E+01
>
> TOWNS A AND B ARE APPROXIMATELY 1.48556387E+01 MILES APART.

The value 1.48556387E+01 (or 14.8556387 in decimal notation) is only an approximation to the square root of the sum of the squares of 13.5 and 6.2. When the program is run on different computers, the computed distance may vary, depending on the precision maintained by each computer when the square root is calculated.

3.1 EXERCISES

1. Trace the evaluation of each of the following expressions. Write a program to check your answers.

   a. 9 − 65 DIV 7
   b. (9 − 65) DIV 7 + 60
   c. 9 − 65 DIV (7 + 60 MOD 26)
   d. 9 − 65 DIV ((7 + 60 MOD 26) + 40)
   e. 4 * 11 DIV 3 − 20 MOD 5 * 8 − 14
   f. (4 * 11 DIV 3 − 20) MOD (5 * 8 − 14)
   g. 4 * ((11 DIV (3 − 20 MOD 5) * 8) − 14)
   h. 4.5 * 3.0 / 0.25 − 0.75
   i. (4.5 * 3.0) / (0.25 − 0.75)
   j. 4.5 * ((3.0 / 0.25 − 0.75) − 8.25)
   k. 20.0 + 5.5 / 0.5 * 10.0 − 15.0
   l. (20.0 + 5.5) / (0.5 * 10.0 − 15.0)
   m. 20.0 + (55.0E1 / 0.5 * (10.0 − 15.0))

2. Some of the following expressions are illegal. Trace the evaluation of each expression and locate the errors:

   a. −62 DIV 27 (DIV 5 + 21)
   b. (8 − 33) DIV (8 − (26 MOD 9))
   c. 2 * (45 MOD 7 + 81) DIV 10
   d. 1195 − 9 * −25 DIV (8 * 15 + 28)
   e. (125 * (−3) − 42)(19 + 432 DIV 66)
   f. 2.5 * (120.0 − 32.5 + 75)
   g. 200.0 / (100.0 − 1E2)
   h. (1.3 * 5) DIV 6 * (9 MOD 2)
   i. 20.0 − (5.5 / (0.5 * 10.0)) + 15.0

3. Remove all the redundant parentheses from the following expressions:

   a. ((9 − (65 DIV 7) + 60) MOD 26) + 40
   b. (9 − 65) DIV (7 + (60 MOD 26 + 40))

   c. ((4 * (− 11) DIV 3) − 20) MOD (5 * 8 − 14)
   d. (4 * (− 11)) DIV 3 − (((20 MOD 5) * 8) − 14)
   e. (4.5 * 3.0) / (0.25 − 0.75) * 6.4
   f. (4.5 * ((3.0 / 0.25) − 0.75)) * (−6.4)
   g. 11.25 / ((7.2 + 8.4) * (194.7 − (1.5 * 8.2)))
   h. 3.16 * (9.0 * (0.35 / (7.0 / 0.3)))

4. Insert the minimum number of parentheses needed in the expression

   22 + 16 * 100 MOD 12 − 25 DIV 4

   to have the operations occur in the sequences indicated below:

Sequence of Operations

	1st	2nd	3rd	4th	5th
a.	+	MOD	*	DIV	−
b.	DIV	−	MOD	+	*
c.	−	MOD	DIV	*	+

5. Insert the minimum number of parentheses needed in the expression

   16.4 − 51.0 / 4.8 * 0.6 + 74.92

   to have the operations occur in the sequences indicated below:

	1st	2nd	3rd	4th
a.	−	+	*	/
b.	*	+	/	−
c.	/	−	+	*

6. Find the value of each of the following functions:

   a. ABS(5 − 25 MOD 9)
   b. ROUND(18.0 / 5.0 − 1.3)
   c. SQR(1.2)
   d. SQRT(25 − 9)
   e. TRUNC(18.0 / 5.0 − 1.3)
   f. ROUND(ABS(7.4 − 10.0)
   g. ABS(ROUND(3.6) − TRUNC(3.6))
   h. ABS(18.0) / (5.0 − 1.3)
   i. ROUND(2.0 * (5.5 − 8.9))
   j. SQR(14 DIV 4 * 3)
   k. SQRT(0.9 * 1.1 − 0.35)
   l. TRUNC(2.0 * (− 3.4))
   m. SQR(2.0 + SQRT(100))
   n. SQR(SQR(3))

7. Some of the following expressions are valid and some are invalid. Trace the evaluation of each expression and find the errors (if any).

   a. 2.8 * 0.7 − ABS(− 10.5 * 3.0 / 5.0)
   b. SQR(2.0 * SQRT(2 * 81 MOD 42))
   c. ((18.5 − 6.2) + 5) MOD TRUNC(4.2 * 0.5)
   d. (8 + TRUNC((4.8 − 2.5) * 2.0)) DIV 3
   e. 75.0 / SQRT(4.5 * 6 − 2) * ROUND(32.0 / 5.0)
   f. 24 DIV (9 / 4.0) − SQR(50 MOD 8)
   g. ABS(ROUND(34 / 10) − ROUND(5.2 * 8)

8. The functions TRUNC and ROUND are supposed to be called with REAL type arguments. Investigate what happens if these functions are called with INTEGER-valued arguments by running some test programs. Can INTEGER type arguments be used in calls to the TRUNC and ROUND functions?

3.2
BOOLEAN EXPRESSIONS

In addition to the data types INTEGER, REAL, and CHAR, there is another standard data type in Pascal, which is termed BOOLEAN. There are only two BOOLEAN data constants and they are represented by the standard identifiers TRUE and FALSE. BOOLEAN type variables may be declared in a variable declaration that takes the form

list-of-variables : BOOLEAN;

For example,

DONE, START : BOOLEAN;

Like all variables in Pascal, BOOLEAN variables do not have values until they are assigned values. The variables DONE and START shown in the variable declaration above can be assigned only TRUE or FALSE values. When the statements

DONE := TRUE;
START := FALSE

are executed, values are assigned to DONE and START as depicted below:

TRUE	FALSE
DONE	START

Pascal provides various operators that can be used to construct expressions that yield BOOLEAN values. Any expression whose value is either TRUE or FALSE is known as a **BOOLEAN expression.** The value of a BOOLEAN expression can be assigned to a BOOLEAN variable by using an assignment statement of the form

BOOLEAN-variable := BOOLEAN-expression

A BOOLEAN constant, variable, or expression can also appear in a WRITELN statement. For instance, the statement

WRITELN(TRUE, FALSE)

will print the constants TRUE and FALSE in consecutive fields on one line. If the standard field width used in printing a BOOLEAN value is ten, the output produced by the WRITELN statement given above will look like this:

■■■■■■TRUE■■■■■FALSE

If DONE and START are BOOLEAN variables whose values are TRUE and FALSE, respectively, then the statement

WRITELN(DONE, START)

will produce exactly the same output as the previous WRITELN statement.

In this section we will consider the operators used to generate BOOLEAN values in expressions and how to form BOOLEAN expressions. An expression that has a BOOLEAN value is useful for decision-making purposes in a program, since that value represents one of two logical states. In Chapter Five we will see that BOOLEAN expressions can be used to place conditions on the execution of a statement, thereby enabling a program to "skip" a statement or choose between two alternative statements. For now, we will be concerned only with the formation of valid BOOLEAN expressions.

RELATIONAL OPERATIONS

In mathematics, any two numbers are comparable in the sense that one of the numbers is always less than or equal to the other number. Furthermore, neither a smallest number nor a largest number exists. In Pascal, both integers and real numbers are limited in magnitude, but the same ordering of numbers is maintained. The INTEGER constants may range from $-$MAXINT to MAXINT, inclusive, in the ordered sequence shown below:

$$-\text{MAXINT}, -\text{MAXINT} + 1, \ldots, -3, -2, -1, 0, 1, 2, 3, \ldots, \text{MAXINT}$$

Suppose that n and m are two integers in this sequence. If n is equal to m, or if n is to the left of m in the sequence, then n is said to be less than or equal to m. If n and m are different integers (not equal), then either n is less than m or m is less than n. For instance, -3 is less than 2, 3 is less than MAXINT, 234 is less than 576, and -56 is less than -7. If m is to the right of n in the ordered sequence, then we say that m is greater than n. Thus 2 is greater than -3, MAXINT is greater than 3, 576 is greater than 234, and -7 is greater than -56. The REAL constants are ordered in a similar fashion. For example, 2.35 is less than 2.542, -5.0 is less than 2.5, 256.75 is greater than 119.0, and -16.3 is greater than -23.64.

In Pascal, an order relationship between two integers or two real numbers is expressed by using a **relational operator.** For instance, the symbol "<" is a relational operator meaning "less than" that can appear between two operands to express an order relationship between the operands, such as 7 < 12. An expression containing one relational operator is termed a **relational expression** or a **simple BOOLEAN expression** and its value is either TRUE or FALSE. The relational expression 7 < 12 has the value TRUE because 7 is less than 12, but the expression 23 < 15 is FALSE since 23 is not less than 15. There are six relational operators in all. Those operators and their meanings are shown in Figure 3–3. A relational expression is TRUE if it gives a correct order relationship between the values of two operands; otherwise it is FALSE. Here are some examples of relational expressions and their values:

Relational Expression	Value of the Expression	Relational Expression	Value of the Expression
$-17 < 8$	TRUE	22.3 > 22.4	FALSE
3.8 >= -9.0	TRUE	125 <> 384	TRUE
11 = 111	FALSE	30.25 <= 3.025	FALSE
8950 > 12752	FALSE	-127.4 <= -75.0	TRUE

Relational Operator	Meaning
<	"is less than"
<=	"is less than or equal to" or "is not greater than"
>	"is greater than"
>=	"is greater than or equal to" or "is not less than"
=	"is equal to" or "equals"
<>	"is not equal to" or "does not equal"

Figure 3–3
The Pascal relational operators.

The CHAR data type is ordered by a one-to-one correspondence between the character set and a subset of the nonnegative integers. By that correspondence, each character is associated with a unique nonnegative integer termed the **ordinal** of the character. Two CHAR values are compared based on their ordinals. The diagram below illustrates the correspondence that exists between the printable characters in the full ASCII character set and integer ordinals ranging from 32 to 126. (Ordinals for the ASCII characters actually range from 0 to 127, inclusive, but the first 31 characters and the character whose ordinal is 127 are unprintable control characters.)

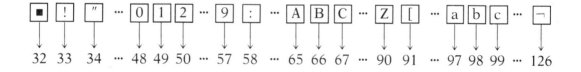

The relational expression '2' < 'B' has the value TRUE for the ASCII character set because the ordinal of '2' is less than the ordinal of 'B'. Similarly, '[' > '!' is TRUE, 'A' < ':' is FALSE, and '■' > 'Z' is FALSE.

Unfortunately, the ordinals associated with CHAR values depend on the character set in use. Ordinals for the EBCDIC character set range from 0 to 255, inclusive, with the first printable character (the blank space character) having ordinal 40 and the last printable character ('9') having ordinal 249. By listing the characters in a character set from left to right in order of increasing ordinals, we get the **collating sequence** for the character set. Three different collating sequences are shown in Figure 3–4. Characters not used in this book have been omitted from these collating sequences. (See Appendix A for a complete list of the ordinals for characters in the ASCII and EBCDIC character sets as well as an ASCII subset with CDC's ordering.) Note that each digit character is less than every capital letter in the ASCII character set (even with CDC's ordering), but the reverse is true for the same characters in the EBCDIC character set. Here are some examples of relational expressions with CHAR type operands and the values the expressions have according to the three orderings given in Figure 3–4:

Relational Expression	ASCII	EBCDIC	ASCII Subset CDC Ordering
'A' < 'Z'	TRUE	TRUE	TRUE
'7' > 'C'	FALSE	TRUE	TRUE
'■' < 'T'	TRUE	TRUE	FALSE
'<' > '&'	TRUE	FALSE	TRUE
'1' <= '9'	TRUE	TRUE	TRUE
'$' >= '/'	FALSE	FALSE	TRUE
'=' < '+'	FALSE	FALSE	FALSE

ASCII Ordering

■!"#$%&'()* + , − ./0123456789:;<=>?@ABCDEFGHIJKLMNOPQRSTUVWX
YZ[\]_↑

EBCDIC Ordering

■.<(+&!$*);−/,%_>?:#@'="ABCDEFGHIJKLMNOPQRSTUVWXYZ0123456
789

CDC's Ordering for an ASCII Subset (see Appendix A)

ABCDEFGHIJKLMNOPQRSTUVWXYZ0123456789+ − */()$ = ■,.#[]:"_!&'?<
>@\↑;

Figure 3–4
*Three collating sequences restricted to the 64 characters
shown in Figure 2–2. (The characters [,], \, and ↑ are
nonstandard EBCDIC characters. Also, % is not available in
this CDC ASCII subset.)*

The standard function ORD can be called to produce the ordinal for a CHAR value. Of course, the value returned by a call to ORD depends on the collating sequence for the character set. For example, ORD('A') has the value 65 if the ASCII ordering applies, 193 if the EBCDIC ordering is used, or 1 if CDC's ordering for an ASCII subset is in force. If *char1* and *char2* are CHAR constants, variables, or expressions, the order relationship between the values of *char1* and *char2* will always be the same as the order relationship between the integers ORD*(char1)* and ORD*(char2)*. For instance, 'A' < '1' is TRUE if and only if ORD('A') < ORD('1') is TRUE. Here are a few relationships that hold in all implementations of Pascal:

1. The digits 0 through 9 appear consecutively in the collating sequence so that '0' is less than '1', '1' is less than '2', and so on.
2. The uppercase letters may not appear consecutively in the collating sequence, but they are ordered so that 'A' is less than 'B', 'B' is less than 'C', and so on.
3. The lowercase letters (if available) may not appear consecutively in the collating sequence, but they are ordered so that 'a' is less than 'b', 'b' is less than 'c', and so on.

The data types INTEGER and CHAR are known as **ordinal data types** because their orderings are defined in terms of the ordering for integers. Any expression having an ordinal type value can be used as the argument for a call to the function ORD. If ORD is called with an INTEGER-valued argument, then that same value is returned as its ordinal. For instance, ORD(28) returns the integer 28 and ORD(-9) has the value -9. When ORD is called with a CHAR-valued argument, it produces a nonnegative integer (the ordinal of the CHAR value). The BOOLEAN data type is also an ordinal data type. In fact, ORD(FALSE) is 0 and ORD(TRUE) is 1, so that FALSE is less than TRUE.

There are four standard functions that return values according to the ordering for ordinal data types. They are described in Figure 3–5. The functions ORD and CHR are inverses of one another with respect to CHAR data. For example, ORD('B') is 66 (assuming the ASCII ordering), and so CHR(66) returns the CHAR value 'B'. Regardless of the ordering for CHAR data, CHR(ORD('B')) returns the value 'B' or, more generally, CHR(ORD(*ch*)) returns the value of *ch*, where *ch* represents any CHAR-valued expression. The argument for a call to the function CHR should have a nonnegative integer value not exceeding the largest ordinal for the character set. If x is a value in an ordinal data type, then PRED(x), x, and SUCC(x) are consecutive values of the same type (assuming that PRED(X) and SUCC(x) both exist). For instance, PRED(10) is 9 and SUCC(10) is 11. Also, PRED(MAXINT) returns the value of MAXINT $-$ 1, but SUCC(MAXINT) is not valid because there are no INTEGER type values larger than MAXINT. The values

Function Call	Argument Type	Type of Result	Value of the Function
ORD*(argument)*	Any ordinal type	INTEGER	The ordinal corresponding to the value of the argument
CHR*(argument)*	INTEGER	CHAR	The character whose ordinal is the value of the argument
PRED*(argument)*	Any ordinal type	Same as the argument type	The ordered predecessor of the value of the argument (if it exists)
SUCC*(argument)*	Any ordinal type	Same as the argument type	The ordered successor of the value of the argument (if it exists)

Figure 3–5
Standard functions that use the ordering for ordinal type data.

of PRED('*') and SUCC('*') depend on the ordering for the character set. Here are some possibilities:

	PRED('*')	SUCC('*')
ASCII Ordering	')'	'+'
EBCDIC Ordering	'$'	')'
CDC's Ordering for an ASCII Subset	'−'	'/'

The BOOLEAN values are ordered so that PRED(TRUE) is FALSE and SUCC(FALSE) is TRUE. Both SUCC(TRUE) and PRED(FALSE) are invalid because TRUE has no successor and FALSE has no predecessor. If *val* is any value in an ordinal data type, then PRED(SUCC*(val)*) is *val* provided that SUCC*(val)* exists, and SUCC(PRED*(val)*) is *val* if PRED*(val)* exists. For instance, PRED(SUCC('H')) and SUCC(PRED('H')) both yield the CHAR value 'H'.

Consider the following program:

```
PROGRAM ORDERING (OUTPUT);
CONST
        CH1 = '4';
        CH2 = 'T';
BEGIN (* PROGRAM ORDERING *)
WRITELN('ORD(''', CH1, ''') =', ORD(CH1));
WRITELN('PRED(''', CH1, ''') = ''', PRED(CH1), '''');
WRITELN('SUCC(''', CH1, ''') = ''', SUCC(CH1), '''');
WRITELN;
WRITELN('ORD(''', CH2, ''') =', ORD(CH2));
WRITELN('PRED(''', CH2, ''') = ''', PRED(CH2), '''');
WRITELN('SUCC(''', CH2, ''') = ''', SUCC(CH2), '''');
WRITELN;
WRITELN('''', CH1, ''' < ''', CH2, ''' IS', CH1 < CH2)
END (* OF PROGRAM ORDERING *).
```

The program ORDERING will produce output that exhibits the order relationship between the CHAR values '4' and 'T' and the relative positions of these characters in the collating sequence. If this program is run on a computer system that uses the ASCII ordering for characters, the output will look like this:

```
ORD('4') =           52
PRED('4') = '3'
SUCC('4') = '5'

ORD('T') =           84
PRED('T') = 'S'
SUCC('T') = 'U'

'4' < 'T' IS         TRUE
```

Note that pairs of consecutive apostrophes are used to represent single apostrophes within strings in the program so that CHAR values will be enclosed in apostrophes in the printed output. If the program ORDERING is run on a computer system that employs the EBCDIC character set, the output will be different:

```
ORD('4') =        244
PRED('4') = '3'
SUCC('4') = '5'

ORD('T') =        226
PRED('T') = 'S'
SUCC('T') = 'U'

'4' < 'T' IS     FALSE
```

Although '4' and 'T' have the same predecessors and successors in both the ASCII and EBCDIC orderings, they do not have the same ordinals in both character sets and their order of appearance in the collating sequence determined by the ASCII ordering is the reverse of their order of appearance in the EBCDIC collating sequence.

LOGICAL OPERATIONS

The logical operations known as **conjugation** (denoted by the keyword AND) and **disjunction** (denoted by the keyword OR) can be applied to BOOLEAN-valued expressions to yield a BOOLEAN result. Expressions that contain one or more logical operators are termed **compound BOOLEAN expressions.** Here are two valid compound BOOLEAN expressions:

$$(100 > 78) \text{ AND } (3.1 < -16.4)$$
$$(100 > 78) \text{ OR } (3.1 < -16.4)$$

The relational subexpressions $100 > 78$ and $3.1 < -16.4$ are evaluated first, yielding the BOOLEAN values TRUE and FALSE, respectively. Thus, the two expressions given above have the same values as the expressions

TRUE AND FALSE
TRUE OR FALSE

Values produced by the operations AND and OR are easily specified because each operand must have either the value TRUE or the value FALSE. The possible results are listed in the following truth tables.

Conjugation (AND)

Value of Operand1	Value of Operand2	Value of the Expression Operand1 AND Operand2
FALSE	FALSE	FALSE
FALSE	TRUE	FALSE
TRUE	FALSE	FALSE
TRUE	TRUE	TRUE

Disjunction (OR)

Value of Operand1	Value of Operand2	Value of the Expression Operand1 OR Operand2
FALSE	FALSE	FALSE
FALSE	TRUE	TRUE
TRUE	FALSE	TRUE
TRUE	TRUE	TRUE

From these truth tables we see that TRUE AND FALSE has the value FALSE and the expression TRUE OR FALSE yields the value TRUE. The evaluation of a compound BOOLEAN expression can be traced by using the method employed previously to trace the evaluation of an arithmetic expression. For example, the value of the expression (100 > 78) AND (3.1 < −16.4) is shown to be FALSE by the following trace:

$$(\underline{100 > 78}) \text{ AND } (3.1 < -16.4)$$
$$\downarrow$$
$$\text{TRUE} \quad \text{AND } (\underline{3.1 < -16.4})$$
$$\downarrow$$
$$\underline{\text{TRUE} \quad \text{AND} \quad \text{FALSE}}$$
$$\downarrow$$
$$\text{FALSE}$$

It can be noted from the truth tables that an AND operation produces the value TRUE only if both operands are TRUE. On the other hand, an OR operation will yield the value TRUE when one or both of the operands are TRUE. There is a third logical operation, known as **negation,** which requires only one BOOLEAN-valued operand. The negation operator is the keyword NOT. Logical negation produces the results shown in the following truth table:

Negation (NOT)

Value of the Operand	Value of the Expression NOT(Operand)
FALSE	TRUE
TRUE	FALSE

Consider the expression NOT(A > B), where A and B are INTEGER variables. If A > B is TRUE, then NOT(A > B) is FALSE. If A > B is FALSE, then NOT(A > B) yields the value TRUE. That is, NOT TRUE has the value FALSE and NOT FALSE has the value TRUE.

If an operand for a logical operation (AND, OR, or NOT) is represented by a relational expression, that expression must be enclosed in parentheses. The relational operators have the lowest priority of all Pascal operators. Thus, in an expression containing both relational and logical operators, the logical operations take precedence over the relational operations unless parentheses are used to force the evaluation of relational subexpressions. Consider the following compound BOOLEAN expression:

'C' < 'K' AND 'L' < 'P'

This expression is illegal because the AND operation must occur first and 'K' and 'L' are not valid operands for logical conjugation (they are not **BOOLEAN** values). However, the expression

('C' < 'K') AND ('L' < 'P')

is legal, since the BOOLEAN-valued subexpressions 'C' < 'K' and 'L' < 'P' must be evaluated before the AND operation occurs. Here is a trace of the evaluation of that expression:

$$('C' < 'K') \text{ AND } ('L' < 'P')$$
$$\downarrow$$
$$\text{TRUE} \quad \text{AND } ('L' < 'P')$$
$$\downarrow$$
$$\text{TRUE} \quad \text{AND} \quad \text{TRUE}$$
$$\downarrow$$
$$\text{TRUE}$$

MORE COMPLEX BOOLEAN EXPRESSIONS

Pascal expressions may contain a variety of arithmetic, relational, and logical operators. As always, subexpressions enclosed in parentheses are evaluated first, starting with the subexpressions nested deepest in the expression. When an expression free of subexpressions is evaluated, the operators are applied from left to right on a priority basis. The operators fall into four distinct priority levels, as shown in Figure 3–6. Logical negation (NOT) has the highest priority. The "high" and "low" priority levels for arithmetic operators discussed earlier in this chapter correspond to levels 2 and 3 in Figure 3–6. Note that logical conjunction (AND) has a higher priority than logical disjunction (OR).

Consider the following expression:

3 + 16 DIV 7 >= 5

Since arithmetic operations have a higher precedence than relational operations, this expression compares the value of the arithmetic expression 3 + 16 DIV 7 to the integer 5. Here is an evaluation trace:

Priority Level	Operators					
1 (highest)	NOT					
2	*	/	DIV	MOD	AND	
3	+	−	OR			
4 (lowest)	<	<=	>	>=	=	<>

Figure 3–6
Priority levels for Pascal operators.

$$3 + \underline{16 \text{ DIV } 7} <= 5$$
$$\underline{3 + \quad \downarrow \atop 2} \quad <= 5$$
$$\underline{5 \atop \downarrow} \qquad\qquad <= 5$$
$$\qquad\qquad\qquad \downarrow$$
$$\qquad\qquad\qquad \text{TRUE}$$

The expression

$$(3 + 16) \text{ DIV } 7 <= 5$$

is also valid and its value is TRUE because the arithmetic expression (3 + 16) DIV 7 has the value 2. Care must be taken to avoid forming subexpressions that make the overall expression invalid. For instance, the expression

$$3 + (16 \text{ DIV } 7 <= 5)$$

contains the valid subexpression 16 DIV 7 <= 5, but the value of that subexpression (TRUE) cannot be added to the integer 3. The error in this expression will be discovered by the Pascal compiler and flagged with an appropriate error message.

We noted earlier that relational expressions that appear as operands for a logical operation must be enclosed in parentheses, since the relational operators have the lowest priority. The expression

$$25 + 17 * 3 >= 100 \text{ OR } 36.0 / 5.0 < 6.3$$

is illegal, as we see by attempting to trace its evaluation:

$$25 + \underline{17 * 3} >= 100 \text{ OR } 36.0 / 5.0 < 6.3$$
$$25 + \quad 51 \quad >= 100 \text{ OR } \underline{36.0 / 5.0} < 6.3$$
$$\underline{25 + \quad 51} \quad >= 100 \text{ OR } \quad 7.2 \quad < 6.3$$
$$76 \qquad\qquad >= \underline{100 \text{ OR}} \qquad 7.2 \quad < 6.3$$
$$\qquad\qquad\qquad\qquad \downarrow$$
$$\qquad\qquad\qquad\qquad \text{error}$$

If the subexpressions on each side of the OR operator are enclosed in parentheses, the expression can be evaluated and is therefore valid:

$$(25 + \underline{17 * 3} >= 100) \text{ OR } (36.0 / 5.0 < 6.3)$$
$$(\underline{25 + \quad 51} \quad >= 100) \text{ OR } (36.0 / 5.0 < 6.3)$$
$$(\quad \underline{76 \qquad\qquad >= 100}) \text{ OR } (36.0 / 5.0 < 6.3)$$
$$\qquad \text{FALSE} \qquad\quad \text{OR } (\underline{36.0 / 5.0} < 6.3)$$
$$\qquad \text{FALSE} \qquad\quad \text{OR } (\quad \underline{7.2 \quad < 6.3})$$
$$\qquad \underline{\text{FALSE} \qquad\quad \text{OR} \qquad\qquad \text{FALSE}}$$
$$\qquad\qquad\qquad\qquad \downarrow$$
$$\qquad\qquad\qquad\qquad \text{FALSE}$$

Since logical negation has the highest priority of all the operations, NOT operators must be carefully positioned in BOOLEAN expressions. Consider the following expression:

$$\text{NOT } (49 <= 95) \text{ AND } (4 < -17)$$

When this expression is evaluated, the NOT operation will precede the AND operation, as illustrated below:

NOT (49 <= 95) AND (4 < -17)

NOT TRUE   AND (4 < -17)

NOT TRUE   AND   FALSE

FALSE   AND   FALSE

FALSE

It is legal to have an AND or an OR operator followed immediately by a NOT. In fact, the expression given above may be written in the equivalent form

$$(4 < -17) \text{ AND NOT } (49 <= 95)$$

because switching the order of the operands for an AND operation does not change the value of the expression. If the NOT operation should be applied after the AND operation, then the expression could be written like this:

$$\text{NOT } ((49 <= 95) \text{ AND } (4 < -17))$$

First the relational subexpressions are evaluated, then the AND operation occurs, and finally the NOT operator is applied.

It is natural to be overwhelmed at first by the complexity of the rules for constructing valid Pascal expressions. However, such rules are necessary to ensure that an expression can be interpreted in only one way. The ability to consistently construct error-free expressions is developed through practice and experience.

3.2 EXERCISES

1. Suppose A, B, C, and D are INTEGER variables whose current values are depicted below.

10	−5	5	2
A	B	C	D

Convert each of the following word expressions into an equivalent Pascal relational expression and tell the value of that expression (TRUE or FALSE).

a. B is greater than or equal to A   b. C equals 5
c. D is less than B   d. B does not equal C
e. A is greater than C   f. C is less than or equal to A

2. Determine the value of each of the following functions, if possible. If a function call is illegal, explain why. (Assume the ASCII ordinals for all CHAR values.)

a. SUCC('*')   b. ORD(TRUE)   c. CHR(74)

d. PRED(28)   e. SUCC(FALSE)   f. ORD('7')

g. CHR(32)   h. PRED(2.0)   i. SUCC(PRED('D'))

j. ORD(CHR(88))   k. CHR(ORD(')') + 5)   l. PRED('A')

3. Suppose the following variables have been declared:

```
VAR
     RV1, RV2, RV3 : REAL;
     IV1, IV2, IV3 : INTEGER;
     CH1, CH2 : CHAR;
```

Determine the value of each of the following BOOLEAN expressions if it is assumed that the variables have the indicated values.

2.4	5.92	−3.6	12
RV1	RV2	RV3	IV1

−8	5	'T'	'P'
IV2	IV3	CH1	CH2

a. (RV1 < RV2) OR (IV2 > IV3)   b. (IV1 >= IV3) AND (IV2 = 8)

c. (CH1 < CH2) OR (RV1 < 0.0)   d. (RV2 <= 6.0) AND (RV2 >= 5.0)

e. NOT (IV3 < IV2) AND (CH2 < 'X')   f. (RV1 > RV3) OR NOT (10 <= IV3)

4. Trace the evaluation of each of the following expressions and then write a program to check your answers. (Assume the ordinals for your character set.)

a. ORD('X') > ORD('P')

b. (15 + 24) MOD 5 <= 3

c. 12.2 * 0.5 < 25.0 / 8.0 + 1.3

d. 5 = ORD('8') − ORD('3')

e. 48 DIV 7 <> 48 MOD 7

f. (16.4 − 10.8) / 2.0 >= 8E−1 + 1.3

g. (−17 < 28 − 49) AND (4.3 >= 2.5)

h. (84 DIV (5 * 3) <= 100 MOD 30) OR ('N' > 'S')

i. ((4.8 + 10.6) * 2.0 > 22.6) AND NOT (60 MOD 9 < 6)

j. NOT (ORD('$') − 10 <= 25) OR (5 > ROUND(0.4 * 12.0))

k. (2E2 > 16E1) AND (76 + ORD('3') < 125) OR (CHR(66) > 'Z')

5. Find the errors (if any) in each of the following expressions:

a. 14 − 50 − CHR(45)

b. NOT ('R' < ',') OR NOT (SUCC(25 MOD 3) > 1)

c. 3.5 * 0.2 − 1.5 > (1.4 / 0.2) OR (−15 + 32) * 3 <= 54

d. 115 DIV 10 + 5 <= TRUNC(40.0 / 2.5)

e. NOT (63 / 6 > 10.0) AND (16 + ORD('T') <= 50

6. A computer can store numbers with only a limited degree of precision. Thus, many numbers are stored in some approximate form. For example, the decimal

number 0.1 is one that a computer cannot store accurately if it must represent a number in binary form. The evaluation of REAL expressions can propagate further inaccuracies. Consider the following program:

```
PROGRAM TESTEQUALITY (OUTPUT);
VAR
    S : REAL;
BEGIN (* PROGRAM TESTEQUALITY *)
S := 0.1 + 0.1 + 0.1 + 0.1 + 0.1 + 0.1 + 0.1 + 0.1 + 0.1 + 0.1;
WRITELN('S =', S);
WRITELN('AND YET, S = 1.0 IS', S = 1.0)
END (* OF PROGRAM TESTEQUALITY *).
```

Run this program on your computer. Do you get the results you expected? What seems out of place? Try summing other numbers and then compare the actual result against the value you expect to get if the arithmetic is accurate. What conclusions do you draw from having made this study?

3.3 PROGRAMMING PROBLEMS

Each of the following problems requires that a program be written. Capitalized words in the problems are suggested constant identifiers and variables. Use the data provided to test the program, and run the program with several sets of your own data as well. The program will have to be modified to accommodate each new data set. Use constant identifiers as needed to simplify program modifications.

1. An automobile will be used to travel a known distance (MILES) between two towns. Given the automobile's fuel mileage rating in miles per gallon (MPG) and the average cost of a gallon of fuel in dollars (PRICE), develop a program that will compute the expected cost of fuel (FUELCOST) for a round trip between the two towns.

Test Data	MILES	MPG	PRICE
Set #1	175	18.5	$1.40
Set #2	422	31.4	$1.52
Set #3	1395	24.0	$1.45

2. Write a program to compute an employee's net SALARY (in dollars) after taxes given the total number of hours worked (TIME), hourly RATE of pay in dollars, and the applicable federal tax rate (FTAXPCT) and state tax rate (STAXPCT). The output should include all information used to compute the net SALARY, the salary before tax deductions (GROSS), the tax amounts deducted, and the net SALARY.

Test Data	TIME	RATE	FTAXPCT	STAXPCT
Set #1	40	$5.50	16.0%	7.0%
Set #2	36	$10.65	18.0%	5.0%
Set #3	54	$7.94	15.0%	4.5%

3. Write a program that will calculate the total selling price (COST) of a QUAN-
TITY of identical items given the regular price (LISTPRICE) of a single item
and the DISCOUNT rate (percentage) that applies to the purchase. The output
should show a complete breakdown of the transaction.

Test Data	QUANTITY	LISTPRICE	DISCOUNT
Set #1	15	$18.95	20%
Set #2	120	$4.45	15%
Set #3	64	$126.50	35%

4. Write a program that will calculate the surface area (SURFACE) and the VOL-
UME of an enclosed box given its LENGTH, WIDTH, and DEPTH measured in
centimeters. (The surface area of an enclosed box is the sum of the areas of its
six faces.)

Test Data	LENGTH	WIDTH	DEPTH
Set #1	50	30	10
Set #2	125	60	35
Set #3	242	115	26

5. A vacuum cleaner company pays its salespersons a certain BASE dollar amount
each month plus a fixed BONUS for every vacuum cleaner they sell during the
month. In addition, the company pays each salesperson a COMMISSION calculated as a fixed percentage (COMRATE) of that person's total SALES (in dollars) for the month. Write a program to compute a salesperson's GROSS salary
for a month in which the QUANTITY of vacuum cleaners sold by that person
and the total dollar SALES are known. The program should output all the information used to compute the GROSS salary.

Test Data	BASE	BONUS	QUANTITY	COMRATE	SALES
Set #1	$250.00	$20.00	12	15%	$1545.00
Set #2	$325.00	$25.00	21	8%	$2438.00
Set #3	$280.00	$16.50	17	22%	$2170.50

6. The distance s in meters traveled in t seconds by a moving body that uniformly
accelerates at m meters per second per second starting from an initial velocity
of v meters per second is determined by the formula

$$s = vt + \frac{mt^2}{2}$$

Write a program to compute the DISTANCE traveled by a moving body during
a period of constant ACCELERATION for which the initial VELOCITY and
elapsed TIME (in seconds) are known.

Test Data	TIME	ACCELERATION	VELOCITY
Set #1	8.5	15.0	25.0
Set #2	16.0	4.6	10.5
Set #3	24.0	9.5	35.0

7. A publishing company must pay a certain COST (in dollars) to have a book printed and bound. The author(s) receive a fixed percentage (ROYALTY) of the WHOLESALE price for each book sold and the unsold books have a certain SALVAGE value per book. Given the NUMBER of copies of a book printed, write a program to compute the PROFIT for the company when the QUANTITY of books sold is known. The output should show all pertinent information used to calculate the PROFIT, including the total royalties paid to the author(s).

Test Data	NUMBER	COST	QUANTITY	WHOLESALE	ROYALTY	SALVAGE
Set #1	5250	$5.45	4320	$11.95	15%	$3.50
Set #2	9000	$6.80	7450	$14.25	13%	$4.30
Set #3	16500	$4.80	16500	$8.75	14%	$1.55

8. The safe load (SAFELOAD) of a rectangular beam varies jointly as the WIDTH of the BEAM and its DEPTH and inversely as the LENGTH of the beam between its supports. Write a program to calculate the safe load of a beam given the LENGTH, WIDTH, and DEPTH in inches and the constant of proportionality (KPROP).

Test Data	WIDTH	DEPTH	LENGTH	KPROP
Set #1	8.10	5.40	56.0	2.5
Set #2	3.25	2.20	115.50	1.8
Set #3	15.50	3.65	29.84	6.6

FOUR/INPUT AND OUTPUT STATEMENTS

Results produced by a program that does not contain any output statements remain hidden in the computer's memory. Consider the following program:

```
PROGRAM AVERAGE (OUTPUT);
VAR
      SCORE1, SCORE2, SCORE3, MEAN : INTEGER;
BEGIN (* PROGRAM AVERAGE *)
SCORE1 := 84;
SCORE2 := 75;
SCORE3 := 91;
MEAN := (SCORE1 + SCORE2 + SCORE3) DIV 3
END (* OF PROGRAM AVERAGE *).
```

The program AVERAGE will run error free, but it will not generate any printed record of its actions. Of course, this situation can be easily remedied by inserting one or more WRITELN statements into the program, as in the program PRINTAVERAGE shown below:

```
PROGRAM PRINTAVERAGE (OUTPUT);
VAR
      SCORE1, SCORE2, SCORE3, MEAN : INTEGER;
BEGIN (* PROGRAM PRINTAVERAGE *)
SCORE1 := 84;
SCORE2 := 75;
SCORE3 := 91;
WRITELN('SCORES:', SCORE1, SCORE2, SCORE3);
MEAN := (SCORE1 + SCORE2 + SCORE3) DIV 3;
WRITELN('AVERAGE SCORE:', MEAN)
END (* OF PROGRAM PRINTAVERAGE *).
```

Each WRITELN statement copies data to the OUTPUT file (a printer or TV monitor) where it is displayed as a line of characters. The program PRINTAVERAGE produces two lines of output:

```
SCORES:         84         75         91
AVERAGE SCORE:         83
```

Printed information appearing in the OUTPUT file is spaced according to its type. The conventional field widths associated with each type of data value often cause unnecessary spaces to appear between successive values. Section 4.3 describes how to control the spacing between data values so that the output will appear in a more readable form.

The use of assignment statements to give values to variables severely limits the usefulness of a program. For instance, the program PRINTAVERAGE always computes the average of the numbers assigned to the variables SCORE1, SCORE2, and SCORE3. To change one of those numbers, we must change the appropriate assignment statement before the program is run. It is possible to construct a more general program in which the numbers to be averaged do not appear. Instead, the program will be able to get the data it needs from a data file named INPUT. Consider the following program:

```
PROGRAM AVERAGESCORE (INPUT, OUTPUT);
VAR
      SCORE1, SCORE2, SCORE3, MEAN : INTEGER;
BEGIN (* PROGRAM AVERAGESCORE *)
READ(SCORE1, SCORE2, SCORE3);
WRITELN('SCORES:', SCORE1, SCORE2, SCORE3);
MEAN := (SCORE1 + SCORE2 + SCORE3) DIV 3;
WRITELN('AVERAGE SCORE:', MEAN)
END (* OF PROGRAM AVERAGESCORE *).
```

If the program AVERAGESCORE is punched on cards, the values for the variables SCORE1, SCORE2, and SCORE3 should appear on one or more data cards at the end of the program deck (see Section 1.4). The data supplied on cards in a batch program deck constitutes the INPUT file. When a READ statement is executed, values are assigned to the variables listed in the statement from data in the INPUT file. If the program AVERAGESCORE is run on an interactive computer system, the contents of the INPUT file is made up of data entered at a keyboard terminal by the program user during the execution of the program. In any case, no modification of the program AVERAGESCORE is necessary to account for particular values that the variables SCORE1, SCORE2, and SCORE3 will be assigned.

Note that the standard identifier INPUT appears along with OUTPUT in the heading for the program AVERAGESCORE. In many versions of Pascal, the word INPUT must appear in the program heading if the program READs any data from the INPUT file. Therefore, the file name INPUT is included in the program headings for all the programs in this book that use the INPUT file. Versions of Pascal that do not specifically require the presence of the identifiers INPUT and OUTPUT in the program heading also do not object to their presence in the program heading.

4.1
BATCH INPUT

The structure of the INPUT file for interactive programs is easier to understand once use of the INPUT file by batch programs has been explained. All the data to be included in the INPUT file for a batch program must appear on data cards in the program deck. This means that the contents of the INPUT file for a batch program is completely established prior to the execution of the program. Such is not the case for interactive programs.

The INPUT file is called a **text file** because it is composed of lines of characters, like the information on this page. However, the characters in the INPUT file are arranged in one continuous sequence with the end of each line marked by a special character referred to as a **line-separator** and the end of the file denoted by an **end-of-file-mark.** As a notational convenience in this book, the symbol "‖" is used to denote the presence of a line-separator and the symbol "●" is used as an end-of-file mark whenever a portion of the INPUT file is illustrated.

Suppose that a batch program deck contains three data cards arranged in the following order:

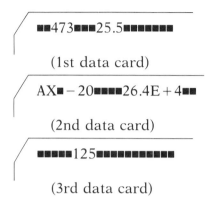

■■473■■■25.5■■■■■■■■

(1st data card)

AX■ − 20■■■■26.4E + 4■■

(2nd data card)

■■■■■125■■■■■■■■■■■■

(3rd data card)

Portions of the data cards not shown above are assumed to be blank. The characters on these cards go into the INPUT file in card sequence with line-separators placed between the characters taken from each card. Some or all of the blank spaces on a card that appear to the right of the last nonblank character may not be included in the INPUT file line that represents the card. For example, some computer systems will keep only enough of the trailing blank spaces on a card to assure that every line in the INPUT file contains an even number of characters. This convention is assumed whenever a portion of the INPUT file is depicted in this book. For instance, the contents of the INPUT file constructed from the three data cards just shown looks like this:

■■473■■■25.5‖AX■ − 20■■■■26.4E + 4■‖■■■■■125‖●

↑

The arrow shown below the simulated INPUT file represents the "INPUT pointer," which keeps track of the leftmost character in the file that has not yet been read. When the contents of the INPUT file is initially established, the INPUT pointer is positioned at the first character in the file. READing data from the file advances the pointer to the right (relative to the diagram above). It is possible that a READ will leave the file pointer positioned at a line-separator or the end-of-file mark.

THE READ STATEMENT

A READ statement must contain a list of one or more variables, as illustrated in Figure 4–1. Consecutive variables are separated by a comma and the entire list must be enclosed in parentheses. When a READ statement is executed, each variable in turn from left to right in the list is assigned the next value available in the INPUT file.

READ(*variable-1, variable-2, . . . , variable-k*)

Figure 4–1
General form of the READ statement.

Let A, B, and N be variables declared as follows:

```
VAR
     A, B : REAL;
     N : INTEGER;
```

Suppose that the INPUT file contains exactly one line of data:

$$\boxed{■18.5■■■■ - 128.36■■75■■■0.625\|●}$$
↑

When an INTEGER or REAL value is read from the INPUT file, blank spaces preceding the number (if any) are ignored. After the number has been read, the INPUT pointer is positioned at the character immediately following the last digit in the number. If the statement

$$\text{READ(A, B, N)}$$

is executed when the status of the INPUT file is as shown above, the variables A, B, and N are assigned the values 18.5, − 128.36, and 75, respectively. The diagrams given below trace the READing process by showing the status of the INPUT file before and after each value is read.

A	B	N	$■18.5■■■■ - 128.36■■75■■■0.625\|●$
			↑
18.5			$■18.5■■■■ - 128.36■■75■■■0.625\|●$
A	B	N	↑
18.5	− 128.36		$■18.5■■■■ - 128.36■■75■■■0.625\|●$
A	B	N	↑
18.5	− 128.36	75	$■18.5■■■■ - 128.36■■75■■■0.625\|●$
A	B	N	↑

It is necessary that consecutive numbers in the INPUT file be separated by one or more blank spaces so that the end of one number and the start of the next number can be determined by the computer. The movement of the INPUT pointer always progresses toward the end of the file. Thus, it is not possible to READ any value from the INPUT file more than once during the run of a program.

READ statements may contain a combination of REAL, INTEGER, and CHAR variables, but BOOLEAN variables are not allowed. A data value read from the INPUT file must be of the same type as the variable to which it is assigned, except that the value read for a REAL variable may appear as an integer. Suppose that the initial status of the INPUT file is

$$\boxed{■■■18.5■■■ - 128■75■\|●}$$
↑

If the statement

READ(A, B, N)

is executed, the values assigned to A, B, and N and the status of the INPUT file will be as shown below when the READing is finished.

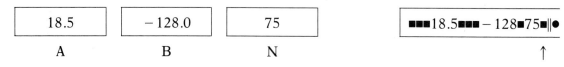

If the statement

READ(N, A, B)

is used instead of the one shown above, then an execution error will result when the program attempts to read a value for A. To understand why an error occurs, consider the status of the INPUT file just after the value for N has been read:

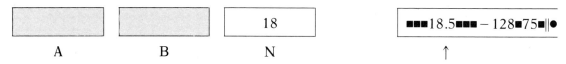

The INPUT pointer is positioned at a period (or decimal point) immediately after the integer 18 has been assigned to N. Since the next variable for which a value must be read is a REAL variable, it is necessary that the next nonblank character in the INPUT file be a sign (+ or −) or a digit. Execution of the program will terminate when an "unexpected character" (such as the period in our example) is encountered during a READ.

A program may contain many READ statements. Consider the following shell of a program that has three READ statements:

```
PROGRAM X (INPUT, OUTPUT);
VAR
     P, Q, R : REAL;
     M, N, K : INTEGER;
BEGIN (* PROGRAM X *)
     .
     .
     .
READ(M, P, N);
     .
     .
     .
READ(K);
     .
     .
     .
READ(Q, R);
     .
     .
     .
END (* OF PROGRAM X *).
```

Suppose that program X is run as a batch program with three data cards so that the initial status of the INPUT file is

863■■ − 42.064‖■■■ − 67■■7■1.25E + 3■‖2.83■■■2509■‖●
↑

Each READ statement gets data from the INPUT file starting at the position of the INPUT pointer following the previous READ (if any). If a line-separator is encountered while a number is being read, it is treated as a blank space. The following diagrams show how the three READs in program X assign values to variables:

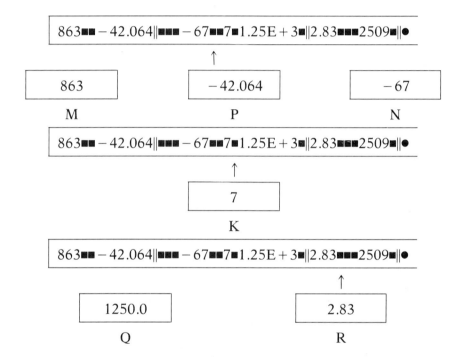

Note that the INPUT pointer has not reached the end-of-file mark when the execution of program X ends. A program need not READ any data from the INPUT file even if there are data available to be read. Normally, the data in the INPUT file are there for a reason and they will all be read by the program at the appropriate times. If the INPUT pointer ever reaches the end-of-file mark, it can be advanced no farther. An **end-of-file condition** exists when the INPUT pointer is at the end-of-file mark and any further attempt to READ from that file will cause an "attempt to read past end of file" error, which terminates execution of the program. Pascal provides two standard functions that produce BOOLEAN values indicating whether or not the INPUT file pointer is positioned at a line-separator or an end-of-file mark. The names of these functions are EOLN (for End Of LiNe) and EOF (for End Of File). Figure 4–2 summarizes the meanings of the values produced by the EOLN and EOF functions with respect to the status of the INPUT file. When either EOLN or EOF is called, the name of a file must appear as an argument; otherwise (i.e., if no file is specified), INPUT is assumed. (In Chapter Ten, the use of EOLN and EOF to determine the status of files other than INPUT is discussed.)

Function Call	Value of the Function
EOLN(INPUT) or EOLN	TRUE if the INPUT pointer is positioned at a line-separator; FALSE otherwise
EOF(INPUT) or EOF	TRUE if the INPUT pointer is positioned at an end-of-file mark; FALSE otherwise

Figure 4–2
*The standard functions EOLN and EOF as applied to the
INPUT file.*

Consider the following program segment in which A is a REAL variable, N is an INTEGER variable, and CH is a CHAR variable:

```
READ(A);
WRITELN('END OF INPUT LINE:', EOLN, '   END OF INPUT FILE:', EOF);
WRITELN;
READ(N);
WRITELN('N =', N);
WRITELN('END OF INPUT LINE:', EOLN, '   END OF INPUT FILE:', EOF);
WRITELN;
READ(CH);
WRITELN('CH =', CH);
WRITELN('END OF INPUT FILE:', EOF)
```

Suppose that the unread portion of the INPUT file looks like this when the foregoing program segment is executed:

■■1.6■‖■■4571‖●
↑

The following diagrams show the status of the INPUT file immediately after each READ statement has been executed:

1.6			■■1.6■‖■■4571‖●
A	N	CH	↑
1.6	4571		■■1.6■‖■■4571‖●
A	N	CH	↑
1.6	4571	'■'	■■1.6■‖■■4571‖●
A	N	CH	↑

Since the INPUT pointer is at a line-separator when the value for the CHAR variable CH is read, CH is assigned a blank space. The program segment produces the following output:

```
A =  1.60000000E+00
END OF INPUT LINE:       FALSE    END OF INPUT FILE:       FALSE

N =        4571
END OF INPUT LINE:       TRUE     END OF INPUT FILE:       FALSE

CH =
END OF INPUT FILE:       TRUE
```

When a CHAR value must be read from the INPUT file, the value assigned to the CHAR variable is the character at which the INPUT pointer is positioned when the READ is attempted (assuming that the INPUT pointer is not at the end-of-file mark). Thus, the INPUT pointer is advanced one character after each CHAR value has been read. Suppose that CH1 and CH2 are CHAR variables and N is an INTEGER variable. The statement

$$\text{READ(CH1, CH2, N)}$$

will READ two CHAR values and then an integer. Assume that this READing occurs when the status of the INPUT file is as shown below:

$$\underline{X\blacksquare23\|364\blacksquare50.5\|\blacksquare\blacksquare-9}$$
$$\uparrow$$

The status of the INPUT file and the values of the variables after the READ statement has been executed are as follows:

'X'	'■'	23	$\underline{X\blacksquare23\|364\blacksquare50.5\|\blacksquare\blacksquare-9}$
CH1	CH2	N	↑

If the same READ statement is executed again, two more characters and an integer are read:

'■'	'3'	64	$\underline{X\blacksquare23\|364\blacksquare50.5\|\blacksquare\blacksquare-9}$
CH1	CH2	N	↑

Needless to say, the data placed in the INPUT file must be arranged very carefully when both numbers and characters are read by the same statement. If an inappropriate character is encountered in the INPUT file when a number is being read, program execution is immediately terminated.

THE READLN STATEMENT

The READLN (pronounced "read line") statement (Figure 4–3) is an extension of the READ statement. Like a READ statement, a READLN statement may contain a list of variables; on the other hand, it may consist solely of the word READLN. Variables listed in a READLN statement are assigned values from the INPUT file in the manner of a READ. The difference between a READ and a READLN is that a READLN positions the INPUT pointer at the beginning of a new line in the file **after** the variables listed in the statement (if any) have been assigned values.

> READLN*(variable-1, variable-2, . . . , variable-k)*

Figure 4–3
General form of the READLN statement.

Suppose the following declarations are made in a program:

```
VAR
      MX, COUNT : INTEGER;
      DEV : REAL;
      P, Q, R, S : CHAR;
```

Assume that the initial status of the INPUT file is as shown below:

> 325■■ − 16.3X■‖*74■■19905‖●
> ↑

The statement

> READ(MX, DEV, P)

gets values for the variables MX, DEV, and P from the INPUT file and leaves the INPUT pointer positioned immediately after the last value read. Here are the values of the variables and the status of the INPUT file after the READ is completed:

325	− 16.3	'X'	325■■ − 16.3X■‖*74■■19905‖●
MX	DEV	P	↑

But suppose the statement

> READLN(MX, DEV, P)

is used to read values for MX, DEV, and P instead of a READ statement. The same values are assigned to the variables, but the READLN statement leaves the INPUT pointer positioned just beyond the next line-separator after the last value read from the file:

> 325■■ − 16.3X■‖*74■■19905‖●
> ↑

Characters skipped when a READLN adjusts the INPUT pointer to the first character of a new line are simply not used. After a READLN statement has been executed, the next input statement (READ or READLN) begins reading data at the start of a new line.

A READLN statement without a list of variables may be used to move the INPUT pointer to the start of a new line. In fact, any READLN statement that contains a list of variables can be replaced by a READ statement containing the same variables followed by a READLN statement without a list of variables. For example, the statement

> READLN(MX, DEV, P)

is equivalent to the pair of statements

```
READ(MX, DEV, P);
READLN
```

Suppose the status of the INPUT file is

325■■ − 16.3X■ ‖ *74■■19905 ‖●
↑

when the following sequence of statements is executed:

```
READLN;
READ(P, MX, DEV)
```

The READLN statement positions the INPUT pointer at the first character of a new line without reading any data:

325■■ − 16.3X■ ‖ *74■■19905 ‖●
            ↑

Thus, the READ statement produces the effects illustrated below:

'*'	74	19905.0	325■■ − 16.3X■ ‖ *74■■19905 ‖●
P	MX	DEV	

                                                       ↑

Again, suppose the status of the INPUT file is

325■■ − 16.3X■ ‖ *74■■19905 ‖●
↑

and this time consider the effects of the statement

```
READ(MX, DEV, P, Q, R, S, COUNT)
```

The values assigned to the variables are illustrated below:

325	− 16.3	74	'X'	'■'	'■'	'*'
MX	DEV	COUNT	P	Q	R	S

After the READing of values for the variables has been completed, the INPUT file looks like this:

325■■ − 16.3X■ ‖ *74■■19905 ‖●
                   ↑

If the statement

```
READLN(MX, DEV, P, Q, R, S, COUNT)
```

is used in place of the READ statement with the same variable list, there is no change in the values assigned to the variables from the INPUT file. However, the

READLN statement leaves the INPUT pointer positioned at the end-of-file mark:

$$325■■-16.3X■\|\!{}^{*}74■■19905\|●$$

↑

When READLN statements are used instead of READ statements in a batch program, it is easier for users of the program to punch the data cards. Knowing that every input statement starts reading data at the beginning of a new line also facilitates coordinating and changing program input.

4.1 EXERCISES

1. The data for the INPUT file are on four data cards, as illustrated below. (The portions of each card that are not shown are assumed to be blank.)

■■ − 75.6■2■■■■■■■■■■■

(1st data card)

4920■$8■■■ − 184■■■■■

(2nd data card)

■■■■10/4■■■■■■■■■■■

(3rd data card)

■1628.293■■■■■■■■■■■

(4th data card)

a. Show what the INPUT file will look like before any data are read. (Assume that every INPUT line will contain an even number of characters or use the convention for your computer system.)

b. Assume the following declarations:

```
VAR
      KEY, KOUNT, NUM, LIMIT, PART : INTEGER;
      AVAL, BVAL, CVAL : REAL;
      MARK1, MARK2, MARK3 : CHAR;
```

Trace the following sequence of READs, showing the values assigned to the variables and the status of the INPUT file after each READ statement has been executed:

```
READ(AVAL, KEY);
READ(KOUNT, MARK1, MARK2, NUM);
READ(BVAL, LIMIT, MARK3, PART, CVAL)
```

2. Suppose that the current status of the INPUT file is

$$■24■ - 13.46T9‖16E3■■999■‖●$$
$$\uparrow$$

Also, assume the following variable declarations:

```
VAR
      DIFF, MAX : REAL;
      T1, T2, T3 : CHAR;
      LOW, HIGH : INTEGER;
```

Find the values assigned to the variables when each of the following READ statements is used to get data from the INPUT file as it is shown above and tell the status of the INPUT file after the READ has been completed. If the READing of data is interrupted by an input error, explain why.

a. READ(LOW, DIFF, T1, T2, MAX, HIGH)
b. READ(MAX, T1, HIGH, T2, LOW)
c. READ(T1, T2, LOW, DIFF, T3, HIGH)
d. READ(HIGH, T1, T2, LOW, MAX, T3, DIFF)

3. For this exercise, use the INPUT file and the variables from Exercise 1. Trace the following sequence of input statements, showing the values assigned to the variables and the status of the INPUT file after each READ or READLN statement has been executed:

```
READLN(AVAL);
READ(KEY, MARK1, MARK2, KOUNT);
READLN(BVAL, NUM);
READ(LIMIT, MARK3, CVAL)
```

4. For this exercise, use the INPUT file and the variables from Exercise 2. Find the values assigned to the variables when each of the following sequences of input statements is used to get data from the INPUT file. Also, show the status of the INPUT file after each READ or READLN statement has been executed. If the READing of data is interrupted by an input error, explain why.

a.
```
READLN(LOW, DIFF);
READ(MAX, HIGH, T1, T2)
```

b.
```
READLN;
READ(MAX, T1, LOW, HIGH)
```

c.
```
READ(MAX);
READLN(LOW, T1);
READLN(HIGH, T2, DIFF)
```

d.
```
READLN(HIGH, DIFF, T1, T2);
READLN(LOW, MAX)
```

4.2
INTERACTIVE INPUT

All the data that a batch program will READ must be in the INPUT file when the program begins execution. Just the opposite is true for an interactive program. The interactive INPUT file is initially empty. Data enter the interactive INPUT file at appropriate times **during the execution of the program.** The person sitting at the terminal (the program user) is the source for these data. When the program attempts to READ values from the INPUT file and finds that all the data previously entered into that file have already been read, it will wait for the user to type in more data.

PROGRAM REQUESTS FOR DATA

When a Pascal program is run in interactive mode, the user of the program is allowed to put data into the INPUT file while the program is being executed. If more data need to be added to the INPUT file to meet the demands of a READ or READLN statement, execution of the program is temporarily suspended until the user of the program types a new line of data and presses the "Return" key (or some equivalent key). How does the user know when the program is waiting for data? Some versions of Pascal will signal the user that the program is waiting for data by printing some character, which is termed an **input prompt.** For example, the question mark character (?) is often used as an input prompt. Consider the following program:

```
PROGRAM PERIPHERY (INPUT, OUTPUT);
VAR
      LENGTH, WIDTH, PERIMETER : REAL;
BEGIN (* PROGRAM PERIPHERY *)
READ(LENGTH, WIDTH);
PERIMETER := 2.0 * (LENGTH + WIDTH);
WRITELN('PERIMETER =', PERIMETER)
END (* OF PROGRAM PERIPHERY *).
```

If the program PERIPHERY is run on an interactive computer system that generates a question mark to prompt the user for input, the printed output displayed at the terminal may look like this:

```
?10.0 7.5
PERIMETER =   3.50000000E+01
```

The READ statement in the program causes the printing of the question mark as an input prompt because the INPUT file is initially empty and two REAL values must be read. After the user has typed the numbers 10.0 and 7.5 (and pressed the "Return" key), those numbers are available in the INPUT file and the READing is then resumed. The status of the INPUT file and the values of the variables LENGTH and WIDTH are affected in the following manner:

Execution of the READ statement begins.

☐	☐	☐
LENGTH	WIDTH	(The INPUT file is empty.)

The user responds to an input prompt by entering data at the terminal.

☐	☐	10.0■7.5‖
LENGTH	WIDTH	↑

Execution of the READ statement is completed.

10.0	7.5	10.0■7.5‖
LENGTH	WIDTH	↑

When the program PERIPHERY is executed, the person sitting at the terminal receives no information from the program concerning how much data should be entered or what type of data is needed. This problem may be complicated by the fact that some versions of Pascal do not print input prompts when data are needed for the INPUT file. To overcome these handicaps, every "silent" or prompted request for data should be preceded by the printing of a message concerning the kind and quantity of data needed in the INPUT file. The message can be generated by one or more WRITELN statements that are executed prior to the READ or READLN statement that needs additional data in the INPUT file. It is the responsibility of the programmer to make sure that such messages clearly indicate the quantity and type of data the program user must enter. Here is an example:

```
PROGRAM BOUNDARYLENGTH (INPUT, OUTPUT);
VAR
      LENGTH, WIDTH, PERIMETER : REAL;
BEGIN (* PROGRAM BOUNDARYLENGTH *)
WRITELN('THIS PROGRAM WILL COMPUTE THE PERIMETER OF A RECTANGLE.');
WRITELN('YOU MUST ENTER THE LENGTH AND WIDTH OF THE RECTANGLE NOW.');
READ(LENGTH, WIDTH);
PERIMETER := 2.0 * (LENGTH + WIDTH);
WRITELN('THE PERIMETER OF YOUR RECTANGLE IS', PERIMETER)
END (* OF PROGRAM BOUNDARYLENGTH *).
```

A typical run of the program BOUNDARYLENGTH on a computer that generates input prompts looks like this:

```
THIS PROGRAM WILL COMPUTE THE PERIMETER OF A RECTANGLE.
YOU MUST ENTER THE LENGTH AND WIDTH OF THE RECTANGLE NOW.
?10.0 7.5
THE PERIMETER OF YOUR RECTANGLE IS  3.50000000E+01
```

If the computer does not generate an input prompt, the message printed by the WRITELN statements is sufficient to prompt the user to enter the appropriate data, and the resulting output looks like this:

```
THIS PROGRAM WILL COMPUTE THE PERIMETER OF A RECTANGLE.
YOU MUST ENTER THE LENGTH AND WIDTH OF THE RECTANGLE NOW.
10.0 7.5
THE PERIMETER OF YOUR RECTANGLE IS   3.50000000E+01
```

Throughout the rest of this book, the example programs are written to be executed on an interactive computer system that generates question marks as prompts for input. The example programs can be converted into batch programs by deleting or suitably modifying the WRITELN statements that print information requesting data input. Although it makes no sense to have a batch program print a message that is designed as a request for data input, it does make sense to have the program print and identify the data after they have been read. For example, here is a modified version of the program BOUNDARYLENGTH that is suitable for a batch run:

```
PROGRAM RECTSIZE (INPUT, OUTPUT);
(*********************************************************************
*                                                                   *
*   A PROGRAM TO COMPUTE THE PERIMETER OF A RECTANGLE GIVEN ITS      *
*   LENGTH AND WIDTH                                                 *
*                                                                   *
*********************************************************************)
VAR                                 (*-------[REAL VARIABLES]--------*)
    LENGTH,                         (* LENGTH OF THE RECTANGLE       *)
    WIDTH,                          (* WIDTH OF THE RECTANGLE        *)
    PERIMETER : REAL;               (* PERIMETER OF THE RECTANGLE    *)
                                    (*-----------------------------*)
(*********************************************************************)
BEGIN (* PROGRAM RECTSIZE *)
(*** GET THE LENGTH AND WIDTH OF THE RECTANGLE ***)
READ(LENGTH, WIDTH);
WRITELN('RECTANGLE LENGTH:', LENGTH);
WRITELN('RECTANGLE WIDTH: ', WIDTH);
PERIMETER := 2.0 * (LENGTH + WIDTH);
WRITELN('THE PERIMETER OF THE RECTANGLE IS', PERIMETER)
END (* OF PROGRAM RECTSIZE *).
```

The data for the program RECTSIZE must appear on one or more data cards in the program deck. Suppose the following data card is used for a batch run of the program:

■■15.0■■6.0■■■

The output generated by the batch run of the program RECTSIZE looks like this:

```
RECTANGLE LENGTH:   1.50000000E+01
RECTANGLE WIDTH:    6.00000000E+00

THE PERIMETER OF THE RECTANGLE IS  4.20000000E+01
```

COORDINATING DATA INPUT FOR
INTERACTIVE PROGRAMS

In an interactive program, requests for data (messages appearing in WRITELN statements that request data input) must be carefully coordinated with the READing of data from the INPUT file. When the program user is prompted to enter data, every character the user types before pressing the "Return" key is entered into the INPUT file. Consider the following segment from the program BOUNDARY-LENGTH (page 109):

```
WRITELN('YOU MUST ENTER THE LENGTH AND WIDTH OF THE RECTANGLE NOW.');
READ(LENGTH, WIDTH)
```

Suppose that the program user responds to the request for a length and a width in the following manner:

```
YOU MUST ENTER THE LENGTH AND WIDTH OF THE RECTANGLE NOW.
?  15.0 8.2   ALL DONE
```

After the "Return" key has been pressed, but prior to the READing of data, the status of the INPUT file is as shown below.

```
■■15.0■8.2■■ALL■DONE‖
```
↑

In this case the extra data entered by the user do not interfere with the READing process and the program is able to compute and print the proper circumference because only the first two numbers are read. That is, the program terminates with the INPUT file looking like this:

```
■■15.0■8.2■■ALL■DONE‖
```
↑

In the last example, the excess input data had no bearing on the performance of the program, but consider what will happen if the user responds to the request for a length and a width as follows:

```
YOU MUST ENTER THE LENGTH AND WIDTH OF THE RECTANGLE NOW.
? 15.0 FEET   8.2 FEET
```

Prior to the READing of values for LENGTH and WIDTH, the INPUT file looks like this:

```
■15.0■FEET■■8.2■FEET‖
```
↑

The value 15.0 is then read and assigned to LENGTH, but an input error occurs when the letter F is encountered as the computer looks for a number to assign to WIDTH. This error will, of course, prematurely terminate execution of the program.

If the program user does not enter a sufficient amount of data to satisfy the demands of a READ statement, more data must be entered before the READing can be completed. Consider the following responses made by a user of the program BOUNDARYLENGTH:

```
YOU MUST ENTER THE LENGTH AND WIDTH OF THE RECTANGLE NOW.
?   15.0
?    8.2
```

When the user types 15.0 (with two leading blank spaces) and presses the "Return" key, the INPUT file takes the following form:

$$\boxed{\blacksquare\blacksquare15.0\|}$$
$$\uparrow$$

Then the value 15.0 is read and assigned to the variable LENGTH, leaving the INPUT file pointer positioned at a line-separator:

$$\boxed{\blacksquare\blacksquare15.0\|}$$
$$\uparrow$$

However, the same READ statement must get a value for the variable WIDTH from the INPUT file. This means that the READing is suspended again, until the user enters another number. After the 8.2 has been entered, the INPUT file looks like this:

$$\boxed{\blacksquare\blacksquare15.0\|\blacksquare\blacksquare\blacksquare8.2\|}$$
$$\uparrow$$

Now the value for WIDTH is read and the program produces the desired results.

Use of the READLN statement in interactive programs can cause some undesirable results. Consider the following program segment:

```
WRITELN('ENTER THREE TEST SCORES.');
READLN(SCORE1, SCORE2, SCORE3);
WRITELN;
WRITELN('AVERAGE OF THE SCORES:', (SCORE1 + SCORE2 + SCORE3) DIV 3)
```

Here is what happens when this segment is executed:

```
ENTER THREE TEST SCORES.
?65 87 79
?
```

It appears that the three numbers that were entered by the user do not satisfy the demands of the READLN statement. To understand why, recall that the READLN statement shown above is equivalent to the following pair of statements:

```
READ(SCORE1, SCORE2, SCORE3);
READLN
```

Thus, the values entered by the user are assigned to the variables listed in the READLN statement, but then the INPUT file pointer must be positioned at the first character of the **next line.** Immediately after the assignments to the variables have been completed, the INPUT file looks like this:

$$65\blacksquare87\blacksquare69\|$$
↑

The user is prompted to enter more data because the INPUT pointer cannot be moved to the first character of the next line until a new line of data has been entered into the INPUT file. Suppose the user (who is undoubtedly confused) types the word HELP and then presses the "Return" key. This enables completion of the READLN statement and computation of the average score:

```
ENTER THREE TEST SCORES.
?65 87 79
?HELP

AVERAGE OF THE SCORES:              77
```

The status of the INPUT file at this point is

$$65\blacksquare87\blacksquare69\|HELP\|$$
↑

If the execution of another READLN or READ statement is attempted and the first variable listed in that statement is REAL or INTEGER type, an input error will occur. In effect, the use of a READLN statement has disrupted the synchronization between input requests and user responses.

Can the use of READLN statements in interactive programs ever be beneficial? If a READLN statement contains one or more variables, then it can cause very undesirable effects, such as those mentioned earlier. However, a READLN statement without a variable list can produce some desirable results. Consider the following program segment:

```
WRITELN('ENTER TWO TEMPERATURES.');
READ(TEMP1, TEMP2);
WRITELN('WHAT TEMPERATURE SCALE APPLIES?');
WRITELN('ENTER F FOR FAHRENHEIT OR C FOR CELSIUS.');
READLN;
READ(SCALE)
```

In this segment, TEMP1 and TEMP2 are INTEGER variables and SCALE is a CHAR variable. Suppose the user's responses to the input requests made by the WRITELN statements look like this:

```
ENTER TWO TEMPERATURES.
? 72 56
WHAT TEMPERATURE SCALE APPLIES?
ENTER F FOR FAHRENHEIT OR C FOR CELSIUS.
?F
```

The effects of each input statement on the status of the INPUT file are depicted in the following diagrams:

After READ(TEMP1, TEMP2)	After READLN	After READ(SCALE)
■72■56‖	■72■56‖F■‖	■72■56‖F■‖
↑	↑	↑

Note that the letter F was entered in response to the prompt generated by the READLN statement and then SCALE was assigned the CHAR value 'F' by the next READ statement. The worth of using a READLN preceding a READ merely to prompt the user to enter input may be seen by examining the following dialogue between the program segment and the user:

```
ENTER TWO TEMPERATURES.
? 72 56 82
WHAT TEMPERATURE SCALE APPLIES?
ENTER F FOR FAHRENHEIT OR C FOR CELSIUS.
?F
```

The values 72 and 56 are assigned to TEMP1 and TEMP2, respectively, as before, and SCALE is assigned the value 'F'. What happened to the 82? The answer to this question can be found by studying the effects of the input statements on the status of the INPUT file, as illustrated in the following diagrams:

After READ(TEMP1, TEMP2)	After READLN	After READ(SCALE)
■72■56■82■‖	■72■56■82■‖F■‖	■72■56■82■‖F■‖
↑	↑	↑

After the values for TEMP1 and TEMP2 have been read, the READLN moves the INPUT pointer past all other characters on the same line. Thus, the problem segment will not accept more than two temperatures; it simply ignores all excess data appearing after the second temperature up to the end of the line.

4.2 EXERCISES

1. Suppose the following declarations have been made in a program:

```
VAR
      BITS, DAYS, WEEKS : INTEGER;
      SEED, DIFF, COST : REAL;
      SYM1, SYM2, SYM3 : CHAR;
```

The INPUT file is empty prior to the execution of a sequence of input statements that result in the input responses shown below:

```
?256■■42.5
?T13■-194.0■9
?-63*■■■483.05
```

Determine whether or not each of the following sequences of input statements could have prompted the responses shown above, and if so, what values were assigned to the variables. Show the status of the INPUT file after each statement has been executed, and if an input error would occur during the reading process, explain why.

a.
```
READ(BITS, SEED);
READ(SYM1, DAYS);
READLN(DIFF);
READ(SYM2, WEEKS, SYM3)
```

b.
```
READLN(DAYS);
READ(SYM2, SYM3, SEED, COST);
READ(WEEKS, BITS, SYM1);
READ(DIFF)
```

c.
```
READ(DAYS, COST, SYM1, SEED);
READLN(BITS, DIFF, WEEKS);
READ(SYM2, SYM3)
```

d.
```
READLN(SYM3, WEEKS, BITS, SYM1);
READLN;
READ(DIFF, SYM2, SEED)
```

2. Assume that the current status of the INPUT file is

$$243\blacksquare\blacksquare6\|22.3\|$$
$$\uparrow$$

Explain what will happen if each of the following input statements or sequences of input statements is executed next. If an input error occurs, explain why. (PT1 and PT2 are CHAR variables, SEATS is an INTEGER variable, and GAUGE is REAL.)

a.
```
READ(SEATS, GAUGE)
```

b.
```
READ(GAUGE, SEATS, PT1, PT2)
```

c.
```
READLN(PT1);
READ(SEATS, PT2, GAUGE)
```

d.
```
READLN;
READ(SEATS, PT2, GAUGE)
```

3. The status of the INPUT file is

$$1620\blacksquare19\blacksquare\|$$
$$\uparrow$$

when a WRITELN statement containing a message is executed. Then input data are requested and the response looks like this

```
ENTER THREE WHOLE NUMBERS
?485∎∎-80∎1217
```

Explain what happens if the input statement (or statements) executed after the message has been printed is

a.   READ(A, B, C)

b.   READ(A, B, C, D)

c.   READLN(A, B, C, D)

d.   READLN;
            READ(A, B, C)

e.   READ(A, B, C);
            READ(D)

f.   READLN(A);
            READ(B, C, D)

4. Consider the following program:

```
PROGRAM MISCELLANEOUS (INPUT, OUTPUT);
VAR
     NUM1, NUM2 : INTEGER;
     L1, L2, L3, L4, L5, L6 : CHAR;
BEGIN (* PROGRAM MISCELLANEOUS *)
WRITELN('ENTER A WHOLE NUMBER AND ANY THREE CHARACTERS');
READLN;
READ(NUM1, L1, L2, L3);
WRITELN('DO IT AGAIN');
READ(NUM2, L4, L5, L6);
WRITELN(NUM1, ' +', NUM2, ' =', NUM1 + NUM2);
WRITELN(L1, L2, L3, L4, L5, L6)
END (* OF PROGRAM MISCELLANEOUS *).
```

Suppose that when this program is executed, the data input proceeds as follows:

```
ENTER A WHOLE NUMBER AND ANY THREE CHARACTERS
?28■DC9
DO IT AGAIN
?■4HAT
```

What will the rest of the output look like?

4.3 OUTPUT

The WRITELN statement we have been using to print information on some output device (line printer, terminal, TV monitor, etc.) is an extension of the fundamental output statement in Pascal, the WRITE statement. It is worthwhile at this point to review what we already know about the WRITELN statement. If a WRITELN statement consists solely of the word WRITELN, it will generate one blank line of output. WRITELN may be followed by a list of items (enclosed in parentheses), where each item is a constant, variable, or expression. When such a WRITELN statement is executed, the values of the items are printed on one line. The following table summarizes the kinds of items that can appear in a WRITELN statement and the corresponding output that will be generated:

WRITELN List Item	Output
An INTEGER, REAL, CHAR, or BOOLEAN constant or constant identifier	The constant or value of the constant identifier
An INTEGER, REAL, CHAR, or BOOLEAN variable	The current value of the variable
An arithmetic or BOOLEAN expression	The value of the expression
A character string enclosed in apostrophes	The character string without the enclosing apostrophes

(There are versions of Pascal—UCSD Pascal for one—that do not allow the use of BOOLEAN constants, variables, and expressions in a WRITELN statement.)

The maximum number of characters that can be printed on one line is determined by the type of output device used. The limit on the number of characters per line is usually set at between 72 and 136. No more than the set maximum number of characters can be printed on one line. If an output line generated by a WRITELN statement contains more than the allowable number of characters, the extra characters at the end of the line **will not** be printed.

Each data value printed consumes a certain field of character positions on a line. The default length of the field depends on the type of value printed. Every version of Pascal employs a default field width for each type of data. A CHAR value is always printed in a one-character field, but the other default widths (for INTEGER, REAL, BOOLEAN, and string data) are implementation dependent. The default field widths we have been using and will continue to use in this book are given below:

Type of Output Value	Default Field Width
INTEGER	10
REAL	16 (including a leading blank space and a signed two-digit exponent)
BOOLEAN	10
CHAR	1
'string'	The length of the string

All values are printed right justified (all the way to the right) in their fields. Blank spaces will fill any unused positions in each field.

THE WRITE AND WRITELN STATEMENTS

The WRITE and WRITELN statements are both used to generate printed output. These two output statements are very similar in form, as shown in Figure 4–4.

WRITE*(item-1, item-2, . . . , item-k)*

WRITELN*(item-1, item-2, . . . , item-k)*

Figure 4-4
General forms of the WRITE and WRITELN statements.

The WRITELN statement can be used without an item list. In fact, a WRITELN statement that includes an item list is equivalent to the pair of statements

WRITE*(item-1, item-2, . . . , item-k);*
WRITELN

WRITE statements put the values of items in a "holding area" of the computer's memory referred to as a **buffer,** where the image of an output line is constructed. WRITELN statements that contain lists of items do the same thing, but after the value of the last item has been placed in the buffer, the line image in the buffer is printed.

Consider the following program, which contains both a WRITE statement and a WRITELN statement:

```
PROGRAM CIRCLEAREA (OUTPUT);
CONST
        PI = 3.14;
        RADIUS = 3.5;
VAR
        AREA : REAL;
BEGIN (* PROGRAM CIRCLEAREA *)
WRITE('RADIUS =', RADIUS);
AREA := PI * SQR(RADIUS);
WRITELN(' AREA =', AREA)
END (* OF PROGRAM CIRCLEAREA *).
```

When execution of the program CIRCLEAREA begins, the output buffer is empty. The WRITE statement stores the string 'RADIUS =' and the value RADIUS in the buffer just as they will appear when they are printed, but they are not printed yet. After the value of AREA has been computed, the WRITELN statement appends the string ' AREA =' and the value of AREA to the previous contents of the buffer and then causes all data currently in the buffer to be printed. Thus, the output produced by the program CIRCLEAREA looks like this:

```
RADIUS =  3.50000000E+00  AREA =  3.84650000E+01
```

The WRITELN statement could be replaced by the pair of statements

```
WRITE(' AREA =', AREA);
WRITELN
```

which illustrates that the printing of a line generated by a WRITELN statement occurs after the values of the items listed in that statement (if any) have been placed in the output buffer.

All output data generated by WRITE statements accumulate in the output buffer until a WRITELN statement is executed. After the execution of a WRITELN statement, the buffer is again empty and available for the construction of a new line image. Consider the following sequence of output statements:

```
WRITE('I NEVER MET');
WRITE(' A COM');
WRITELN('PUTER I DID''NT LIKE.');
WRITELN;
WRITE('HAVE ');
WRITELN('YOU?')
```

This program segment generates three lines of output:

> I NEVER MET A COMPUTER I DIDN'T LIKE.
>
> HAVE YOU?

Here is an equivalent form of the same program segment in which each WRITELN statement containing a list of items is replaced by a WRITE statement containing that list of items followed by a WRITELN statement without an item list:

```
WRITE('I NEVER MET');
WRITE(' A COM');
WRITE('PUTER I DIDN''T LIKE.');
WRITELN; (* PRINT A LINE *)
WRITELN; (* PRINT A BLANK LINE *)
WRITE('HAVE ');
WRITE('YOU?');
WRITELN   (* PRINT A LINE *)
```

The comments that appear in this segment indicate when lines are printed. Note that the output buffer is empty after the first line is printed, and so the second WRITELN statement generates a blank line of printed output.

Consider the following interactive version of the program CIRCLEAREA, which allows the user to input a value for RADIUS:

```
PROGRAM AREAOFCIRCLE (INPUT, OUTPUT);
(*******************************************************************
 *                                                                 *
 *          A PROGRAM TO CALCULATE THE AREA OF A CIRCLE            *
 *                                                                 *
 ******************************************************************)
CONST                                   (*----------[CONSTANTS]----------*)
      PI = 3.14;                        (* AN APPROXIMATION TO THE       *)
                                        (* MATHEMATICAL CONSTANT "PI"    *)
                                        (*-------------------------------*)
VAR                                     (*-------[REAL VARIABLES]--------*)
      RADIUS,                           (* THE RADIUS OF THE CIRCLE      *)
      AREA : REAL;                      (* THE AREA OF THE CIRCLE        *)
                                        (*-------------------------------*)
(*******************************************************************)
BEGIN (* PROGRAM AREAOFCIRCLE *)
WRITELN('THIS PROGRAM WILL COMPUTE THE AREA OF A CIRCLE.');
```

```
WRITELN('PLEASE ENTER THE RADIUS NOW.');
READ(RADIUS);
WRITELN;
WRITE('WITH PI =', PI, ', THE AREA OF THE ');
AREA := PI * SQR(RADIUS);
WRITELN('CIRCLE IS', AREA)
END (* OF PROGRAM AREAOFCIRCLE *).
```

Here is the output from a typical run of the program AREAOFCIRCLE; it shows that the four WRITELN statements in the program each generate one line of output:

```
THIS PROGRAM WILL COMPUTE THE AREA OF A CIRCLE.
PLEASE ENTER THE RADIUS NOW.
?3.5

WITH PI =  3.14000000E+00, THE AREA OF THE
CIRCLE IS  3.84650000E+01
```

In summary, WRITE statements are used to store data in the output buffer for later printing. When a WRITELN statement is executed, the values of the items listed in that statement (if any) are stored in the output buffer and then the entire line image recorded in the buffer is printed. Immediately after a WRITELN statement has been executed, the output buffer is empty. If it happens that the last output statement executed before a program ends is a WRITE statement, the contents of the output buffer are automatically printed, as if that statement were a WRITELN. For instance, suppose the last WRITELN statement in the program AREAOFCIRCLE is changed to a WRITE statement:

```
WRITE('CIRCLE IS', AREA)
```

This change will have no effect on the output generated by the program because the contents of the output buffer are automatically printed when the program ends if the buffer is not empty. Thus, a program always begins and ends with the output buffer empty.

FORMAT-CONTROLLED OUTPUT

An **output format** may be attached to any item appearing in a WRITE or WRITELN list. The purpose of an output format is to specify the field width to be used when the value of an item is printed. A format consists of a colon followed by an INTEGER constant, variable, or expression. Consider the following pair of output statements:

```
WRITELN('UNFORMATTED OUTPUT:', 252, 25.2);
WRITELN('FORMATTED OUTPUT:':19, 252:4, 25.2:10)
```

These two statements produce the following output:

```
UNFORMATTED■OUTPUT:■■■■■■■252■■2.52000000E+01
■■FORMATTED■OUTPUT:■252■■2.52E+01
```

The format ":19" that appears after the string 'FORMATTED OUTPUT:' specifies that the string should be printed in a field of width 19. Since the string contains only 17 characters, it is printed right justified in a 19-character field whose first two characters are blank spaces. Similarly, the constants 252 and 25.2 are printed right justified in fields of sizes four and ten, respectively. Note that the real number 25.2 is still printed in exponential form, but only two digits are shown after the decimal point so that the printed value will fit into a ten-character field with a leading blank space.

When CHAR-valued items are listed in an output statement, they are treated as character strings of length one. The minimum field width necessary to print a BOOLEAN value is either four (for TRUE) or five (for FALSE). Consider the following program:

```
PROGRAM FORMATS (INPUT, OUTPUT);
VAR
     INT1, INT2 : INTEGER;
     CH1, CH2 : CHAR;
     BVAL : BOOLEAN;
BEGIN (* PROGRAM FORMATS *)
WRITELN('ENTER TWO WHOLE NUMBERS.');
READ(INT1, INT2);
BVAL := INT1 > INT2;
WRITELN('THE EXPRESSION ':25, INT1:4, ' > ', INT2:4, ' IS ', BVAL:5);
WRITELN;
WRITELN('ENTER TWO CHARACTERS.');
READLN;
READ(CH1, CH2);
BVAL := CH1 > CH2;
WRITELN('THE EXPRESSION':24, CH1:2, ' >', CH2:2, ' IS ', BVAL:5)
END (* OF PROGRAM FORMATS *).
```

Here is the output from a typical run of the program FORMATS:

```
ENTER TWO WHOLE NUMBERS.
?37■1059
■■■■■■■■■THE■EXPRESSION■■■37■> ■1059■IS■FALSE

ENTER■TWO■CHARACTERS.
?RG
■■■■■■■■■THE■EXPRESSION■R■> ■G■IS■■TRUE
```

Note how the formats are used to control the spacing between items on an output line. Format-controlled output can be much more readable than the output produced by using the default field widths.

It is not necessary that every item appearing in an output statement be formatted. A WRITE or WRITELN statement may contain a mixture of formatted and unformatted items. Formats are used to improve the readability of program output, and sometimes the default field widths provide satisfactory formatting. The programmer should carefully plan the layout of the output for a program before the program is written.

The format for a REAL-valued item in a output list may include two field widths so that the number printed will appear in decimal notation. For example, the statement

WRITELN(23.5:7:2, 0.25:8:3, -1825.0:10:3)

produces one line of output, which looks like this:

| ■■23.50■■■0.250■-1825.000

The first field width is the overall size of the field in which the number is printed (right justified) and the second field width indicates how many digits should be shown after the decimal point. Thus, the formatted item 23.5:6:2 means that the number 23.5 should be printed in a field of size six with exactly two digits shown after the decimal point. Since the values of output items are always printed right justified in the default or specified fields, one or more blank spaces may fill out the left side of a field. When a real number is printed in decimal notation, it may only be an approximation to the actual value of a constant, variable, or expression. For instance, suppose the value of the REAL variable A is 62.4375 when the statement

WRITELN(A:10:1, A:10:2, A:10:3, A:10:4, A:10:5)

is executed. The resulting output looks like this:

| ■■■■■■62.4■■■■■62.44■■■■62.438■■■62.4375■■62.43750

The first three times the value of A is printed, it is rounded to the exact number of decimal places specified by the second field widths in the formats. Use of a second field width in a format is valid only if the item to which the format applies has a REAL value.

What happens if the value of a formatted item will not fit into a field of the size specified in the format? For example, suppose the INTEGER variable CHOICES has the value 23470 when the statement

WRITELN(CHOICES:3)

is executed. The number 23470 cannot be printed in a three-character field since it contains five digits. Usually, the field width is automatically expanded to the minimum size needed to print the value of an item if the specified or default field width is too small. In this case, the value of CHOICES would be printed in a field of size five:

| 23470

However, some versions of Pascal will hold fast to the specified or default field width and print only a part of the value of an item when the field width is not large enough to show the entire value.

A modified form of the program AREAOFCIRCLE (Program 4.8) is presented next to show how formatting can improve the appearance of program output.

```
PROGRAM AREAOFACIRCLE (INPUT, OUTPUT);
(*******************************************************************
 *                                                                 *
 *          A PROGRAM TO CALCULATE THE AREA OF A CIRCLE            *
 *                                                                 *
 *******************************************************************)
```

```
CONST                             (*---------[CONSTANTS]---------*)
     PI = 3.14;                   (* AN APPROXIMATION TO THE     *)
                                  (* MATHEMATICAL CONSTANT "PI"   *)
                                  (*-----------------------------*)
VAR                               (*------[REAL VARIABLES]-------*)
     RADIUS,                      (* THE RADIUS OF THE CIRCLE    *)
     AREA : REAL;                 (* THE AREA OF THE CIRCLE      *)
                                  (*-----------------------------*)
(*****************************************************************)
BEGIN (* PROGRAM AREAOFACIRCLE *)
WRITELN('THIS PROGRAM WILL COMPUTE THE AREA OF A CIRCLE.');
WRITELN('PLEASE ENTER THE RADIUS NOW.');
READ(RADIUS);
WRITELN;
AREA := PI * SQR(RADIUS);
WRITELN;
WRITELN('-------------------------------------':42);
WRITELN;
WRITELN('2':29);
WRITELN('AREA = PI(RADIUS)':28);
WRITELN;
WRITELN('PI':8, 'RADIUS':15, 'AREA':15);
WRITELN('******':10, '**********':15, '***********':17);
WRITELN(PI:10:3, RADIUS:15:3, AREA:17:4);
WRITELN;
WRITELN('-------------------------------------':42)
END (* OF PROGRAM AREAOFACIRCLE *).
```

Here is the output from a sample run of the program AREAOFACIRCLE:

```
THIS PROGRAM WILL COMPUTE THE AREA OF A CIRCLE.
PLEASE ENTER THE RADIUS NOW.

?12.5

        -------------------------------------

                              2
            AREA = PI(RADIUS)

          PI          RADIUS           AREA
        ******      **********      ***********
        3.140         12.500         490.6250

        -------------------------------------
```

A table like this one can be produced by a program only when the output is format controlled.

The field widths used in the examples so far are all constants. More generally, a format may appear as a colon followed by a constant, constant identifier, variable, or expression whose value is a positive integer. Suppose that N and K are INTEGER variables and X is a REAL variable. If the values of N and K are greater than zero and the value of X is greater than or equal to 1.0, then all of the following output statements are valid:

```
WRITELN('SALARY: $':N, AMOUNT:8:2)

WRITE('AMOUNT =':N + 10, AMOUNT:K:2)

WRITELN(AMOUNT:N + 10:N, DEV:K:1 + K DIV 4, KEY:TRUNC(X))
```

The values of the field widths in formats like those shown above are set during the execution of the program. This gives more flexibility to the format control, but it also adds more complexity to the program. A person reading a program in which variables and expressions containing variables are used in formats must study the program very carefully to determine the layout of the output.

Suppose OFFSET is an INTEGER variable or a constant identifier for an integer and the value of OFFSET is greater than or equal to zero. OFFSET can be used to position a table printed by a program. For instance, replace the last ten statements in the program AREAOFACIRCLE with the following sequence of statements:

```
WRITELN('----------------------------------':OFFSET + 42);
WRITELN;
WRITELN('2':OFFSET + 29);
WRITELN('AREA = PI(RADIUS)':OFFSET + 28);
WRITELN;
WRITELN('PI':OFFSET + 8, 'RADIUS':15, 'AREA':15);
WRITELN('*****':OFFSET + 10, '**********':15, '************':17);
WRITELN(PI:OFFSET + 10:3, RADIUS : 15:3, AREA:17:4);
WRITELN;
WRITELN('----------------------------------':OFFSET + 42)
```

If the value of OFFSET is zero, then the table will appear in the same position as it does when the original version of AREAOFACIRCLE is run. Suppose OFFSET has the value 10 when the table is printed. All the entries in the table will be shifted ten character positions to the right:

```
THIS PROGRAM WILL COMPUTE THE AREA OF A CIRCLE.
PLEASE ENTER THE RADIUS NOW.

?8.0

                   ----------------------------------
                                        2
                       AREA = PI(RADIUS)

             PI           RADIUS            AREA
          ******       **********      ************
          3.140          8.00           200.9600

                   ----------------------------------
```

The appearance of a program's output can be greatly enhanced by using formats in WRITE and WRITELN statements. Character strings can easily be centered on a line or spaced at uniform intervals to serve as column headings for a table. Numeric values can be aligned in specific columns and printed in either exponential or decimal notation. In short, a program can control the spacing between all output data on a line.

4.3
EXERCISES

1. The REAL variables A and E and the INTEGER variable P have the values illustrated below:

− 135.482	0.0005	425
A	E	P

Show the exact output that the following sequences of output statements will produce:

a.
```
WRITE (A:9:1, P:5);
WRITELN ('ERROR:':20, E:12)
```

b.
```
WRITELN ('A =', A:12:5);
WRITE ('P =':5, P:3, ' ':3, 'E =', E:15:2);
WRITELN (A + 3.0 * P:20:3)
```

c.
```
WRITE (P:15, P - 500:7);
WRITE (A:10);
WRITELN;
WRITE ('ERROR =':8, E:8:4);
WRITELN (' ':5, A:7:2)
```

d.
```
WRITELN ('RESULTS':18);
WRITELN;
WRITELN ('A':6, 'P':10, 'E':15);
WRITE (A:10:2, P:10);
WRITELN (' ':6, E:14)
```

2. The values of the REAL variables X and Y and the INTEGER variables T and R are as shown below:

47.8062	− 0.00438	27	− 1705
X	Y	T	R

Prepare a sequence of output statements to produce each of the following outputs:

a.
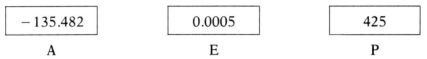
```
  ▪▪47.806▪▪▪T▪=▪27▪▪▪-1705
  ▪-4.3800E-03
```

b.
```
47.8■■■■■27
■■■■■■Y■=■-0.0044
-1705
```

c.
```
■■■■****■DATA■****
■■■■■■■27■■■■-1705
■■■■■■4.780620E+01
■■■■■-4.4E-03
```

d.
```
■VALUES:■■47.806,■-0.004,■27,■-1705
```

3. Variables N, K, C1, C2, P1, and P2 have been declared and given values as shown below:

```
VAR
    N, K : INTEGER;
    C1, C2 : CHAR;
    P1, P2 : REAL;
```

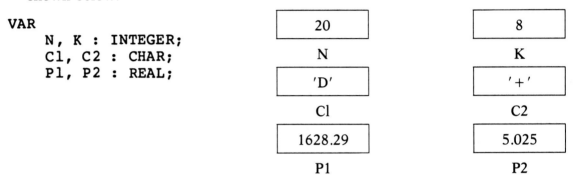

Show the exact output that the following sequences of output statements will produce:

a.
```
WRITE(P1:N:3, ' ':K, P2);
WRITELN(C2:10, C1:N DIV K);
WRITELN(N:K, K:N)
```

b.
```
WRITELN((P1 + P2)/10.0:N - 5);
WRITELN((P1 + P2)/100.0:N - 5:N MOD K);
WRITE(C1:K, C2);
WRITELN(N + K:N - K, K - N:2*K)
```

4. Assume the same variable declarations given in Exercise 3 and tell what (if anything) is wrong with each of the following output statements:

a.
```
WRITE(P2:10, 'P1 =:5', P1:16:5)
```

b.
```
WRITELN(N - M * 3:P1, C1:N, C2:4:1)
```

c.
```
WRITELN(K * P1, ROUND(P2 / P1):7, K DIV N * N)
```

d.
```
WRITE('***':K, C1:2, C2:3, :K + M, P1:52:6)
```

e.
```
WRITELN(P1,:12, K:8, '(', N:3, ')')
```

5. What is the purpose of the READLN statement in the program FORMATS (Program 4.9)? Could that READLN statement be deleted from the program? Should it be deleted from the program? Explain.

4.4
PROGRAMMING PROBLEMS

The problems in this section are basically the same as those given at the end of Chapter Three. This time, however, some of the data must be read from the INPUT file rather than assigned to variables by using assignment statements. Refer to the problem with the same number in Section 3.3 for test data. Also, use formatted output when formatting will make the output more readable.

1. The expected cost of fuel (FUELCOST) for a trip between two towns can be determined from the length of the trip (MILES), the mileage rating of the automobile (MPG), and the average cost of a gallon of fuel in dollars (PRICE). Write a program to compute the expected cost of fuel for a round trip between the two towns after reading the data necessary to compute that cost.

2. Write a program that will compute an employee's net SALARY (in dollars) after reading the total number of hours worked (TIME), the hourly RATE of pay in dollars, and the applicable federal tax rate (FTAXPCT) and state tax rate (STAXPCT). The output should include all the input data (appropriately labeled) as well as the employee's net SALARY, the salary before tax deductions (GROSS), and the tax amounts deducted.

3. Write a program that will calculate the total selling price (COST) of a QUANTITY of identical items given the regular selling price (LISTPRICE) of a single item and the DISCOUNT rate (percentage) that applies to the purchase. All data used to compute the COST should be read as input to the program. The output should show a complete breakdown of the transaction.

4. The SURFACE area of an enclosed box (the sum of the areas of its faces) can be calculated by using the dimensions of the box. Write a program that will compute the SURFACE area of a box after reading its LENGTH, WIDTH, and DEPTH measured in centimeters. The program should print the dimensions of the box and the SURFACE area appropriately labeled.

5. A vacuum cleaner company pays its salespersons a certain BASE dollar amount each month plus a fixed BONUS for every vacuum cleaner they sell during the month. In addition, the company pays each salesperson a COMMISSION calculated as a fixed percentage (COMRATE) of that person's total SALES (in dollars) for the month. Write a program to compute a salesperson's gross salary for a month. The QUANTITY of vacuum cleaners sold and the total dollar SALES for the person should be read as input. The program should output all information used to compute the GROSS salary.

6. The distance s in meters traveled in t seconds by a moving body that uniformly accelerates at m meters per second per second starting from an initial velocity of v meters per second is determined by the formula

$$s = vt + \frac{mt^2}{2}$$

Write a program to compute the DISTANCE traveled by a moving body during a period of constant ACCELERATION. The duration of the acceleration (TIME) in seconds and the initial VELOCITY of the body should be read as input.

7. A publishing company must pay a certain COST (in dollars) to have a book printed and bound. The author(s) receive a fixed percentage (ROYALTY) of the WHOLESALE price for each book sold and the unsold books have a certain SALVAGE value per book. Write a program that will read the NUMBER of copies of a book printed and the QUANTITY sold and then compute the PROFIT for the company. Also, have the program print the total royalties paid to the author(s) and all other pertinent data used to compute the company's PROFIT.

8. The safe load (SAFELOAD) of a rectangular beam varies jointly as the WIDTH of the beam and its DEPTH and inversely as the LENGTH of the beam between its supports. Write a program that will read the LENGTH, WIDTH, and DEPTH in inches as well as the constant of proportionality (KPROP) and then compute the safe load of the beam.

FIVE/CONDITIONAL CONTROL STRUCTURES

In all the programs we have constructed up to this point, the order in which the statements are executed is completely determined by the physical arrangement of those statements in the program. Each statement is executed once and only once. All programming languages provide **control statements,** which add flexibility to this sequential structure. In this chapter we will study the Pascal control statements, which are used to select and execute a statement or sequence of statements based on the value of an expression.

Consider the following variable declarations:

```
VAR
        BALANCE, AMOUNT : REAL;
        TRANSACTION : CHAR;
```

Suppose that the value of BALANCE is a dollar amount representing the current balance in a checking account and the value of AMOUNT is a dollar amount that should either be deposited in the account or withdrawn from the account. Furthermore, assume that the value of TRANSACTION is 'D' if the dollar AMOUNT should be deposited in the account or 'W' if the dollar AMOUNT should be withdrawn from the account. An IF statement can be used to select and execute the appropriate transaction:

```
IF TRANSACTION = 'D'
   THEN BALANCE := BALANCE + AMOUNT    (* TRUE ALTERNATIVE *)
   ELSE BALANCE := BALANCE - AMOUNT    (* FALSE ALTERNATIVE *)
```

The condition that determines whether to credit or debit the checking BALANCE is embodied in the BOOLEAN expression TRANSACTION = 'D'. If the value of this expression is TRUE, then the statement BALANCE := BALANCE + AMOUNT is executed. Otherwise, the value of the expression must be FALSE, in which case the statement BALANCE := BALANCE − AMOUNT is executed. The IF statement is a **structured statement,** meaning that it contains one or more other statements within its structure. When an IF statement is executed, only one of the embedded statements is executed.

5.1 COMPOUND STATEMENTS

The entire executable section of a Pascal program is a sequence of statements forming one functional unit referred to as a **compound statement.** Any sequence of statements in a program may be grouped between the keywords BEGIN and END to form a compound statement, as illustrated in Figure 5–1. Consecutive statements embedded in a compound statement must be separated by a semicolon.

```
                    BEGIN
                    statement-1;
                    statement-2;
                         •
                         •
                         •
                    statement-k
                    END
```

Figure 5-1
Structure of a compound statement.

When a compound statement is executed, the embedded statements are executed in sequential order.

All statements in the executable section of a program must be embedded in a compound statement. Thus it may be said that a Pascal program consists of a heading, a declaration section, and a compound statement, in that order. Consider the following program:

```
PROGRAM ADD2NUMBERS (INPUT, OUTPUT);
VAR
      A, B : REAL;
BEGIN (* PROGRAM ADD2NUMBERS *)
WRITELN('ENTER TWO NUMBERS.');
READ(A, B);
WRITELN(A:8:2, ' + ', B:8:2, ' = ', A + B:10:2)
END (* OF PROGRAM ADD2NUMBERS *).
```

The compound statement representing the executable section of the program ADD2NUMBERS is the only compound statement in the program. A typical run of this program produces the following output:

```
ENTER TWO NUMBERS.
?45.6 70.2
   45.60 +    70.20 =       115.80
```

Now consider a slightly different form of the same program:

```
PROGRAM SUM2NUMBERS (INPUT, OUTPUT);
VAR
      A, B : REAL;
BEGIN (* PROGRAM SUM2NUMBERS *)
  BEGIN (* DATA INPUT *)
   WRITELN('ENTER TWO NUMBERS.');
   READ(A, B)
   END (* OF DATA INPUT *);
WRITELN(A:8:2, ' + ', B:8:2, ' = ', A + B:10:2)
END (* OF PROGRAM SUM2NUMBERS *).
```

The program SUM2NUMBERS contains two compound statements: the entire executable section, which starts at the first BEGIN and extends to the last END, and the first statement in the executable section (the indented portion of the executable section). Since the statements within a compound statement are executed sequentially, the program SUM2NUMBERS produces exactly the same results as the program ADD2NUMBERS. In other words, embedding the first two statements in the program ADD2NUMBERS in a compound statement is redundant, since doing so does not affect the order in which those statements are executed. Even a single statement like the WRITELN statement at the end of the program SUM2NUMBERS can be placed within a BEGIN and END, thereby turning it into a compound statement:

```
BEGIN (* DATA OUTPUT *)
WRITELN(A:8:2, ' + ', B:8:2, ' = ', A + B:10:2)
END (* OF DATA OUTPUT *)
```

The value of compound statements lies in their use within IF statements and other structured statements. Consider the following IF statement, which is a modification of the IF statement presented at the beginning of this chapter:

```
IF TRANSACTION = 'D'
  THEN BEGIN (* DEPOSIT TRANSACTION *)
       BALANCE := BALANCE + AMOUNT;
       WRITELN('DEPOSIT: $', AMOUNT:7:2)
       END (* OF DEPOSIT TRANSACTION *)
  ELSE BEGIN (* WITHDRAWAL TRANSACTION *)
       BALANCE := BALANCE - AMOUNT;
       WRITELN('WITHDRAWAL: $', AMOUNT:7:2)
       END (* OF WITHDRAWAL TRANSACTION *)
```

If the value of the variable TRANSACTION is 'D', then the compound statement whose BEGIN is followed by the comment "DEPOSIT TRANSACTION" is executed. If the value of TRANSACTION is 'W', then the compound statement BEGINning after the keyword ELSE is executed. A compound statement structure should be used for a sequence of statements that must be executed as a unit.

Since there may be many BEGINs and ENDs in a program, it is important to be able to locate the matching END for each BEGIN easily while reading the program. In this book, the BEGINs and ENDs are followed by short comments that are easily matched, like those shown in the example above. Also, a BEGIN and its matching END are always indented the same number of spaces so that they line up vertically in the program. Another common practice (which is not followed in this book) is to indent the statements within a compound statement one or more spaces to the right so that they are not vertically aligned with the BEGIN and END of that compound statement, as in the following example:

```
BEGIN (* WITHDRAWAL TRANSACTION *)
  BALANCE := BALANCE - AMOUNT;
  WRITELN('WITHDRAWAL: $', AMOUNT:7:2)
END (* OF WITHDRAWAL TRANSACTION *)
```

Style conventions such as these should be consistently employed in a program so that the range of each compound statement is clearly visible.

5.2
IF STATEMENTS

We have already noted that an IF statement can be used to select one of two mutually exclusive courses of action in a program. The selection criteria are embodied in a BOOLEAN expression following the keyword IF. This BOOLEAN expression constitutes one or more conditions that must be met in order for the execution of the statement following the keyword THEN to occur. Thus, IF statements are often termed **conditional control statements.** The conditions are met when the value of the BOOLEAN expression is TRUE. If the value of the BOOLEAN expression is FALSE, the statement following THEN is not executed. What happens next depends on whether or not the optional ELSE portion of an IF statement is present.

THE IF STATEMENT WITHOUT AN ELSE OPTION

An IF statement may be used simply to place a precondition on the execution of a statement. Figure 5–2 shows the structure of an IF statement of this type, which we will refer to as an **IF-THEN statement.** The *statement* indicated after THEN in Figure 5–2 can be any structured or unstructured statement, including a compound statement. (Throughout the remainder of this book, the word "statement" is

```
                    IF BOOLEAN expression
                    THEN statement
```

Figure 5–2
Structure of an IF-THEN statement.

used in the general sense to include compound statements and other structured statements.) Consider the following example, in which LIMIT is an INTEGER variable:

```
            READ(LIMIT);
            IF LIMIT > 10
               THEN LIMIT := LIMIT - 5;
            WRITELN(LIMIT)
```

When the IF-THEN statement is executed, the relational expression LIMIT > 10 (the condition) is evaluated and tested. If this expression is found to be TRUE, then the TRUE alternative represented by the statement following the keyword THEN is executed and after that the statement following the entire IF-THEN statement (the WRITELN statement) is executed. If the expression is FALSE, the statement LIMIT := LIMIT − 5 is not executed, but the WRITELN statement following the IF-THEN statement is executed. In other words, the FALSE alternative for an IF-THEN statement is to proceed onward in the program without executing the embedded statement present after the keyword THEN.

Flowcharts are used in this chapter and in Chapter Six to illustrate the effects of control statements. Diamond-shaped nodes in a flowchart represent evaluation and testing of conditions that are described by BOOLEAN expressions in a program. Here, for instance, is a flowchart that shows the effects of the IF statement in our last example:

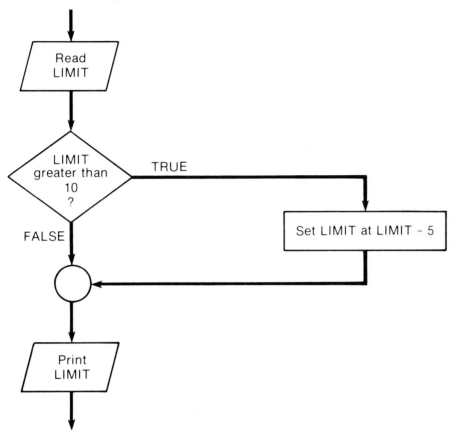

The small circle in this diagram is referred to as a "collection" node. Collection nodes appear in the flowcharts where two or more flow lines join. The flowchart in Figure 5–3 illustrates the general effects of an IF-THEN statement.

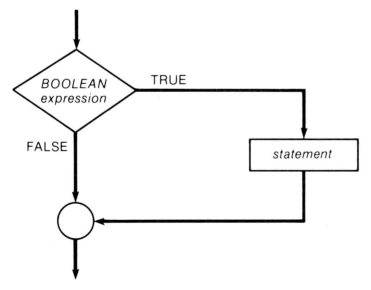

Figure 5–3
Flowchart of the IF-THEN statement.

The placement of the "THEN clause" on a line below the BOOLEAN expression in an IF-THEN statement is a matter of style rather than necessity. IF statements that are not too long can appear on one line by themselves or with other statements, as illustrated in the following examples:

```
READ(LIMIT);
IF LIMIT > 10 THEN LIMIT := LIMIT - 5;
WRITELN
```

```
READ(LIMIT); IF LIMIT > 10 THEN LIMIT := LIMIT - 5; WRITELN(LIMIT)
```

In this book, a THEN clause is placed on the line below that which contains the word IF and the BOOLEAN expression and it is indented two spaces. This style of coding for IF-THEN statements is used to emphasize that the statement in the THEN clause is executed only on condition that the BOOLEAN expression is TRUE.

Consider the following program segment, in which the TRUE alternative for the IF-THEN statement is represented by a compound statement:

```
READ(LIMIT);
IF LIMIT > 10
  THEN BEGIN (* MODIFICATION *)
        LIMIT := LIMIT - 5;
        WRITELN('INPUT LIMIT MODIFIED')
        END (* OF MODIFICATION *);
WRITELN(LIMIT)
```

Note that the semicolon appearing after the END of the compound statement in the THEN clause separates the IF-THEN statement from the WRITELN statement. The effects of this program segment are illustrated in the flowchart on page 135: The compound statement in the THEN clause is executed if and only if LIMIT > 10 is TRUE. After execution of the IF-THEN statement is complete, the WRITELN statement that prints the value of LIMIT is executed.

A sequence of IF-THEN statements may be used in a program to select one of a collection of alternative actions. Suppose that the commission earned by a a salesperson for a certain accounting period is determined by using the person's total sales (in dollars) for that period as described by the following pseudocode:

IF the SALES total does not exceed $1000.00
  THEN calculate the COMMISSION as 5% of SALES
IF the SALES total exceeds $1000.00 but is less than or equal
  to $5000.00
  THEN calculate the COMMISSION as $50.00 plus 8% of
  SALES in excess of $1000.00
IF the SALES total exceeds $5000.00
  THEN calculate the COMMISSION as $370.00 plus 10% of
  SALES in excess of $5000.00

Each of the three alternative ways to calculate the COMMISSION has a precondition, and only one of the conditions can be satisfied for a given SALES total.

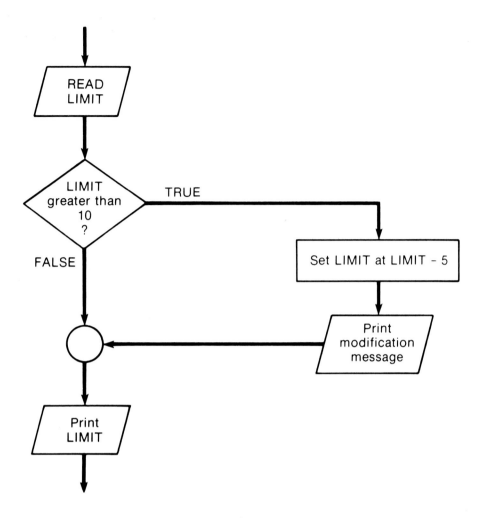

Here is a program segment that will compute the appropriate COMMISSION:

```
IF SALES <= 1000.0
   THEN COMMISSION := 0.05 * SALES;
IF (SALES > 1000.0) AND (SALES <= 5000.0)
   THEN COMMISSION := 50.0 + 0.08 * (SALES - 1000.0);
IF SALES > 5000.0
   THEN COMMISSION := 370.0 + 0.10 * (SALES - 5000.0)
```

Exactly one of the assignment statements in the THEN clauses will be executed because only one of the conditions appearing after the IFs will be TRUE for a given SALES total.

The way in which IF-THEN statements are used in the example above is rather inefficient, since the value of SALES must always be tested three times. In reality, it is not necessary to test SALES further once a TRUE condition is encountered. Note that the COMMISSION will always be at least 5% of SALES. An additional 3% of SALES exceeding $1000.00 and an additional 2% of SALES exceeding $5000.00 must be added to the COMMISSION when appropriate. Thus another way to compute the COMMISSION is illustrated in the following flowchart:

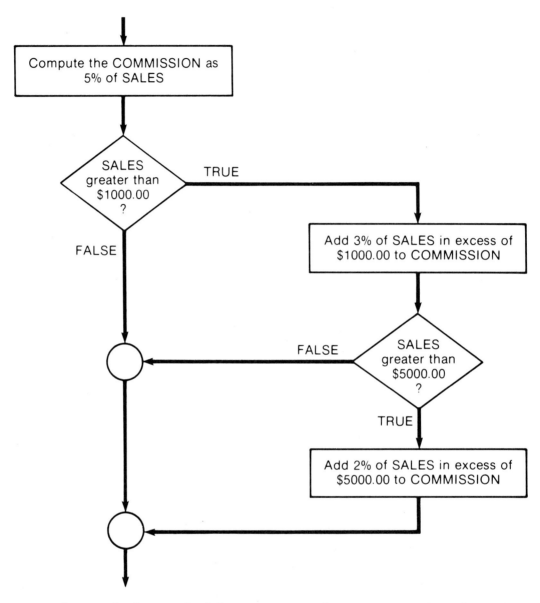

Note that with this method for computing the COMMISSION, the SALES total will be tested at most two times and the second test is necessary only when the first condition is satisfied.

In the following pseudocode description of a program to compute a salesperson's COMMISSION, the method described above is implemented:

```
Constants: BASERATE = 0.05; RATEINC1 = 0.03; RATEINC2 = 0.02;
           LEVEL1 = 1000.0; LEVEL2 = 5000.0
BEGIN program PAYDAY
Print program information and directions
Print a request for total SALES
READ the SALES
Calculate the base COMMISSION as BASERATE * SALES
IF the total SALES exceeds LEVEL1
   THEN BEGIN adjustments
        Add RATEINC1 * (SALES − LEVEL1) to the COMMISSION
```

```
            IF the total SALES exceeds LEVEL2
                THEN add RATEINC2 * (SALES - LEVEL2) to the COMMISSION
            END of adjustments
        Print the total SALES and the COMMISSION
    END of program PAYDAY
```

The commission rates and sales levels are represented by constant identifiers to make it easy to change these values if necessary. Also, note that the value of SALES must be tested within a compound statement that is executed only if the total SALES exceeds $1000.00. Here is the program PAYDAY:

```
PROGRAM PAYDAY (INPUT, OUTPUT);
(**********************************************************************
*                                                                    *
*   A PROGRAM TO COMPUTE A SALES COMMISSION BASED ON ESTABLISHED      *
*   SALES LEVELS AND COMMISSION RATES                                 *
*                                                                    *
**********************************************************************)
CONST                                   (*----------[CONSTANTS]----------*)
        BASERATE = 0.05;                (* BASE RATE OF COMMISSION       *)
                                        (* (FRACTION)                    *)
        RATEINC1 = 0.03;                (* RATE INCREMENT FOR SALES IN   *)
                                        (* EXCESS OF LEVEL1 (FRACTION)   *)
        RATEINC2 = 0.02;                (* RATE INCREMENT FOR SALES IN   *)
                                        (* EXCESS OF LEVEL2 (FRACTION)   *)
        LEVEL1 = 1000.0;                (* FIRST SALES LEVEL CUTOFF      *)
        LEVEL2 = 5000.0;                (* SECOND SALES LEVEL CUTOFF     *)
                                        (*------------------------------*)
VAR                                     (*-------[REAL VARIABLES]--------*)
        SALES,                          (* TOTAL SALES (DOLLARS)         *)
        COMMISSION : REAL;              (* TOTAL COMMISSION ON SALES     *)
                                        (*------------------------------*)
(**********************************************************************)
BEGIN (* PROGRAM PAYDAY *)
WRITELN('THIS PROGRAM WILL COMPUTE A SALES COMMISSION BASED ON ',
        'TOTAL DOLLAR');
WRITELN('SALES. THE MINIMUM COMMISSION IS', BASERATE * 100.0:4:1,
        ' PERCENT OF THE TOTAL SALES.');
WRITELN('IF THE SALES AMOUNT EXCEEDS $', LEVEL1:8:2, ', THEN AN ',
        'EXTRA',  RATEINC1 * 100.0:4:1, ' PERCENT OF');
WRITELN('THE SALES OVER $', LEVEL1:8:2, ' IS ADDED TO THE BASIC ',
        'COMMISSION. IF THE');
WRITELN('SALES AMOUNT EXCEEDS $', LEVEL2:8:2, ', THEN ANOTHER',
        RATEINC2 * 100.0:4:1, ' PERCENT OF THE');
WRITELN('SALES OVER $', LEVEL2:8:2, ' IS ADDED TO THE ACCUMULATED ',
        'COMMISSION.');
WRITELN;
WRITELN('ENTER THE TOTAL DOLLAR SALES TO BE USED:');
READ(SALES);
COMMISSION := BASERATE * SALES;
IF SALES > LEVEL1
   THEN BEGIN (* COMMISSION ADJUSTMENTS *)
        COMMISSION := COMMISSION + RATEINC1 * (SALES - LEVEL1);
```

```
      IF SALES > LEVEL2
         THEN COMMISSION := COMMISSION + RATEINC2 * (SALES - LEVEL2)
      END (* OF COMMISSION ADJUSTMENTS *);
WRITELN;
WRITELN('THE COMMISSION ON TOTAL SALES OF $', SALES:8:2, ' IS $',
        COMMISSION:7:2, '.')
END (* OF PROGRAM PAYDAY *).
```

Here is the output from a typical run of the program PAYDAY:

```
THIS PROGRAM WILL COMPUTE A SALES COMMISSION BASED ON TOTAL DOLLAR
SALES. THE MINIMUM COMMISSION IS 5.0 PERCENT OF THE TOTAL SALES.
IF THE SALES AMOUNT EXCEEDS $ 1000.00, THEN AN EXTRA 3.0 PERCENT OF
THE SALES OVER $ 1000.00 IS ADDED TO THE BASIC COMMISSION. IF THE
SALES AMOUNT EXCEEDS $ 5000.00, THEN ANOTHER 2.0 PERCENT OF THE
SALES OVER $ 5000.00 IS ADDED TO THE ACCUMULATED COMMISSION.

ENTER THE TOTAL DOLLAR SALES TO BE USED:
?1400.00

THE COMMISSION ON TOTAL SALES OF $ 1400.00 IS $   82.00.
```

The COMMISSION computed in this example is based on SALES of $1400.00. Thus, the basic commission is $70.00 (5.0% of 1400.00) and an adjustment of $12.00 (3.0% of 400.00) is added to the basic commission to give a total commission of $82.00. The second adjustment (for sales exceeding $5000.00) is not made.

THE IF STATEMENT WITH THE ELSE OPTION

An IF statement may have both a THEN clause and an ELSE clause, as illustrated in Figure 5–4. The statement following THEN is executed if and only if the value of the BOOLEAN expression is TRUE. When the value of the BOOLEAN expression is FALSE, the statement following ELSE is executed. Thus, the statements in the THEN and ELSE clauses of an IF statement represent two distinct alternatives, only one of which is chosen, based on the value of the BOOLEAN expression. The process by which an alternative is selected is depicted in Figure 5–5.

Suppose we want to write a program that will convert a temperature given in degrees Fahrenheit to its equivalent in degrees Celsius or a Celsius temperature to degrees Fahrenheit, depending on which type of temperature is input to the program. The program will read a temperature (TEMP) and a SCALE designation whose value may be 'F' for Fahrenheit or 'C' for Celsius. Selection of the appro-

```
                 IF BOOLEAN expression
                 THEN statement-1
                 ELSE statement-2
```

Figure 5–4
Structure of an IF-THEN-ELSE statement.

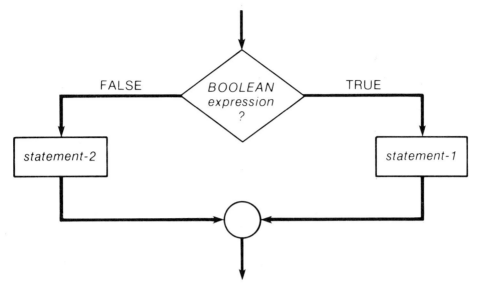

Figure 5–5
Flowchart of the IF-THEN-ELSE statement.

priate temperature conversion can be controlled by an IF-THEN-ELSE statement, as described in the flowchart shown below.

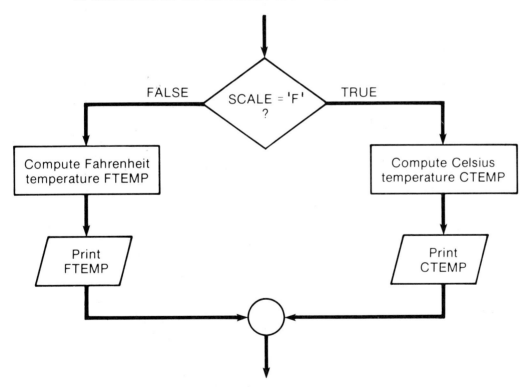

The temperature conversion formulas are

$$C = \frac{5}{9}(F - 32) \quad \text{and} \quad F = \frac{9}{5}C + 32$$

where F represents a Fahrenheit temperature and C represents a Celsius temperature. From the flowchart we see that regardless of the value of SCALE, a temperature must be computed and then printed. Thus, both alternatives in the IF-THEN-ELSE statement must appear as compound statements.

A pseudocode description of a program to convert a temperature from degrees Fahrenheit to degrees Celsius or degrees Celsius to degrees Fahrenheit is given below. Since the fraction $^9/_5$ is equal to 1.8, this value is used when a Fahrenheit temperature is computed.

```
Constants: FAHRENHEIT = 'F'; CELSIUS = 'C'
BEGIN program CONVERT
Print program information and directions
Print a request for a TEMPerature and a SCALE indicator
READ the TEMPerature and SCALE
IF the SCALE is FAHRENHEIT
    THEN BEGIN conversion to CELSIUS
        Compute CTEMP as 5.0 / 9.0 * (TEMPerature − 32.0)
        Print the input TEMPerature and CTEMP
        END of conversion to Celsius
    ELSE  BEGIN conversion to Fahrenheit
        Compute FTEMP as 1.8 * TEMPerature + 32.0
        Print the input TEMPerature and FTEMP
        END of conversion to Fahrenheit
END of program CONVERT
```

Here is the program CONVERT:

```
PROGRAM CONVERT (INPUT, OUTPUT);
(******************************************************************
*                                                                *
*   A PROGRAM TO CONVERT A FAHRENHEIT TEMPERATURE TO CELSIUS OR A *
*   CELSIUS TEMPERATURE TO FAHRENHEIT                             *
*                                                                *
******************************************************************)
CONST                                (*---------[CONSTANTS]---------*)
        FAHRENHEIT = 'F';            (* FAHRENHEIT SCALE SYMBOL     *)
        CELSIUS = 'C';               (* CELSIUS SCALE SYMBOL        *)
                                     (*----------------------------*)
VAR                                  (*-------[REAL VARIABLES]-------*)
        TEMP,                        (* THE INPUT TEMPERATURE       *)
        CTEMP,                       (* INPUT TEMPERATURE AFTER     *)
                                     (* CONVERSION TO DEGREES CELSIUS *)
        FTEMP : REAL;                (* INPUT TEMPERATURE AFTER     *)
                                     (* CONVERSION TO FAHRENHEIT    *)
                                     (*----------------------------*)
                                     (*-------[CHAR VARIABLES]-------*)
        SCALE : CHAR;                (* TEMPERATURE SCALE SYMBOL    *)
                                     (*----------------------------*)
(******************************************************************)
BEGIN (* PROGRAM CONVERT *)
WRITELN('ENTER A TEMPERATURE FOLLOWED IMMEDIATELY (NO SPACES) BY');
WRITELN('THE LETTER ', FAHRENHEIT, ' FOR FAHRENHEIT OR THE LETTER ',
        CELSIUS, ' FOR CELSIUS');
WRITELN('WHICH INDICATES THE SCALE FOR THE TEMPERATURE. THIS');
```

```
WRITELN('TEMPERATURE WILL BE CONVERTED TO ITS EQUIVALENT ON THE');
WRITELN('OTHER SCALE.');
WRITELN;
WRITELN('ENTER TEMPERATURE AND SCALE:');
READ(TEMP, SCALE);
IF SCALE = FAHRENHEIT
   THEN BEGIN (* CONVERSION TO CELSIUS *)
          CTEMP := 5.0 / 9.0 * (TEMP - 32.0);
          WRITELN(TEMP:20:2, ' DEGREES F = ', CTEMP:6:2, ' DEGREES C.')
          END (* OF CONVERSION TO CELSIUS *)
   ELSE BEGIN (* CONVERSION TO FAHRENHEIT *)
          FTEMP := 1.8 * TEMP + 32.0;
          WRITELN(TEMP:20:2, ' DEGREES C = ', FTEMP:6:2, ' DEGREES F.')
          END (* OF CONVERSION TO FAHRENHEIT *)
END (* OF PROGRAM CONVERT *).
```

Here is the output from a sample run of the program CONVERT:

```
ENTER A TEMPERATURE FOLLOWED IMMEDIATELY (NO SPACES) BY
THE LETTER F FOR FAHRENHEIT OR THE LETTER C FOR CELSIUS
WHICH INDICATES THE SCALE FOR THE TEMPERATURE. THIS
TEMPERATURE WILL BE CONVERTED TO ITS EQUIVALENT ON THE
OTHER SCALE.

ENTER TEMPERATURE AND SCALE:
? 23.5C
                    23.50 DEGREES C =  74.30 DEGREES F.
```

Note that the semicolons that appear in the IF statement of the program CONVERT are necessary to separate two consecutive statements within each of the compound statements. No semicolon appears after the END of the compound statement in the THEN clause because there is an ELSE clause for the IF statement. A semicolon preceding ELSE would signify that ELSE marks the beginning of a new statement, which is not correct. No Pascal statement begins with the keyword ELSE. Hence, the appearance of a semicolon immediately preceding ELSE is a syntax error. A semicolon could be placed after the END of the compound statement in the ELSE clause to separate the entire IF statement from the next statement in the program. However, the IF statement in the program CONVERT is followed by the END of the program, and so a semicolon following the IF statement is unnecessary (but not illegal).

5.2 EXERCISES

1. Find the errors (if any) in each of the following IF-THEN statements. Assume that all the variables have been declared and assigned values.

a.
```
IF A + B < C AND B >= 0.0
   THEN WRITELN(B)
```

b.
```
IF (C >= D + 2.0) OR (B < 0.0)
   THEN A := B * C - 1.5
```

c.
```
IF C <= B
   THEN BEGIN
          C := B - 2.0 * C
          B := 0.0
          END
```

d.
```
IF A * B + C
   THEN BEGIN
          WRITELN (A, B, C);
          D := A + B / C;
          C := C + 1.0
          END
```

2. Draw a flowchart for the following program segment:

```
READ (K, M);
IF (K <= M) OR (M < 0)
   THEN BEGIN
          M := K - M;
          K := K + 1
          END;
K := K + 2;
WRITELN (K, M)
```

What values will be printed for K and M if the values 5 and 10 are read in that order? What values are printed if 10 is read first and then 5?

3. Write a pseudocode description of the program segment depicted in each of the flowcharts on pages 143 and 144 and then write the program segment. Assume A and B are REAL variables.

4. What values will be printed for the variables A and B by the program segments described in Exercise 3 if the values read for A and B are 15.5 and 24.2, respectively? What will the output be if the values read for A and B are 20.0 and 6.5, respectively?

a.

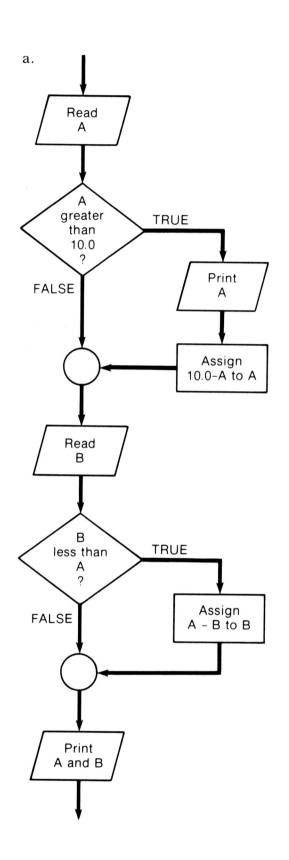

b.

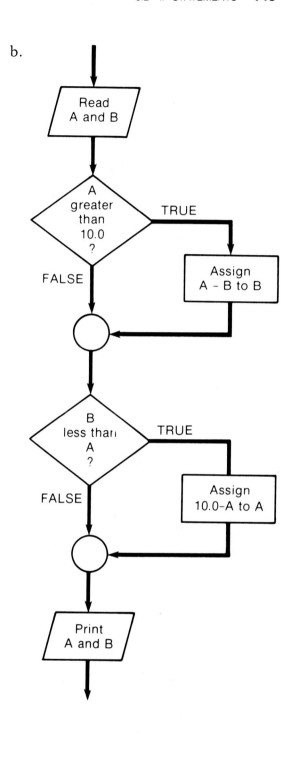

c.

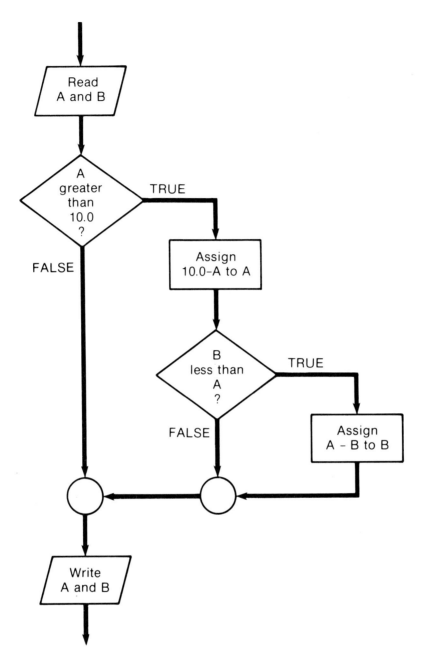

5. Find the errors (if any) in each of the IF-THEN-ELSE statements given below. Assume that all the variables have been declared and given values.

a.
```
IF DAY > 31
    THEN WRITELN('ERROR');
    ELSE WRITELN('DAY: ', DAY:2)
```

b.
```
IF (GAME <= 4) AND (SCORE < 100.0)
    THEN BEGIN
            GAME := GAME + 1;
            WRITELN('NEW GAME')
         END
    ELSE WRITELN('GAME OVER.',
            ' SCORE =', SCORE:6:2)
```

```
c.          IF COST <= 50.0
              THEN WRITELN('COST: $', COST:5:2)
              ELSE DISCOUNT := COST * RATE;
                   COST := COST - DISCOUNT;
                   WRITELN('DISCOUNTED COST: $',
                           COST:6:2)
              END
```

```
d.          IF (DIMENSION < 0) OR (DIMENSION > 3)
              THEN BEGIN
                   SEGMENT := 1;
                   IF (DIMENSION <= 1)
                     THEN SEGMENT := SEGMENT
                             + 2 * DIMENSION
                     ELSE SEGMENT := SEGMENT
                             + 3 * DIMENSION
                   END
              ELSE BEGIN
                   SEGMENT := 0;
                   DIMENSION := 0
                   END
```

6. Draw a flowchart for the following program segment.

```
              READ(K, M);
              IF K <= M
                THEN BEGIN
                     K := K + 3;
                     IF M < 0
                       THEN M := M - K
                       ELSE BEGIN
                            M := 5 - M;
                            K := M + K
                            END
                     END
                ELSE BEGIN
                     M := K - M;
                     K := K + 1
                     END;
              WRITELN(K, M)
```

What values will be printed for K and M if the values 12 and 20 are read by the segment in that order? What values will be printed if 20 is read first and then 12? What will the output be if −12 and −20 are read in that order?

7. Show how an IF-THEN statement in the form

> IF *(BOOLEAN-expression-1)* OR *(BOOLEAN-expression-2)*
>   THEN *statement*

can be replaced by an equivalent IF-THEN-ELSE statement that does not contain a compound BOOLEAN expression. (You may assume that *BOOLEAN-expression-1* and *BOOLEAN-expression-2* are relational expressions.)

8. Write a pseudocode description of the program segment depicted in each of the following flowcharts and then write the program segment. Assume A and B are REAL variables.

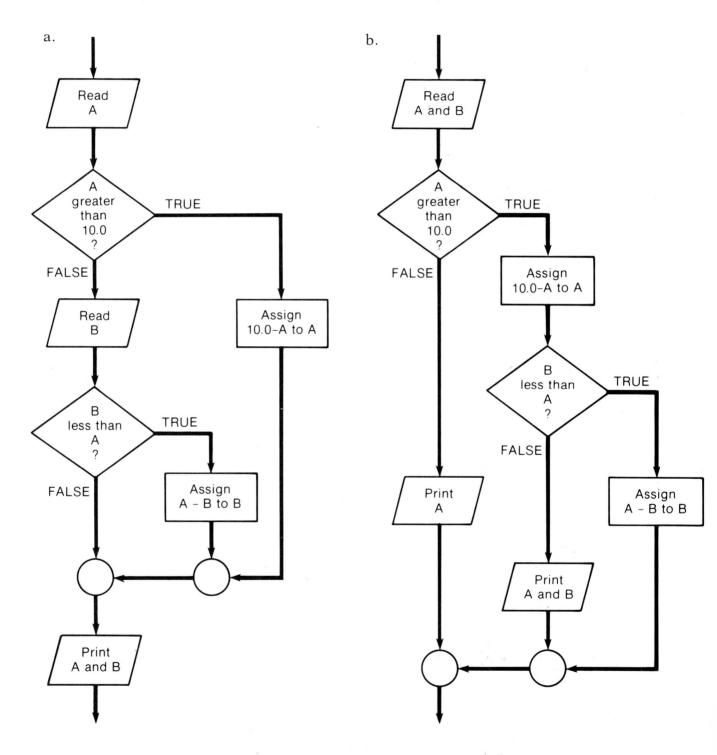

a.

b.

9. Show by examples using specific values for A and B how the various combinations of TRUE and FALSE paths taken in the flowcharts in Exercise 8 produce changes in the values of A and B.

10. Write a program segment to calculate a salesman's commission as described in Section 5.2, but use an IF-THEN-ELSE statement.

5.3
NESTED IF STATEMENTS

The statement after THEN or ELSE in an IF statement can be another IF statement. When an IF statement follows the keyword THEN or the keyword ELSE in a prior IF statement, it is said to be "nested" inside that prior IF statement. Many levels of nesting for IF statements (with or without ELSE clauses) are possible. First, we will consider nesting IF-THEN statements.

NESTING IF STATEMENTS WITHOUT THE ELSE CLAUSE

The simplest type of nesting for IF statements occurs when an IF-THEN statement is nested inside a previous IF-THEN statement, as illustrated in the following example:

```
IF ALPHA <= BETA
    THEN IF COUNT < 100
            THEN ALPHA := BETA - ALPHA
```

In this statement it appears that two preconditions are placed on the execution of the statement ALPHA := BETA − ALPHA, and indeed that is the case. However, the value of ALPHA <= BETA must be TRUE or the nested IF statement will not be executed. The effects of the nesting are illustrated in the following flowchart:

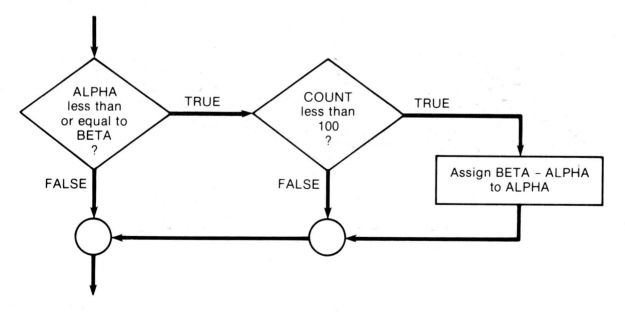

It is possible to achieve the same results without nesting IF statements by having both relational expressions in a compound BOOLEAN expression in a single IF statement:

```
IF (ALPHA <= BETA) AND (COUNT < 100)
    THEN ALPHA := BETA - ALPHA
```

However, the value of (ALPHA <= BETA) AND (COUNT < 100) can be determined only after **both** relational subexpressions have been evaluated. When the relational expressions ALPHA <= BETA and COUNT < 100 are placed in a nesting of two IF statements, only the relational expression in the "outer" IF statement will be evaluated when its value is FALSE.

IF-THEN statements may be nested to any desired depth. The structure of the nesting is outlined below.

IF *BOOLEAN expression-1*
   THEN IF *BOOLEAN expression-2*
      THEN IF *BOOLEAN expression-3*
         THEN IF *BOOLEAN expression-4*
            .
            .
            .
               THEN IF *BOOLEAN expression-n*
                 THEN *statement*

The *statement* appearing within a nesting of IF-THEN statements as illustrated here will be executed only if the value of every *BOOLEAN expression* is TRUE. Furthermore, these expressions are evaluated in the order *BOOLEAN expression-1*, *BOOLEAN expression-2*, *BOOLEAN expression-3*, and so on, and if any one of the expressions proves to be FALSE, no further execution of IF-THEN statements within the nesting occurs.

Consider the following example:

```
IF X >= 0
    THEN IF X <= 100
            THEN IF X MOD 2 = 0
                    THEN BEGIN (* TASK *)
                         Y := 2 * X;
                         Z := Y + 1
                         END (* OF TASK *)
```

The compound statement representing a "TASK" is executed only if the value of X is an even integer between 0 and 100 inclusive. Even if the order in which the relational expressions are evaluated and tested is changed, the net effects of the nesting remain the same. For instance, the statement

```
IF X MOD 2 = 0
    THEN IF X >= 0
            THEN IF X <= 100
                    THEN BEGIN (* TASK *)
                         Y := 2 * X;
                         Z := Y + 1
                         END (* OF TASK *)
```

imposes the same preconditions on the performance of the TASK as the previous nesting of IF statements. It should be noted, however, that approximately one-fourth of the possible values for X make both X MOD 2 = 0 and X >= 0 TRUE, while only 101 different values for X make both X >= 0 and X <= 100 TRUE. This means that using X <= 100 as the third precondition, as in the second nesting of IF statements, is less efficient than using X MOD 2 = 0 as the third precondition when all the possible values for X are equally likely. The point is that the BOOLEAN expressions should be placed in a nesting of IF-THEN statements in an order that generally requires that as few of these expressions as possible be evaluated in order to determine that not all of the preconditions given in the nesting are satisfied.

NESTING IF STATEMENTS WITH THE ELSE CLAUSE

When an ELSE clause is used in a nested IF statement, the nesting must be carefully structured to produce the desired effects. Consider the following nesting of IF statements:

```
IF X < 0 THEN IF Y > 5 THEN Z := X + Y ELSE Z := 0
```

The logic involved in this statement is not clear because there are two THENs and only one ELSE. But the statement is valid the way it is written. The flowchart below describes the effects of this statement.

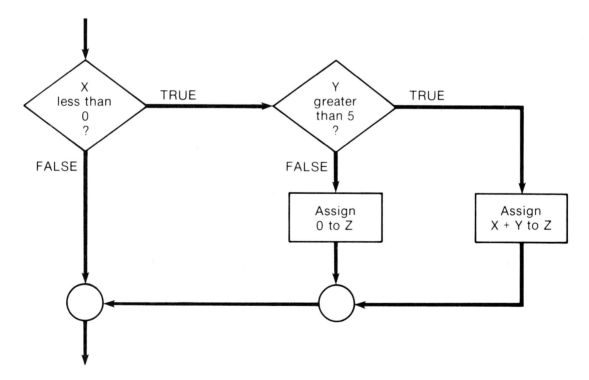

This interpretation is more apparent if the statement is written as follows:

```
IF X < 0
    THEN IF Y > 5
            THEN Z := X + Y
            ELSE Z := 0
```

The other reasonable (but incorrect) interpretation of the nested IF statement shown above is illustrated in the following flowchart.

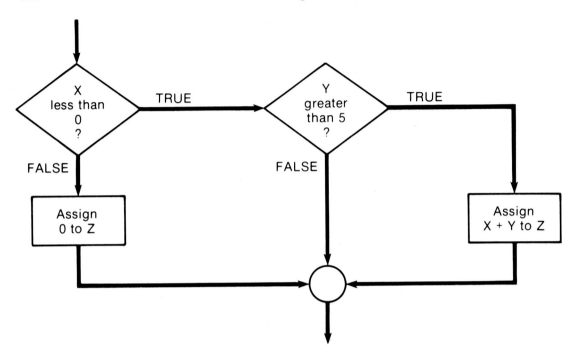

We can write a statement that will produce the effects described in this flowchart. Forcing the ELSE clause to be matched by the first THEN is accomplished by enclosing the second IF statement in a BEGIN-END pair, thereby making it a compound statement:

```
IF X < 0
    THEN BEGIN
             IF Y > 5
                 THEN Z := X + Y
         END
    ELSE Z := 0
```

There may be as many ELSE clauses in a nesting of IF statements as there are THEN clauses or there may be fewer (as in the example above). The rule for determining the proper matching of THENs and ELSEs for a nesting of IF statements where none of the IF statements is enclosed in a BEGIN-END pair is as follows:

When a nesting of IF statements is read from left to right, each occurrence of an ELSE is matched with the most recently encountered THEN that has not yet been matched with an ELSE.

This matching principle for THENs and ELSEs is illustrated in the following example:

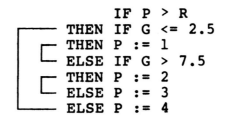

```
            IF  P  >  R
      THEN  IF  G  <=  2.5
      THEN  P  :=  1
      ELSE  IF  G  >  7.5
      THEN  P  :=  2
      ELSE  P  :=  3
      ELSE  P  :=  4
```

The appropriate association of THENs and ELSEs is much more apparent in the following indented form of this statement:

```
IF  P  >  R
   THEN  IF  G  <=  2.5
            THEN  P  :=  1
            ELSE  IF  G  >  7.5
                     THEN  P  :=  2
                     ELSE  P  :=  3
   ELSE  P  :=  4
```

A sales commission can be computed according to the specifications given in Section 5.2 by using a nesting of IF statements with ELSE clauses. The following flowchart describes the appropriate procedure:

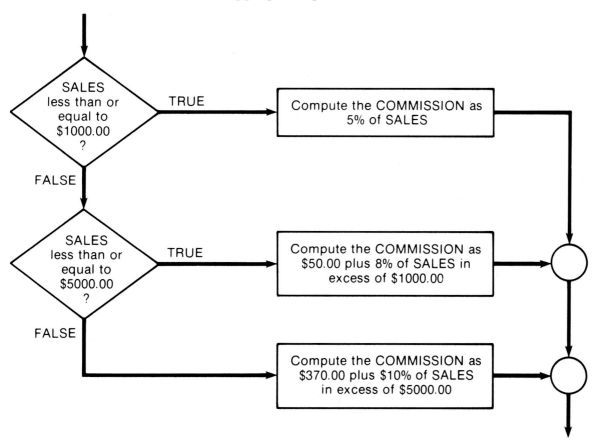

The procedure outlined here is easy to implement by using a nesting of IF-THEN-ELSE statements:

```
IF SALES <= 1000.0
   THEN COMMISSION := 0.05 * SALES
   ELSE IF SALES <= 5000.0
           THEN COMMISSION := 50.0 + 0.08 * (SALES - 1000.0)
           ELSE COMMISSION := 370.0 + 0.1 * (SALES - 5000.0)
```

Often a variety of different nested IF statements can be used to perform a desired task. Suppose that a letter grade must be assigned to a test score between 0 and 100 inclusive according to the following procedure: 90 to 100 is an A, 80 to 89 is a B, 70 to 79 is a C, 60 to 69 is a D, and 0 to 59 is an F. Let SCORE be an INTEGER variable whose value is between 0 and 100 inclusive, and let GRADE be a CHAR variable. The nesting of IF statements shown below will produce the proper GRADE assignment.

```
IF SCORE >= 60
   THEN IF SCORE >= 70
           THEN IF SCORE >= 80
                   THEN IF SCORE >= 90
                           THEN GRADE := 'A'
                           ELSE GRADE := 'B'
                   ELSE GRADE := 'C'
           ELSE GRADE := 'D'
   ELSE GRADE := 'F'
```

The following flowchart illustrates the effects of the nested IF statements:

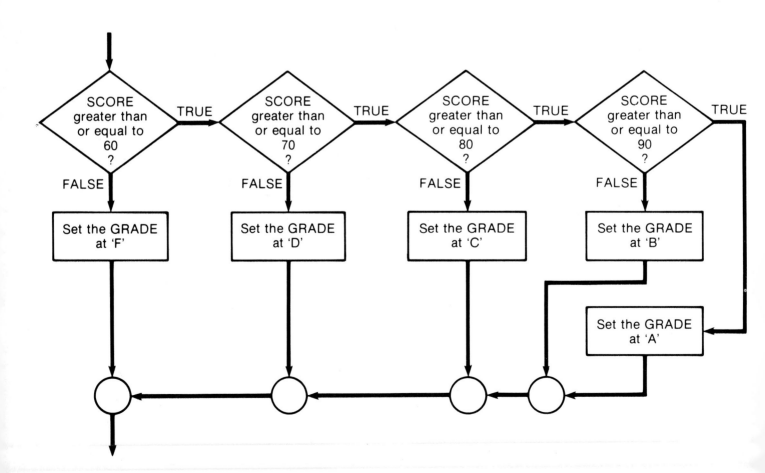

The nested IF structure presented above requires that four conditions be tested when SCORE is 90 or larger. A maximum of three conditions will be tested if the program segment shown next is used to assign GRADEs:

```
IF SCORE >= 70
  THEN IF SCORE >= 80
         THEN IF SCORE >= 90
                THEN GRADE := 'A'
                ELSE GRADE := 'B'
         ELSE GRADE := 'C'
  ELSE IF SCORE >= 60
         THEN GRADE := 'D'
         ELSE GRADE := 'F'
```

In this nesting of IF statements, the first test of SCORE is used to determine if the SCORE is high (70 or greater) or low. Low scores and high scores are processed as different alternatives of the outer IF statement. There are many other nestings of IF statements that can be constructed to generate an appropriate letter GRADE.

When a choice of alternative actions is called for in a program, the IF statement is a natural form in which to represent the selection process. In order to choose an IF structure that is both effective and efficient, it is important that the programmer be aware of all the valid forms for an IF statement and the rules that govern the nesting of IF statements. A given programming situation that necessitates a choice of alternative actions can usually be represented effectively by many different IF structures. The programmer should be mindful of the efficiency of those IF structures in order to implement a structure that will minimize the testing needed to select an alternative.

5.3 EXERCISES

1. Rewrite each of the following statements in an equivalent form without using any compound conditions or compound statements:

   a.
   ```
   IF (A > B) OR (B > C)
      THEN WRITELN('SUCCESS')
      ELSE WRITELN('FAILURE')
   ```

   b.
   ```
   IF ((A <= B) OR (X = '$')) AND (C > 0)
      THEN WRITELN('SUCCESS')
      ELSE WRITELN('FAILURE')
   ```

   c.
   ```
   IF ((A <= B) AND (X = '$')) OR (C > 0)
      THEN WRITELN('SUCCESS')
      ELSE WRITELN('FAILURE')
   ```

   d.
   ```
   IF (A <= B) OR ((X = '$') AND (C > 0))
      THEN WRITELN('SUCCESS')
      ELSE WRITELN('FAILURE')
   ```

2. In Section 5.3 two program segments were written to assign a letter grade based on a test score. Write two more different segments to perform that task.

3. Draw a flowchart for the following program segment:

```
READ(K, M);
IF K >= M
   THEN IF M > 0
            THEN BEGIN
                    K := K - 5;
                    M := M + K
                 END
            ELSE M := 10 -M
   ELSE IF M - K > 5
            THEN M := M - 10
            ELSE K := M - K;
WRITELN(K, M)
```

What values will be printed for K and M if the values 15 and 8 are read in that order? What values will be printed if 8 is read first and then 15? What will the output be if the values 6 and −4 are read in that order?

4. Why might the following program segment generate an execution error?

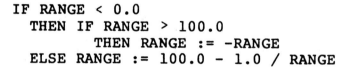

```
IF RANGE < 0.0
   THEN IF RANGE > 100.0
            THEN RANGE := -RANGE
   ELSE RANGE := 100.0 - 1.0 / RANGE
```

a.

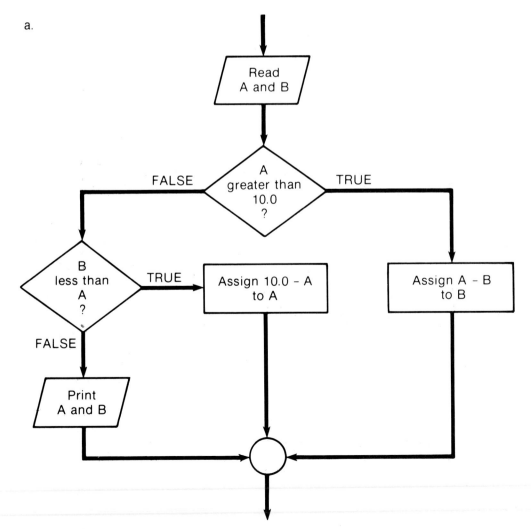

b.

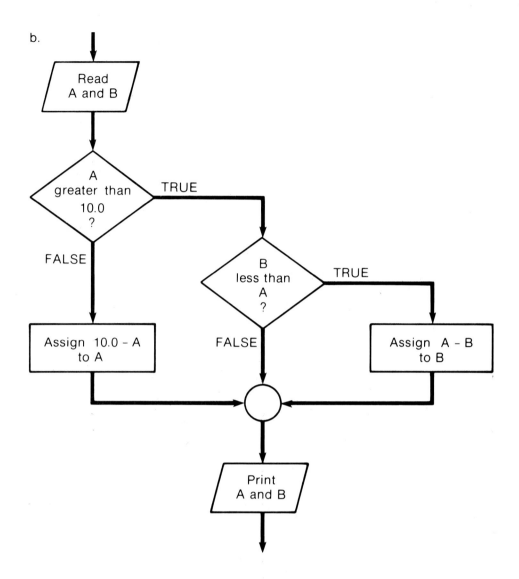

5. Write a pseudocode description of the program segment depicted in each of the flowcharts (page 154 and above) and then write the program segment. Assume A and B are REAL variables.

6. What values will be printed for the variables A and B by the program segments described in Exercise 5 if the values read for A and B are 20.0 and 6.5, respectively? What will the output be if the values read for A and B are 8.4 and 15.8, respectively?

5.4
CASE STATEMENTS

When one of several alternatives must be selected, it is generally possible to design a program segment that uses IF statements to control the selection. The complexity of such an IF structure increases dramatically as the number of alternatives increases, reducing both the efficiency and readability of the program. It may be more suitable to select an alternative by using a CASE statement.

THE STANDARD CASE STATEMENT

A CASE statement may be used to assign the proper letter GRADE for a test SCORE according to the specifications given in Section 5.3. If the INTEGER variable SCORE has a value between 0 and 100 inclusive, then the value of the expression SCORE DIV 10 must be an integer between 0 and 10 inclusive. This expression can be used as a **CASE selector** to choose a proper GRADE assignment alternative, as shown in the following CASE statement:

```
CASE SCORE DIV 10 OF
           10, 9 : GRADE := 'A';
               8 : GRADE := 'B';
               7 : GRADE := 'C';
               6 : GRADE := 'D';
   0, 1, 2, 3, 4, 5 : GRADE := 'F'
END (* OF SCORE GRADING CASES *)
```

The CASE statement is a structured statement that controls the selection of one statement to be executed based upon the value of a CASE selector expression. Each of the statements that could be selected must be embedded within the CASE statement and be prefixed by a list, termed a **CASE label list,** of one or more possible values for the CASE selector. In the example just shown, for instance, the integers 10 and 9 appear as CASE labels in a list preceding the statement GRADE := 'A'. This means that when the CASE statement is executed, GRADE is assigned the value 'A' if and only if the value of the CASE selector (SCORE DIV 10) is 10 or 9. Only one of the GRADE assignments is selected when the CASE statement is executed, namely, the one whose CASE label list contains the value of the CASE selector.

The selector in a CASE statement can be any variable or expression that has an ordinal type value; no REAL variable or REAL-valued expression can be used as a CASE selector. Figure 5–6 shows the standard form of a CASE statement. Note that an END keyword must be used to mark the end of the list of labeled alternatives. This is one of the few instances in Pascal in which END is used without a matching BEGIN. Each *label-list* must contain one or more constants (or constant identifiers), which are possible values of the CASE *selector*. When a CASE statement is executed, the value of the *selector* is computed and then matched with a corresponding label in a *label-list* to determine which *statement* embedded within the CASE statement should be executed. This selection process is illustrated in the flowchart shown in Figure 5–7. In order to guarantee that the CASE selection be well defined, no label (value for the CASE selector) may appear in more than one *label-list* within the same CASE statement. A colon must separate a *statement* from its *label-list* and every *statement* except the last one must be followed by a semi-colon to separate the alternatives.

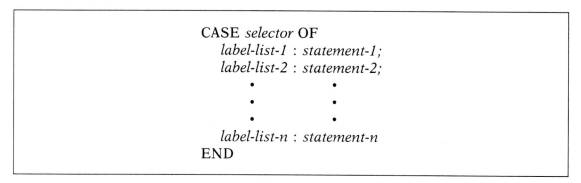

Figure 5–6
Structure of a standard CASE statement.

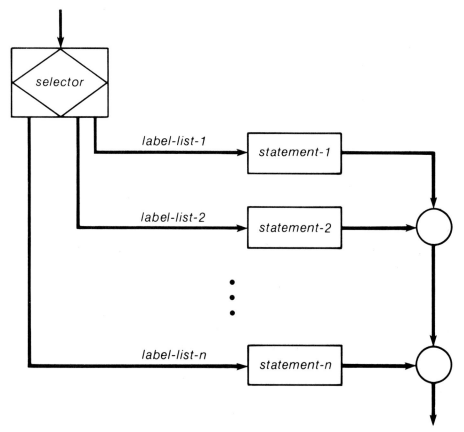

Figure 5–7
Flowchart of the standard CASE statement.

It is not necessary that all the possible values of a CASE selector be listed as labels in a CASE statement. For example, in the CASE statement that assigns a letter GRADE based on the value of a SCORE, not all of the possible values of the selector SCORE DIV 10 appear as labels. If SCORE happens to be less than 0 or greater than 109, the value of SCORE DIV 10 is either a negative integer or an integer greater than 10. Some versions of Pascal would consider this an execution error, but others (UCSD Pascal, for instance) would merely assume that none of the CASE alternatives should be selected and continue on to the next statement after the END of the CASE statement. Inappropriate CASEs can be handled by placing suitable preconditions on the execution of the CASE statement. For example,

```
IF (SCORE >= 0) AND (SCORE <= 100)
   THEN CASE SCORE DIV 10 OF
                     10, 9 : GRADE := 'A';
                         8 : GRADE := 'B';
                         7 : GRADE := 'C';
                         6 : GRADE := 'D';
          0, 1, 2, 3, 4, 5 : GRADE := 'F'
             END (* OF SCORE GRADING CASES *)
   ELSE WRITELN('INVALID SCORE:', SCORE:4)
```

or

```
IF (SCORE < 0) OR (SCORE > 100)
   THEN WRITELN('INVALID SCORE:', SCORE:4)
   ELSE CASE SCORE DIV 10 OF
                     10, 9 : GRADE := 'A';
                         8 : GRADE := 'B';
                         7 : GRADE := 'C';
                         6 : GRADE := 'D';
          0, 1, 2, 3, 4, 5 : GRADE := 'F'
             END (* OF SCORE GRADING CASES *)
```

The effects of the first IF statement shown above are illustrated in the flowchart on page 159.

The temperature conversion program named CONVERT in Section 5.2 (page 140) will convert an input TEMPerature from Fahrenheit to Celsius or Celsius to Fahrenheit, depending on an input SCALE code. If SCALE has the value 'F', then the program calculates the Celsius equivalent of the input TEMPerature. Although the directions printed by the program say to enter the letter C for a conversion from Celsius to Fahrenheit, note that the user may enter any character except F as a signal that the input TEMPerature is measured in degrees Celsius. One way to make sure that an appropriate temperature scale is entered is to have the program check the value of SCALE after it has been read. If an appropriate SCALE has been entered, the program may use the value of SCALE for a CASE selection. Otherwise, the program should print a message to the user indicating that an improper scale was entered. This process is described by the following pseudocode:

```
IF the SCALE is 'F' or 'C'
   THEN CASE for SCALE OF
            'F' : BEGIN conversion to Celsius
                  Compute CTEMP as 5.0 / 9.0 * (TEMPerature - 32.0)
                  Print the input TEMPerature and CTEMP
                  END of conversion to Celsius
            'C' : BEGIN conversion to Fahrenheit
                  Compute FTEMP as 1.8 * TEMPerature + 32.0
                  Print the input TEMPerature and FTEMP
                  END of conversion to Fahrenheit
         END of scale cases
   ELSE Print a message indicating the SCALE is invalid
```

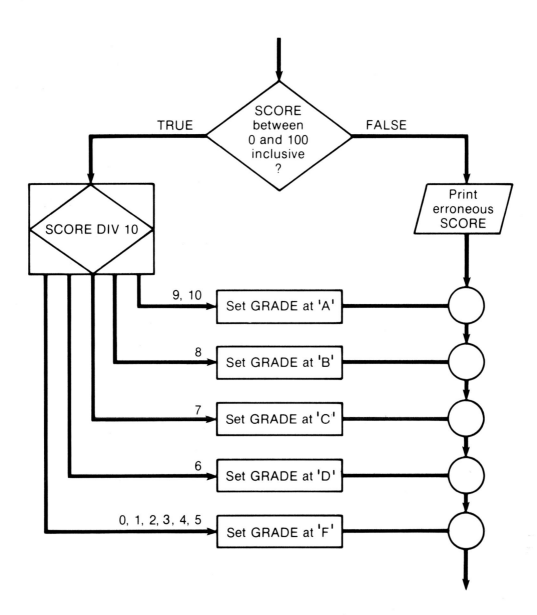

The program TEMPCONVERT shown below uses CASE selection to convert a TEMPerature from Fahrenheit to Celsius or Celsius to Fahrenheit. Constant identifiers FAHRENHEIT and CELSIUS are used to represent the CHAR constants 'F' and 'C', respectively, to document the CASEs, and to make it easy to modify the program if different SCALE indicators are desired.

```
PROGRAM TEMPCONVERT (INPUT, OUTPUT);
(*******************************************************************
 *                                                                 *
 *   A PROGRAM TO CONVERT A FAHRENHEIT TEMPERATURE TO CELSIUS OR A *
 *   CELSIUS TEMPERATURE TO FAHRENHEIT                             *
 *                                                                 *
 *******************************************************************)
```

```
CONST                                  (*---------[CONSTANTS]----------*)
       FAHRENHEIT = 'F';               (* FAHRENHEIT SCALE SYMBOL      *)
       CELSIUS = 'C';                  (* CELSIUS SCALE SYMBOL         *)
                                       (*-----------------------------*)
VAR                                    (*-------[REAL VARIABLES]-------*)
       TEMP,                           (* THE INPUT TEMPERATURE        *)
       CTEMP,                          (* INPUT TEMPERATURE AFTER      *)
                                       (* CONVERSION TO DEGREES CELSIUS*)
       FTEMP : REAL;                   (* INPUT TEMPERATURE AFTER      *)
                                       (* CONVERSION TO FAHRENHEIT     *)
                                       (*-----------------------------*)
                                       (*-------[CHAR VARIABLES]-------*)
       SCALE : CHAR;                   (* TEMPERATURE SCALE SYMBOL     *)
                                       (*-----------------------------*)
(********************************************************************)
BEGIN (* PROGRAM TEMPCONVERT *)
WRITELN('ENTER A TEMPERATURE FOLLOWED IMMEDIATELY (NO SPACES) BY');
WRITELN('THE LETTER ', FAHRENHEIT, ' FOR FAHRENHEIT OR THE LETTER ',
        CELSIUS, ' FOR CELSIUS');
WRITELN('WHICH INDICATES THE SCALE FOR THE TEMPERATURE. THIS');
WRITELN('TEMPERATURE WILL BE CONVERTED TO ITS EQUIVALENT ON THE');
WRITELN('OTHER SCALE.');
WRITELN;
WRITELN('ENTER TEMPERATURE AND SCALE:');
READ(TEMP, SCALE);
IF (SCALE = FAHRENHEIT) OR (SCALE = CELSIUS)
   THEN CASE SCALE OF
           FAHRENHEIT : BEGIN (* CONVERSION TO CELSIUS *)
                        CTEMP := 5.0 / 9.0 * (TEMP - 32.0);
                        WRITELN(TEMP:20:2, ' DEGREES F = ', CTEMP:6:2,
                                ' DEGREES C.')
                        END (* OF CONVERSION TO CELSIUS *);
              CELSIUS : BEGIN (* CONVERSION TO FAHRENHEIT *)
                        FTEMP := 1.8 * TEMP + 32.0;
                        WRITELN(TEMP:20:2, ' DEGREES C = ', FTEMP:6:2,
                                ' DEGREES F.')
                        END (* OF CONVERSION TO FAHRENHEIT *)
        END (* OF SCALE CASES *)
   ELSE WRITELN('"':15, SCALE, '" IS NOT A VALID SCALE.')
END (* OF PROGRAM TEMPCONVERT *).
```

Here is a sample of what the output produced by the program TEMPCONVERT looks like when an invalid SCALE is entered:

```
ENTER A TEMPERATURE FOLLOWED IMMEDIATELY (NO SPACES) BY
THE LETTER F FOR FAHRENHEIT OR THE LETTER C FOR CELSIUS
WHICH INDICATES THE SCALE FOR THE TEMPERATURE. THIS
TEMPERATURE WILL BE CONVERTED TO ITS EQUIVALENT ON THE
OTHER SCALE.

ENTER TEMPERATURE AND SCALE:
?37G
              "G" IS NOT A VALID SCALE.
```

CASE labels merely serve as identification tags for the various alternatives represented in a CASE statement. The labels used in a CASE statement pertain only to that CASE statement. That is, a particular value may appear as a label in more than one CASE statement in the same program, but not in more than one label list within the same CASE statement. Also, CASE labels must always be constants or constant identifiers of an ordinal type (REAL excluded), never variables or expressions.

THE OTHERWISE OPTION FOR THE CASE STATEMENT†

We have already noted that it may or may not be an execution error for the value of a CASE selector not to be one of the labels listed in the label lists for the CASE statement in which that selector is used. Some versions of Pascal provide an OTHERWISE option for the CASE statement to give an explicit alternative in CASEs where the selector's value is not in one of the label lists. The OTHERWISE portion of a CASE statement (if allowed) is placed after the last labeled alternative, as shown in Figure 5–8. One or more statements appearing after the keyword OTHERWISE up to the END of the CASE statement constitute the OTHERWISE alternative. These statements are executed only if none of the labeled alternatives is selected.

An IF statement is used in the program TEMPCONVERT (page 159) to make sure that the variable SCALE has an appropriate value when it is used as the selector in a CASE statement. The IF structure may be replaced by a CASE statement that has an OTHERWISE option:

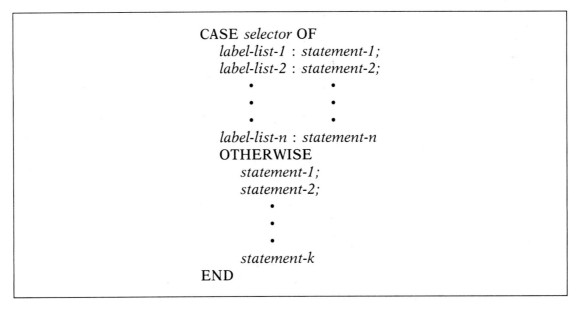

```
CASE selector OF
    label-list-1 : statement-1;
    label-list-2 : statement-2;
         •              •
         •              •
         •              •
    label-list-n : statement-n
OTHERWISE
    statement-1;
    statement-2;
         •
         •
         •
    statement-k
END
```

Figure 5–8
Structure of a CASE statement with the OTHERWISE option.

†The OTHERWISE option for CASE statements is not available in many versions of Pascal. This section can be skipped without loss of continuity.

```
CASE SCALE OF
   FAHRENHEIT : BEGIN (* CONVERSION TO CELSIUS *)
                CTEMP := 5.0 / 9.0 * (TEMP - 32.0);
                WRITELN(TEMP:20:2, ' DEGREES F = ', CTEMP:6:2,
                        ' DEGREES C.')
                END (* OF CONVERSION TO CELSIUS *)
      CELSIUS : BEGIN (* CONVERSION TO FAHRENHEIT *)
                FTEMP := 1.8 * TEMP + 32.0;
                WRITELN(TEMP:20:2, ' DEGREES C = ', FTEMP:6:2,
                        ' DEGREES F.')
                END (* OF CONVERSION TO FAHRENHEIT *)
   OTHERWISE (* SCALE ERROR *)
      WRITELN('"':15, SCALE, '" IS NOT A VALID SCALE.')
END (* OF SCALE CASES *)
```

When SCALE has any CHAR value except 'F' or 'C' (the values of the constant identifiers FAHRENHEIT and CELSIUS), the WRITELN statement after OTHER-WISE is executed.

A CASE statement with an OTHERWISE option may be used to assign a letter GRADE based on the value of the test SCORE:

```
CASE SCORE DIV 10 OF
                 9 : GRADE := 'A';
                 8 : GRADE := 'B';
                 7 : GRADE := 'C';
                 6 : GRADE := 'D';
   0, 1, 2, 3, 4, 5 : GRADE := 'F'
   OTHERWISE
      IF SCORE = 100
         THEN GRADE := 'A'
         ELSE WRITELN('INVALID SCORE:', SCORE:4)
END (* OF SCORE GRADING CASES *)
```

Note that a SCORE of 100 is treated as a "special case" when the OTHERWISE alternative is selected. The IF statement in the OTHERWISE clause is executed only if the value of SCORE is less than 0 or greater than 99.

5.4 EXERCISES

1. Find the errors (if any) in each of the following CASE statements. Assume that all the variables used have been appropriately declared and given values.

a.
```
CASE COUNT OF
          1, 2 : POINTS := POINTS + 1;
          3, 4 : POINTS := POINTS + 2;
    5, 6, 7, 8 : POINTS := POINTS + 3;
       8, 9, 10 : POINTS := POINTS + 4
END
```

b.
```
CASE SYMBOL OF
  '(', ')' : WRITE(SYMBOL);
  '$', '#' : BEGIN
               READ(VALUE)
               WRITE(VALUE)
             END;
       '/' : WRITELN
```

c.
```
CASE A > B OF
    'TRUE' : BEGIN
               C := B - A;
               B := B + 1.0
             END
   'FALSE' : BEGIN
               C := A - B;
               IF A < B
                  THEN A := A + 1.0
             END
END
```

d.
```
CASE (P + Q) / R OF
  1.84 : P := P-R;
  4.25 : BEGIN
           Q := P * R + 5.0;
           P := P + 1.0
         END;
   3.3 : WRITELN(P, Q)
END
```

2. Develop a program segment that uses a CASE statement to find a salesperson's commission according to the specifications given in Section 5.2. Would it be advantageous to use the OTHERWISE option? Explain.

3. In the School of Science at a small college, every course has a four-digit number: the first digit is the code number of the department and the last three digits represent the sequence number for the course. The departments and their code numbers are as follows:

> 1 Biology
> 2 Chemistry
> 3 Computer Science
> 4 Geology
> 5 Mathematics
> 6 Physics

Develop a CASE statement with alternatives that will print the name of the department offering a course and the code number of the course given the course number.

4. Shown below is a flowchart of a program segment to process a cash Withdrawal or Deposit TRANSaction of a specified AMOUNT. Write a pseudocode description of the program segment and then write the program segment.

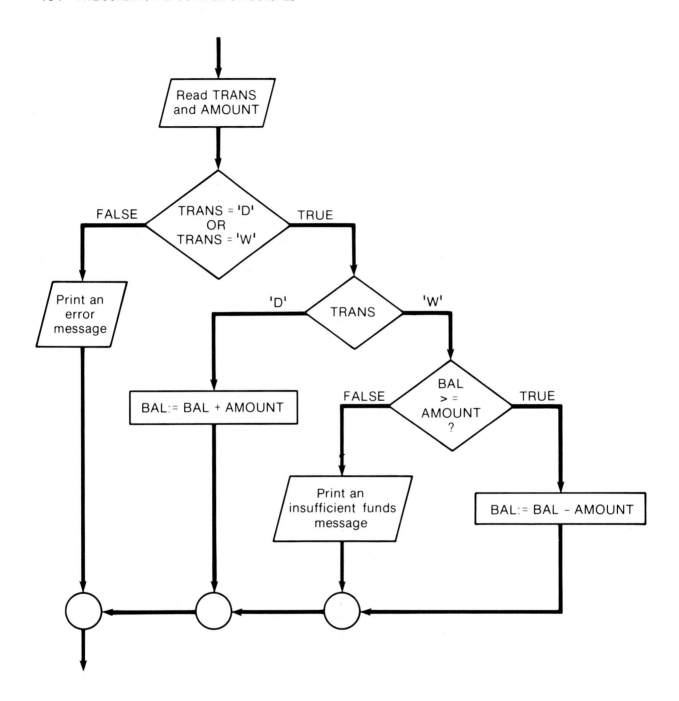

5.5
PROGRAMMING PROBLEMS

Design and write a program according to the specifications given in the following problems. Sample data sets are provided with each program description. Use these data sets and several sets of your own data to test your program. Information in the data sets should be read as input by the program. Use constant identifiers for data that stay the same for every run of the program.

1. Write a program that will read an integer representing the time of day on a 24-hour clock and print the equivalent time in hours and minutes. (For example, if the input time is 1635, the output should be 4:35 P.M.)

Test Data	24-Hour Clock Time
Set #1	2215
Set #2	348
Set #3	1372

2. Write a program that will read a value x and then evaluate the following mathematical function:

$$f(x) = \begin{cases} x(x + 2.0) & \text{if} \quad 2.0 < x \leq 10.0 \\ 2.0x & \text{if} \quad -1.0 < x \leq 2.0 \\ x - 1.0 & \text{if} \quad x \leq -1.0 \end{cases}$$

If x is greater than 10.0, the program should print a message indicating that f(x) does not exist.

Test Data	x
Set #1	2.0
Set #2	7.85
Set #3	-12.5
Set #4	15.3

3. Viking Athletic Supply Company is running a special on its best football uniform. The trousers normally sell for $42.50 each and the jerseys sell for $64.95 each, but the complete uniform is on sale for only $79.95 if 50 or more are purchased. Single jerseys or trousers still sell for regular price. Write a program that will read the number of jerseys and the number of trousers in an order and then compute the charges. The output should consist of an itemized list of the charges and the total amount billed.

Test Data	Number of Trousers	Number of Jerseys
Set #1	75	62
Set #2	50	84
Set #3	38	47
Set #4	65	65

4. The regular hourly wages for workers in each of four job classifications at a small factory are shown in the following table:

Classification	Hourly Rate
A	$10.25
B	$8.50
C	$6.30
D	$4.65

An employee who works more than 40 hours in a week earns one and one-half times the regular rate for all hours in excess of 40. Federal tax is withheld from the weekly gross salary on a percentage basis as follows:

Tax Rate	Gross Salary Ranges
12%	Gross ≤ $200.00
15%	$200.00 < Gross ≤ $350.00
18%	Gross > $350.00

Write a program that will read an employee's job classification and the number of hours worked for a week and then compute the gross salary, federal tax withheld, and the net salary.

Test Data	Classification	Hours Worked
Set #1	A	40.0
Set #2	C	32.0
Set #3	B	48.5
Set #4	D	44.5

5. Given the values a, b, c, d, e, and f, the system of linear equations

$$ax + by = c$$
$$dx + ey = f$$

has a unique solution when ae − bd is not zero. This solution is given by the formulas

$$x = \frac{ce - bf}{ae - bd} \quad \text{and} \quad y = \frac{af - cd}{ae - bd}$$

Write a program that will read the values of a, b, c, d, e, and f and then compute the solution when ae − bd is not zero. If ae − bd = 0, an appropriate message should be printed. Otherwise, the solution to the system of equations should be printed.

Test Data	a	b	c	d	e	f
Set #1	2.0	5.0	8.0	−4.0	2.0	5.0
Set #2	3.5	−12.25	6.4	0.6	7.0	9.5
Set #3	−5.4	18.0	4.5	2.7	−9.0	13.3

6. A service station with a car wash sells three grades of gasoline: regular at $1.359 per gallon, premium at $1.479 per gallon, and lead-free at $1.429 per gallon. A car wash normally costs $2.00, but the station offers a 10% reduction on the price of a wash for every full gallon of gasoline purchased in excess of 10 gallons. When 20 or more gallons are purchased, the car wash is free. Write a program that reads the number of gallons purchased by a customer and a character indicating the grade of gasoline purchased. The program should print the cost of the gasoline and the price of a wash and then read another character indicating whether or not the customer wants a car wash before it prints the total charges.

Test Data	Grade of Gasoline	Gallons Purchased	Wash Wanted?
Set #1	Premium	15.0	No
Set #2	Regular	21.4	Yes
Set #3	Lead-Free	7.5	Yes
Set #4	Regular	17.9	Yes

7. The city of Hillsdale bills its residents for sewage disposal and water, electric power, and sanitation services. Sewage disposal and water are billed every other month (starting in February) according to the number of gallons of water used:

Water (gallons)	Rates
1500 or less	$0.0125 per gallon
Over 1500	$18.75 plus $0.0142 for every gallon over 1500

Electric power is billed every three months (beginning in March) according to the number of kilowatt-hours (kwh) used:

Electricity (kwh)	Rates
400 or less	$0.053 per kwh
700 or less	$21.20 plus $0.061 per kwh in excess of 400
Over 700	$39.50 plus $0.073 per kwh in excess of 700

The sanitation charge is a flat $5.50 per month billed every month. Write a program that will read an integer between 1 and 12 inclusive, indicating the billing month, and then solicit the water and / or electric power usage for a customer as required. The program should compute the charges due for the month and print an itemized bill.

Test Data	Month Number	Water (gallons)	Electricity (kwh)
Set #1	1	—	—
Set #2	6	1290	360
Set #3	9	—	725
Set #4	10	1854	—

8. A certain game requires that two dice be rolled one at a time. If p and q are the numbers rolled on the first and second die, respectively, the value of the roll in the game is determined as follows:

p	q	Value of the Roll	
even	odd	$2p + q$	
odd	even	$p + 2q$	
even	even	$\begin{cases} p + q \\ 3p \end{cases}$	if $p \neq q$ if $p = q$
odd	odd	$\begin{cases} p + q \\ 3q \end{cases}$	if $p \neq q$ if $p = q$

Write a program that will read a pair of values p and q and then compute and print the value of the roll.

Test Data	p	q
Set #1	2	5
Set #2	4	4
Set #3	6	2
Set #4	1	3

9. Write a program that will read the radius (r) of a circle and then compute either the circumference (c) of the circle (c = $2\pi r$) or the area of the circle (area = πr^2) or both, depending on a signal character that is also read. (Use 3.14159 as an approximation for π.)

Test Data	r	Signal
Set #1	2.5	Area
Set #2	15.0	C
Set #3	8.8	Both

10. National Parcel Service (NPS) specializes in nationwide delivery of small packages. NPS will not accept any package whose largest dimension is greater than 3 feet or whose weight exceeds 50 pounds. The charge for shipping a parcel is $0.75 plus an amount based on package weight as follows:

Weight (lb.)	Rate
20 or less	$0.08 per lb.
40 or less	$0.10 per lb.
Over 40	$0.15 per lb.

There is an additional $1.00 charge if the volume of the package exceeds 18 cubic feet. Write a program that will read the dimensions of a parcel (in feet) and its weight (in pounds) and then compute and print the postage due. If the package is rejected, an appropriate message should be printed.

Test Data	Length	Width	Depth	Weight
Set #1	1.5	1.2	0.8	6.0
Set #2	3.0	2.7	2.3	25.6
Set #3	2.4	1.0	4.4	45.8
Set #4	2.6	2.6	2.6	40.5
Set #5	4.0	2.0	2.0	63.2

SIX/CONTROL STRUCTURES FOR PROGRAM LOOPS

Most programming applications involve activities that are repetitive by nature. For example, the simple process of summing three or more numbers requires repeated addition. If exactly three numbers must be summed, one of the following program segments could be used:

```
READ(A, B, C);              SUM := 0;
SUM := A + B + C            READ(X);
                           SUM := SUM + X;
                           READ(X);
                           SUM := SUM + X;
                           READ(X);
                           SUM := SUM + X
```

Both of these program segments depend on the fact that exactly three numbers are to be summed. Notice that the segment on the right has three identical pairs of statements following one another. The statement SUM := SUM + X is used after each number is read to add that number to the accumulated SUM. This repetition of the same process suggests the concept of a "loop," as illustrated in the following flowchart:

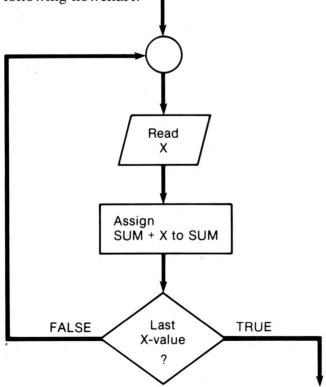

In order to implement a loop in a program, it must be possible to execute a sequence of statements repeatedly until some conditions for termination of the loop are satisfied.

All programming languages provide control statements that can be used to modify the normal sequential flow of execution through a program. **A program loop** consists of a sequence of one or more statements, known as the **body of the loop,** and some form of control, which directs the repeated execution of that sequence of statements. Each time the body of a loop is executed, one **loop cycle** is completed. Pascal provides various control statements that are structured to regulate the number of times a loop cycles.

There are two general structures for controlled program loops: the **entrance-controlled structure** and the **exit-controlled structure.** The loop control provided by these two structures is illustrated by the flowcharts in Figure 6–1. In an entrance-controlled loop, the control conditions are tested prior to the beginning of each cycle. The body of an entrance-controlled loop will not be executed if the entrance conditions are not satisfied. The control conditions for an exit-controlled loop are tested at the conclusion of each loop cycle. This means that the body of an exit-controlled loop is executed unconditionally the first time.

The assumption with regard to a controlled loop is that the control conditions will eventually result in an exit from the loop. If this is not the case, then an **infinite loop** results. When execution of a program is "caught" in an infinite loop, the same sequence of statements is executed over and over again with no chance that the program will reach normal completion. Time-sharing computer systems normally place a time limit on the execution of a program so that any program caught in an infinite loop is prematurely terminated once its execution time exceeds the limit.

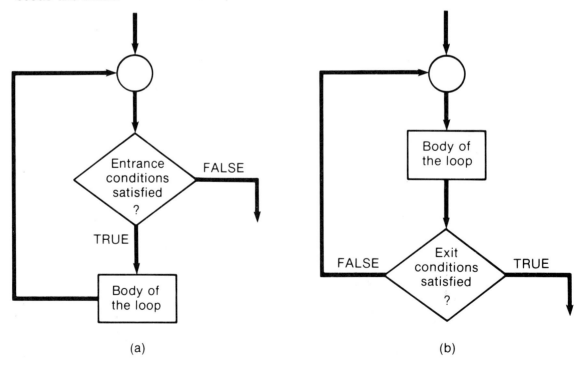

(a)   (b)

Figure 6–1
Flowchart description of the two basic loop structures. (a)
Entrance-controlled loop. (b) Exit-controlled loop.

6.1
THE WHILE STATEMENT

The WHILE statement is a structured statement that is used to implement an entrance-controlled loop. Consider the following example:

```
I := 1;
SUM := 0;
WHILE I <= 6
   DO BEGIN (* SUM ACCUMULATION *)
         READ(X);
         SUM := SUM + X;
         WRITELN('SUBTOTAL:', SUM:8);
         I := I + 1
         END (* OF SUM ACCUMULATION *);
WRITELN;
WRITELN('GRAND TOTAL:', SUM:8)
```

The body of the WHILE loop is the compound statement that BEGINs after the word DO and the relational expression $I <= 6$ is the condition that controls the number of times the loop will cycle. Note that the value of I is 1 the first time the control condition is tested and the value of I is incremented by 1 during each loop cycle so that $I <= 6$ will eventually be FALSE (when $I = 7$). A flowchart of the entire program segment is shown on page 172.

A total of six numbers are read and their SUM is accumulated. Here is the output produced by a sample run of the program segment:

```
?34
SUBTOTAL:         34
?166
SUBTOTAL:        200
?4218
SUBTOTAL:       4418
?3
SUBTOTAL:       4421
?75
SUBTOTAL:       4496
?504
SUBTOTAL:       5000

GRAND TOTAL:      5000
```

The general form of the WHILE statement and a flowchart showing the effects of a WHILE loop are given in Figure 6–2. Prior to each cycle of the loop, the *BOOLEAN expression* that appears after the keyword WHILE is evaluated and tested. A new cycle is started if and only if the value of the *BOOLEAN expression* is TRUE. Otherwise, the next statement after the WHILE statement is executed. The *statement* following the keyword DO represents the body of the loop. It is imperative that this *statement* eventually cause the value of the *BOOLEAN expression* to be FALSE when it is evaluated prior to beginning a new cycle so that the loop will be terminated after a finite number of cycles. In the example given ear-

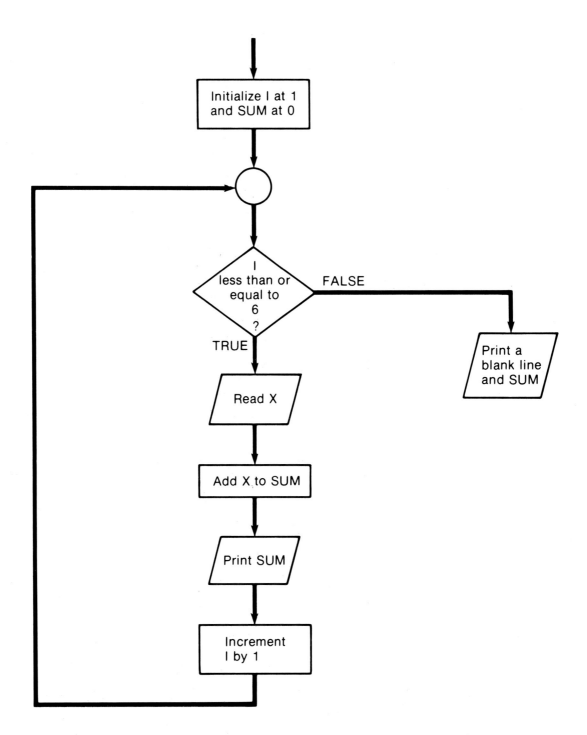

lier, the incrementation of I by 1 within the body of the loop guarantees that I <= 6 will eventually be FALSE.

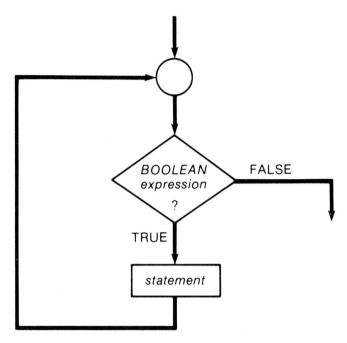

WHILE *BOOLEAN expression*
DO *statement*

Figure 6–2
General structure of the WHILE statement and a flowchart
description of a WHILE loop.

WHILE LOOPS

The body of a WHILE loop may be one simple statement, as illustrated in the following example:

```
READ(CH);
WHILE CH = ' '
    DO READ(CH);
WRITELN(CH)
```

If the input value read for the CHAR variable CH by the READ statement preceding the WHILE statement is not a blank space, then the WHILE loop is not entered and the value of CH is printed. Otherwise, the WHILE loop READs values for CH one by one until a nonblank value has been read. When this occurs, the loop is exited and the value of CH is printed. The effects of the WHILE loop are shown in the flowchart on page 174.

Here is another example of a WHILE statement, but this time the body of the loop is represented by a compound statement:

```
READLN;
WHILE NOT EOLN
    DO BEGIN
        READ(CH);
        WRITE(CH)
        END;
WRITELN
```

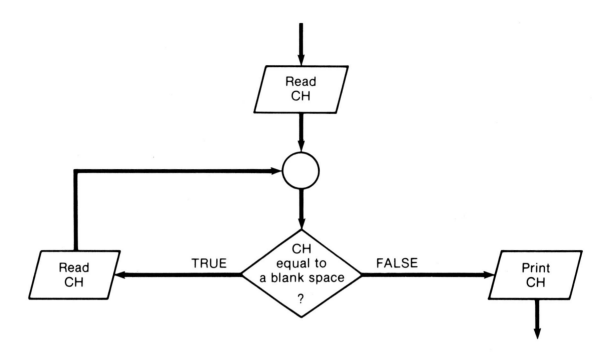

The purpose of this program segment is to print all characters on an input line. Prior to the reading and printing of each character, the value of NOT EOLN is determined and tested. When the EOLN function returns the value TRUE, NOT EOLN is FALSE and the loop is terminated. A sample of the effects of this program segment is shown next:

```
?SMITH, JOHN    18
SMITH, JOHN    18
```

A number may be raised to a positive integer power by successive multiplication. For instance, $(5.0)^3$ means $(5.0)(5.0)(5.0)$ which has the value 125.0. The following pseudocode describes a program segment that can be used to compute the value of X^N when N is a nonnegative integer and X is a real number. (By definition, $X^0 = 1.0$ when X is not zero.)

```
READ values for X and N
Initialize the multiplication ACCUMulator at 1.0
Initialize the multiplication COUNTer at 0
WHILE the COUNT is less than N
    DO BEGIN a multiplication
        Multiply the ACCUMulator by X
        Increment the COUNTer by 1
        END of a multiplication
Print the ACCUMulated product
```

The ACCUMulator is initially set at 1.0 and then it is multiplied exactly N times by the value of X in a loop that is controlled by a COUNTer. This pseudocode easily translates into the following program segment:

```
READ(X, N);
ACCUM := 1.0;
```

```
COUNT := 0;
WHILE COUNT < N
    DO BEGIN (* A MULTIPLICATION *)
        ACCUM := ACCUM * X;
        COUNT := COUNT + 1
        END (* OF A MULTIPLICATION *);
WRITELN (ACCUM)
```

In the examples that have been presented, the DO clause of each WHILE statement is indented on the line below WHILE. This style for the WHILE statement is used to stress that the execution of the body of the loop given in the DO clause is controlled by the BOOLEAN expression present after the word WHILE. The WHILE statement in the last program segment could be written in the form

```
WHILE COUNT < N DO BEGIN ACCUM := ACCUM * X; COUNT := COUNT + 1 END
```

However, a WHILE statement is much more readable if the body of the loop is not crowded onto the same line as the BOOLEAN expression that controls its execution.

A complete program is described by the pseudocode given below. The purpose of this program is to count "yes" and "no" responses signified by the presence of the letters Y and N, respectively, in the INPUT file. The counting stops when the letter S is read:

```
Constants: YES = 'Y'; NO = 'N'; STOP = 'S'
BEGIN program SURVEY
Print program information and directions
Initialize YESCOUNT and NOCOUNT at 0
Print a request for RESPONSEs
READ the first RESPONSE
WHILE the RESPONSE is not STOP
    DO BEGIN counting process
        IF the RESPONSE is YES
            THEN increment the YESCOUNT by 1
            ELSE IF the RESPONSE IS NO
                    THEN increment the NOCOUNT by 1
        READ the next RESPONSE
        END of counting process
Print YESCOUNT and NOCOUNT
END of program SURVEY
```

Although the program SURVEY employs two variables (YESCOUNT and NOCOUNT) as counters, neither of them is used to control the WHILE loop that manages the counting process. Exit from the loop occurs after the value 'S' has been read for the CHAR variable RESPONSE. Note that only the letters Y, N, and S in the INPUT file affect the counting process. Here is the program:

```
PROGRAM SURVEY (INPUT, OUTPUT);
(*********************************************************************
*                                                                   *
*           A PROGRAM TO COUNT YES AND NO RESPONSES                  *
*                                                                   *
*********************************************************************)
```

```
CONST                                   (*---------[CONSTANTS]----------*)
      YES = 'Y';                        (* A "YES" RESPONSE             *)
      NO = 'N';                         (* A "NO" RESPONSE              *)
      STOP = 'S';                       (* THE SIGNAL TO "STOP" COUNTING *)
                                        (*------------------------------*)
VAR                                     (*------[INTEGER VARIABLES]------*)
      YESCOUNT,                         (* COUNTER FOR "YES" RESPONSES  *)
      NOCOUNT : INTEGER;                (* COUNTER FOR "NO" RESPONSES   *)
                                        (*------------------------------*)
                                        (*-------[CHAR VARIABLES]--------*)
      RESPONSE : CHAR;                  (* AN INPUT CHARACTER           *)
                                        (*------------------------------*)
(*************************************************************************)
BEGIN (* PROGRAM SURVEY *)
WRITELN('THIS PROGRAM COUNTS YES AND NO RESPONSES SIGNIFIED BY');
WRITELN('THE LETTERS ', YES, ' AND ', NO, ', RESPECTIVELY. THE ',
        'RESPONSES CAN');
WRITELN('BE SEPARATED BY ANY NUMBER OF BLANK SPACES. USE AS');
WRITELN('MANY LINES AS NECESSARY AND ENTER THE LETTER ', STOP,
        ' AS A');
WRITELN('SIGNAL THAT ALL THE RESPONSES HAVE BEEN ENTERED. THE');
WRITELN('COUNTS OF YES AND NO RESPONSES WILL THEN BE PRINTED.');
WRITELN;
YESCOUNT := 0;
NOCOUNT := 0;
WRITELN('BEGIN ENTERING THE RESPONSES NOW.');
READ(RESPONSE);
WHILE RESPONSE <> STOP
   DO BEGIN (* COUNTING PROCESS *)
      IF RESPONSE = YES
         THEN YESCOUNT := YESCOUNT + 1
         ELSE IF RESPONSE = NO
                 THEN NOCOUNT := NOCOUNT + 1;
      READ(RESPONSE)
      END (* OF COUNTING PROCESS *);
WRITELN;
WRITELN('TOTAL COUNTS':20);
WRITELN('------------':20);
WRITELN('YES:':14, YESCOUNT:4);
WRITELN('NO:':14, NOCOUNT:4);
WRITELN('------------':20)
END (* OF PROGRAM SURVEY *).
```

The output from a typical run of the program SURVEY follows:

```
THIS PROGRAM COUNTS YES AND NO RESPONSES SIGNIFIED BY
THE LETTERS Y AND N, RESPECTIVELY. THE RESPONSES CAN
BE SEPARATED BY ANY NUMBER OF BLANK SPACES. USE AS
MANY LINES AS NECESSARY AND ENTER THE LETTER S AS A
SIGNAL THAT ALL THE RESPONSES HAVE BEEN ENTERED. THE
COUNTS OF YES AND NO RESPONSES WILL THEN BE PRINTED.
```

```
BEGIN ENTERING THE RESPONSES NOW.
? Y Y N Y N NY Y  Y N NNN Y  N YY Y  N S

          TOTAL COUNTS
          ------------
          YES:  10
          NO:    9
          ------------
```

The counting process in the program is designed in such a way that the input characters representing responses may appear consecutively on a line or there may be blank spaces between consecutive responses. Characters other than Y, N, and S that may appear by chance in the INPUT file are simply not counted. This is illustrated in the following output produced by a run of the program SURVEY:

```
THIS PROGRAM COUNTS YES AND NO RESPONSES SIGNIFIED BY
THE LETTERS Y AND N, RESPECTIVELY. THE RESPONSES CAN
BE SEPARATED BY ANY NUMBER OF BLANK SPACES. USE AS
MANY LINES AS NECESSARY AND ENTER THE LETTER S AS A
SIGNAL THAT ALL THE RESPONSES HAVE BEEN ENTERED. THE
COUNTS OF YES AND NO RESPONSES WILL THEN BE PRINTED.

BEGIN ENTERING THE RESPONSES NOW.
?NY N  N YN Y U YY  NNN N
?  Y Y NNB Y Y   Y N
? 4 N  NY *N  YY N S Y NN

          TOTAL COUNTS
          ------------
          YES:  13
          NO:   15
          ------------
```

6.1 EXERCISES

1. Assume that the INTEGER variables A and B have the values 3 and 100, respectively. Analyze each of the program segments that follow and determine how many times the body of each WHILE loop will be executed. Also tell what values will be printed for A and B.

a.
```
WHILE A <= B
   DO A := 2 * A;
WRITELN(A, B)
```

b.
```
WHILE A * B <> 500
   DO B := B + 25;
WRITELN(A, B)
```

c.
```
WHILE B DIV A > 5
    DO IF B - A > 25
           THEN A := A + 1
           ELSE B := B DIV 2;
WRITELN(A, B)
```

d.
```
WHILE B - 20 * A >= 0
    DO CASE B MOD A OF
               0 : B := B - 25;
            1, 2 : B := B + 2
           END;
WRITELN(A, B)
```

2. Find the errors (if any) in each of the following program segments. Assume that all the variables have been defined and given values.

a.
```
WHILE X < 100
    DO BEGIN
       X := X - 2;
       WRITELN(X)
       END
```

b.
```
IF X > 10 + Y
   THEN WHILE X > Y
            DO X := X - 10;
   ELSE WHILE Y > X
            DO Y := Y - 10
```

c.
```
TOTAL := 0;
WHILE (X < 20) OR (Y < 20)
    DO BEGIN
       X := X - 1;
       Y := Y - 2;
       TOTAL := TOTAL + X - Y
       END;
WRITELN(X, Y, TOTAL)
```

d.
```
Z := 0;
WHILE Y * X + 3
    DO BEGIN
       Z := Y + Z DIV X;
       Y := Y + 5
       END
WRITELN(X, Y, Z)
```

3. Examine the following program segment and tell what it does. In particular, tell what output is produced if the following sequence of characters is read:

LOOK■TO■THE■EAST■AT■DAWN.■THE■SUN■IS■RISING.

```
READ(CH);
WHILE CH <> '.'
```

```
DO BEGIN
   IF CH = ' '
     THEN WRITELN
     ELSE WRITE(CH);
   READ(CH)
   END
```

4. Show how the program SURVEY given in Section 6.1 can be modified to print every invalid response (a character other than Y, N, or S) along with a suitable message.

5. Write a program segment that uses a WHILE loop to balance a checkbook. First, read the starting balance. Then successively read and process any number of transactions (deposits and withdrawals). The program segment should use some signal character to determine when to exit the transaction processing loop. Output should consist of the total number of each type of transaction and the ending balance in the checking account.

6. The program segment to compute the value of X^N given in Section 6.1 works properly only when the value of N is a nonnegative integer. Suppose X can be any real number and N can be any integer. Write a program segment that will calculate the value of X^N. (If N is negative, the value of X^N is 1.0 divided by X^{-N}.)

6.2
THE REPEAT STATEMENT

The REPEAT statement is a structured control statement used to implement an exit-controlled loop. Consider the following example:

```
SUM := 0;
REPEAT
   READ(X);
   SUM := SUM + X;
   WRITELN('SUBTOTAL:', SUM:8)
UNTIL X = 0;
WRITELN;
WRITELN('GRAND TOTAL:', SUM:8)
```

The sequence of statements between the keyword REPEAT and the keyword UNTIL constitutes the body of a loop that is controlled by the relational expression X = 0 given after the word UNTIL. X-values are read and their sum is accumulated until an input value for X is zero. Here is a sample of the output produced when the program segment above is executed:

```
?34
SUBTOTAL:        34
?166
SUBTOTAL:       200
?4218
SUBTOTAL:      4418
?3
```

```
SUBTOTAL:         4421
?0
SUBTOTAL:         4421

GRAND TOTAL:          4421
```

The general form of the REPEAT statement and a flowchart showing the effects of a REPEAT loop are given in Figure 6–3. After each loop cycle, the *BOOLEAN expression* specified following the word UNTIL is evaluated and tested to determine whether or not another loop cycle should be started. This *BOOLEAN expression* gives the loop exit criteria. The sequence of statements (*statement-1* through *statement-k*) listed after the word REPEAT is executed every time evaluation of the *BOOLEAN expression* produces the value FALSE. This sequence of statements must eventually cause the value of the *BOOLEAN expression* to be TRUE or an infinite loop will result. Consecutive statements in the body of the loop must be separated by a semicolon.

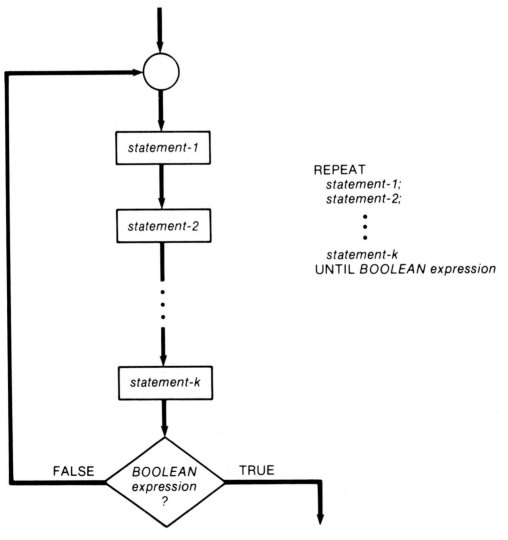

```
REPEAT
    statement-1;
    statement-2;
        •
        •
        •
    statement-k
UNTIL BOOLEAN expression
```

Figure 6–3
General structure of the REPEAT statement and a flowchart description of a REPEAT loop.

REPEAT LOOPS

Any loop implemented by using a WHILE statement can also be implemented by using a REPEAT statement. The reverse is also true. However, in most situations where either a WHILE loop or a REPEAT loop could be used, one form of loop control will be more efficient than the other. Consider the two program segments shown below, both of which are designed to read input characters and print them on one line until an asterisk has been read (but not printed).

```
READ(CH);                          REPEAT
WHILE CH <> '*'                        READ(CH);
    DO BEGIN                           IF CH <> '*'
        WRITE(CH);                         THEN WRITE(CH)
        READ(CH)                   UNTIL CH = '*';
        END;                       WRITELN
WRITELN
```

The following sample output could have resulted from the execution of either of these program segments:

```
?THE ASTERISK (*) MEANS STOP.
THE ASTERISK (
```

Since the value of CH is tested in the body of the REPEAT loop and again after every cycle of the REPEAT loop, the WHILE structure is more efficient. If the asterisk should be printed after it is read, then a REPEAT structure for the loop is more efficient:

```
READ(CH);                          REPEAT
WHILE CH <> '*'                        READ(CH);
    DO BEGIN                           WRITE(CH)
        WRITE(CH);                 UNTIL CH = '*';
        READ(CH)                   WRITELN
        END;
WRITELN(CH)
```

In this book, the keyword REPEAT and the UNTIL portion of a REPEAT statement are placed on separate lines and the sequence of statements representing the body of the loop is indented on lines in between. It is possible for the body of a REPEAT loop to consist of a single statement, as in the following example:

```
REPEAT
    READ(CH)
UNTIL CH <> ' '
```

This loop reads characters from the INPUT file until a nonblank character has been read. Since the REPEAT statement is rather short, it could appear entirely on one line:

```
REPEAT READ(CH) UNTIL CH <> ' '
```

To clarify the purpose of a REPEAT loop, a short comment may be inserted prior to the body of the loop. For instance,

```
REPEAT (* SKIP A SPACE *)
   READ(CH)
UNTIL CH <> ' '
```

Suppose a dollar amount (INITIALAMOUNT) is invested in an account that pays a certain average RATE of interest (a fraction) compounded each MONTH. The following program segment will determine the number of months it will take for the value of the investment to at least double the dollar amount initially invested:

```
READ(INITIALAMOUNT, RATE);
NEWAMOUNT := INITIALAMOUNT;
MONTH := 0;
REPEAT (* EARN A MONTH'S INTEREST *)
   NEWAMOUNT := NEWAMOUNT + RATE * NEWAMOUNT;
   MONTH := MONTH + 1
UNTIL NEWAMOUNT >= 2.0 * INITIALAMOUNT;
WRITELN('AN INITIAL INVESTMENT OF $', INITIALAMOUNT:8:2,
        ' IN AN ACCOUNT');
WRITELN('WHICH EARNS ', 100.0 * RATE:4:2, ' PERCENT ',
        'INTEREST COMPOUNDED');
WRITELN('EACH MONTH WILL BE WORTH $', NEWAMOUNT:8:2,
        ' IN ', MONTH:2, ' MONTHS.')
```

Here is a sample of the output produced by this program segment:

```
? 1000.0  0.0075
AN INITIAL INVESTMENT OF $ 1000.00 IN AN ACCOUNT
WHICH EARNS 0.75 PERCENT INTEREST COMPOUNDED
EACH MONTH WILL BE WORTH $ 2003.50 IN 93 MONTHS.
```

Consider a program to process the payroll for a company. An employee's gross salary (salary before deductions) is based on an hourly rate. If an employee works more than 40 hours in a pay period, some overtime factor (for instance, 1.5) is multiplied by the regular hourly rate to determine an overtime rate that applies only to the hours worked in excess of 40. The only deductions to be considered are federal and state taxes, union dues, and credit union savings. It is desirable that the program process as many employee salaries as necessary and that the salary calculations be summarized in the output. Here is a pseudocode description of a program that meets these requirements:

```
Constants: YES = 'Y'; NO = 'N'
           REGULARHRS = 40
BEGIN program PAYDAY
Print program information and directions
Initialize the total PAYROLL at 0.0
REPEAT employee salary processing
     READ an employee IDentification number, hourly PAYRATE, OVERTIME
          factor, and HOURS worked
     IF the HOURS worked exceeds REGULARHRS
        THEN compute GROSSPAY as
               REGULARHRS * PAYRATE + (HOURS - REGULARHRS)
                 * OVERTIME * PAYRATE
```

```
          ELSE compute GROSSPAY as
                    HOURS * PAYRATE
          Add GROSSPAY to the total PAYROLL
          READ the FEDERALRATE and STATERATE for taxes
          Calculate the FEDERALTAX deduction as FEDERALRATE * GROSSPAY
          Calculate the STATETAX deduction as STATERATE * GROSSPAY
          READ the CREDITUNION and UNIONDUES deductions
          Compute the total DEDUCTIONS as
                    FEDERALTAX + STATETAX + CREDITUNION + UNIONDUES
          Calculate the NETPAY as GROSSPAY − DEDUCTIONS
          Print a summary of the salary calculations
          READ a RESPONSE (YES or NO) indicating whether or not there are
                    more salaries to be processed
      UNTIL the RESPONSE is NO
      Print the total PAYROLL
      END of program PAYDAY
```

The program PAYDAY is given next. It was written after further refinement of the pseudocode to give a more detailed explanation of how a RESPONSE is processed. Note that a REPEAT loop and a WHILE loop are used in the program to ensure that only valid RESPONSEs are accepted.

```
PROGRAM PAYDAY (INPUT, OUTPUT);
(**************************************************************
*                                                           *
*          A PROGRAM TO PROCESS WORKERS' SALARIES           *
*                                                           *
**************************************************************)
CONST                            (*---------- [CONSTANTS] -----------*)
      YES = 'Y';                 (* A "YES" RESPONSE                *)
      NO = 'N';                  (* A "NO" RESPONSE                 *)
      REGULARHRS = 40;           (* LIMIT ON HOURS AT REGULAR       *)
                                 (* PAYRATE                         *)
                                 (*--------------------------------*)

VAR                              (*------ [INTEGER VARIABLES] -------*)
      ID : INTEGER;              (* EMPLOYEE IDENTIFICATION NO.     *)
                                 (*--------------------------------*)

      PAYRATE,                   (* HOURLY RATE OF PAY ($/HR)       *)
      HOURS,                     (* TOTAL HOURS FOR THE PAY PERIOD  *)
      OVERTIME,                  (* PAYRATE OVERTIME FACTOR         *)
      FEDERALRATE,               (* FEDERAL TAX RATE (FRACTION)     *)
      STATERATE,                 (* STATE TAX RATE (FRACTION)       *)
      CREDITUNION,               (* CREDIT UNION DEDUCTION ($)      *)
      UNIONDUES,                 (* UNION DUES DEDUCTION ($)        *)
      FEDERALTAX,                (* FEDERAL TAX DEDUCTION ($)       *)
      STATETAX,                  (* STATE TAX DEDUCTION ($)         *)
      GROSSPAY,                  (* SALARY BEFORE DEDUCTIONS ($)    *)
      NETPAY,                    (* SALARY AFTER DEDUCTIONS ($)     *)
      DEDUCTIONS,                (* TOTAL DEDUCTIONS ($)            *)
      PAYROLL : REAL;            (* TOTAL OF GROSS SALARIES ($)     *)
                                 (*--------------------------------*)
```

```
                                    (*-------[CHAR VARIABLES]---------*)
          RESPONSE : CHAR;          (* AN INPUT "YES" OR "NO" RESPONSE*)
                                    (*--------------------------------*)
(***********************************************************************)
BEGIN (* PROGRAM PAYDAY *)
WRITELN('THIS PROGRAM CAN BE USED TO DETERMINE THE PAYROLL FOR');
WRITELN('ANY NUMBER OF EMPLOYEES. THE INPUT DATA CONSIST OF AN');
WRITELN('EMPLOYEE NUMBER, AN HOURLY RATE OF PAY ($/HOUR), NUMBER');
WRITELN('OF HOURS WORKED, AN OVERTIME FACTOR, FEDERAL AND STATE');
WRITELN('TAX RATES (FRACTIONS), A CREDIT UNION DEDUCTION ($), AND');
WRITELN('A UNION DUES DEDUCTION ($). ENTER DATA FOR EACH EMPLOYEE');
WRITELN('AS THEY ARE REQUESTED. THE SALARY CALCULATIONS WILL BE');
WRITELN('SHOWN IN A PRINTED SUMMARY AFTER EACH EMPLOYEE''S DATA');
WRITELN('IS PROCESSED.');
PAYROLL := 0.0;
REPEAT (* EMPLOYEE SALARY PROCESSING *)
  WRITELN;
  WRITELN('EMPLOYEE IDENTIFICATION NUMBER:');
  READ(ID);
  WRITELN('HOURLY RATE     HOURS WORKED     OVERTIME FACTOR');
  READ(PAYRATE, HOURS, OVERTIME);
  IF HOURS > REGULARHRS
     THEN GROSSPAY := REGULARHRS * PAYRATE
                        + (HOURS - REGULARHRS) * OVERTIME * PAYRATE
     ELSE GROSSPAY := HOURS * PAYRATE;
  PAYROLL := PAYROLL + GROSSPAY;
  WRITELN('FED. TAX RATE    STATE TAX RATE    (FRACTIONS)');
  READ(FEDERALRATE, STATERATE);
  FEDERALTAX := FEDERALRATE * GROSSPAY;
  STATETAX := STATERATE * GROSSPAY;
  WRITELN('CREDIT UNION ($)     UNION DUES ($)');
  READ(CREDITUNION, UNIONDUES);
  DEDUCTIONS := FEDERALTAX + STATETAX + CREDITUNION + UNIONDUES;
  NETPAY := GROSSPAY - DEDUCTIONS;
  (**** SUMMARY OF SALARY CALCULATIONS ****)
  WRITELN;
  WRITELN('EMPLOYEE #', ID:5, ':');
  WRITELN('GROSS PAY':20, '$':2, GROSSPAY:7:2);
  WRITELN('DEDUCTIONS':20, '$':2, DEDUCTIONS:7:2);
  WRITELN('-------':29);
  WRITELN('NET PAY':20, '$':2, NETPAY:7:2);
  WRITELN;
  (**** END OF SALARY SUMMARY ****)
  WRITELN('MORE EMPLOYEES TO BE PROCESSED (Y MEANS YES, N MEANS NO)');
  REPEAT (* RESPONSE ANALYSIS *)
    READLN; (* NEW INPUT LINE *)
    READ(RESPONSE);
    WHILE RESPONSE = ' '
       DO READ(RESPONSE);
    IF (RESPONSE <> YES) AND (RESPONSE <> NO)
      THEN WRITELN(RESPONSE, ' IS INVALID. ENTER Y OR N.')
  UNTIL (RESPONSE = YES) OR (RESPONSE = NO);
  WRITELN
```

```
UNTIL RESPONSE = NO;
WRITELN('TOTAL OF GROSS SALARIES: $':30, PAYROLL:10:2)
END (* OF PROGRAM PAYDAY *).
```

The output from a sample run of the program PAYDAY is given next. When data are requested, column headings are printed so that the user knows the order in which the data should be entered.

```
THIS PROGRAM CAN BE USED TO DETERMINE THE PAYROLL FOR
ANY NUMBER OF EMPLOYEES. THE INPUT DATA CONSIST OF AN
EMPLOYEE NUMBER, AN HOURLY RATE OF PAY ($/HOUR), NUMBER
OF HOURS WORKED, AN OVERTIME FACTOR, FEDERAL AND STATE
TAX RATES (FRACTIONS), A CREDIT UNION DEDUCTION ($), AND
A UNION DUES DEDUCTION ($). ENTER DATA FOR EACH EMPLOYEE
AS THEY ARE REQUESTED. THE SALARY CALCULATIONS WILL BE
SHOWN IN A PRINTED SUMMARY AFTER EACH EMPLOYEE'S DATA
IS PROCESSED.

EMPLOYEE IDENTIFICATION NUMBER:
?  56347
HOURLY RATE      HOURS WORKED      OVERTIME FACTOR
?  13.45             45                 1.5
FED. TAX RATE     STATE TAX RATE     (FRACTIONS)
?  0.18              0.05
CREDIT UNION ($)     UNION DUES ($)
?  35.00             18.00

EMPLOYEE #56347:
          GROSS PAY: $ 638.87
          DEDUCTIONS: $ 199.94
                      -------
          NET PAY: $ 438.93

MORE EMPLOYEES TO BE PROCESSED (Y MEANS YES, N MEANS NO)
?  T
T IS INVALID. ENTER Y OR N.
?  Y


EMPLOYEE IDENTIFICATION NUMBER:
?  37540
HOURLY RATE      HOURS WORKED      OVERTIME FACTOR
?   3.45             37                 1.0
FED. TAX RATE     STATE TAX RATE     (FRACTIONS)
?  0.16              0.07
CREDIT UNION ($)     UNION DUES ($)
?  15.50              0.00

EMPLOYEE #37540:
            GROSS PAY: $ 127.65
            DEDUCTIONS: $  44.86
                        -------
              NET PAY: $  82.79
```

```
MORE EMPLOYEES TO BE PROCESSED (Y MEANS YES, N MEANS NO)
? N

    TOTAL OF GROSS SALARIES: $      766.52
```

Although the program PAYDAY appears to function properly, some modifications are needed. When the gross pay and taxes are computed, more than two digits after the decimal point will be maintained. Since the results of these calculations represent dollars and cents, they should be rounded to the nearest whole cent. Otherwise, some of the numbers in the printed summaries and the total of gross salaries may be incorrect. The necessary adjustments are left as an exercise (see Exercise 6 below).

6.2 EXERCISES

1. Assume that the INTEGER variables A and B have the values 3 and 100, respectively. Analyze each of the following program segments and determine how many times the body of each REPEAT loop will be executed. Also tell what values will be printed for A and B.

   a.
   ```
   REPEAT
      A := 2 * A
   UNTIL A >= B;
   WRITELN(A, B)
   ```

   b.
   ```
   REPEAT
      A := B DIV A;
      B := B - A
   UNTIL A < B;
   WRITELN(A, B)
   ```

   c.
   ```
   REPEAT
      B := B DIV A - 1;
      IF B >= A
         THEN B := A
   UNTIL B < 1;
   WRITELN(A, B)
   ```

   d.
   ```
   REPEAT
      CASE B MOD A OF
           0 : B := B - 25;
         1, 2 : B := B + 2
      END
   UNTIL (B - 20) * A <= 150;
   WRITELN(A, B)
   ```

2. Find the errors (if any) in each of the following program segments. Assume that all the variables have been declared and given values.

a.
```
P := 100;
REPEAT
   P := P - 3
UNTIL P = 0
```

b.
```
IF P > 10 + R
   THEN REPEAT
           P := P - 10;
           WRITELN(P)
        UNTIL P < R
   ELSE R := R - 10;
WRITELN(P, R)
```

c.
```
REPEAT
   WRITELN(P MOD 2);
   R := R - 1;
   P := P + 5
UNTIL R <= 0 OR P >= 1000
```

d.
```
TOTAL := 0;
REPEAT;
   TOTAL := TOTAL + ABS(P - R);
   R := R -1
UNTIL TOTAL > 500
```

3. Examine the following program segment and tell what it does. In particular, tell what output is produced if the following sequence of characters is read:

LOOK■TO■THE■EAST■AT■DAWN.■THE■SUN■IS■RISING.

```
REPEAT
   READ(CH);
   IF CH = ' '
      THEN WRITELN
      ELSE WRITE(CH)
UNTIL CH = '.';
WRITELN
```

4. Rewrite the program segment given in Section 6.1 to calculate the value of X^N, but use a REPEAT loop instead of a WHILE loop. Is it more appropriate to use a REPEAT loop in this case?

5. The numbers in the sequence
1 1 2 3 5 8 13 21 34 . . .
are called Fibonacci numbers. After the first two numbers in the sequence, each number is the sum of the two preceding numbers. Thus, the next Fibonacci number in the sequence after 34 is 55. Using a REPEAT loop, write a program segment that will calculate and print the first N Fibonacci numbers. The value of N (a positive integer) should be read by the program segment. (Caution: even when N is rather small, the Nth Fibonacci number can be very large.)

6. Explain how the program PAYDAY given in Section 6.2 can be modified to produce exact dollar and cent values for the salary calculations. Do you see any other ways that the program PAYDAY could be changed so that it will be more versatile?

7. Write a program segment to balance a checkbook as described in Exercise 5, Section 6.1. This time use a REPEAT loop instead of a WHILE loop. Is a REPEAT loop more appropriate to use in this situation than a WHILE loop? Explain.

6.3
FOR STATEMENTS

We have seen that a variable can be used as a counter to control the number of times a WHILE or REPEAT loop cycles. A variable used for this purpose is termed a **control variable.** Consider the following program segment:

```
I := 1;
WHILE I <= 6
   DO BEGIN
      WRITELN(I:5, I * I:5);
      I := I + 1
   END
```

The purpose of this program segment is to print the integers from 1 through 6, inclusive, and their squares:

```
1     1
2     4
3     9
4    16
5    25
```

The INTEGER variable I is used as a control variable for the WHILE loop. During each cycle of the loop, I is incremented by 1 so that the control expression I <= 6 is eventually FALSE when it is evaluated and tested. Here is another example:

```
I := ORD('A');
REPEAT
   WRITE(CHR(I));
   I := I + 1
UNTIL CHR(I) = 'Z';
WRITELN
```

Again the value of I controls the number of times the loop cycles, but the CHAR values from 'A' through 'Z' inclusive actually provide the counting mechanism. The output produced by this program segment (assuming the ASCII ordering) is

```
ABCDEFGHIJKLMNOPQRSTUVWXYZ
```

In both of the preceding examples, the value of I is incremented by 1 during each loop cycle. More generally, a counter is incremented by 1 when its value is replaced by the SUCCessor of that value. The SUCC function can be used to construct program segments that produce the same effects as the two given above:

```
I := 1;                         LETTER := 'A'
WHILE I <= 6                    REPEAT
   DO BEGIN                        WRITE(LETTER);
      WRITELN(I:5, I * I:5);       LETTER := SUCC(LETTER)
      I := SUCC(I)              UNTIL LETTER > 'Z';
      END                       WRITELN
```

It is often appropriate to control the number of times a loop cycles by employing a control variable as a counter. In fact, programming languages usually provide special statements that feature automatic updating of the control variable after each loop cycle. In Pascal, the FOR statements are structured to provide loop control by using a control variable with the automatic updating feature.

FOR–TO LOOPS

In a FOR statement, the following information must be specified: the control variable, the initial and final values for the control variable, and the statement that represents the body of the loop. Here, for instance, is a FOR statement that can be used to print the integers 1 through 6 and their squares:

```
FOR I := 1 TO 6
   DO WRITELN(I:5, I * I:5)
```

Note how much simpler the FOR statement is when compared to the program segments (shown earlier) containing WHILE statements. Those program segments and the FOR statement all perform the same task. The initialization, incrementation, and testing of I at the appropriate times occur automatically, as illustrated in the following flowchart:

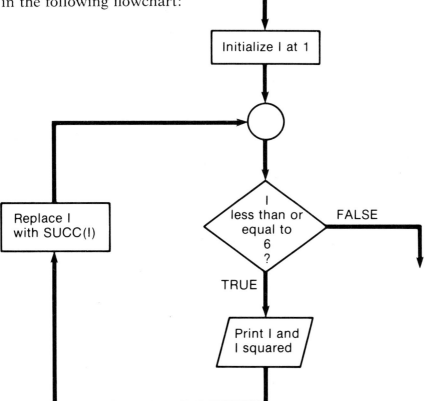

The control variable (I) SUCCessively takes on the values 1 through 6, and for each value of I the body of the loop (the WRITELN statement) is executed. Here is another example:

```
FOR LETTER := 'A' TO 'Z'
  DO WRITE(LETTER);
WRITELN
```

The FOR–TO loop in this program segment causes the value of the control variable LETTER to be printed as LETTER SUCCessively takes on the CHAR values from 'A' through 'Z' inclusive. The letters A through Z will all be printed on one line because the WRITELN statement is not executed until after the FOR loop is finished.

All of the loop control information appears after the keyword FOR and then the body of the loop is given in a DO clause, as illustrated in Figure 6–4. The *control-variable* may be any ordinal type variable (INTEGER, CHAR, or BOOLEAN, but **not REAL**). The *initial-value* and *final-value* may be given as constants, constant identifiers, variables, or expressions whose values are of the same type as the *control-variable*. Before the *statement* is executed the first time, the following events occur:

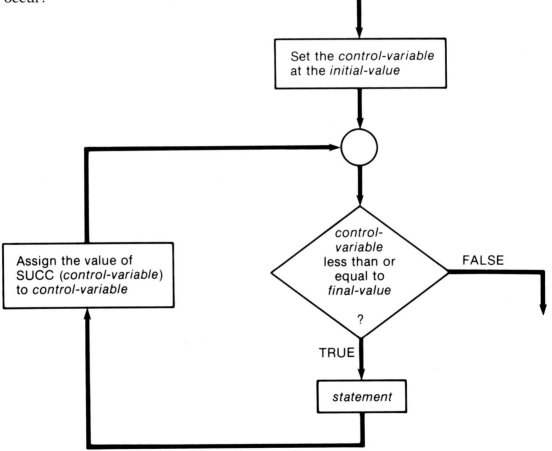

FOR *control-variable* := *initial-value* TO *final-value*
  DO *statement*

Figure 6–4
General structure of the FOR–TO statement and a flowchart description of a FOR–TO loop.

1. The *initial-value* is assigned to the *control-variable*. (If the *initial-value* is represented by an expression, the expression is evaluated first.)

2. The *final-value* is determined (by evaluating an expression, if necessary) and then the *initial-value* is compared to the *final-value*. If the *initial-value* is greater than the *final-value*, the loop will not be entered.

3. The *final-value* is remembered so that it can be compared to the value of the *control-variable* prior to the start of each subsequent loop cycle.

The events just described indicate that a FOR–TO statement is used to generate an entrance-controlled loop.

Consider the following example, in which Y is a REAL variable and K is an INTEGER variable:

```
Y := 1.0;
FOR K := 1 TO 5
  DO BEGIN
      Y := Y / 2.0;
      WRITE(Y:10:5)
      END;
WRITELN
```

In this example, K is used as a control variable in a FOR statement that generates a loop that divides the value of Y by 2.0 and prints the result five times. The output produced by the program segment looks like this:

```
0.50000   0.25000   0.12500   0.06250   0.03125
```

It may appear that the variable K will have the value 6 immmediately after the FOR loop is exited, but this is not the case. **When a FOR loop is exited, the control variable is left undefined.** That is, it still exists and can be used again in the program, but it retains no useful value, much like a variable that has been declared but not yet assigned a value. All variables used to control FOR loops in a program should be used only as control variables for FOR loops in that program.

A program segment to calculate a power of a number was presented in Section 6.1. The same segment is shown below, along with an equivalent program segment that uses a FOR–TO loop:

```
READ(X, N);                       READ(X, N);
ACCUM := 1.0;                     ACCUM := 1.0;
COUNT := 0;                       FOR I := 1 TO N
WHILE COUNT < N                     DO ACCUM := ACCUM * X;
    DO BEGIN                      WRITELN(ACCUM)
        ACCUM := ACCUM * X;
        COUNT := COUNT + 1
        END;
WRITELN(ACCUM)
```

The segment containing the FOR statement is much simpler. Neither segment produces the correct value when N is negative or when both X and N are zero (zero raised to the zero power is illegal). Since X^N is mathematically equal to $1.0/X^{-N}$, either of these two program segments can easily be generalized so that they will compute X^N for any integer N. For example,

```
READ(X, N);
IF (X = 0.0) AND (N = 0)
  THEN WRITELN('ZERO TO THE ZERO POWER IS ILLEGAL.')
  ELSE BEGIN
         ACCUM := 1.0;
         FOR COUNT := 1 TO N
          DO ACCUM := ACCUM * X;
         IF N < 0
           THEN ACCUM := 1.0 / ACCUM;
         WRITELN(ACCUM)
       END
```

The number of times a WHILE or REPEAT loop may cycle may not be known when the loop is first entered. This is not the case with FOR loops because the final value for the control variable is set before the loop is entered and it cannot be changed by any statement in the body of the loop. Consider the following program segment:

```
READ(M);
FOR K := M + M TO M * M
 DO BEGIN
      WRITELN('K =':5, K:2, 'M =':5, M:2);
      M := M - 2
    END;
WRITELN('FINAL VALUE OF M =', M:2)
```

Suppose 3 is read as the input value for M. The initial value for the control variable K is 6 and the final value is 9. When the program segment is executed, the following output is produced:

```
? 3
  K = 6   M = 3
  K = 7   M = 1
  K = 8   M =-1
  K = 9   M =-3
FINAL VALUE OF M =-5
```

Note that the changes made to the value of M in the body of the loop have no effect on the final value of the control variable.

Although a control variable for a FOR loop may appear in statements in the body of the loop, no statement in the body of the loop should modify the control variable's value. READ, READLN, and assignment statements that change the value of a control variable within the body of the loop it controls disrupt the normal control mechanism and defeat the purpose of a FOR loop. Furthermore, the loop may turn out to be infinite, as in the following example:

```
FOR J := -5 TO 5
 DO BEGIN
      WRITELN(J);
      J := J - 2
    END
```

Since the assignment statement in the body of the FOR loop reduces the value of J by 2 just before it is automatically incremented by 1, the value of J at the start of each loop cycle decreases by 1. Thus, the final value given in the FOR statement is unreachable. To avoid problems such as this, never use in the body of a FOR loop READ, READLN, or assignment statements that can change the value of the loop's control variable.

It is possible for a FOR loop to be nested inside another FOR loop. That is, the body of a FOR loop may consist entirely of another FOR loop. Consider the following nesting of FOR statements.

```
FOR I := 1 TO 3
  DO FOR LETTER := 'D' TO 'G'
       DO WRITE(LETTER:2);
    WRITELN
```

In this program segment, the "outer" loop is controlled by the INTEGER variable I and the "inner" loop is controlled by the CHAR variable LETTER. The effects of this program segment are illustrated in the flowchart on page 194:

The loop controlled by LETTER completes all of its cycles for each value of the control variable I. This means that the LETTERs D through G inclusive are printed a total of three times (once for each value of I), all on one line:

D E F G D E F G D E F G

Suppose the WRITELN is moved inside the body of the outer loop:

```
FOR I := 1 TO 3
  DO BEGIN
       FOR LETTER := 'D' TO 'G'
        DO WRITE(LETTER:2);
       WRITELN
     END
```

In this case, a line is printed each time the inner FOR loop is exited. The result is three lines of output:

D E F G
D E F G
D E F G

When two FOR loops are nested, the inner loop is reinitialized and completes all of its cycles during every cycle of the outer loop.

In a nesting of FOR loops, the same control variable must not be used to control both loops because the initialization of that variable in the inner loop constitutes changing the value of the control variable for the outer loop. Consider the following example:

```
FOR J := 1 TO 3
  DO FOR J := 2 TO 5
       DO WRITE(J:4);
    WRITELN
```

After J is set to its initial value of 1 for the outer loop, its value is changed to 2 by the initialization in the inner loop. After the inner loop has completed its four

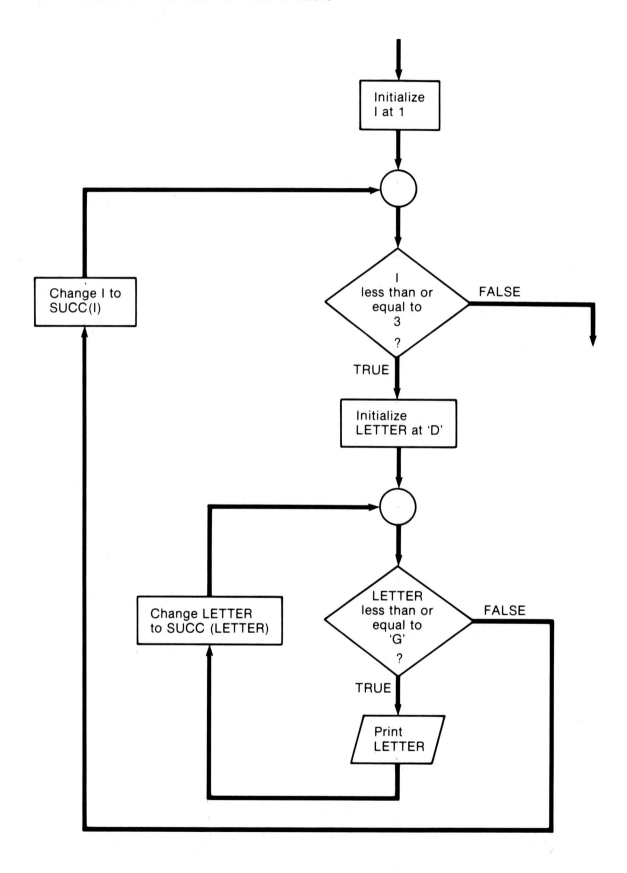

cycles, the value of J is left undefined. Thus, J cannot be properly incremented in the outer loop. This will probably result in an execution error. In any case, the nesting of FOR statements constructed above is illogical.

It is convenient to use a FOR loop structure to trace the yearly growth of population given the average yearly birth and death rates. Here is the pseudocode description of a program that will perform this task:

```
BEGIN program POPGROWTH
Print program information and directions
READ the FIRST and LAST years of the study, the INITIAL POPulation,
      the BIRTHRATE, and the DEATHRATE
Initialize the current POPULATION at INITIALPOP
Print table headings
FOR the YEARs from FIRST to LAST
  DO BEGIN the population adjustments
      Compute the number of BIRTHS as the whole part of BIRTHRATE
        * POPULATION
      Compute the number of DEATHS as the whole part of DEATH-
        RATE * POPULATION
      Set the new POPULATION at POPULATION + BIRTHS − DEATHS
      Print the current YEAR, BIRTHS, DEATHS, and POPULATION
      END of adjustments to population
Print the net change in POPULATION from the FIRST year to the LAST year
END of program POPGROWTH
```

The BIRTHRATE and DEATHRATE must be fractions (for example, a BIRTHRATE of 0.06 means that the number of births will be equal to 6% of the current POPULATION). The program POPGROWTH is given next.

```
PROGRAM POPGROWTH (INPUT, OUTPUT);
(*********************************************************************
 *                                                                  *
 *   A PROGRAM TO CHART THE YEAR BY YEAR POPULATION GROWTH OR        *
 *   DECLINE GIVEN AN INITIAL POPULATION AND PROJECTED ANNUAL BIRTH  *
 *   AND DEATH RATES                                                 *
 *                                                                  *
 ********************************************************************)
VAR                              (*------[INTEGER VARIABLES]------*)
    FIRST,                       (* FIRST YEAR OF THE STUDY       *)
    LAST,                        (* LAST YEAR OF THE STUDY        *)
    INITIALPOP,                  (* THE POPULATION STARTING THE   *)
                                 (* FIRST YEAR                    *)
    POPULATION,                  (* UPDATED POPULATION            *)
    BIRTHS,                      (* NUMBER OF BIRTHS IN A YEAR    *)
    DEATHS,                      (* NUMBER OF DEATHS IN A YEAR    *)
    YEAR : INTEGER;              (* CURRENT YEAR IN THE STUDY     *)
                                 (*-----------------------------*)
                                 (*------[REAL VARIABLES]--------*)
    BIRTHRATE,                   (* ANNUAL BIRTH RATE (FRACTION)  *)
    DEATHRATE : REAL;            (* ANNUAL DEATH RATE (FRACTION)  *)
                                 (*-----------------------------*)
(*********************************************************************)
```

```
BEGIN (* PROGRAM POPGROWTH *)
WRITELN('THIS PROGRAM WILL CHART POPULATION GROWTH FOR ANY NUMBER ',
        'OF');
WRITELN('CONSECUTIVE YEARS. YOU MUST SUPPLY THE FIRST AND LAST ',
        'YEARS');
WRITELN('OF THE STUDY, THE POPULATION AT THE START OF THE FIRST ',
        'YEAR');
WRITELN('AND THE ANNUAL BIRTH AND DEATH RATES (FRACTIONS WHICH ',
        'WILL');
WRITELN('BE THE SAME FOR ALL YEARS OF THE STUDY).');
WRITELN;
WRITELN('FIRST YEAR    LAST YEAR');
READ(FIRST, LAST);
WRITELN('POPULATION AT THE START OF ', FIRST:4);
READ(INITIALPOP);
WRITELN('BIRTH RATE    DEATH RATE');
READ(BIRTHRATE, DEATHRATE);
POPULATION := INITIALPOP;
WRITELN;
WRITELN('YEAR':9);
WRITELN('ENDING':10, 'BIRTHS':10, 'DEATHS':10, 'POPULATION':15);
WRITELN('******':10, '******':10, '******':10, '**********':15);
FOR YEAR := FIRST TO LAST
  DO BEGIN (* ADJUSTMENTS TO POPULATION *)
     BIRTHS := TRUNC(BIRTHRATE * POPULATION);
     DEATHS := TRUNC(DEATHRATE * POPULATION);
     POPULATION := POPULATION + BIRTHS - DEATHS;
     WRITELN(YEAR:9, BIRTHS:11, DEATHS:10, POPULATION:15)
     END (* OF ADJUSTMENTS TO POPULATION *);
WRITELN;
WRITELN('THE CHANGE IN POPULATION FROM ', FIRST:4, ' TO ', LAST:4,
        ': ', POPULATION - INITIALPOP:8)
END (* OF PROGRAM POPGROWTH *).
```

Here is the output from a sample run of the program POPGROWTH:

```
THIS PROGRAM WILL CHART POPULATION GROWTH FOR ANY NUMBER OF
CONSECUTIVE YEARS. YOU MUST SUPPLY THE FIRST AND LAST YEARS
OF THE STUDY, THE POPULATION AT THE START OF THE FIRST YEAR,
AND THE ANNUAL BIRTH AND DEATH RATES (FRACTIONS WHICH WILL
BE THE SAME FOR ALL YEARS OF THE STUDY).
FIRST YEAR    LAST YEAR
? 1980         1985
POPULATION AT THE START OF 1980
? 12563
BIRTH RATE    DEATH RATE
? 0.095        0.067

        YEAR
      ENDING    BIRTHS    DEATHS    POPULATION
      ******    ******    ******    **********
       1980      1193       841         12915
```

```
1981      1226      865      13276
1982      1261      889      13648
1983      1296      914      14030
1984      1332      940      14422
1985      1370      966      14826
```

THE CHANGE IN POPULATION FROM 1980 TO 1985:   2263

FOR–DOWNTO LOOPS

The control variable in a FOR–TO loop is given SUCCessively larger values until the final value is exceeded. In a FOR–DOWNTO loop, the value of the control variable is automatically made smaller after each loop cycle, and termination of the loop occurs when the value of the control variable is less than the final value. The structure of a FOR–DOWNTO statement is the same as that of a FOR–TO statement except that the word TO is replaced by the word DOWNTO. Consider the following example:

```
FOR I := 10 DOWNTO 0
  DO WRITE(I:3);
WRITELN
```

Prior to the start of each loop cycle after the first, the value of I is changed to the PREDecessor of I. Exit from the loop occurs when the value of I is less than 0. Thus, this program segment produces the following output:

```
 10  9  8  7  6  5  4  3  2  1  0
```

The effects of the program segment given above are the same as those produced by the following program segment, in which a WHILE loop is used:

```
I := 10;
WHILE I >= 0
  DO BEGIN
     WRITE(I:3);
     I := PRED(I)
     END;
WRITELN
```

The flowchart in Figure 6–5 describes the control structure of a FOR–DOWNTO loop. As with a FOR–TO loop, the *control-variable* must be an ordinal type variable (INTEGER, CHAR, or BOOLEAN, but **not REAL**) and the *initial-value* and *final-value* must be constants, constant identifiers, variables, or expression whose values can be assigned to the *control-variable*. Before the *statement* representing the body of the loop is executed the first time, the following events occur:

1. The *initial-value* is assigned to the *control-variable*. (If the *initial-value* is represented by an expression, the expression is evaluated first.)
2. The *final-value* is determined (by evaluating an expression, if necessary) and then the *initial-value* is compared to the *final-value*. If the *initial-value* is less than the *final-value*, the loop will not be entered.
3. The *final-value* is remembered so that it can be compared to the value of the *control-variable* prior to the start of each subsequent loop cycle.

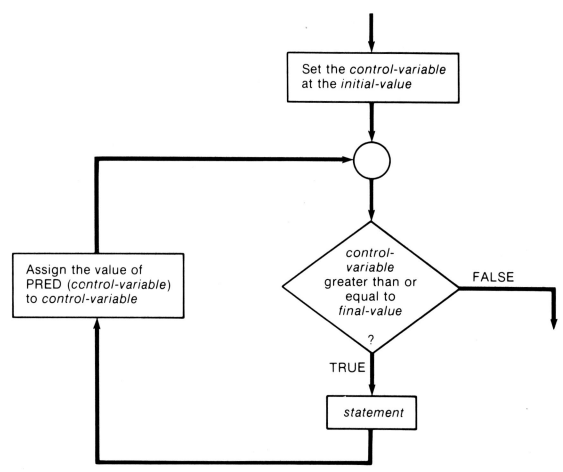

FOR *control-variable* := *initial-value* DOWNTO *final-value*
    DO *statement*

Figure 6–5
*General structure of the FOR–DOWNTO statement and a
flowchart description of a FOR–DOWNTO loop.*

The events described here indicate that a FOR–DOWNTO loop, like a FOR–TO loop, is entrance controlled.

In some cases it may be just as appropriate to use a FOR–DOWNTO loop as a FOR–TO loop. For instance, to sum all the integers between N and M (where the value of N is assumed to be less than or equal to the value of M), either of the following program segments can be used:

```
SUM := 0;                    SUM := 0;
FOR I := N TO M              FOR I := M DOWNTO N
   DO SUM := SUM + I            DO SUM := SUM + I
```

There are situations in which a FOR–DOWNTO statement provides a more efficient loop structure than a FOR–TO statement. Suppose the integers from 90 through 100 inclusive must be printed on one line so that they appear in decreasing order from left to right. Both of the following program segments will perform this task:

```
FOR L := 0 TO 10                FOR L := 100 DOWNTO 90
  DO WRITE(100 - L:5);            DO WRITE(L:5);
WRITELN                         WRITELN
```

Since the FOR–TO loop is actually imitating a FOR–DOWNTO loop, it makes more sense to use a FOR–DOWNTO loop.

FOR loops are very useful for printing tables or charts. The following program segment will print a temperature conversion chart (Fahrenheit to Celsius) after reading the lowest (LOWTEMP) and highest (HIGHTEMP) Fahrenheit temperatures to be represented in the chart.

```
READ(HIGHTEMP, LOWTEMP);
WRITELN('DEGREES        DEGREES':30);
WRITELN('FAHRENHEIT      CELSIUS':30);
FOR FAHRENHEIT := HIGHTEMP DOWNTO LOWTEMP
  DO BEGIN (* CONVERSION *)
     WRITELN(':':20);
     CELSIUS := 5.0 / 9.0 * (FAHRENHEIT - 32.0);
     WRITELN(FAHRENHEIT:15, '--+--':7, CELSIUS:8:2)
     END (* OF CONVERSION *)
```

If the INTEGER values read for HIGHTEMP and LOWTEMP are 75 and 70, respectively, the chart printed by the program segment looks like this:

```
        DEGREES        DEGREES
        FAHRENHEIT      CELSIUS
                     :
           75     --+--   23.89
                     :
           74     --+--   23.33
                     :
           73     --+--   22.78
                     :
           72     --+--   22.22
                     :
           71     --+--   21.67
                     :
           70     --+--   21.11
```

By simply changing the FOR–DOWNTO statement to a FOR–TO statement with LOWTEMP as the initial value for the control variable FAHRENHEIT and HIGHTEMP as the final value, the program segment will print the chart with the temperatures going from low to high (top to bottom in the chart).

6.3 EXERCISES

1. Write each of the following program segments in an equivalent form by using a FOR loop instead of a WHILE loop. Assume that all variables are INTEGER.

a.
```
X := 1;
WHILE X < 25
    DO BEGIN
        Y := Y + X * X;
        X := X + 1
        END
```

b.
```
I := B;
WHILE (I >= A) AND (I <= B)
    DO BEGIN
        WRITELN((B - A) MOD I);
        I := I - 1
        END
```

c.
```
S := 0;
K := 2;
WHILE K <= N
    DO BEGIN
        S := S + K;
        WRITELN(S);
        K := K + 2
        END
```

d.
```
T := 100;
K := 0;
WHILE T - K >= 0
    DO BEGIN
        WRITELN(T - K);
        K := K + 5
        END
```

2. What output will the following program segment produce?

```
FOR I := 4 DOWNTO 1
  DO BEGIN
      WRITE('*':I);
      FOR J := 1 TO 4 - I
        DO WRITE('*');
      WRITELN
      END
```

3. Trace the output produced by each of the following program segments when M = 10 and N = 25. Assume that all variables are INTEGER.

a.
```
A := 100;
FOR K := M + 5 TO N - M DIV 2
  DO BEGIN
      A := A - K;
      IF A < 50
        THEN M := M - 1;
      WRITELN(A, K, M, N)
      END
```

b.
```
                A := 0;
                FOR K := N DIV M TO M
                 DO BEGIN
                    CASE K MOD 3 OF
                      0 : A := A + 1;
                      1 : A := A - 2;
                      2 : IF K > M DIV 2
                            THEN A := A - 1
                            ELSE A := A + 2
                    END (* OF CASES *);
                    WRITELN(A, K, M, N)
                 END
```

4. Explain what is wrong with each of the following program segments.

a.
```
                READ(F, N);
                FOR J := 1 TO N
                 DO F := F + F MOD J;
                WRITELN(F, J)
```

b.
```
                T := 0;
                READ(K, N);
                FOR I := K TO N
                 DO BEGIN
                    IF I MOD 3 = 0
                      THEN T := T + I
                      ELSE I := K;
                    WRITELN(I, T)
                 END
```

5. Write a FOR loop that will print all the letters of the alphabet in order from A to Z on the same line. Write another program segment to print the letters in reverse order. (Hint: Use the ORD and CHR functions.)

6. A sequence of Fibonacci numbers is described in Exercise 5, Section 6.2. Write a program segment that will print the first N numbers in this sequence. Assume that N is an integer greater than 2 and use a FOR loop.

7. Use FOR loops to print each of the following designs. Each output statement in your program segment should print at most one asterisk.

```
a.                        b.                              c.
   *                         **      **                         *
   **                        **      **                        ***
   ***                       **      **                       *****
   ****                         ****                         *******
   *****                         **                         *********
```

8. Write a program segment that will READ a REAL number A and a positive integer N and then round A to N decimal places.

9. In Section 6.3 there is a program segment to print a temperature conversion chart given a range of Fahrenheit temperatures. The Fahrenheit temperatures are whole numbers in the specified range. Modify this program segment so that a REAL Fahrenheit temperature and a REAL increment will be read, and N

Fahrenheit temperatures (beginning with the input temperature) the specified increment apart will be converted to Celsius. Assume that the increment is greater than zero.

6.4
TRANSFER OF CONTROL TO LABELED STATEMENTS

All of the control statements presented so far provide conditional control since the effects they produce depend on the value of a BOOLEAN expression or CASE selector. It is possible for control to be passed to a program statement without testing any conditions. This unconditional transfer of control can be generated by a GOTO statement. It is necessary that every statement that is the "target" of a GOTO have a **statement label** so that it can be referenced in the GOTO statement.

LABEL DECLARATIONS

Any unsigned integer between 1 and 9999 inclusive may serve as a statement label. (Some implementations of a Pascal permit a much broader range of statement labels, which includes the unsigned integers in the range 1 through 9999.) Even though statement labels look like numbers, they are merely sequences of digits used to mark certain program statements. Every statement label used in a program must appear in the LABEL declaration part of the declaration section. The LABEL declaration part is the first part of the declaration section and it has the form illustrated in Figure 6–6. There is no significance to the order in which the

LABEL *label-1, label-2, . . . , label-k;*

Figure 6–6
General form of the LABEL declaration part.

labels are listed when they are declared. Here is an example of a properly constructed LABEL declaration part:

LABEL 27, 3512, 160;

Consecutive labels must be separated by a comma, and a semicolon must appear after the last label. A statement label must appear immediately in front of the statement it labels and be separated from that statement by a colon. Here are some statements that are validly labeled:

```
27 : WRITELN(X, Y, Z)

160: WHILE A < B
        DO BEGIN
            READ(C);
            A := A + ABS(C)
        END

3512:IF M = N
        THEN WRITELN(M)
```

No blank spaces or any number of blank spaces may appear on either side of the colon that separates a statement from its label. Since statement labels are identification tags, each one must be attached to only one statement. In a program that does not contain any GOTO statements, statement labels have no purpose.

THE GOTO STATEMENT

A GOTO statement consists of the keyword GOTO followed by one declared statement *label*, as illustrated in Figure 6–7. That *label* must also appear as a prefix on one statement in the program, as described above. When the GOTO statement is executed, control is passed immediately and unconditionally to the statement whose *label* is specified. This unconditional "jump" may result in a forward or a backward movement in the program and one or more statements may be skipped in the process.

GOTO *label*

Figure 6–7
General form of the GOTO statement.

As a rule, GOTO statements detract from the readability of a program and so they should be used sparingly or not at all. The appearance of several GOTO statements in a Pascal program is often symptomatic of poor program design. Consider the following program segment:

```
        READ(A, B);
        GOTO 425;
   128: WRITELN(SUM);
        DIFFERENCE := A - B;
        GOTO 9;
   425: SUM := A + B;
        GOTO 128;
     9: WRITELN(DIFFERENCE)
```

This program segment is much more complicated than it needs to be. A flowchart showing the effects produced by this segment appears on page 204.

The GOTO statements are needed because of the order in which the other statements appear. Looking at the flowchart, we see that there is no need for GOTO statements if the order of the other statements is changed. Here is how the program segment should have been written:

```
        READ(A, B);
        SUM := A + B;
        WRITELN(SUM);
        DIFFERENCE := A - B;
        WRITELN(DIFFERENCE)
```

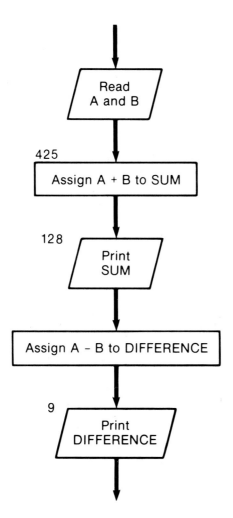

The unwarranted use of GOTO statements can be avoided by careful and logical planning during the design phase of program development.

Statement labels and CASE labels are two different forms of identification for program statements. CASE labels have significance only within the structure of the CASE statement in which they are used and they are not declared in the LABEL declaration part of a program. Consider the following shell of a program:

```
PROGRAM Z (INPUT, OUTPUT);
LABEL 2;
VAR
     KEY, J : INTEGER;
     .
     .
     .
BEGIN (* PROGRAM Z *)
     .
     .
     .
  2: READ(KEY);
     .
     .
     .
```

```
CASE KEY MOD 4 OF
  0, 3 : J := J + 1;
     2 : J := J - 1;
     1 : GOTO 2
END (* OF KEY CASES *);
     .
     .
     .
END (* OF PROGRAM Z *).
```

The CASE option whose label is 2 (the assignment statement $J := J - 1$) is executed when the CASE selector KEY MOD 4 is evaluated and has the value 2. When the CASE selector's value is 1, the GOTO statement is selected and executed, which causes control to be passed to the READ statement, whose label is 2. The label referenced in a GOTO statement must always be a declared statement label.

A GOTO statement can be used to create a program loop. Since the transfer of control resulting from the execution of a GOTO statement is unconditional, the loop may well be infinite, as illustrated in the following example:

```
      TOTAL := 0;
  84: READ(X);
      TOTAL := TOTAL + X;
      GOTO 84;
      WRITELN(TOTAL)
```

After a value is read for X and added to TOTAL, another value is always sought for X. The WRITELN statement can never be reached. Suppose we want to accumulate the TOTAL of X-values until a nonpositive value has been read for X. To accomplish this task, a GOTO statement may be used in conjunction with an IF statement, as illustrated in the following program segment:

```
       TOTAL := 0;
   84: READ(X);
       IF X <= 0
         THEN GOTO 135;
       TOTAL := TOTAL + X;
       GOTO 84;
  135: WRITELN(TOTAL)
```

The same effects can be achieved by employing a WHILE loop, which is much easier to read:

```
      TOTAL := 0;
      READ(X);
      WHILE X > 0
        DO BEGIN (* ACCUMULATION *)
           TOTAL := TOTAL + X;
           READ(X)
           END (* OF ACCUMULATION *);
      WRITELN(TOTAL)
```

In Pascal, programs it is never necessary to construct a program loop by using IF and GOTO statements because any loop can be implemented by using a WHILE, REPEAT, of FOR statement. Furthermore, the WHILE, REPEAT, and

FOR statements more clearly represent the logical structure of a loop than any IF–GOTO combination. The following table shows various IF–GOTO controlled loops and how they can be structured as WHILE, REPEAT, or FOR loops:

IF–GOTO Controlled Loop	Equivalent Form Using a Structured Repetitive Control Statement

1: IF NOT (*BOOLEAN expression*)
    THEN GOTO 2;
statement-1;
statement-2;
    •
    •
    •
statement-k;
GOTO 1;
2: . . .
	WHILE *BOOLEAN expression*
	    DO BEGIN
	        statement-1;
	        statement-2;
	            •
	            •
	            •
	        statement-k
	    END

1: *statement-1;*
statement-2;
    •
    •
    •
statement-k;
IF NOT(*BOOLEAN expression*)
    THEN GOTO 1
	REPEAT
	    statement-1;
	    statement-2;
	        •
	        •
	        •
	    statement-k
	UNTIL *BOOLEAN expression*

I := n;
1: IF I > m
    THEN GOTO 2;
statement-1;
statement-2;
    •
    •
    •
statement-k;
GOTO 1;
2: . . .
	FOR I := n TO m
	    DO BEGIN
	        statement-1;
	        statement-2;
	            •
	            •
	            •
	        statement-k
	    END

I := n
1: IF I < m
    THEN GOTO 2;
statement-1;
statement-2;
    •
    •
    •
statement-k;
GOTO 1;
2: . . .
	FOR I := n DOWNTO m
	    DO BEGIN
	        statement-1;
	        statement-2;
	            •
	            •
	            •
	        statement-k
	    END

6.4
EXERCISES

1. Draw a flowchart of each of the following program segments and then write each segment in an equivalent form without using any GOTO statements and statement labels. Tell what output will be produced by each segment if X is 2904.

   a.
   ```
                       READ(X);
              10: WRITE(X MOD 10:1);
                  X := X DIV 10;
                  IF X > 0
                    THEN GOTO 10;
                  WRITELN
   ```

   b.
   ```
                       READ(X);
              10: IF X DIV 10 < 10
                      THEN GOTO 20;
                  WRITE(X MOD 10:1);
                  X := X DIV 10;
                  GOTO 10;
              20: WRITELN(X MOD 10:1)
   ```

2. Draw a flowchart of each of the following program segments and then write each segment in an equivalent form using a FOR statement to generate the loop. Tell what output will be produced by each segment if X is 6.

   a.
   ```
                       READ(X);
                  T := 1;
              10: IF X < 0
                      THEN GOTO 20;
                  T := T * X;
                  X := X - 1;
                  GOTO 10;
              20: WRITELN(T)
   ```

   b.
   ```
                       READ(X);
                  Y := 1;
                  T := 2;
              10: IF T > X
                      THEN GOTO 20;
                  Y := Y * T;
                  T := T + 1;
                  GOTO 10;
              20: WRITELN(T)
   ```

3. The following program segment can be replaced by nested FOR loops. Draw a flowchart of the segment and then write the appropriate nested FOR loops. What output will the program segment generate?

```
            M := 1;
    10:     N := 1;
    20:     WRITE(M * N:3);
            N := N + 1;
            IF N < 6
                THEN GOTO 20;
            WRITELN;
            M := M + 1;
            IF M <= 4
                THEN GOTO 10
```

6.5
PROGRAMMING PROBLEMS

1. Write a program to read a line of text and print it out with all the blank spaces deleted. Use the EOLN function to test for the end of the text. The program should also print out the number of nonblank characters read and printed.

2. Write a program that will encode a line of text by replacing each letter by the letter directly opposite it in the order A through Z. That is, each A is replaced by a Z and each Z is replaced by an A, each B is replaced by a Y and each Y is replaced by a B, and so on. Characters other than letters should not be changed.

3. An integer greater than 1 is prime if its only divisors are 1 and itself. Write a program that will read a positive integer n and print all the prime numbers less than or equal to n.

4. For large positive integers n, $[1 + (1/n)]^n$ is a good approximation for the number e that is used as the base for the natural logarithms. Write a program that computes the value of $[1 + (1/n)]^n$ for consecutive values of n starting with n = 1. The program should read some small positive value (for example, 0.001) and stop the computations when two consecutive approximations for e differ by less than the input amount. The program should print only the last approximation for e that was computed and the value of n used for that computation.

5. Write a program to compute the average of a group of test scores. A valid score will be between 0 and 100 inclusive. All the scores should be read by the program and a signal value (for example, a negative number) should be entered after the last score to mark the end of input. Any score that is less than 0 or greater than 100 should be considered an invalid score, and the program should print a message indicating that it will not be counted in the average. The output should include the total count of valid test scores, the largest score, the smallest score, and the average.

6. A woman has x dollars to deposit in a savings account on the first day of a year. She has two choices: an account at the local bank that earns 5.25% annual interest compounded quarterly (1.3125% every three months), or a credit union shares account that earns a guaranteed 5.5% interest at the end of each year. The woman plans to deposit 10% more money at the start of each succeeding year than she did before. Write a program that will print the amount

of money in each type of account at the end of each year for n consecutive years. The values of x and n should be read by the program.

7. Binary numbers are represented by using only the digits 0 and 1. The "bits" (short for binary digits) in the binary form of a nonnegative whole number are the coefficients when that number is written as a sum of powers of 2. Here is an example:

$$1(2^5) + 0(2^4) + 0(2^3) + 1(2^2) + 0(2^1) + 1(2^0) = 37$$

1 0 0 1 0 1   (binary representation of 37)

The bits can be generated by repeatedly dividing the original number and the successive quotients by 2 and saving the remainder (which must be 0 or 1) after each division. Use of this technique is illustrated in the following diagrams, which show how the binary representation of 37 is generated:

Quotients:

$$\frac{18}{2)37} \quad \frac{9}{2)18} \quad \frac{4}{2)9} \quad \frac{2}{2)4} \quad \frac{1}{2)2} \quad \frac{0}{2)1}$$

Remainders:
(bits)

1   0   1   0   0   1

Note that the bits are generated in reverse order of their appearance in the binary representation of 37 and the divisions are finished when a 0 quotient occurs. Write a program that will read a nonnegative whole number (integer) and then find and print its binary representation.

8. A television rating service makes a telephone survey of the viewing audience to sample the popularity of TV shows. When a call is made concerning a particular show, the sex and age of the person called, as well as whether or not that person watches the show regularly, are recorded. Write a program that will process the data gathered for a show. The total number of people called, the number who said they watch the show regularly, and the percentage of those called who watch the show on a regular basis should be printed. The program should also print a table showing the percentages of those who watch the show by sex and age categories. The output table should look something like the sample table shown here.

SEX	UNDER 18	18 TO 35	36 TO 55	OVER 55
MALE	12.2%	47.5%	34.3%	6.0%
FEMALE	18.5%	32.4%	35.6%	13.5%

Set up the program so that after the data for one show have been processed and the results printed, the user has the opportunity to enter data for another show.

9. If a and b are positive numbers, the graph of the equation

$$\frac{(x - p)^2}{a} + \frac{(y - q)^2}{b} = 1$$

using a rectangular x–y coordinate system is an ellipse centered at the point (p, q). The axis of the ellipse parallel to the x axis has length $\sqrt{a}$ and the axis of the ellipse parallel to the y axis has length $\sqrt{b}$. The coordinates of points on an ellipse can be generated by using the equation

$$y = q \pm \sqrt{b - b(x - p)^2/a}$$

where $p - \sqrt{a} \leqslant x \leqslant p + \sqrt{a}$. Write a program to generate the coordinates of points on an ellipse. The values a, b, p, and q should be read by the program. The program should also read a positive integer n greater than 3 and determine the n equally spaced values of x between $p - \sqrt{a}$ and $p + \sqrt{a}$ for which points will be determined.

10. Write the program to compute a salesman's commission described in Problem 5 of Section 3.3, but permit the user to enter data for as many salesmen as desired.

11. Write the program to compute the salary of a factory worker as described in Problem 4, Section 5.5, but this time set up the program to process the salary information for any number of workers.

12. Problem 7, Section 5.5, describes a program for generating a utilities bill for a resident of the city of Hillside. Write that program in such a way that a sequence of bills can be generated in one run of the program.

SEVEN/INTRODUCTION TO USER-DEFINED DATA TYPES

The standard identifiers INTEGER, REAL, CHAR, and BOOLEAN are names for four predefined data types in Pascal. A variety of other data types can be defined in the TYPE definition part of a program. For example,

```
TYPE
        DIRECTIONS = (NORTH, SOUTH, EAST, WEST);
```

This TYPE definition part contains only one data type definition: the identifier DIRECTIONS is specified as the name of a new data type consisting of four constants known by the identifiers NORTH, SOUTH, EAST, and WEST. In this case the data specifications for the new type are given in the form of a list, but there are many other ways to construct valid data specifications. Some of them are presented in this chapter. A type definition always consists of an identifer, which serves as the name of the new data type, followed by the symbol "=" and the data specifications for the new type. These type definitions are listed one after the other in the TYPE definition part of the declaration section, as illustrated in Figure 7–1. A semicolon must be placed after every type definition.

```
TYPE
        type-identifier-1  =  data-specifications-1;
        type-identifier-2  =  data-specifications-2;
                            •
                            •
                            •
        type-identifier-k  =  data-specifications-k;
```

FIGURE 7–1
General structure of the TYPE definition part of the declaration section.

7.1 SIMPLE DATA TYPES

A simple data type consists of an ordered collection of data constants. The types INTEGER, REAL, CHAR, and BOOLEAN are all simple data types. The type REAL stands alone as a real type, while the types INTEGER, CHAR, and BOOLEAN are ordinal types. Other ordinal data types may be defined by type definitions in which the name of the data type and the constants of that types are specified (as for the type DIRECTIONS defined above).

USER-DEFINED ORDINAL TYPES

The constants of a user-defined ordinal data type are represented by identifiers that are listed when that type is defined. These identifiers constitute the data specifications for the type definition. Here is an example of a TYPE definition part in which three ordinal data types are defined:

```
TYPE
    SCIENCES = (BIOLOGY, MATHEMATICS, PHYSICS, CHEMISTRY,
                COMPUTERSCIENCE, GEOLOGY);
    WEATHER = (CLEAR, CLOUDY, RAIN, SNOW);
    CARDS = (TWO, THREE, FOUR, FIVE, SIX, SEVEN, EIGHT,
             NINE, TEN, JACK, QUEEN, KING, ACE);
```

The general structure of a type definition for an ordinal type is depicted in Figure 7–2. Each *constant* must be a valid identifier and the entire list of *constants* in a definition must be enclosed in parentheses. The constants of a user-defined ordinal type look like variables, but they are not. PHYSICS and COMPUTERSCIENCE are SCIENCES type values in the same sense that TRUE and FALSE are BOOLEAN values.

---

type-identifier = (constant-1, constant-2, . . . , constant-n);

Figure 7–2
General form of a type definition for a user-defined ordinal type.

The number of distinct constants of an ordinal data type is referred to as the **cardinality of the data type.** In the examples given above, SCIENCES has cardinality 6, WEATHER has cardinality 4, and CARDS has cardinality 13. Each constant is associated with an ordinal (nonnegative integer) that is determined by its position in the data specification list. If an ordinal data type has cardinality $n + 1$ (where n is some nonnegative integer), then its constants have ordinals that range from 0 through n. The first constant listed in the definition has ordinal 0, the second constant has ordinal 1, the third has ordinal 2, and so on. The ordinals associated with the constants of the ordinal types SCIENCES, WEATHER, and CARDS are show in the following table:

Ordinal	SCIENCES	WEATHER	CARDS
0	BIOLOGY	CLEAR	TWO
1	MATHEMATICS	CLOUDY	THREE
2	PHYSICS	RAIN	FOUR
3	CHEMISTRY	SNOW	FIVE
4	COMPUTERSCIENCE		SIX
5	GEOLOGY		SEVEN
6			EIGHT
7			NINE
8			TEN
9			JACK
10			QUEEN
11			KING
12			ACE

Two constants of the same ordinal type can be compared by using the relational operators. The result of a comparison is based on the ordinal values of the operands, as described for the data type CHAR in Section 3.2. For instance, the relational expression CLOUDY < SNOW has the value TRUE because the ordinal value of CLOUDY (1) is less than the ordinal value of SNOW (3). Two ordinal type constants can be compared only if they are of the same type. The expression GEOLOGY > CLOUDY is invalid, since GEOLOGY is a constant of the type SCIENCES and CLOUDY is a constant of the type WEATHER. Here are some examples of valid relational expressions and their values:

Relational Expression	Value of the Expression
GEOLOGY > MATHEMATICS	TRUE
FOUR >= JACK	FALSE
PHYSICS <> CHEMISTRY	TRUE
RAIN <= CLEAR	FALSE

Constants of a user-defined ordinal type may be used as arguments in calls to the standard functions ORD, PRED, and SUCC. An ordinal type value whose ordinal is 0 has no PREDecessor and a value that has the largest ordinal for data of its type has no SUCCessor. For example, PRED(CLEAR) and SUCC(SNOW) are invalid function calls (given the type WEATHER defined earlier). The ORD function always returns the ordinal value of its argument. Here are some valid calls to the functions ORD, PRED, and SUCC, and the values they return:

Expression	Value of the Expression
ORD(EIGHT)	6
ORD(SNOW)	3
(5 + ORD(PHYSICS)) DIV 3	2
PRED(COMPUTERSCIENCE)	CHEMISTRY
PRED(SNOW)	RAIN
SUCC(TEN)	JACK
SUCC(BIOLOGY)	MATHEMATICS
PRED(SUCC(CLOUDY))	CLOUDY
SUCC(PRED(ACE))	ACE

The type identifier for a user-defined data type is used like the standard type identifiers INTEGER, REAL, CHAR, and BOOLEAN to declare variables. Consider the following definitions and declarations:

```
CONST
      MAXSCORE = 100;
TYPE
      STATUS = (GO, ERROR, STOP);
VAR
      SCORE, SUM, COUNT : INTEGER;
      AVERAGE : REAL;
      ACTION : STATUS;
```

STATUS is the name of an ordinal data type whose constants are GO, ERROR, and STOP. Since ACTION is declared as a STATUS type variable, the only values it can be assigned are GO, ERROR, and STOP.

It is not necessary that a user-defined data type be given a name. A type definition may appear within a variable declaration in place of a type identifier. For example, the variable ACTION can be declared as shown in the following VAR declaration part:

```
VAR
      SCORE, SUM, COUNT : INTEGER;
      AVERAGE : REAL;
      ACTION : (GO, ERROR, STOP);
```

One reason for defining a data type in a TYPE definition is to give that new data type a name that can be used in declaring variables. However, type identifiers are also very useful in defining other data types and there are times when it is absolutely necessary to refer to a data type by name only. These situations are discussed later in this chapter and in subsequent chapters.

The ordinal data type STATUS is defined and used in the program MEAN-SCORE, which follows. In this program, the order in which the STATUS type values GO, STOP, and ERROR are listed in the data specifications list is not important because the program never compares these values.

```
PROGRAM MEANSCORE (INPUT,OUTPUT);
(*******************************************************************
*                                                                 *
*   A PROGRAM WHICH WILL SUM ANY NUMBER OF TEST SCORES AND PRINT   *
*   THE AVERAGE                                                    *
*                                                                 *
*******************************************************************)
CONST                                 (*----------[CONSTANTS]----------*)
      MAXSCORE = 100;                 (* HIGHEST POSSIBLE TEST SCORE   *)
                                      (*-------------------------------*)
TYPE
      STATUS = (GO, ERROR, STOP);

VAR                                   (*------[INTEGER VARIABLES]------*)
      SCORE,                          (* AN INPUT TEST SCORE           *)
      SUM,                            (* THE SUM OF SCORES ACCUMULATOR *)
      COUNT : INTEGER;                (* THE NUMBER OF SCORES ENTERED  *)
                                      (*-------------------------------*)
                                      (*-------[REAL VARIABLES]--------*)
      AVERAGE : REAL;                 (* AVERAGE OF THE SCORES         *)
                                      (*-------------------------------*)
                                      (*------[STATUS VARIABLES]-------*)
      ACTION : STATUS;                (* PROCESSING SIGNAL             *)
                                      (*-------------------------------*)
(*******************************************************************)
BEGIN (* PROGRAM MEANSCORE *)
COUNT := 0;
SUM := 0;
WRITELN('THIS PROGRAM WILL ACCUMULATE TEST SCORES BETWEEN 0 AND');
```

```
WRITELN(MAXSCORE:3, ' AND THEN CALCULATE THE AVERAGE SCORE. ',
        'ENTER AS MANY');
WRITELN('SCORES PER LINE AS YOU WISH. TO SIGNAL THE END OF INPUT,');
WRITELN('ENTER ANY NEGATIVE WHOLE NUMBER.');
WRITELN('BEGIN ENTERING THE SCORES NOW.');
REPEAT (* SCORE PROCESSING *)
  ACTION := GO;
  READ(SCORE);
  IF SCORE > MAXSCORE
    THEN ACTION := ERROR
    ELSE IF SCORE < 0
            THEN ACTION := STOP;
  CASE ACTION OF
      GO : BEGIN (* SCORE ACCUMULATION *)
             COUNT := COUNT + 1;
             SUM := SUM + SCORE
           END (* OF SCORE ACCUMULATION *);
   ERROR : WRITELN('SCORE ', SCORE:3, ' IGNORED. MAXIMUM ALLOWED ',
                   'IS ', MAXSCORE:3, '.');
    STOP : BEGIN (* CALCULATE AND OUTPUT THE AVERAGE *)
             AVERAGE := SUM / COUNT;
             WRITELN(COUNT:3, ' SCORES PROCESSED. AVERAGE = ',
                     AVERAGE:5:2)
           END (* OF CALCULATE AND OUTPUT THE AVERAGE *)
  END (* OF ACTION CASES *)
UNTIL ACTION = STOP
END (* OF PROGRAM MEANSCORE *).
```

Here is the output from a sample run of the program MEANSCORE:

```
THIS PROGRAM WILL ACCUMULATE TEST SCORES BETWEEN 0 AND
100 AND THEN CALCULATE THE AVERAGE SCORE. ENTER AS MANY
SCORES PER LINE AS YOU WISH. TO SIGNAL THE END OF INPUT,
ENTER ANY NEGATIVE WHOLE NUMBER.
BEGIN ENTERING THE SCORES NOW.
? 34 78 82 76 75
? 64 78 105 99
SCORE 105 IGNORED. MAXIMUM ALLOWED IS 100.
? 62 53 64 85 86 88
? 47 93 -1
 16 SCORES PROCESSED. AVERAGE = 72.75
```

In the program MEANSCORE, the STATUS type values are used primarily to enhance the readability of the program. The use of user-defined ordinal data in a program is never absolutely required, but such data can often add clarity to a program. It is not possible to READ or WRITE user-defined ordinal data. If ACTION is a STATUS type variable as defined in the program MEANSCORE, the statements READ(ACTION), READLN(ACTION), WRITE(ACTION), and WRITELN(ACTION) are all illegal. When it is necessary or desirable that an ordinal type value be printed, a CASE statement can be used to select an output statement that will print a string image of the appropriate identifier. For example, the identifier for the appropriate ACTION value is printed when the following CASE statement is executed:

```
CASE ACTION OF
     GO : WRITELN('GO');
  ERROR : WRITELN('ERROR');
   STOP : WRITELN('STOP')
END (* OF ACTION CASES *)
```

The control variable in a FOR statement may be any ordinal type variable. If the control variable has a user-defined type, it will take on all values of that type whose ordinals are between the ordinal of the initial value and the ordinal of the final value. Suppose the ordinal type WEEKDAY is defined as

```
WEEKDAY = (MONDAY, TUESDAY, WEDNESDAY, THURSDAY, FRIDAY);
```

If DAY is a WEEKDAY type variable, then a FOR statement like the following one is valid:

> FOR DAY := MONDAY TO FRIDAY
> DO *statement*

Since there are five WEEKDAY type values between MONDAY and FRIDAY inclusive, the *statement* will be executed five times. Similarly, a FOR statement of the form

> FOR DAY := TUESDAY TO THURSDAY
> DO *statement*

generates a loop that cycles three times as DAY SUCCessively takes on the values TUESDAY, WEDNESDAY, and THURSDAY. If the ordinal of the initial value for the control variable in a FOR–TO statement is greater than the ordinal of the final value, the body of the loop is not executed at all. For instance, the statement

> FOR DAY := WEDNESDAY TO MONDAY
> DO *statement*

is valid, but the *statement* is not executed even once because the relational expression DAY <= MONDAY is FALSE when DAY has the initial value WEDNESDAY. On the other hand, the statement

> FOR DAY := WEDNESDAY DOWNTO MONDAY
> DO *statement*

generates a loop in which the *statement* is executed three times as the variable DAY takes on the values WEDNESDAY, TUESDAY, and MONDAY, in that order. Here is an example of a program that uses a WEEKDAY type variable to control a FOR loop:

```
PROGRAM ACCOUNTUPDATE (INPUT,OUTPUT);
(********************************************************************
*                                                                  *
*       A PROGRAM TO UPDATE AN ACCOUNT BALANCE ON A DAILY BASIS     *
*                                                                  *
********************************************************************)
TYPE
      WEEKDAY = (MONDAY, TUESDAY, WEDNESDAY, THURSDAY, FRIDAY);

VAR                                  (*------[INTEGER VARIABLES]------*)
      I,                             (* LOOP CONTROL VARIABLE         *)
      TRANCOUNT : INTEGER;           (* NUMBER OF TRANSACTIONS PER DAY*)
                                     (*------------------------------*)
                                     (*-------[CHAR VARIABLES]--------*)
      SIGNAL : CHAR;                 (* SIGNAL FOR END OF INPUT       *)
                                     (*------------------------------*)
                                     (*-------[REAL VARIABLES]--------*)
      AMOUNT,                        (* A TRANSACTION AMOUNT          *)
      BALANCE : REAL;                (* THE RUNNING BALANCE           *)
                                     (*------------------------------*)
                                     (*------[WEEKDAY VARIABLES]------*)
      DAY : WEEKDAY;                 (* A DAY OF THE WEEK             *)
                                     (*------------------------------*)
(********************************************************************)
BEGIN (* PROGRAM ACCOUNTUPDATE *)
WRITELN('THIS PROGRAM WILL UPDATE THE BALANCE FOR AN ACCOUNT ON');
WRITELN('A DAY BY DAY BASIS. ENTER AS MANY TRANSACTION DOLLAR');
WRITELN('AMOUNTS ON A LINE AS YOU WISH. A POSITIVE NUMBER IS A');
WRITELN('CREDIT AND A NEGATIVE NUMBER IS A DEBIT. AFTER YOU HAVE');
WRITELN('ENTERED ALL THE TRANSACTION AMOUNTS FOR A PARTICULAR DAY,');
WRITELN('TYPE AN ASTERISK (*) IMMEDIATELY AFTER THE LAST NUMBER AS');
WRITELN('A SIGNAL TO MOVE TO THE NEXT DAY.');
WRITELN('ENTER THE STARTING BALANCE');
READ(BALANCE);
WRITELN;
FOR DAY := MONDAY TO FRIDAY
  DO BEGIN (* A DAY'S TRANSACTIONS *)
     CASE DAY OF
           MONDAY : WRITE('MONDAY');
          TUESDAY : WRITE('TUESDAY');
        WEDNESDAY : WRITE('WEDNESDAY');
         THURSDAY : WRITE('THURSDAY');
           FRIDAY : WRITE('FRIDAY')
     END (* OF DAY CASES *);
     WRITELN(': ENTER TRANSACTIONS');
     TRANCOUNT := 0;
     REPEAT (* TRANSACTION PROCESSING *)
       READ(AMOUNT, SIGNAL);
       BALANCE := BALANCE + AMOUNT;
       TRANCOUNT := TRANCOUNT + 1
     UNTIL SIGNAL = '*';
     WRITELN;
     WRITELN(TRANCOUNT:2, ' TRANSACTIONS');
```

```
      WRITELN('CURRENT BALANCE: $', BALANCE:7:2);
      FOR I := 1 TO 25
       DO WRITE('-');
      WRITELN; WRITELN
      END (* OF A DAY'S TRANSACTIONS *)
 END (* OF PROGRAM ACCOUNTUPDATE *).
```

The output from a typical run of the program ACCOUNTUPDATE follows:

```
THIS PROGRAM WILL UPDATE THE BALANCE FOR AN ACCOUNT ON
A DAY BY DAY BASIS. ENTER AS MANY TRANSACTION DOLLAR
AMOUNTS ON A LINE AS YOU WISH. A POSITIVE NUMBER IS A
CREDIT AND A NEGATIVE NUMBER IS A DEBIT. AFTER YOU HAVE
ENTERED ALL THE TRANSACTION AMOUNTS FOR A PARTICULAR DAY,
TYPE AN ASTERISK (*) IMMEDIATELY AFTER THE LAST NUMBER AS
A SIGNAL TO MOVE TO THE NEXT DAY.
ENTER THE STARTING BALANCE
? 250.00

MONDAY: ENTER TRANSACTIONS
? 25.45 89.30 -50.00*

  3 TRANSACTIONS
CURRENT BALANCE: $ 314.75
-------------------------
TUESDAY: ENTER TRANSACTIONS
? -25.20 56.75 130.00
? 66.10 -260.95
? 69.70*

  6 TRANSACTIONS
CURRENT BALANCE: $ 351.15
-------------------------
WEDNESDAY: ENTER TRANSACTIONS
? 165.00*

  1 TRANSACTIONS
CURRENT BALANCE: $ 516.15
-------------------------
THURSDAY: ENTER TRANSACTIONS
? -352.17 42.80*

  2 TRANSACTIONS
CURRENT BALANCE: $ 206.78
-------------------------
FRIDAY: ENTER TRANSACTIONS
? -16.62
? 82.60*

  2 TRANSACTIONS
CURRENT BALANCE: $ 272.76
-------------------------
```

SUBRANGE TYPES

A collection of successive constants of an already defined ordinal type may be given its own identity as a **subrange** type. Subranges may be defined and named in the TYPE definition part of a program. Consider the following examples:

```
TYPE
      TESTSCORE = 0 .. 100;
      LETTER = 'A' .. 'Z';
      DIGIT = '0' .. '9';
```

The subrange type TESTSCORE consists of all INTEGER values between 0 and 100 inclusive. In this case, the predefined data type INTEGER is the **associated ordinal type** for the subrange TESTSCORE. LETTER is the type name of a subrange of CHAR values from 'A' through 'Z' inclusive, and DIGIT is a subrange consisting of the CHAR values between '0' and '9' inclusive.

The general form of a type definition for a subrange is illustrated in Figure 7–3. Both the *first-value* and the *last-value* specified in a subrange definition must be constants or constant identifiers of the same predefined or user-defined ordinal type, and the symbol ".." (two consecutive periods) must appear between these two values. A subrange consists of all constants that are less than or equal to the *last-value* and greater than or equal to the *first-value* in the ordering determined by the associated ordinal type. It is necessary that the *first-value* be less than or equal to the *last-value*.

> *type-identifier = first-value..last-value;*

Figure 7–3
General form of a type definition for a subrange.

The names of defined subrange types may be used to declare variables, as illustrated in the following examples in which TESTSCORE, LETTER, and DIGIT are the subranges defined above:

```
VAR
      SCORE, HIGHSCORE, LOWSCORE : TESTSCORE;
      TOTAL : INTEGER;
      CH : CHAR;
      CH1 : LETTER;
      CH2 : DIGIT;
```

A subrange value can be used anywhere that a value of the associated ordinal type is allowed. Given the variable declarations shown here, all the following statements are valid:

```
TOTAL := TOTAL + SCORE


IF SCORE > HIGHSCORE
   THEN HIGHSCORE := SCORE
   ELSE IF SCORE < LOWSCORE
           THEN LOWSCORE := SCORE
```

```
          CASE CH2 OF
                '0', '2', '4' : CH1 := 'A';
          '1', '5', '7', '8' : CH1 := 'E';
                '3', '6', '9' : CH1 := 'I'
          END (* OF CH2 CASES *)
```

Only integers in the subrange TESTSCORE may be assigned to the variables SCORE, HIGHSCORE, and LOWSCORE. CH1 and CH2 can take on CHAR values, but CH1 is restricted to the subrange LETTER and CH2 is restricted to the subrange DIGIT. The following statements are valid only when the values assigned to SCORE, CH1, and CH2 are in the appropriate subranges:

```
          SCORE := TOTAL

          CH1 := CH

          READ(CH1, CH2)
```

If the value of TOTAL (an INTEGER variable) is less than 0 or greater than 100, then it cannot be assigned to the TESTSCORE type variable SCORE. The value of CH must be in the subrange LETTER and the values read for CH1 and CH2 must be in the subranges LETTER and DIGIT, respectively.

It is not absolutely necessary that a subrange type be defined in the TYPE definition part of a program. Like an ordinal type, a subrange can be defined in a variable declaration. For instance,

```
     VAR
          SCORE, HIGHSCORE, LOWSCORE : 0 .. 100;
          TOTAL : INTEGER;
          CH : CHAR;
          CH1 : 'A' .. 'Z';
          CH2 : '0' .. '9';
```

When a user-defined ordinal type has been defined, any subrange of that type can also be defined. Consider the following type definitions:

```
TYPE
     LEVEL = (POOR, FAIR, GOOD, VERYGOOD, EXCELLENT, SUPERIOR);
     MIDRANGE = FAIR .. EXCELLENT;
     TOPNOTCH = VERYGOOD .. SUPERIOR;
     SAMPLESTATE = (NY, PENN, NJ, FLA, OHIO, ILL, MICH, MO,
                    WISC, TEX, ARIZ, CALIF);
     EAST = NY .. FLA;
     MIDWEST = OHIO .. WISC;
     WEST = TEX .. CALIF;
     POLLSTATE = FLA .. MICH;
```

The subranges and their associated types are listed in the following table:

Subrange Type	Associated Type	Values in the Subrange
MIDRANGE	LEVEL	FAIR, GOOD, VERYGOOD, EXCELLENT
TOPNOTCH	LEVEL	VERYGOOD, EXCELLENT, SUPERIOR
EAST	SAMPLESTATE	NY, PENN, NJ, FLA
MIDWEST	SAMPLESTATE	OHIO, ILL, MICH, MO, WISC
WEST	SAMPLESTATE	TEX, ARIZ, CALIF
POLLSTATE	SAMPLESTATE	FLA, OHIO, ILL, MICH

If the values for a variable should always be in some subrange of ordinal type values, it is best to restrict this variable to the appropriate subrange. This provides a convenient way to assure that the variable will not take on unexpected values. In the next section, we will see how ordinal data types and subranges are used to define a more complex data type.

7.1 EXERCISES

1. Define an ordinal data type for the days in a week so that a subrange consisting of Monday, Wednesday, and Friday identifiers and a subrange composed of the Tuesday, Thursday, and Saturday identifiers can also be defined. Construct the appropriate subrange definitions.

2. Tell what (if anything) is wrong with each of the following type definitions.

   a. COUNTER = (1, 2, 3, 4, 5);
   b. UNKNOWNS = 'X'..'T';
   c. SCOPE = 1.. MAXINT;
   d. TREES = (MAPLE, OAK, BIRCH, FIR, OAK, SPRUCE, WILLOW);
   e. GRADES = (AAA, A1, B, C);

3. Given the data types METAL and SLED defined as follows, tell whether each relational expression is TRUE or FALSE. If any expression is invalid, explain why.

   METAL = (ZINC, IRON, SILVER, GOLD, PLATINUM, ALUMINUM, TIN);
   SLED = (AUST1, USA1, ITALY2, USA2, GDR2, GDR1, AUST2, ITALY1);

   a. SILVER <= TIN   b. IRON = METAL
   c. USA2 > GDR1   d. (GOLD > IRON) OR (ITALY2 < USA1)
   e. TIN <> AUST2   f. (ZINC < PLATINUM) AND (GDR2 <= AUST1)
   g. ITALY1 < AUST1   h. NOT(ALUMINUM >= SILVER)

4. Evaluate each of the following expressions, if possible. If an expression cannot be evaluated, explain why. The types METAL and SLED are as defined in Exercise 3.

   a. ORD(AUST2)   b. SUCC(ORD(ITALY2))
   c. PRED(PLATINUM)   d. ORD(TIN) MOD ORD(USA1)
   e. SUCC(USA1)   f. PRED(SUCC(ITALY1))
   g. ORD(PRED(IRON))   h. ORD(SUCC(IRON) + PRED(TIN))

5. Using the identifiers ALPHA, BETA, DELTA, GAMMA, and OMEGA (not necessarily in that order), define ordinal data types that will satisfy each of the following sets of criteria.

a. PRED(DELTA) is GAMMA
   OMEGA < GAMMA is FALSE
   ORD(BETA) is 2
   SUCC(OMEGA) is ALPHA

b. GAMMA < BETA is TRUE
   ORD(BETA) − ORD(ALPHA) equals 3
   DELTA > OMEGA is FALSE
   PRED(OMEGA) is GAMMA

6. Assume that the following definitions and declarations have been made.

```
TYPE
      CATEGORY = 'C' .. 'I';
      ANIMAL = (CAT, DOG, BIRD, PIG, COW, HORSE);
VAR
      K : CATEGORY;
      A : ANIMAL;
```

Show the output that will be produced by each of the following program segments.

a.
```
FOR K := 'C' TO 'I'
   DO CASE K OF
         'C', 'G', 'H' : WRITE(K, SUCC(K));
                'E', 'I' : WRITELN(K, PRED(K));
                'D', 'H' : WRITE(K, ORD(K):1)
   END (* OF K CASES *)
```

b.
```
FOR A := DOG TO HORSE
   DO CASE A OF
         HORSE, DOG : WRITELN(ORD(PRED(A)));
                 PIG : WRITE(ORD(A));
          BIRD, COW : WRITE(ORD(SUCC(A)) + 1)
   END (* OF A CASES *)
```

7.2
ONE-DIMENSIONAL ARRAYS

Each variable of a real or ordinal type represents an individual memory location that is capable of storing a single value. Such variables are termed simple or unstructured. A structured variable represents an organized collection of memory locations, each of which is the equivalent of a simple variable. The values of a structured variable can be accessed individually, but the form of this access varies according to the type of structure the variable has. Some of the simplest and most useful types of structured variables, one-dimensional arrays, are introduced in this section.

ARRAY TYPES AND VARIABLES

When an array variable (or, simply, an array) is declared, its structure must be specified by an explicit definition or by a type identifier for an array structure defined in the TYPE definition part of a program. Consider the following example:

```
TYPE
     SUBSCRIPT = 1 .. 5;
     LIST = ARRAY [SUBSCRIPT] OF INTEGER;
VAR
     X, Y : LIST;
```

The variables X and Y are both declared as LIST type arrays. A LIST type array is composed of five memory locations, one corresponding to each SUBSCRIPT type constant, and each of those memory locations (referred to as **array components**) can store one INTEGER type value. The array components are referenced by using the name of the array followed by a SUBSCRIPT type value that is enclosed in square brackets. This is illustrated in the following diagrams, which show the individual components of the arrays X and Y:

X[1] ▢   Y[1] ▢

X[2] ▢   Y[2] ▢

X[3] ▢   Y[3] ▢

X[4] ▢   Y[4] ▢

X[5] ▢   Y[5] ▢

Every integer in the subrange SUBSCRIPTS is employed as an **index** for exactly one component of each LIST type array. Thus, identifiers like X[2] and Y[5], which serve as names for array components, are termed **indexed variables.** All values assigned to the components of an array must be of the same data type, referred to as the **base type** of the array, which for the arrays X and Y is the ordinal type INTEGER. The boxes representing the components of the arrays X and Y in the diagrams above are shaded to indicate that none of these components (indexed variables) has been assigned a value yet. Since only one index (SUBSCRIPT type value) is needed to reference each component of the arrays X and Y, they are one-dimensional arrays.

The composition of a definition for an array structure is formally illustrated in Figure 7–4. Two data types must be specified when an array structure is defined: an *index-type*, which defines the collection of indices for the components, and a *base-type*, which defines the type of values that can be stored in the components. The *index-type* may be CHAR, BOOLEAN, a user-defined ordinal type, or a subrange of any ordinal type. (Note that the type INTEGER cannot be specified as the *index-type*, but a subrange whose associated type is INTEGER, like SUBSCRIPT in the example presented earlier, is allowed.) The *base-type* can be any data type, although in this section we will consider only arrays that have a real,

---

type-identifier = ARRAY [*index-type*] OF *base-type*;

Figure 7–4
General form of a type definition for an array structure.

ordinal, or subrange *base-type*. Other possible *base-types* for arrays are examined later in this chapter and in subsequent chapters. Both the *index-type* and the *base-type* can be specified by using type identifiers or explicit type definitions.

Indexed variables can be used like simple variables in program statements. For example, the following assignment statements can be used to give values to various components of the arrays X and Y whose structures are defined above:

```
X[2] := 18;   X[4] := 125;
Y[4] := 0;    Y[3] := -15;
X[5] := -256; Y[1] := 6452
```

After these assignment statements have been executed, the components of the arrays X and Y will have the values indicated in the following diagrams:

X[1]			Y[1]	6452
X[2]	18		Y[2]	
X[3]			Y[3]	-15
X[4]	125		Y[4]	0
X[5]	-256		Y[5]	

Since no values are assigned to the indexed variables X[1], X[3], Y[2], and Y[5], they retain their previous values (if values have been assigned to these components yet). Indexed variables can also be assigned values via READ and READLN statements. For instance, the statement

```
READ(X[2], X[4], Y[4], Y[3], X[5], Y[1])
```

will produce the same effects as the six assignment statements shown earlier if six input values are read in the order 18, 125, 0, -15, -256, and 6452.

The index specified in a reference to an array component need not appear as a constant. It can be represented by a variable or expression that yields an appropriate index type value. Suppose I, J, and K are SUBSCRIPT type variables and consider the following FOR loop.

```
FOR I := 1 TO 3
  DO BEGIN
       J := 2 * I - 1;
       X[J] := 10 - I;
       K := I DIV 2 + 1;
       Y[K] := 10 + I
     END
```

During each cycle of the loop, J and K are assigned values in the subrange SUBSCRIPT, which are then used to identify particular components of X and Y. More precisely, J takes on the values 1, 3, and 5 while K takes on the values 1, 2, and 2 again. If X and Y had previously been assigned the values depicted in the last diagram, the contents of those arrays after the FOR loop has been executed will be as follows:

X[1]	9	Y[1]	11
X[2]	18	Y[2]	13
X[3]	8	Y[3]	−15
X[4]	125	Y[4]	0
X[5]	7	Y[5]	

Note that Y[2] is assigned the value 12 during the second loop cycle and then its value is changed to 13 during the third loop cycle. Since the index for an array component can be represented by an arithmetic expression, the FOR loop given above could be written in the following shorter form.

```
FOR I := 1 TO 3
  DO BEGIN
      X[2 * I - 1] := 10 - I;
      Y[I DIV 2 + 1] := 10 + I
  END
```

FOR loops are very useful for processing a known number of components in an array. Suppose N is an INTEGER variable to which a value has already been assigned, and let SUM be an INTEGER variable. Consider the following program segment.

```
SUM := 0;
FOR I := 1 TO N
  DO BEGIN
      READ(X[I]);
      SUM := SUM + X[I]
  END
```

If the value of N is between 1 and 5 inclusive, values for components 1 through N of the array X will be read and their SUM will be accumulated. The value of N should not be less than 1 nor greater than 5. If it is, an execution error will occur. For instance, suppose N has the value 8. Values for all five components of X will be read and their SUM accumulated, but an error will occur at the end of the fifth cycle when I should be incremented to 6. Recall that I is restricted to the subrange SUBSCRIPT. If I is declared as an INTEGER variable instead, an error will still occur. This time it will be an "array index out of range" type error, which results when an attempt is made to read a value for X[6] during the sixth loop cycle. If an array component is referenced by using a constant index that is not of the appropriate type, the compiler should note the error and print a suitable message. When a variable or expression is used to represent the index value for an indexed variable, any "out of range" error for the index will occur at execution time.

It is not absolutely necessary that array structures be defined in TYPE definitions. Nor is it necessary that the index type and the base type for an array be specified by using type identifiers. For instance, the subrange 1..5 may appear explicitly as the index type, as shown below.

```
TYPE
      LIST = ARRAY [1 .. 5] OF INTEGER;
VAR
      X, Y : LIST;
```

The name of the array structure for X and Y need not be specified in a TYPE definition; instead the structure for the array may appear in a VAR declaration such as

```
VAR
      X, Y : ARRAY [1 .. 5] OF INTEGER;
```

or

```
TYPE
      SUBSCRIPT = 1 .. 5;
VAR
      X, Y : ARRAY [SUBSCRIPT] OF INTEGER;
```

An array can have hundreds or thousands of components, depending on the number of distinct values of its index type. There will always be as many components for the array as there are distinct values of its index type. Any reference to a component of an array must include the array name and an appropriate index value, with the index enclosed in brackets after the name. Here are some valid array declarations:

```
TYPE
      COLOR = (WHITE, YELLOW, BLUE, GREEN, ORANGE, BLACK);
VAR
      R : ARRAY [1 .. 200] OF REAL;
      G : ARRAY ['A' .. 'T'] OF BOOLEAN;
      B : ARRAY [COLOR] OF 10 .. 25;
      C : ARRAY [-150 .. 150] OF YELLOW .. GREEN;
```

The structure for each of these arrays is described in the following table:

Array Name	Composition of the Array
R	200 components identified by the indexed variables R[1], R[2], R[3], . . . , R[199], R[200]. Each component may be assigned a REAL value.
G	20 components identified by the indexed variables G['A'], G['B'], G['C'], . . . , G['S'], G['T']. Each component may be assigned a BOOLEAN value (TRUE or FALSE).
B	6 components identified by the indexed variables B[WHITE], B[YELLOW], B[BLUE], B[GREEN], B[ORANGE], and B[BLACK]. Each component may be assigned a value in the subrange 10..25.
C	301 components identified by the indexed variables C[-150], C[-149], C[-148], . . . , C[149], C[150]. Each component may be assigned a value in the subrange YELLOW . . GREEN.

USE OF ARRAYS IN PROGRAMS

An array is suitable for storing a quantity of data of the same type that must be available to the program on demand. The ability to specify the indices in indexed variables by using variables and expressions has advantages that are not available when simple variables are used. For instance, the contents of an entire array can easily be printed by using a FOR loop.

Suppose we want to develop a program that will count the frequency of occurrence of the letters that appear in a single line of input to the program. The program must maintain 26 counters, one for each letter. These counters will be indexed variables that are components of the array FREQUENCY. In fact, we can use the subrange 'A'..'Z' as the index type for that array. The base type for the array will be 0..136, where we are assuming that no more than 136 characters will appear in the input line. Here is a pseudocode description of the counting process.

```
Initialize the TOTAL character count at 0
FOR LETTERs ranging from 'A' TO 'Z'
  DO Initialize FREQUENCY[LETTER] at 0
WRITE a request for input
WHILE there is a character to be read
     DO  BEGIN a frequency update
         READ a CHaracter
         Increment the TOTAL character count by 1
         IF the CHaracter is a letter
            THEN increment FREQUENCY[CHaracter] by 1
         END of a frequency update
FOR LETTERs ranging from 'A' to 'Z'
  DO WRITE the LETTER and FREQUENCY[LETTER]
WRITE the TOTAL character count
```

Since the components of the array FREQUENCY will be used as accumulators, they must all be initialized at 0. If a CHaracter other than a letter is read, the TOTAL character count will be updated, but the frequency counters will be unaffected. The program LETTERCOUNT given next will produce the required frequencies.

```
PROGRAM LETTERCOUNT (INPUT,OUTPUT);
(*********************************************************************
*                                                                   *
*   A PROGRAM TO COUNT THE FREQUENCY OF EACH LETTER IN AN INPUT      *
*   LINE                                                             *
*                                                                   *
*********************************************************************)
CONST                                   (*---------- [CONSTANTS] ----------*)
      MAXLINELENGTH = 136;              (* LIMIT ON THE NUMBER OF INPUT  *)
                                        (* CHARACTERS                    *)
                                        (*-------------------------------*)
TYPE
      ALPHABET = 'A' .. 'Z';
      COUNTS = 0 .. MAXLINELENGTH;
      COUNTERS = ARRAY [ALPHABET] OF COUNTS;
```

```
VAR                                    (*-----[ALPHABET VARIABLES]------*)
        LETTER : ALPHABET;             (* A LETTER CHARACTER           *)
                                       (*------------------------------*)
                                       (*-------[CHAR VARIABLES]--------*)
        CH : CHAR;                     (* A CHARACTER                  *)
                                       (*------------------------------*)
                                       (*------[COUNTS VARIABLES]-------*)
        J,                             (* CONTROL VARIABLE FOR OUTPUT  *)
                                       (* LOOP                         *)
        TOTAL : COUNTS;                (* TOTAL CHARACTERS INPUT       *)
                                       (*------------------------------*)
                                       (*-------[COUNTERS ARRAY]--------*)
        FREQUENCY : COUNTERS;          (* THE FREQUENCIES OF THE LETTERS*)
                                       (*------------------------------*)
(*****************************************************************************)
BEGIN (* PROGRAM LETTERCOUNT *)
TOTAL := 0;
FOR LETTER := 'A' TO 'Z'
 DO FREQUENCY[LETTER] := 0;
WRITELN('THIS PROGRAM WILL ACCEPT ONE LINE OF INPUT AND THEN PRINT ',
        'THE');
WRITELN('FREQUENCY OF OCCURRENCE OF THE LETTERS IN THAT LINE.');
WRITELN('ENTER THE INPUT LINE NOW.');
WHILE NOT EOLN
    DO BEGIN (* A FREQUENCY UPDATE *)
       READ(CH);
       TOTAL := TOTAL + 1;
       IF (CH >= 'A') AND (CH <= 'Z')
          THEN FREQUENCY[CH] := FREQUENCY[CH] + 1
       END (* OF A FREQUENCY UPDATE *);
WRITELN;
WRITELN('** TABLE OF FREQUENCIES **':46);
WRITELN;
FOR J := 1 TO 4
 DO WRITE('LETTER   COUNT':16);
WRITELN;
FOR J := 1 TO 4
 DO WRITE('------   -----':16);
WRITELN;
FOR LETTER := 'A' TO 'Z'
 DO BEGIN (* FREQUENCY OUTPUT *)
    WRITE(LETTER:7, FREQUENCY[LETTER]:8, ' ');
    IF (ORD(LETTER) - ORD('A') + 1) MOD 4 = 0
       THEN WRITELN

    END (* OF FREQUENCY OUTPUT *);
WRITELN; WRITELN;
WRITELN('A TOTAL OF ':25, TOTAL:3, ' CHARACTERS WERE ENTERED.')
END (* OF PROGRAM LETTERCOUNT *).
```

In the loop that prints the frequencies, the value of the expression

$$(ORD(LETTER) - ORD('A') + 1) \bmod 4$$

will be 0 every fourth LETTER past 'A' so that only four frequencies are printed per line. Here is the output from a sample run of the program LETTERCOUNT.

```
THIS PROGRAM WILL ACCEPT ONE LINE OF INPUT AND THEN PRINT THE
FREQUENCY OF OCCURRENCE OF THE LETTERS IN THAT LINE.
ENTER THE INPUT LINE NOW.
?I NEVER MET A MAN I DIDN'T LIKE.

              ** TABLE OF FREQUENCIES **

  LETTER  COUNT   LETTER  COUNT   LETTER  COUNT   LETTER  COUNT
  ------  -----   ------  -----   ------  -----   ------  -----
    A       2       B       0       C       0       D       2
    E       4       F       0       G       0       H       0
    I       4       J       0       K       1       L       1
    M       2       N       3       O       0       P       0
    Q       0       R       1       S       0       T       2
    U       0       V       1       W       0       X       0
    Y       0       Z       0

        A TOTAL OF   32 CHARACTERS WERE ENTERED.
```

The number of components an array will have is fixed when the array is declared, but the program is under no obligation to use all the components. The actual array storage that a program will use from run to run can vary. It is the responsibility of the programmer to anticipate the sizes of the arrays that a program will normally need. The constant identifier MAXLINELENGTH was used in the program LETTERCOUNT to make it easier to change the maximum number of characters that will be read. Changing the definition of MAXLINELENGTH will automatically change the last value for the subrange COUNTS. By using constant identifiers to represent the first and last values for subranges we can easily modify the subranges. This procedure is particularly useful for subranges that are used as array index types.

An array is a convenient structure to use for storing values of the same type that need to be sorted. Suppose V is an array declared by

```
VAR
    V : ARRAY [0 .. 100] OF INTEGER;
```

The array V can store up to 101 integers. In order to sort values that are in the array V, it is convenient to have these values in consecutive components of the array. The basic sorting process is

> Read values for the array
> Sort the values in the array
> Print the list of sorted values

The component V[0] is used for special purposes in the sorting process described below. The values to be sorted are assumed to be in consecutive components of V, starting with the component V[1]. A count of the number of values to be sorted will be maintained in the INTEGER variable N. Once all the values have been inserted into the array, they will occupy components V[1] through V[N]. A special SIGNALVALUE will be used to signal the end of data input.

It is convenient to use the component V[0] to temporarily hold each input value while it is determined whether that value belongs in the array or whether it is the SIGNALVALUE. Here is a pseudocode description of the input process we will use.

```
Initialize N at 0
READ a value for V[0]
WHILE V[0] does not equal the SIGNALVALUE
    DO BEGIN insertion into the array
        Increment N by 1
        Copy V[0] to V[N]
        Read the next value for V[0]
    END of insertion into the array
```

We will assume that V has enough components to store all the input values.

Suppose that only five values are read before the SIGNALVALUE is encountered. The array components whose indices range from 6 through 100 inclusive will still be undefined. If the five values read are 32, 115, 56, −16, and 43 (in this order), components V[1] through V[5] will contain the following values.

V[1]	32
V[2]	115
V[3]	56
V[4]	− 16
V[5]	43

Sorting an array consists of rearranging the values stored in the array so that they will end up in ascending order (increasing as the index values increase) or descending order (decreasing as the index values increase). These two orders are illustrated here for the case of an array V that contains five numbers:

Array V Sorted in Ascending Order		Array V Sorted in Descending Order	
V[1]	− 16	V[1]	115
V[2]	32	V[2]	56
V[3]	43	V[3]	43
V[4]	56	V[4]	32
V[5]	115	V[5]	− 16

Suppose that array V contains N values in components V[1] through V[N] and we want to sort V in ascending order. Our first objective could be to move the smallest value in the entire array into POSition 1 (array component V[1]). To do this, we will have to LOCate the index of the component containing the smallest value and then interchange the values of V[1] and V[LOCation]. This procedure is illustrated below for the case when N is 5.

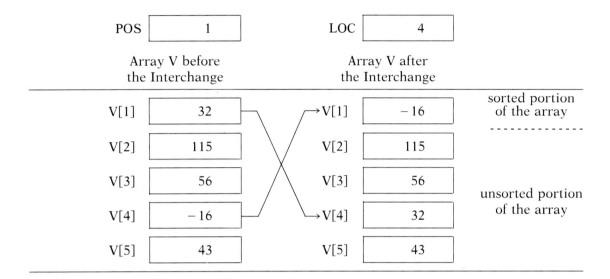

Now only components V[2] through V[N] are left to be sorted. The next objective is to move the smallest value in the unsorted portion of the array into POSition 2 (component V[2]). To do this we will have to LOCate the component in the unsorted portion of the array that contains the smallest value and then interchange the values of V[2] and V[LOCation], as illustrated in the following diagram:

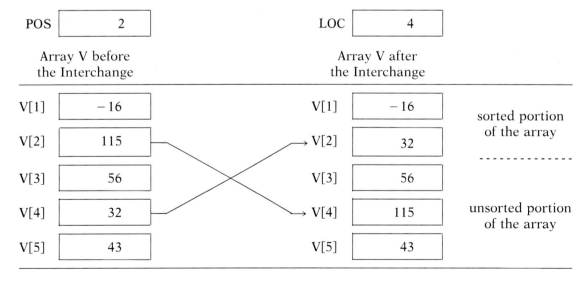

If we continue in this manner, the array V will be sorted in N − 1 steps. At each step we select a value from the unsorted portion of the array and then put it in the array component it must occupy in the sorted array. This method of sorting an array is known as a **selection sort.** If at each step we select the largest value in the unsorted portion of the array instead of the smallest value, the array will end up sorted in descending order.

Each cycle in a selection sort consists of finding a value in the unsorted portion of the array and then moving it to the position it will occupy in the sorted array, as described by the following pseudocode:

> FOR POSitions ranging from 1 to N − 1
>   DO BEGIN a selection cycle
>   Search for the LOCation of the smallest value in the unsorted portion of array V
>   Interchange the values of V[POSition] and V[LOCation]
>   END of a selection cycle

A search through the unsorted portion of the array for the smallest value must scan components V[POSition] through V[N]:

> Initialize the LOCation at POSition
> FOR J ranging from POSition + 1 to N
> DO IF V[J] is less than V[LOCation]
>   THEN Change the LOCation to J

In order to interchange the values of two array components, a "save" variable must be used to temporarily store one of two values so that it is not lost when the value of one component is copied to the other component. The component V[0] will be used for this purpose. Since the LOCation of the smallest value in the unsorted portion of the array could already be at the POSition in which it belongs in the sorted array, an interchange is necessary only when the LOCation and POSition indices are not identical:

> IF the cycle POSition and the selected LOCation are not the same
>   THEN BEGIN an interchange
>   Save the value of V[POSition] in V[0]
>   Copy the value of V[LOCation] into V[POSition]
>   Copy the value of V[0] into V[LOCation]
>   END of an interchange

Now that we have refined the sorting process, a more thorough description of the entire program can be given.

> BEGIN program SELECTIONSORT
> WRITE directions
> Initialize N at 0
> Read a value for V[0]
> WHILE V[0] does not equal the SIGNALVALUE
>   DO BEGIN insertion into the array
>   Increment N by 1
>   Copy V[0] to V[N]
>   READ the next value for V[0]
>   END of insertion into the array

```
          FOR POSitions ranging from 1 to N − 1
           DO  BEGIN a selection cycle
                  Initialize the LOCation at POSition
                  FOR J ranging from POSition + 1 to N
                     DO IF V[J] is less than V[LOCation]
                           THEN Change the LOCation to J
                  IF POSition and LOCation are not the same
                     THEN  BEGIN an interchange
                              Save the value of V[POSition] in V[0]
                              Copy the value of V[LOCation] into V[POSition]
                              Copy the value of V[0] into V[LOCation]
                              END of an interchange
                  END of a selection cycle
           FOR J ranging from 1 to N
            DO WRITE the value of V[J]
           END of program SELECTIONSORT
```

The program just described will arrange the values in the array V into ascending order. To sort these values into descending order, simply replace the words "less than" by the words "greater than" in a selection cycle.

The SELECTIONSORT program is given next. Note the use of the constant identifier MAXINDEX. This makes it possible to change the declared size of the array V by simply changing the definition of MAXINDEX.

```
PROGRAM SELECTIONSORT (INPUT, OUTPUT);
(******************************************************************
*                                                                *
*   A PROGRAM WHICH SELECTION SORTS AN ARRAY OF INTEGERS AND PRINTS *
*   THE NUMBERS IN ASCENDING ORDER                                *
*                                                                *
******************************************************************)
CONST                             (*----------[CONSTANTS]----------*)
      MAXINDEX = 100;             (* MAXIMUM INDEX FOR ARRAY V       *)
      SIGNALVALUE = 999999;       (* SIGNAL FOR END OF INPUT         *)
                                  (*-------------------------------*)

TYPE
      INDICES = 0 .. MAXINDEX;
      LISTOFVALUES = ARRAY [INDICES] OF INTEGER;

VAR                               (*------[INDICES VARIABLES]------*)
      N,                          (* NUMBER OF VALUES TO BE SORTED  *)
      POS,                        (* POSITION TO FILL IN SORTED     *)
                                  (* PORTION OF ARRAY V             *)
      LOC,                        (* SELECTED LOCATION IN A SORT    *)
                                  (* CYCLE                          *)
      J : INDICES;                (* INDEX USED IN SCANNING THE     *)
                                  (* ARRAY V                        *)
                                  (*-------------------------------*)
                                  (*-----[LISTOFVALUES ARRAY]------*)
      V : LISTOFVALUES;           (* VALUES TO BE SORTED            *)
                                  (*-------------------------------*)
(******************************************************************)
```

```
BEGIN (* PROGRAM SELECTIONSORT *)
N := 0;
WRITELN('THIS PROGRAM WILL SORT A LIST OF WHOLE NUMBERS AND THEN');
WRITELN('PRINT THEM OUT FROM LOW TO HIGH. YOU MAY ENTER NO MORE');
WRITELN('THAN ', MAXINDEX:3, ' NUMBERS. PUT AS MANY NUMBERS ON A ',
        'LINE AS YOU');
WRITELN('WISH AND USE AS MANY LINES AS NECESSARY. TO SIGNAL THE');
WRITELN('END OF INPUT, ENTER THE NUMBER ', SIGNALVALUE:6, '.');
WRITELN('ENTER THE NUMBERS TO BE SORTED NOW.');
READ(V[0]);
WHILE V[0] <> SIGNALVALUE
    DO BEGIN (* INSERTION INTO THE ARRAY *)
        N := N + 1;
        V[N] := V[0];
        READ(V[0])
        END (* OF INSERTION INTO ARRAY *);
FOR POS := 1 TO N - 1
 DO BEGIN (* A SELECTION CYCLE *)
    LOC := POS;
    FOR J := POS + 1 TO N
     DO IF V[J] < V[LOC]
          THEN LOC := J;
    IF LOC <> POS
      THEN BEGIN (* AN INTERCHANGE *)
            V[0] := V[POS];
            V[POS] := V[LOC];
            V[LOC] := V[0]
            END (* OF AN INTERCHANGE *)
    END (* OF A SELECTION CYCLE *);
WRITELN;
WRITELN('THE SORTED LIST:');
FOR J := 1 TO N
 DO WRITELN(V[J]:9)
END (* OF PROGRAM SELECTIONSORT *).
```

Here is a sample run of the program SELECTIONSORT.

```
THIS PROGRAM WILL SORT A LIST OF WHOLE NUMBERS AND THEN
PRINT THEM OUT FROM LOW TO HIGH. YOU MAY ENTER NO MORE
THAN 100 NUMBERS. PUT AS MANY NUMBERS ON A LINE AS YOU
WISH AND USE AS MANY LINES AS NECESSARY. TO SIGNAL THE
END OF INPUT, ENTER THE NUMBER 999999.
ENTER THE NUMBERS TO BE SORTED NOW.
?184 54 -39 7 219 55
?-104 177 54 555
? 38 375 -1 999999

THE SORTED LIST:
     -104
      -39
       -1
        7
```

```
        38
        54
        54
        55
       177
       184
       219
       375
       555
```

ARRAY VARIABLES IN ASSIGNMENT STATEMENTS

An assignment statement can be used to copy the entire contents of one array into the corresponding components of another array provided that both arrays are of the same type. Consider the following array declarations.

```
    VAR
        P, Q : ARRAY [1 .. 6] OF INTEGER;
        R, S : ARRAY [1 .. 6] OF CHAR;
        T : ARRAY [1 .. 10] OF INTEGER;
```

The assignment statement

$$P := Q$$

is valid and will have the same effect as the loop

```
        FOR I := 1 TO 6
        DO P[I] := Q[I]
```

Array assignments like the one shown above are valid only when both arrays have the same structure. Even though arrays P and T have the same base type, the statement

$$P := T$$

is illegal because P and T have different index types. In fact, T has 10 components while P has only 6. In order to copy the values in the first 6 components of T into the first 6 components of P, we could use the loop

```
        FOR I := 1 TO 6
        DO P[I] := T[I]
```

Since R and S are arrays of the same type, the statements

$$R := S$$

and

$$S := R$$

are both valid. The first one will copy the entire contents of S into R and the second one will copy the entire contents of R into S. A statement like

$$R := Q$$

is not valid because the arrays R and Q have different base types.

7.2 EXERCISES

1. Find the errors (if any) in each of the following sets of declarations.

a.
```
TYPE
        SECTION = (A, B, C, D, E, F, G, H);
        NUMBER = [100 .. 499];
        SEATS = ARRAY [SECTION] OF NUMBER;
    VAR
        BLEACHER, RESERVED : SEATS;
        UTILIZATION : ARRAY [SECTION] OF 0.0 .. 100.0;
```

b.
```
TYPE
        SPORT = (GOLF, TENNIS, BASEBALL, BASKETBALL,
                FOOTBALL, HOCKEY);
        CLASS = (C, B, A, AA, AAA);
    VAR
        MEMBER : ARRAY [CLASS] OF 0 .. 500;
        SCHOOL : ARRAY [250] OF CLASS;
        COST, RECEIPTS : ARRAY [SPORT] OF REAL;
```

2. Give the necessary definitions and declarations that will create the arrays described here.

a. Array BUDGET has one component for each month in a year and its components will store monthly expenses in dollars and cents.
b. Array POP has one component for each year in the twentieth century and each component will store the population for a town in a given year.
c. Array REPORTCARD has a component for each of the school subjects Algebra, English, History, Biology, and French, and the value of each component is a letter grade (A, B, C, D, or F).

3. Assume that the following declarations have been made.
```
TYPE
        MONTH = 1 .. 12;
        TEMPERATURES = -50 .. 120;
        SEASONS = (SPRING, SUMMER, FALL, WINTER);
        EXTREMES = ARRAY [SEASONS] OF TEMPERATURES;
        AVERAGES = ARRAY [MONTH] OF REAL;
    VAR
        LOWTEMP, HIGHTEMP : EXTREMES;
        MEANTEMP : AVERAGES;
        I : SEASONS;
        TEMP : TEMPERATURES;
        FIRST, LAST, K : MONTH;
```

Check the following statements for errors and correct any you find.

a. `WRITELN(MEANTEMP:12)`

b. ```
FOR I := SPRING TO WINTER
  DO WRITELN(MEANTEMP[I])
```

c.  ```
CASE SEASON OF
   SPRING : WRITELN(LOWTEMP[SPRING]:5, HIGHTEMP[SPRING]:5);
   SUMMER : WRITELN(LOWTEMP[SUMMER]:5, HIGHTEMP[SUMMER]:5);
     FALL : WRITELN(LOWTEMP[FALL]:5, HIGHTEMP[FALL]:5);
   WINTER : WRITELN(LOWTEMP[WINTER]:5, HIGHTEMP[WINTER]:5)
END (* OF SEASON CASES *)
```

d. ```
READ(TEMP);
WHILE TEMP > -99
   DO BEGIN
       MEANTEMP[K] := MEANTEMP[K] + TEMP;
       READ(TEMP)
       END
```

**4.** Assume that the following declarations have been made.

```
TYPE
      COLORS = (WHITE, RED, BLUE, YELLOW, GREEN, PINK, BLACK);
VAR
      ALPHA, OMEGA : ARRAY [1 .. 10] OF INTEGER;
      PART : ARRAY ['A' .. 'Z'] OF 'A' .. 'Z';
      BLEND : ARRAY [COLORS] OF BOOLEAN;
      SHADE : COLORS;
      I, J, K : INTEGER;
      L : CHAR;
```

Tell what values will be assigned to the arrays ALPHA, OMEGA, PART, and BLEND by the following program segments.

a. ```
FOR I := 10 DOWNTO 1
  DO OMEGA[I] := I DIV 2
```

b. ```
FOR K := 2 TO 10
  DO BEGIN
     ALPHA[K - 1] := K * 5;
     ALPHA[K] := ALPHA[K - 1] MOD 4
     END
```

c.  ```
FOR SHADE := WHITE TO BLACK
  DO CASE SHADE OF
```

```
              RED,
              PINK  : BLEND[PRED(SHADE)]  := FALSE;
            BLACK,
            WHITE,
          YELLOW  : BLEND[SHADE]  := TRUE;
            BLUE,
           GREEN  : BLEND[SUCC(SHADE)]  := TRUE
        END (* OF SHADE CASES *)
```

d.
```
      J := 0;
      FOR L := 'A' TO 'E'
        DO BEGIN
           PART[L] := CHR(ORD(L) + J);
           J := J + 1
           END
```

5. The program LETTERCOUNT uses an array of counters to accumulate frequencies for letters in an input line of characters. Another approach is to read all the characters into an array and then use a single counter and loops to accumulate the frequency of each letter. Write a program that implements this approach. Which of the two letter counting methods do you think is better and why?

6. Show how the program SELECTIONSORT must be modified if the index type for the array V is some subrange of CHAR.

7.3 PACKED ARRAYS AND STRING DATA TYPES

Since an array stores values of only one type (the base type), an equal amount of storage is allocated for every component. In some cases, the storage allocated to each component far exceeds the amount of storage actually needed. Consider the case of a CHAR value. The amount of memory needed to store one character is known as a **byte,** but the fundamental unit of storage for one data value is one **word,** which may consist of two or more bytes depending on the type of computer. (For small microcomputers, the terms "byte" and "word" are synonymous.) CDC Cyber Series computers, for instance, use words that consists of ten bytes of storage. Suppose CH is a CHAR variable whose value is 'P'. We have depicted the contents of the memory word represented by the variable CH by using a rectangle like this one:

CH ['P'   ]

Actually, the value 'P' occupies only the first byte of the storage word allocated to the variable CH, and the remaining bytes of that word are unused. This is illustrated in the following diagram, which shows a blowup of a 10-byte word sectioned into bytes.

CH ['P' | | | | | | | | |]

Thus 90% of the storage word allocated to the variable CH is wasted. Even if a word of storage consists of only two bytes (as is the case for most minicomputers), 50% of a word is wasted if it is used to store a single character.

Suppose that instead of being a simple variable, CH is an array whose base type is CHAR:

```
VAR
     CH : ARRAY [1 .. 6] OF CHAR;
```

One word of storage is allocated to each component of CH. Now suppose the following assignment statements are executed.

```
CH[1] := 'P';   CH[2] := 'A';   CH[3] := 'S';
CH[4] := 'C';   CH[5] := 'A';   CH[6] := 'L'
```

If one word consists of 10 bytes of storage, the contents of the array CH may be depicted as shown here.

CH[1]	'P'									
CH[2]	'A'									
CH[3]	'S'									
CH[4]	'C'									
CH[5]	'A'									
CH[6]	'L'									

Sixty bytes of storage are allocated to the array CH (10 bytes per component), but only 6 of those bytes are used to store CHAR values. Again, 90% of the storage space allocated to the array variable CH is wasted.

Other types of data may also require less than a full word of storage. For example, many computers need to use only one byte of storage for an integer in the subrange 0..63. If one word of storage is allocated to such a value, at least 50% of the word will not be used.

In Pascal, an array may be "packed" in order to conserve storage. This is accomplished by placing keyword PACKED in front of the word ARRAY when the array's type is defined, as illustrated in Figure 7–5. The amount of storage saved by packing an array varies according to the *base-type* for the array as well as the word and byte capacities on the computer. In some cases a considerable amount of storage can be saved, but in others there is no savings at all. In any case, it is always permissible to define an array as PACKED.

---

type-identifier = PACKED ARRAY [*index-type*] OF *base-type;*

Figure 7–5
General form of the type definition for a PACKED array.

PACKED ARRAYS OF CHARACTERS

The types of arrays that benefit the most from packed structures are arrays of CHAR, BOOLEAN, or subrange base types. A character string is a constant of a particular PACKED ARRAY of CHAR type. For example, the string 'PASCAL' is stored in the computer as a packed array composed of six CHAR values. Those CHAR values are packed into six consecutive bytes of one word if that word consists of six or more bytes. For instance, in a 10-byte word the string 'PASCAL' would be stored as shown here.

'P'	'A'	'S'	'C'	'A'	'L'				

The 4 bytes at the end of the word simply remain unused. A string consisting of more than 10 characters will require more than one 10-byte word. For instance, the string constant 'PASCAL PROGRAMMING IS FUN.' requires three 10-byte words of storage, as illustrated below.

'P'	'A'	'S'	'C'	'A'	'L'	'■'	'P'	'R'	'O'
'G'	'R'	'A'	'M'	'M'	'I'	'N'	'G'	■	'I'
'S'	■	'F'	'U'	'N'	'.'				

This time two full words (20 bytes) and 6 bytes of a third word are needed. The 4 bytes at the end of the third word remain unused.

The storage arrangement for a variable whose declared type is a packed array of characters follows the pattern shown earlier for string constants. Consider the following declaration.

```
VAR
     C : PACKED ARRAY [1 .. 8] OF CHAR;
```

If a storage word consists of 10 bytes, each component of the array C will be allocated one byte of storage in the same word. The storage arrangement for C is depicted below.

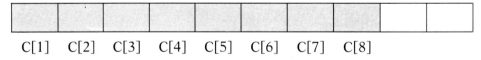

C[1]   C[2]   C[3]   C[4]   C[5]   C[6]   C[7]   C[8]

Had the array C not been packed, each component of C would have been allocated a full word of storage. Even though two bytes of a 10-byte word are not utilized when C is packed, the fact that only one word of storage is needed versus the eight words that would have been required had C not been packed results in an 87.5% savings in storage.

The packing of an array does not reduce a program's ability to access individual components of that array. All of the following statements will produce essentially the same effects whether or not the array C is packed.

```
C[5] := '*'

FOR LETTER := 'A' TO 'H'
  DO C[ORD(LETTER) - ORD('A') + 1] := CH

IF C[3] > C[7]
   THEN WRITELN(C[3])
   ELSE WRITELN(C[7])
```

Some storage may be conserved when an array is packed, but the components are still individually accessible in the normal manner. However, it does take the computer longer to process components of a packed array because more time is needed to locate a component in a packed array. In some cases, the savings in storage realized by packing arrays may be offset by a substantial increase in execution time for the program.

The relational operators may be used to compare two character strings that have the same length (same number of characters). A comparison between two strings of the same length is made on a character-by-character basis, starting with the leftmost character in each string. The order of one string with respect to another string of the same length is determined by the order of the leftmost characters in each string that are different. For example, the relational expression

$$\text{'GEORGE'} < \text{'GERALD'}$$

has the value TRUE because the first two characters in both strings are the same and the third character in 'GEORGE' ('O') is less than the third character in 'GERALD' ('R') in any character set. In Pascal, it is not possible to compare two character strings that have different lengths. For instance, the string 'GERALD', whose length is six, and the string 'GERONIMO', whose length is eight, cannot be compared by using any of the relational operators. However, the expression

$$\text{'GERALD■■'} > \text{'GERONIMO'}$$

is valid because every blank space in a character string counts as a character. The value of this expression is FALSE, since the first three characters in each string are identical and 'A' > 'O' is FALSE.

Comparisons between character strings may not yield the same results in every version of Pascal because the order of one character string with respect to another depends on the collating sequence for the available character set. For instance, the relational expression

$$\text{'GERALD■■■'} < \text{'GERALDINE'}$$

has the value TRUE if the full ASCII or EBCDIC character sets are used, but it has the value FALSE if the CDC ASCII subset shown in Appendix A (Table A.2) is used. The reason for this is that the blank space character precedes all letters in both the ASCII and the EBCDIC collating sequences, but the letters precede the blank space character in CDC's ordering for the ASCII subset. Here are some more examples of string comparisons and the values they yield when the full ASCII ordering applies:

Relational Expression	Value of the Expression
'BALLOONS' > 'BALONEY'	FALSE
'COTTON■■■■' < ' COTTONBALL'	TRUE
'YES,■I■CAN!' >= 'YESTERDAY■■'	FALSE
'■■DO■IT' <= 'I■CAN' 'T'	TRUE
'3142■-■27' = ' 3142-27■■'	FALSE

A variable declared as a packed array of characters is called a **string variable.** Consider the following declarations:

```
TYPE
     INDICES = 1 .. 20;
VAR
     I : INDICES;
     PHRASE, SAYING : PACKED ARRAY [INDICES] OF CHAR;
```

There are several advantages to packing arrays of characters. One is that a string variable can be assigned a string value by using an assignment statement, provided that the length of the string and the number of components in the string variable are the same. From here on, a single box will be used to represent the storage allocated for a character string. The assignment statements

```
PHRASE := 'GET TO WORK NOW      ';
SAYING := ' TIME IS RUNNING OUT'
```

are both valid and they have the effects shown here:

PHRASE   `'GET■TO■WORK■NOW■■■■■'`

SAYING   `'■TIME■IS■RUNNING■OUT'`

Remember that a string variable is actually an array. When a string value is assigned to a string variable, each component of that variable receives one character. The characters in the string are assigned to the string variable in order of their appearance in the string. When 'GET TO WORK NOW' is assigned to PHRASE, PHRASE[1] gets the value 'G', PHRASE[2] gets the value 'E', PHRASE[3] gets the value 'T', PHRASE[4] gets the value '■', and so on. Since PHRASE has 20 components, only strings containing exactly 20 characters can be assigned to PHRASE by using assignment statements. The statement

```
PHRASE := 'GET TO WORK NOW'
```

is illegal because 'GET TO WORK NOW' contains only 15 characters.

Each component of a string variable is individually accessible by referencing the appropriate indexed variable. Consider the following program segment:

```
FOR I := 1 TO 10
  DO BEGIN
     IF PHRASE[I] := 'O'
       THEN PHRASE[I] := 'A';
     WRITE (PHRASE[I])
     END;
FOR I := 11 TO 20
  DO WRITE (PHRASE[I]);
WRITELN
```

The first FOR loop will change every occurrence of 'O' in the first 10 components of PHRASE to 'A' before printing each component's value. The second FOR loop simply prints the characters stored in the last 10 components of PHRASE. All the output produced by this program segment appears on one line:

     GET TA WARK NOW

We can get the same effects by using the following program segment:

```
FOR I := 1 TO 10
  DO IF PHRASE[I] = 'O'
        THEN PHRASE[I] := 'A';
WRITELN(PHRASE)
```

When the name of a string variable (packed array of characters) appears in a WRITE or WRITELN list, the entire string stored in the array is printed. This is another one of the advantages of using an array of characters that is packed. Normally it is not legal to list the name of an array in a WRITE or WRITELN statement in order to have the contents of the array printed; string variables are the exception to this rule.

It is not permissible to read a string of characters by using statements like READ(PHRASE) or READLN(PHRASE). A character string must be read from the INPUT file character by character. A string value can be read for PHRASE by using the the loop

```
FOR I := 1 TO 20
  DO READ(PHRASE[I])
```

This loop will read exactly 20 characters from the INPUT file so that every component of PHRASE will have a value. When there are blank spaces at the end of a string, it is convenient to have the program assign the trailing blank space characters automatically, as illustrated below.

```
WRITELN('ENTER THE MESSAGE (20 CHARACTERS OR LESS).');
READLN; (* NEW INPUT LINE *)
FOR I := 1 TO 20
  DO IF NOT EOLN
        THEN READ(PHRASE[I])
        ELSE PHRASE[I] := ' '
```

If a string containing fewer than 20 characters is read, the remaining components of PHRASE will be padded with blanks. It is not advisable to assign fewer characters to a string variable than the variable can hold because then the value of the string variable is not fully defined. If a string variable's value has been only partially established before it is printed, the output may look very strange because some character value will be printed for every component (even the undefined components).

PACKING AND UNPACKING

When the components of a packed array are processed individually, the computer may spend a considerable amount of time just accessing those components. It may therefore be worthwhile, when many operations are to be performed on the data stored in a packed array, to move the contents of that array to an array that does not have a packed structure. This is known as "unpacking" an array. Suppose the arrays P and U are declared as shown here:

```
VAR
    P : PACKED ARRAY [1 .. 8] OF CHAR;
    U : ARRAY [1 .. 8] OF CHAR;
```

Even though P and U have the same index and base types, it is not possible to copy the contents of one of these arrays to corresponding components in the other array by using either P := U or U := P because P is packed and U is not. We could assign the values in one of these arrays to the corresponding components in the other array component by component in a loop. For example,

```
FOR I := 1 TO 8
  DO U[I] := P[I]
```

This is allowed because the individual components of the P and U arrays are of the same type even though the amount of storage used for components of P may be less than the storage allocated to each component of U.

In order to facilitate packing and unpacking arrays, Pascal provides two **standard procedures,** named PACK and UNPACK. A standard procedure is "called" to perform tasks by specifying its name and then a list of arguments that represent the data that the procedure should process. The procedures PACK and UNPACK each require three arguments, which must appear in parentheses after the name of the procedure in a **procedure statement.** The general forms of the procedure statements used to call PACK and UNPACK are given in Figure 7–6. When PACK or UNPACK is called, *unpacked-array* and *packed-array* must be the names of an unpacked array and a packed array, respectively. The *index* may be any constant, constant identifier, variable, or expression whose value is of the index type for the *unpacked-array*. Note that the procedures PACK and UNPACK require the same number and kind of arguments, but the order in which the arguments must appear in each procedure statement is different.

PACK(*unpacked-array, index, packed-array*)

UNPACK(*packed-array, unpacked array, index*)

Figure 7–6
General forms of the procedure statements for PACKing and UNPACKing arrays.

Suppose that the components of array U have been assigned the following values:

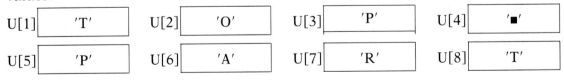

If the procedure PACK is called by using the statement

PACK(U, 1, P)

all the characters in the array U will be copied into the corresponding components of the packed array P. The contents of P after this call to PACK will be as depicted here:

P | 'TOP■PART'

The index value 1 specified in the call to PACK indicates that all characters from the first component of the array U to the eighth component are to be copied into the corresponding components in array P. In other words, the PACKing that results is equivalent to that produced by the loop

```
FOR I := 1 TO 8
   DO P[I] := U[I]
```

In the last example, the arrays P and U have the same number of components. The procedure PACK may be used to assign data from an unpacked array to a packed array when the unpacked array has more components than the packed array. Suppose the array PK is declared by

```
VAR
     PK : PACKED ARRAY [1 .. 4] OF CHAR;
```

PACK may be called to assign the values in four consecutive components of U to the array PK. For instance, the statement

```
PACK(U, 3, PK)
```

will assign the values of U[3], U[4], U[5], and U[6] to the array components PK[1], PK[2], PK[3], and PK[4], respectively. There are four other calls to PACK that can be made by using the arrays U and PK. The effects that these five possible calls to PACK will have on the contents of array PK are shown next.

		Contents of PK after PACKing
PACK(U, 1, PK)	PK	'TOP■'
PACK(U, 2, PK)	PK	'OP■P'
PACK(U, 3, PK)	PK	'P■PA'
PACK(U, 4, PK)	PK	'■PAR'
PACK(U, 5, PK)	PK	'PART'

The procedure UNPACK produces the opposite effects of a PACK. Suppose that the arrays U and PK have the following values.

PK | 'JUMP'

U[1]	'2'		U[5]	'R'
U[2]	'■'		U[6]	'■'
U[3]	'F'		U[7]	'1'
U[4]	'O'		U[8]	'■'

If the procedure UNPACK is called by using the statement

UNPACK(PK, U, 3)

the characters in array components PK[1], PK[2], PK[3], and PK[4] will be assigned to the array components U[3], U[4], U[5], and U[6], respectively. The index value specified in UNPACKing an array refers to the first component in the unpacked array that will receive a value from the packed array. The effects of an UNPACK for three different index values are depicted next.

UNPACK(PK, U, 1)		UNPACK(PK, U, 3)		UNPACK(PK, U, 4)	
U[1]	'J'	U[1]	'2'	U[1]	'2'
U[2]	'U'	U[2]	'■'	U[2]	'■'
U[3]	'M'	U[3]	'J'	U[3]	'F'
U[4]	'P'	U[4]	'U'	U[4]	'J'
U[5]	'R'	U[5]	'M'	U[5]	'U'
U[6]	'■'	U[6]	'P'	U[6]	'M'
U[7]	'1'	U[7]	'1'	U[7]	'P'
U[8]	'■'	U[8]	'■'	U[8]	'■'

7.3 EXERCISES

1. Determine the values of each of the following relational expressions, assuming that the collating sequence for the full ASCII character set applies. Do the same thing for the EBCDIC character set and the CDC ASCII subset (Appendix A), and compare your answers.

  a. 'WASHINGTON' < 'WASTEFULLY'   b. '$453' > '#453'
  c. 'IN■THE■BAG' <= 'IN■3■STEPS'   d. 'A■+■B■*■C' > 'A■*■B■+■C'
  e. 'FORMULA■200' >= 'FORMULA■20X' f. '■■"I' 'VE" ' = '■I■HAVE'

2. Assume that the following declarations have been made.

```
TYPE
      ASTRING = PACKED ARRAY [1 .. 25] OF CHAR;
      BSTRING = PACKED ARRAY [1 .. 50] OF CHAR;
VAR
      X, Y : ASTRING;
      Z : BSTRING;
```

Locate the errors (if any) in each of the following program segments and show how they can be corrected.

  a.
```
      READ(X);
      WRITELN(X)
```

  b.
```
      FOR I := 1 TO 25
        DO READ(X[I]);
      Y := X;
      WRITELN(X)
```

  c.
```
      FOR I := 1 TO 50
        DO BEGIN
            READ(Z[I]);
            IF I <= 25
              THEN X[I] := Z[I]
              ELSE Y[I] := Z[I]
            END;
      WRITELN(X, Y:30)
```

  d.
```
      FOR I := 1 TO 25
        DO READ(Z[I]);
      X := Z;
      WRITELN(X)
```

3. In the following program segments, T is a one-dimensional array declared as

```
VAR
      T : PACKED ARRAY [1 .. 20] OF CHAR;
```

Each segment reads some input string. Suppose that the input entered in each case is

> ?THE SKY IS FALLING

(where the question mark is a prompt, not part of the string). Show the output that each program segment will generate.

a.
```
FOR I := 1 TO 20
  DO IF NOT EOLN
        THEN READ(T[I])
        ELSE T[I] := ' ';
WRITELN(T)
```

b.
```
FOR I := 1 TO 10
  DO IF NOT EOLN
        THEN READ(T[I], T[10 + I])
        ELSE BEGIN
             T[I] := '*';
             T[10 + I] := '$'
             END;
WRITELN(T)
```

c.
```
FOR I := 1 TO 25
  DO IF NOT EOLN
        THEN READ(T[21 - I]);
WRITE(T);
FOR I := 20 DOWNTO 1
  DO WRITE(T[I]);
WRITELN
```

d.
```
FOR I := 1 TO 20
  DO IF NOT EOLN
        THEN REPEAT
                READ(T[I])
             UNTIL T[I] <> ' '
        ELSE T[I] := '*';
WRITELN(T)
```

4. Assume that the following declarations have been made.

```
VAR
     F, G : PACKED ARRAY [1 .. 10] OF CHAR;
     H : ARRAY [1 .. 20] OF CHAR;
```

Show the output that each of the following program segments will generate if the input is

ABCDEFGHIJKLMNOPQRST

a.
```
FOR I := 1 TO 20
  DO READ(H[I]);
PACK(H, 7, F);
WRITELN(F);
PACK(H, 11, G);
WRITELN(G)
```

b.
```
FOR I := 1 TO 10
  DO BEGIN
      READ(F[I]);
      H[I] := '1';
      H[10 + I] := '2'
      END;
UNPACK(F, H, 5);
FOR I := 1 TO 20
  DO WRITE(H[I]);
WRITELN
```

c.
```
FOR I := 1 TO 20
  DO READ(H[I]);
FOR J := 1 TO 4
  DO BEGIN
      PACK(H, J * 2, G);
      WRITELN(G)
      END
```

d.
```
FOR I := 1 TO 10
  DO READ(G[I]);
FOR J := 1 TO 11
  DO UNPACK(G, H, J);
FOR I := 1 TO 20
  DO WRITE(H[I]);
WRITELN
```

7.4
MULTIDIMENSIONAL ARRAYS

Although a collection of data that are all of the same type can be stored in a one-dimensional array, it is not always appropriate to do so. Consider the following data table, which shows the cost (in dollars) of transporting each of four items from a wholesaler to one of three distributors:

	Distributor		
	Apex	Acme	Century
Item #1	2.54	3.75	2.95
Item #2	3.10	2.25	3.62
Item #3	1.80	1.65	1.70
Item #4	4.35	3.95	3.50

Since there are 12 transportation costs, they could be stored in a one-dimensional array, named COST, declared by

```
VAR
    COST : ARRAY [1 .. 12] OF REAL;
```

Values from the table could be assigned to the array COST by columns so that the contents of COST would be as shown below.

COST[1]	2.54	COST[5]	3.75	COST[9]	2.95
COST[2]	3.10	COST[6]	2.25	COST[10]	3.62
COST[3]	1.80	COST[7]	1.65	COST[11]	1.70
COST[4]	4.35	COST[8]	3.95	COST[12]	3.50

The problem with using a one-dimensional array to store values from a table is that the index values for the components do not reflect the positions of the values in the table. For instance, the index value 7 does not indicate that COST[7] is a cost for transporting item 3 to ACME. We could define the type

```
ROUTE = (APEX1, APEX2, APEX3, APEX4, ACME1, ACME2, ACME3,
         ACME4, CENTURY1, CENTURY2, CENTURY3, CENTURY4);
```

and then declare the array COST by

```
VAR
    COST : ARRAY [ROUTE] OF REAL;
```

With the array COST having ROUTE type indices, the component formerly known as COST[7] is now known as COST[ACME3]. Now the index values give some indication of the significance of each value stored in the array COST.

Another way to store the transportation costs is to use three separate one-dimensional arrays, one for each distributor:

```
VAR
    APEX, ACME, CENTURY : ARRAY [1 .. 4] OF REAL;
```

The costs from the table can be assigned to the arrays in item number order by using the statement

```
FOR I := 1 TO 4
    DO READ(APEX[I], ACME[I], CENTURY[I])
```

If the costs are entered by rows from the table, the contents of the arrays will be as shown below.

APEX[1]	2.54	ACME[1]	3.75	CENTURY[1]	2.95
APEX[2]	3.10	ACME[2]	2.25	CENTURY[2]	3.62
APEX[3]	1.80	ACME[3]	1.65	CENTURY[3]	1.70
APEX[4]	4.35	ACME[4]	3.95	CENTURY[4]	3.50

The costs are stored as three essentially separate lists, one for each distributor. This arrangement is certainly an improvement over one list that we would be forced to view as having three sections.

Although a data table like the one considered in the preceding examples has two dimensions (row and column), the use of one or more one-dimensional arrays to store the data does not truly maintain the table's two-dimensional structure. However, it is possible in Pascal to define two-dimensional arrays whose structures are appropriate for storing tables of data when each table contains data of only one type.

TWO-DIMENSIONAL ARRAYS

A two-dimensional array is defined as a one-dimensional array whose base type is a one-dimensional array type. Consider the following example:

```
TYPE
     DISTRIBUTOR = (APEX, ACME, CENTURY);
     ITEMNUMBER = 1 .. 4;
     TRANSPORTCOSTS = ARRAY [DISTRIBUTOR] OF REAL;
     COSTTABLE = ARRAY [ITEMNUMBER] OF TRANSPORTCOSTS;
VAR
     COST : COSTTABLE;
```

COST is a two-dimensional array composed of COST[1], COST[2], and COST[3], each of which is a one-dimensional array. The array COST[1], for instance, has components COST[1,APEX], COST[1,ACME], and COST[1,CENTURY]. Suppose we want the data in the transportation cost table presented earlier to be stored in the array COST as depicted below.

2.54	3.75	2.95
COST[1,APEX]	COST[1,ACME]	COST[1,CENTURY]
3.10	2.25	3.62
COST[2,APEX]	COST[2,ACME]	COST[2,CENTURY]
1.80	1.65	1.70
COST[3,APEX]	COST[3,ACME]	COST[3,CENTURY]
4.35	3.95	3.50
COST[4,APEX]	COST[4,ACME]	COST[4,CENTURY]

The costs from the table can be read row by row and assigned to the appropriate components of the array COST by using the following nesting of FOR statements:

```
FOR ITEM := 1 TO 4
  DO FOR DESTINATION := APEX TO CENTURY
       DO READ(COST[ITEM, DESTINATION])
```

Alternately, the costs may be read column by column by using

```
FOR DESTINATION := APEX TO CENTURY
  DO FOR ITEM := 1 TO 4
       DO READ(COST[ITEM, DESTINATION])
```

The array type COSTTABLE can be defined by the following type definition:

```
COSTTABLE = ARRAY [ITEMNUMBER]
              OF ARRAY [DISTRIBUTOR]
                  OF REAL;
```

In this definition, the type identifier TRANSPORTCOSTS is replaced by the appropriate array type definition. More generally, a two-dimensional array type may be defined as shown in Figure 7–7. Both *index-type-1* and *index-type-2* must be ordinal data types. The total number of *base-type* components the array will have is deter-

```
type-identifier = ARRAY [index-type-1]
                    OF ARRAY [index-type-2]
                        OF base-type;
```

Figure 7–7
A general form for the definition of a two-dimensional array type.

mined by multiplying the number of distinct *index-type-1* values by the number of distinct *index-type-2* values. For example, the array COST has 12 REAL type components because there are 4 ITEMNUMBER type values and 3 DISTRIBUTOR type values. Each of these components has a unique name of the form COST[i,j], where i is 1, 2, 3, or 4 and j is APEX, ACME, or CENTURY. The type definition of COSTTABLE can also be constructed in the following abbreviated form:

```
COSTTABLE = ARRAY [ITEMNUMBER, DISTRIBUTOR]
              OF REAL;
```

Figure 7–8 shows the general structure of this abbreviated form.

```
type-identifier = ARRAY [index-type-1, index-type-2]
                    OF base-type;
```

Figure 7–8
An alternate form for the definition of a two-dimensional array type.

Suppose an array T is declared as follows:

```
TYPE
      TABLE = ARRAY [1 .. 3]
                OF ARRAY [-1 .. 2]
                    OF INTEGER;
VAR
      T : TABLE;
```

The definition of the array type TABLE shown here is constructed according to the general form shown in Figure 7–7. This TABLE type can also be defined by using the general form given in Figure 7–8:

```
TYPE
     TABLE = ARRAY [1 .. 3, -1 .. 2]
              OF INTEGER;
VAR
     T : TABLE;
```

In either case, T is a two-dimensional array variable whose components are referenced by using indexed variables of the form $T[i,j]$ where i is in the subrange 1..3 and j is in the subrange $-1..2$. Each component of T can store one INTEGER type value. It is convenient to think of the components $T[i,j]$ as being arranged in rows and columns with i serving as the **row index** and j serving as the **column index**, as depicted below.

$T[1,-1]$	$T[1,0]$	$T[1,1]$	$T[1,2]$
$T[2,-1]$	$T[2,0]$	$T[2,1]$	$T[2,2]$
$T[3,-1]$	$T[3,0]$	$T[3,1]$	$T[3,2]$

Note that the order in which the index values are specified in an indexed variable that represents a component of a two-dimensional array is significant. For instance, T[1,2] and T[2,1] are two different components of the array T. Also, T[3,2] is a valid reference to a component of T, but T[2,3] is not valid because 3 is not in the subrange $-1..2$.

There are many ways to define a two-dimensional array. For example, the array type TABLE and both of the index types can be specified in type definitions:

```
TYPE
     ROWINDEX = 1 .. 3;
     COLINDEX = -1 .. 2;
     TABLE = ARRAY [ROWINDEX, COLINDEX]
              OF INTEGER;
VAR
     T : TABLE;
```

An array type definition may appear in a variable declaration, as in the following declaration of the two-dimensional array T:

```
TYPE
     ROWINDEX = 1 .. 3;
     COLINDEX = -1 .. 2;
VAR
     T : ARRAY [ROWINDEX, COLINDEX]
         OF INTEGER;
```

If the index types are not TYPE defined, then the array T can be declared as

```
VAR
     T : ARRAY [1 .. 3, -1 .. 2]
              OF INTEGER;
```

All of the ways to declare the array T presented here give T the same array structure. It is often advantageous to use type definitions in the TYPE definition part of a program to associate names with ordinal data types used as index types for arrays, particularly when the same index type is used to define more than one array.

Suppose a company wants to measure the effectiveness of its advertising campaign for a new product. In particular, it is interested in finding out which age groups are most influenced to purchase the product as a result of newspaper ads, radio commercials, and television commercials. A telephone survey will be conducted and each person called will be asked whether he (or she) has heard of the new product and, if so, which form of advertising was responsible for calling his (or her) attention to the product. Each person surveyed will be asked to indicate his (or her) age. The data collected from the telephone survey is to be processed by a program that will produce a table showing the influence of the advertising campaign on various age groups by advertising medium. There will be six age groups: under 20 years, 20 to 29 years, 30 to 39 years, 40 to 49 years, 50 to 59 years, and 60 years or more. The table will also include a column for people who have not heard of the product through advertising.

A two-dimensional array will be appropriate for storing the statistics accumulated from the advertising effectiveness survey. The first index may indicate an age category and the second an advertising medium:

```
TYPE
     AGERANGE = 1 .. 6;
     ADCATEGORY = (NEWSPAPER, RADIO, TELEVISION, NONE);
     STATS = ARRAY [AGERANGE, ADCATEGORY]
             OF 0 .. MAXINT;
VAR
     SURVEY : STATS;
```

Each component of the array SURVEY will serve as an accumulator. The value of SURVEY[i,j] will be incremented by 1 when a person in the ith age range first heard of the new product via advertising medium j. All components of SURVEY must initially be set to 0. The input data will consist of a letter to indicate a form of advertising (N for newspaper, R for radio, T for television, or X for none) and an age for each person surveyed. A pseudocode description of the program is provided below.

```
BEGIN program ADSURVEY
Initialize all SURVEY accumulators at 0
WRITE directions
READ an ADvertising CODE letter
WHILE the ADvertising CODE is not 'S'
     DO BEGIN a survey update
          READ an AGE
          CASE ADvertising CODE OF
```

> 'N' : Establish NEWSPAPER as the ADvertising FORM
> 'R' : Establish RADIO as the ADvertising FORM
> 'T' : Establish TELEVISION as the ADvertising FORM
> 'X' : Establish NONE as the ADvertising FORM
> END of ADvertising CODE cases
> IF the AGE is 60 or greater
>   THEN set the AGE INDEX at 6
>   ELSE set the AGE INDEX at the AGE DIVided by 10
> Increment SURVEY[AGE INDEX, ADvertising FORM] by 1
> READ the next ADvertising CODE letter
> END of a survey update
> WRITE the table headings
> FOR the AGE INDEX ranging from 1 to 6
> DO WRITE a row of SURVEY totals
> END of program ADSURVEY.

As many lines as necessary may be used to enter the data for each person. The input information must alternate between advertising code and age until the letter S is entered to signal the end of input. Program ADSURVEY is shown below.

```
PROGRAM ADSURVEY (INPUT, OUTPUT);
(*********************************************************************
*                                                                   *
*   A PROGRAM TO ACCUMULATE STATISTICS FROM A TELEPHONE SURVEY TO    *
*   MEASURE THE EFFECTIVENESS OF THE ADVERTISING CAMPAIGN FOR A      *
*   NEW PRODUCT                                                      *
*                                                                   *
*********************************************************************)
TYPE
     AGERANGE = 1 .. 6;
     ADCATEGORY = (NEWSPAPER, RADIO, TELEVISION, NONE);
     STATS = ARRAY [AGERANGE, ADCATEGORY]
               OF 0 .. MAXINT;

VAR                              (*------[INTEGER VARIABLES]------*)
     AGE : INTEGER;             (* A PERSON'S AGE                 *)
                                 (*------------------------------*)
                                 (*-------[CHAR VARIABLES]--------*)
     ADCODE : CHAR;             (* AN ADVERTISING CODE            *)
                                 (*------------------------------*)
                                 (*-----[AGERANGE VARIABLES]------*)
     AGEINDEX : AGERANGE;       (* AN AGE CATEGORY NUMBER         *)
                                 (*------------------------------*)
                                 (*----[ADCATEGORY VARIABLES]-----*)
     ADFORM : ADCATEGORY;       (* NAME OF ADVERTISING MEDIUM     *)
                                 (*------------------------------*)
                                 (*---------[STATS ARRAY]---------*)
     SURVEY : STATS;            (* ACCUMULATED SURVEY STATISTICS *)
                                 (*------------------------------*)
(*********************************************************************)
BEGIN (* PROGRAM ADSURVEY *)
FOR AGEINDEX := 1 TO 6
```

```
    DO FOR ADFORM := NEWSPAPER TO NONE
        DO SURVEY[AGEINDEX, ADFORM] := 0;
WRITELN('THIS PROGRAM WILL PRODUCE A TABLE OF STATISTICS FROM DATA');
WRITELN('DERIVED FROM A TELEPHONE SURVEY TO MEASURE THE EFFECTIVE-');
WRITELN('NESS OF THE ADVERTISING CAMPAIGN FOR A NEW PRODUCT. FOR');
WRITELN('EACH PERSON SURVEYED, YOU WILL NEED TO ENTER THE CODE FOR');
WRITELN('AN ADVERTISING MEDIUM AND THE AGE OF THE PERSON, IN THAT');
WRITELN('ORDER. THE VALID ADVERTISING CODES ARE SINGLE LETTERS:');
WRITELN;
WRITELN(' ':20, 'N STANDS FOR NEWSPAPER');
WRITELN(' ':20, 'R STANDS FOR RADIO');
WRITELN(' ':20, 'T STANDS FOR TELEVISION');
WRITELN(' ':20, 'X STANDS FOR NONE');
WRITELN;
WRITELN('YOU MAY USE AS MANY LINES AS NECESSARY TO ENTER THE DATA,');
WRITELN('ALTERNATING BETWEEN AN ADVERTISING CODE LETTER AND AN AGE.');
WRITELN('TO SIGNAL THE END OF INPUT, ENTER THE LETTER S IN PLACE');
WRITELN('OF AN ADVERTISING CODE.');
WRITELN('START ENTERING YOUR DATA NOW.');
REPEAT
  READ(ADCODE)
UNTIL ADCODE <> ' ';
WHILE ADCODE <> 'S'
  DO BEGIN (* A SURVEY UPDATE *)
      READ(AGE);
      CASE ADCODE OF
        'N' : ADFORM := NEWSPAPER;
        'R' : ADFORM := RADIO;
        'T' : ADFORM := TELEVISION;
        'X' : ADFORM := NONE
      END (* OF ADCODE CASES *);
      IF AGE >= 60
        THEN AGEINDEX := 6
        ELSE AGEINDEX := AGE DIV 10;
      SURVEY[AGEINDEX, ADFORM] := SURVEY[AGEINDEX, ADFORM] + 1;
      REPEAT
        READ(ADCODE)
      UNTIL (ADCODE = 'N') OR (ADCODE = 'R') OR (ADCODE = 'T')
            OR (ADCODE = 'X') OR (ADCODE = 'S')
    END (* OF A SURVEY UPDATE *);
WRITELN; WRITELN;
WRITELN('AGE RANGE':10, 'NEWSPAPER':16, 'RADIO':9, 'TELEVISION':14,
        'NONE':8);
WRITELN('=========':10, '---------':16, '-----':9, '----------':14,
        '----':8);
FOR AGEINDEX := 1 TO 6
  DO BEGIN (* TABLE OUTPUT *)
      CASE AGEINDEX OF
            1 : WRITE('LESS THAN 20');
      2,3,4,5 : WRITE(AGEINDEX * 10:5, ' -', AGEINDEX * 10 + 9:3,
                      ' ':2);
            6 : WRITE('MORE THAN 60')
      END (* OF AGEINDEX CASES *);
```

```
      FOR ADFORM := NEWSPAPER TO NONE
       DO WRITE(SURVEY[AGEINDEX, ADFORM]:11);
      WRITELN
      END (* OF TABLE OUTPUT *)
END (* OF PROGRAM ADSURVEY *).
```

A sample run of the program ADSURVEY is shown below.

```
THIS PROGRAM WILL PRODUCE A TABLE OF STATISTICS FROM DATA
DERIVED FROM A TELEPHONE SURVEY TO MEASURE THE EFFECTIVE-
NESS OF THE ADVERTISING CAMPAIGN FOR A NEW PRODUCT. FOR
EACH PERSON SURVEYED, YOU WILL NEED TO ENTER THE CODE FOR
AN ADVERTISING MEDIUM AND THE AGE OF THE PERSON, IN THAT
ORDER. THE VALID ADVERTISING CODES ARE SINGLE LETTERS:

                N STANDS FOR NEWSPAPER
                R STANDS FOR RADIO
                T STANDS FOR TELEVISION
                X STANDS FOR NONE

YOU MAY USE AS MANY LINES AS NECESSARY TO ENTER THE DATA,
ALTERNATING BETWEEN AN ADVERTISING CODE LETTER AND AN AGE.
TO SIGNAL THE END OF INPUT, ENTER THE LETTER S IN PLACE
OF AN ADVERTISING CODE.
START ENTERING YOU DATA NOW.
?T 27 R 45 T 35 N 47 T 17 X 57 R 44 T 35 R 68 N 57 R 29
?T 19 R 47 N 39 R 61 T 25 T 31 R 41 T 34 N 49 T 29 R 57
?X 72 R 43 T 27 R 19 R 52 X 37 T 19 R 47 R 74 T 62 R 37
?T 35 S


    AGE RANGE        NEWSPAPER      RADIO     TELEVISION      NONE
    =========        ---------      -----     ----------      ----
 LESS THAN 20            0            1           3            0
     20 - 29             0            1           4            0
     30 - 39             1            1           5            1
     40 - 49             2            6           0            0
     50 - 59             1            2           0            1
 MORE THAN 60            0            3           1            1
```

As a final example of the use of two-dimensional arrays, consider a program to sort a list of character strings. The program will be a modified version of the program SELECTIONSORT (from Section 7.2). This time the array to be sorted will be an array of string variables.

```
PROGRAM STRINGSORT (INPUT,OUTPUT);
(*************************************************************
 *                                                           *
 *  A PROGRAM THAT SELECTION SORTS AN ARRAY OF CHARACTER STRINGS  *
 *  AND PRINTS THEM OUT IN ASCENDING ORDER                   *
 *                                                           *
 *************************************************************)
```

```
CONST                                 (*---------- [CONSTANTS] ----------*)
      MAXSTRINGLENGTH = 50;           (* MAXIMUM NUMBER OF CHARACTERS   *)
                                      (* IN A STRING                    *)
      MAXINDEX = 100;                 (* MAXIMUM NUMBER OF STRINGS      *)
                                      (* THAT CAN BE SORTED             *)
                                      (*-------------------------------*)
TYPE
      STRINGINDICES = 0 .. MAXINDEX;
      CHARPOSITION = 1 .. MAXSTRINGLENGTH;
      STRING = PACKED ARRAY [CHARPOSITION] OF CHAR;
      STRINGLIST = ARRAY [STRINGINDICES] OF STRING;

VAR                                   (*---[STRINGINDICES VARIABLES]---*)
      N,                              (* NUMBER OF STRINGS TO BE SORTED*)
      POS,                            (* POSITION TO FILL IN SORTED     *)
                                      (* PORTION OF NAMES ARRAY         *)
      LOC,                            (* SELECTED NAMES LOCATION IN A   *)
                                      (* SORT CYCLE                     *)
      J : STRINGINDICES;              (* INDEX USED IN SCANNING THE     *)
                                      (* NAMES ARRAY                    *)
                                      (*-------------------------------*)
                                      (*--- [CHARPOSITION VARIABLES]----*)
      CHARPTR : CHARPOSITION;         (* CHARACTER INDEX IN A STRING    *)
                                      (*-------------------------------*)
                                      (*------ [STRINGINDEX ARRAY]------*)
      NAMES : STRINGLIST;             (* THE LIST OF STRINGS THAT WILL *)
                                      (* BE SORTED                      *)
                                      (*-------------------------------*)
(*****************************************************************************)
BEGIN (* PROGRAM STRINGSORT *)
N := 0;
WRITELN('THIS PROGRAM WILL SORT A LIST OF CHARACTER STRINGS AND');
WRITELN('THEN PRINT THE SORTED LIST. YOU MAY ENTER NO MORE THAN');
WRITELN(MAXINDEX:3, ' STRINGS, ONE PER LINE. EACH STRING CAN ',
        'CONTAIN AT');
WRITELN('MOST ', MAXSTRINGLENGTH:2, ' CHARACTERS. TO SIGNAL THE',
        ' END OF INPUT, SIMPLY');
WRITELN('PRESS THE "RETURN" KEY WITHOUT ENTERING A NEW STRING.');
WRITELN('BEGIN ENTERING THE STRINGS NOW.');
READLN; (* NEW INPUT LINE *)
WHILE NOT EOF
   DO BEGIN (* STRING INPUT *)
      N := N + 1;
      FOR CHARPTR := 1 TO MAXSTRINGLENGTH
        DO IF NOT EOLN
             THEN READ(NAMES[N, CHARPTR])
             ELSE NAMES[N, CHARPTR] := ' ';
      READLN (* NEW INPUT LINE *)
      END (* OF STRING INPUT *);
FOR POS := 1 TO N - 1
  DO BEGIN (* A SELECTION CYCLE *)
     LOC := POS;
     FOR J := POS + 1 TO N
```

```
      DO IF NAMES[J] < NAMES[LOC]
            THEN LOC := J;
      IF LOC <> POS
        THEN BEGIN (* AN INTERCHANGE *)
              NAMES[0] := NAMES[POS];
              NAMES[POS] := NAMES[LOC];
              NAMES[LOC] := NAMES[0]
              END (* OF AN INTERCHANGE *)
      END (* OF A SELECTION CYCLE *);
WRITELN;
WRITELN('THE SORTED LIST OF STRINGS:');
FOR J := 1 TO N
 DO WRITELN(NAMES[J])
END (* OF PROGRAM STRINGSORT *).
```

Even though NAMES is a two-dimensional array, the indexed variable NAMES [J] is valid when J is greater than 1 and less than N. NAMES [J] is a one-dimensional packed array of characters of the type STRING. Here is the output from a sample run of the program STRINGSORT:

```
THIS PROGRAM WILL SORT A LIST OF CHARACTER STRINGS AND
THEN PRINT THE SORTED LIST. YOU MAY ENTER NO MORE THAN
100 STRINGS, ONE PER LINE. EACH STRING CAN CONTAIN AT
MOST 50 CHARACTERS. TO SIGNAL THE END OF INPUT, SIMPLY
PRESS THE "RETURN" KEY WITHOUT ENTERING A NEW STRING.
BEGIN ENTERING THE STRINGS NOW.
?WASHINGTON MONUMENT
?LINCOLN MEMORIAL
?WHITE HOUSE
?ARLINGTON NATIONAL CEMETARY
?SMITHSONIAN INSTITUTE
?CAPITOL BUILDING
?POTOMAC RIVER
?SENATE OFFICE BUILDING
?PENNSYLVANIA AVENUE
?

THE SORTED LIST OF STRINGS:
ARLINGTON NATIONAL CEMETARY
CAPITOL BUILDING
LINCOLN MEMORIAL
PENNSYLVANIA AVENUE
POTOMAC RIVER
SENATE OFFICE BUILDING
SMITHSONIAN INSTITUTE
WASHINGTON MONUMENT
WHITE HOUSE
```

ARRAYS OF THREE OR MORE DIMENSIONS

We have seen that a two-dimensional array is constructed as an array of one-dimensional arrays. In a similar fashion, we can define an array of two-dimensional arrays to get a three-dimensional array, an array of three-dimensional arrays to get a four-dimensional array, and so on. Consider the following example:

```
TYPE
     TABLENUMBER = 1 .. 3;
     ROWNUMBER = 1 .. 4;
     COLNUMBER = 1 .. 6;
     TABLES = ARRAY [TABLENUMBER]
                 OF ARRAY [ROWNUMBER]
                      OF ARRAY [COLNUMBER]
                           OF INTEGER;
VAR
     CHART : TABLES;
```

CHART is a three-dimensional array variable whose components are identified by the indexed variables of the form CHART[i,j,k] where i must be in the subrange TABLENUMBER, j must be in the subrange ROWNUMBER, and k must be in the subrange COLNUMBER. The array type TABLES can also be defined by

```
TABLES = ARRAY [TABLENUMBER, ROWNUMBER, COLNUMBER]
           OF INTEGER;
```

CHART is actually an array consisting of three two-dimensional arrays identified by the indexed variables CHART[1], CHART[2], and CHART[3]. Since each of these two-dimensional arrays contains 24 components (why?), the array CHART is composed of 72 INTEGER type components. For instance, one third of the components of CHART are components of CHART[1], and they are referenced by indexed variables of the form CHART[$1,j,k$] where j is 1, 2, 3, or 4 and k is 1, 2, 3, 4, 5, or 6.

Pascal imposes no restrictions on the number of dimensions an array may have. However, the storage space needed for arrays and all other variables used in a program is always limited by the amount of memory allocated to the program for data storage. The basic form of a type definition for an n-dimensional array is shown in Figure 7–9. Note that this general form is an extension of the one given in Figure 7–7. This form is used in the first definition of the array type TABLES given earlier. The second definition of TABLES follows the abbreviated form for the definition of an n-dimensional array type illustrated in Figure 7–10.

```
type-identifier = ARRAY [index-type-1]
                     OF ARRAY [index-type-2]
                          OF
                                   .
                                   .
                                   .
                              ARRAY [index-type-n]
                                 OF base-type;
```

Figure 7–9
A general form for the definition of an n-*dimensional array type.*

$$type\text{-}identifier = \text{ARRAY } [index\text{-}type\text{-}1, \; index\text{-}type\text{-}2,$$
$$\ldots, \; index\text{-}type\text{-}n]$$
$$\text{OF } base\text{-}type;$$

Figure 7–10
An alternate form for the definition of an n-*dimensional array type.*

Consider the array KEYINFO, which is defined as follows:

```
TYPE
    CATEGORY = (SINGLE, MARRIED, DIVORCED, WIDOWED);
    TABLENUMBER = 1 .. 3;
    ROWNUMBER = 1 .. 4;
    COLNUMBER = 1 .. 6;
    CHARTS = ARRAY [CATEGORY, TABLENUMBER, ROWNUMBER, COLNUMBER]
            OF INTEGER;
VAR
    KEYINFO : CHARTS;
```

KEYINFO is a four-dimensional array consisting of four three-dimensional arrays identified by indexed variables of the form KEYINFO[SINGLE,i,j,k], KEYINFO-[MARRIED,i,j,k], KEYINFO[DIVORCED,i,j,k], and KEYINFO[WIDOWED,i,j,k]. Since these three-dimensional arrays are all of the type TABLES defined earlier, the four-dimensional array type CHARTS can also be defined by

```
    TYPE
        CATEGORY = (SINGLE, MARRIED, DIVORCED, WIDOWED);
        TABLENUMBER = 1 .. 3;
        ROWNUMBER = 1 .. 4;
        COLNUMBER = 1 .. 6;
        TABLES = ARRAY [TABLENUMBER, ROWNUMBER, COLNUMBER]
                OF INTEGER;
        CHARTS = ARRAY [CATEGORY] OF TABLES;
```

Indexed variables of the form KEYINFO[t,i,j,k] are used to identify each INTEGER type component of KEYINFO where t, i, j, and k are values of the types CATEGORY, TABLENUMBER, ROWNUMBER, and COLNUMBER, respectively. Since KEYINFO consists of four TABLE type arrays, each having 72 components, the entire four-dimensional array has 288 components.

7.4 EXERCISES

1. Find the errors (if any) in each of the following sets of declarations.

```
    a.      TYPE
                INDEX1 = 1 .. 5;
                INDEX2 = 'A' .. 'H';
                INDEX3 = (DOG, CAT, HORSE, COW, PIG);
```

```
VAR
        A : ARRAY [INDEX1, INDEX3]
                OF REAL;
        B : ARRAY [INDEX2 OF ARRAY INDEX1]
                OF INTEGER;
        C : ARRAY [INDEX1]
                OF ARRAY [INDEX2]
                        OF INDEX3;
        D : ARRAY [INDEX1 .. INDEX2]
                OF CHAR;
```

b.
```
    TYPE
        TIME = (PAST, PRESENT, FUTURE);
        YEARS = 1940 .. 1990;
        PERIODS = ARRAY [1 .. 4] OF YEARS;
    VAR
        E : ARRAY [TIME] OF PERIODS;
        F : ARRAY [PERIODS] OF TIME;
        G : ARRAY [1 .. 4]
                OF ARRAY [TIME]
                        OF YEARS;
        H : ARRAY [YEARS, TIME]
                OF 1 .. 4;
```

2. Suppose the array X is declared by

```
    VAR
        X : ARRAY [1 .. 5, 1 .. 3] OF INTEGER;
```

Determine the values that will be assigned to the components of X by the following program segments. (Draw rectangles to represent the components and fill in the rectangles with the appropriate values.)

a.
```
        FOR I := 1 TO 5
          DO FOR J := 3 DOWNTO 1
              DO X[I,J] := I + J
```

b.
```
        FOR I := 5 DOWNTO 1
          DO FOR J := 1 TO 3
              DO IF I = J
                    THEN X[I,J] := 0
                    ELSE X[I,J] := I - J
```

c.
```
        FOR I := 1 TO 5
          DO BEGIN
              K := I * 2;
              FOR J := 1 TO 3
                DO X[I,J] := K
          END
```

d.
```
FOR I := 1 TO 3
   DO BEGIN
      K := 0;
      FOR J := 1 TO 5
       DO BEGIN
          K := K + 1;
          X[J,I] := K
          END
      END
```

3. Assume that the arrays R and P are declared by

```
VAR
   R : ARRAY [2 .. 6, 1 .. 5] OF REAL;
   P : ARRAY [1 .. 5, 2 .. 6] OF INTEGER;
```

Find the errors (if any) in the following program segments.

a.
```
FOR I := 2 TO 6
   DO BEGIN
      FOR J := 1 TO 5
       DO WRITE(P[J,I]);
      WRITELN
      END
```

b.
```
FOR I := 1 TO 5
   DO FOR J := 2 TO 6
         DO WRITELN(R[I,J], P[I,J])
```

c.
```
FOR I := 2 TO 6
   DO BEGIN
      J := I - 1;
      R[I,J] := P[J,I]
      END
```

d.
```
FOR I := 5 DOWNTO 1
   DO FOR J := 2 TO 6
         DO P[I,J] := R[J,I] + 1.0
```

4. Consider the following definitions and declarations

```
TYPE
     DAYS = (MONDAY, TUESDAY, WEDNESDAY, THURSDAY, FRIDAY);
     TEAMS = (BASEBALL, FOOTBALL, BASKETBALL);
     LEVELS = (D, C, B, A, AA, AAA);
     LEAGUE = ARRAY [LEVELS, TEAMS]
                 OF INTEGER;
VAR
     RED : LEAGUE;
     BLUE : ARRAY [LEVELS] OF TEAMS;
     GOLD : ARRAY [DAYS] OF LEAGUE;
     GREEN : ARRAY [1 .. 10]
                 OF ARRAY [TEAMS]
                     OF ARRAY [DAYS]
                         OF BOOLEAN;
```

Determine the dimensions of the arrays RED, BLUE, GOLD, and GREEN and tell how many components each array has.

5. The program ADSURVEY prints a table that shows the number of people in each age range per advertising medium. What adjustment need to be made to the program to have those numbers replaced by percentages determined by dividing each number by the total number of people surveyed?

7.5
PROGRAMMING PROBLEMS

1. Write a program that will accept lines of text as input (as many as the user cares to enter) and then produces a frequency table showing each word that appears in the text and how many times it appears. Assume that the end of a word will be marked by the appearance of a blank space or some punctuation character or some combination of blank spaces and punctuation characters.

2. Write the same program as described in Problem 1, except have the words in the frequency table printed out in alphabetical order.

3. A list of data values can be sorted as it is read. The first value read can be inserted into the first component of a one-dimensional array. If k values have been inserted in the first k components of the array so that they are ordered, the next value read can be inserted into its proper position in the first k + 1 components of the array. This may require that one or more values be shifted to make room for the new value. Write a program to sort a list of REAL numbers as they are read so that they will end up in descending order in an array. The program should print the contents of the sorted array.

4. If n is a positive integer, the number n! (called "n factorial") is given by the mathematical formula n! = (n)(n − 1)(n − 2) · · · (2)(1). Also, zero factorial (0!) is defined to be 1. For example, 5! = (5)(4)(3)(2)(1) = 120. Note that 5! = 5(4!). In general, n! may be computed as n multiplied by (n − 1)!. Even for relatively small values of n, n! is rather large. For instance,

$$10! = 3628800$$
$$25! = 15511210043330985984000000$$

An INTEGER type memory location can be used to store the value of n! only for small values of n. One way to overcome this problem is to store each digit in the value of n! in a separate component of a one-dimensional array whose base type is the subrange 0..9. Using this technique, write a program that will read a value of n and then print a table of factorials from 0! to n!. Allow at least 100 components in the array, but define the array in such a way that it will be easy to increase the number of components.

5. Write a program that will read a list of at most 100 student names and a test score for each student. The program should average the test scores and then print the names and corresponding scores in columns so that the scores are ordered from high to low.

6. Krantz, Inc. operates three department stores in the midwest, one each in Chicago, Milwaukee, and Minneapolis. At the end of each week, a report is sent to the regional headquarters in Chicago giving a breakdown of the total sales by each department per day. Every Krantz store has four departments: clothing, hardware, toys, and cosmetics. Write a program that will read the weekly data from the stores, store it in arrays (or consider using a three-dimensional array), and generate a composite report to be sent to the national headquarters in New York. The report should contain tables that show the sales per department per day for each store as well as the total weekly sales of each store, the total weekly sales for each department (all three stores combined), the total sales per day (all three stores combined), and the total sales for the week (all departments in all stores).

7. It often happens that a college student inadvertently schedules two courses that meet at the same time on a given day. Write a program that will read course information for a student and print that student's schedule if there are no course conflicts. The input information for each course should consist of a four-character department code, a three-digit course number, the days of the week on which the course meets (use M for Monday, T for Tuesday, W for Wednesday, R for Thursday, and F for Friday), and the hour when the class begins. Assume that all classes start on the hour and last for 50 minutes. The earliest class starts at 8:00 A.M. and the latest class starts at 3:00 P.M. For example, the dialogue between the program and the student could look like this:

```
WHAT'S YOUR NAME
?JOHNNY JONES
ENTER INFORMATION FOR EACH COURSE
?MATH  150  MWF   10
?HIST  224  MTRF  12
?ENGL  112  TWF   3
?PHYE  180  R  10
?BIOL  210  MTWRF  1
```

The schedule that the program prints should look something like this one:

SCHEDULE FOR JOHNNY JONES

TIME	MONDAY	TUESDAY	WEDNESDAY	THURSDAY	FRIDAY
8					
9					
10	MATH 150		MATH 150	PHYE 180	MATH 150
11					
12	HIST 224	HIST 224		HIST 224	HIST 224
1	BIOL 210	BIOL 210	BIOL 210	BIOL 210	BIOL 210
2					
3		ENGL 112	ENGL 112		ENGL 112

TOTAL HOURS SCHEDULED : 16

Your program should check for course conflicts and print reports on them.

8. The airplanes used by Trans-City Airlines for commuter service have a capacity of 28 passengers each. The seats are arranged in seven rows (marked A through G) with four seats per row, as illustrated in the accompanying diagram. Write a program that will read the names of passengers as they make their reservations and indicate their seat preference (row letter and seat number). If the seat a person wants is already filled, assign that person any other seat in the same row. If this is not possible, assign a seat in the nearest row moving toward the back of the airplane (toward the G row). If all the seats in the requested row and all rows behind it are filled, try to find a seat for the person by starting at row A and moving toward the rear of the airplane. The seats are available on a first-come, first-served basis. When all seats on the airplane have been filled or the last reservation has been entered, print a seating chart in table form that shows each person's name in the proper seating arrangement (four names per row, seven rows).

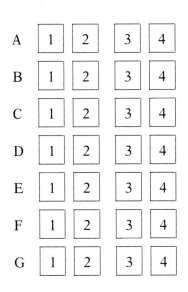

9. Suppose Trans-City Airlines (see Problem 8) has three airplanes leaving within an hour for the same destination: Flight 700 leaves on the hour, Flight 720 leaves at 20 minutes past the hour, and Flight 740 at 40 minutes past the hour. Write a program that will handle reservations for all three planes. When a requested flight is full, reserve a seat on the next flight (if possible). After all flights have been filled or the last reservation has been processed, the program should print out seating charts for all three flights.

10. Write a program to print a course schedule as in Problem 7, but this time allow for a building code and room number for each course, as well as for the possibility that a course may meet for more than one hour on a given day.

11. An n-by-m ($n \times m$) matrix is a rectangular arrangement of numbers that has n rows and m columns. Two matrices that have the same number of rows and columns (they are known as square matrices) can be multiplied to produce a third matrix. Consider two general 3×3 matrices A and B:

$$A = \begin{pmatrix} a_{11} & a_{12} & a_{13} \\ a_{21} & a_{22} & a_{23} \\ a_{31} & a_{32} & a_{33} \end{pmatrix} \qquad B = \begin{pmatrix} b_{11} & b_{12} & b_{13} \\ b_{21} & b_{22} & b_{23} \\ b_{31} & b_{32} & b_{33} \end{pmatrix}$$

Each a_{ij} and b_{ij} represent a number, the subscripts i and j indicating the row and column, respectively, in which the number appears in the matrix. The product of A and B is a 3 × 3 matrix C with components of the form c_{ij} where

$$c_{ij} = (a_{i1})(b_{1j}) + (a_{i2})(b_{2j}) + (a_{i3})(b_{3j})$$

Write a program that will read values for the components of matrices A and B and then compare the product matrix C. the matrices can be represented in the program by two-dimensional arrays. All three matrices should be printed out after the components of C have been calculated.

12. The matrix multiplication described in Problem 11 can be extended to matrices that have n rows and n columns where n is any positive integer. If A and B are n × n matrices, the product matrix C has components c_{ij}, which are determined by

$$c_{ij} = (a_{i1})(b_{1j}) + (a_{i2})(b_{2j}) + \cdots + (a_{in})(b_{nj})$$

Write a program that will compute the product of any two n × n matrices. (In designing the program, assume that n will not exceed 10, but make it easy to accommodate larger values of n.)

EIGHT/SUBPROGRAMS: FUNCTIONS AND PROCEDURES

Early in the design phase of program development, simple flowcharts or outlines are used to give an overview of the sequence of major tasks that the program must perform. Each task should be well defined, although it can be described in very broad terms. An initial outline or flowchart of an algorithm has a certain simplicity that can easily be lost during later stages of refinement. Consider the following outline for a program to average and order a list of test scores:

> BEGIN program SCORER
> Print directions
> Input the test scores
> Order the scores high to low
> Print the ordered list of scores
> Calculate the average score
> Print the average score
> END of program SCORER

This outline is not detailed enough to serve as a pattern for coding the program, but it does list the sequence of all major tasks to be performed by the program in a simple and straightforward manner.

Suppose that a one-dimensional array named SCORES will be used by the program SCORER to store the test scores and that the variable COUNT will be used to store the number of test scores to be processed. Here is a refined outline of the program SCORER in which some pseudocode is used:

> BEGIN program SCORER
> Print directions
>
> (ACCESS) the test SCORES and COUNT them
>
> (SORT) the SCORES from high to low

FOR the Index ranging from 1 to COUNT
DO Print SCORES[Index]

Compute the test MEAN as the (AVERAGE)
of the SCORES
Print the test MEAN
END of program SCORER

Only the activities implied by the circled identifiers ACCESS, SORT, and AVER-AGE require further clarification before the entire program can be constructed.

In earlier chapters we saw that Pascal provides functions like SQRT, ROUND, and ORD and procedures such as PACK and UNPACK that can be called by a program to perform various tasks. These functions and procedures are precoded **subprograms** that are automatically available to all Pascal programs. Pascal also allows programmers to code and use their own subprograms (functions and procedures). For instance, a function named AVERAGE could be defined to compute the arithmetic average of a collection of numbers stored in components of a one-dimensional *array* whose indices range from 1 through n inclusive; this function would be called by a reference of the form AVERAGE(*array, n*). The function AVERAGE could then be used to compute the test MEAN in program SCORER. Similarly, user-defined procedures named ACCESS and SORT can be constructed to meet the needs of program SCORER when they are called by procedure statements of the form ACCESS(*array, n*) and SORT(*array, n*). All user-defined functions and procedures used by a program must be coded in the declaration section. A possible structure for the program SCORER that uses the user-defined subprograms AVERAGE, ACCESS, and SORT is shown below.

The program SCORER will, of course, not be complete until the subprograms ACCESS, SORT, and AVERAGE have been coded. However, we have considerably simplified the task of developing the program by postponing consideration of activities that will be implemented as subprograms. Our efforts have produced the **main program.** We can now focus our attention on developing the individual subprograms ACCESS, SORT, and AVERAGE. These subprograms can be designed and written independently, since the task delegated to each subprogram is well defined.

This chapter is devoted to the design and construction of user-defined functions and procedures. The use of subprograms is a natural outgrowth of top-down program development that enhances the structure of a program. A task that must be performed at various times during the execution of a program may be coded as a subprogram that can be called as needed. Thus, the use of subprograms helps avoid repetitious coding of similar sequences of statements in a program, thereby reducing the program's size and increasing its efficiency. It is beneficial to design and code as a subprogram a task that must be performed only once. As we saw in the development of the program SCORER, it is possible to design and code all of the major activities of a program as a main program with some of the tasks delegated to subprograms yet to be constructed. This enables the programmer to focus attention on the development of small parts of a program one at a time without losing sight of the overall structure of the program. A program constructed in this manner is bound to be logically structured and highly readable.

```
PROGRAM SCORER (INPUT, OUTPUT);
(*******************************************************************
 *                                                                *
 *   A PROGRAM TO COMPUTE THE ARITHMETIC AVERAGE OF A LIST OF TEST *
 *   SCORES ORDERED FROM HIGH TO LOW                              *
 *                                                                *
 *****************************************************************)
CONST                              (*--------- [CONSTANTS] ----------*)
        MINSCORE = 0;              (* LOWEST POSSIBLE TEST SCORE    *)
        MAXSCORE = 100;            (* HIGHEST POSSIBLE TEST SCORE   *)
        MAXSTUDENTS = 200;         (* LIMIT ON THE NUMBER OF SCORES *)
                                   (*------------------------------*)

TYPE
        STUDENTCOUNT = 0 .. MAXSTUDENTS;
        TESTSCORES = 0 .. 100;
        TESTRESULTS = ARRAY [STUDENTCOUNT] OF TESTSCORES;

VAR                                (*------- [REAL VARIABLES] --------*)
        MEAN : REAL;               (* ARITHMETIC AVERAGE OF SCORES  *)
                                   (*------------------------------*)
                                   (*------ [TESTRESULTS ARRAY] ------*)
        SCORES : TESTRESULTS;      (* THE TEST SCORES               *)
                                   (*------------------------------*)
                                   (*--- [STUDENTCOUNT VARIABLES] ----*)
        COUNT,                     (* NUMBER OF SCORES              *)
        I : STUDENTCOUNT;          (* LOOP CONTROL VARIABLE         *)
                                   (*------------------------------*)


(*================================================================*)
(*                                                                *)
(*              INSERT PROCEDURE ACESS HERE.                      *)
(*                                                                *)
(*================================================================*)
```

```
(*==================================================================*)
(*                                                                  *)
(*                  INSERT PROCEDURE SORT HERE.                     *)
(*                                                                  *)
(*==================================================================*)


(*==================================================================*)
(*                                                                  *)
(*                  INSERT FUNCTION AVERAGE HERE.                   *)
(*                                                                  *)
(*==================================================================*)

(********************************************************************)
BEGIN (* PROGRAM SCORER *)
WRITELN('THIS PROGRAM WILL COMPUTE THE ARITHMETIC AVERAGE OF UP TO ',
        MAXSTUDENTS:3);
WRITELN('TEST SCORES WHICH RANGE BETWEEN ', MINSCORE:1, ' AND ',
        MAXSCORE:3, ', INCLUSIVE.');
WRITELN('THE SCORES WILL ALSO BE PRINTED FROM HIGH TO LOW.');
WRITELN('USE AS MANY LINES AS NECESSARY WHEN ENTERING THE TEST ',
        'SCORES.');
WRITELN('ENTER AN ASTERISK (*) IMMEDIATELY AFTER THE LAST NUMBER ',
        'TO');
WRITELN('SIGNAL THE END OF INPUT. ENTER YOUR SCORES NOW.');
ACCESS(SCORES, COUNT);
SORT(SCORES,COUNT);
WRITELN;
WRITELN('TEST SCORES');
FOR I := 1 TO COUNT
  DO WRITELN(SCORES[I]:7);
MEAN := AVERAGE(SCORES, COUNT);
WRITELN;
WRITELN('ARITHMETIC AVERAGE = ', MEAN:5:2)
END (* OF PROGRAM SCORER *).
```

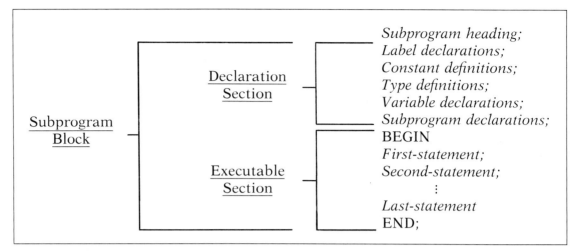

Figure 8–1
An overview of a Pascal subprogram.

8.1
USER-DEFINED SUBPROGRAMS

Except for the heading, the structure of a Pascal function or procedure is identical to the structure of a Pascal program, as can be seen by comparing Figure 8–1 to the overview of a Pascal program given in Figure 2–1. Note, in particular, that a subprogram may have subprograms declared within its own declaration section. The effects and implications of definitions and declarations made in the declaration section of a subprogram are explored in detail in Section 8.3. In this section we will examine simple functions and procedures that contain a few subprogram declarations. It is also worth noting that the END of the executable section of a subprogram must be followed by a semicolon because the subprogram appears as a declaration. Even though subprograms declared in the main block of a program precede the executable section of the main block, execution of the program always starts at the first statement in the executable section of the main block (the main program). The execution of a subprogram does not start until that subprogram is called by the main program or some other subprogram that was previously called. Once a subprogram has been activated by a call, the statements in its executable section are executed and then the execution of the calling program is resumed. This transfer of control between the calling program and the subprogram that is called will be made clearer in the examples presented below.

FUNCTIONS

Suppose that a REAL variable named CASH declared in the main block is assigned a value that constitutes a dollar amount. If the value of CASH is the result of some arithmetic computations, it is likely that the stored value will have three or more significant digits after the decimal point. Let PENNIES be an INTEGR variable that has also been declared in the main block. Here is a function that can be called to round the value of CASH to two significant digits after the decimal point:

```
FUNCTION DOLLARSANDCENTS : REAL;
   BEGIN
   PENNIES := ROUND(CASH * 100.0);
   DOLLARSANDCENTS := PENNIES / 100
   END;
```

The heading for this function follows the form for the simplest of all possible headings for a user-defined function:

FUNCTION *name* : *type-identifier;*

In this case, the function's *name* is declared to be DOLLARSANDCENTS and the *type-identifier* REAL specifies that the function will return a real number as its value. Consider the following sequence of statements in the main program, where PAYCHECK and TAX are REAL variables:

```
PAYCHECK := 235.24;
CASH := 0.07 * PAYCHECK;
TAX := DOLLARSANDCENTS
```

The reference to DOLLARSANDCENTS in the last assignment statement is a call to the function named DOLLARSANDCENTS. When that statement is executed, the function DOLLARSANDCENTS is executed and the value produced by the function is then assigned to TAX. Once this has been done, the values of the variables PAYCHECK, CASH, TAX and PENNIES will be as shown here.

235.24	18.4668	18.47	1847
PAYCHECK	CASH	TAX	PENNIES

  In the function DOLLARSANDCENTS, the variables PENNIES and CASH are **global variables,** which means that they are declared outside the subprogram block but retain their meanings within the function block. Although PENNIES is intended to be used only in the function, it may also be used in the main program. The main program will be unable to use PENNIES if it is declared in the declaration section of the function rather than outside the function, as follows:

```
FUNCTION DOLLARSANDCENTS : REAL;
   VAR
        PENNIES : INTEGER;
   BEGIN
   PENNIES := ROUND(CASH * 100.0);
   DOLLARSANDCENTS := PENNIES / 100
   END;
```

What we have done here is make PENNIES a **local variable** for the private use of the function DOLLARSANDCENTS. It is illegal for any statement outside the function block to make reference to this variable PENNIES.

This version of the function DOLLARSANDCENTS still relies on the global variable CASH having the value to be rounded when it is called. This limits the usefulness of the function because each value to be rounded by DOLLARSANDCENTS must be assigned to CASH before the function is called. The way to remove this limitation is to specify the value needed by the function by using an argument in the function call, as is done when Pascal-supplied functions like SQRT and ROUND are called. For instance, consider the following pair of statements:

```
PAYCHECK := 235.24;
TAX := DOLLARSANDCENTS(0.07 * PAYCHECK)
```

Now a special kind of local variable known as a **formal parameter** must be declared in the heading for the function DOLLARSANDCENTS. The purpose of this formal parameter is to "receive" the value of the argument specified in the function call. Consider the following version of DOLLARSANDCENTS:

```
FUNCTION DOLLARSANDCENTS (CASH : REAL) : REAL;
   VAR
        PENNIES : INTEGER;
   BEGIN
   PENNIES := ROUND(CASH * 100.0);
   DOLLARSANDCENTS := PENNIES / 100
   END;
```

Here CASH is declared a formal parameter of the type REAL. This makes CASH a local variable within the function DOLLARSANDCENTS, but more important is that it automatically ensures that CASH will receive the value of the argument that now must be specified in the function call.

In every version of the function DOLLARSANDCENTS presented above, the value of the function is returned to the calling program via the function name DOLLARSANDCENTS. The purpose of a function is to generate one REAL or ordinal type value (according to the function type specified in the heading), and that value must be assigned to the name of the function via an assignment statement prior to the END of the function. If this is not done, an execution error will result when the calling program is resumed.

Suppose we want to write a program that will compute the federal and state taxes applicable to a collection of gross salaries. For the sake of simplicity, assume that the federal and state tax rates are fixed at 0.16 and 0.05, respectively. A negative or zero salary may be input as a signal to stop the tax computations. Here is a pseudocode description of a program that will perform the required tasks:

Constants: FEDRATE = 0.16; STATERATE = 0.05
BEGIN program COMPUTETAXES
Print directions
READ a gross SALARY
WHILE the gross SALARY is greater than zero
    DO BEGIN tax computations

        Compute FEDTAX as ⟨DOLLARSANDCENTS(FEDRATE * SALARY)⟩

        Compute STATETAX as ⟨DOLLARSANDCENTS (STATERATE * SALARY)⟩

```
               Print FEDTAX and STATETAX
               READ another gross SALARY
               END of tax computations
          END of program COMPUTETAXES
```

Note that the function DOLLARSANDCENTS is called twice during each cycle of the WHILE loop, and that a different argument is specified each time. Thus, the function must have declared in its heading a REAL type formal parameter to receive the value of the argument given in the call. We have already constructed such a function—the last version of DOLLARSANDCENTS presented above. Here is the program COMPUTETAXES, complete with the function DOLLARSAND-CENTS:

```
PROGRAM COMPUTETAXES (INPUT, OUTPUT);
(***********************************************************************
 *                                                                    *
 *   A PROGRAM TO COMPUTE THE FEDERAL AND STATE TAXES APPLICABLE TO   *
 *   A COLLECTION OF GROSS SALARIES                                   *
 *                                                                    *
 ********************************************************************* )
CONST                             (*---------- [CONSTANTS]----------*)
        FEDRATE = 0.16;           (* FEDERAL TAX RATE (FRACTION)   *)
        STATERATE = 0.05;         (* STATE TAX RATE (FRACTION)     *)
                                  (*------------------------------*)
VAR                               (*------- [REAL VARIABLES]--------*)
        SALARY,                   (* A GROSS SALARY (DOLLARS)      *)
        FEDTAX,                   (* A COMPUTED FEDERAL TAX        *)
        STATETAX : REAL;          (* A COMPUTED STATE TAX          *)
                                  (*------------------------------*)

FUNCTION DOLLARSANDCENTS
   (*===========================================================*)
   (*            ROUND A DOLLAR AMOUNT TO THE NEAREST CENT      *)
   (*===========================================================*)
                                  (*---------- [PARAMETERS]----------*)
   (CASH : REAL)                  (* AMOUNT TO BE ROUNDED          *)
                    : REAL;       (*------------------------------*)
      VAR                         (*------ [INTEGER VARIABLES]------*)
         PENNIES : INTEGER;       (* NUMBER OF PENNIES IN ROUNDED  *)
                                  (* DOLLAR AMOUNT                 *)
                                  (*------------------------------*)
   (*===========================================================*)
   BEGIN (* FUNCTION DOLLARSANDCENTS *)
   PENNIES := ROUND(CASH * 100.0);
   DOLLARSANDCENTS := PENNIES / 100
   END (* OF FUNCTION DOLLARSANDCENTS *);

(***********************************************************************)
BEGIN (* PROGRAM COMPUTETAXES *)
WRITELN('THIS PROGRAM WILL COMPUTE THE FEDERAL AND STATE TAXES');
WRITELN('FOR A COLLECTION OF GROSS SALARIES WHICH YOU SUPPLY.');
WRITELN('THE FEDERAL AND STATE TAX RATES ARE FIXED AT ',
        FEDRATE:4:2, ' AND');
```

```
WRITELN(STATERATE:4:2, ', RESPECTIVELY. ENTER ONE SALARY PER LINE ',
       'AS IT');
WRITELN('IS REQUESTED. TO TERMINATE INPUT, ENTER 0 OR ANY');
WRITELN('NEGATIVE NUMBER WHEN A SALARY IS REQUESTED.');
WRITELN;
WRITELN('FIRST SALARY:');
READ(SALARY);
WHILE SALARY > 0.0
   DO BEGIN (* TAX COMPUTATIONS *)
      FEDTAX := DOLLARSANDCENTS(FEDRATE * SALARY);
      STATETAX := DOLLARSANDCENTS(STATERATE * SALARY);
      WRITELN('FEDERAL TAX: $':20, FEDTAX:6:2, 'STATE TAX: $':15,
              STATETAX:6:2);
      WRITELN;
      WRITELN('NEXT SALARY:');
      READ(SALARY)
      END (* OF TAX COMPUTATIONS *)
END (* OF PROGRAM COMPUTETAXES *).
```

Here is the output from a sample run of the program COMPUTETAXES:

```
THIS PROGRAM WILL COMPUTE THE FEDERAL AND STATE TAXES
FOR A COLLECTION OF GROSS SALARIES WHICH YOU SUPPLY.
THE FEDERAL AND STATE TAX RATES ARE FIXED AT 0.16 AND
0.05, RESPECTIVELY. ENTER ONE SALARY PER LINE AS IT
IS REQUESTED. TO TERMINATE INPUT, ENTER 0 OR ANY
NEGATIVE NUMBER WHEN A SALARY IS REQUESTED.

FIRST SALARY:
? 275.50
        FEDERAL TAX: $ 44.08   STATE TAX: $ 13.78

NEXT SALARY:
? 468.79
        FEDERAL TAX: $ 75.01   STATE TAX: $ 23.44

NEXT SALARY:
? 146.20
        FEDERAL TAX: $ 23.39   STATE TAX: $  7.31

NEXT SALARY:
? 836.16
        FEDERAL TAX: $133.79   STATE TAX: $ 41.81

NEXT SALARY:
? 0.0
```

At the beginning of this chapter, we developed a program named SCORER that uses subprograms named ACCESS, SORT, and AVERAGE. ACCESS and SORT should be constructed as procedures because they must return more than one value when called. However, the subprogram AVERAGE should be a function, since it must produce only the arithmetic average of a collection of numbers stored in an array. The function AVERAGE may be written like this:

```
FUNCTION AVERAGE
 (*==============================================================*)
 (*                   COMPUTE THE TEST AVERAGE                   *)
 (*==============================================================*)
                                    (*---------[PARAMETERS]----------*)
 (X : TESTRESULTS;                  (* ARRAY OF TEST SCORES          *)
  N : STUDENTCOUNT)                 (* NUMBER OF SCORES              *)
                      : REAL;       (*-------------------------------*)
  VAR                               (*-------[REAL VARIABLES]--------*)
      SUM : REAL;                   (* SUM OF THE TEST SCORES        *)
                                    (*-------------------------------*)
                                    (*---[STUDENTCOUNT VARIABLES]----*)
       J : STUDENTCOUNT;            (* LOOP CONTROL VARIABLE         *)
                                    (*-------------------------------*)
 (*==============================================================*)
 BEGIN (* FUNCTION AVERAGE *)
 SUM := 0.0;
 FOR J := 1 TO N
  DO SUM := SUM + X[J];
 AVERAGE := SUM / N
 END (* OF FUNCTION AVERAGE *);
```

The two parameters declared in the function heading (X and N) are necessary because two arguments are specified when AVERAGE is called by the program SCORER (namely, SCORES and COUNT). The number of parameters and their types must match the number of arguments in the call and the types of values for the arguments. For instance, the variable SCORES must be the first argument specified so that the array parameter X in the function AVERAGE will receive the collection of values to be averaged. This correspondence between the arguments in the call to a function and the parameters declared for the function is depicted in the following diagram:

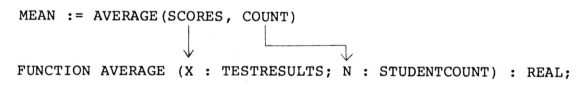

```
MEAN := AVERAGE(SCORES, COUNT)



FUNCTION AVERAGE (X : TESTRESULTS; N : STUDENTCOUNT) : REAL;
```

Also, note that the declarations of the two parameters must be separated by a semicolon. Whenever the function AVERAGE is called, exactly two arguments must be specified. The first argument must be a TESTRESULTS type array and the second argument must be a constant, constant identifier, variable, or arithmetic expression that has a STUDENTCOUNT type value.

The two functions presented so far in this section both produce REAL type values. A function's type can also be INTEGER, CHAR, BOOLEAN, a user-defined ordinal type, or a subrange type. It is necessary that the function type and the types of all parameters declared in the function heading be specified by means of type identifiers. Therefore, the function type and the types of its parameters must be defined outside the function block if they are not standard types. Suppose ACTION is the name of an ordinal data type defined by

ACTION = (STOP, PROCEED);

and consider the following function:

```
FUNCTION SIGNALCHECK (STOPFLAG : CHAR) : ACTION;
   VAR
       CH : CHAR;
   BEGIN (* FUNCTION SIGNALCHECK *)
   REPEAT
     READ(CH)
   UNTIL CH <> ' ';
   IF CH = STOPFLAG
      THEN SIGNALCHECK := STOP
      ELSE SIGNALCHECK := PROCEED
   END (* OF FUNCTION SIGNALCHECK *);
```

The purpose of this function is to read input characters one at a time until a nonblank character has been read. If the last character read is the same as the value of the parameter STOPFLAG (which is established by a CHAR type argument that must be specified when the function is called), the function returns the ACTION type value STOP. Otherwise, the ACTION type value PROCEED is established as the value of the function.

PROCEDURES

Procedure subprograms are used to perform tasks that do not require that exactly one value be returned to the calling program. The simplest form of a procedure heading is

PROCEDURE *name;*

No data type is associated with the *name* of a procedure because this *name* is used only to identify the procedure. It is not possible to return a value to the calling program through the name of a procedure. Consider the following PROCEDURE declaration:

```
PROCEDURE EXCHANGE;
   BEGIN (* PROCEDURE EXCHANGE *)
   SAVE := X;
   X := Y;
   Y := SAVE
   END (* OF PROCEDURE EXCHANGE *);
```

Assume that X, Y, and SAVE are INTEGER variables declared in the program that calls the procedure EXCHANGE. The purpose of this procedure is to interchange the values of X and Y. It is called by a procedure statement consisting solely of the identifier EXCHANGE, as illustrated in the following program segment:

```
X := 75;
Y := 256;
WRITELN(X:5, Y:5);
EXCHANGE;
WRITELN(X:5, Y:5)
```

The output that is generated looks like this:

```
          75   256
         256    75
```

The variables X, Y, and SAVE are global with respect to the procedure EX-CHANGE since they are declared in the calling program. EXCHANGE can be used to interchange only the values of X and Y. This procedure can be made more useful by declaring parameters in its heading. However, the kind of parameters used in the functions we considered previously are not suitable for use by the procedure EXCHANGE. They are known as **value parameters** and are used for one-way communication of data from a calling program to a subprogram. Formal parameters that allow a subprogram to communicate data back to a calling program as well as to receive data from the calling program are known as **variable parameters.** Consider the following version of the procedure EXCHANGE:

```
PROCEDURE EXCHANGE (VAR A, B : INTEGER);
   VAR
       SAVE : INTEGER;
   BEGIN (* PROCEDURE EXCHANGE *)
   SAVE := A;
   A := B;
   B := SAVE
   END (* OF PROCEDURE EXCHANGE *);
```

A and B are declared as variable parameters for EXCHANGE. Note that a list of variable parameters must be preceded by the keyword VAR. When EXCHANGE is called, the procedure statement must contain the identifier EXCHANGE followed by a list of exactly two variables as arguments for the call. A call to EXCHANGE is illustrated in the following program segments:

```
X := 75;
Y := 256;
WRITELN(X:5, Y:5);
EXCHANGE(X, Y);
WRITELN(X:5, Y:5)
```

This program segment produces exactly the same results as the program segment that calls the first version of EXCHANGE. When EXCHANGE is called, the arguments X and Y are associated with the variable parameters A and B, respectively, in such a way that changes made to the values of A and B during execution of the procedure are reflected in the values of X and Y when execution of the calling program is resumed. Thus, variable parameters provide two-way channels for the passing of data between a procedure and the calling program, as depicted in the following diagram:

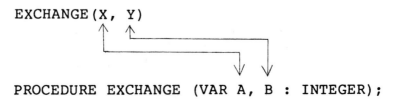

The differences between value parameters and variable parameters are examined more closely in Section 8.2.

The subprogram ACCESS needed for the program SCORER should be constructed as a procedure because it must get the test scores for the program. Here is one way that ACCESS can be written:

```
PROCEDURE ACCESS
  (*==================================================================*)
  (*                     INPUT THE TEST SCORES                        *)
  (*==================================================================*)
                                    (*---------[PARAMETERS]----------*)
  (VAR LIST : TESTRESULTS;          (* THE ARRAY OF SCORES           *)
   VAR NUM : STUDENTCOUNT);         (* NUMBER OF INPUT SCORES        *)
                                    (*------------------------------*)
  VAR                               (*-------[CHAR VARIABLES]--------*)
       SYMBOL : CHAR;               (* END-OF-INPUT SIGNAL           *)
                                    (*------------------------------*)
  (*==================================================================*)
  BEGIN (* PROCEDURE ACCESS *)
  NUM := 0;
  REPEAT (* SCORE INPUT *)
    NUM := NUM + 1;
    READ(LIST[NUM], SYMBOL)
  UNTIL SYMBOL = '*'
  END (* OF PROCEDURE ACCESS *);
```

Both the array LIST and NUM must be variable parameters, but they are declared in separate sections of the parameter list since their types are different. When ACCESS is called by the program SCORER via the procedure statement

ACCESS(SCORES, COUNT)

the array SCORES and the variable COUNT have not been assigned values. However, the procedure does not assume that values have been assigned to the corresponding parameters (LIST and NUM). The purpose of the procedure ACCESS is to read values for the array LIST and establish the NUMber of values read so that values for the array SCORES and the variable COUNT are returned to the program SCORER. Since the CHAR variable SYMBOL is for the local use of the procedure ACCESS, it has been declared in the procedure.

The SORT subprogram used by the program SCORER should also be constructed as a procedure because it can alter the arrangement of the values stored in the SCORES array. Here is a SORT procedure that performs a selection sort on the array V whose values are contained in the components indexed from 1 through K:

```
PROCEDURE SORT
  (*==================================================================*)
  (*                     SORT THE SCORES                              *)
  (*==================================================================*)
```

```
(VAR V : TESTRESULTS;        (*--------[PARAMETERS]----------*)
 K : STUDENTCOUNT);          (* SCORES TO BE SORTED          *)
                             (* NUMBER OF SCORES             *)
                             (*------------------------------*)
 VAR                         (*---[STUDENTCOUNT VARIABLES]----*)
      POS,                   (* POSITION TO BE FILLED IN THE *)
                             (* SORTED PORTION OF ARRAY V    *)
      LOC,                   (* SELECTED LOCATION IN A SORT  *)
                             (* CYCLE                        *)
      J : STUDENTCOUNT;      (* LOOP CONTROL VARIABLE        *)
                             (*------------------------------*)
(*===============================================================*)
BEGIN (* PROCEDURE SORT *)
FOR POS := 1 TO K - 1
  DO BEGIN (* A SELECTION CYCLE *)
     LOC := POS;
     FOR J := POS + 1 TO K
      DO IF V[J] > V[LOC]
           THEN LOC := J;
     IF POS <> LOC
       THEN BEGIN (* AN EXCHANGE *)
            V[0] := V[POS];
            V[POS] := V[LOC];
            V[LOC] := V[0]
            END (* OF AN EXCHANGE *)
     END (* OF A SELECTION CYCLE *)
END (* OF PROCEDURE SORT *);
```

(Compare the procedure SORT with the SELECTIONSORT program presented in Section 7.2.) Since POS, LOC, and J are used only in the procedure SORT, they are declared as local variables in the procedure's declaration section.

Program SCORER and all of its subprograms have now been written. The entire program can be constructed according to the structure outlined at the beginning of this chapter (see Exercise 5). In the outline, the positions at which the subprograms should be inserted are marked. However, the order in which the subprograms ACCESS, SORT, and AVERAGE are declared in the main block is actually insignificant. Any of the six possible orders will suffice. (As we will see later, this is not always the case.)

8.1 EXERCISES

1. Tell which of the following subprogram headings are valid and which are invalid. If a heading is invalid, explain why.

   a. FUNCTION TOTAL;
   b. PROCEDURE A − B;
   c. PROCEDURE SUMALLTHENUMBERS;
   d. FUNCTION BUS45 : 0..60;
   e. PROCEDURE 3HIGH;

f. PROCEDURE FINDER : INTEGER;
g. FUNCTION DIFFERENCE : REAL;
h. FUNCTION DIV : CHAR;

2. Assume that all the variables in the following subprograms are INTEGER variables.

```
FUNCTION THREES : INTEGER;
   BEGIN (* FUNCTION THREES *)
   N := 0;
   D := 2 * X;
   WHILE D >= X
      DO BEGIN
            D := D DIV 3;
            N := N + 1
            END;
   THREES := N
   END (* OF FUNCTION THREES *);


PROCEDURE SPLIT;
   BEGIN (* PROCEDURE SPLIT *)
   D1 := A - B;
   D2 := B - C;
   IF D1 < D2
      THEN M := D2 DIV D1
      ELSE M := D1 MOD D2
   END (* OF PROCEDURE SPLIT *);
```

Determine the output that will be generated by each of the following program segments. If an error will occur, explain why.

a.
```
A := 8;
B := 15;
C := 45;
SPLIT;
WRITELN(D1, D2, M)
```

b.
```
X := 21;
R := (THREES + 5) * 2;
WRITELN(X, R);
WRITELN(X, THREES)
```

c.
```
X := 1;
REPEAT
   X := 2 * X
UNTIL THREES > 3;
WRITELN(X)
```

d.
```
A := 5;
B := A * 4;
C := A * (B + 3);
T := SPLIT;
WRITELN(D1, D2, M, T)
```

e.
```
X := 12;
R := THREES * THREES;
WRITELN(X, R);
R := X;
THREES;
WRITELN(X, R)
```

f.
```
            A := 18;
            B := 5;
            C := 62;
            SPLIT;
            IF D2 - D1 > 0
              THEN SPLIT
              ELSE BEGIN
                   B := B + 20;
                   SPLIT
                   END;
            WRITELN(D1, D2, M)
```

3. Rewrite the function THREES and the procedure SPLIT given in Exercise 2 using parameters and local variables. Show how the calls to these subprograms appearing in the program segments given in Exercise 2 must be modified.

4. Suppose that M is an INTEGER variable whose value is greater than zero and CH is a CHAR variable. Construct a subprogram that will print the value of CH a total of M times on one line. (You may set some upper limit on the magnitude of M.) Show how your subprogram can be used to print each letter of the alphabet ten times on successive lines. Could this subprogram be written as either a function or a procedure? Explain.

5. A program named SCORER is outlined in the introduction to Chapter 8 and all of its subprograms appear in Section 8.1. Test this program on your computer system and suggest possible improvements.

8.2
PARAMETERS FOR SUBPROGRAMS

In the preceding section, parameters were introduced as local variables for functions and procedures that serve as vehicles for the transfer of data between a subprogram and a program that calls it. Two kinds of formal parameters that can be declared in a subprogram heading were discussed: value parameters and variable parameters. This section gives a more detailed description of how value and variable parameters are declared and used.

VALUE PARAMETERS

Value parameters for a subprogram are declared in one or more formal parameter sections in the subprogram heading. Each formal parameter section used to declare value parameters takes the form

parameter-1, parameter-2, . . . , parameter-n : type-identifier

where each *parameter* is a valid identifier and *type-identifier* is the name of a standard or user-defined data type. For instance, the function heading

```
FUNCTION MATCH (ALIST, BLIST : IDNUMBERS;
                LENGTH : INTEGER) : INTEGER;
```

contains two formal parameter sections. The first one declares ALIST and BLIST as IDNUMBERS type parameters and the second one declares LENGTH as an INTEGER parameter. Consecutive formal parameter sections in a subprogram heading (if there is more than one) must be separated by a semicolon and the entire sequence of parameter sections must be enclosed in parentheses, as illustrated in the example above.

Suppose that the purpose of the function MATCH is to count the number of components of an array whose values are identical to those stored in the corresponding components of another array, where both arrays are of the type

`IDNUMBERS = ARRAY [1 .. 100] OF INTEGER;`

The contents of the two arrays will be communicated to the function MATCH via the parameters ALIST and BLIST and the number of components of the arrays to be MATCHed will be the value established for the parameter LENGTH. Here is the entire function:

```
FUNCTION MATCH (ALIST, BLIST : IDNUMBERS; LENGTH : INTEGER) : INTEGER;
  VAR
      I, SAME : INTEGER;
  BEGIN (* FUNCTION MATCH *)
  SAME := 0;
  FOR I := 1 TO LENGTH
   DO IF ALIST[I] = BLIST[I]
         THEN SAME := SAME + 1;
  MATCH := SAME
  END (* OF FUNCTION MATCH *);
```

When MATCH is called, exactly three arguments (also referred to as **actual parameters**) must be specified as the sources for the data that the function needs. The form of this call is

MATCH (*actual-parameter-1*, *actual-parameter-2*, *actual-parameter-3*)

where *actual-parameter-1* and *actual-parameter-2* are the names of the arrays containing the values to be MATCHed and *actual-parameter-3* is a constant, constant identifier, variable, or expression whose value is the number of components of the arrays to be MATCHed. Say, for instance, RANK1 and RANK2 are both arrays of the type IDNUMBERS and LAST is an INTEGER variable. Assuming that components 1 through LAST of the arrays RANK1 and RANK2 have been assigned values, the call to MATCH in the following WRITELN statement is valid:

```
WRITELN(MATCH(RANK1, RANK2, LAST), ' COMPONENTS HAVE BEEN MATCHED.')
```

The order in which the actual parameters are listed in a call to a subprogram is significant because it determines the values the formal parameters for the subprogram will have when execution of the subprogram begins. The function call MATCH(RANK1, RANK2, LAST) establishes the following correspondence between the actual parameters listed and the formal parameters of the function:

RANK1 $\longrightarrow$ ALIST

RANK2 $\longrightarrow$ BLIST

LAST $\longrightarrow$ LENGTH

The arrows in this diagram indicate that the formal parameters ALIST, BLIST, and LENGTH are assigned the values stored in RANK1, RANK2, and LAST, respectively. In the case of function MATCH, the call MATCH(RANK2, RANK1, LAST) produces the same value as MATCH(RANK1, RANK2, LAST) because it does not matter in the function which of the two arrays is ALIST and which is BLIST. The correspondence between the actual parameters in the call MATCH(RANK2, RANK1, LAST) and the formal parameters of the function is as follows:

$$RANK2 \longrightarrow ALIST$$
$$RANK1 \longrightarrow BLIST$$
$$LAST \longrightarrow LENGTH$$

Every formal parameter declared in a subprogram heading must be associated with an actual parameter of the same type. The function call MATCH(RANK1, LAST, RANK2) is illegal, since the correspondence between the actual parameters in the call and the formal parameters of the function would have the INTEGER variable LAST associated with the IDNUMBERS type array BLIST, and RANK2, which is an IDNUMBERS type array, would be associated with the INTEGER parameter LENGTH. An error of this kind is noted by an appropriate error message generated by the Pascal compiler.

A value parameter cannot be used as a vehicle for passing data generated by a subprogram back to the calling program through its association with an actual parameter. Suppose the data type DEVIATIONS is defined by

```
DEVIATIONS = ARRAY [1 .. 50] OF REAL;
```

and consider the following function:

```
FUNCTION AVRPOSITIVE (X : DEVIATIONS; N : INTEGER) : REAL;
  VAR
      TOTAL : REAL;
      K : INTEGER;
  BEGIN (* FUNCTION AVRPOSITIVE *)
  TOTAL := 0.0;
  FOR K := 1 TO N
   DO IF X[K] >= 0.0
        THEN BEGIN (* ACCUMULATION *)
             TOTAL := TOTAL + X[K];
             N := N - 1
             END (* OF ACCUMULATION *);
  IF N <> 0
    THEN AVRPOSITIVE := TOTAL / N
    ELSE AVRPOSITIVE := 0.0
  END (* OF FUNCTION AVRPOSITIVE *);
```

The purpose of this function is to compute the average of all the positive real numbers stored in components 1 through N of array X. If only negative numbers and zeros are stored in the array, the function will return the value 0.0. The value of N is initially the value passed to the function as the value of the second parameter listed in the call. However, the function subtracts 1 from N each time a nonpositive value is excluded from the TOTAL so that the value of N will be the number of positive values whose sum is TOTAL when the summing ends. No matter what value N has when the function ends, the value of the second parameter listed in the call is no different than it was when the call was made.

Since the purpose of a function is to return a single REAL or ordinal type value through the name of the function, it is appropriate that the formal parameters for functions be value parameters. A procedure, on the other hand, must be able to pass data back to a calling program by using global variables or some of its parameters. Consider, for instance, the following version of the procedure EXCHANGE, whose intended purpose is to interchange the values of two INTEGER variables:

```
PROCEDURE EXCHANGE (A, B : INTEGER);
   VAR
        SAVE : INTEGER;
   BEGIN (* PROCEDURE EXCHANGE *)
   SAVE := A;
   A := B;
   B := SAVE;
   WRITELN('A =', A:5, ' B =', B:5)
   END (* OF PROCEDURE EXCHANGE *);
```

Now suppose that X and Y are INTEGER variables and the following sequence of statements is executed:

```
X := 75;
Y := 256;
WRITELN('X =', X:5, ' Y =', Y:5);
EXCHANGE(X, Y);
WRITELN('X =', X:5, ' Y =', Y:5)
```

The output generated by this program segment is

```
X =     75  Y =    256
A =    256  B =     75
X =     75  Y =    256
```

When EXCHANGE is called, the parameters A and B do, in fact, receive the values 75 and 256, respectively. Furthermore, the values of A and B are interchanged, as evidenced by the output that the procedure generates. But the values of X and Y remain unaffected by interchange performed by the procedure EXCHANGE. The procedure is capable of interchanging "copies" of the values of two variables, but it cannot cause the values of the variables themselves to be interchanged. We did not encounter this problem with the other two versions of EXCHANGE presented in Section 8.1 because one of them uses global variables and the other uses variable parameters to communicate with the calling program.

Is it ever appropriate to use value parameters in a procedure? The answer to this question is yes, but only to receive data from the calling program. A procedure often uses a mixture of value parameters and variable parameters. However, useful procedures whose only parameters are value parameters can be constructed. Here, for example, is a procedure whose only task is data output:

```
PROCEDURE PRINTARRAY (D : DEVIATIONS; M : INTEGER);
VAR
    I : INTEGER;
BEGIN (* PROCEDURE PRINTARRAY *)
WRITELN;
WRITELN('----------');
FOR I := 1 TO M
 DO WRITELN(D[I]);
WRITELN('----------');
WRITELN
END (* OF PROCEDURE PRINTARRAY *);
```

Procedures with value parameters may also be constructed to print table headings, error messages, and other program-generated information.

VARIABLE PARAMETERS

Variable parameters are used in a procedure to provide two-way communication of data between the procedure and a program that calls it. A formal parameter section in which variable parameters are declared must take the form

VAR *parameter-1*, *parameter-2*, . . . , *parameter-n* : *type-identifier*

Only variable parameters of the same type can be declared in any one formal parameter section, but a subprogram may contain as many formal parameter sections declaring variable parameters as necessary. Variable parameters and value parameters can be declared in the same subprogram heading, but of course a variable parameter cannot be declared in the same formal parameter section as a value parameter. Let the data type CODELIST be defined by

```
CODELIST = ARRAY [1 .. 1000] OF INTEGER;
```

and consider the following procedure:

```
PROCEDURE COMPRESS (CODESIN : CODELIST; COUNTIN : INTEGER;
                    VAR CODESOUT : CODELIST; VAR COUNTOUT : INTEGER);
VAR
    I, J : INTEGER;
BEGIN (* PROCEDURE COMPRESS *)
COUNTOUT := 0;
FOR I := 1 TO COUNTIN
 DO IF COUNTOUT = 0
     THEN BEGIN (* INITIALIZE CODESOUT *)
         CODESOUT[1] := CODESIN[1];
         COUNTOUT := 1
         END (* OF INITIALIZE CODESOUT *)
     ELSE BEGIN (* SCAN CODESOUT *)
         J := 1;
         WHILE (J <= COUNTOUT) AND (CODESIN[I] <> CODESOUT[J])
            DO J := J + 1;
         IF J > COUNTOUT
           THEN BEGIN (* UPDATE CODESOUT *)
                COUNTOUT := COUNTOUT + 1;
```

```
                    CODESOUT[COUNTOUT] := CODESIN[I]
                    END (* OF UPDATE CODESOUT *)
              END (* OF SCAN CODESOUT *)
    END (* OF PROCEDURE COMPRESS *);
```

Procedure COMPRESS creates an array of integers CODESOUT that contains every integer stored in the array CODESIN, but no duplicates. Components 1 through COUNTIN of array CODESIN are assumed to contain the collection of integers to be COMPRESSed into array CODESOUT. After the array CODESOUT has been constructed, it will contain the COMPRESSed collection of integers in components 1 through COUNTOUT.

When the procedure COMPRESS is called, four actual parameters must be specified. The first two will be associated with the value parameters CODESIN and COUNTIN and the second two will be associated with the variable parameters CODESOUT and COUNTOUT. Suppose X is a CODELIST type array containing integers in components 1 through N and Y is another CODELIST type array. Let M, like N, be an INTEGER variable. Here is a procedure statement that makes a valid call to COMPRESS:

$$COMPRESS(X, N, Y, M)$$

The association between the actual parameters given in the procedure statement and the formal parameters for the procedure COMPRESS is depicted as follows:

$$
\begin{array}{ll}
X \longrightarrow & CODESIN \\
N \longrightarrow & COUNTIN \\
Y \longleftarrow\!-\!-\!\rightarrow & CODESOUT \\
M \longleftarrow\!-\!-\!\rightarrow & COUNTOUT
\end{array}
$$

The contents of X and N are "passed by value" to the parameters CODESIN and COUNTIN, respectively. Values stored in X and N cannot be changed by the procedure COMPRESS because they are associated with value parameters. On the other hand, Y and M are associated with variable parameters in the procedure that establishes CODESOUT and COUNTOUT as alternate names for Y and M, respectively, while the procedure is executed. All values assigned to variable parameters by the procedure are, in effect, assigned to the corresponding actual parameters. The phrase "pass by reference" is used to describe the form of data transfer that exists between variable parameters and associated actual parameters. Since a variable parameter serves as a substitute name for an actual parameter, **it is necessary that every actual parameter associated with a variable parameter be a variable.**

Parameters used by a subprogram merely to receive data from a calling program should be declared as value parameters rather than variable parameters so that the values of the associated actual parameters remain undisturbed when the subprogram is executed. Since the general purpose of a function is to compute a single value that is returned to the calling program via the function's name, it is inappropriate (although not illegal) for a function to use variable parameters. If a parameter is used by a procedure only to return data to a calling program, it must be declared as a variable parameter. Likewise, a parameter used both to receive data from a calling program and to return data to that program must be a variable parameter. The heading for the procedure SORT presented in Section 8.1 is

```
PROCEDURE SORT (VAR V : TESTRESULTS; VAR K : STUDENTCOUNT);
```

It is necessary that V be declared as a variable parameter because the initial contents of the array V must be established when SORT is called and the contents of V after the SORTing is complete must be returned to the calling program. However, K is used by the procedure SORT only to receive a value from the calling program and should therefore be declared as a value parameter to protect the value of its associated actual parameter. Suppose the heading for SORT is changed to

```
PROCEDURE SORT (VAR V : TESTRESULTS; K : STUDENTCOUNT);
```

No other changes need be made to the procedure to compensate for the fact that K is now a value parameter. A call to SORT must contain a TESTRESULTS type array as the first actual parameter, but now the second actual parameter can be any constant, constant identifier, variable, or expression having a STUDENT-COUNT type value. For instance, the procedure statement

```
SORT(SCORES, 30)
```

is valid when K is a value parameter and invalid when K is a variable parameter.

8.2
EXERCISES

1. Assume that the following declarations have been made.

```
CONST
        N = 50;
TYPE
        RANGE = 1 .. N;
        LINE = PACKED ARRAY [RANGE] OF CHAR;
VAR
        NAME, SUMMARY, UPDATE : LINE;
        M, K, I : RANGE;
        X, SEC : INTEGER;
        CH : CHAR;
```

The heading for the function PICK is

```
FUNCTION PICK (INFO : LINE; LEFT, RIGHT : RANGE) : INTEGER;
```

Determine the validity of each of the following statements. If a statement is invalid, explain why.

```
a.          X := 5 * PICK(NAME, M + 1, N)
b.          READ(PICK(NAME, M, K))
c.          SEC := PICK(M, K, SUMMARY)
d.          WRITELN(PICK(UPDATE, 1, N):5)
e.          FOR I := 1 TO N
              DO X := X + PICK(NAME, CH, I)
```

f.
```
    REPEAT
      M := M + 1
    UNTIL PICK(SUMMARY, M, M) = '*'
```

2. Assume the same declarations as in Exercise 1. The heading for the procedure ISOLATE is

```
PROCEDURE ISOLATE (TITLE : LINE; FIRST, LAST : RANGE;
                   VAR SECTION : LINE; VAR LENGTH : INTEGER);
```

Determine the validity of each of the following statements. If a statement is invalid, explain why.

a.   `ISOLATE(NAME, K + 1, M, UPDATE, X)`
b.   `ISOLATE(SUMMARY, M, K, NAME)`
c.   `FOR I := 1 TO N`
        `  DO ISOLATE(UPDATE, I, N, NAME, SEC)`
d.   `ISOLATE(SUMMARY, 1, K, NAME, X + 1)`
e.   `WRITELN(ISOLATE(NAME, 1, N, SECTION, SEC))`
f.   `ISOLATE(UPDATE, M, K, NAME, X) + 1`

8.3 IDENTIFIERS DECLARED IN SUBPROGRAMS

Formal parameters declared in the heading for a subprogram may be used only in that subprogram's block. The use of formal parameters in subprograms gives those subprograms a certain degree of flexibility and independence. When a subprogram relies on global variables to communicate with a calling program, there is a danger that the subprogram will change the value of a variable that some other module will need to use later. A change in the value of a global variable made in a subprogram is known as a "side effect." We have already noted that any side effects produced by a function are totally inconsistent with the philosophy of a function. Procedures, on the other hand, must be able to channel information back to a calling program through variable parameters or global variables.

When a subprogram uses any global variables, it loses some of its autonomy. Consider the case of the function DOLLARSANDCENTS in which PENNIES is a global variable:

```
FUNCTION DOLLARSANDCENTS (CASH : REAL) : REAL;
   BEGIN (* FUNCTION DOLLARSANDCENTS *)
   PENNIES := ROUND(CASH * 100.0);
   DOLLARSANDCENTS := PENNIES / 100
   END (* OF FUNCTION DOLLARSANDCENTS *);
```

PENNIES clearly exists for the local use of the function DOLLARSANDCENTS, but it is declared outside that function's block. This means that some other program module can use PENNIES; in particular, it can use a value that PENNIES has been assigned in the function DOLLARSANDCENTS. Furthermore, DOLLARSANDCENTS changes the value of PENNIES each time it is called. The point here is that the sharing of the variable PENNIES by two or more program blocks poses a threat to the effectiveness of the program as a whole.

In this section we will see that there are ways to prevent the main program and its subprograms from interfering with one another. The use of formal parameters is a step in the right direction, but parameters alone may not be sufficient in all cases.

THE DECLARATION SECTION OF A SUBPROGRAM

The declaration section of a function or a procedure has the same five order-dependent parts as the declaration section of a main program (see Figure 8–1). All identifiers defined or declared in a subprogram block are said to be **local identifiers.** This includes all labels, constant identifiers, names of data types, variables, and names of functions and procedures defined or declared in the declaration section of the subprogram, as well as all parameters declared in the subprogram heading. Since the meanings of local identifiers are established in a subprogram block, they apply only to that block.

Suppose we want to write a program that will generate the selling prices for items whose regular unit prices are discounted when the items are purchased in quantity. Each item has a four-digit code number whose first digit signifies a pricing category (1, 2, or 3). The following table shows how items in each of the three categories are discounted for bulk purchases:

Category	Unit Discount
1	8% per unit, if the number of units purchased is at least 1000
2	3% per unit, if the number of units purchased is at least 500;
	8% per unit, if the number of units purchased is at least 2000
3	14% per unit, if the number of units purchased is at least 500

Here is a pseudocode description of a program to calculate bulk prices for any number of items purchased in quantity:

BEGIN program PRICER

Use (PRINTINFO) to print directions

Use (GETITEMCODE) to read and validate an ITEMNUMBER

WHILE ITEMNUMBER is not 0
    DO BEGIN bulk pricing
        READ the UNITPRICE and the purchase QUANTITY
        Calculate the unit PRICEREDUCTION

          using (DISCOUNT(ITEMNUMBER, UNITPRICE, QUANTITY))

        Print PRICEREDUCTION
        Compute SELLINGPRICE as UNITPRICE − PRICEREDUCTION
        Print the unit SELLINGPRICE
        Print the bulk price as QUANTITY * SELLINGPRICE

Use ⟨GETITEMCODE⟩ to read and validate an ITEMNUMBER

END of bulk pricing
END of program PRICER

The program PRICER will call the procedure PRINTINFO to give directions and information about the program and a function named DISCOUNT to calculate the discounted unit price for an item. A third subprogram named GETITEMCODE will be used to read an item code number and test its validity. GETITEMCODE could be constructed as a function that returns a value for the variable ITEM-NUMBER, but it will be constructed as a procedure that uses ITEMNUMBER as a global variable. The structure of the program PRICER is outlined next.

```
PROGRAM PRICER (INPUT, OUTPUT);
(*****************************************************************
 *                                                             *
 *   A PROGRAM TO DETERMINE THE DISCOUNT PRICES FOR ITEMS THAT ARE  *
 *   PURCHASED IN BULK                                         *
 *                                                             *
 *****************************************************************)
CONST                              (*---------[CONSTANTS]----------*)
       LOWCODE = 1000;             (* LOWEST ITEM CODE NUMBER      *)
       HIGHCODE = 4000;            (* HIGHEST ITEM CODE NUMBER     *)
                                   (*------------------------------*)
TYPE
       CODERANGE = LOWCODE .. HIGHCODE;
       SIZERANGE = 1 .. MAXINT;

VAR                                (*-----[CODERANGE VARIABLES]-----*)
       ITEMNUMBER : CODERANGE;     (* AN ITEM CODE NUMBER          *)
                                   (*------------------------------*)
                                   (*-----[SIZERANGE VARIABLES]-----*)
       QUANTITY : SIZERANGE;       (* NUMBER OF UNITS IN AN ORDER  *)
                                   (*------------------------------*)
                                   (*-------[REAL VARIABLES]--------*)
       UNITPRICE,                  (* REGULAR PRICE PER UNIT       *)
       PRICEREDUCTION,             (* UNIT DISCOUNT                *)
       SELLINGPRICE : REAL;        (* DISCOUNTED PRICE PER UNIT    *)
                                   (*------------------------------*)


(*=============================================================*)
(*                                                             *)
(*            INSERT PROCEDURE PRINTINFO HERE.                 *)
(*                                                             *)
(*=============================================================*)


(*=============================================================*)
(*                                                             *)
(*            INSERT PROCEDURE GETITEMCODE HERE.               *)
(*                                                             *)
(*=============================================================*)
```

```
(*====================================================================*)
(*                                                                    *)
(*                INSERT FUNCTION DISCOUNT HERE.                      *)
(*                                                                    *)
(*====================================================================*)

(********************************************************************)
BEGIN (* PROGRAM PRICER *)
PRINTINFO;
GETITEMCODE;
WHILE ITEMNUMBER < HIGHCODE
   DO BEGIN (* BULK PRICING *)
      WRITELN('ENTER THE UNIT PRICE AND THE PURCHASE QUANTITY:');
      READ(UNITPRICE, QUANTITY);
      PRICEREDUCTION := DISCOUNT(ITEMNUMBER, UNITPRICE, QUANTITY);
      WRITELN('THE DISCOUNT PER UNIT FOR ITEM #', ITEMNUMBER:4,
            ' IS $', PRICEREDUCTION:6:2);
      SELLINGPRICE := UNITPRICE - PRICEREDUCTION;
      WRITELN(QUANTITY:5, ' UNITS AT $', SELLINGPRICE:6:2,
            ' PER UNIT: $', QUANTITY * SELLINGPRICE:8:2);
      WRITELN;
      WRITELN('CODE NUMBER FOR NEXT ITEM:');
      GETITEMCODE
      END (* OF BULK PRICING *)
END (* OF PROGRAM PRICER *).
```

The purpose of the procedure PRINTINFO is merely to print instructions for the program user:

```
PROCEDURE PRINTINFO;
  (*====================================================================*)
  (*           PRINT PROGRAM INFORMATION AND DIRECTIONS                 *)
  (*====================================================================*)
  BEGIN (* PROCEDURE PRINTINFO *)
  WRITELN('THIS PROGRAM WILL PRICE QUANTITIES OF ITEMS WHOSE UNIT ',
          'PRICES');
  WRITELN('ARE DISCOUNTED FOR BULK PURCHASES. YOU MUST SUPPLY AN ',
          'ITEM');
  WRITELN('CODE NUMBER, REGULAR UNIT PRICE (IN DOLLARS), AND THE ',
          'PURCHASE');
  WRITELN('QUANTITY AS THEY ARE REQUESTED. ONLY WHOLE NUMBERS ',
          'BETWEEN');
  WRITELN(LOWCODE:4, ' AND ', HIGHCODE - 1:4, ', INCLUSIVE, ARE ',
          'VALID ITEM CODES. TO TERMINATE');
  WRITELN('THE PROGRAM, ENTER THE NUMBER ', HIGHCODE:4, ' WHEN AN ',
          'ITEM CODE NUMBER');
  WRITELN('IS REQUESTED.');
  WRITELN;
  WRITELN('ENTER AN ITEM CODE NUMBER:')
  END (* OF PROCEDURE PRINTINFO *);
```

The procedure GETITEMCODE will allow the program user to enter any integer, but it will print an error message and request another number when the input value is not in the subrange 1000..4000. Each input item code is assigned to a local variable CODE so that its validity can be tested. Here is the procedure GETITEMCODE:

```
PROCEDURE GETITEMCODE;
 (*==================================================================*)
 (*          READ AND VALIDATE THE CODE NUMBER FOR AN ITEM           *)
 (*==================================================================*)
    VAR                            (*------[INTEGER VARIABLES]------*)
       CODE : INTEGER;             (* AN INPUT CODE NUMBER           *)
                                   (*-------------------------------*)
 (*==================================================================*)
    BEGIN (* PROCEDURE GETITEMCODE *)
    READ(CODE);
    WHILE (CODE < LOWCODE) OR (CODE > HIGHCODE)
       DO BEGIN (* REJECT CODE *)
          WRITELN('INVALID CODE NUMBER.');
          WRITELN('ENTER A NUMBER BETWEEN ', LOWCODE:4, ' AND ',
                  HIGHCODE:4, ':');
          READ(CODE)
          END (* OF REJECT CODE *);
    ITEMNUMBER := CODE
    END (* OF PROCEDURE GETITEMCODE *);
```

Reading and validating an item code number is coded as a procedure because there are two different places in the program at which an item code is read. This avoids duplication of code in the program. Note that ITEMCODE is global with respect to the procedure GETITEMCODE; that is, the procedure may use ITEMCODE because it has been declared in the main block.

Function DISCOUNT will use three formal parameters: ITEMCODE, ORDERSIZE, and REGULARPRICE. Since this function computes a dollar amount, it is appropriate that the value returned via DISCOUNT be rounded to the nearest cent. A version of the function DOLLARSANDCENTS (see Section 8.1) is used for the rounding. Here is the structure of the function DISCOUNT:

```
FUNCTION DISCOUNT
 (*==================================================================*)
 (*          COMPUTE THE DISCOUNTED UNIT PRICE FOR AN ITEM           *)
 (*==================================================================*)
                                   (*--------[PARAMETERS]----------*)
 (ITEMCODE : CODERANGE;            (* CODE NUMBER FOR THE ITEM       *)
  REGULARPRICE : REAL;             (* UNIT PRICE FOR THE ITEM        *)
  ORDERSIZE : SIZERANGE)           (* QUANTITY ORDERED               *)
                       : REAL;     (*-------------------------------*)
    CONST                          (*----------[CONSTANTS]----------*)
         LOWRATE = 0.03;           (* LOW DISCOUNT RATE/UNIT         *)
         MEDRATE = 0.08;           (* MEDIUM DISCOUNT RATE/UNIT      *)
         HIGHRATE = 0.14;          (* HIGH DISCOUNT RATE/UNIT        *)
         LEVEL1 = 500;             (* LOW ORDER LEVEL                *)
         LEVEL2 = 1000;            (* MEDIUM ORDER LEVEL             *)
         LEVEL3 = 2000;            (* HIGH ORDER LEVEL               *)
```

```
                                    (*-------------------------------*)
VAR                                 (*------[REAL VARIABLES]--------*)
        RATE : REAL;                (* DISCOUNT RATE PER UNIT        *)
                                    (*-------------------------------*)
                                    (*------[INTEGER VARIABLES]------*)
        CATEGORY : INTEGER;         (* ITEM DISCOUNT CATEGORY        *)
                                    (*-------------------------------*)


(*===============================================================*)
(*                                                               *)
(*            INSERT FUNCTION DOLLARSANDCENTS HERE.              *)
(*                                                               *)
(*===============================================================*)


(*===============================================================*)
BEGIN (* FUNCTION DISCOUNT *)
CATEGORY := ITEMCODE DIV 1000;
CASE CATEGORY OF
   1 : IF ORDERSIZE >= LEVEL2
          THEN RATE := MEDRATE
          ELSE RATE := 0.0;
   2 : IF ORDERSIZE >= LEVEL3
          THEN RATE := MEDRATE
          ELSE IF ORDERSIZE >= LEVEL1
                THEN RATE := LOWRATE
                ELSE RATE := 0.0;
   3 : IF ORDERSIZE >= LEVEL1
          THEN RATE := HIGHRATE
          ELSE RATE := 0.0
END (* OF CATEGORY CASES *);
DISCOUNT := DOLLARSANDCENTS(RATE * REGULARPRICE)
END (* OF FUNCTION DISCOUNT *);
```

Note that the function DOLLARSANDCENTS is declared in the DISCOUNT block. Actually, DOLLARSANDCENTS can be declared in the main block preceding the function DISCOUNT and the program will still run properly. The implications of nesting subprogram blocks within other subprogram blocks are discussed later. Now that the program PRICER and all of the subprograms it uses have been constructed, the entire program is complete. A sample of the output produced by this program is shown here.

```
THIS PROGRAM WILL PRICE QUANTITIES OF ITEMS WHOSE UNIT PRICES
ARE DISCOUNTED FOR BULK PURCHASES. YOU MUST SUPPLY AN ITEM
CODE NUMBER, REGULAR UNIT PRICE (IN DOLLARS), AND THE PURCHASE
QUANTITY AS THEY ARE REQUESTED. ONLY WHOLE NUMBERS BETWEEN
1000 AND 3999, INCLUSIVE, ARE VALID ITEM CODES. TO TERMINATE
THE PROGRAM, ENTER THE NUMBER 4000 WHEN AN ITEM CODE NUMBER
IS REQUESTED.

ENTER AN ITEM CODE NUMBER:
? 2534
ENTER THE UNIT PRICE AND THE PURCHASE QUANTITY:
? 1.95  672
```

```
THE DISCOUNT PER UNIT FOR ITEM #2534 IS $   0.06
  672 UNITS AT $   1.89 PER UNIT: $ 1270.08

CODE NUMBER FOR NEXT ITEM:
? 5610
INVALID CODE NUMBER.
ENTER A NUMBER BETWEEN 1000 AND 4000:
? 3025
ENTER THE UNIT PRICE AND THE PURCHASE QUANTITY:
? 1.63   1724
THE DISCOUNT PER UNIT FOR ITEM #3025 IS $   0.23
  1724 UNITS AT $   1.40 PER UNIT: $ 2413.60

CODE NUMBER FOR NEXT ITEM:
? 4000
```

One advantage to using a local variable like CODE (declared in the procedure GETITEMCODE) in a subprogram is that it gives the subprogram some privacy. For instance, program PRICER cannot use the variable CODE that is declared in the GETITEMCODE block. Of course, the main program does not need access to CODE. Had CODE been declared in the main block, outside the GETITEMCODE block, the program would run just as it does with CODE declared local to the procedure. However, it would then be legal to use CODE both in the main program and in any subprogram declared in the main block. In this case CODE would be global with respect to the procedure GETITEMCODE. Since only this procedure ever uses CODE, it is appropriate that CODE be declared within the procedure block. ITEMNUMBER, on the other hand, is a variable whose value is established in the procedure GETITEMCODE and then used in the main program. Therefore, ITEMNUMBER has been declared in the main block so that it is global with respect to the procedure. The alternative would be to have the main program use ITEMNUMBER as an actual parameter in a revised version of GETITEMCODE that has one formal parameter that it uses in place of ITEMCODE.

BLOCK STRUCTURE AND THE SCOPES OF IDENTIFIERS

A main block and all subprogram blocks have the same basic structure: a five-part declaration section followed by an executable section. The subprogram blocks are physically within the main block. Hence, the main block is often referred to as the **outer block** of a program and each subprogram block is said to be an **inner block.** A typical arrangement of program blocks is illustrated in the following diagram:

PROGRAM MAIN (INPUT, OUTPUT);

FUNCTION A : INTEGER;

BEGIN (* FUNCTION A *)
 •
 •
 •
END (* OF FUNCTION A *);

```
PROCEDURE B;
    BEGIN (* PROCEDURE B *)
        •
        •
        •
    END (* OF PROCEDURE B *);
PROCEDURE C;
    BEGIN (* PROCEDURE C *)
        •
        •
        •
    END (* OF PROCEDURE C *);
BEGIN (* MAIN PROGRAM *)
    •
    •
    •
END (* OF MAIN PROGRAM *).
```

The subprograms A, B, and C are independent program units that are once removed from the main program. It may be said that these subprograms are at level 1 of the program, while the main program is at level 0.

Program execution always begins in the main program at level 0 and continues there until a level 1 subprogram is called. Any level 1 subprogram can be called by the main program. Execution of the main program is temporarily suspended when a subprogram is called and execution of the subprogram is initiated. Since only one program module can be active at a time, a call to a subprogram is said to pass control of the program to that subprogram. When a subprogram ends, control of the program is passed back to the block that called the subprogram and program execution resumes there. Once a level 1 subprogram has been activated, it can call another level 1 subprogram. Such a call will temporarily suspend execution of the first subprogram and initiate execution of the second subprogram. Suppose that the MAIN program calls procedure C and then procedure C calls function A. When function A ends, program control is passed back to procedure C and execution of procedure C is resumed. Execution of the MAIN program remains suspended until procedure C ends and passes control back to MAIN program. Function A will return control directly to the MAIN program only if the MAIN program issued the call that activated function A. **When a subprogram ends, it always returns control to the program block from which it was called.**

The block structure of a program is not limited to only two levels because the declaration section for a subprogram may contain FUNCTION and PROCEDURE declarations. A subprogram declared in any level 1 subprogram is termed a level 2 subprogram, a subprogram declared in any level 2 subprogram is referred to as a level 3 subprogram, and so on. The only subprograms that a main program can call directly are those that are at level 1, since subprogram names are identifiers that are known only in the blocks in which those subprograms are declared. The level 1 subprograms are declared at level 0, but level 2 subprograms are declared at level 1. A level 2 subprogram is two levels "deeper" in the block structure of a program than the main program, and a call to a subprogram can "penetrate" only one level deeper than the level from which the call originates.

Consider the program block structure shown here:

PROGRAM MAIN (INPUT, OUTPUT);

FUNCTION A : INTEGER;

PROCEDURE C;

BEGIN (* PROCEDURE C *)
.
.
.
END (* OF PROCEDURE C *);

BEGIN (* FUNCTION A *);
.
.
.
END (* OF FUNCTION A *);

PROCEDURE B;

BEGIN (* PROCEDURE B *)
.
.
.
END (* OF PROCEDURE B *);

BEGIN (* MAIN PROGRAM *)
.
.
.
END (* OF MAIN PROGRAM *).

The MAIN program can call only function A or procedure B, the two level 1 subprograms. Procedure B can call function A because they are both declared in the same block at level 0. Function A can call procedure C because that procedure is declared in the function A block. Neither the MAIN program nor procedure B can call procedure C, since such a call would have to penetrate more than one block. The name of procedure C is an identifier declared in the declaration section for function A, and so it is local to the function A block. The MAIN program and procedure B have only indirect access to procedure C; that is, the MAIN program or procedure B can call function A and then function A can call procedure C. When procedure C ends, it will always return control to function A.

The effects of the block structure we have just examined can be seen more clearly by studying the output generated by the following program.

```
PROGRAM MAINPROG (OUTPUT);

VAR
    I, N : INTEGER;
    X : ARRAY [1 .. 5] OF INTEGER;

FUNCTION APROG : INTEGER;

    VAR
        TOTAL, HI : INTEGER;

    PROCEDURE CPROG;

        BEGIN (* PROCEDURE CPROG *)
        WRITELN('--->':10, 'BEGINNING CPROG');
        TOTAL := X[1];
        HI := X[1];
        FOR I := 1 TO 5
         DO BEGIN
            TOTAL := TOTAL + X[I];
            IF X[I] > HI
              THEN HI := X[I]
            END;
        WRITELN(' ':10, 'TOTAL =', TOTAL:4, 'HI =':5, HI:3);
        WRITELN('<---':10, 'END OF CPROG')
        END (* OF PROCEDURE CPROG *);

    BEGIN (* FUNCTION APROG *)
    WRITELN('--->':5, 'BEGINNING APROG');
    CPROG;
    APROG := TOTAL DIV HI;
    WRITELN('<---':5, 'END OF APROG')
    END (* OF FUNCTION APROG *);

PROCEDURE BPROG;

    VAR
        M : INTEGER;
    BEGIN (* PROCEDURE BPROG *)
    WRITELN('--->':5, 'BEGINNING BPROG');
    FOR I := 1 TO 5
     DO X[I] := X[I] + I;
    M := APROG * 3;
    WRITELN(' ':5, 'M =', M:3);
    WRITELN('<---':5, 'END OF BPROG')
    END (* OF PROCEDURE BPROG *);

BEGIN (* PROGRAM MAINPROG *)
WRITELN('BEGINNING MAINPROG');
X[1] := 25; X[2] := 32; X[3] := 10; X[4] := 4; X[5] := 17;
WRITE('ARRAY X:');
FOR I := 1 TO 5
 DO WRITE(X[I]:5);
```

```
WRITELN;
N := APROG;
WRITELN('N =', N:3);
BPROG;
WRITE('ARRAY X:');
FOR I := 1 TO 5
  DO WRITE(X[I]:5);
WRITELN;
WRITELN('END OF MAINPROG')
END (* OF PROGRAM MAINPROG *).
```

The WRITE and WRITELN statements in the program MAINPROG trace the progress of the program. Here is the output that will be produced.

```
BEGINNING MAINPROG
ARRAY X:    25    32    10     4    17
 --->BEGINNING APROG
     --->BEGINNING CPROG
         TOTAL = 113 HI = 32
     <---END OF CPROG
 <---END OF APROG
N =   3
 --->BEGINNING BPROG
 --->BEGINNING APROG
     --->BEGINNING CPROG
         TOTAL = 129 HI = 34
     <---END OF CPROG
 <---END OF APROG
     M = 9
 <---END OF BPROG
ARRAY X:    26    34    13     8    22
END OF MAINPROG
```

Identifiers used in subprograms have been termed local or global several times in this chapter. These designations refer to the relative **scope of an identifier** in a program. The scope of an identifier is the program block in which it is defined. For instance, the scope of the identifier TOTAL used in the program MAINPROG is the APROG block and TOTAL is said to be local to the function APROG. The procedure CPROG may use TOTAL because the CPROG block is nested inside the APROG block. Since the procedure CPROG has access to TOTAL because TOTAL has been defined in a block that contains the CPROG block, the identifier TOTAL is global with respect to the procedure CPROG. In general, an identifier used in a subprogram block is global with respect to that subprogram if its meaning has been established in some outer block containing the subprogram. The variables X and I used in the CPROG block are global with respect to the CPROG block because the meanings they have in the procedure CPROG were established in the MAINPROG block.

We have already noted that the names of formal parameters are local identifiers for the subprogram in which they are declared. A subprogram that uses only its formal parameters and local identifiers defined in its declaration section is virtually independent of any outer block in which it resides. When local identifiers are defined for subprograms, there is a possibility that two or more program blocks will have different definitions for the same identifier. One such case is illustrated in the following diagram.

PROGRAM MAIN (INPUT, OUTPUT);

```
VAR
        A : ARRAY [1..20] OF REAL;
PROCEDURE SUBPROG;

    VAR
            A : CHAR;
    BEGIN (* PROCEDURE SUBPROG *)
        •
        •
        •
    END (* OF PROCEDURE SUBPROG *);

BEGIN (* MAIN PROGRAM *)
    •
    •
    •
END (* OF MAIN PROGRAM *).
```

Within the MAIN block, A is an array with 20 REAL components. The procedure SUBPROG cannot reference this array because the identifier A has been redefined in the SUBPROG block. While the procedure SUBPROG is active, the identifier A serves as the name of a local CHAR variable. The array named A still exists and it contains whatever values it has been assigned by the MAIN program, but it cannot be accessed because the identifier A has a different meaning in the procedure SUBPROG. When SUBPROG ends and control is passed back to the MAIN program, the array named A is available again and the CHAR variable named A is not. The general rule is that a local definition for an identifier in a subprogram block supersedes any global definition that identifier might otherwise have had in that block.

The use of several definitions for the same identifier in a program is a poor programming practice. Such programs are more difficult to read and more likely to contain errors than those in which every identifier has a unique meaning. Examine the program MISSINGLETTERS shown next. MISSINGLETTERS does not violate any Pascal language rules; it will execute without error.

```
PROGRAM MISSINGLETTERS (INPUT, OUTPUT);
TYPE
     STRING100 = ARRAY [1 .. 100] OF CHAR;
VAR
     N, M : INTEGER;
     I : CHAR;
     X : STRING100;

PROCEDURE GETSTRING (VAR Y : STRING100; VAR L : INTEGER);
  BEGIN (* PROCEDURE GETSTRING *)
```

```
    L := 0;
    WRITELN('ENTER ANY STRING OF UP TO 100 CHARACTERS.');
    WHILE (NOT EOLN) AND (L <= 100)
        DO BEGIN (* CHARACTER INPUT *)
            L := L + 1;
            READ(Y[L])
            END (* OF CHARACTER INPUT *);
    WRITELN
    END (* OF PROCEDURE GETSTRING *);

FUNCTION FINDLETTER (L : CHAR; M : STRING100; N : INTEGER) : BOOLEAN;
    TYPE
        STATUS = (NOTFOUND, FOUND);
    VAR
        C : INTEGER;
        X : STATUS;
    BEGIN (* FUNCTION FINDLETTER *)
    C := 0;
    X := NOTFOUND;
    REPEAT
        C := C + 1;
        IF M[C] = L
            THEN X := FOUND
    UNTIL (X = FOUND) OR (C = N);
    IF X = FOUND
        THEN FINDLETTER := TRUE
        ELSE FINDLETTER := FALSE
    END (* OF FUNCTION FINDLETTER *);

BEGIN (* PROGRAM MISSINGLETTERS *)
GETSTRING(X, N);
M := 0;
FOR I := 'A' TO 'Z'
 DO IF NOT FINDLETTER(I, X, N)
        THEN BEGIN
            M := M + 1;
            WRITE(I:2)
            END;
WRITELN;
WRITELN('THE', M:3, ' LETTERS SHOWN ABOVE ARE NOT IN THE INPUT ',
        'STRING.')
END (* OF PROGRAM MISSINGLETTERS *).
```

MISSINGLETTERS will accept up to 100 characters as input and will then print all the letters that do not appear at least once in the input string. Here is the output from a sample run of the program.

```
ENTER ANY STRING OF UP TO 100 CHARACTERS.
?THE EVENING STARS ARE SHINING BRIGHTLY IN THE SKY.

C D F J M O P Q U W X Z
THE 12 LETTERS SHOWN ABOVE ARE NOT IN THE INPUT STRING.
```

The identifiers L, M, N, and X are all defined twice in MISSINGLETTERS. While the procedure GETSTRING is active, L identifies an INTEGER variable. After GETSTRING has ended, that meaning for L no longer applies. Within the main program L has no meaning at all, but in the function FINDLETTER L is a CHAR variable. The input characters are stored in an array that the main program knows as X. However, the characters are read by the procedure GETSTRING and assigned to the array M, which is a formal parameter for that procedure. The variable X is matched with the parameter M when GETSTRING is called so that the main program will get the string of characters in the array X. Within the main program M is an integer variable, and in the function FINDLETTER X is a variable of the user-defined type STATUS. The identifier N is the name for an INTEGER variable in the main program, but N is an INTEGER parameter for the function FINDLETTER. Does this sound confusing? You bet it does! Of course, that the program contains insufficient documentation makes matters worse. MISSINGLETTERS is a terrible program. It was presented here merely to dramatize how difficult it can be to read a program in which the meanings of identifiers vary from block to block. Such confusion can be avoided by using more descriptive names as identifiers.

8.3 EXERCISES

1. The following questions concern the program MAINPROG (page 299):

   a. Would the program MAINPROG execute without error if the procedure CPROG were declared in the main block rather than in the APROG block? If so, would the output be the same? Explain your answers.

   b. How would the program MAINPROG be affected if the procedure CPROG were declared in the BPROG block instead of in the APROG block?

   c. At the beginning of MAINPROG, the components of the array X are assigned the values 25, 32, 10, 4, and 17. Show how the output would appear if X were assigned the values 15, 48, 29, 37, and 8 instead.

2. Discuss the feasibility and desirability of nesting the subprograms that appear in the programs SCORER (page 270) and PRICER (page 292).

3. Two different block structures for a program are depicted here. Tell which subprograms the main program and each subprogram can and cannot call. Give reasons for your answers.

a.

PROGRAM MAIN1 (INPUT,OUTPUT);

> PROCEDURE A;
>
> > FUNCTION B : CHAR;
> >
> > PROCEDURE C;
> >
> > FUNCTION D : REAL;
> >
> > PROCEDURE E;
> >
> > > PROCEDURE F;

b.

PROGRAM MAIN2 (INPUT,OUTPUT);

> PROCEDURE A;
>
> FUNCTION B : CHAR;
>
> > PROCEDURE C;
>
> FUNCTION D : REAL;
>
> > PROCEDURE E;
> >
> > PROCEDURE F;

4. Revise the program MISSINGLETTERS (page 301) to make it more readable. Insert comments at appropriate places and avoid defining identifiers more than once in the program.

5. Suppose that the following subprograms appear in the main block of a program in the order shown.

```
        PROCEDURE GAMMA (K : INTEGER);

           FUNCTION DELTA : CHAR;
             BEGIN (* FUNCTION DELTA *)
             DELTA := 'D'
             END (* OF FUNCTION DELTA *);

           BEGIN (* PROCEDURE GAMMA *)
           IF K > 0
             THEN WRITE(DELTA, 'G')
             ELSE WRITE('G', DELTA)
           END (* OF PROCEDURE GAMMA *);

        PROCEDURE ALPHA (N : INTEGER);

           PROCEDURE BETA;
             BEGIN (* PROCEDURE BETA *)
             WRITE('B')
             END (* OF PROCEDURE BETA *);

           BEGIN (* PROCEDURE ALPHA *)
           WRITE('A');
           IF N > 0
             THEN BETA
             ELSE GAMMA(10 - N)
           END (* OF PROCEDURE ALPHA *);
```

Assume that each of the following program segments appears in the main program and show the output that each will generate:

a.   ALPHA(20);   b.   ALPHA(5);
              GAMMA(20);   GAMMA(0);
              WRITELN   WRITELN

c.   GAMMA(-5);   d.   GAMMA(7);
              ALPHA(0);   ALPHA(-5);
              WRITELN   WRITELN

e.   ALPHA(2);   f.   GAMMA(-10);
              WRITELN;   WRITELN;
              GAMMA(25);   ALPHA(-5);
              WRITELN   WRITELN

8.4
FURTHER USES FOR FUNCTIONS AND PROCEDURES

In this section we will examine some features of Pascal subprograms that are not used as frequently as those we have already studied.

RECURSION

When an activity can be defined in a manner that makes reference to a simpler form of the same activity, the definition is said to be **recursive.** There are many activities that have recursive definitions. One of these is the raising of a number to a whole number power. Suppose we want to calculate the value of X^N where X is any number and N is a nonnegative integer. If X is not 0.0 at the same time that N = 0 (zero raised to the zero power is not defined), the value of X^N is defined recursively by the mathematical equations

$$X^0 = 1.0$$

and

$$X^N = (X^{N-1})X$$

when N is greater than 0. This definition is recursive because X raised to the power N is defined in terms of X raised to the power N − 1. A nonrecursive definition of X^N is that it is 1.0 multiplied by X a total of N times. This definition is easy to implement in the form of a function subprogram:

```
FUNCTION POWER (X : REAL; N : INTEGER) : REAL;
   VAR
        I : INTEGER;
        PRODUCT : REAL;
   BEGIN (* FUNCTION POWER *)
   PRODUCT := 1.0;
   FOR I := 1 TO N
    DO PRODUCT := PRODUCT * X;
   POWER := PRODUCT
   END (* OF FUNCTION POWER *);
```

In order for the recursive definition of X^N to be implemented, it must be possible for a function to call itself in order to calculate a reduced power of X. A subprogram that calls itself is said to be a **recursive subprogram.** Many of the more popular programming languages do not allow subprograms to be recursive, but in Pascal both functions and procedures may be recursive. In essence, a subprogram's call to itself is a call to an exact, yet distinct, copy of that subprogram. Despite this fact, the subprogram need be declared only once.

The ability to understand recursion and to develop recursive subprograms does not come easily to many programmers. It is a skill that often takes many hours of careful study as well as trial and error to learn.

A recursive function to generate the value of X^N is given next. As you read this subprogram, keep in mind that POWERIZE, X, and N identify new memory locations every time the function is called.

```
FUNCTION POWERIZE (X : REAL; N : INTEGER) : REAL;
   BEGIN (* FUNCTION POWERIZE *)
   IF N = 0
     THEN POWERIZE := 1.0
     ELSE POWERIZE := X * POWERIZE(X, N - 1)
   END (* OF FUNCTION POWERIZE *);
```

Execution of one copy of POWERIZE is temporarily suspended when a call to another copy of POWERIZE is made. Each call to POWERIZE specifies a power that is reduced by 1. That is, when POWERIZE makes a call to itself, new value parameters X and N are allocated and the value passed to N is 1 less than the value of N received by the copy of POWERIZE that issued the call. Eventually, POWERIZE will receive a 0 value for N and that value will trigger the actual calculation of the value of X^N. In order to understand how POWERIZE can be used, consider the following program.

```
PROGRAM POWERTEST (OUTPUT);
VAR
    Y, Z : REAL;
    K : INTEGER;

FUNCTION POWERIZE (X : REAL; N : INTEGER) : REAL;
  BEGIN (* FUNCTION POWERIZE *)
  WRITELN(' ':3*N, 'BEGINNING POWERIZE WITH N =', N:2);
  IF N = 0
    THEN POWERIZE := 1.0
    ELSE POWERIZE := X * POWERIZE(X, N - 1);
  WRITELN(' ':3*N, 'END OF POWERIZE WITH N =', N:2)
  END (* OF FUNCTION POWERIZE *);

BEGIN (* PROGRAM POWERTEST *)
Y := 2.0;
K := 3;
Z := POWERIZE(Y, K);
WRITELN;
WRITELN(Y:4:1, ' RAISED TO THE POWER ', K:1, ' EQUALS ', Z:4:2)
END (* OF PROGRAM POWERTEST *).
```

The output generated by the program POWERTEST is

```
            BEGINNING POWERIZE WITH N = 3
          BEGINNING POWERIZE WITH N = 2
        BEGINNING POWERIZE WITH N = 1
      BEGINNING POWERIZE WITH N = 0
      END OF POWERIZE WITH N = 0
        END OF POWERIZE WITH N = 1
          END OF POWERIZE WITH N = 2
            END OF POWERIZE WITH N = 3

2.0 RAISED TO THE POWER 3 EQUALS 8.00
```

There are several reasons why the nonrecursive function POWER is superior to the recursive function POWERIZE. First, POWER is much easier to read and understand. The ability to work comfortably with recursion and recursive programs is developed through practice. Another disadvantage to using POWERIZE is that storage must be allocated to the parameters X and N every time POWERIZE calls itself. In general, use of a recursive subprogram can be very costly in terms of storage.

Any function or procedure that is recursive can be replaced by a nonrecursive subprogram that employs one or more loops. However, there are tasks for which recursive subprograms are preferable to the nonrecursive alternatives. Suppose we want to write a subprogram that will print the binary representation of any nonnegative integer. (See Problem 7, Section 6.5, for details concerning the binary representation of integers.) The binary form of an integer consists of a sequence of 1's and 0's referred to as bits. For instance, the integer 37 is the value of $1(2^5) + 0(2^4) + 0(2^3) + 1(2^2) + 0(2^1) + 1(2^0)$, which makes 100101 the binary representation of 37. The bits can be generated sequentially, right to left, by successively DIViding the integer to be converted and the resulting quotients by 2 until a zero quotient is achieved. The following table illustrates this process for the integer 37.

Sequence of Divisions	Remainders	
$\dfrac{18}{2\overline{)37}}$	1	(rightmost bit)
$\dfrac{9}{2\overline{)18}}$	0	
$\dfrac{4}{2\overline{)9}}$	1	
$\dfrac{2}{2\overline{)4}}$	0	
$\dfrac{1}{2\overline{)2}}$	0	
$\dfrac{0}{2\overline{)1}}$	1	(leftmost bit)

Note that the bits are generated in reverse order of their presence in the binary form of 37. The procedure CONVERTTOBINARY that follows utilizes an array to store the remainders and then prints the bits stored in the array in reverse order of their generation.

```
PROCEDURE CONVERTTOBINARY (X : INTEGER);
  TYPE
        INDICES = 1 .. 50;
  VAR
        N, K : INTEGER;
        BITS : ARRAY [INDICES] OF 0 .. 1;
BEGIN (* PROCEDURE CONVERTTOBINARY *)
N := 0;
REPEAT
  N := N + 1;
  BITS [N] := X MOD 2;
  X := X DIV 2
UNTIL X = 0;
FOR K := 1 TO N
  DO WRITE (BITS [K]:1);
WRITELN
END (* OF PROCEDURE CONVERTTOBINARY *);
```

When the procedure CONVERTTOBINARY is called, storage is allocated for the entire array BITS even when the binary form of X consists of only a few binary digits. Also, each bit is stored in one component of the array BITS, and so the total number of remainders generated cannot exceed the number of components in the array. Now consider the following nested procedures:

```
PROCEDURE BINARYFORM (X : INTEGER);
   PROCEDURE PRINTBITS (QUOTIENT : INTEGER);
      BEGIN (* PROCEDURE PRINTBITS *)
      IF QUOTIENT DIV 2 <> 0
        THEN PRINTBITS(QUOTIENT DIV 2);
      WRITE(QUOTIENT MOD 2:1)
      END (* OF PROCEDURE PRINTBITS *);
   BEGIN (* PROCEDURE BINARYFORM *)
   PRINTBITS(X);
   WRITELN
   END (* OF PROCEDURE BINARYFORM *);
```

The recursive procedure PRINTBITS generates the binary form of X when it is called by the procedure BINARYFORM. No array is needed to store the bits because they will be generated in the proper order. It is true that storage for a new QUOTIENT parameter will be allocated each time PRINTBITS is called, but note that there is no limit on how many binary digits may be generated.

All the recursive subprograms we have looked at up to now call themselves directly. It is possible for a subprogram to call another subprogram that in turn calls the first subprogram. This is known as **mutual recursion.** In many versions of Pascal a subprogram can call another subprogram that is declared in the same block only if the subprogram to be called is declared before the subprogram that makes the call. Suppose procedures A and B are declared in the order depicted here.

```
PROCEDURE B (VAR X : REAL; Y, Z : INTEGER);

   BEGIN (* PROCEDURE B *)
       .
       .
       .

   END (* OF PROCEDURE B *);

PROCEDURE A (CH : CHAR; VAR I : INTEGER);

   BEGIN (* PROCEDURE A *)
       .
       .
       .


   END (* OF PROCEDURE A *);
```

Procedure A will be able to call procedure B because the declaration of B precedes the declaration of A. Depending on the version of Pascal, procedure B may or may not be able to call procedure A. If not, it appears that the procedures A and B cannot be mutually recursive. This situation can be remedied by making a **forward declaration** of the procedure A prior to the declaration of procedure B. A forward declaration for a subprogram consists of that subprogram's heading followed immediately by a single statement consisting solely of the keyword FORWARD. When the actual declaration of the subprogram is made later in the same declaration section, its formal parameters need not be specified again in the heading. The use of a forward declaration is illustrated next.

```
PROCEDURE A (CH : CHAR; VAR I : INTEGER);
  FORWARD;

PROCEDURE B (VAR X : REAL; Y, Z : INTEGER);

  BEGIN (* PROCEDURE B *)
      .
      .
      .


  END (* OF PROCEDURE B *);

PROCEDURE A;

  BEGIN (* PROCEDURE A *)
      .
      .
      .


  END (* OF PROCEDURE A *);
```

With this arrangement it is possible for procedure B to call procedure A. Thus, procedures A and B may be mutually recursive.

PROCEDURE AND FUNCTION PARAMETERS †

We know that a formal parameter section in a function or procedure heading may contain a declaration of either a value parameters or variable parameters. It is also possible for functions and procedures to be passed as parameters to other functions and procedures. Consider the following two functions, each of which may be used to compute a gross salary for a salesperson that is based on the person's total sales for a pay period:

†This section describes the use of formal parameters of the types FUNCTION and PROCEDURE in subprograms according to the Pascal standard proposed by the International Standards Organization.

```
FUNCTION SALARY1 (TOTALSALES : REAL) : REAL;
  BEGIN (* FUNCTION SALARY1 *)
  IF TOTALSALES > 10000.00
    THEN SALARY1 := 1750.00 + 0.2 * (TOTALSALES - 10000.00)
    ELSE IF TOTALSALES > 5000.00
           THEN SALARY1 := 1000.00 + 0.15 * (TOTALSALES - 5000.00)
           ELSE SALARY1 := 1000.00
  END (* OF FUNCTION SALARY1 *);
```

```
        FUNCTION SALARY2 (SALESTOTAL : REAL) : REAL;
          BEGIN (* FUNCTION SALARY2 *)
          IF SALESTOTAL > 12000.00
            THEN SALARY2 := 0.25 * SALESTOTAL
            ELSE IF SALESTOTAL > 7500.00
                   THEN SALARY2 := 0.2 * SALESTOTAL
                   ELSE SALARY2 := 0.15 * SALESTOTAL
          END (* OF FUNCTION SALARY2 *);
```

Suppose a procedure named PAYROLLER will compute the gross salary, tax deductions, and net salary for a salesperson and return these values to the calling program. The procedure PAYROLLER must receive the state and federal tax rates, sales amount, and the appropriate salary computation function (SALARY1 or SALARY2) from the calling program. For instance, either of the following procedure statements would constitute a valid call to PAYROLLER:

```
PAYROLLER(SALARY1, SALESAMOUNT, STATEPCT, FEDPCT, TAXSTATE, TAXFED,
          GROSSPAY, NETPAY)
```

```
PAYROLLER(SALARY2, SALESAMOUNT, STATEPCT, FEDPCT, TAXSTATE, TAXFED,
          GROSSPAY, NETPAY)
```

In order for the procedure PAYROLLER just described to process a salesperson's salary correctly, it must recognize the first actual parameter in the call as the name of a function. This requires that the first formal parameter in the procedure heading be a FUNCTION type parameter that consists of a function heading, as illustrated here.

```
PROCEDURE PAYROLLER (FUNCTION PAY (X : REAL) : REAL;
                     SALES, STATERATE, FEDRATE : REAL;
                     VAR STATETAX, FEDTAX, GROSS, NET : REAL);
  BEGIN (* PROCEDURE PAYROLLER *)
  GROSS := PAY(SALES);
  STATETAX := STATERATE * GROSS;
  FEDTAX := FEDRATE * GROSS;
  NET := GROSS - STATETAX - FEDTAX
  END (* OF PROCEDURE PAYROLLER *);
```

Within the procedure PAYROLLER, PAY is the formal name of the function used to compute a GROSS salary. Note that when the function parameter PAY is declared in the procedure heading, X is specified as the formal parameter for the function PAY. Just as PAY is the formal name for an actual function specified in a call to the procedure PAYROLLER, X is the formal name of the one parameter that function must have. That is, the first actual parameter specified in a call to PAYROLLER must be a function that has one REAL type value parameter and returns a REAL result.

A PROCEDURE type parameter is declared in a formal parameter section that takes the form of a procedure heading. Consider the following heading for a procedure in which the procedure parameter MATCH is declared:

```
PROCEDURE SCAN (PROCEDURE MATCH (SYMBOL : CHAR; VAR COUNT : INTEGER);
           LENGTH : INTEGER; VAR G : STRING);
```

When SCAN is called, the first actual parameter specified must be the name of a procedure that has two formal parameters, a CHAR type value parameter and an INTEGER type variable parameter. The second and third actual parameters must correspond properly to the formal parameters LENGTH and G, respectively.

8.4 EXERCISES

1. Write a recursive subprogram that will print a row of asterisks, one asterisk per call. The number of asterisks to be printed should be specified as a parameter in the initial call to the subprogram.

2. The factorial of a nonnegative integer n (denoted by n!) is defined recursively as $0! = 1$ and $n! = n(n - 1)!$. (See Problem 4, Section 7.5.) Write a recursive function that will generate the factorial of a nonnegative integer.

3. The Fibonacci numbers are defined recursively by the formulas $F_1 = 1$, $F_2 = 1$, and $F_n = F_{n-1} + F_{n-2}$ for n greater than 2. (See Exercise 5, Section 6.2.) Write a recursive subprogram that will generate and print the first n Fibonacci numbers.

8.5 PROGRAMMING PROBLEMS

Problems 1 through 10 involve writing specific subprograms. Some of these problems indicate whether the subprogram should be a function or a procedure and others do not. In the latter case, choose the form of the subprogram that best meets the requirements of the problem.

1. Write a function that will count the number of times a particular character appears in a character string.

2. Suppose that two one-dimensional arrays with REAL components have been ordered so that the component values are in ascending order. The two arrays do not necessarily contain the same number of values, but they both have the same index type. Write a procedure that will form one sorted array by merging the two sorted arrays.

3. Write a function that will round a REAL number to an indicated decimal place. That decimal place will be specified as an INTEGER value, say n. If n is positive, the decimal place is to the left of the decimal point. For instance, when n is 2 and the number is 4076.36, the rounding should occur at the tens place (two places to the left of the decimal point) and the result should be the number 4080.0. If n is negative, the rounding should occur to the right of the decimal point. For example, when n is -1 and the number is 4076.36, the rounding should occur at the tenths place (one place to the right of the decimal point), which yields the value 4076.4.

4. The multiplication of two $n \times n$ matrices is described in Problem 12 of Section 7.5. Write a procedure that will find the product of two $n \times n$ matrices.

5. Write a subprogram that will scan a character string passed as a parameter and determine the set of letters that are in the string and the set of digits that are in the string.

6. The commission earned by a salesperson is determined by the dollar amount of sales for that person according to the following table:

Total Sales	Commission
Less than $1000	5% of the total sales
$1000 or more up to $5000	$50 plus 8% of the sales over $1000
$5000 or more	$370 plus 12% of the sales over $5000

Write a subprogram that will calculate the commission for a salesperson given the total sales for that person.

7. When the values of a, b, and c are known, the equation

$$ax^2 + bx + c = 0$$

can be solved for x by using the quadratic formula:

$$x = \frac{-b + \sqrt{b^2 - 4ac}}{2a}$$

and

$$x = \frac{-b - \sqrt{b^2 - 4ac}}{2a}$$

There will be two distinct REAL solutions when $b^2 - 4ac$ is greater than zero, but only one solution when $b^2 - 4ac$ equals zero. If $b^2 - 4ac$ is less than zero there are no REAL solutions. Write a subprogram that will solve a quadratic equation given the values a, b, and c. When $b^2 - 4ac$ is negative, the subprogram should have some way of indicating to the calling program that there are no REAL solutions.

8. Write a subprogram to solve a quadratic equation as described in Problem 8, but handle the case when $b^2 - 4ac$ is less than zero in a different manner. If $b^2 - 4ac$ is negative, the solutions to the equation are the complex numbers

$$\frac{-b}{2a} + \frac{d}{2a}i \quad \text{and} \quad \frac{-b}{2a} - \frac{d}{2a}i$$

where i represents $\sqrt{-1}$ and d equals $\sqrt{-(b^2 - 4ac)}$. The subprogram should indicate to the calling program whether there are two distinct REAL solutions, one REAL solution, or two complex solutions, and it should find those solutions.

9. The bubble sort is a method for sorting an array. It is based on the principle that in a sorted array the values of any two consecutive components will be in the proper order. The bubble sorting process consists of a series of passes through the array during which the values of consecutive components are compared and, when they are out of order, interchanged. A single pass through an array containing eight values is depicted below for the case in which the array must be sorted in ascending order.

→ 45 ₁	38	38	38	38	38	38	38
→ 38	→ 45	45	45	45	45	45	45
75	→ 75	→ 75 ₁	57	57	57	57	57
57	57	→ 57	→ 75	75	75	75	75
91	91	91	→ 91	→ 91 ₁	57	57	57
57	57	57	57	→ 57	→ 91 ₁	68	68
68	68	68	68	68	→ 68	→ 91 ₁	83
83	83	83	83	83	83	→ 83	91

The arrows indicate the pairs of values that are compared during the pass, and the letter I indicates that a pair is out of order and should be interchanged. Note that a pass through an array containing eight values requires seven comparisons. In the pass depicted here, five interchanges were required and the array still is not sorted. The subprogram should continue to make passes through the array until no interchanges are required during a pass. Write a subprogram that will bubble sort an array of INTEGER values.

10. An integer can be represented in hexadecimal (base 16) form by using the digits 0 through 9 and the letters A through F. For instance, the hexadecimal number 2B8E represents the decimal (base 10) number 11150, since

$$11150 = 2(16)^3 + 11(16)^2 + 8(16)^1 + 14(16)^0$$

In a hexadecimal number, A represents 10, B represents 11, C represents 12, D represents 13, E represents 14, and F represents 15. The hexadecimal form of an integer can be generated by successively DIViding that number by 16 and retaining the remainders. These remainders yield the required hexadecimal digits in reverse order, as illustrated below.

Quotients:	696	43	2	0
	16)11150	16)696	16)43	16)2
Remainders:	14	8	11	2
Hexadecimal:	E	8	B	2

Write a subprogram that will convert a nonnegative integer into hexadecimal form. Create the hexadecimal form as a character string.

Problems 11 through 15 require that complete programs be written. Each of these programs should make use of appropriate subprograms.

11. Write the program to generate a sales report for Krantz, Inc., as described in Problem 6, Section 7.5.

12. Write the program to generate a class schedule for a student as described in Problems 7 and 10, Section 7.5.

13. Write the program to process flight reservations for Trans-City Airlines as described in Problems 8 and 9, Section 7.5.

14. In a cryptogram, each letter stands for some other letter. One way to create a cryptogram is simply to rotate the letters in the alphabet, as shown here.

Alphabet: A B C D E F G H I J K L M N O P Q R S T U V W X Y Z
Rotation: I J K L M N O P Q R S T U V W X Y Z A B C D E F G H

Each letter in a message can then be replaced by the letter that is in the same position in the rotation. For instance, the rotation just shown would be used to code a message as follows.

Original message: ON A CLEAR DAY, YOU CAN SEE FOREVER.
Coded message: WV I KTMIZ LIG, GWC KIV AMM NWZMDMZ.

To make the coded message more confusing, the punctuation can be removed:

WV I KTMIZ LIG GWC KIV AMM NWZMDMZ

Since the message can still be decoded by simple replacement, let's switch successive pairs of letters or letter and blank space pairs, starting from the left side:

VWI K MTZIL GIG CWK VIA MMN ZWDMZM

Finally, place the character corresponding to A (an I) at the beginning of the message so that the coder knows which rotation was used:

IVWI K MTZIL GIG CWK VIA MMN ZWDMZM

Write a program that will encode a message by the process just described. The program should read the message and a number between 1 and 26 that indicates the rotation to use. If the number read is N, the Nth letter in the alphabet should be used as the letter corresponding to A. (Note that if N is 1, A will correspond to A and there will be no rotation.)

15. Write a program that will decode a message that has been encoded by the method described in Problem 14. The first letter in the coded message will be the letter corresponding to A in the rotation.

NINE/SETS AND RECORDS

Arrays are very useful for storing quantities of data. The indexing feature provides ready access to individual values stored in array components. There are many other varieties of structured data types that can be defined in Pascal programs and used to declare variables. Two of these varieties, set types and record types, are discussed in this chapter.

9.1
SETS

In Pascal a set is a collection of scalar values of the same type. Each component of a set is called an **element.** A set is represented by enclosing a list of its elements in brackets. For example, the set whose elements are the integers 5, 12, and 28 could be represented by [5, 12, 28]. The order in which the elements of a set are listed is unimportant. Two sets are considered equal when they have exactly the same elements regardless of the order in which those elements are listed. Hence, the set containing 5, 12, and 28 can be represented in any one of the following forms:

[5, 12, 28]	[5, 28, 12]	[12, 5, 28]
[12, 28, 5]	[28, 5, 12]	[28, 12, 5]

A Pascal set is fundamentally the same as the mathematical notion of a set, although in mathematics the elements of a set are usually enclosed in braces instead of brackets. Another difference is that a Pascal set may contain elements of only a single ordinal type (for example, all integers). The basic set operations in mathematics, such as set union and intersection, are implemented in the Pascal language.

SET TYPES AND VARIABLES

A set type can be established by a TYPE definition of the form

type-identifier = SET OF *base-type;*

The *base-type* for a set specifies the data type for the elements. As noted, this *base-type* must be an ordinal data type (it cannot be REAL). Consider the following set types:

```
TYPE
      SEGMENTS = SET OF 3 .. 9;
      GRADES = SET OF 'A' .. 'E';
```

The identifier SEGMENTS is the name for all possible sets whose elements come from the subrange 3..9 and the identifier GRADES is the name for all possible sets whose elements come from the subrange 'A'..'E'. One set of the type SEGMENTS is the set containing all values in the subrange 3..9, which is known as the **universal set** of the type SEGMENTS. The universal sets of the types SEGMENTS and GRADES are [3, 4, 5, 6, 7, 8, 9] and ['A', 'B', 'C', 'D', 'E'], respectively. Every element of a SEGMENTS type set must be an element of the universal set of that type. When one set contains only elements that are also in a second set, the first set is said to be a **subset** of the second set. For instance, [4, 6, 7] is a subset of the universal set of the type SEGMENTS. In fact, every SEGMENTS type set is a subset of the set [3, 4, 5, 6, 7, 8, 9]. It turns out that the seven-element set [3, 4, 5, 6, 7, 8, 9] has a total of 2^7 (or 128) different subsets. One of those subsets is the universal set itself (because any set qualifies as a subset of itself) and another subset is the one that is void of any elements. This set is known as the **empty set** or **null set** and it is denoted by [ ]. In general, the number of elements in the universal set of a particular set type is the cardinality of its base type. If a universal set contains n elements, it will have 2^n different subsets, including itself and the empty set. If follows that there are 2^5 (or 32) distinct sets of the type GRADES.

The base type for a set may be a user-defined ordinal data type. Consider the following definitions:

```
TYPE
      DARKCOLORS = (ORANGE, PURPLE, BROWN, BLACK);
      COLORCOMBOS = SET OF DARKCOLORS;
```

Since there are four constants of the type DARKCOLORS, there must be 2^4 (or 16) different sets of the type COLORCOMBOS. These sets are listed below.

Sets of the Type COLORCOMBOS

0-element set:	[ ]
1-element sets:	[ORANGE] [PURPLE] [BROWN] [BLACK]
2-element sets:	[ORANGE, PURPLE] [ORANGE, BROWN]
	[ORANGE, BLACK] [PURPLE, BROWN]
	[PURPLE, BLACK] [BROWN, BLACK]
3-element sets:	[ORANGE, PURPLE, BROWN] [ORANGE, PURPLE, BLACK]
	[ORANGE, BROWN, BLACK] [PURPLE, BROWN, BLACK]
4-element set:	[ORANGE, PURPLE, BROWN, BLACK]

Remember that one set is distinguished from another by comparing the contents of the sets. Two sets with exactly the same elements, regardless of the order in which the elements are listed, are equal. Thus [ORANGE, PURPLE] and [PURPLE, ORANGE] are simply two representations of the same set.

Subrange notation can be used to abbreviate the representations of some sets. For example, the set whose elements are 4, 5, 6, and 7 can be represented in the usual form [4, 5, 6, 7] or in the equivalent form [4..7]. Similarly, the set [3, 4, 5, 7, 8, 9] can be represented as [3..5, 7..9] and the set [4, 7, 8, 9] is equivalent to [4, 7..9].

We have already mentioned that the base type for a set cannot be REAL. Most versions of Pascal impose a limit on the number of elements a set can have and it is likely that this limit will exclude the types INTEGER and CHAR as base types for sets. Of course, a subrange of INTEGER or CHAR may serve as the base type for a set, as is the case for sets of the types SEGMENTS and GRADES. It is also possible that a set of integers cannot contain any elements that are negative or outside some subrange of type INTEGER that starts at 0, such as 0..58. This statement means that the subranges − 5..20 and 34..72 cannot be used as base types for sets when the elements of sets of integers are restricted to the subrange 0..58. Since these restrictions vary from one version of Pascal to another, programs that use sets may not be compatible with every implementation of the Pascal language.

Set types are normally defined so that set variables can be declared. A set variable may have as its value any set of the type specified for that variable. Consider the following definitions and declarations.

```
TYPE
    FRUITS = (APPLE, PEACH, PLUM, CHERRY, GRAPE, BANANA, PEAR);
    APPETIZERS = SET OF FRUITS;
    AGERANGE = 15 .. 55;
    AGEGROUP = SET OF AGERANGE;
VAR
    SUPPER, LUNCH : APPETIZERS;
    I, J : AGERANGE;
    MARRIED, SINGLE, DIVORCED : AGEGROUP;
```

Like all other kinds of variables, a set variable has no value until it is assigned a value. One way to assign a set to a set variable is by using an assignment statement. Here are some examples.

```
        SUPPER := [APPLE, CHERRY, BANANA]

        LUNCH := [PEACH .. GRAPE]

        MARRIED := [19 .. 25, 29, 32, 40 .. 49]

        SINGLE := [18 .. 29, 35 .. 41, 45, 48, 52 .. 55]

        DIVORCED := []
```

The variables SUPPER and LUNCH may be assigned any sets whose elements are of the type FRUITS, and the variables MARRIED, SINGLE, and DIVORCED may be assigned any sets whose elements are of the type AGERANGE. It should be noted that a one-element set such as [27] is not the same as the INTEGER value 27. The assignment statement SINGLE := [27] is valid, but SINGLE := 27 is illegal because the variable SINGLE may be assigned only a set value.

So far, when listing the elements of a set we have used only constants. In a program, any set element can appear as an expression whose value is of the base type for the set. Suppose the AGERANGE type variables I and J have values when the following assignment statement is executed.

```
        MARRIED := [J, I + J, 38, J - 2, 3 * (I MOD J)]
```

The set assigned to the variable MARRIED depends on the values of I and J. Here are some examples.

Value of I	Value of J	Set Assigned to MARRIED
33	18	[18, 51, 38, 16, 45]
29	22	[22, 51, 38, 20, 21]
22	17	[17, 39, 38, 15]

In the last example, the value of J − 2 is 15 and the value of 3 * (I MOD J) is 15. Thus 15 is an element of the set assigned to MARRIED, but it need appear only once in a representation of that set. When a set element is specified by using an expression, there is a danger that the value of the expression will not be of the desired base type. For instance, if I = 23 and J = 24, the assignment statement shown earlier will be equivalent to

MARRIED := [24, 47, 38, 22, 69]

This assignment is illegal because MARRIED may be assigned only a set whose elements are in the subrange AGEGROUP, and 9 is not in this subrange.

SET OPERATIONS

A simple set expression consists of two sets or set-valued variables that are separated by a set operator. There are three operations that can be performed on a pair of sets to produce a new set: **union, intersection,** and **difference.** The symbols used to denote these operations and the effects of each operation are described in Figure 9–1.

The union of two sets forms a third set by combining the first two sets. An element will be in the union of two sets only if it is in at least one of those sets. In contrast, the intersection of two sets produces a set containing only those values that are in both sets. Here are some examples.

Simple Set Expression	Value of the Expression
[2, 8, 13] + [3, 5, 8, 12]	[2, 3, 5, 8, 12, 13]
[2, 8, 13] * [3, 5, 8, 12]	[8]
[6, 7, 11, 20] + [3, 6, 9, 11, 20]	[3, 6, 7, 9, 11, 20]
[6, 7, 11, 20] * [3, 6, 9, 11, 20]	[6, 11, 20]
[4..14] + [1..3, 20..25]	[1..14, 20..25]
[4..14] * [1..3, 20..25]	[ ]

When the union or intersection of two sets is specified, the order in which the sets are listed is not signficant. For instance, the value of the set expression [2, 8, 13] + [3, 5, 8, 12] is the same as the value of the set expression [3, 5, 8, 12] + [2, 8, 13]. This is not the case for set difference. The difference of two sets depends on which of the two sets is given to the left of the difference operator. The difference [5, 8..11, 15] − [8, 10..14] produces the set [5, 9, 15], since 5, 9, and 15 are the only elements of [5, 8..11, 15] that are not in [8, 10..14]. On the other hand, [8, 10..14] − [5, 8..11, 15] yields the set [12..14] because 12, 13, and 14 are the only elements of [8, 10..14] that are not elements of [5, 8..11, 15]. Some other examples are given below.

Operation	Expression Form	Value of the Expression
Union	*set1* + *set2*	The set containing elements that are either in *set1* or in *set2* or in both of those sets
Intersection	*set1* * *set2*	The set containing elements that are in both *set1* and *set2*
Difference	*set1* − *set2*	The set containing elements that are in *set1* but not in *set2*

Figure 9–1
Set operations used to form new sets.

Simple Set Expression	Value of the Expression
[2, 8, 13] − [3, 5, 8, 12]	[2, 13]
[3, 5, 8, 12] − [2, 8, 13]	[3, 5, 12]
[7..11] − [4..9, 15..20]	[10, 11]
[4..9, 15..20] − [7..11]	[4..6, 15..20]
[1..7, 16] − [8, 10..14]	[1..7, 16]
[8, 10..14] − [1..7, 16]	[8, 10..14]

Set expressions, like arithmetic expressions, may contain several operators and operands. For instance, the expression

$$[2, 5..8] * [2..5, 8] + [3, 6, 8..10]$$

is valid and yields the set [2, 3, 5, 6, 8..10]. The set operators +, −, and * have the same priorities in the evaluation of a set expression as their counterparts have in the evaluation of an arithmetic expression; that is, intersection(*) takes precedence over both union(+) and difference (−). Below we illustrate the evaluation of a set expression by the same method that was used to evaluate an arithmetic expression in Chapter Three.

$$
\begin{array}{l}
[2, 5..8] * [2..5, 8] + [3, 6, 8..10] \\
\underline{\quad [2, 5, 8] \quad} + [3, 6, 8..10] \\
\underline{\quad [2, 3, 5, 6, 8..10] \quad}
\end{array}
$$

When a set expression contains no subexpressions enclosed in parentheses, the expression is evaluated from left to right in two passes, the first pass resolving all intersections and the second pass resolving all unions and differences as they are encountered. Parentheses can be used to force the operations to occur in a particular order. For example,

$$
\begin{array}{l}
[2, 5..8] * ([2..5, 8] + [3, 6, 8..10]) \\
[2, 5..8] * \underline{\quad [2..6, 8..10] \quad} \\
\underline{\quad [2, 5, 6, 8] \quad}
\end{array}
$$

There are four relational operators that can be used to make comparisons between pairs of sets. These operators and their meanings are given in Figure 9–2.

Relational Operator	Meaning
=	"Equals" or "is equal to"
<>	"Does not equal" or "is not equal to"
<=	"Is a subset of"
>=	"Contains" or "is a superset of"

Figure 9–2
Relational operations that can be applied to sets.

The value of a relational expression is either TRUE or FALSE. If A and B are two set variables that have been assigned values, A = B will be TRUE if and only if the sets A and B contain precisely the same elements; otherwise, A = B will be FALSE and A <> B will be TRUE. If every element of A is also an element of B, then A is a subset of B and A <= B has the value TRUE; otherwise, some element of A is not an element of B and A <= B is FALSE. The set B will be a superset of the set A if and only if A is a subset of B. Thus B >= A if and only if A <= B. Here are some examples of simple relational expressions involving sets and their values.

Relational Expression	Value of the Expression
[2, 6, 8, 9] = [6, 8, 9, 2]	TRUE
[7, 9, 13] <> [5, 7, 9]	TRUE
[5..8, 10] <= [5, 7..12]	FALSE
[3, 8] <= [1..4, 7..10]	TRUE
[2, 6, 9, 12, 15] >= [6, 8, 12]	FALSE
[2, 6, 9, 12, 15] >= [6, 12]	TRUE

Each of the set operators we have studied so far is applied to a pair of sets. The operator denoted by the keyword IN may be used in an expression of the form

element **IN** *set*

where *element* may be any constant, constant identifier, variable, or expression whose value is a possible member of the *set* specified. The value of such an expression is TRUE if the element is a component of the set; otherwise, the value of the expression is FALSE. Here are some examples.

Expression	Value of the Expression
5 IN [2, 3, 5, 9]	TRUE
11 IN [8..13] * [10..15]	TRUE
5 + 9 IN ([1..4, 9] + [5..8])	FALSE
'D' IN ['B'..'F']	TRUE
'G' IN ['A', 'C'..'E', 'J']	FALSE

Several of these expressions contain more than one operator. An expression may contain a variety of arithmetic, relational, logical, and set operators, provided that the arrangement of the operators and operands forms a well-defined expression.

Priority Level	Operators
1	NOT
2	* / DIV MOD AND
3	+ − OR
4	< <= > >= <> IN

Figure 9–3
Priority levels for all Pascal operators.

In order to recognize when such an expression is properly formed, we need to know the priority of each operator. These priorities are given in Figure 9–3. Note that the IN operator and all the relational operators have the lowest priority. Here is another example of the evaluation of an expression containing sets.

$$
\begin{array}{ccc}
[3, 5, 9, 12] * [1, 5, 7, 9] & <= & [4..6] + [7, 9, 12, 20] \\
\hline
[5, 9] & <= & [4..6] + [7, 9, 12, 20] \\
\hline
[5, 9] & <= & [4..7, 9, 12, 20] \\
\hline
& \text{TRUE} &
\end{array}
$$

USING SETS IN PROGRAMS

The elements of a set cannot be printed by specifying the set in a WRITE or WRITELN statement. A loop can be used to look for elements IN a set and and then print them individually. Suppose the following definitions and declarations have been made:

```
TYPE
      LETTERS = 'A' .. 'Z';
      LETTERSET = SET OF LETTERS;
VAR
      ALPHABET, STRINGLETTERS : LETTERSET;
      CH : CHAR;
      I : LETTERS;
```

The following program segment will read a line of characters and build a set containing all letters that appear at least once in the input line. Then the elements of the set will be printed.

```
ALPHABET := ['A' .. 'Z'];
STRINGLETTERS := [];
WRITELN('ENTER A NEW LINE OF CHARACTERS.');
WHILE NOT EOLN
    DO BEGIN
       READ(CH);
       IF CH IN ALPHABET
         THEN STRINGLETTERS := STRINGLETTERS + [CH]
       END;
```

```
WRITELN;
WRITELN('THE FOLLOWING LETTERS OCCUR AT LEAST ONCE ',
         'IN THE STRING:');
FOR I := 'A' TO 'Z'
  DO IF I IN STRINGLETTERS
       THEN WRITE(I : 2);
WRITELN
```

The variable STRINGLETTERS must be assigned the empty set as its initial value before any characters are processed. A letter is added to the set STRINGLETTERS by forming the union of STRINGLETTERS and a set containing the one letter to be inserted into STRINGLETTERS. Here is a sample of the output produced by the program segment.

```
ENTER A NEW LINE OF CHARACTERS.
?EVERYBODY LOVES A PARADE. DON'T YOU?

THE FOLLOWING LETTERS OCCUR AT LEAST ONCE IN THE STRING:
 A  B  D  E  L  N  O  P  R  S  T  U  V  Y
```

It is often simpler to test for membership in a set rather than to use a complex Boolean expression. Consider the case in which a program user is asked to respond with a Y for Yes, N for No, or U for Undecided. A loop can be employed to reject inappropriate responses as in the following program segment:

```
WRITELN('WHAT IS YOUR RESPONSE');
CONTINUE := TRUE;
REPEAT (* READING RESPONSES *)
  READ(RESPONSE);
  IF (RESPONSE = 'Y') OR (RESPONSE = 'N') OR (RESPONSE = 'U')
    THEN CONTINUE := FALSE
    ELSE BEGIN
           WRITELN('PLEASE ENTER Y, N, OR U.');
           READLN (* NEW LINE OF INPUT *)
         END
UNTIL NOT CONTINUE
```

The compound Boolean expression in the IF statement can be replaced by an expression that checks the RESPONSE for membership in the set ['Y', 'N', 'U']:

```
WRITELN('WHAT IS YOUR RESPONSE');
CONTINUE := TRUE;
REPEAT (* READING RESPONSES *)
  READ(RESPONSE);
  IF RESPONSE IN ['Y', 'N', 'U']
    THEN CONTINUE := FALSE
    ELSE BEGIN
           WRITELN('PLEASE ENTER Y, N, OR U.');
           READLN (* NEW LINE OF INPUT *)
         END
UNTIL NOT CONTINUE
```

Sets can also be used to test whether a group of responses is appropriate. Suppose that three one-digit positive integers are supposed to be input. The following program segment will reject inappropriate groups of input data.

```
CONTINUE := TRUE;
REPEAT (* READING NUMBERS *)
  READ(NUM1, NUM2, NUM3);
  IF [NUM1, NUM2, NUM3] <= [0 .. 9]
    THEN CONTINUE := FALSE
    ELSE WRITELN('1-DIGIT INTEGERS ONLY. RE-ENTER ALL DATA.')
UNTIL NOT CONTINUE
```

Testing for set membership can also provide a way to escape invalid CASE alternatives. This is particularly useful when the OTHERWISE clause is not available.

Parameters for a subprogram may have SET types. For instance, the function SIZEOFSET given here can be used to count the number of elements in a set of the type LETTERSET.

```
FUNCTION SIZEOFSET (ASET:LETTERSET) : INTEGER;
  VAR
      LETTER : 'A' .. 'Z';
      COUNT : INTEGER;
  BEGIN (* FUNCTION SIZEOFSET *)
  COUNT := 0;
  FOR LETTER := 'A' TO 'Z'
    DO IF LETTER IN ASET
        THEN COUNT := COUNT + 1;
  SIZEOFSET := COUNT
  END (* OF FUNCTION SIZEOFSET *)
```

Since sets are not scalar types, a function cannot return a set as its value. However, a procedure can modify or generate a set and return it to a calling program through a variable parameter. Suppose NUMBERS0TO9 identifies a set type defined as SET OF 0..9. The following procedure will generate a set whose elements are those numbers in the subrange 0..9 that appear as digits in a positive integer that is passed to the procedure as a parameter.

```
PROCEDURE PICKDIGITS (INTVAL : INTEGER; VAR DIGITSET : NUMBERS0TO9);
  VAR
      DIGIT : 0 .. 9;
  BEGIN (* PROCEDURE PICKDIGITS *)
  IF INTVAL = 0
    THEN DIGITSET := [0]
    ELSE DIGITSET := [];
  WHILE INTVAL <> 0
    DO BEGIN (* ISOLATING A DIGIT *)
      DIGIT := INTVAL MOD 10;
      DIGITSET := DIGITSET + [DIGIT];
      INTVAL := INTVAL DIV 10
      END (* OF ISOLATING A DIGIT *)
  END (* OF PROCEDURE PICKDIGITS *);
```

Note that PICKDIGITS will reduce the value of INTVAL to zero, but the value of the actual parameter corresponding to INTVAL will not be affected because INT-VAL is a value parameter.

9.1 EXERCISES

1. List all sets of the types PEOPLE, BITS, and MARKERS where

```
TYPE
     PEOPLE = SET OF (MAN, WOMAN, CHILD);
     BITS = SET OF 0 .. 1;
     MARKERS = SET OF 'W' .. 'Z';
```

2. For each pair of sets A and B, find A + B, A * B, A − B, and B − A.

a. A := [4, 7..15, 20] and B := [1..5, 12..18]
b. A := [8, 12, 15..22] and B := [1..7, 9..11, 14]
c. A := [1..6, 8, 11..14, 19] and B := [2, 4..8, 13]
d. A := [3, 8, 10..15] and B := [ ]

3. Suppose the set variables A, B, C, and D are assigned the following values.

$$A := [3 .. 7, 10, 12, 18]$$

$$B := [1, 5 .. 8, 12]$$

$$C := [3, 6 .. 9, 14 .. 20]$$

$$D := [2, 3, 9 .. 11, 15, 16]$$

Evaluate each of the following expressions.

a. A + B * C
c. A + C * B + D
e. A * C − B * D
g. C * (A + B − D)

b. (A + B) * C
d. A + C * (B + D)
f. A * (C − B) * D
h. (C * (A + B)) − D

4. Assume that the set variables A, B, C, and D have been assigned the sets shown in Exercise 3. Determine the value of each of the following expressions.

a. C <= [3 .. 20]
c. D * B = [ ]
e. A * D <= B
g. (10 IN D) AND (15 IN A − D)

b. [1..5, 8..12] >= B
d. A − C <> [4, 5, 10, 12]
f. 7 IN B
h. NOT (5 IN A)

5. Suppose that X, Y, and Z are set variables and E and F are variables whose type is the same as the base type for the sets. Find the errors (if any) in each of the following expressions. Give a corrected version of each erroneous expression.

a. X >= Y AND Z   b. E NOT IN X
c. X * Y + Y / Z   d. [E, F] <= X
e. X + Y * E   f. (X − Y) * ([E] + [F])
g. Y + (X >= Z)   h. Y − [F]

6. Write a subprogram that will find the set of all consonants and the set of all vowels in a character string passed to it as a parameter. Assume that the string is of the type

```
SENTENCE = PACKED ARRAY [1 .. 120] OF CHAR;
```

7. Write a subprogram that will return the value TRUE if an integer value passed to it contains only the digits 2, 3, 5, 7, and 9; otherwise, the subprogram should return the value FALSE.

8. Give an example that shows how testing for set membership can be used to escape invalid alternatives in a CASE statement.

9.2 RECORDS

An array may be used to store related information only if that information is representable by a single data type. Suppose that a program is used to process a book inventory and the information for each book consists of the title, the author's name, the price per copy, and the number of copies. The book data can be stored in variables like those declared here.

```
VAR
     TITLE : PACKED ARRAY [1 .. 30] OF CHAR;
     AUTHOR : PACKED ARRAY [1 .. 30] OF CHAR;
     PRICE : REAL;
     COPIES : 0 .. MAXINT;
```

Although TITLE, AUTHOR, PRICE, and COPIES are distinct variables, they will be used as a unit to provide a description for one book. It would add to the clarity of the program if the entire description could be stored in a single data structure. In Pascal, data that are not all of the same type can be stored in a data structure known as a record. A record has components that are individually accessible, but they need not all contain data of the same type.

RECORDS WITH FIXED PARTS

The components of a record are called **fields** and each field has a data type associated with it. A record may have two parts: a **fixed part**, which contains fields that are always available; and a **variant part**, whose composition can change depending on how the record is used. For the present, we will consider only records that have fixed parts.

Information on a book can be stored in a record variable named BOOK whose structure is defined as follows:

```
TYPE
     BOOKINFO = RECORD
                    TITLE, AUTHOR : PACKED ARRAY [1 .. 30] OF CHAR;
                    PRICE : REAL;
                    COPIES : 0 .. MAXINT
                END (* OF BOOKINFO RECORD *);
VAR
     BOOK : BOOKINFO;
```

The variable BOOK has four fields: TITLE, AUTHOR, PRICE, and COPIES. Each of these fields is a component of BOOK that can store data of the type specified in the definition of a BOOKINFO type record. Using a large rectangle to represent the entire BOOK record and smaller rectangles to represent its fields, we can depict the structure of BOOK as shown here.

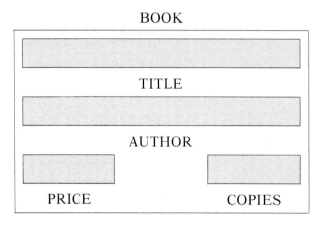

The sizes of the rectangles used in this diagram to represent the fields of the record variable BOOK are not meant to reflect the relative amount of storage allocated to each field. All the smaller rectangles are shaded to signify that a field of a record, like a simple variable or array component, has no value until it has been assigned a value.

The general form of a type definition for a record structure that has only a fixed part is shown in Figure 9–4. Each *field-identifier-list* is a list of one or more identifiers to serve as field names. Every field identifier must be unique within a given record, but it is possible for fields in two different record type definitions to have the same name. The fields of a record variable are not indexed like the components

```
        type-identifier = RECORD
                          field-identifier-list-1 : data-type-1;
                          field-identifier-list-2 : data-type-2;
                                        ⋮
                          field-identifier-list-n : data-type-n
                          END;
```

Figure 9–4
*General form of a type definition for a record having only a
fixed part.*

of an array. Instead, a record field is identified by the name of the record variable followed immediately by a period and then a field identifier (for example, BOOK.PRICE and BOOK.AUTHOR).

BOOK is only one record of the type BOOKINFO. A program may declare and use many record variables of the type BOOKINFO and each one will have fields named TITLE, AUTHOR, PRICE, and COPIES. Thus, a field identifier alone may not uniquely identify a record field. As noted above, the full name of a field in a record is represented by a **field designator** that consists of the name of a record variable and the name of a field within the specified record separated by a period. The four fields of the BOOK record are

> BOOK.TITLE
> BOOK.AUTHOR
> BOOK.PRICE
> BOOK.COPIES

The prefix BOOK used in front of a field name in a field designator is termed a **field qualifier.** If GUIDE is another BOOKINFO type record variable, the field designators for its fields are GUIDE.TITLE, GUIDE.AUTHOR, GUIDE.PRICE, and GUIDE.COPIES. Since the TITLE and AUTHOR fields of every BOOKINFO type record are arrays, the field designators for these fields can be indexed. For instance, the fifth component of BOOK.TITLE is identified by BOOK.TITLE[5].

Field designators are used like variables in a program. For example, values can be assigned to the fields of BOOK by using assignment statements like

```
BOOK.TITLE := 'THE RED BADGE OF COURAGE      ';
BOOK.AUTHOR := 'STEPHEN CRANE                ';
BOOK.PRICE := 14.95;
BOOK.COPIES := 8
```

When values for the fields of a record need to be read as input, the appropriate field designators may be used in READ statements, as illustrated in the following program segment:

```
WRITELN('ENTER THE BOOK INFORMATION AS REQUESTED.');
WRITELN('TITLE:');
READLN; (* NEW LINE OF INPUT *)
FOR I := 1 TO 30
  DO IF NOT EOLN
        THEN READ(BOOK.TITLE[I])
        ELSE BOOK.TITLE[I] := ' ';
WRITELN('AUTHOR''S NAME:');
READLN; (* NEW LINE OF INPUT *)
FOR I := 1 TO 30
  DO IF NOT EOLN
        THEN READ(BOOK.AUTHOR[I])
        ELSE BOOK.AUTHOR[I] := ' ';
WRITELN('PRICE PER COPY AND NUMBER OF COPIES:');
READLN; (* NEW LINE OF INPUT *)
READ(BOOK.PRICE, BOOK.COPIES)
```

The input prompted by this program segment might look like this:

```
ENTER THE BOOK INFORMATION AS REQUESTED.
TITLE:
?THE RED BADGE OF COURAGE
AUTHOR'S NAME:
?STEPHEN CRANE
PRICE PER COPY AND NUMBER OF COPIES:
?14.95  8
```

After the fields of BOOK have been assigned values, the contents of BOOK can be depicted as shown here.

BOOK

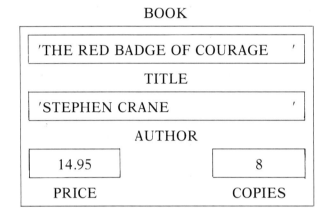

The contents of record fields can be printed by listing the appropriate field designators in WRITE or WRITELN statements. Since BOOK.TITLE and BOOK.AUTHOR are both string fields, and string variables can be listed in WRITE and WRITELN statements, no array indices are needed when referring to those fields. Here is a program segment that will print the entire contents of the BOOK record.

```
WRITELN('TITLE: ':8, BOOK.TITLE);
WRITELN('AUTHOR: ':8, BOOK.AUTHOR);
WRITELN(BOOK.COPIES:3, ' COPIES AVAILABLE AT $',
        BOOK.PRICE:5:2, ' EACH.')
```

Given that BOOK contains the information depicted above, the output produced by this program segment will be

```
  TITLE: THE RED BADGE OF COURAGE
 AUTHOR: STEPHEN CRANE
   8 COPIES AVAILABLE AT $14.95 EACH.
```

Any number of record variables of the type BOOKINFO can be declared in a program. The type BOOKINFO may be defined and then the identifier BOOKINFO may be used to declare variables, or the record structure for the variables may appear explicitly when the variables are declared, as shown here.

```
VAR
    BOOK,
    GUIDE,
    USEDBOOK : RECORD
                TITLE : PACKED ARRAY [1 .. 30] OF CHAR;
                AUTHOR : PACKED ARRAY [1 .. 30] OF CHAR;
                PRICE : REAL;
                COPIES : 0 .. MAXINT
            END;
```

Since it is likely that the types of fields used in records will also be used to declare other program variables, it is usually preferable to make TYPE definitions and use type identifiers when defining record fields and record variables. For instance,

```
TYPE
        NAME = PACKED ARRAY [1 .. 30] OF CHAR;
        COPYCOUNT = 0 .. MAXINT;
        BOOKINFO = RECORD
                    TITLE, AUTHOR : NAME;
                    PRICE : REAL;
                    COPIES : COPYCOUNT
                END (* OF BOOKINFO RECORD *);
    VAR
        BOOK, GUIDE, USEDBOOK : BOOKINFO;
```

When the entire contents of a record variable has to be copied to the corresponding fields of another record variable of the same type, it is not necessary to copy field by field. Suppose we want to copy the contents of BOOK to USEDBOOK. This can be accomplished by using the assignment statement

```
            USEDBOOK := BOOK
```

Similarly, to interchange the entire contents of the records BOOK and GUIDE, we could use the sequence of statements

```
            USEDBOOK := BOOK;
            BOOK := GUIDE;
            GUIDE := USEDBOOK
```

Copying the contents of one record variable to another record variable by using assignment statements like those shown above is possible only when both variables are of the same type. Suppose COMICBOOK is a record variable of the type

```
        BOOKDATA = RECORD
                    TITLE : NAME;
                    PRICE : REAL;
                    COPIES : COPYCOUNT;
                    AUTHOR : NAME
                END (* OF BOOKDATA RECORD *);
```

Even though COMICBOOK and BOOK have the same number and kinds of fields, the arrangement of those fields within each record is different, as depicted here.

BOOK

COMICBOOK

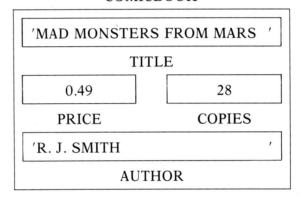

BOOK and COMICBOOK are not records of the same type, and so it is not legal to use a statement such as

BOOK := COMICBOOK

To copy the entire contents of COMICBOOK to BOOK, the contents of each field of COMICBOOK must be copied to the corresponding field of BOOK individually:

```
BOOK.TITLE   := COMICBOOK.TITLE;
BOOK.AUTHOR  := COMICBOOK.AUTHOR;
BOOK.PRICE   := COMICBOOK.PRICE;
BOOK.COPIES  := COMICBOOK.COPIES
```

Here are some other record declarations:

```
TYPE
    TEAM = RECORD
            NAME : PACKED ARRAY [1 .. 40] OF CHAR;
            WINS, LOSSES, TIES, TOTALGAMES : INTEGER;
            GAMESWON : SET OF 1 .. 16;
            WINPCT : REAL
          END (* OF TEAM RECORD *);
    REPORT = RECORD
            NAME : PACKED ARRAY [1 .. 30] OF CHAR;
            TEST : ARRAY [1 .. 3] OF 0 .. 100;
            TESTCOUNT : 0 .. 3;
```

```
                AVERAGE : REAL;
                GRADE : 'A' .. 'E'
              END (* OF REPORT RECORD *);
     VAR
          HOME : TEAM;
          STUDENT : REPORT;
```

The following diagrams show the structures of the HOME and STUDENT records and their contents after values have been assigned to the fields.

HOME

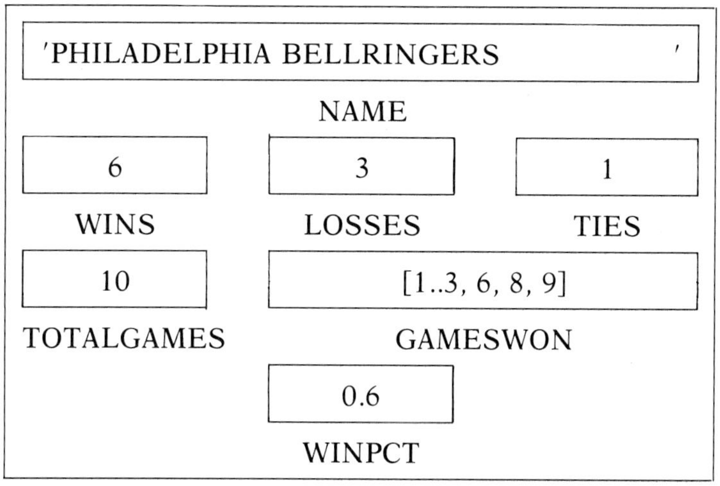

STUDENT

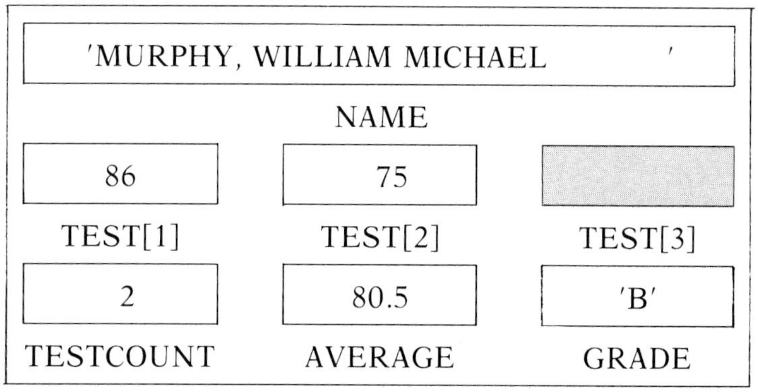

THE WITH STATEMENT

Having to repeat fully qualified field designators for records over and over again in a program segment can be quite tedious. Consider the following program segment, which can be used to read information for a STUDENT record.

```
WRITELN('ENTER THE STUDENT''S NAME.');
FOR I := 1 TO 30
 DO IF NOT EOLN
     THEN READ(STUDENT.NAME[I])
     ELSE STUDENT.NAME[I] := ' ';
WRITELN('HOW MANY TESTS (MAXIMUM OF 3).');
```

```
READ(STUDENT.TESTCOUNT);
IF STUDENT.TESTCOUNT > 0
   THEN BEGIN (* TEST INPUT AND AVERAGING *)
        STUDENT.AVERAGE := 0.0;
        WRITELN('ENTER THE TEST SCORES.');
        FOR J := 1 TO STUDENT.TESTCOUNT
          DO BEGIN (* READ A TEST SCORE *)
             READ(STUDENT.TEST[J]);
             STUDENT.AVERAGE := STUDENT.AVERAGE + STUDENT.TEST[J]
             END (* OF READ A TEST SCORE *);
        STUDENT.AVERAGE := STUDENT.AVERAGE / STUDENT.TESTCOUNT
        END (* OF TEST INPUT AND AVERAGING *)
```

A WITH statement can be used to eliminate the need to specify the record identifier STUDENT each time a STUDENT field is referenced. The general form of the WITH statement is shown in Figure 9–5. A *record-identifier-list* consists of one or more names of record variables separated by commas. A field of a record whose name appears after the keyword WITH can be referenced by using only the appropriate field name in the simple or compound statement following the DO. Using a WITH statement, we can write this program segment in the following equivalent form:

```
WRITELN('ENTER THE STUDENT''S NAME.');
WITH STUDENT
   DO BEGIN (* INPUT FOR A STUDENT RECORD *)
      FOR I := 1 TO 30
        DO IF NOT EOLN
             THEN READ(NAME[I])
             ELSE NAME[I] := ' ';
      WRITELN('HOW MANY TESTS (MAXIMUM OF 3).');
      READ(TESTCOUNT);
      IF TESTCOUNT > 0
         THEN BEGIN (* TEST INPUT AND AVERAGING *)
              AVERAGE := 0.0;
              WRITELN('ENTER THE TEST SCORES.');
              FOR J := 1 TO TESTCOUNT
                DO BEGIN (* READ A TEST SCORE *)
                   READ(TEST[J]);
                   AVERAGE := AVERAGE + TEST[J]
                   END (* OF READ A TEST SCORE *);
              AVERAGE := AVERAGE / TESTCOUNT
              END (* OF TEST INPUT AND AVERAGING *)
      END (* OF INPUT FOR A STUDENT RECORD *)
```

WITH *record-identifier-list*
DO *statement*

Figure 9–5
General form of the WITH statement.

Sometimes two or more records are processed in the same section of a program. Suppose STATS and INFO are two record variables and consider a WITH statement of the form

WITH STATS, INFO
DO statement

In the simple or compound statement following DO, the identifiers STATS and INFO need not be used to qualify the fields of the STATS record or the INFO record provided that each field referred to by only its field name is unique to one of the records. If both STATS and INFO have a field by the same name, the use of that field name without a qualifier is ambiguous. For instance, suppose STATS and INFO both have fields named IDNUMBER, and consider a WITH statement that has the form

```
WITH STATS, INFO
   DO BEGIN
         .
         .
         .

      WRITELN(IDNUMBER);
         .
         .
         .

   END
```

In the compound statement after DO, the identifiers STATS and INFO are used as implicit qualifiers in references to fields of the records named STATS and INFO. However, the reference to IDNUMBER in the WRITELN statement cannot be resolved because both records have an IDNUMBER field. The WRITELN statement is invalid in its present form. It must be changed to WRITELN(STATS.IDNUMBER) or WRITELN(INFO.IDNUMBER).

RECORD VARIANTS

The fields specified in the fixed part of a TYPE definition for a record are available in all record variables of that type. It is possible for records to be of the same type and yet not have exactly the same fields. Suppose we want to use record variables that always have fields for the MAKE, MODEL, and YEAR of an automobile, but may have some additional fields depending on the kind of transmission (manual or automatic) an automobile has. The MAKE, MODEL, and YEAR fields constitute the fixed part of the record. All fields dependent on the kind of transmission will appear in the variant part of the record. Let AUTOTRANS be the data type defined by

```
AUTOTRANS = (MANUAL, AUTOMATIC);
```

Here is an example of a variant part for a record.

```
CASE TRANSMISSION : AUTOTRANS OF
      MANUAL : (FORWARDSPEEDS : 3 .. 5;
                  SHIFT : (FLOOR, COLUMN);
                  MANPRICE : REAL);
   AUTOMATIC : (AUTOPRICE : REAL)
```

The identifier TRANSMISSION is the name of a **tag field** whose value determines the composition of the variant part for a particular record. TRANSMISSION values are restricted to the type AUTOTRANS. If the value of TRANSMISSION is MANUAL, the variant fields FORWARDSPEEDS, SHIFT, and MANPRICE will be available along with all the fields in the fixed part of the record. When TRANSMISSION has the value AUTOMATIC, the variant field AUTOPRICE will be available along with the fixed fields. Although the variant part of a record is defined in a form that is similar to a CASE statement, note that the word END is not used to mark the end of the variant fields. The END that marks the physical end of the record suffices to mark the end of the variant part as well.

A complete definition of the record type we have just described is given next, and two such records are declared.

```
TYPE
     STRING20 = PACKED ARRAY [1 .. 20] OF CHAR;
     MODELYEARS = 1920 .. 1999;
     AUTOTRANS = (MANUAL, AUTOMATIC);
     SHIFTLOCATION = (FLOOR, COLUMN);
     AUTOSTATS = RECORD
                    MAKE, MODEL : STRING20;
                    YEAR : MODELYEARS;
                    CASE TRANSMISSION : AUTOTRANS OF
                          MANUAL : (FORWARDSPEEDS : 3 .. 5;
                                      SHIFT : SHIFTLOCATION;
                                      MANPRICE : REAL);
                       AUTOMATIC : (AUTOPRICE : REAL)
                 END (* OF AUTOSTATS RECORD *);
VAR
     CAR1, CAR2 : AUTOSTATS;
```

The record variables will always have fixed fields named MAKE, MODEL, and YEAR. After CAR1.TRANSMISSION and CAR2.TRANSMISSION have been assigned values (either MANUAL or AUTOMATIC), the appropriate variant fields will be available. Suppose that CAR1.TRANSMISSION has been assigned the value MANUAL and CAR2.TRANSMISSION has been assigned the value AUTOMATIC. The structure of the records CAR1 and CAR2 will be as depicted in the following diagrams.

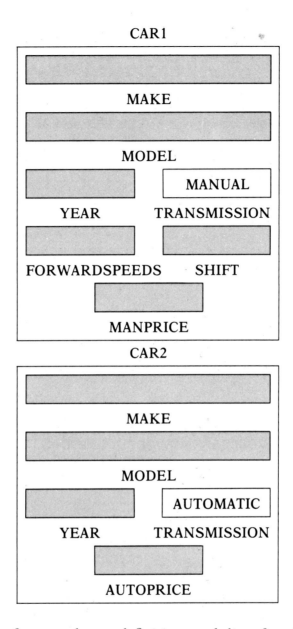

In the variant part of a record type definition, each list of variants corresponding to a tag field value is enclosed in parentheses and labeled with that value. We refer to such a list as a **variant field list,** and the collection of all fields in the fixed part will be called the **fixed field list.**

A record type definition may have only a fixed part, only a variant part, or both parts. When a fixed part is used, it must appear before the variant part (if any). The general structure of a record definition that includes both a fixed part and a variant part is shown in Figure 9–6. Each label list may contain only values of the data type specified for the tag field, and none of those values may appear in more than one label list in the same variant part. Also, each field identifier in the variant part can appear in only one variant field list, and of course it may not be identical to any of the fixed field identifiers.

$$
\begin{aligned}
\textit{type-identifier} = \text{RECORD} \\
\textit{fixed-field-list;} \\
\text{CASE } \textit{tag-field} : \textit{type-identifier} \\
\textit{label-list-1} : \textit{(variant-field-list-1);} \\
\textit{label-list-2} : \textit{(variant-field-list-2);} \\
\bullet \\
\bullet \\
\textit{label-list-n} : \textit{(variant-field-list-n)} \\
\text{END;}
\end{aligned}
$$

Figure 9–6
*General form of a record TYPE definition that includes both a
fixed part and a variant part.*

A record that has a variant part is often processed by using CASE statements so that only the appropriate variant fields are referenced. Consider the procedure AUTODATA, which can be used to read values for an AUTOSTATS type record:

```
PROCEDURE AUTODATA (VAR CAR : AUTOSTATS);
  CONST
          YES = 'Y';
          NO = 'N';
  PROCEDURE STRINGREAD (VAR NAME : STRING20);
    VAR
          I := 1 .. 20;
    BEGIN (* PROCEDURE STRINGREAD *)
    READLN; (* NEW LINE OF INPUT *)
    FOR I := 1 TO 20
      DO IF NOT EOLN
           THEN READ(NAME[I])
           ELSE NAME[I] := ' '
    END (* OF PROCEDURE STRINGREAD *);
  FUNCTION RESPONSE : CHAR;
    VAR
          ANSWER : CHAR;
    BEGIN (* FUNCTION RESPONSE *)
    REPEAT
      WRITELN('ENTER YES OR NO.');
      READLN; (* NEW LINE OF INPUT *)
      READ(ANSWER)
    UNTIL ANSWER IN [YES, NO];
    RESPONSE := ANSWER
    END (* OF FUNCTION RESPONSE *);
  BEGIN (* PROCEDURE AUTODATA *)
  WITH CAR
    DO BEGIN (* DATA INPUT *)
       WRITELN('WHAT MAKE OF AUTOMOBILE');
       STRINGREAD(MAKE);
```

```
    WRITELN('WHICH MODEL');
    STRINGREAD(MODEL);
    WRITELN('MODEL YEAR');
    READLN; (* NEW LINE OF INPUT *)
    READ(YEAR);
    WRITELN('AUTOMATIC TRANSMISSION?');
    CASE RESPONSE OF
       YES : TRANSMISSION := AUTOMATIC;
        NO : BEGIN (* MANUAL TRANSMISSION INPUT *)
             TRANSMISSION := MANUAL;
             WRITELN('HOW MANY FORWARD SPEEDS (3, 4, OR 5)');
             READLN; (* NEW LINE OF INPUT *)
             READ(FORWARDSPEEDS);
             WRITELN('SHIFT ON THE COLUMN?');
             CASE RESPONSE OF
                YES : SHIFT := COLUMN;
                 NO : SHIFT := FLOOR
             END (* OF SHIFT CASES *)
             END (* OF MANUAL TRANSMISSION INPUT *)
    END (* OF TRANSMISSION CASES *)
END (* OF PROCEDURE AUTODATA *);
```

Suppose AUTODATA is called by means of the statement

AUTODATA(CAR1)

The input for CAR1 will be entered as shown here:

```
WHAT MAKE OF AUTOMOBILE
?CHEVROLET
WHICH MODEL
?CHEVETTE
WHICH YEAR
?1981
AUTOMATIC TRANSMISSION?
ENTER YES OR NO.
?MANUAL
ENTER YES OR NO.
?NO
HOW MANY FORWARD SPEEDS (3, 4, OR 5)
?4
SHIFT ON THE COLUMN?
ENTER YES OR NO.
?YES
```

In this example, the TRANSMISSION field of CAR1 is set to MANUAL, indicating that the FORWARDSPEEDS, SHIFT, and MANPRICE fields of CAR1 will be used. The contents of CAR1 after the input information has been read are depicted in the diagram below.

CAR1

It is not necessary that every possible value for the tag field appear as a label on one of the variant field lists, but it is advisable that this be the case in order to protect the program from errors. Should there be values for the tag field that indicate no need for any variant fields, they can be listed as labels on an empty variant field list that will have the form

label-list : ( )

Use of a variant field list that is empty is illustrated in the following example.

```
TYPE
     STRING30 = PACKED ARRAY [1 .. 30] OF CHAR;
     GRADELEVEL = (FRESHMAN, SOPHOMORE, JUNIOR, SENIOR);
     JOBCATEGORY = (STUDENT, EMPLOYED, UNEMPLOYED);
     YEARRANGE = 1900 . 1999;
     JOBFILE = RECORD
                    NAME : STRING30;
                    AGE : 16 .. 99;
                 CASE JOBSTATUS : JOBCATEGORY OF
                       STUDENT : (SCHOOL : STRING30;
                                  GRADE : GRADELEVEL);
                      EMPLOYED : (EMPLOYER : STRING30;
                                  YEARHIRED : YEARRANGE);
                    UNEMPLOYED : ()
                 END (* OF JOBFILE RECORD *);
```

The tag field of a record is used as a selector to determine which variant fields will be used. It is not absolutely necessary that the variant part specify a tag field. Only a data type for the labels need be present, as demonstrated in the following version of the record type JOBFILE.

```
JOBFILE = RECORD
             NAME : STRING30;
             AGE : 16 .. 99;
                CASE JOBCATEGORY OF
                      STUDENT : (SCHOOL : STRING30;
                                   GRADE : GRADELEVEL);
                     EMPLOYED : (EMPLOYER : STRING30;
                                   YEARHIRED : YEARRANGE);
                  UNEMPLOYED : ()
             END (* OF JOBFILE RECORD *);
```

If this form of JOBFILE is used, there is no tag field that can be employed to control which variant fields are used. There are not many instances when a variant part of this kind is useful. It is important that a tag field be utilized to make sure that the variant fields are used correctly.

9.2 EXERCISES

1. Write definitions and declarations for record variables that meet the following criteria:

   a. A variable named CLIENT has fields for a name, address, social security number, telephone number, age, and marital status.

   b. A variable named HOUSE has fields location, number of rooms, lot size, type of heating system, and price.

   c. A variable named BANKACCOUNT has fields for an account number, depositor's name, current balance, and year-to-date interest accumulated.

   d. A variable named INVENTORYITEM has fields for an item description, inventory number, quantity in stock, wholesale price, and retail price.

2. Consider the following definitions and declarations.

```
TYPE
    STRING40 = PACKED ARRAY [1 .. 40] OF CHAR;
    TIMEPERIOD = (DAILY, WEEKLY, BIWEEKLY, MONTHLY,
                  BIMONTHLY);
    RATES = ARRAY [1 .. 3] OF REAL;
    PERIODICAL = RECORD
                    TITLE : STRING40;
                    PUBLISHER : STRING40;
                    CIRCULATION : 0 .. MAXINT;
                    DISTRIBUTION : TIMEPERIOD;
                    COPYPRICE : REAL;
                    SUBSCRIPTION : RATES
                 END (* OF PERIODICAL RECORD *);
VAR
    I : INTEGER;
    INCOME : REAL;
    NEWSPAPER, MAGAZINE, JOURNAL : PERIODICAL;
```

Tell whether the field references for the record variables NEWSPAPER, MAGA-ZINE, and JOURNAL made in the following program segments are always valid, sometimes valid, or never valid. If a field reference is sometimes valid or never valid, explain why.

a. `READ(NEWSPAPER.TITLE)`

b.
```
FOR I := 1 TO 40
  DO WRITE(MAGAZINE.PUBLISHER[I])
```

c. `CIRCULATION := CIRCULATION + 1`

d.
```
WITH JOURNAL, MAGAZINE
  DO IF COPYPRICE > 1.50
      THEN WRITELN(TITLE)
```

e. `INCOME := PERIODICAL.CIRCULATION * PERIODICAL.COPYPRICE`

f.
```
WITH NEWSPAPER
  DO FOR I := 1 TO 3
      DO WRITE(SUBSCRIPTION[I])
```

g.
```
CASE MAGAZINE.DISTRIBUTION OF
      DAILY : YEARCOST := 365 * MAGAZINE.COPYPRICE;
     WEEKLY : YEARCOST := 52 * MAGAZINE.COPYPRICE;
   BIWEEKLY : YEARCOST := 26 * MAGAZINE.COPYPRICE;
    MONTHLY : YEARCOST := 12 * MAGAZINE.COPYPRICE;
  BIMONTHLY : YEARCOST := 6 * MAGAZINE.COPYPRICE
END (* OF MAGAZINE.DISTRIBUTION CASES *)
```

9.3 DATA STRUCTURES FORMED BY USING RECORDS

We have seen that the data type for a field in a record may be a scalar, subrange, array, or set type. It is also possible for a record field to have a record type; that is, the data type specified for a field of a record may give that field a record structure. When a field of a record is itself a record, these records are said to be nested. A record may contain a variety of pertinent facts about some entity such as a person or an item. To store information about a collection of similar entities, an array of records may be constructed. The formation of nested records and arrays of records will be discussed in this section.

NESTED RECORDS

Suppose that we need a data structure to store the catalog number, description, and quantity of an item as well as the name of a supplier for the item and the unit price of the item. Two distinct record variables may be declared, one for information about the item and one for information about the supplier:

```
TYPE
      NUMBERRANGE = 1000 .. 9999;
      STRING30 = PACKED ARRAY [1 .. 30] OF CHAR;
      COUNT = 0 .. MAXINT;
      INVENTORY = RECORD
                     CATNUMBER : NUMBERRANGE;
                     QUANTITY : COUNT;
                     DESCRIPTION : STRING30
                  END (* OF INVENTORY RECORD *);
      SOURCE = RECORD
                     COMPANY : STRING30;
                     PRICE : REAL
                  END (* OF SOURCE RECORD *);
   VAR
      ITEM : INVENTORY;
      SUPPLIER : SOURCE;
```

Even though ITEM and SUPPLIER are distinct record variables, the two records will be used to store information about one item. The field designators for the ITEM record are ITEM.CATNUMBER, ITEM.QUANTITY, and ITEM.DESCRIPTION, while the field designators for the SUPPLIER record are SUPPLIER.COMPANY and SUPPLIER.PRICE. ITEM and SUPPLIER are depicted in the following diagrams.

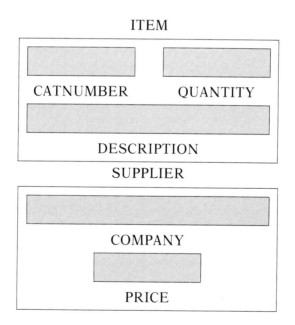

Since the SUPPLIER information supplements the ITEM information, it would be appropriate to have COMPANY and PRICE as fields in the ITEM record. However, it is still possible to maintain the SUPPLIER record within the ITEM record. Consider the following definitions and declarations.

```
TYPE
      NUMBERRANGE = 1000 .. 9999;
      STRING30 = PACKED ARRAY [1 .. 30] OF CHAR;
```

```
COUNT = 0 .. MAXINT;
SOURCE = RECORD
             COMPANY : STRING30;
             PRICE : REAL
         END (* OF SOURCE RECORD *);
INVENTORY = RECORD
                CATNUMBER : NUMBERRANGE;
                QUANTITY : COUNT;
                DESCRIPTION : STRING30;
                SUPPLIER : SOURCE
            END (* OF INVENTORY RECORD *);
    VAR
        ITEM : INVENTORY;
```

In the ITEM record, the field ITEM.SUPPLIER exists and that field is itself a record that has the fields ITEM.SUPPLIER.COMPANY and ITEM.SUPPLIER.PRICE. The SUPPLIER record is nested in the ITEM record, and so COMPANY and PRICE are in fact fields of ITEM. However, the references ITEM.COMPANY and ITEM.PRICE are not valid because they do not trace the heritage of COMPANY and PRICE fields. The field designators ITEM.SUPPLIER.COMPANY and ITEM.SUPPLIER.PRICE are the fully qualified names for the COMPANY and PRICE fields of the record ITEM. A diagram showing the the nesting of SUPPLIER within ITEM is given next.

ITEM

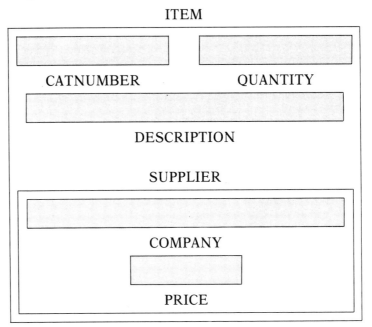

The field designator ITEM.SUPPLIER is valid, but it will refer to the entire "subrecord" of ITEM whose name is SUPPLIER.

When records are nested, the levels of nesting are traced by the fully qualified field designators that identify fields at the innermost level. A diagram like the following one for the ITEM record is helpful in determining the heritage of each field.

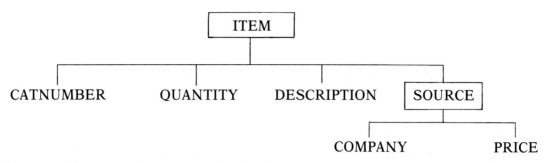

This "tree diagram" shows not only the level of each field within the ITEM record, but also the structure of an INVENTORY type record. That is, the arrangement of the fields at each level moving from left to right gives the order in which these fields appear in the record.

Suppose that the record type INVENTORY2 is defined by

```
INVENTORY2 = RECORD
                DESCRIPTION : STRING30;
                CATNUMBER : NUMBERRANGE;
                SUPPLIER : SOURCE;
                QUANTITY : COUNT
             END (* OF INVENTORY2 RECORD *);
```

Let ITEM2 be a variable of the type INVENTORY2. The record ITEM2 will contain the same number and kinds of fields that the record ITEM contains, but the arrangement of the fields in those two records is different. This may be seen by comparing the tree diagram of ITEM with the tree diagram of ITEM2, which is shown next.

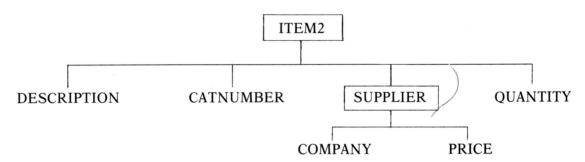

If ITEMA and ITEMB are both INVENTORY type records or both INVENTORY2 type records, the entire contents of ITEMB can be copied to ITEMA by using the assignment statement

$$\text{ITEMA := ITEMB}$$

When ITEMA and ITEMB are not records of the same type, this assignment statement is invalid. The copying of all information in ITEM to ITEM2 can be accomplished on a field-by-field basis:

```
      ITEM2.DESCRIPTION := ITEM.DESCRIPTION;
      ITEM2.CATNUMBER := ITEM.CATNUMBER;
      ITEM2.QUANTITY := ITEM.QUANTITY;
      ITEM2.SUPPLIER.COMPANY := ITEM.SUPPLIER.COMPANY;
      ITEM2.SUPPLIER.PRICE := ITEM.SUPPLIER.PRICE
```

Since the SUPPLIER fields of both records each have a SOURCE type structure, the last two assignment statements can be replaced by the single assignment statement

```
        ITEM2.SUPPLIER := ITEM.SUPPLIER
```

A WITH statement can be used to simplify the assignments even further:

```
    WITH ITEM
      DO BEGIN (* COPYING *)
         ITEM2.DESCRIPTION := DESCRIPTION;
         ITEM2.CATNUMBER := CATNUMBER;
         ITEM2.QUANTITY := QUANTITY;
         ITEM2.SUPPLIER := SUPPLIER
         END (* OF COPYING *)
```

It is not possible to list both ITEM and ITEM2 after the keyword WITH in order to eliminate the need to qualify the fields of both records because ITEM and ITEM2 have fields with the same names.

Several records of the same type may be nested within one record. Consider the following definitions and declarations.

```
    TYPE
         STRING30 = PACKED ARRAY [1 .. 30] OF CHAR;
         NUMBERRANGE = 1000 .. 9999;
         COUNT = 0 .. MAXINT;
         SOURCE = RECORD
                     COMPANY : STRING30;
                     PRICE : REAL
                 END (* OF SOURCE RECORD *);
         TRANSACTION = RECORD
                     CATNUMBER : COUNT;
                     DESCRIPTION : STRING30;
                     QUANTITY : COUNT;
                     SUPPLIER,
                     DESTINATION : SOURCE
                 END (* OF TRANSACTION RECORD *);
    VAR
         WAREHOUSE : TRANSACTION;
         CUSTOMER, DEALER : SOURCE;
```

The CUSTOMER and DEALER records each have COMPANY and PRICE fields, as shown below.

WAREHOUSE has five fields at the first level (CATNUMBER, DESCRIPTION, QUANTITY, SUPPLIER, and DESTINATION) and four fields at the second level (SUPPLIER.COMPANY, SUPPLIER.PRICE, DESTINATION.COMPANY, and DESTINATION.PRICE), as illustrated in the following tree diagram.

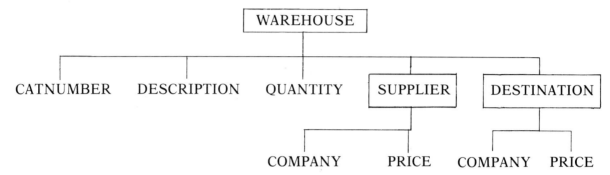

The DESCRIPTION, SUPPLIER.COMPANY, and DESTINATION.COMPANY fields are all arrays of the type STRING30. If I has an integer value in the subrange 1..30, then DESCRIPTION[I], SUPPLIER.COMPANY[I], and DESTINATION.COMPANY[I] are all valid references to the Ith components of those arrays. For example, the following loop can be used to read a character string for the field WAREHOUSE.DESTINATION.COMPANY.

```
FOR I := 1 TO 40
  DO IF NOT EOLN
       THEN READ(WAREHOUSE.DESTINATION.COMPANY[I])
       ELSE WAREHOUSE.DESTINATION.COMPANY[I] := ' '
```

The array references can be shortened by using a WITH statement that specifies the record names WAREHOUSE and DESTINATION:

```
WITH WAREHOUSE.DESTINATION
  DO FOR I := 1 TO 40
       DO IF NOT EOLN
            THEN READ(COMPANY[I])
            ELSE COMPANY[I] := ' '
```

Records may be nested within records to any desired depth. Of course, the more levels of nesting there are in a record structure, the more complex this structure becomes. It is not a good programming practice to nest records more than two or three levels deep because the complexity of such a structure tends to detract from the readability of a program. For instance, consider the following definitions and declarations.

```
TYPE
    DATAINFO = RECORD
                    DAY : 1 .. 31;
                    MONTH : 1 .. 12;
                    YEAR : 1850 .. 1999
               END (* OF DATEINFO RECORD *);
    WINDSTATS = RECORD
                    DIRECTION : 0 .. 359;
                    SPEED : 0 .. 100
               END (* OF WINDSTATS RECORD *);
    BASICINFO = RECORD
                    TEMPERATURE : INTEGER;
                    BAROMETER : REAL;
                    WIND : WINDSTATS
               END (* OF BASICINFO RECORD *);
    SKY = (CLEAR, PARTLYCLOUDY, OVERCAST, STORM);
    PRECIP = (SNOW, RAIN, SLEET, HAIL);
    RATE = (LIGHT, MODERATE, HARD);
    WEATHERSTATS = RECORD
                    DATE : DATEINFO;
                    CONDITIONS : BASICINFO;
                    CASE CLOUDS : SKY OF
                        CLEAR : ();
                    PARTLYCLOUDY : (CLOUDLEVEL : 0 .. MAXINT);
                        OVERCAST : (CEILING : 0 .. MAXINT;
                                    VISIBILITY : REAL);
                        STORM : (INTENSITY : RATE;
                                CASE VARIETY : PRECIP OF
                                    SNOW : (DEPTH : REAL);
                                    RAIN : (INCHES : REAL);
                                    SLEET : (FREEZE : BOOLEAN);
                                    HAIL : (DIAMETER : REAL))
               END (* OF WEATHERSTATS RECORD *);
VAR
    WEATHER : WEATHERSTATS;
```

Note that the variant part whose tag field is CLOUDS has nested within it a variant part whose tag field is VARIETY. When CLOUDS has the value STORM, the WEATHER record will include the variant field INTENSITY as well as one of the nested variant fields SNOW, RAIN, SLEET, and HAIL, depending on the value of VARIETY. Since there are four possible values for VARIETY, the WEATHER record can have seven different forms. A tree diagram of WEATHER is shown next. Tag fields are enclosed in boxes and the "branches" for the possible variants are numbered.

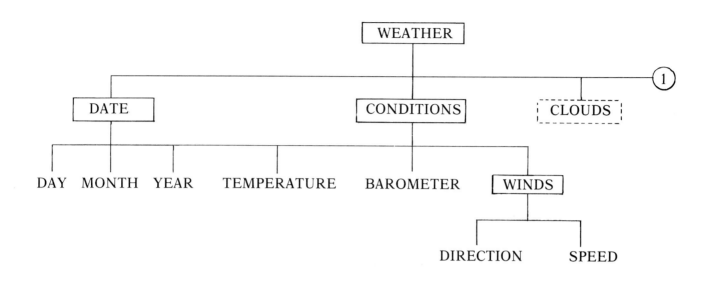

CLOUDS *Variants:*

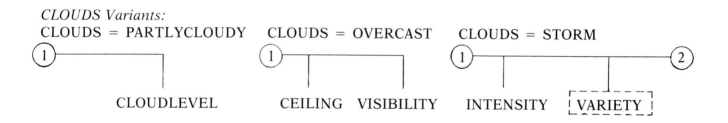

VARIETY *Variants:*

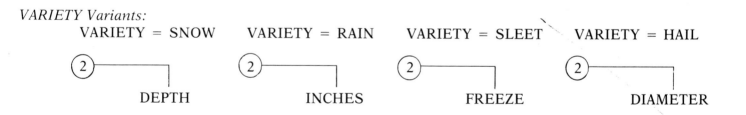

The fully qualified field designators for the fixed fields in the record WEATHER are:

WEATHER.DATE.DAY	WEATHER.CONDITIONS.TEMPERATURE
WEATHER.DATE.MONTH	WEATHER.CONDITIONS.BAROMETER
WEATHER.DATE.YEAR	WEATHER.CONDITIONS.WINDS.DIRECTION
	WEATHER.CONDITIONS.WINDS.SPEED

WEATHER.DATE and WEATHER.CONDITIONS are records and WEATHER.CONDITIONS.WINDS is a record nested in the WEATHER.CONDITIONS record. The field designator for the tag field CLOUDS is WEATHER.CLOUDS and the variant part whose tag field is CLOUDS includes the variant fields WEATHER.CLOUDLEVEL, WEATHER.CEILING, WEATHER.VISIBILITY, WEATHER.INTENSITY, and WEATHER.VARIETY. Since VARIETY is the tag field for the nested variant part, there may be additional variant fields named WEATHER.DEPTH, WEATHER.INCHES, WEATHER.FREEZE, and WEATHER.DI-AMETER.

A WEATHERSTATS type record such as WEATHER is rather complex. It would perhaps be better to simplify the structure of a WEATHERSTATS record by not including as many nested records. DATAINFO, WINDSTATS, or BASICINFO type records could be maintained separate from the WEATHERSTATS type records.

ARRAYS OF RECORDS

When the base type specified for an array is a record type, every component of that array will have a record structure. That is, each subscripted variable representing a component of that array will be a record variable. Consider the following definitions and declarations.

```
TYPE
PERSONALDATA = RECORD
                NAME : PACKED ARRAY [1 .. 30] OF CHAR;
                AGE : 16 .. 65;
                SEX : (MALE, FEMALE);
                RACE : (CAUCASIAN, NEGRO, ORIENTAL, OTHER);
                 CASE MARRIED : BOOLEAN OF
                   TRUE : (CHILDREN : 0 .. 20);
                  FALSE : ()
               END (* OF PERSONALDATA RECORD *);
SURVEY = ARRAY [1 .. 200] OF PERSONALDATA;
VAR
PERSON : SURVEY;
```

The array PERSON has 200 components of the type PERSONALDATA. If k represents any integer in the subrange 1..200, the component PERSON[k] will be a record variable that has the structure depicted here.

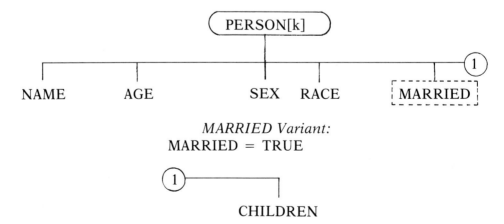

MARRIED Variant:
MARRIED = TRUE

The field designators for the fixed part of the kth PERSON are PERSON[k]. NAME, PERSON[k].AGE, PERSON[k].SEX, and PERSON[k].RACE. When the tag field designated by PERSON[k].MARRIED has the value TRUE, the variant field PERSON[k].CHILDREN is available.

The array PERSON is simply an indexed collection of records, each of which has the PERSONALDATA type structure. PERSON[25] is the 25th component in this collection and PERSON[25].AGE is the age field in that component. Since each of the components in the array PERSON has the same record type structure, it is possible to copy the entire contents of one component to another component by using a single assignment statement. For example, the statement

```
PERSON[42] := PERSON[25]
```

will copy the contents of PERSON[25] to the corresponding fields of the record PERSON[42]. If I and J are variables whose values are in the subrange 1..200 and if SAVERECORD is a record variable of the type PERSONALDATA, the entire contents of the records PERSON[I] and PERSON[J] can be interchanged by using the statements

```
SAVERECORD := PERSON[I];
PERSON[I]  := PERSON[J];
PERSON[J]  := SAVERECORD
```

The NAME field of each PERSON record is an array consisting of 30 components. PERSON[I].NAME represents the entire array and PERSON[I].NAME[N] is the Nth component of the array. Actually, PERSON[I].NAME is a string variable. If a string is to be read as input for PERSON[I].NAME, it must be read character by character. This can be accomplished by using a FOR loop:

```
FOR N := 1 TO 30
  DO IF NOT EOLN
       THEN READ(PERSON[I].NAME[N])
       ELSE PERSON[I].NAME[N] := ' '
```

Since PERSON[I] is a record, a WITH statement could be used so that the components of NAME can be specified without the qualifier PERSON[I]:

```
WITH PERSON[I]
  DO FOR N := 1 TO 30
       DO IF NOT EOLN
            THEN READ(NAME[N])
            ELSE NAME[N] := ' '
```

Suppose we want to read NAMEs for the first ten PERSONs. We can do so by using this program segment in a FOR loop that varies the value of I:

```
FOR I := 1 TO 10
  DO WITH PERSON[I]
       DO FOR N := 1 TO 30
            DO IF NOT EOLN
                 THEN READ(NAME[N])
                 ELSE NAME[N] := ' '
```

The WITH statement is positioned so that the value of I will properly vary the index value for the array PERSON. Examine the following program segment.

```
      (* ERRONEOUS USE OF A WITH STATEMENT *)
      WITH PERSON [I]
        DO FOR I := 1 TO 10
            DO FOR N := 1 TO 30
                DO IF NOT EOLN
                    THEN READ(NAME[N])
                    ELSE NAME[N] := ' '
```

The WITH statement establishes PERSON[I] as a qualifier before the nested FOR loops are executed, and the varying of I in the outer loop cannot change this qualifier. If I has been given no value prior to the WITH statement, then the reference PERSON[I] is not even valid. Even if I has a value in the subrange 1..200, the nested FOR loops will establish a value for that one NAME field a total of ten times.

9.3 EXERCISES

1. Two ways to define a record variable called INVOICE are shown below. In each case draw a tree diagram showing the structure of INVOICE and give the full names of its fields.

a.
```
TYPE
    ALFA20 = PACKED ARRAY [1 .. 20] OF CHAR;
    ALFA30 = PACKED ARRAY [1 .. 30] OF CHAR;
    IDENTIFICATION = RECORD
                    NAME : ALFA30;
                    HOUSENUMBER : 1 .. 99999;
                    STREET,
                    CITY,
                    STATE : ALFA20;
                    ZIPCODE : 0 .. 99999
                END (* OF IDENTIFICATION RECORD *);
    INVOICE = RECORD
            ITEM : ALFA30;
            ITEMCODE : 100 .. 9999;
            PURCHASER : IDENTIFICATION;
            PAYMENT : (NONE, CASH, CHARGE);
            QUANTITY : 0 .. MAXINT;
            UNITPRICE,
            TOTALPRICE : REAL
        END (* OF INVOICE RECORD *);
VAR
    ORDER : INVOICE;
```

b.
```
TYPE
    ALFA20 = PACKED ARRAY [1 .. 20] OF CHAR;
    ALFA30 = PACKED ARRAY [1 .. 30] OF CHAR;
    SPECIFICATIONS = RECORD
```

```
                        DESCRIPTION : ALFA30;
                        CODE : 100 .. 9999;
                        QUANTITY : 0 .. MAXINT;
                        UNITPRICE,
                        TOTALPRICE : REAL
                     END (* OF SPECIFICATIONS RECORD *);
        LOCATION = RECORD
                     HOUSENUMBER : 1 .. 99999;
                     STREET,
                     CITY,
                     STATE : ALFA20;
                     ZIPCODE : 0 .. 99999
                  END (* OF LOCATION RECORD *);
        IDENTIFICATION = RECORD
                     NAME : ALFA30;
                     ADDRESS : LOCATION;
                     PAYMENT : (NONE, CASH, CHARGE)
                  END (* OF IDENTIFICATION RECORD *);
        INVOICE = RECORD
                     ITEM : SPECIFICATIONS;
                     PURCHASER : IDENTIFICATION
                  END (* OF INVOICE RECORD *);
   VAR
        ORDER : INVOICE;
```

2. Define data structures that meet the following specifications.

   a. Create an information structure that can store the following data for a state: the name of the governor, the names of its senators, the number of representatives it has, the year in which it was admitted to the union, and its current population.
   b. Extend the structure described in part a to include all 50 states.
   c. Extend the structure described in part b to cover each election year from 1900 to the present.

3. Develop data structures that could be used to store information about the following:

   a. The books in a library.
   b. A fleet of rental automobiles.
   c. The students in a university.
   d. Teams in a bowling league.

9.4
PROGRAMMING PROBLEMS

All of the following programming problems encourage the use of sets and records. Make use of appropriate sets or records whenever possible.

1. Write a program that will read two character strings and then print the following information:

   a. A list of all letters and digits that occur at least once in each string.

b. A list of all letters and digits that occur at least once in both strings.

c. A list of all letters and digits that occur in one of the two strings but not in the other.

d. A list of all letters and digits that do not appear in either of the two strings.

2. A REAL number in exponential form consists of a mantissa (in INTEGER or REAL form) followed by the letter E and an INTEGER exponent. Both the mantissa and the exponent may have a sign. Write a program that will read a character string that is supposed to represent a REAL number in exponential form and determine if it is validly constructed. If the input string does not represent a valid number, the program should indicate why it is improper by printing an appropriate message.

3. In mathematics a complex number is written in the form a + bi where a and b are real numbers (known as the real and imaginary parts of the complex number, respectively) and i represents $\sqrt{-1}$. Suppose a + bi and c + di are two complex numbers. Addition, subtraction, multiplication, and division of two complex numbers are each defined to yield a result that is also a complex number. These operations are defined in terms of the usual arithmetic operations applied to the real and imaginary parts of the complex numbers involved as described below.

Sum of a + bi and c + di: (a + c) + (b + d)i
Difference of a + bi and c + di: (a − c) + (b − d)i
Product of a + bi and c + di: (ac − bd) + (ad + bc)i
Quotient of a + bi divided by c + di: $\left(\dfrac{ac + bd}{c^2 + d^2}\right) + \left(\dfrac{bc - ad}{c^2 + d^2}\right)i$

The arithmetic indicated inside the parentheses is the usual arithmetic for real numbers. Write a program that will read the real and imaginary parts of two complex numbers and then compute the sum, difference, product, and quotient of those numbers. The program should print the results in the normal complex number form:

(real part) + (imaginary part)I

4. In a professional baseball league there are five teams, each of which will draft four players from a list of 20 eligible players. The five teams in their drafting order are the Omaha Tigers, the Wichita Lions, the Tulsa Cowboys, the Denver Spikes, and the Santa Fe Steamers. Each team will draft one player at a time until each has chosen four players. Every team has a list of the eligible players that includes pertinent data. The players' names, ages (ranging from 17 to 25), and positions (pitcher, catcher, infielder, outfielder) are given, along with certain other information that depends on a player's position. A catcher, infielder, or outfielder will have a batting average, number of home runs, and number of errors committed. A pitcher will have the number of games won, the number of games lost, an earned run average, number of strikeouts, and number of walks. All player statistics are for last year's season. Write a program that will accept player information as input and then conduct the draft. The program must keep track of those players who have already been drafted and the teams

that drafted them so that no player is drafted more than once. After the draft is complete, the program should print out the lists of players drafted by each team along with the data for those players.

5. Write a program that will create and maintain bank accounts for as many as 50 people. Each bank account must include the account number, name of the person holding the account, and a transaction record showing all deposits and withdrawals. The program should be able to read a person's name and a dollar amount (positive for a deposit, negative for a withdrawal) and then record the transaction. When the name of a person does not match an existing account, the program should open a new account. In no circumstances are withdrawals allowed to reduce the funds available in an account below zero. After all accounts have been updated, the program should print a history of each account that traces all deposits and withdrawals and their effect on the account balance.

6. Suppose that the students in a college course take up to six hour-long tests and a final examination. Each hour test may have a maximum point value in the range 75 to 150 and the final examination may be worth from 150 to 250 points. A student's grade is based on total accumulated points. The instructor maintains a record of each student's name, Social Security number, test scores, and final examination score. Letter grades (A, B, C, D, or E) are awarded according to a scale that provides a cutoff percentage for each grade, such as 93% for an A, 85% for a B, and so on. Write a program that will accept student records as input and then produce a class roster showing the input information for each student as well as the total points accumulated, percentage of the total possible points, and a letter grade. The roster should be sorted so that the student records are listed in decreasing order of total points accumulated. The point values of each test and the final examination and the cutoff percentages should also be read as input.

7. A company owns three identical machines that are shared by each of its departments. These machines must be scheduled for use a day in advance. The scheduling is made on a first-come, first-served basis. No department may schedule a machine for more than a 2-hour block of time between 8:00 A.M. and 5:00 P.M., nor can a machine be scheduled for less than 15 minutes. Write a program that will schedule the machines. Requests will consist of a starting time, an ending time, and the name and department of the person making the request. Since the company does not want any one of the machines running constantly while another is unused most of the time, the program should attempt to distribute the workload between the machines so that each will be busy for approximately the same length of time during the day. When a requested block of time cannot be accommodated on any of the machines, the program should ask for an alternate block of time. Once the scheduling is complete, each machine's schedule, showing the hours in use and the user's name as well as the idle times, should be printed.

8. During various times of the year, the machines described in Problem 7 are not used at all by the company. On such days, they are rented by other businesses outside the company. However, the machines must still be scheduled one day in advance of their use. There is no limit on the length of time a user may have a machine, except that the machines are available only between 8:00 A.M. and

5:00 P.M. The rates charged by the company vary according to the length of time requested:

Length of Time	Charge per Minute
Less than 30 minutes	$2.60
30 minutes to 59 minutes	$2.45
60 minutes to 239 minutes	$2.25
240 minutes or more	$2.10

Write a program that will schedule the machines as outlined in Problem 7 with the exceptions noted above. The program should print the schedule for each machine and a billing list that shows the name of each company that rented the machines, machine time, and amounts to be charged.

9. A certain state penitentiary houses people convicted of first-degree murder, second-degree murder, rape, or armed robbery. A summary record is maintained for each inmate which shows the inmate's name, type of offense, age when convicted, date of entry into the penitentiary, and length of sentence (in years and months). The prisoners are housed in three cell blocks according to length of sentence:

Cell Block	Length of Sentence
I	20 years or less
II	20 years and 1 month to 50 years
III	More than 50 years

Write a program that will read the information for the prisoners and then print a list of the prisoners in each building. The lists should be ordered by increasing length of sentence. A projected release date (year and month) should be determined for each prisoner and printed in the listing. The program should also compute and print the average age of the persons who have committed each type of offense.

10. Write a program that will isolate individual words in line after line of input text and record new words in word-length categories (one-letter words, two-letter words, three-letter words, etc.). Assume that consecutive words will be separated by one or more blank spaces, a combination of blank spaces and punctuation marks, or the end of an input line. The program should keep track of all 1-letter to 15-letter words encountered and should have a catchall category for words more than 15 letters long. After all the input text has been read, the words should be printed by their categories.

11. This problem is a variation of Problem 10. Have the program print the words in each category in alphabetical order and show the frequency of occurrence of each word in the input text.

TEN/FILES

Simple variables, arrays, sets, and records are all used to store data during the execution of a program, but they do not retain values from one run of the program to the next. They exist only while the program in which they are declared is executed; the memory space allocated to them is released when the program ends. There is often a need to retain data in the computer's memory so that it can be accessed at a later time. These data can be stored in a **file** that has been created in mass storage (on a magnetic tape or disk).

The main advantage that a file has over other data structures such as arrays and records is that it is not limited to a predefined size. In Pascal a file is a structured variable, but it does not have a fixed number of components. Data files may exist either internally or externally to a program. An **internal file** is a structured variable that, like arrays and records, exists only during an execution of the program in which it is declared. An **external file** does not rely on a program for its existence. A program may create or use an external file as it does an internal file, but an external file does not disappear when the program ends. Thus, external files may serve as sources of data for many different programs. The way that external files are differentiated from internal files in a program is explained toward the end of Section 10.1.

The two standard files named INPUT and OUTPUT are external files, but they cannot be used in quite the same manner as user-defined files. In general, it is possible for a program to get data from a file as well as to put data into a file. However, the INPUT file is always associated with a device that is capable only of reading data from the file, thereby preventing a program from writing data into the INPUT file. On the other hand, a program may put data into the OUTPUT file, but it cannot read data from that file.

10.1
BASIC FILE CONCEPTS

In Pascal a file is a structured variable. Unlike arrays and records, files have components that do not have names and the components are not randomly accessible. Each component of a file has the same base type, but the number of components a file may have is not fixed. The components are arranged in a sequence, and only one component at a time is available to a program. All file variables except INPUT and OUTPUT must be declared in a variable declaration in the declaration section of the program that uses them. A name may be associated with a file by a TYPE definition of the form

type-identifier = FILE OF *base-type;*

The *base-type* for a file may be a simple data type or it may be a structured type such as an array or record. In this section we will restrict our attention to files with simple base types, although what will be said applies to files with structured components as well.

PUTTING DATA INTO A FILE

Access to a file is provided by a **buffer variable** that is created when the file is declared. The buffer variable's type is the same as the base type for the file. It serves as a "window" to the file through which exactly one file component is visible. Suppose that SCOREFILE is a file consisting of INTEGER components that is declared by

```
TYPE
      NUMBERLIST = FILE OF INTEGER;
VAR
      SCOREFILE : NUMBERLIST;
```

The buffer variable associated with SCOREFILE is identified as SCOREFILE ↑. In general, the name of the buffer variable for a file is the name of the file followed by an up-arrow (or a circumflex). Since SCOREFILE has INTEGER type components, SCOREFILE ↑ is an INTEGER variable.

A program is able to put data into a file only after that file has been opened for output by a call to the standard procedure REWRITE that takes the form

REWRITE(*file-identifier*)

For instance, SCOREFILE may be opened for output by using the statement

REWRITE (SCOREFILE)

A call to REWRITE destroys any existing data in the file specified so that a new file can be constructed. Suppose we want to put the integers 68, 84, and 75 into SCOREFILE. Each integer must be assigned to the buffer variable SCOREFILE ↑ and then the contents of SCOREFILE ↑ must be entered into SCOREFILE by a call to the standard procedure PUT that takes the form

PUT(*file-identifier*)

Here is a sequence of statements that will put 68, 84, and 75 into SCOREFILE.

```
REWRITE (SCOREFILE);
SCOREFILE^ := 68;
PUT (SCOREFILE);
SCOREFILE^ := 84;
PUT (SCOREFILE);
SCOREFILE^ := 75;
PUT (SCOREFILE)
```

Note that each value is assigned to SCOREFILE ↑ and then the value of SCOREFILE ↑ is PUT into the file. After each call to PUT, SCOREFILE ↑ is undefined (has no meaningful value). The status of SCOREFILE and its buffer variable after the three values have been entered into the file is depicted below.

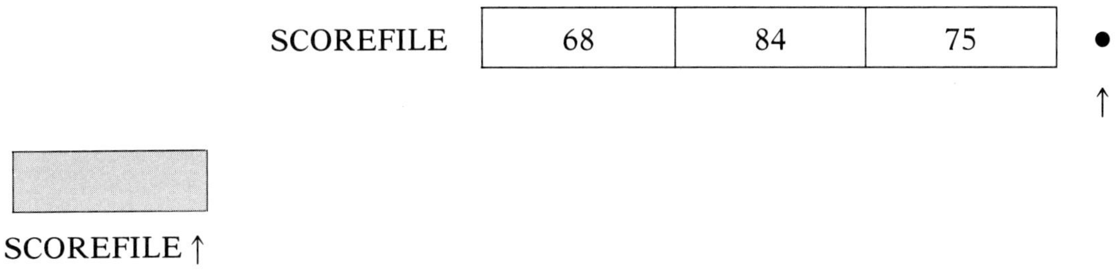

SCOREFILE | 68 | 84 | 75 | •
↑

SCOREFILE ↑

In this diagram, the symbol "•" marks the current end of the file and the symbol "↑" represents the file pointer that marks the position in the file where the next value can be PUT. While a file is open for output, the file pointer will always be positioned at the current end of the file.

It is worthwhile to examine the effects of each statement used to insert the values 68, 84, and 75 into SCOREFILE. The following diagrams trace the status of SCOREFILE and its buffer variable as each statement is executed.

```
REWRITE (SCOREFILE);
```
SCOREFILE •
↑

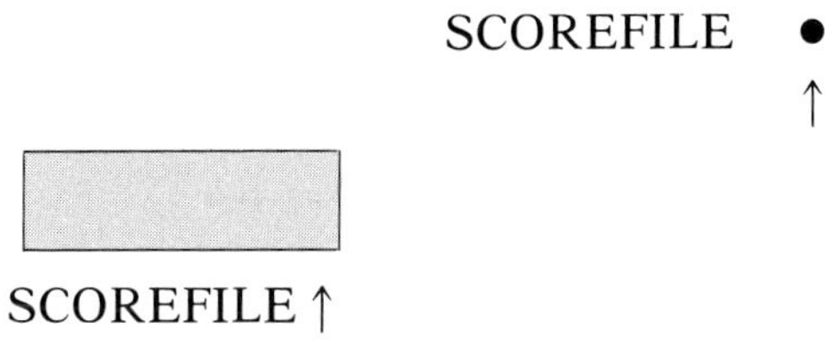

SCOREFILE ↑

```
SCOREFILE^ := 68;
```
SCOREFILE •
↑

| 68 |

SCOREFILE ↑

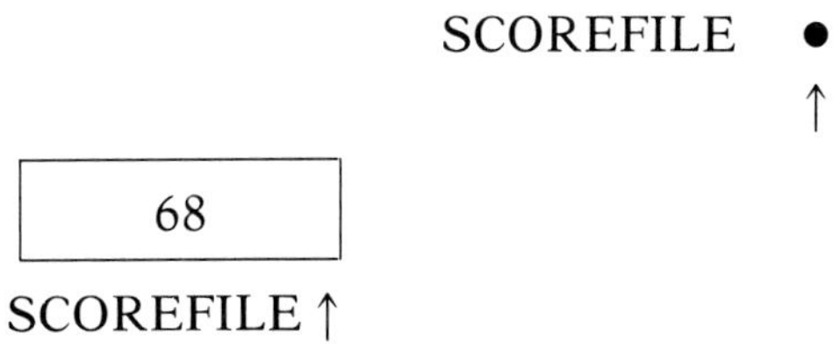

```
PUT (SCOREFILE);
```
SCOREFILE | 68 | • 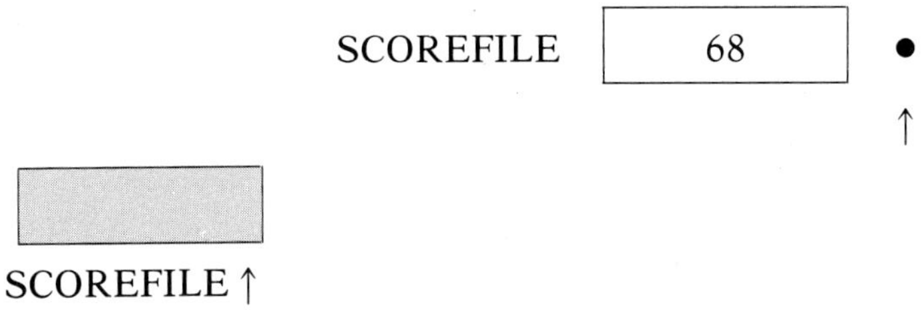
↑

SCOREFILE ↑

```
SCOREFILE^ := 84;
```
SCOREFILE | 68 | •
↑

| 84 |

SCOREFILE ↑

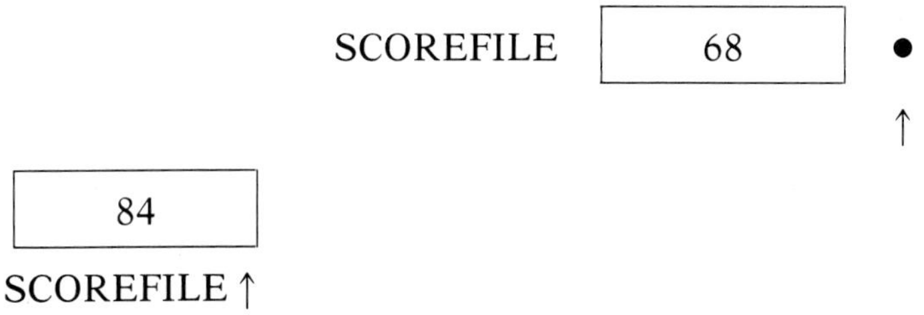

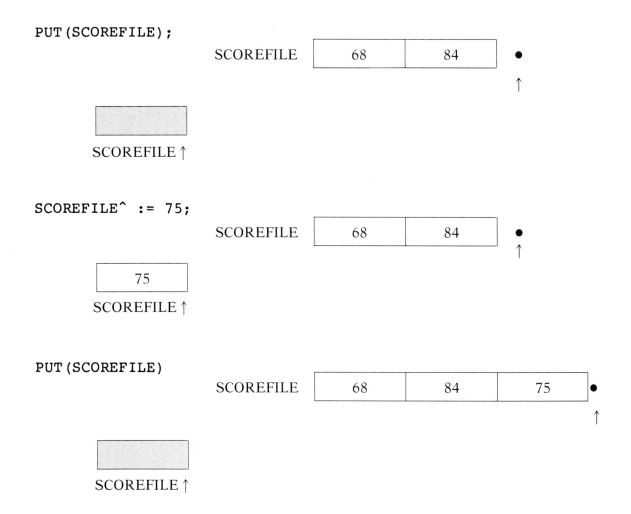

Although each value must be assigned to the buffer variable before it can be PUT into the file, the standard procedure WRITE can be used to accomplish both tasks. A call to WRITE the value of an *item* into a file takes the form

$$\text{WRITE}(\textit{file-identifier, item})$$

When a WRITE statement is used to send information to the OUTPUT file, the file identifier OUTPUT is optional and one or more items may be listed. If WRITE is called to send information to any other file except OUTPUT, the name of the file must be listed first. The standard procedure WRITELN may only be used to write data into a file whose base type is CHAR. Such files are known as TEXT files and they will be discussed in Section 10.2. When the procedure WRITE is called to generate output to any file except a TEXT file, only one *item* may be listed. That *item* may appear as a constant, variable, or expression whose value has the same base type as the file, and WRITE produces the same effects as the pair of statements

$$\textit{file-identifier} \uparrow := \textit{item};$$
$$\text{PUT}(\textit{file-identifier})$$

Thus the sequence of statements used earlier to PUT the values 68, 84, and 75 into SCOREFILE can be replaced by the the program segment

```
REWRITE(SCOREFILE);
WRITE(SCOREFILE, 68);
WRITE(SCOREFILE, 84);
WRITE(SCOREFILE, 75)
```

A procedure to CREATE a file of integer values is given next. Note that the only parameter for this procedure is a file of the type NUMBERLIST and that it is a variable parameter. A file cannot be created solely for the local use of a subprogram. **In Pascal all formal parameters for functions and procedures that are files must be declared as variable parameters.**

```
PROCEDURE CREATE (VAR AFILE : NUMBERLIST);
  CONST
          FLAGVALUE = -99999;
  VAR
          NUMBER : INTEGER;
  BEGIN (* PROCEDURE CREATE *)
  REWRITE(AFILE);
  WRITELN('THE FILE IS NOW READY TO BE WRITTEN. ENTER THE INTEGERS');
  WRITELN('ON AS MANY LINES AS NECESSARY. TO SIGNAL THE END OF DATA');
  WRITELN('INPUT, ENTER THE VALUE ', FLAGVALUE:6, ' AFTER THE LAST');
  WRITELN('NUMBER WHICH IS TO BE PUT INTO THE FILE.');
  WRITELN('BEGIN ENTERING YOUR DATA NOW.');
  WRITELN;
  READ(NUMBER);
  WHILE NUMBER <> FLAGVALUE
     DO BEGIN (* PUTTING A NUMBER INTO THE FILE *)
        WRITE(AFILE, NUMBER);
        READ(NUMBER)
        END (* OF PUTTING A NUMBER INTO THE FILE *);
  WRITELN;
  WRITELN('FILE CREATION IS NOW COMPLETE.')
  END (* OF PROCEDURE CREATE *);
```

Suppose CREATE is called by using the statement

CREATE(SCOREFILE)

The following dialogue between the procedure and the program user may take place:

```
THE FILE IS NOW READY TO BE WRITTEN. ENTER THE INTEGERS
ON AS MANY LINES AS NECESSARY. TO SIGNAL THE END OF DATA
INPUT, ENTER THE VALUE -99999 AFTER THE LAST
NUMBER WHICH IS TO BE PUT INTO THE FILE.
BEGIN ENTERING YOUR DATA NOW.

? 68 84 75 -28 165 -99999

FILE CREATION IS NOW COMPLETE.
```

After CREATE has returned control to the calling program, the status of SCORE-FILE and its buffer variable will be as depicted here.

SCOREFILE	68	84	75	−28	165	●

↑

SCOREFILE ↑

Furthermore, SCOREFILE is still open for output, and so the main program or one of its subprograms could write more data to the end of the file without destroying the data already in the file. It is not possible to insert a new value between two values already in the file. All data written in a file will be inserted at the end of the file in the sequence in which they are written.

GETTING DATA FROM A FILE

A file that is opened for output (established by a call to the procedure REWRITE) cannot be simultaneously used as a source of input for the program. In order for a program to use a file as a source of data, that file must first be opened for input by a call to the standard procedure RESET that takes the form

RESET(*file-identifier*)

The standard files INPUT and OUTPUT can never be RESET. A call to RESET a file will position the file pointer at the first component of the file (assuming the file is not empty) and the contents of that component will be copied to the file's buffer variable. Suppose SCOREFILE is a file of the type NUMBERLIST that is not empty. SCOREFILE may contain many values, but the statement

RESET(SCOREFILE)

will open the file for input by positioning the file pointer at the very first component and placing the value of that component in the buffer variable SCOREFILE ↑ as depicted here.

SCOREFILE	245	13	−18	. . .	66	●

↑

245

SCOREFILE ↑

When a file is open for input, the only file value available to the program is the one in that file's buffer variable. The file pointer can be advanced to the next component in the file by a call to the standard procedure GET that takes the form

GET(*file-identifier*)

GET also causes the contents of the next file component to be copied into the buffer variable. Thus the contents of the buffer variable always match the contents of the file component at which the file pointer is positioned, unless the file pointer has reached the end-of-file mark. If a GET moves the file pointer to the end of the file, the buffer variable will be undefined and it will be impossible to GET another value from that file until it has been RESET again. The standard function EOF that we have been using to test for the end of the INPUT file may be called in the form

$$\text{EOF}(\textit{file-identifier})$$

to produce the value TRUE when the file pointer for the specified file is at the end-of-file mark, or FALSE otherwise. When EOF is called without specifying a file, the file INPUT is automatically assumed. The following loop can be used to print the entire contents of the file named SCOREFILE.

```
RESET(SCOREFILE);
WHILE NOT EOF(SCOREFILE)
    DO BEGIN
        WRITELN(SCOREFILE^);
        GET(SCOREFILE)
    END
```

The function EOF can also be used to test the status of a file that is open for output, but it should always return the value TRUE because the file pointer is always at the end of a file that is being written.

Suppose we want to RESET the SCOREFILE and then assign the first two values in that file to the INTEGER variables A and B. This can be accomplished by using the following sequence of statements.

```
RESET(SCOREFILE);
A := SCOREFILE^;
GET(SCOREFILE);
B := SCOREFILE^;
GET(SCOREFILE)
```

The following diagrams trace the effects of this program segment statement by statement. Only the first few components of SCOREFILE are shown in the diagrams.

`RESET(SCOREFILE);`

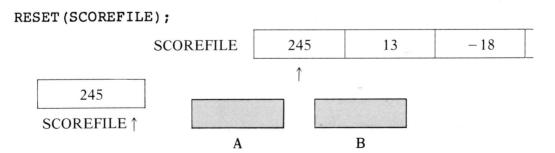

`A := SCOREFILE^;`

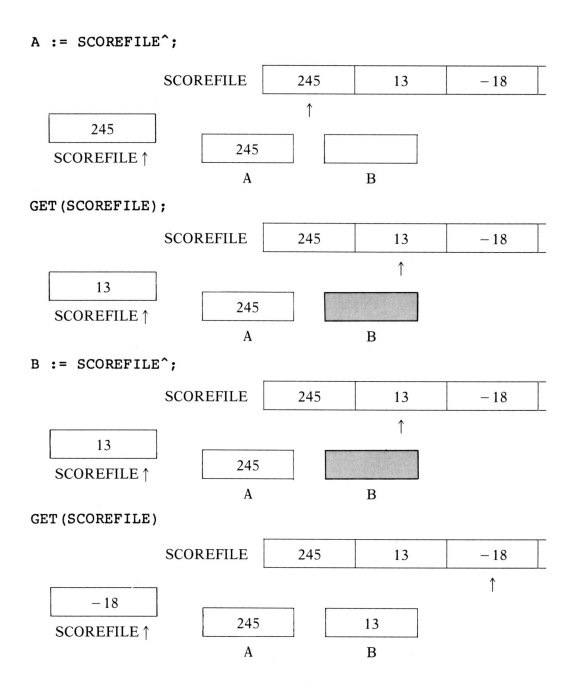

`GET(SCOREFILE);`

`B := SCOREFILE^;`

`GET(SCOREFILE)`

The last call to GET is used to have a new file value ready in the buffer variable when it is needed. We could continue sequentially to GET values from the file until the EOF(SCOREFILE) is TRUE. Any time RESET(SCOREFILE) is executed, the file pointer will be repositioned to the first component of the file SCOREFILE and the value of that component will also be the value of the file's buffer variable.

READ is the name of a standard procedure used to get input from a file that is open for input. We have used READ statements in the past to get data from the INPUT file, but a more general call to READ takes the form

READ(*file-identifier, variable*)

When READing data from the INPUT file, listing the file identifier INPUT is optional. If a READ statement is used to get input from any other data file, the name of the file must be specified first and then the name of a variable that is to receive the input value. READing a file value for a variable is equivalent to the pair of statements

$$variable := file\text{-}identifier\uparrow;$$
$$\text{GET}(file\text{-}identifier)$$

The program segment used previously to assign values from the beginning of the file SCOREFILE to the variables A and B can be replaced by the sequence of statements

```
RESET(SCOREFILE);
READ(SCOREFILE, A);
READ(SCOREFILE, B)
```

Only one variable may be specified in a call to READ unless the file to be read is a TEXT file. Use of the standard procedure READLN is restricted to TEXT files and will be discussed in Section 10.2

It is not possible to alternate between reading and writing components of the same file in Pascal because a file cannot be open for input and output at the same time. A program may utilize many files, some of them open for input and some of them open for output. An attempt to WRITE to a file that is open for input or READ from a file that is open for output is an execution error. It is also an execution error to attempt to READ from a file that is open for input but has its file pointer positioned at the end of the file. It is very important to check the status of a file by using the EOF function before attempting to GET or READ a value from that file. Consider the following procedure, which can be used to print the entire contents of a NUMBERLIST type file.

```
PROCEDURE DUMP (VAR THEFILE : NUMBERLIST);
   VAR
        NUMBER : INTEGER;
   BEGIN (* PROCEDURE DUMP *)
   RESET(THEFILE);
   WHILE NOT EOF(THEFILE)
      DO BEGIN (* PRINTING A NUMBER *)
         READ(THEFILE, NUMBER);
         WRITELN(NUMBER)
         END (* OF PRINTING A NUMBER *)
   END (* OF PROCEDURE DUMP *);
```

If GET is used in place of READ in the procedure DUMP, the values to be printed will be available in the buffer variable THEFILE↑, and so the WHILE loop could be written in the form

```
WHILE NOT EOF(THEFILE)
   DO BEGIN (* PRINTING A VALUE *)
      NUMBER := THEFILE^;
      WRITELN(NUMBER);
      GET(THEFILE)
      END (* OF PRINTING A VALUE *)
```

Actually, the variable NUMBER is not needed because the name of the buffer variable can be used in the WRITELN statement:

```
WHILE NOT EOF (THEFILE)
    DO BEGIN (* PRINTING A VALUE *)
        WRITELN (THEFILE^);
        GET (THEFILE)
        END (* OF PRINTING A VALUE *)
```

INTERNAL AND EXTERNAL FILES

The names of all external files used by a program must appear in the program heading. All files except INPUT and OUTPUT, whether they are internal files or external files, must also be declared as variables in the declaration section of the program. When a program uses a file whose name does not appear in the program heading, it will be an internal file that exists only while the program is being executed. An internal file, like records, arrays, and simple variables that a program may use, does not contain any values when the program begins and it will not be available after the program has ended. External files used by a program may exist both before and after the execution of the program.

Internal files are commonly used to store temporarily information that will be copied to one or more external files before the program ends. Suppose that SCORES is an external file of integers that already exists and we want to be able to update the file by appending additional data to the end of the file. It is not appropriate to REWRITE(SCORES) because doing so will erase the contents of SCORES before opening that file for output. The proper way to update SCORES requries three processing steps:

Use COPY(SCORES, SCRATCH, TESTCOUNT) to create a working file
    named SCRATCH that is a copy of the file SCORES
Put the new data into the SCRATCH file

Use COPY(SCRATCH, SCORES, TESTCOUNT) to copy the updated
    SCRATCH file to the master SCORES file

COPY is a procedure that will REWRITE a DESTINATION file, RESET a SOURCE file, and then copy the contents of the SOURCE file into the DESTINATION file:

REWRITE the DESTINATION file
RESET the SOURCE file
WHILE there is another value in the SOURCE file
    DO BEGIN a read and copy
        READ a COMPONENT value from the SOURCE file
        WRITE the COMPONENT value to the DESTINATION file
        END of a read and copy

The TESTFILEUPDATE program shown next can be used either to create a SCORES file or to update a SCORES file that already exists. SCORES is an external file and so it will retain its values after the program has ended. The program will insert a negative integer into the file before any new SCOREs are appended to the file so that the sequences of integers entered from one run of the program to the next will be marked by negative integers. Furthermore, these negative integers will appear in the sequence -1, -2, -3, etc., so that their absolute values will serve as data set numbers.

```
PROGRAM TESTFILEUPDATE (INPUT, OUTPUT, SCORES);
(***************************************************************
*                                                             *
*       A PROGRAM TO CREATE OR UPDATE A FILE OF TEST SCORES    *
*                                                             *
***************************************************************)
TYPE
      TESTMARKS = FILE OF INTEGER;

VAR                                 (*------[INTEGER VARIABLES]------*)
      TESTCOUNT,                    (* COUNT OF TESTS IN SCORES FILE *)
      NEWSCORE : INTEGER;           (* NEW VALUE FOR THE SCORES FILE *)
                                    (*-----------------------------*)
                                    (*-------[TESTMARKS FILES]-------*)
      SCORES,                       (* MASTER FILE OF TEST SCORES    *)
      SCRATCH : TESTMARKS;          (* TEMPORARY FILE FOR TEST SCORES*)
                                    (*-----------------------------*)

PROCEDURE COPY
   (*==========================================================*)
   (*   COPY A SOURCE FILE CONTAINING DATA SETS OF NONNEGATIVE  *)
   (*   INTEGERS WHICH ARE SEPARATED BY NEGATIVE INTEGERS       *)
   (*==========================================================*)
                                    (*---------[PARAMETERS]----------*)
   (VAR SOURCE,                     (* FILE TO BE COPIED            *)
        DESTINATION : TESTMARKS;    (* NEW COPY OF THE SOURCE FILE   *)
    VAR COUNT : INTEGER);           (* COUNT OF THE DATA SETS        *)
                                    (*-----------------------------*)
    VAR                             (*------[INTEGER VARIABLES]------*)
        COMPONENT : INTEGER;        (* A FILE COMPONENT             *)
                                    (*-----------------------------*)
   (*==========================================================*)
   BEGIN (* PROCEDURE COPY *)
   REWRITE(DESTINATION);
   RESET(SOURCE);
   COUNT := 0;
   WHILE NOT EOF(SOURCE)
      DO BEGIN (* A READ AND COPY *)
         READ(SOURCE, COMPONENT);
         WRITE(DESTINATION, COMPONENT);
         IF COMPONENT < 0
           THEN COUNT := ABS(COMPONENT)
         END (* OF A READ AND COPY *)
   END (* OF PROCEDURE COPY *);


(***************************************************************)
```

```
BEGIN (* PROGRAM TESTFILEUPDATE *)
COPY(SCORES, SCRATCH, TESTCOUNT);
WRITE(SCRATCH, -1 - TESTCOUNT);
WRITELN('THIS PROGRAM WILL CREATE A FILE NAMED SCORES OR ADD ',
        'ANOTHER DATA');
WRITELN('SET TO AN EXISTING SCORES FILE. IT IS ASSUMED THAT ',
        'THE NUMBERS');
WRITELN('IN A DATA SET WILL BE NONNEGATIVE INTEGERS. THERE ARE ',
        'CURRENTLY');
WRITELN(TESTCOUNT:2, ' DATA SETS IN THE SCORES FILE.');
WRITELN;
WRITELN('YOU MAY ENTER AS MANY NUMBERS ON A LINE AS YOU WISH. ',
        'TO SIGNAL THE');
WRITELN('END OF DATA INPUT, ENTER ANY NEGATIVE INTEGER.');
WRITELN('READY FOR THE NEW DATA SET.');
READ(NEWSCORE);
WHILE NEWSCORE >= 0
   DO BEGIN (* APPEND VALUE TO END OF FILE *)
      WRITE(SCRATCH, NEWSCORE);
      READ(NEWSCORE)
      END (* OF APPEND VALUE TO END OF FILE *);
WRITELN('END OF NEW DATA SET.');
COPY(SCRATCH, SCORES, TESTCOUNT);
WRITELN('THERE ARE NOW ', TESTCOUNT:2, ' DATA SETS IN THE SCORES ',
        'FILE.')
END (* OF PROGRAM TESTFILEUPDATE *).
```

To make an existing SCORES file available to the program TESTFILEUPDATE, it may be necessary to issue one or more control commands. The need for such commands and their exact forms vary from one implementation of Pascal to the next. If no existing SCORES file is made available to the program, then a SCORES file will be created. Suppose that this is the situation when TESTFILEUPDATE is executed, resulting in the following dialogue.

```
THIS PROGRAM WILL CREATE A FILE NAMED SCORES OR ADD ANOTHER DATA
SET TO AN EXISTING SCORES FILE. IT IS ASSUMED THAT THE NUMBERS
IN A DATA SET WILL BE NONNEGATIVE INTEGERS. THERE ARE CURRENTLY
 0 DATA SETS IN THE SCORES FILE.

YOU MAY ENTER AS MANY NUMBERS ON A LINE AS YOU WISH. TO SIGNAL THE
END OF DATA INPUT, ENTER ANY NEGATIVE INTEGER.
READY FOR THE NEW DATA SET.
? 78 94 76 -99
END OF NEW DATA SET.
THERE ARE NOW  1 DATA SETS IN THE SCORES FILE.
```

When TESTFILEUPDATE has ended, the file SCORES still exists and it contains the information depicted here.

SCORES	−1	78	94	76	●

Now suppose TESTFILEUPDATE is executed again to append another data set to the end of the SCORES file:

```
THIS PROGRAM WILL CREATE A FILE NAMED SCORES OR ADD ANOTHER DATA
SET TO AN EXISTING SCORES FILE. IT IS ASSUMED THAT THE NUMBERS
IN A DATA SET WILL BE NONNEGATIVE INTEGERS. THERE ARE CURRENTLY
 1 DATA SETS IN THE SCORES FILE.

YOU MAY ENTER AS MANY NUMBERS ON A LINE AS YOU WISH. TO SIGNAL THE
END OF DATA INPUT, ENTER ANY NEGATIVE INTEGER.
READY FOR THE NEW DATA SET.
? 86 57 -7
END OF THE NEW DATA SET.
THERE ARE NOW  2 DATA SETS IN THE SCORES FILE.
```

Now the SCORES file looks like this:

SCORES	−1	78	94	76	−2	86	57	●

To simplify the foregoing examples, only small data sets were used. A program user may enter as many numbers for the file as desired. Note how the negative integers have been inserted by the program to separate the data sets. They also serve to number the data sets. A program could be written to access any particular data set or combination of data sets. Such a program would simply READ or GET numbers from the SCORES file until it encountered a negative number whose absolute value is the sequence number for the desired data set. The file must be scanned sequentially from its beginning; there is no way to cause an automatic jump to a particular file component other than the first component.

10.1 EXERCISES

1. Suppose MONEY and CASH are variables declared by

```
VAR
       CASH : REAL;
       MONEY : FILE OF REAL;
```

The file MONEY is open for output. Tell what (if anything) is wrong with each of the following program segments, which attempt to PUT a CASH value into the file.

a.
```
READ(CASH;
PUT(MONEY, CASH)
```

b.
```
READ(CASH);
PUT(MONEY);
MONEY^ := CASH
```

c.
```
READ(CASH);
MONEY^ := CASH;
PUT(MONEY)
```

d.
```
READ(CASH);
CASH := MONEY^;
PUT(CASH)
```

2. Consider the following declarations.

```
VAR
      I : INTEGER;
      C : CHAR;
      NUMBERS : FILE OF INTEGER;
      LETTERS : FILE OF CHAR;
```

Each of the following program segments will construct a file. Draw a diagram that shows the contents of each file after it has been constructed.

```
a.  REWRITE (NUMBERS);
    FOR I := 1 TO 10
      DO IF I MOD 3 = 0
          THEN WRITE (NUMBERS, 11 - I)
          ELSE WRITE (NUMBERS, I)
```

```
b.  REWRITE (LETTERS);
    FOR C := 'A' TO 'G'
      DO CASE C OF
              'A','E' : WRITE (LETTERS, C);
          'B','D','G' : WRITE (LETTERS, 'C');
              'C','F' : WRITE (LETTERS, CHR(ORD(C) - 1))
          END (* OF C CASES *);
    WRITELN
```

3. Suppose OURDATA is a FILE OF INTEGER that contains the values depicted below.

OURDATA	116	29	− 13	82	47	12	− 34	●

Each of the program segments that follow will get values from the OURDATA file and print some output. Show the status of the file after a program segment has been executed (including the contents of OURDATA ↑) and show the output that is produced. Also, rewrite each segment using READ instead of GET to access file data. (Assume that SUM is an INTEGER variable.)

```
a.          RESET (OURDATA);
            WHILE NOT EOF (OURDATA)
                DO BEGIN
                    IF OURDATA^ MOD 2 = 0
                      THEN WRITE (OURDATA^:4)
                      ELSE WRITE ('***':4);
                    GET (OURDATA)
                    END;
            WRITELN
```

```
b.          RESET (OURDATA);
            SUM := 0;
            REPEAT
              SUM := SUM + OURDATA^;
              GET (OURDATA)
            UNTIL SUM > 150;
            WRITELN ('SUM =', SUM:4)
```

4. Consider the following definitions and declarations.

```
TYPE
        CODES = 100 .. 99999;
        CODEFILE = FILE OF CODES;
VAR
        LIST1, LIST2 : CODEFILE;
```

LIST1 is an existing file that is not empty.

a. Write a subprogram that will return the number of times a particular CODES value appears in the file LIST1.
b. Write a subprogram that will copy all values in LIST1 that are greater than a particular CODES value into a new LIST2 file.

10.2 TEXT FILES

A file that has CHAR type components is known as a text file. The standard procedures PUT, GET, READ, and WRITE can be used with text files, as described in Section 10.1. Both INPUT and OUTPUT are text files, but we know that it is possible to READ from the INPUT file and WRITE into the OUTPUT file data that are not necessarily CHAR type. When the procedures READ and WRITE are used with text files, they can assemble a sequence of one or more characters to form other types of data. For instance, it is possible to READ a REAL number form the INPUT file or WRITE such a number into the OUTPUT file. Pascal automatically takes care of the conversion between a sequence of characters and a data value represented by that sequence.

Text files are used more often than any other type of file. Pascal provides a standard data type named TEXT whose definition is

TEXT = FILE OF CHAR;

Since TEXT is the name of a standard data type, it may be used like the type identifiers INTEGER, REAL, CHAR, and BOOLEAN to define variables. A TEXT variable will be a file with CHAR components.

WRITING TEXT FILES

A TEXT file, like any file, is opened for output by a call to the standard procedure REWRITE. It is not legal for a program to REWRITE either the INPUT file or the OUTPUT file. The INPUT file cannot be used as an output file and the OUTPUT file is automatically opened for output when a program begins. A WRITE statement of the form

WRITE(*file-identifier, item*)

can be used to put the value of an item into a specified TEXT file, where the item may be any constant, variable, or expression whose value is of the type INTEGER, REAL, CHAR, BOOLEAN, or PACKED ARRAY of CHAR. (Some versions of Pascal will not allow BOOLEAN values to be written to the OUTPUT file or any other TEXT file.) Writing the value of an item into a TEXT file causes the sequence of characters representing that value to be placed into the file. The default field widths used to WRITE values into the OUTPUT file apply to all TEXT files, but a specific field width may be established for an item in the usual manner. For instance, the statement

```
WRITE(FILEX, 378)
```

will put seven spaces followed by the characters 3, 7, and 8 into the TEXT file FILEX if the default field width used to print INTEGER values into the OUTPUT file is ten. The statement

```
WRITE(FILEX, 378:5)
```

will put two blank spaces followed by the characters 3, 7, and 8 into FILEX because a field width of 5 is specified. As for the OUTPUT file, a REAL value will be inserted into any TEXT file in exponential form unless two field widths are specified.

When a WRITE statement is used to put data into a TEXT file, more than one item may be listed after the name of the file. A statement of the form

WRITE(*file-identifier, item-1, item-2, . . . , item-n*)

is equivalent to the sequence of statements

WRITE(*file-identifier, item-1*);
WRITE(*file-identifier, item-2*);
•
•
•
WRITE(*file-identifier, item-n*)

As before, if no file identifier is specified in a WRITE statement, OUTPUT is automatically assumed. Suppose the following declarations have been made:

```
VAR
      A : INTEGER;
      B : REAL;
      FILEX : TEXT;
```

Assume that the variables A and B have been assigned the values 12 and 7.35, respectively. Here is a program segment that puts some data into FILEX.

```
REWRITE(FILEX);
WRITE(FILEX, 'A=', A:3);
WRITE(FILEX, ' B=', B:6:3);
WRITE(FILEX, 2.0 * B + 1.5:6:1)
```

The status of FILEX after this program segment has been executed is depicted below.

FILEX | A | = | ■ | 1 | 2 | ■ | B | = | ■ | 7 | . | 3 | 5 | 0 | ■ | ■ | 1 | 6 | . | 2 | ●

↑

Each component of FILEX may contain one character. In order to simplify diagrams that show portions of TEXT files, we will not box the components from here on. For instance, the contents of FILEX will be shown as a stream of characters, as depicted here.

FILEX | A = ■12■B = ■7.350■■16.2 ●

↑

The standard procedure WRITELN may be called to insert a line separator into a TEXT file that is open for output. A call to WRITELN takes the form

WRITELN(*file-identifier*)

When WRITELN is called with no file identifier specified, OUTPUT is assumed and a printed line is generated on the OUTPUT device. For other TEXT files, the procedure WRITELN is used to organize the file into segments called lines. The way that a line separator is represented in a TEXT file varies from computer to computer. When a portion of a TEXT file is depicted, we will use the symbol "‖" to denote the presence of a line separator. Consider the following program segment.

```
REWRITE(FILEX);
WRITE(FILEX, 'A=', A:2);
WRITE(FILEX, ' B=', B:7:2);
WRITELN(FILEX);
WRITE(FILEX, 3.0 * B:12);
WRITELN(FILEX)
```

The status of FILEX after this program segment has been executed is depicted in the following diagram.

FILEX | A = 12■B = ■■■7.35‖■■2.2050E + 01‖ ●

↑

Suppose that the same data had been written in the OUTPUT file:

```
WRITE('A=', A:2);
WRITE(' B=', B:7:2);
WRITELN;
WRITE(3.0 * B:12);
WRITELN
```

A total of two lines of output would appear on the OUTPUT device, as shown below.

```
A=12 B=   7.35
   2.2050E+01
```

In some implementations of Pascal, the lines of a TEXT file may have to contain an even number of characters. This was noted in Chapter Four with respect to the INPUT file. When this is the case, a call to WRITELN will cause an "extra" blank space to be inserted into the file immediately before the line separator if it is needed to give the line an even number of characters.

A WRITELN statement may contain an item list:

WRITELN(*file-identifier, item-1, item-2, . . ., item-n*)

This form of the WRITELN statement is equivalent to the pair of statements

WRITE(*file-identifier, item-1, item-2, . . ., item-n*);
WRITELN(*file-identifier*)

The program segment given above to write data into FILEX can appear in the equivalent form

```
REWRITE(FILEX);
WRITELN(FILEX, 'A=', A:2, ' B=', B:7:2);
WRITELN(FILEX, 3.0 * B:12)
```

We can construct a file of integers by using a file whose base type is INTEGER (see Section 10.1) or by using a TEXT file. In a TEXT file, the integers can be organized by lines. For example, we could arrange the integers in a TEXT file so that each line contains the same number of integers. The procedure BUILD given next will construct just such a file. The parameter LIMIT is used to determine how many integers will appear in each line of INTFILE and PADVALUE will be the integer value that will be used to fill out a line that would be short of the LIMIT. Values to be inserted into INTFILE are read from the INPUT file.

```
PROCEDURE BUILD (VAR INTFILE : TEXT; LIMIT, PADVALUE : INTEGER);
  CONST
          ENDSIGNAL = '*';
  VAR
          CH : CHAR;
          COUNT, NUMBER, I : INTEGER;
  BEGIN (* PROCEDURE BUILD *)
  REWRITE(INTFILE);
  WRITELN('ENTER AS MANY INTEGERS ON A LINE AS YOU WISH. TYPE AN ',
          ENDSIGNAL);
  WRITELN('IMMEDIATELY AFTER THE LAST NUMBER YOU ENTER TO SIGNAL THE');
  WRITELN('END OF INPUT.');
  WRITELN('BEGIN ENTERING THE NUMBERS NOW.');
  COUNT := 0;
  REPEAT (* A FILE INSERTION *)
    READ(NUMBER, CH);
    COUNT := COUNT + 1;
    WRITE(INTFILE, NUMBER:4);
    IF COUNT = LIMIT
      THEN BEGIN (* INSERTING LINE SEPARATOR *)
             WRITELN(INTFILE);
             COUNT := 0
             END (* OF INSERTING LINE SEPARATOR *)
  UNTIL CH = ENDSIGNAL;
```

```
IF COUNT < LIMIT
   THEN BEGIN (* PADDING LAST FILE LINE *)
        FOR I := COUNT + 1 TO LIMIT
          DO WRITE(INTFILE, PADVALUE:4);
          WRITELN(INTFILE)
          END (* OF PADDING LAST FILE LINE *)
END (* OF PROCEDURE BUILD *);
```

Suppose that BUILD is called a construct a TEXT file named SCORES using the statement

BUILD(SCORES, 5, -1)

Here is a sample of input entered in response to the request made by the procedure BUILD.

> ENTER AS MANY INTEGERS ON A LINE AS YOU WISH. TYPE AN *
> IMMEDIATELY AFTER THE LAST NUMBER YOU ENTER TO SIGNAL THE
> END OF INPUT.
> BEGIN ENTERING THE NUMBERS NOW.
> ? 73 48 89 99 62 53 37 75 67 73 68
> ? 82 93 75 62 37 49 62 71 83 74 77
> ? 90 85 66 100 72*

Since 27 numbers are read from the INPUT file, the SCORES file will have a total of six lines and the last line will be padded with − 1 three times, as illustrated below.

SCORES ▪▪73▪▪48▪▪89▪▪99▪▪62‖▪▪53▪ . . . ▪66‖▪100▪▪72▪▪ − 1▪▪ − 1▪▪ − 1‖ ●

READING TEXT FILES

The procedure READ is used to get data from a user-defined TEXT file in basically the same way that it is used to get data from the INPUT file. The file must first be opened for input. File INPUT is automatically opened when a program begins, but any other file to be used as a source of input data must be opened by a call to the procedure RESET. It is illegal for a program to RESET the INPUT file. A value for a single variable of the type INTEGER, REAL, or CHAR may be read from a TEXT file by using a statement of the form

READ(file-identifier, variable)

The value assigned to the variable will be assembled from the next available characters in the specified file, as described in Chapter Four. If no file identifier is specified in a READ statement, INPUT is the assumed file. Another form of the READ statement, which can be used only with a TEXT file, is

READ(file-identifier, variable-1, variable-2, . . ., variable-n)

This form of the READ statement is equivalent to the following sequence of statements.

$$READ(\textit{file-identifier, variable-1});$$
$$READ(\textit{file-identifier, variable-2});$$
$$\bullet$$
$$\bullet$$
$$\bullet$$
$$READ(\textit{file-identifier, variable-n})$$

Suppose that TFILE is a TEXT file that has been RESET and that some data have already been read from that file. The following diagram shows a portion of TFILE with the file pointer positioned where the last READ left it.

TFILE   . . . $-4.6\blacksquare15\blacksquare\|\blacksquare37.25\|-275BIN\blacksquare84$ · · ·
                              ↑

Assume that N and M are INTEGER variables, C and D are CHAR variables, and Y is a REAL variable. The next READ statement is

```
READ(TFILE, N, Y, C, M, D)
```

When INTEGER or REAL values are read from a TEXT file, leading blank spaces are ignored and a line separator is treated as a blank space. Values are read for the variables in the order in which those variables are listed in the READ statement. The following diagrams show the values assigned to the variables and the status of TFILE immediately after each value has been read.

| 15 | TFILE | . . . $-4.6\blacksquare15\blacksquare\|\blacksquare37.25\|-275BIN\blacksquare84$ · · · |

N   ↑

| 37.25 | TFILE | . . . $-4.6\blacksquare15\blacksquare\|\blacksquare37.25\|-275BIN\blacksquare84$ · · · |

Y   ↑

| '■' | TFILE | . . . $-4.6\blacksquare15\blacksquare\|\blacksquare37.25\|-275BIN\blacksquare84$ · · · |

C   ↑

| −275 | TFILE | . . . $-4.6\blacksquare15\blacksquare\|\blacksquare37.25\|-275BIN\blacksquare84$ · · · |

M   ↑

| 'B' | TFILE | . . . $-4.6\blacksquare15\blacksquare\|\blacksquare37.25\|-275BIN\blacksquare84$ · · · |

D   ↑

As with the INPUT file, nonblank characters in a TEXT file are not ignored when a value is being assembled. If a character is encountered that cannot be in a representation of the value being assembled, an error will occur and the program will be stopped. For instance, an INTEGER or a REAL value cannot be read from TFILE while the file pointer is positioned at the letter I as depicted above.

While a TEXT file is open for input, its file pointer may be advanced to the first character of a new line by a call to the standard procedure READLN that takes the form

READLN(file-identifier)

If no file identifier is specified in a READLN statement, INPUT is assumed. READLN causes the specified file's pointer to be moved just beyond the next line separator in the file. Another form of the READLN statement is

READLN(file-identifier, variable-1, variable-2, . . ., variable-n)

which produces the same effects as the statement pair

READ(file-identifier, variable-1, variable-2, . . ., variable-n);
READLN(file-identifier)

Suppose that the current status of the TEXT file named TFILE is

TFILE   . . . $-4.6\blacksquare15\blacksquare\|\blacksquare37.25\|-275BIN\blacksquare84$ $\cdots$

↑

Consider the following sequence of statements.

```
READLN(TFILE);
READLN(TFILE, N, C, M);
READ(TFILE, D, Y)
```

The first READLN statement causes the file pointer to move to the blank space character immediately following the next line separator:

TFILE   . . . $-4.6\blacksquare15\blacksquare\|\blacksquare37.25\|-275BIN\blacksquare84$ $\cdots$

↑

After values are read for N, C, and M, the second READLN statement again moves the file pointer past the next line separator. Since the values assigned to N, C, and M are 37, '.', and 25, respectively, the file pointer will be positioned at a line separator and then it is moved one position so that the status of TFILE will be

TFILE   . . . $-4.6\blacksquare15\blacksquare\|\blacksquare37.25\|-275BIN\blacksquare84$ $\cdots$

↑

Now the READ statement will assign the CHAR value $'-'$ to the variable D and the INTEGER value 275 will be converted to 275.0 and assigned to the variable Y. This leaves TFILE in the state

TFILE   . . . $-4.6\blacksquare15\blacksquare\|\blacksquare37.25\|-275BIN\blacksquare84$ $\cdots$

↑

The standard function EOF may be used to test for the end of a TEXT file and another standard function, named EOLN, may be used to test for the end of a line in a TEXT file. A call to EOLN takes the form

EOLN(file-identifier)

If no file identifier is specified, INPUT is the assumed file; otherwise the specified file must be a TEXT file. A call to EOLN produces a BOOLEAN value: TRUE if the specified file's pointer is positioned at a line separator or FALSE if it is not. Suppose that THEDATA is a TEXT file that has just been RESET and it contains the information depicted here.

THEDATA | ■18.8■■LBS‖53■ − 6■■999‖■■HALLELUJAH‖ ● |
          ↑

Let CH be a CHAR variable and consider the following program segment.

```
WHILE NOT EOF(THEDATA)
   DO BEGIN (* READ AND PRINT A LINE *)
      WHILE NOT EOLN(THEDATA)
         DO BEGIN (* READ AND PRINT A CHARACTER *)
            READ(THEDATA, CH);
            WRITE(CH)
            END (* OF READ AND PRINT A CHARACTER *);
      WRITELN;
      READLN(THEDATA)
      END (* OF READ AND PRINT A LINE *)
```

This program segment will print the entire contents of THEDATA file character by character, starting a new line of output after each line separator is encountered in that file:

```
18.8  LBS
53 -6  999
   HALLELUJAH
```

By slightly modifying the program segment given above, we can construct a procedure that will print the entire contents of any TEXT file, starting a new line of output each time a line separator is encountered. In THEDATA file depicted above, a line separator appears immediately before the end of the file. A TEXT file may not always end in this fashion. Thus it is necessary to test for the end of the file before attempting to advance the file pointer beyond the next line separator. Otherwise, a call to READLN may result in an attempt to move the file pointer beyond the end of the file, which is an execution error. Here is a procedure that will successfully output all characters in any TEXT file line by line.

```
PROCEDURE TEXTFILEDUMP (VAR THEFILE : TEXT);
   VAR
        CH : CHAR;
   BEGIN (* PROCEDURE TEXTFILEDUMP *)
   RESET(THEFILE);
   WHILE NOT EOF(THEFILE)
```

```
      DO BEGIN (* READ AND PRINT A LINE *)
          WHILE NOT EOLN(THEFILE) AND NOT EOF(THEFILE)
              DO BEGIN (* READ AND PRINT A CHARACTER *)
                  READ(THEFILE, CH);
                  WRITE(CH)
                  END (* OF READ AND PRINT A CHARACTER *);
          IF NOT EOF(THEFILE)
              THEN READLN(THEFILE);
          WRITELN
          END (* OF READ AND PRINT A LINE *)
    END (* OF PROCEDURE TEXTFILEDUMP *);
```

10.2 EXERCISES

1. Write a program that will create a TEXT file with your name, address, age, sex, and marital status in it. Then have the program RESET the file and print out the contents of the file in some orderly fashion.

2. Write a subprogram that will create a file with INTEGER type components using the data in a TEXT file that contains integers.

3. Suppose that an existing TEXT file contains lines composed of between 1 and 100 characters. Write a procedure that will construct a new TEXT file by adding blank spaces to the lines of the original file so that each line of the new file will contain exactly 100 characters.

4. Write a procedure that will create a TEXT file using a file with REAL components as its data source. The numbers entered into the text file should appear five per line (except possibly the last line) and they should each have three digits after the decimal point.

10.3 FILES WITH STRUCTURED COMPONENTS

The base type for a file may be a structured type such as an array or record. It may even be possible to define an array of files or a file of files. However, many implementations of Pascal do not allow files to be components of other structured data types. The use of files of files and arrays of files is beyond the scope of this book. In this section, we will examine files with array type components and files with record type components.

ARRAYS AS FILE COMPONENTS

When the base type for a file is an array type, each component of the file and the file's buffer variable will have an array structure. This means that the procedures GET and PUT may be used to copy an entire array from a file to the buffer variable and from the buffer variable to the file. Consider the following declarations.

```
TYPE
      PARTS = ARRAY [1 .. 4] OF 0 .. MAXINT;
      INVENTORY = FILE OF PARTS;
VAR
      HARDWARE : INVENTORY;
```

HARDWARE is a file variable whose components will each have a PARTS type structure. These components and the buffer variable HARDWARE are all arrays consisting of four components whose values are restricted to the subrange 0 . . MAXINT. A typical HARDWARE file and its buffer variable are depicted next.

HARDWARE

2340	6759	3662	14802	9005	12900
16	5	0	34	10	2
8	10	3	25	12	2
0	8	5	0	0	3

HARDWARE ↑

HARDWARE ↑ [1]	
HARDWARE ↑ [2]	
HARDWARE ↑ [3]	
HARDWARE ↑ [4]	

These diagrams show the status of the HARDWARE file and its buffer variable as they might appear while the file is being written. Each component of the file is an array whose component values (from top to bottom in the diagram) represent a part identification number, the quantity currently in stock, the stock level at which the part should be reordered, and the quantity currently on order.

Suppose PARTINFO is an array variable of the type PARTS. A program may get values for the components of PARTINFO from the INPUT file:

```
WRITELN('ENTER THE PART NUMBER, QUANTITY CURRENTLY IN STOCK,');
WRITELN('THE REORDER LEVEL, AND QUANTITY ON ORDER.');
FOR I := 1 TO 4
 DO READ(PARTINFO[I])
```

PARTINFO and the buffer variable HARDWARE ↑ are arrays of the same type and so the entire contents of PARTINFO can be copied to HARDWARE ↑ by means of a single assignment statement. Thus the information in PARTINFO can be copied to the HARDWARE file by using the statements

```
HARDWARE^ := PARTINFO;
PUT(HARDWARE)
```

When the procedure WRITE is used to print array values in the OUTPUT file, the value of each component must be printed individually unless the array is a packed array of characters (character string). However, an entire array may be put into a file with array type components by listing the name of the array in a WRITE statement that references that file. For instance, the contents of PARTINFO can be copied into the HARDWARE file by using the statement

```
WRITE(HARDWARE, PARTINFO)
```

This WRITE statement causes the contents of PARTINFO to be copied into the buffer variable HARDWARE↑ and then the contents of the buffer variable are copied into the file. We have used the array PARTINFO to store input information that is subsequently copied into the HARDWARE file. If this is the sole purpose of PARTINFO, it is not really needed because the input information can be read directly into the components of HARDWARE↑ and then the contents of HARD-WARE can be PUT into the file:

```
FOR I := 1 TO 4
  DO READ(HARDWARE^[I]);
PUT(HARDWARE)
```

Suppose that the HARDWARE file has been RESET and is currently being used as a source of input for a program. After two file components have been read, the status of the HARDWARE file and its buffer variable will be as shown here.

HARDWARE

2340	6759	3662	14802	9005	12900
16	5	0	34	10	2
8	10	3	25	12	2
0	8	5	0	0	3

↑

HARDWARE↑

HARDWARE↑[1]	3662
HARDWARE↑[2]	0
HARDWARE↑[3]	3
HARDWARE↑[4]	5

The statement

```
READ(HARDWARE, PARTINFO)
```

is equivalent to the pair of statements

```
PARTINFO := HARDWARE^;
GET(HARDWARE)
```

After the READ statement is executed, the status of the HARDWARE file, its buffer variable, and the array variable PARTINFO will be as depicted below.

Consider a program that will adjust the HARDWARE file to reflect new part orders. The program will assume that the components of HARDWARE are sequenced in increasing part-number order and it will maintain this order when making adjustments. All part orders entered by the program user will initially be stored in an array of records named ORDER where each record has a PARTNUM-BER field and a QUANTITY field. These ORDERs will be COUNTed as they are entered. A negative QUANTITY for an order will signal the end of input. Here is a pseudocode description of the main program:

```
Constants: LOWPARTNUMBER = 1000; HIGHPARTNUMBER = 99999
          ORDERLIMIT = 500
BEGIN program NEWORDERS
Initialize the order COUNT at 0
Set the CONTINUE flag at YES
Print program information and directions
REPEAT order input
```

```
                WITH record ORDER[COUNT + 1]
                    DO  BEGIN
                            READ a PARTNUMBER and QUANTITY ordered
                            IF the QUANTITY is not negative
                                THEN Increment the order COUNT by 1
                                ELSE Set the CONTINUE flag at NO
                            END
                    UNTIL the CONTINUE flag is NO

            Use SORT(ORDER, COUNT) to arrange the ORDERs high to low

            Use INSERTORDERS(HARDWARE, SCRATCH, ORDER, COUNT) to
                insert ORDERs into the HARDWARE file
            END of program NEWORDERS
```

The composition of the program NEWORDERS without the procedures SORT and INSERTORDERS follows.

```
PROGRAM NEWORDERS (INPUT, OUTPUT, HARDWARE);
(****************************************************************
*                                                              *
*   A PROGRAM WHICH WILL ADD NEW PART ORDERS TO THE HARDWARE FILE  *
*                                                              *
****************************************************************)
CONST                               (*---------[CONSTANTS]----------*)
        LOWPARTNUMBER = 1000;       (* LOWEST PART NUMBER ALLOWED   *)
        HIGHPARTNUMBER = 99999;     (* HIGHEST PART NUMBER ALLOWED  *)
        ORDERLIMIT = 500;           (* LIMIT ON THE NUMBER OF ORDERS *)
                                    (*------------------------------*)

TYPE
        RESPONSE = (YES, NO);
        CODERANGE = LOWPARTNUMBER .. HIGHPARTNUMBER;
        UNITORDER = RECORD
                        PARTNUMBER : CODERANGE;
                        QUANTITY : INTEGER
                    END (* OF UNITORDER RECORD *);
        PARTS = ARRAY [1 .. 4] OF INTEGER;
        TRANSACTIONS = ARRAY [1 .. ORDERLIMIT] OF UNITORDER;
        INVENTORY = FILE OF PARTS;

VAR                                 (*------[INTEGER VARIABLES]------*)
        COUNT : INTEGER;            (* TOTAL COUNT OF ORDERS TO BE  *)
                                    (* PROCESSED                    *)
                                    (*------------------------------*)
                                    (*-----[RESPONSE VARIABLES]------*)
        CONTINUE : RESPONSE;        (* SIGNAL TO CONTROL ORDER INPUT *)
                                    (*------------------------------*)
                                    (*-----[TRANSACTIONS ARRAY]------*)
        ORDER : TRANSACTIONS;       (* THE ORDERS TO BE FILLED      *)
                                    (*------------------------------*)
                                    (*-------[INVENTORY FILES]-------*)
        HARDWARE,                   (* MASTER PARTS INVENTORY       *)
        SCRATCH : INVENTORY;        (* WORKING UPDATED FILE         *)
                                    (*------------------------------*)
```

```
(*================================================================*)
(*                                                                *)
(*                 INSERT PROCEDURE SORT HERE.                    *)
(*                                                                *)
(*================================================================*)

(*================================================================*)
(*                                                                *)
(*             INSERT PROCEDURE INSERTORDERS HERE.                *)
(*                                                                *)
(*================================================================*)

(******************************************************************)
BEGIN (* PROGRAM NEWORDERS *)
COUNT := 0;
CONTINUE := YES;
WRITELN('THIS PROGRAM WILL ADD NEW PART ORDERS TO THE HARDWARE ',
        'FILE.');
WRITELN('FOR EACH PART ORDERED YOU MUST SUPPLY A PART NUMBER ',
        'AND THE');
WRITELN('QUANTITY ORDERED. A PART NUMBER MUST BE BETWEEN ',
        LOWPARTNUMBER:4, ' AND');
WRITELN(HIGHPARTNUMBER:5, '. TO SIGNAL THE END OF INPUT, ENTER ANY ',
        'PART NUMBER');
WRITELN('WITH A NEGATIVE QUANTITY.');
WRITELN;
WRITELN(' PART ');
WRITELN('NUMBER     QUANTITY');
WRITELN('------     --------');
REPEAT
  WITH ORDER[COUNT + 1]
    DO BEGIN (* PART DATA INPUT *)
       READ(PARTNUMBER, QUANTITY);
       IF QUANTITY < 0
         THEN CONTINUE := NO
         ELSE COUNT := COUNT + 1
       END (* OF PART DATA INPUT *)
UNTIL CONTINUE = NO;
SORT(ORDER, COUNT);
INSERTORDERS(HARDWARE, SCRATCH, ORDER, COUNT)
END (* OF PROGRAM NEWORDERS *).
```

The procedure SORT will simply be a modified version of the selection sort procedure introduced in Chapter Seven. SORT will put the ORDERs in increasing order by part numbers and then the procedure INSERTORDERS will be used to merge the ORDERs into the HARDWARE file. Here is the SORT procedure:

```
PROCEDURE SORT
  (*================================================================*)
  (*   SELECTION SORT THE ARRAY IN ASCENDING ORDER BY PART NUMBERS   *)
  (*================================================================*)
                                        (*---------[PARAMETERS]----------*)
  (VAR V : TRANSACTIONS;                 (* ARRAY TO BE SORTED            *)
   N : INTEGER);                         (* NUMBER OF ARRAY COMPONENTS    *)
                                         (* USED                          *)
                                         (*------------------------------*)
   VAR                                   (*------[INTEGER VARIABLES]------*)
       POS,                              (* BOTTOM OF SORTED PORTION OF V *)
       LOC,                              (* LOCATION OF NEXT INSERTION    *)
       L : INTEGER;                      (* ARRAY INDEX FOR LOOP CONTROL  *)
                                         (*------------------------------*)
                                         (*------[UNITORDER RECORDS]------*)
       SAVE : UNITORDER;                 (* TEMPORARY RECORD STORAGE      *)
                                         (*------------------------------*)
  (*================================================================*)
  BEGIN (* PROCEDURE SORT *)
  FOR POS := 1 TO N-1
    DO BEGIN (* A SELECTION CYCLE *)
       LOC := POS;
       FOR L := POS + 1 TO N
         DO IF V[L].PARTNUMBER < V[LOC].PARTNUMBER
              THEN LOC := L;
       SAVE := V[POS];
       V[POS] := V[LOC];
       V[LOC] := SAVE
       END (* OF A SELECTION CYCLE *)
  END (* OF PROCEDURE SORT *);
```

In the procedure INSERTORDERS, the file HARDWARE will be known as IN-FILE and the updated file produced by the procedure will be known as OUTFILE. The array ORDER will be known in the procedure as ORDERLIST After OUTFILE has been created, a new INFILE is created that is an exact copy of OUTFILE so that the associated actual parameter HARDWARE will contain all the updates. As OUTFILE is copied to INFILE, it will also be copied to the OUTPUT file so that a printed copy of the new contents of the HARDWARE file is produced. Here is a pseudocode description of the procedure INSERTORDERS:

```
BEGIN procedure INSERTORDERS
RESET the INFILE
REWRITE the OUTFILE
Initialize ORDERINDEX at 1
WHILE EOF (INFILE) is FALSE and ORDERINDEX is not greater than LASTORDER
      DO WITH ORDERLIST [ORDERINDEX]
           DO IF INFILE↑[1] is less than PARTNUMBER

               THEN Use (COPYPARTINFO) to copy a record from INFILE to OUTFILE

               ELSE BEGIN an insertion
                    IF INFILE↑[1] equals PARTNUMBER
```

THEN Use (UPDATEPARTINFO) to update a record from INFILE

ELSE Use (NEWPARTINFO) to create a record in OUTFILE

Increment ORDERINDEX by 1
END of an insertion
IF EOF(INFILE) is TRUE
   THEN FOR J ranging from ORDERINDEX to LASTORDER
    DO WITH ORDERLIST[J]

DO Use (NEWPARTINFO) to create a new record in OUTFILE

ELSE WHILE EOF(INFILE) is FALSE

DO Use (COPYPARTINFO) to copy a record from INFILE to OUTFILE

RESET the OUTFILE
REWRITE the INFILE
WHILE EOF(OUTFILE) is FALSE
   DO Copy OUTFILE ↑ to INFILE and to OUTPUT
END of procedure INSERTORDERS

The procedure INSERTORDERS uses three procedures: COPYPARTINFO, UPDA-TEPARTINFO, and NEWPARTINFO. The positions for these procedures are shown below.

```
PROCEDURE INSERTORDERS
  (*================================================================*)
  (*           MERGE ORDERS INTO THE MASTER PARTS FILE              *)
  (*================================================================*)
                                      (*-------- [PARAMETERS] ----------*)
  (VAR INFILE,                        (* MASTER PARTS INVENTORY FILE    *)
       OUTFILE : INVENTORY;           (* WORKING INVENTORY FILE         *)
   ORDERLIST : TRANSACTIONS;          (* ORDERS TO BE FILED             *)
   LASTORDER : INTEGER);              (* NUMBER OF NEW ORDERS           *)
                                      (*------------------------------- *)
   VAR                                (*------ [INTEGER VARIABLES] ------*)
       ORDERINDEX,                    (* INDEX FOR A SELECTED ORDER     *)
        J : INTEGER;                  (* INDEX FOR THE ORDERLIST        *)
                                      (*------------------------------- *)
                                      (*-------- [PARTS ARRAY] ---------*)
       PARTINFO : PARTS;              (* INVENTORY DATA FOR ONE PART    *)
                                      (*------------------------------- *)


  (*================================================================*)
  (*                                                                *)
  (*           INSERT PROCEDURE COPYPARTINFO HERE.                  *)
  (*                                                                *)
  (*================================================================*)
```

```
(*================================================================*)
(*                                                                *)
(*            INSERT PROCEDURE UPDATEPARTINFO HERE.               *)
(*                                                                *)
(*================================================================*)

(*================================================================*)
(*                                                                *)
(*            INSERT PROCEDURE NEWPARTINFO HERE.                  *)
(*                                                                *)
(*================================================================*)

(*================================================================*)
BEGIN (* PROCEDURE INSERTORDERS *)
RESET(INFILE);
REWRITE(OUTFILE);
ORDERINDEX := 1;
WHILE NOT EOF(INFILE) AND (ORDERINDEX <= LASTORDER)
    DO WITH ORDERLIST[ORDERINDEX]
        DO IF INFILE^[1] < PARTNUMBER
            THEN COPYPARTINFO
            ELSE BEGIN (* A FILE UPDATE *)
                IF INFILE^[1] = PARTNUMBER
                    THEN UPDATEPARTINFO(QUANTITY)
                    ELSE NEWPARTINFO(ORDERLIST[ORDERINDEX]);
                ORDERINDEX := ORDERINDEX + 1
                END (* OF A FILE UPDATE *);
IF EOF(INFILE)
  THEN FOR J := ORDERINDEX TO LASTORDER
        DO NEWPARTINFO(ORDERLIST[J])
  ELSE WHILE NOT EOF(INFILE)
        DO COPYPARTINFO;
RESET(OUTFILE);
REWRITE(INFILE);
WRITELN;
WRITELN('** CURRENT HARDWARE FILE **':35);
WRITELN;
WRITELN('PART':9, 'QUANTITY':14, 'REORDER':9, 'QUANTITY':11);
WRITELN('NUMBER':10, 'IN STOCK':13, 'LEVEL':8, 'ON ORDER':12);
WRITELN('*****':10, '********':13, '*****':8, '********':12);
WHILE NOT EOF(OUTFILE)
    DO BEGIN (* REWRITING THE MASTER FILE *)
       READ(OUTFILE, PARTINFO);
       FOR J := 1 TO 4
        DO WRITE(PARTINFO[J]:10);
       WRITELN;
       WRITE(INFILE, PARTINFO)
       END (* OF REWRITING THE MASTER FILE *)
END (* OF PROCEDURE INSERTORDERS *);
```

The procedures COPYPARTINFO, UPDATEPARTINFO, and NEWPARTINFO are declared in the INSERTORDERS block because they are called by the procedure INSERTORDERS. These three procedures are given below.

```
PROCEDURE COPYPARTINFO;
 (*=============================================================*)
 (*   COPY DATA FOR ONE PART FROM MASTER FILE TO WORKING FILE    *)
 (*=============================================================*)
 BEGIN (* PROCEDURE COPYPARTINFO *)
 READ(INFILE, PARTINFO);
 WRITE(OUTFILE, PARTINFO)
 END (* OF PROCEDURE COPYPARTINFO *);


PROCEDURE UPDATEPARTINFO
 (*=============================================================*)
 (*   UPDATE THE QUANTITY ON ORDER FOR A PART ALREADY LISTED IN  *)
 (*   THE MASTER FILE                                            *)
 (*=============================================================*)
                                  (*-------- [PARAMETERS] ----------*)
 (ORDERQUANTITY : INTEGER);        (* QUANTITY ORDERED              *)
                                  (*-------------------------------*)
 (*=============================================================*)
 BEGIN (* PROCEDURE UPDATEPARTINFO *)
 READ(INFILE, PARTINFO);
 PARTINFO[4] := PARTINFO[4] + ORDERQUANTITY;
 WRITE(OUTFILE, PARTINFO)
 END (* OF PROCEDURE UPDATEPARTINFO *);


PROCEDURE NEWPARTINFO
 (*=============================================================*)
 (*           ENTER NEW PART DATA INTO THE WORKING FILE          *)
 (*=============================================================*)
                                  (*-------- [PARAMETERS] ----------*)
 (ORDERPART : UNITORDER);          (* NEW PART DATA                 *)
                                  (*-------------------------------*)
 (*=============================================================*)
 BEGIN (* PROCEDURE NEWPARTINFO *)
 WITH ORDERPART
   DO BEGIN (* NEW PART COMPONENT *)
      PARTINFO[1] := PARTNUMBER;
      PARTINFO[2] := 0;
      PARTINFO[3] := QUANTITY DIV 2;
      PARTINFO[4] := QUANTITY
      END (* OF NEW PART COMPONENT *);
 WRITE(OUTFILE, PARTINFO)
 END (* OF PROCEDURE NEWPARTINFO *);
```

If no external HARDWARE file is made available to the program NEWORDERS, the program will create a HARDWARE file. NEWORDERS does not modify any file entry that represents a supply already available. The only time it affects the reorder level for a part is when the part is not already listed in the file. In such a case the reorder level is set on one half the amount ordered (neglecting any fraction of a part). A sample run of NEWORDERS is shown next for the case in which a new HARDWARE file is created.

```
THIS PROGRAM WILL ADD NEW PART ORDERS TO THE HARDWARE FILE.
FOR EACH PART ORDERED YOU MUST SUPPLY A PART NUMBER AND THE
QUANTITY ORDERED. A PART NUMBER MUST BE BETWEEN 1000 AND
99999. TO SIGNAL THE END OF INPUT, ENTER ANY PART NUMNER
WITH A NEGATIVE QUANTITY.

   PART
 NUMBER      QUANTITY
 ------      --------
 ? 4789         25
 ?10456         20
 ? 5960         15
 ? 1015         38
 ? 7506          9
 ? 1000         -1

        ** CURRENT HARDWARE FILE **

     PART       QUANTITY   REORDER    QUANTITY
   NUMBER       IN STOCK   LEVEL      ON ORDER
   ******       ********   *****      ********
     1015          0         19         38
     4789          0         12         25
     5960          0          7         15
     7506          0          4          9
    10456          0         10         20
```

Now that a HARDWARE file exists outside the program, it can be used when the program is executed again. Note that the parts are filed by part number. Here is another run of NEWORDERS that is used to update the existing HARDWARE file.

```
THIS PROGRAM WILL ADD NEW PART ORDERS TO THE HARDWARE FILE.
FOR EACH PART ORDERED YOU MUST SUPPLY A PART NUMBER AND THE
QUANTITY ORDERED. A PART NUMBER MUST BE BETWEEN 1000 AND
99999. TO SIGNAL THE END OF INPUT, ENTER ANY PART NUMBER
WITH A NEGATIVE QUANTITY.

   PART
 NUMBER      QUANTITY
 ------      --------
 ? 2968         28
 ? 7506          5
 ? 5332          7
 ?43044         43
 ? 8625         12
 ? 1975         60
 ? 1000         -1
```

```
        ** CURRENT HARDWARE FILE **

   PART       QUANTITY   REORDER   QUANTITY
  NUMBER      IN STOCK    LEVEL    ON ORDER
 * * * * *   * * * * * * * *   * * * * *   * * * * * * * *
   1015          0          19         38
   1975          0          30         60
   2968          0          14         28
   4789          0          12         25
   5332          0           3          7
   5960          0           7         15
   7506          0           4         14
   8625          0           6         12
  10456          0          10         20
  43044          0          21         43
```

The program NEWORDERS is just one program that can be used to keep a HARDWARE file current. A different program can be written to adjust the supply of a part in stock when new parts arrive or when parts are removed from stock. There are various modifications that can be made to NEWORDERS to make it a more versatile program. For instance, the program user could be required to supply an explicit reorder level for new parts or could be given the option of changing any reorder level. Also, the printing of the entire HARDWARE file after adjustments are made can be suppressed at the option of the user. The program NEWORDERS has been presented to demonstrate how a program can process a file that has array components. We have assumed that all file information can be represented by integers. If this is not the case, then perhaps the file should have record type components. We will examine such files in the next section.

Although a TEXT file is usually more suitable for storing character data than other types of files, there are times when it may be convenient to store character strings in a file with array components. Consider the following definitions and declarations.

```
TYPE
      STRING100 = PACKED ARRAY [1 .. 100] OF CHAR;
      DESCRIPTIONS = FILE OF STRING100;
VAR
      SLIDES : DESCRIPTIONS;
```

A character string stored in a TEXT file must be read from that file character by character. Since the components of the SLIDES file are arrays each of which can store 100 characters, the procedure READ is used to get an entire array of 100 characters. Suppose that ITEM is a string variable of the type STRING100 that has been assigned a value. The following program segment can be used to scan the SLIDES file to see if ITEM matches a component in the file. This program segment will leave the matching array in the buffer variable SLIDES ↑ if a match is found; otherwise, the scanning will be stopped when the end of the file is reached.

```
RESET(SLIDES);
MATCH := FALSE;
WHILE NOT EOF(SLIDES) AND (MATCH <> TRUE)
   DO IF SLIDES^ = ITEM
         THEN MATCH := TRUE
         ELSE GET(SLIDES);
IF MATCH = TRUE
   THEN WRITELN('ITEM MATCH WAS SUCCESSFUL.')
   ELSE WRITELN('ITEM MATCH FAILED.')
```

If SLIDES were a TEXT file having 100 characters per line, the matching could be conducted by the following program segment.

```
RESET(SLIDES);
MATCH := FALSE;
WHILE NOT EOF(SLIDES) AND (MATCH <> TRUE)
   DO BEGIN (* SEARCH FOR ITEM MATCH *)
      FOR I := 1 TO 100
        DO READ(SLIDES, ONELINE[I]);
      IF ONELINE = ITEM
         THEN MATCH := TRUE
         ELSE READLN(SLIDES)
      END (* OF SEARCH FOR ITEM MATCH *);
IF MATCH = TRUE
   THEN WRITELN('ITEM MATCH WAS SUCCESSFUL.')
   ELSE WRITELN('ITEM MATCH FAILED.')
```

If any line in SLIDES as a TEXT file does not contain at least 100 characters, this program segment could miss a possible match because the READing ignores line boundaries.

A file with array components that are strings can be used to advantage to store strings that are all of the same length. When the strings to be stored in a file vary greatly in length, it is generally better to use a TEXT file and let line separators mark the end of one string and the beginning of another. The choice of a file type should be guided by the kinds of processing activities in which the file will be used. Although TEXT files are the most versatile of all files in Pascal, they should not be viewed as the best file storage structures for all programming applications.

RECORDS AS FILE COMPONENTS

If the components of a file are records, a program can GET or READ an entire record from the file and PUT or WRITE an entire record into the file because the file's buffer variable is a record variable with the same structure as a file component. Consider the following definitions and declarations.

```
TYPE
      STOCK = RECORD
                  NAME : PACKED ARRAY [1 .. 15] OF CHAR;
                  NUMBER : 10000 .. 99999;
                  COLOR : (WHITE, GOLD, GREEN, BROWN);
                  INSTOCK : 0 .. MAXINT;
                  PRICE : REAL
              END (* OF STOCK RECORD *);
      CATALOG = FILE OF STOCK;
VAR
      APPLIANCE : CATALOG;
```

Each component of the APPLIANCE file will be a STOCK type record. When the file is open for input, the file pointer will be positioned at one component and a copy of that component will be available in the file's buffer variable. The following diagrams depict a portion of the APPLIANCE file while it is being read and the buffer variable's contents given the existing status of the file.

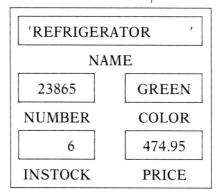

When the file pointer is not at the end of the file, the fields of the component at which it is positioned are available through the buffer variable. The buffer variable's fields have the names APPLIANCE↑.NAME, APPLIANCE↑.NUMBER, APPLIANCE↑.COLOR, APPLIANCE↑.INSTOCK, and APPLIANCE↑.PRICE. Since the NAME field of APPLIANCE↑ has an array structure, the individual components of that field may be referenced. For instance, the eighth character in the string variable APPLIANCE↑.NAME is in the component named APPLIANCE↑.NAME[8]. A call to the procedure GET that specifies the APPLIANCE file will advance the file pointer to the next component of the file and cause the entire contents of that component to be copied into the buffer variable APPLIANCE↑. Suppose STOCKITEM is a record variable of the type STOCK. The statement

READ(APPLIANCE, STOCKITEM)

will assign the contents of APPLIANCE ↑ to STOCKITEM and then the file pointer will be moved to the next file component as in a GET. Given the status of the APPLIANCE file depicted above, the following diagrams demonstrate the effects of this READ.

'REFRIGERATOR '	'REFRIGERATOR '	'MICROWAVE OVEN '
23864 / WHITE	23865 / GREEN	28016 / WHITE
14 / 449.50	6 / 474.95	24 / 289.95

APPLIANCE   ↑

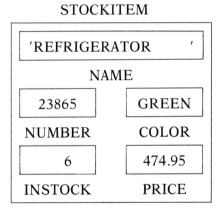

APPLIANCE ↑

'MICROWAVE OVEN   '
NAME
28016 / WHITE
NUMBER / COLOR
24 / 289.95
INSTOCK / PRICE

STOCKITEM

'REFRIGERATOR   '
NAME
23865 / GREEN
NUMBER / COLOR
6 / 474.95
INSTOCK / PRICE

Suppose that a program is creating the APPLIANCE file and the current end of the file looks like this

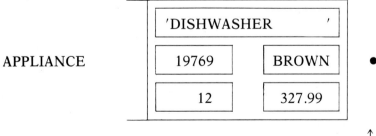

APPLIANCE

'DISHWASHER   '
19769 / BROWN
12 / 327.99

                                                                                         ↑

The program may assign values to the fields of the buffer variable and then cause the contents of APPLIANCE ↑ to be copied into the file by using PUT(APPLIANCE). Another way to accomplish the same task is to assign values to the record STOCK-ITEM and then WRITE(APPLIANCE, STOCKITEM), since this call to WRITE is equivalent to the pair of statements

```
APPLIANCE^ := STOCKITEM;
PUT(APPLIANCE)
```

Here is a program segment that can be used to get STOCKITEM values from the
INPUT file and then copy the contents of STOCKITEM into the APPLIANCE file.

```
WITH STOCKITEM
   DO BEGIN (* DATA INPUT *)
      WRITELN('NAME OF THE APPLIANCE:');
      READLN; (* NEW INPUT LINE *)
      FOR I := 1 TO 15
        DO IF NOT EOLN(INPUT)
             THEN READ(NAME[I])
             ELSE NAME[I] := ' ';
      WRITELN('THE CATALOG NUMBER:');
      READLN; (* NEW INPUT LINE *)
      READ(NUMBER);
      WRITELN('COLOR NUMBER (1 = WHITE, 2 = GOLD, ',
              '3 = GREEN, 4 = BROWN):');
      READ(COLORNUMBER);
      CASE COLORNUMBER OF
         1 : COLOR := WHITE;
         2 : COLOR := GOLD;
         3 : COLOR := GREEN;
         4 : COLOR := BROWN
      END (* OF COLORNUMBER CASES *);
      WRITELN('QUANTITY NOW IN STOCK:');
      READ(INSTOCK);
      WRITELN('UNIT PRICE:');
      READ(PRICE)
      END (* OF DATA INPUT *);
   WRITE(APPLIANCE, STOCKITEM)
```

Typical data input given in response to requests made by this program segment is
shown below.

```
NAME OF THE APPLIANCE:
?DELUXE BLENDER
THE CATALOG NUMBER:
?20003
COLOR NUMBER (1 = WHITE, 2 = GOLD, 3 = GREEN, 4 = BROWN):
? 2
QUANTITY NOW IN STOCK:
? 37
UNIT PRICE:
? 79.95
```

After the new STOCKITEM has been inserted at the end of the APPLIANCE file,
the status of the file will be as depicted here.

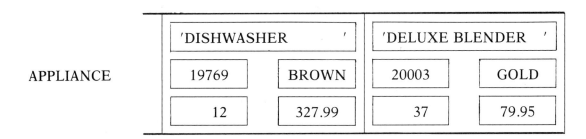

As with any Pascal file, it is possible to WRITE to a file that has record type components only after that file has been opened for output by a call to the procedure REWRITE. A call to REWRITE a file will, of course, clear the file of all components it may have had so that a new file can be constructed. To make additions to an existing APPLIANCE file, a temporary file of the type CATALOG must be used to construct the updated version of APPLIANCE in the same way that the SCRATCH file is used by the program NEWORDERS (page 383) to update the HARDWARE file. Since the program will have only sequential access to the file components, processing the file would be easier if the components were ordered based on the value in some "key field" within each record. For instance, the components of the APPLIANCE file can be ordered by catalog number. When an ordering of the file components is not maintained, the entire file may have to be searched sequentially before it can be determined that a particular record is or is not in the file.

Consider another example. The file PROFILE defined next can be used to store pertinent facts about college professors.

```
TYPE
     STATUS = (LOOKING, NOTFOUND, FOUND);
     ALFA30 = PACKED ARRAY [1 .. 30] OF CHAR;
     RANK = (INSTRUCTOR, ASSISTANTPROFESSOR,
             ASSOCIATEPROFESSOR, PROFESSOR);
     YEARS = 0 .. 50;
     EMPLOYEE = RECORD
                   NAME : ALFA30;
                   TTITLE : RANK;
                   DEPARTMENT : ALFA30;
                   SSN : INTEGER;
                   EXPERIENCE : YEARS;
                   SALARY : REAL
                END (* OF EMPLOYEE RECORD *);
     VITALINFO = FILE OF EMPLOYEE;
VAR
     PROFILE : VITALINFO;
```

Suppose that PROFILE has been created and its components are ordered by Social Security number (SSN) from low to high. The following procedure can be used to try to locate a particular TEACHER record in a VITALINFO type file.

```
PROCEDURE SEARCH (TEACHER : EMPLOYEE; VAR FACULTY : VITALINFO;
                    VAR RESULT : STATUS);
 BEGIN (* PROCEDURE SEARCH *)
 RESET(FACULTY);
 RESULT := LOOKING;
 WHILE NOT EOF(FACULTY) AND (RESULT = LOOKING)
    DO IF FACULTY^.SSN < TEACHER.SSN
          THEN GET(FACULTY)
          ELSE IF FACULTY^.SSN = TEACHER.SSN
                THEN RESULT := FOUND
                ELSE RESULT := NOTFOUND;
 IF EOF(FACULTY)
    THEN RESULT := NOTFOUND
 END (* OF PROCEDURE SEARCH *);
```

If the RESULT of a SEARCH is that a match is FOUND, the buffer variable PRO-FILE will contain the matching record when the procedure SEARCH returns from the call

```
                SEARCH(PERSON, PROFILE, OUTCOME)
```

and the value of OUTCOME will be FOUND. Furthermore, PROFILE will be open for input.

If the purpose of a search through PROFILE is to locate a record so that it can be updated, the components passed over during the search should be copied to a new VITALINFO type file, which will be the updated version of PROFILE. Consider the following procedure.

```
PROCEDURE SEARCHANDCOPY (TEACHER : EMPLOYEE;
                        VAR INFACULTY, OUTFACULTY : VITALINFO;
                        VAR RESULT : STATUS);
  BEGIN (* PROCEDURE SEARCHANDCOPY *)
  RESULT := LOOKING;
  WHILE NOT EOF(INFACULTY) AND (RESULT = LOOKING)
    DO IF INFACULTY^.SSN < TEACHER.SSN
          THEN BEGIN (* COPY *)
              WRITE(OUTFACULTY, INFACULTY^);
              GET(INFACULTY)
              END (* OF COPY *)
          ELSE IF INFACULTY^.SSN = TEACHER.SSN
                THEN RESULT := FOUND
                ELSE RESULT := NOTFOUND
 END (* OF PROCEDURE SEARCHANDCOPY *);
```

The procedure SEARCHANDCOPY does not RESET the file INFACULTY or RE-WRITE the file OUTFACULTY. It is up to the calling program to make sure that the files passed to SEARCHANDCOPY have been properly opened. Suppose that the procedure is called by the statement

SEARCHANDCOPY(PERSON, PROFILE, NEWPROFILE, OUTCOME)

The search for a PERSON match commences at the position in the file PROFILE at which the last search left off. If the OUTCOME is LOOKING when the procedure returns control to the calling program, the end of PROFILE has been reached.

Suppose that STAFF is an array whose type is

ROSTER = ARRAY [1 .. 200] OF EMPLOYEE;

and suppose that the first N components of STAFF contain EMPLOYEE type records that need to be inserted into PROFILE or matched with existing PROFILE records so that updates can be made. Since PROFILE is sorted by Social Security numbers in its components, the changes to be made to PROFILE will be easier to accomplish if the array STAFF is also sorted by Social Security number in ascending order. The following program fragment shows how the STAFF records can be merged with the records in PROFILE to form the updated file NEWPROFILE.

```
RESET(PROFILE);
REWRITE(NEWPROFILE);
STAFFCOUNT := 1;
REPEAT (* A STAFF UPDATE *)
   SEARCHANDCOPY(STAFF[STAFFCOUNT], PROFILE, NEWPROFILE, OUTCOME);
   CASE OUTCOME OF
     NOTFOUND : BEGIN (* INSERT NEW RECORD *)
                   WRITE(NEWPROFILE, STAFF[STAFFCOUNT]);
                   STAFFCOUNT := STAFFCOUNT + 1
                END (* OF INSERT NEW RECORD *);
        FOUND : BEGIN (* UPDATES TO CURRENT RECORD *)
                    .
                    .
                    .

                   WRITE(NEWPROFILE, PROFILE^);
                   STAFFCOUNT := STAFFCOUNT + 1
                END (* OF UPDATES TO CURRENT RECORD *);
      LOOKING : FOR K := STAFFCOUNT TO N
                   DO WRITE(NEWPROFILE, STAFF[K])
   END (* OF OUTCOME CASES *)
UNTIL (OUTCOME = LOOKING) OR (STAFFCOUNT > N)
```

10.3
EXERCISES

1. In the program TESTFILEUPDATE (Section 10.1), a file named SCORES that has INTEGER components is used to store data sets. Each data set is separated from the next one by a negative number, since the data sets contain only nonnegative integers. Suppose that no data set will contain more than 100 integers.

Define a file with array components such that an array can store a complete data set and then revise TESTFILEUPDATE so that it will use this new structure for the SCORES file.

2. A survey questionnaire contains 25 questions and the response to each question must be either true or false. Define a file that can be used to store the responses from the survey questionnaires and write a subprogram that can be used to create or update the file.

3. Write a procedure that will copy a TEXT file containing only REAL numbers into a file that has array components such that each array will contain exactly five numbers.

4. A teacher wants to establish a data file for a class so that the following information can be stored for each student: name, number of tests taken (maximum of 10), the test scores (which are in the range from 0 to 100), and the average score for all tests taken. Define a suitable file and then write a procedure that can be used to create the file. The only information to be inserted into the file when it is created is the name of each student and zeros for the number of tests taken.

5. Write a procedure that will update the student file described in Exercise 4 by adding additional test scores for the students. The procedure will need to increment the number of tests taken and recompute the average of the tests.

6. A file with record components of type shown below already exists.

```
TYPE
    VOTER = RECORD
              NAME : PACKED ARRAY [1 .. 30] OF CHAR;
              ADDRESS : PACKED ARRAY [1 .. 40] OF CHAR;
              AGE : 18 .. 120;
              PARTY : (REPUBLICAN, DEMOCRAT, INDEPENDENT)
            END (* OF VOTER RECORD *);
```

Write a procedure that will use this file to construct three new files, one for REPUBLICANs, one for DEMOCRATs, and one for INDEPENDENTs.

10.4 PROGRAMMING PROBLEMS

1. A program is stored in the computer's memory as a TEXT file. Each line of an interactive Pascal program may begin with a line number. Suppose that the line numbers can range from 1 to 99999 inclusive. Write a program that will scan a TEXT file containing a program with numbered lines and create another TEXT file that contains the same program with the line numbers deleted.

2. Write a program that will add line numbers to all lines of TEXT file. The line numbers must be in the range from 1 to 99999 and each line number should be separated from the remainder of the line by a blank space. Allow the program user to input the lowest line number to be used and the increment between consecutive line numbers. Before attempting to number the lines of a

file, the program must first determine whether it is possible to give each line a number according to the established requirements.

3. Only so many characters can be printed per line on a line printer or terminal. When the contents of a TEXT file are printed, it is possible that some lines in the file cannot physically appear on one line of the OUTPUT device. This problem can be alleviated by establishing a margin for each printed line. For example, if the margin is set at 72, then at most 72 characters can be printed on one line. Write a program that will print the contents of a TEXT file within the margin established as input to the program. No word or number should be split between two lines and no new line of output should be started until it is impossible to print more information on the current line without exceeding the margin. Assume that the end of a word or a number will be marked by the presence of a blank space, some punctuation character (comma, period, semicolon, etc.), or a line separator.

4. Write the program described in Problem 3, except allow both a left-hand and a right-hand margin to be established. For instance, if the left-hand margin is set at 21 and the right-hand margin is set at 100, each output line will begin with 20 blank spaces and contain a maximum of 100 characters.

5. A summer softball league is composed of six teams: Eddie's Rent-All, Southtown Motors, Jones Plumbing, Twin Oaks Supper Club, Green Acres Lodge, and Simmons Drugs. Each team plays once a week during a ten-week season. This enables a team to play all the other teams twice. Write a program that will create a week-by-week schedule of games for the league and record this schedule in a file. Space should also be reserved in the file for the scores of the games. Once the file has been created, the program should print out the schedule for the season. Assume that there is only one softball field available on the night the games are played and that the games begin on the hour starting at 5:00 P.M.

6. The file described in Problem 5 will need to be updated after the softball games for a week have been played. Write a program that will insert a week's scores into the file and then produce the league standings.

7. A file containing information on courses completed could be very useful to a college student in planning future coursework. Write a program that will create or update a file of this type. The entries for each course should include the name of the course, the name of the department that offers the course, the course number, credits, term in which the course was taken (for example, fall, winter, spring, summer), year in which the course was taken, and grade received. The program should be capable of printing out a table showing all information recorded in the file or information on specific courses. The program user should be allowed to make changes to existing information in the file or to add information for new courses. It would also be helpful to have the program compute a grade point average, total number of credits earned, and credits earned by department.

8. The file described in Problem 7 could also include information about courses that a student is planning to take or is currently enrolled in. Write a program that will create or update a student course file of this type. The program should allow changes to be made to existing entries in the file and the addition

of entries for new courses. When the entire contents of the file are printed, the courses should be categorized as completed courses, courses in progress, or courses planned for the future.

9. Suppose that a file contains records of the type

```
ITEM = RECORD
        DESCRIPTION : PACKED ARRAY [1 .. 40] OF CHAR;
        CODENUMBER : 1 .. 99999
      END (* OF ITEM RECORD *);
```

These records may not appear in any particular order in the file. It would be helpful if the file components were ordered low to high or high to low by CODENUMBER. A sorted file could be created by copying each component of the unsorted file into an array, sorting the array, and then copying the contents of the array into a new file. However, the original file could contain as many as 99999 records, and sorting an array with that many components would generally be very time consuming. Also, storage limitations might prevent the program from using an array with 99999 components. These difficulties can be avoided by sorting the file components into smaller groups and then merging the components in each group into a file that contains only records that have previously been sorted. Write a program that will use a sort and merge process to build a file of ITEM type records sorted by CODENUMBER.

10. A file can serve as a dictionary for word and phrases. For instance, a file could contain technical words and phrases and the definitions that apply to them in medicine, engineering, or computer science. Write a program that can create and update a technical dictionary. Assume that each word or phrase will have no more than one definition. The program should be able to produce an alphabetical listing of the dictionary.

ELEVEN/DYNAMIC VARIABLES AND DATA STRUCTURES

Variables used in a Pascal program may be either **static** or **dynamic.** A static variable is one that is declared in a program block and has memory space allocated to it for the entire execution of that block. All the variables we have used up to now have been static variables. A dynamic variable does not exist until it is created during the execution of a program. All variables declared in the declaration section of a program block are static variables. Unlike static variables, dynamic variables do not have specific names. A reference to a dynamic variable must be made indirectly through the use of a **pointer variable.** The value of a pointer variable is the memory address of the storage space allocated to a dynamic variable when it is created. The symbol ''☆'' is used to denote the memory address of a dynamic variable in the following diagram, which depicts the relationship between a pointer variable and a dynamic variable.

Pointer Variable   Dynamic Variable

Pointer variables are used to create (allocate storage for) dynamic variables when the latter are needed and to destroy (release storage allocated to) them when they are of no further use. This creation and destruction of dynamic variables occurs during the execution of a program. Thus a program can build data structures if and when they are required, and the storage space allocated to these structures need not be committed for the entire run of the program. Storage is allocated to dynamic variables on demand, but the amount of computer memory that can be utilized for dynamic variables will always be limited by the total amount of memory available to a program. In this chapter we will study a few of the more common kinds of data structures that can be constructed by using dynamic variables.

11.1 POINTER VARIABLES AND HOW TO USE THEM

When a pointer variable is declared, the data type for a dynamic variable must be specified. A TYPE definition for a pointer type takes the form

$$type\text{-}identifier = \uparrow base\text{-}type;$$

where the *base-type* may be any standard or user-defined data type. Consider the following example.

```
TYPE
        AREALPOINTER = ^REAL;
VAR
        VALUEPTR : AREALPOINTER;
```

VALUEPTR is a pointer variable of the type AREALPOINTER. Since the *base-type* specified in the definition of type identifier AREALPOINTER is REAL, VALUEPTR may be used only to point to a dynamic REAL variable. The value of VALUEPTR (when one is assigned) will be a memory address of a dynamically created variable that can be assigned only a REAL value.

Pointer values are constants of a standard type that is different from all the other standard data types we have considered. It is not possible to READ or WRITE a pointer value and pointer values may not be used in arithmetic expressions. The value of a pointer variable is an "address" that points to a dynamic variable whose type is the base type declared for the pointer variable. For instance, VALUEPTR may be assigned a value that serves as the address of a REAL type dynamic variable.

CREATING AND DESTROYING DYNAMIC VARIABLES

Like any variable, a pointer variable has no value until it is assigned one. It is possible to copy the value of one pointer variable to another pointer variable by using an assignment statement, but to create a new dynamic variable and assign its address to a pointer variable requires a call to the standard procedure NEW:

NEW(*pointer-variable*)

When NEW is called, one pointer variable must be specified as an actual parameter. NEW will create a dynamic variable whose type is the base type to which the pointer variable is bound and the memory address of that dynamic variable will be assigned to the pointer variable. For instance, the procedure statement

NEW(VALUEPTR)

will cause the allocation of memory for a dynamic REAL variable and the memory address of that REAL variable will become the value of VALUEPTR. The relationship between VALUEPTR and the NEWly created dynamic variable is depicted in this diagram:

VALUEPTR

Although VALUEPTR now has a value, the dynamic variable to which it points does not (as indicated by the shading).

A dynamic variable has no explicit name, but it can be referenced by using any pointer variable that contains its memory address. The general form of such a reference is

pointer-variable ↑

For example, when VALUEPTR has a value, VALUEPTR ↑ identifies the dynamic REAL variable whose memory address is stored in VALUEPTR. To assign a value to the dynamic variable we could use an assignment statement like

$$\text{VALUEPTR\textasciicircum} := 17.5$$

The result of this value assignment is illustrated below.

VALUEPTR

As long as VALUEPTR has a value, VALUEPTR ↑ serves as the name for a REAL variable and it can appear anywhere that a REAL variable is allowed. For instance, all of the following statements are valid.

```
WRITELN(VALUEPTR^)

READ(VALUEPTR^)

IF VALUEPTR^ <= 10.0
   THEN X := VALUEPTR^

WHILE VALUEPTR^ >= 3.5
   DO BEGIN
      WRITE(VALUEPTR^:8:2);
      VALUEPTR^ := VALUEPTR^ / 2.0
      END
```

Note the distinction between VALUEPTR and VALUEPTR ↑. The statement

$$\text{VALUEPTR} := 17.5$$

is illegal because VALUEPTR is not a REAL variable. There are only a few operations that can be applied to pointer variables. Suppose NUMBERPTR is another pointer variable of the type AREALPOINTER. The value of VALUEPTR can be copied into the variable NUMBERPTR by using the assignment statement

$$\text{NUMBERPTR} := \text{VALUEPTR}$$

After that assignment, NUMBERPTR and VALUEPTR both contain the same memory address and so NUMBERPTR ↑ and VALUEPTR ↑ both refer to the same dynamic REAL variable.

The values of two pointer variables can be compared by using the relational operators "=" and "<>". Consider the following declarations.

```
TYPE
      INTPOINTER = ^INTEGER;
VAR
      PTR1, PTR2 : INTPOINTER;
```

Both PTR1 and PTR2 are pointer variables and each can be assigned the memory address of some dynamic INTEGER variable. Here is a program segment that uses PTR1 and PTR2.

```
NEW(PTR1);
WRITELN('ENTER ANY INTEGER');
READ(PTR1^);
IF PTR1^ < 10
   THEN BEGIN
        NEW(PTR2);
        WRITELN('ENTER ANOTHER INTEGER');
        READ(PTR2^)
        END
   ELSE PTR2 := PTR1;
IF PTR1 = PTR2
   THEN WRITELN('TWO POINTERS EXIST TO THE SAME VARIABLE.')
   ELSE WRITELN('TWO POINTERS EXIST, EACH POINTING TO A ',
               'DIFFERENT VARIABLE.')
```

Suppose that the following dialogue takes place when this program segment is executed.

```
ENTER ANY INTEGER
? 7
ENTER ANOTHER INTEGER
? -12
TWO POINTERS EXIST, EACH POINTING TO A DIFFERENT VARIABLE.
```

The following diagrams show the relationships created between the pointers PTR1 and PTR2 and the two INTEGER variables dynamically created by the program segment.

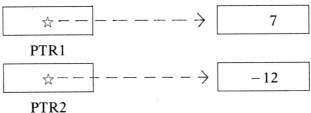

Now suppose that the program segment is executed and only one integer is read:

```
ENTER ANY INTEGER
? 15
TWO POINTERS EXIST TO THE SAME VARIABLE.
```

Only one dynamic variable is created by a call to the procedure NEW and its memory address is left in PTR1. However, the value of PTR1 is copied into PTR2 so that pointers will point to the same dynamic variable, as depicted here.

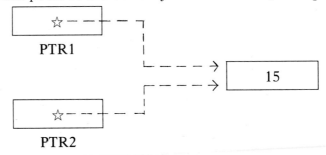

The value of PTR1 ↑ and the value of PTR2 ↑ are both 15, since PTR1 = PTR2.

An existing dynamic variable can be destroyed by a call to the standard procedure named DISPOSE, which takes the form

DISPOSE(pointer-variable)

The pointer variable specified as the actual parameter in a call to DISPOSE must contain the memory address of the dynamic variable to be destroyed. DISPOSE will release the storage allocated to the designated variable and cause the value of the pointer variable to be left undefined. Suppose that PTR1 contains the memory address of a dynamic INTEGER variable that has been assigned the value 604, as depicted in the following diagram.

PTR1

The statement

```
DISPOSE(PTR1)
```

destroys the INTEGER variable previously known as PTR1↑. PTR1 still exists, but it has no value. Thus the reference PTR1 ↑ is now meaningless.

The only pointer variable whose value is lost when DISPOSE is called is that pointer variable which is specified in the call. If two or more pointer variables contain the memory address of the same dynamic variable, any one of them may be used to DISPOSE of that dynamic variable. The other pointer variables will still contain the address of that dynamic variable, but they are now "dangling pointers" because the dynamic variable no longer exists. Suppose that PTR1 and PTR2 both point to a dynamic variable whose value is 604, as depicted below.

After the statement

```
DISPOSE(PTR1)
```

has been executed, PTR1 will no longer contain a value and the dynamic variable it had previously pointed to will no longer exist. However, PTR2 still contains the former address of that dynamic variable, as illustrated in the following diagram.

PTR2 is now a dangling pointer and it cannot be used to refer to a dynamic variable until it has been assigned the memory address of an existing dynamic variable. If PTR2 had been used to DISPOSE of the dynamic variable instead of PTR1, then PTR1 would have been a dangling pointer.

LINKING DYNAMIC VARIABLES BY USING POINTERS

Dynamic variables can be used effectively to conserve storage. Of course, for every dynamic variable there must be a pointer whose value is the memory address of that dynamic variable or it will be impossible to access that variable. Structured variables are much more useful as dynamic variables than simple variables. Consider the following declarations:

```
TYPE
      STRING30 = PACKED ARRAY [1 .. 30] OF CHAR;
      STATS = RECORD
                  NAME : STRING30;
                  SSN : INTEGER;
                  AGE : 1 .. 99;
              END (* OF STATS RECORD *);
      STATSPTR = ^STATS;
      POINTERLIST = ARRAY [1 .. 100] OF STATSPTR;
VAR
      INFO : POINTERLIST;
```

INFO is an array consisting of 100 indexed pointer variables, each of which can be assigned the memory address of a dynamically generated STATS type record. None of these records exist until they are created by calls to the procedure NEW. The array INFO effectively replaces a static array whose components would be STATS type records. While all the record type components of the static array would be available at the same time, the records pointed to by the components of INFO may be created if and when they are needed.

Any of the 100 pointer variables in the array INFO can be used to create a dynamic record variable. Suppose INFO[1] is specified in a call to the procedure NEW. The STATS type record that is created can be referred to by using the identifier INFO[1]↑. That record has three fields: INFO[1]↑.NAME, INFO[1]↑.SSN, and INFO[1]↑.AGE. Since the NAME field of a STATS type record has an array structure, a component's index can be specified in brackets after INFO[1]↑.NAME. For instance, INFO[1]↑.NAME[12] refers to the twelfth character in the NAME field of the record pointed to by INFO[1]. Suppose INFO[1] has just been used to create a dynamic STATS type record and none of the other pointers in the array have yet been assigned pointer values. The fields of that dynamic record will not contain any values until they are assigned values, but the record exists and may be referred to as INFO[1]↑. The relationship of the array INFO to that dynamic record is depicted below.

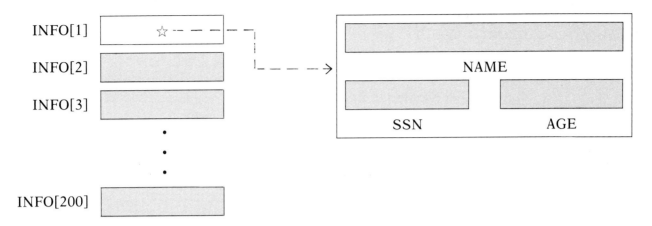

The word NIL is a constant identifier that represents a pointer value that can be assigned to any pointer variable. NIL is not the memory address of any dynamic variable. It is often assigned to a pointer variable that needs to have a value in order for the program to function properly. Consider the following program segment.

```
WRITELN('ENTER INFORMATION FOR EACH PERSON AS IT IS REQUESTED.');
WRITELN('TO SIGNAL THAT THERE IS NO MORE INFORMATION TO BE');
WRITELN('ENTERED, TYPE THE WORD HALT WHEN A NEW NAME IS REQUESTED.');
STOP := 'HALT';
N := 0;
MOREDATA := TRUE;
REPEAT (* RECORD CREATION *)
  N := N + 1;
  NEW(INFO[N]);
  WITH INFO[N]^
    DO BEGIN (* DATA INPUT *)
       WRITELN('NAME:');
       READLN; (* NEW INPUT LINE *)
       FOR I := 1 TO 30
         DO IF NOT EOLN
              THEN READ(NAME[I])
              ELSE NAME[I] := ' ';
       IF NAME = STOP
         THEN BEGIN (* ESTABLISH MARKER IN INFO ARRAY *)
              DISPOSE(INFO[N]);
              INFO[N] := NIL;
              MOREDATA := FALSE
              END (* OF ESTABLISH MARKER IN INFO ARRAY *)
         ELSE BEGIN (* INPUT FOR A PERSON *)
              WRITELN('SOCIAL SECURITY NUMBER AND AGE:');
              READLN; (* NEW INPUT LINE *)
              READ(SSN, AGE)
              END (* OF INPUT FOR A PERSON *)
       END (* OF DATA INPUT *)
UNTIL MOREDATA = FALSE;
WRITELN;
WRITELN('NAME':17, 'SOC. SEC. NUM.':30, 'AGE':6);
FOR I := 1 TO 30
```

```
 DO WRITE('-');
WRITELN('--------------':17, '---':6);
N := 1;
WHILE INFO[N] <> NIL
   DO WITH INFO[N]^
        DO BEGIN (* PRINT A RECORD *)
           WRITELN(NAME, SSN:15, AGE:8);
           N := N + 1
           END (* OF PRINT A RECORD *)
```

Here is a sample of the dialogue between this program segment and the user.

```
ENTER INFORMATION FOR EACH PERSON AS IT IS REQUESTED.
TO SIGNAL THAT THERE IS NO MORE INFORMATION TO BE
ENTERED, TYPE THE WORD HALT WHEN A NEW NAME IS REQUESTED.
NAME:
?JONES, JOHN L.
SOCIAL SECURITY NUMBER AND AGE:
?234567890  35
NAME:
?SMITH, ABRAHAM JEFFERSON
SOCIAL SECURITY NUMBER AND AGE:
?987654321  52
NAME:
?JOHNSON, CINDY LOUISE
SOCIAL SECURITY NUMBER AND AGE:
?111223333  18
NAME:
?HALT

                     NAME                   SOC. SEC. NUM.   AGE
        ------------------------------      --------------   ---
        JONES, JOHN L.                         234567890      35
        SMITH, ABRAHAM JEFFERSON               987654321      52
        JOHNSON, CINDY LOUISE                  111223333      18
```

The records used to store the input information are generated as they are needed. Just after all the information has been entered, the contents of the array INFO and the records pointed to by its components are as illustrated below.

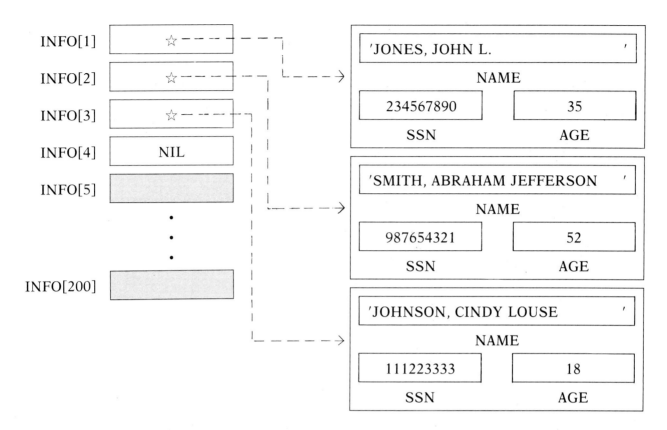

When a static array like INFO is used to store pointers to dynamic variables, the number of dynamic variables that can be generated is limited to the number of components in the array. In some situations, like the example shown above, the vast majority of the array components are not needed. A program can create pointer variables as they are needed. Consider the following declarations.

```
TYPE
      STRING30 = PACKED ARRAY [1 .. 30] OF CHAR;
      STATSPTR = ^STATS;
      STATS = RECORD
                 NAME : STRING30;
                 SSN : INTEGER;
                 AGE : 1 .. 99;
                 NEXTPTR : STATSPTR
              END (* OF STATS RECORD *);
VAR
      TOPPTR, UTILITYPTR : STATSPTR;
```

Note that the STATS type is defined after the pointer type STATSPTR for which STATS is the base type. Normally, a "forward reference" of this type is not allowed, but Pascal makes an exception in the case of a base type for pointer type definition. If a STATS type record is created by using TOPPTR or UTILITYPTR, this record will have a pointer field of the type STATSPTR, namely, NEXTPTR. The NEXTPTR field of one dynamic STATS type record can be used to create another **STATS** type record. This enables the dynamic records to be "chained" as illustrated below.

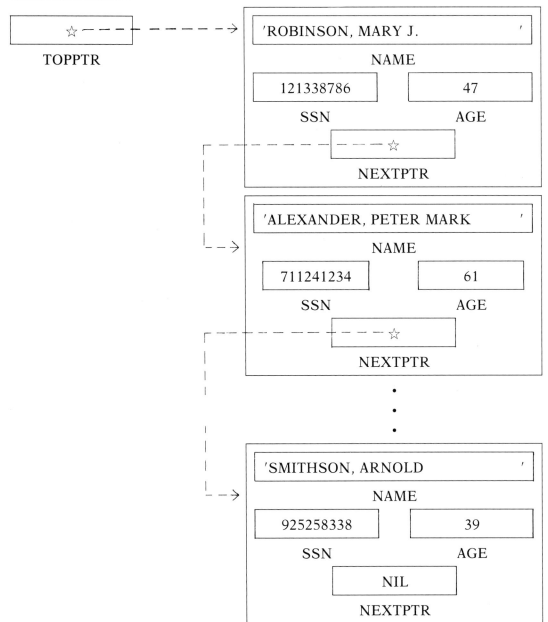

This data structure is a simple **linked list.** Each record is a link in the list and the pointer field within the records is used to establish the linkage. A pointer variable (**TOPPTR** in our example) contains the pointer to the first or top link, and thereafter a pointer field in each link contains the pointer to the next link in the list. The last or bottom link has a NIL pointer to signify that there are no more links in the list.

In order to build a linked list, two pointer variables must be used: one that always points to the top of the list and one that is used to create new links. The list is initialized and the first link is created by the statements

```
TOPPTR := NIL;
NEW(UTILITYPTR)
```

When TOPPTR has the value NIL, the list is empty. UTILITYPTR points to a new STATS type record, but it has not yet become part of the list, as illustrated below.

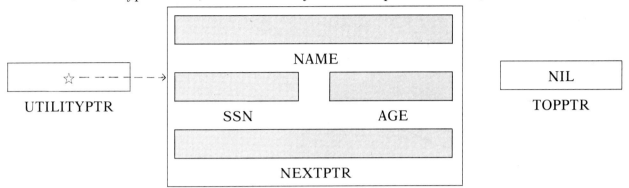

Two statements are needed to insert the record UTILITYPTR↑ into the list:

```
UTILITYPTR^.NEXTPTR := TOPPTR;
TOPPTR := UTILITYPTR
```

When a new record enters the list, it becomes the top link. The first statement establishes the linkage between the new link and the record that was previously at the top of the list. The second statement establishes the new record as the top link. The effects produced by the two statements are depicted in the following diagram.

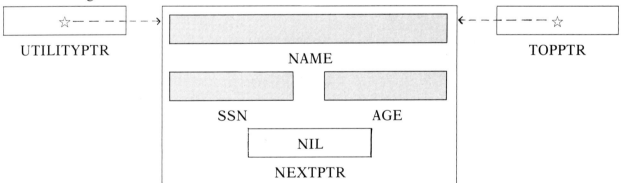

Either UTILITYPTR↑ or TOPPTR↑ may serve as the name of the record that is now at the top of the list, but UTILITYPTR will be used to generate the next link when it is needed. Information can be assigned to the fields of the new record in the list by using a program segment like the one shown below.

```
WITH TOPPTR^
   DO BEGIN (* DATA INPUT FOR A RECORD *)
      WRITELN('NAME:');
      READLN; (* NEW LINE OF INPUT *)
      FOR I := 1 TO 30
         DO IF NOT EOLN
             THEN READ(NAME[I])
             ELSE NAME[I] := ' ';
```

```
WRITELN('SOCIAL SECURITY NUMBER AND AGE:');
READLN; (* NEW LINE OF INPUT *)
READ(SSN, AGE)
END (* OF DATA INPUT FOR A RECORD *)
```

Now suppose that UTILITYPTR is used again to generate another STATS type record:

```
NEW(UTILITYPTR)
```

This new record will be linked to the existing list by means of the same two statements employed to place the first link in the list. The first of these statements is

```
UTILITYPTR^.NEXT := TOPPTR
```

and it establishes the linkage between the new record and the record currently at the top of the list, as illustrated in the following diagram.

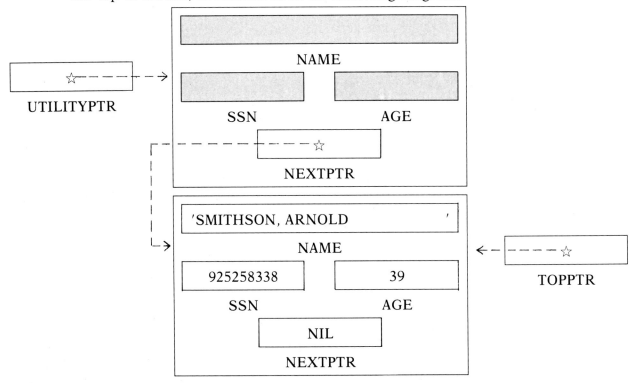

The statement

```
TOPPTR := UTILITYPTR
```

makes the new record the top link in the list, as shown in the next diagram. Again, both TOPPTR and UTILITYPTR point to the top of the list and so UTILITYPTR is available for use when another STATS type record has to be created. The type of linked list we are building is also known as a **stack** because the records in the list appear to be stacked one on top of the other. New records added to the list are always placed one on top of the other. New records added to the list are always placed on top of the stack and only the topmost record is immediately accessible. However, it is possible to access any record in the stack by tracing the pointers from the top of the list down, as we will soon see. The important thing is that none of the pointers to the records in the list have been lost.

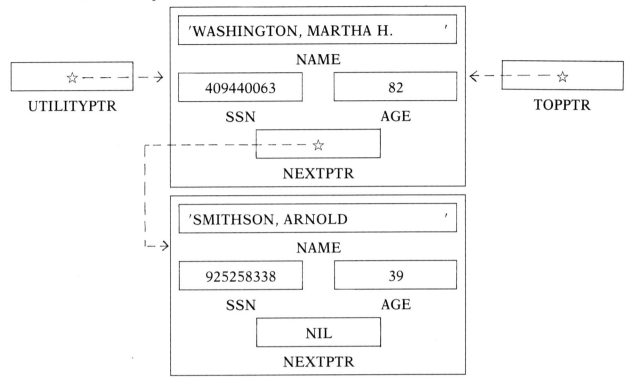

The process of building a linked list composed of STATS type records when the data for those records are read from the INPUT file is described by the following pseudocode.

```
Initialize TOPPTR to NIL
WHILE there is a record to be added to the list
     DO BEGIN record creations and linkage
          Create a NEW record using UTILITYPTR
          Copy TOPPTR to UTILITYPTR↑.NEXTPTR
          READ information for the TOPPTR↑ record
          END of record creation and linkage
```

Since the address of the dynamic record at the top of a stack is readily available, it is possible to visit the records in reverse order of their entry into the stack. For instance, the following procedure will print the contents of every STATS type record in a stack from the topmost record down. The local pointer variable PTR is used to move from link to link.

```
PROCEDURE TOPDOWNPRINT (PTR : STATSPTR);
   VAR
        PTR : STATSPTR;
   BEGIN (* PROCEDURE TOPDOWNPRINT *)
   PTR := TOP;
   WHILE PTR <> NIL
      DO WITH PTR^
```

```
            DO BEGIN (* PRINTING ONE RECORD *)
                WRITELN('NAME: ':10, NAME);
                WRITELN('SSN: ':10, SSN:9);
                WRITELN('AGE: ':10, AGE:2);
                WRITELN;
                PTR := NEXTPTR
            END (* OF PRINTING ONE RECORD *)
      END (* OF PROCEDURE TOPDOWNPRINT *);
```

Since TOP is a value parameter, it could be used in place of PTR to trace through the list. The top of the list passed to the procedure as the actual parameter cannot be affected by values that the procedure assigns to TOP.

It is also possible to print the contents of records in a stack from the bottom up. The easiest way to accomplish this task is to use a recursive procedure like this one:

```
      PROCEDURE BOTTOMUPPRINT (PTR : STATSPTR);
         BEGIN (* PROCEDURE BOTTOMUPPRINT *)
         WITH PTR^
            DO BEGIN (* PRINT ONE RECORD *)
                IF NEXTPTR <> NIL
                  THEN BOTTOMUPPRINT(NEXTPTR);
                WRITELN('NAME: ':10, NAME);
                WRITELN('SSN: ':10, SSN:9);
                WRITELN('AGE: ':10, AGE:2);
                WRITELN
            END (* OF PRINT ONR RECORD *)
         END (* OF PROCEDURE BOTTOMUPPRINT *);
```

BOTTOMUPPRINT calls itself to move the pointer PTR down the stack until the bottom record (whose NEXTPTR field must contain the value NIL) is reached. Then the contents of the bottom record are printed, followed by the other records moving up the stack as each call to BOTTOMUP is completed. Note that the procedure BOTTOMUP assumes that the stack is not empty. The value of the pointer to the top of the stack should be tested immediately before BOTTOMUPPRINT is called to make sure that it is not NIL. Otherwise the first reference to PTR ↑ .NEXTPTR will not be valid.

There are two major advantages to forming a linked list of dynamic records as opposed to maintaining an array of static pointers to a collection of dynamic records. First, since only the pointers that are actually used will exist, storage can be conserved. Second, the number of pointers that will be required need not be known in advance. In this section we examined only one type of linked data structure (a stack) that can be formed by means of dynamic variables. There are many other kinds of dynamic data structures that can be formed by linking dynamic variables. Some of these data structures will be presented in the next section.

**11.1
EXERCISES**

1. Eight pointer variables are declared as follows:

```
VAR
      BPTR1, BPTR2 : ^BOOLEAN;
      CPTR1, CPTR2 : ^CHAR;
      IPTR1, IPTR2 : ^INTEGER;
      RPTR1, RPTR2 : ^REAL;
```

Suppose each pointer variable has been assigned a non-NIL value. Some or all of the following statements illegally use the pointers declared above or make invalid references to them. Find the errors and explain why they are errors.

a.   `IPTR2 := IPTR2 + 1`

b.   `READ(BPTR1^)`

c.   `WRITELN(IPTR1^:4, RPTR^:15:4)`

d.   `IPTR2^ := RPTR1^`

e.   `IF CPTR1 <> CPTR2`
            `THEN WRITELN(CPTR1^, CPTR2^)`

f.   `IF CPTR2^ = CPTR1^`
            `THEN WRITELN(CPTR1, CPTR2)`

g.   `IF BPTR^ AND BPTR2^`
            `THEN IPTR1 := IPTR2`
            `ELSE NEW(IPTR1^)`

h.   `IPTR2^ := TRUNC(RPTR1^ * RPTR2^)`

2. Three pointer variables are declared as follows:

```
VAR
      PTR1, PTR2, PTR3 : ^INTEGER;
```

Show the output that will be produced by each of the following program segments.

a.
```
NEW(PTR1);
PTR1^ := 5;
NEW(PTR2);
PTR2^ := 8;
PTR1^ := PTR1^ + PTR2^;
WRITELN(PTR1^, PTR2^)
```

b.
```
NEW(PTR1);
PTR1^ := 12;
PTR2 := PTR1;
NEW(PTR1);
PTR1^ := PTR2^ + 7;
WRITELN(PTR1^, PTR2^)
```

c.
```
NEW(PTR1);
NEW(PTR2);
PTR1^ := 9;
PTR2^ := 5 * (PTR1^ MOD 5);
PTR3 := PTR1;
PTR1 := PTR2;
PTR2 := PTR3;
WRITELN(PTR1^, PTR2^, PTR3^)
```

d.
```
NEW(PTR1);
PTR1^ := 25;
PTR3^ := PTR1^;
NEW(PTR2);
PTR2^ := 3;
PTR3^ := PTR3^ DIV PTR2^;
PTR2^ := PTR1^ DIV PTR3^;
WRITELN(PTR1^, PTR2^, PTR3^)
```

3. Give the definitions and declarations necessary to construct a linked list of PART type records, where each record contains the description of the part, its code number (a whole number greater than 999), and its unit price. Draw a diagram showing a typical linked list consisting of three PARTs records.

4. Write a procedure that will create a linked list of PARTs as described in Exercise 3.

5. Write a procedure that will print the contents of all records in a linked list composed of PARTs records as described in Exercise 3.

6. Write a procedure that will search the PARTs records in a linked list (as described in Exercise 3) to determine if there is a record containing a particular part number specified as a parameter for the procedure. If the search is successful, the procedure should return the pointer to the desired record. Otherwise, the procedure should return the pointer value NIL.

11.2
LINKED LISTS USED TO REPRESENT QUEUES

The insertion of a new link into a linked list and the removal of a link from the list is usually governed by rules that are intended to maintain some sort of discipline. For instance, a new link added to a linked list that has a stack structure is always placed at the top of the stack. Furthermore, only the link at the top of the stack can be removed from the stack. This is known as a last-in, first-out (LIFO) discipline. A stack is treated as a waiting line or **queue** that is governed by a LIFO discipline. It is also possible to structure a linked list as a queue that is governed by a first-in, first-out (FIFO) discipline. This means that links enter the list at one end and are removed at the other end. In this section we will study the fundamental operations that can be performed on linked lists that are structured as LIFO or FIFO queues.

LIFO AND FIFO QUEUES

Suppose that basketballs are lent out at an equipment window in a gymnasium and each basketball is marked with an identification number that is between 1 and 10. The basketballs available at the checkout window form a waiting line (queue) and the person working at the window determines the rules (queue discipline) to be followed in lending out the balls (for example, LIFO, FIFO, random selection). Consider the following declarations:

```
TYPE
      BALLPTR = ^BASKETBALL;
      BASKETBALL = RECORD
                      IDNUMBER : 1 .. 10;
                      NEXTBALL : BALLPTR
                   END (* OF BASKETBALL RECORD *);
VAR
      TOPBALL : BALLPTR;
```

If the policy followed in lending out basketballs is that the ball most recently returned is the first one to be lent out, the basketballs available at the window form a stack (LIFO queue). For instance, the basketballs could be placed in a cylindrical tube that is open at the top and has a platform attached to its bottom by a spring so that the weight of the balls in the tube makes only the topmost ball available. A physical realization of this stack and its representation as a linked list are both depicted in the following diagrams.

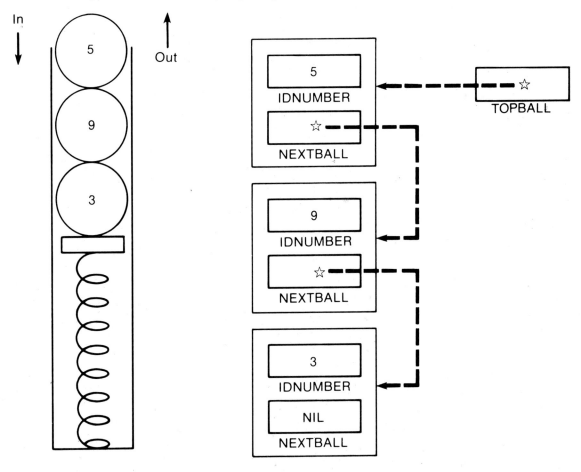

When a basketball is turned in, it is placed on top of the stack. This operation is known as a "push." With respect to the linked list structure, a new BASKETBALL type record is created and linked at the top of the list. A procedure that can be used to generate a push is shown below.

```
PROCEDURE BALLPUSH (VAR CURRENTTOP : BALLPTR);
  VAR
        BALLIN : BALLPTR;
  BEGIN (* PROCEDURE BALLPUSH *)
  NEW(BALLIN);
  BALLIN^.NEXTBALL := CURRENTTOP;
  CURRENTTOP := BALLIN;
  WRITELN('THE BALL''S ID NUMBER:');
  READ(CURRENTTOP^.IDNUMBER)
  END (* OF PROCEDURE BALLPUSH *);
```

The removal of a ball from the stack corresponds to deleting the topmost record from the linked list. This operation is known as a "pop." A pop is essentially the reverse of a push. The statements used to generate a pop reflect this fact, as can be seen by comparing the following program segments.

```
(* A PUSH *)
NEW(BALLIN);
BALLIN^.NEXTBALL := CURRENTTOP;
CURRENTTOP := BALLIN


(* A POP *)
BALLOUT := CURRENTTOP;
CURRENTTOP := BALLOUT^.NEXTBALL;
DISPOSE(BALLOUT)
```

Before the topmost record is DISPOSEd of, the pointer to the top of the stack (CURRENTTOP) must be changed so that it will point to the next record in the stack. First, the pointer to the topmost ball must be copied to the pointer variable BALLOUT, which will be used to destroy that record.

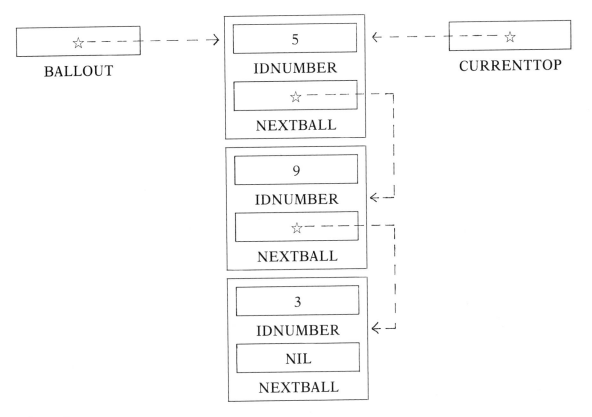

Then the statement

$$\text{CURRENTTOP} := \text{BALLOUT}^\wedge.\text{NEXTBALL}$$

will reposition the CURRENTTOP pointer to the new topmost record for the stack.

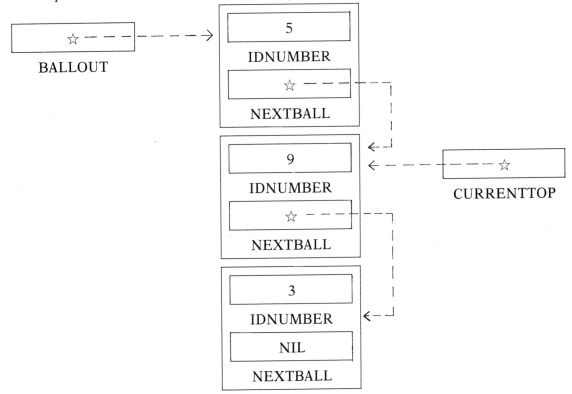

Now the procedure DISPOSE can be called to destroy the record popped off the stack. A complete procedure that can be used to pop a BASKETBALL type record off a stack is given below.

```
PROCEDURE BALLPOP (VAR CURRENTTOP : BALLPTR);
  VAR
        BALLOUT : BALLPTR;
  BEGIN (* PROCEDURE BALLPOP *)
  BALLOUT := CURRENTTOP;
  CURRENTTOP := BALLOUT^.NEXTBALL;
  WRITELN('BALL #', BALLOUT^.IDNUMBER:2, ' CHECKED OUT.');
  DISPOSE(BALLOUT)
  END (* OF PROCEDURE BALLPOP *);
```

Suppose the basketballs are kept in a first-in, first-out waiting line (FIFO queue). The physical realization of this kind of queue could be a gravity-feed tube in which balls are inserted at the top and removed from the bottom. A linked list representation of a FIFO queue requires two special pointers, one pointing to the top (or rear) of the queue and one pointing to the bottom (or front) of the queue. The following diagrams depict a physical and a linked list representation for a FIFO queue.

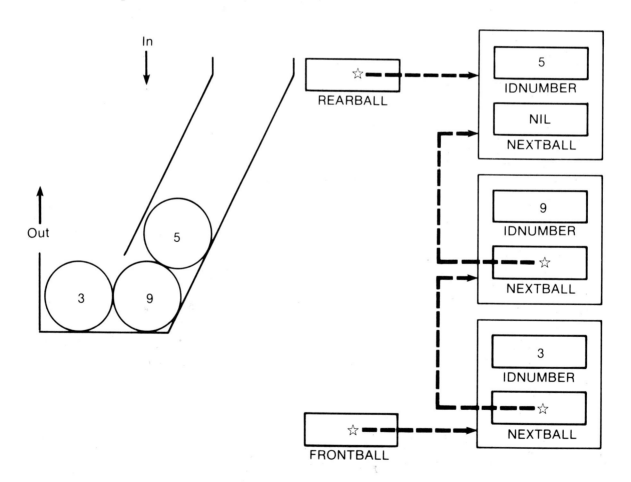

Note that the NEXTBALL pointer in the record at the rear of the queue is NIL. Also, when the queue is empty, both the REARBALL and FRONTBALL pointers should be NIL.

A new BASKETBALL type record is created and inserted at the rear of the FIFO queue by using the REARBALL pointer and another pointer variable referenced in the call to the procedure NEW:

```
NEW(BALLIN);
REARBALL^.NEXTBALL := BALLIN;
REARBALL := BALLIN;
REARBALL^.NEXTBALL := NIL
```

However, this program segment will not be valid if REARBALL is NIL (i.e. the queue is currently empty). When REARBALL is NIL, FRONTBALL should also be NIL. In that case, FRONTBALL should be assigned the value of BALLIN. These changes are incorporated in the following procedure, which can be used to insert a new BASKETBALL type record into the queue.

```
PROCEDURE INQUEUE (VAR REARBALL, FRONTBALL : BALLPTR);
  VAR
       BALLIN : BALLPTR;
  BEGIN (* PROCEDURE INQUEUE *)
  NEW(BALLIN);
  IF REARBALL = NIL
    THEN FRONTBALL := BALLIN
    ELSE REARBALL^.NEXTBALL := BALLIN;
  REARBALL := BALLIN;
  REARBALL^.NEXTBALL := NIL;
  WRITELN('THE BALL''S ID NUMBER:');
  READ(REARBALL^.IDNUMBER)
  END (* OF PROCEDURE INQUEUE *);
```

The deletion of a record from the front of our FIFO queue is basically the same as popping a record from a stack:

```
BALLOUT := FRONTBALL;
FRONTBALL := BALLOUT^.NEXTBALL;
DISPOSE(BALLOUT)
```

Of course this program segment is not valid when the queue is empty (FRONT-BALL is NIL). If FRONTBALL is not NIL, but it is equal to REARBALL, then there is only one record in the queue and REARBALL must be set to NIL when that record is deleted. Here is the complete procedure for removing a BASKETBALL type record from a FIFO queue.

```
PROCEDURE OUTQUEUE (VAR REARBALL, FRONTBALL : BALLPTR);
  VAR
       BALLOUT : BALLPTR;
  BEGIN (* PROCEDURE OUTQUEUE *)
```

```
    IF FRONTBALL = REARBALL
      THEN REARBALL := NIL;
    BALLOUT := FRONTBALL;
    FRONTBALL := BALLOUT^.NEXTBALL;
    WRITELN('BALL #', BALLOUT^.IDNUMBER:2, ' CHECKED OUT.');
    DISPOSE(BALLOUT)
    END (* OF PROCEDURE OUTQUEUE *);
```

When a linked list is used to form a queue, insertions and deletions occur at one or both ends of the queue, depending on the queue discipline. However, it is possible to search a queue in order to determine whether or not a particular record is in the queue. If the desired record is located, then it can be examined for particular information or some information in the record can be changed without removing the record from the queue. A search through a queue normally attempts to match some value to the value of a field in a record that is in the queue. Consider the following procedure.

```
PROCEDURE LOCATE (BALLID : INTEGER; TOP : BALLPTR;
                  VAR LOCATION : BALLPTR);
  BEGIN (* PROCEDURE LOCATE *)
  LOCATION := TOP;
  IF LOCATION <> NIL
    THEN WHILE (LOCATION <> NIL) AND (LOCATION^.IDNUMBER <> BALLID)
         DO LOCATION := LOCATION^.NEXTBALL
  END (* OF PROCEDURE LOCATE *);
```

The procedure LOCATE seeks to match the number of a ball (BALLID) to one that appears in the queue whose top pointer or front pointer is TOP. If the matching is successful, LOCATION will contain the pointer to the desired record. If the matching is unsuccessful then LOCATION will have the value NIL. LOCATE may be used to search either a LIFO or FIFO queue whose links are BASKETBALL type records. Suppose BALLNUMBER is a variable whose value is to be matched to the IDNUMBER field of a record in the queue. For a LIFO queue (stack), the appropriate call to LOCATE is

<code>LOCATE(BALLNUMBER, TOPBALL, POSITION)</code>

where TOPBALL is the pointer to the top of the queue. For a FIFO queue, the proper call is

<code>LOCATE(BALLNUMBER, FIRSTBALL, POSITION)</code>

where FIRSTBALL is the pointer to the front of the queue. In either case, POSITION will point to the desired record in the queue after LOCATE has ended. If POSITION is NIL, then the matching was unsuccessful.

USING A QUEUE IN A PROGRAM

Suppose that a file named STATEDATA has been created so that it can be used by a program that will quiz the user on state capitals and the years in which the states were admitted to the union. The components of the file STATEDATA will be records of the type STATEINFO, as defined below:

```
TYPE
     STRING25 = PACKED ARRAY [1 .. 25] OF CHAR;
     STATEINFO = RECORD
                     NAME : STRING25;
                     CAPITAL : STRING25;
                     YEAR : 1776 .. 2000
                 END (* OF STATEINFO RECORD *);
```

After a component of the STATEDATA file is read, the program must identify the state to the user and then ask the user to name its capital. If the user's response is correct, the program will ask for the year in which the state was admitted to the union. If the response to either question is incorrect, a copy of the state's data record will be pushed onto a stack. When the file has been exhausted, the program will begin a second round of questioning using the data stored in the stack. Here is a pseudocode description of the main program:

BEGIN program STATESQUIZ
RESET the STATEDATA file
Initialize the stack pointer TOPSTATE at NIL
Initialize the number of CORRECT answers at 0
Print program information and directions
WHILE EOF (STATEDATA) is FALSE
    DO BEGIN first round questions for a state
        READ a STATE record from the STATEDATA file
        Use (ASKQUESTIONS (RESULT)) to ask the questions for a state and
           then set the RESULT flag at SUCCESS or FAILURE
        IF the RESULT = FAILURE
          THEN Use (PUSH(STATE)) to push the STATE record onto the stack
          ELSE Increment the number CORRECT by 1
        END of first round questions for a state
Print the number of states for which questions were answered CORRECTly
IF the TOPSTATE pointer to the top of the deferred questions stack is NIL
   THEN Print a congratulatory message
   ELSE BEGIN the second round of questioning
        REPEAT questions for a state
          Use (POP(STATE)) to pop a data record off the stack
          Use (ASKQUESTIONS(RESULT)) to ask the questions for a state and
            then set the RESULT flag at SUCCESS or FAILURE
        IF the RESULT = SUCCESS
          THEN Increment the number CORRECT by 1
        UNTIL the TOPSTATE pointer is NIL
        Print the number of states for which both questions were answered
          CORRECTly after both rounds of questioning
        END of second round of questioning
END of program STATESQUIZ

Here is the shell of the program STATESQUIZ with the procedures PUSH, POP, and ASKQUESTIONS absent:

```
PROGRAM STATESQUIZ (INPUT, OUTPUT, STATEDATA);
(******************************************************************
 *                                                              *
 *    THIS PROGRAM GENERATES A QUIZ ON STATE CAPITALS AND THE YEARS  *
 *    IN WHICH THE STATES JOINED THE UNION                      *
 *                                                              *
 ******************************************************************)
CONST                               (*---------[CONSTANTS]----------*)
        LOWYEAR = 1776;             (* LOWEST YEAR ALLOWED          *)
        HIGHYEAR = 2000;            (* HIGHEST YEAR ALLOWED         *)
                                    (*------------------------------*)
TYPE
        STRING25 = PACKED ARRAY [1 .. 25] OF CHAR;
        YEARRANGE = LOWYEAR .. HIGHYEAR;
        STATEINFO = RECORD
                        NAME : STRING25;
                        CAPITAL : STRING25;
                        YEAR : YEARRANGE
                    END (* OF STATEINFO RECORD *);
        QUESTIONGRADE = (SUCCESS, FAILURE);
        STATEPTR = ^STATESTATS;
        STATESTATS = RECORD
                        STACKSTATE : STATEINFO;
                        NEXTSTATE : STATEPTR
                     END (* OF STATESTATS RECORD *);
        STATESQUESTIONS = FILE OF STATEINFO;


VAR                                 (*------[INTEGER VARIABLES]------*)
        CORRECT : INTEGER;          (* NUMBER OF STATES FOR WHICH   *)
                                    (* BOTH ANSWERS ARE CORRECT     *)
                                    (*------------------------------*)
                                    (*---[QUESTIONGRADE VARIABLES]---*)
        RESULT : QUESTIONGRADE;     (* SIGNAL FOR CORRECTNESS OF    *)
                                    (* THE ANSWERS TO QUESTIONS     *)
                                    (*------------------------------*)
                                    (*------[STATEINFO RECORDS]------*)
        STATE : STATEINFO;          (* QUESTION INFORMATION FOR ONE *)
                                    (* STATE                        *)
                                    (*------------------------------*)
                                    (*-----[STATEPTR VARIABLES]------*)
        TOPSTATE : STATEPTR;        (* POINTER TO THE TOP OF THE    *)
                                    (* STACK CONTAINING STATE DATA  *)
                                    (*------------------------------*)
                                    (*----[STATESQUESTIONS FILE]-----*)
        STATEDATA : STATESQUESTIONS; (* SOURCE FILE FOR QUESTIONS AND *)
                                    (* ANSWERS                      *)
                                    (*------------------------------*)


(*==============================================================*)
(*                                                              *)
(*                INSERT PROCEDURE PUSH HERE.                   *)
(*                                                              *)
(*==============================================================*)
```

```
(*============================================================*)
(*                                                            *)
(*               INSERT PROCEDURE POP HERE.                   *)
(*                                                            *)
(*============================================================*)

(*============================================================*)
(*                                                            *)
(*            INSERT PROCEDURE ASKQUESTIONS HERE.             *)
(*                                                            *)
(*============================================================*)

(************************************************************)
BEGIN (* PROGRAM STATEQUIZ *)
RESET(STATEDATA);
TOPSTATE := NIL;
CORRECT := 0;
WRITELN('THIS IS A QUIZ ON STATE CAPITALS AND THE YEARS IN WHICH');
WRITELN('STATES JOINED THE UNION. FIRST YOU WILL BE ASKED TO ENTER');
WRITELN('THE NAME OF A STATE''S CAPITAL CITY. IF YOU GIVE THE');
WRITELN('CORRECT ANSWER, YOU WILL BE ASKED FOR THE YEAR IN WHICH');
WRITELN('THE STATE JOINED THE UNION. SHOULD YOU FAIL TO ANSWER');
WRITELN('EITHER ONE OF THESE QUESTIONS CORRECTLY, YOU WILL HAVE');
WRITELN('FAILED THE QUIZ FOR THAT STATE. LATER ON YOU WILL HAVE A');
WRITELN('SECOND CHANCE TO GIVE THE CORRECT ANSWERS.');
WRITELN;
WRITELN('HERE COMES THE FIRST ROUND OF QUESTIONS!');
WRITELN;
WHILE NOT EOF(STATEDATA)
   DO BEGIN (* QUESTIONS FOR A STATE *)
      READ(STATEDATA, STATE);
      ASKQUESTIONS(RESULT);
      IF RESULT = FAILURE
        THEN PUSH(STATE)
        ELSE CORRECT := CORRECT + 1;
      WRITELN
      END (* OF QUESTIONS FOR A STATE *);
WRITELN('THE FIRST ROUND OF QUESTIONING IS OVER. YOU HAVE GIVEN');
WRITELN('THE CORRECT ANSWERS TO THE QUESTIONS FOR ', CORRECT:2,
        ' STATES.');
WRITELN;
WRITELN('SECOND CHANCES BEGIN NOW.');
WRITELN;
IF TOPSTATE = NIL
  THEN WRITELN('CONGRATULATIONS! YOU GAVE ALL THE CORRECT ANSWERS.')
  ELSE BEGIN (* SECOND ROUND OF QUESTIONING *)
       REPEAT (* QUESTIONS FOR A STATE *)
          POP(STATE);
          ASKQUESTIONS(RESULT);
          IF RESULT = SUCCESS
            THEN CORRECT := CORRECT + 1;
          WRITELN
       UNTIL TOPSTATE = NIL;
```

```
            WRITELN('THE QUIZ IS OVER. IN ALL, YOU HAVE ANSWERED THE');
            WRITELN('QUESTIONS FOR ', CORRECT:2, ' STATES CORRECTLY.')
            END (* OF SECOND ROUND OF QUESTIONING *)
END (* OF PROGRAM STATESQUIZ *).
```

The records that are PUSHed onto the stack must contain an appropriate pointer field. They will be of the type defined below.

```
        TYPE
                STATEPTR = ^STATESTATS;
                STATESTATS = RECORD
                                    STACKSTATE : STATEINFO;
                                    NEXTSTATE : STATEPTR
                            END (* OF STATESTATS RECORD *);
```

The pointer to the top of the stack will be a STATEPTR type variable. Note that a STATEINFO type record is nested inside each STATESTATS type record. A typical record in the stack is depicted below.

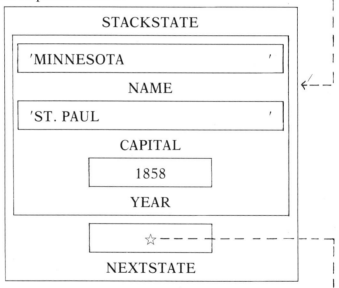

The nesting of the STACKSTATE record inside each stack record facilitates the copying of STATE information into a stack record.

Procedures POP and PUSH are similar in structure to the procedures BALLPOP and BALLPUSH presented earlier in this section:

```
PROCEDURE PUSH
  (*==============================================================*)
  (*         CREATE AND PUSH A STATE RECORD ONTO THE STACK        *)
  (*==============================================================*)
                                    (*---------[PARAMETERS]--------*)
  (INSTATE : STATEINFO);            (* STATE INFORMATION RECORD    *)
                                    (*-----------------------------*)
   VAR                              (*-----[STATEPTR VARIABLES]-----*)
        INPTR : STATEPTR;           (* POINTER TO NEW STACK RECORD  *)
                                    (*-----------------------------*)
  (*==============================================================*)
```

```
BEGIN (* PROCEDURE PUSH *)
NEW(INPTR);
INPTR^.NEXTSTATE := TOPSTATE;
TOPSTATE := INPTR;
TOPSTATE^.STACKSTATE := INSTATE
END (* OF PROCEDURE PUSH *);


PROCEDURE POP
  (*================================================================*)
  (*          POP THE TOPMOST STATE RECORD OFF OF THE STACK         *)
  (*================================================================*)
                                 (*---------- [PARAMETERS] ---------*)
                                 (* STATE INFORMATION RECORD        *)
  (VAR OUTSTATE : STATEINFO);     (*--------------------------------*)
                                 (*----- [STATEPTR VARIABLES] ------*)
   VAR                           (* POINTER TO RECORD REMOVED       *)
       OUTPTR : STATEPTR;        (* FROM THE STACK                  *)
                                 (*--------------------------------*)
  (*================================================================*)
  BEGIN (* PROCEDURE POP *)
  OUTSTATE := TOPSTATE^.STACKSTATE;
  OUTPTR := TOPSTATE;
  TOPSTATE := OUTPTR^.NEXTSTATE;
  DISPOSE(OUTPTR)
  END (* OF PROCEDURE POP *);
```

The procedure ASKQUESTIONS will conduct the quiz for each state. ASKQUESTIONS must set a result FLAG at SUCCESS if both questions are answered correctly. Otherwise, the result FLAG must be set at FAILURE. Here is the procedure ASKQUESTIONS:

```
PROCEDURE ASKQUESTIONS
  (*================================================================*)
  (*     ASK QUESTIONS FOR ONE STATE AND SET THE RESULT FLAG        *)
  (*================================================================*)
                                 (*---------- [PARAMETERS] ---------*)
                                 (* RESULT OF THE QUESTIONING       *)
  (VAR  FLAG : QUESTIONGRADE);    (*--------------------------------*)
                                 (*----- [STRING25 VARIABLES] ------*)
   VAR                           (* STATE CAPITAL RESPONSE          *)
       CITY : STRING25;          (*--------------------------------*)
                                 (*----- [YEARRANGENVARIABLES] -----*)
       JOINYEAR : YEARRANGE;     (* RESPONSE FOR YEAR ADMITTED TO   *)
                                 (* THE UNION                       *)
                                 (*--------------------------------*)
                                 (*------ [INTEGER VARIABLES] ------*)
       I : INTEGER;              (* RESPONSE STRING INDEX           *)
                                 (*--------------------------------*)
  (*================================================================*)
  BEGIN (* PROCEDURE ASKQUESTIONS *)
  WRITELN('WHAT CITY IS THE CAPITAL OF ', STATE.NAME);
  READLN; (* NEW LINE OF INPUT *)
```

```
FOR I := 1 TO 25
 DO IF NOT EOLN
      THEN READ(CITY[I])
      ELSE CITY[I] := ' ';
IF CITY = STATE.CAPITAL
  THEN BEGIN (* SECOND QUESTION *)
       WRITELN('CORRECT!');
       WRITELN('IN WHAT YEAR DID THAT STATE JOIN THE UNION');
       READLN; (* NEW LINE OF INPUT *)
       READ(JOINYEAR);
       IF JOINYEAR = STATE.YEAR
          THEN BEGIN (* SUCCESS ACTIONS *)
               WRITELN('CORRECT, AGAIN!');
               FLAG := SUCCESS
               END (* OF SUCCESS ACTIONS *)
          ELSE BEGIN (* FAILURE ACTIONS *)
               WRITELN('INCORRECT!');
               FLAG := FAILURE
               END (* OF FAILURE ACTIONS *)
       END (* OF SECOND QUESTION *)
  ELSE BEGIN (* ACTIONS FOR INCORRECT STATE CAPITAL *)
       WRITELN('SORRY, THAT''S THE WRONG CITY.');
       FLAG := FAILURE
       END (* OF ACTION FOR INCORRECT STATE CAPITAL *)
END (* OF PROCEDURE ASKQUESTIONS *);
```

A FIFO queue could be used in place of a stack in the program STATESQUIZ. The pointer variable TOPSTATE would be replaced by two pointer variables, say FRONTSTATE and REARSTATE. Both FRONTSTATE and REARSTATE should initially be NIL and each reference to TOPSTATE in the main program should be replaced by a reference to FRONTSTATE. The procedure PUSH would be replaced by the procedure ENTERQUEUE shown below.

```
PROCEDURE ENTERQUEUE (INSTATE : STATEINFO);
  VAR
      INPTR : STATEPTR;
  BEGIN (* PROCEDURE ENTERQUEUE *)
  NEW(INPTR);
  IF REARSTATE = NIL
    THEN FRONTSTATE := INPTR
    ELSE REARSTATE^.NEXTSTATE := INPTR;
  REARSTATE := INPTR;
  REARSTATE^.NEXTSTATE := NIL;
  REARSTATE^.STACKSTATE := INSTATE
  END (* OF PROCEDURE ENTERQUEUE *);
```

The procedure POP would be replaced by the following procedure:

```
PROCEDURE LEAVEQUEUE (VAR OUTSTATE : STATEINFO);
  VAR
      OUTPTR : STATEPTR;
  BEGIN (* PROCEDURE LEAVEQUEUE *)
```

```
IF FRONTSTATE = REARSTATE
  THEN REARSTATE := NIL;
OUTPTR := FRONTSTATE;
FRONTSTATE := OUTPTR^.NEXTSTATE;
OUTSTATE := OUTPTR^.STACKSTATE;
DISPOSE(OUTPTR)
END (* OF PROCEDURE LEAVEQUEUE *);
```

When the program uses a FIFO queue, it can easily be modified so that the user can get more than two chances to answer the questions for a state. If either one of the questions for a state is answered incorrectly during the second round, simply enter the state's record at the rear of the queue again. This would give the program user as many chances as necessary to give all the correct answers. Since there may be some answers that the user simply does not know, it would be better to place a limit on the number of times the same questions are asked.

11.2 EXERCISES

1. In many cases some limit must be imposed on the capacity of a queue. For instance, when basketballs are stored in a tube as described in Section 11.2, the size of the tube determines how many basketballs it can contain. If a LIFO or FIFO queue composed of BASKETBALL type records is used to represent the contents of such a tube, the number of records in the queue must not exceed some limit. Revise the procedures BALLPUSH and INQUEUE to accommodate a limited capacity. The revised procedures should have some way of notifying a calling program that an insertion is not possible when the queue is full.

2. The procedures BALLPOP and OUTQUEUE as given in Section 11.2 may not be used when the queue is empty. Modify those procedures so that they may be called when the queue is empty. In this case, they should notify the calling program that a deletion is impossible.

3. Suppose that a linked list of BASKETBALL type records is used to represent a FIFO queue, but no pointer is maintained for the rear of the queue. Insertions must still occur at the rear of the queue. Write a procedure that will insert a new record into the queue. Discuss the advantages and disadvantages of using a FIFO queue with only a pointer to the front of the queue.

4. Suppose that a FIFO queue is to be formed by using a linked list consisting of PERSON type records defined as follows:

```
TYPE
     ALFA25 = PACKED ARRAY [1 .. 25] OF CHAR;
     ALFA8 = PACKED ARRAY [1 .. 8] OF CHAR;
     AGERANGE = 18 .. 65;
     PERSONPTR = ^PERSON;
     PERSON = RECORD
               NAME : ALFA25;
               TELEPHONE : ALFA8;
               AGE : AGERANGE;
               NEXTPERSON : PERSONPTR
            END (* OF PERSON RECORD *);
```

Declare suitable pointer variables and describe the structure of the queue by drawing a diagram showing three or four links.

5. Write procedures to insert and delete records from the FIFO queue consisting of PERSON type records as described in Exercise 4.

6. It is possible to search a linked list formed as a FIFO queue to determine whether or not a particular record appears in the list. For instance, the queue described in Exercise 4 can be searched for a record whose NAME field contains a particular character string. The procedure that conducts the search would return the pointer to the desired record if it is found; otherwise, a NIL pointer should be returned. Write two different procedures, one recursive and the other nonrecursive, to search for a match for a particular character string of the type ALFA25 in the NAME field of a PERSON type record within a FIFO queue composed of PERSON type records.

11.3
ORDERED LISTS

The linkage for a queue is determined by when a link enters the queue, not by any information that the link contains. Another way to form a linked list is to base the linkage on the contents of some key information field in each link. Suppose that PTR1 and PTR2 are pointers to any two consecutive records in a linked list, where each record has a field named KEYFIELD and possibly some other information fields.

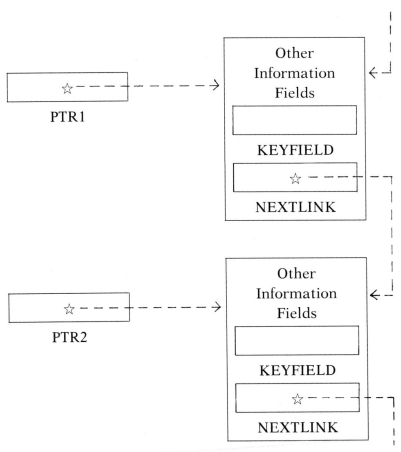

The list is said to be ordered if one of the following two conditions is TRUE for every pair of consecutive links PTR1↑ and PTR2↑:

$$\text{a. PTR1} \uparrow \text{.KEYFIELD} <= \text{PTR2} \uparrow \text{.KEYFIELD}$$
$$\text{b. PTR1} \uparrow \text{.KEYFIELD} >= \text{PTR2} \uparrow \text{.KEYFIELD}$$

When a new link is inserted into an ordered list, the order is maintained by locating the links that should come before and after the new link and adjusting the pointers appropriately.

ORDERED LISTS THAT ARE SINGLY LINKED

When only one pointer field in each link is used to establish the linkage, the list is said to be **singly linked**. The LIFO and FIFO queues we examined in Section 11.2 are examples of singly linked lists. In this section, we will study singly linked lists that are ordered. Consider the following declarations.

```
TYPE
      STRING25 = PACKED ARRAY [1 .. 25] OF CHAR;
      GRADES = 0 .. 100;
      STUDENTPTR = ^STUDENT;
      STUDENT = RECORD
                     NAME : STRING25;
                     SCORE : GRADES;
                     NEXTLINK : STUDENTPTR
                  END (* OF STUDENT RECORD *);
VAR
      FIRST : STUDENTPTR;
```

If a singly linked list is formed by using STUDENT type records as links, a typical link in the list will look like this:

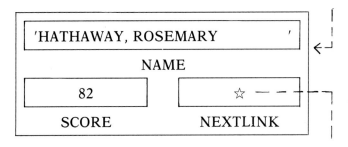

An ordering for the list could be based on either the NAME field or the SCORE field of a link. Suppose the SCOREs in the links are used to determine the way the linkage is established. The links could be arranged so that the scores increase or decrease as the list is traversed from top to bottom. Let FIRST be a pointer to the link containing the lowest SCORE in a singly linked list that is ordered from the lowest SCORE to the highest SCORE, as depicted in the following diagram.

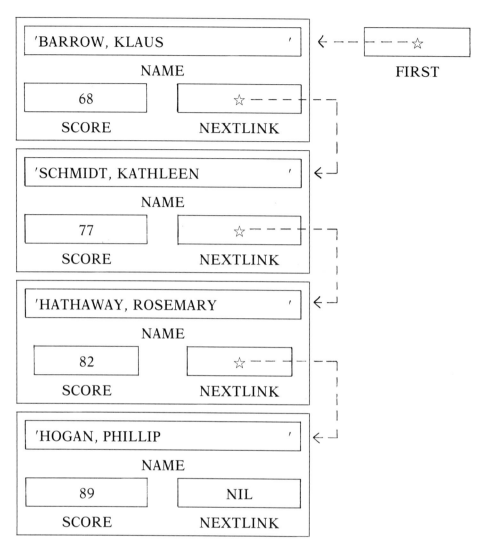

In order to maintain the ordering for this list when a new link is added, the SCORE field of the new link must be used to determine where the link will be inserted. This necessitates a search of the list. Let BEFORE and AFTER be two pointer variables of the type STUDENTPTR and let PTR be a pointer to a NEW dynamic record of the type STUDENT. Suppose PTR↑.SCORE has been assigned a value. If values for BEFORE and AFTER can be determined so that BEFORE↑ is the link that should immediately precede PTR↑ and AFTER↑ is the link that should immediately follow PTR↑, then it is possible to establish the proper linkage by using just two statements. The first statement causes the list to be temporarily "unlinked":

```
BEFORE^.NEXTLINK := PTR
```

The effects this statement will have on the linked list shown above when the new link's SCORE is 80 are illustrated in the following diagram.

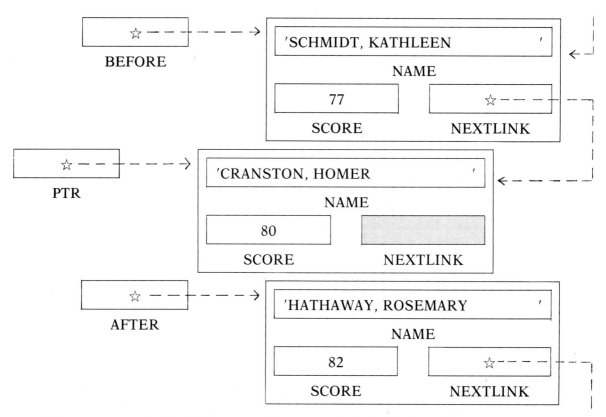

The new record PTR↑ has now been properly linked to the record BEFORE↑. Now PTR↑.NEXTLINK must be set to link the new reocrd with the remainder of the linked list. AFTER points to the link that should immediately follow PTR↑. Thus the appropriate linkage is established by the statement

$$\text{PTR\^.NEXTLINK := AFTER}$$

Locating the proper pointer values for BEFORE and AFTER requires a search of the linked list. The search may begin at the FIRST↑ record and proceed downward through the list. Consider the following procedure.

```
PROCEDURE LOCATE (NEWSCORE : GRADES; VAR BEFORE, AFTER : STUDENTPTR);
  TYPE
        SEARCHSTATUS = (GO, STOP);
  VAR
        ACTION : SEARCHSTATUS;
  BEGIN (* PROCEDURE LOCATE *)
  BEFORE := NIL;
  AFTER := FIRST;
  ACTION := GO;
  WHILE (ACTION = GO) AND (AFTER <> NIL)
     DO IF AFTER^.SCORE >= NEWSCORE
           THEN ACTION := STOP
           ELSE BEGIN (* POINTER ADJUSTMENTS *)
                   BEFORE := AFTER;
                   AFTER := BEFORE^.NEXTLINK
                END (* OF POINTER ADJUSTMENTS *)
  END (* OF PROCEDURE LOCATE *);
```

BEFORE and AFTER always point to consecutive links in the list. LOCATE attempts to find a link AFTER ↑ whose SCORE field contains a value that equals or exceeds the value of NEWSCORE. If both AFTER and BEFORE are not NIL when the procedure ends, the new link should be inserted between the links BEFORE ↑ and AFTER ↑. If BEFORE is NIL and AFTER is not, the new link should be inserted at the top of the list. If AFTER is NIL and BEFORE is not, the new link should be inserted at the bottom of the list. It is possible for both BEFORE and AFTER to be NIL, but only if the list is currently empty.

Once values for BEFORE and AFTER have been established, the rearrangement of pointers required to insert the new link is relatively straightforward. Suppose a new STUDENT type record is created and assigned values as follows:

```
NEW(PTR);
WRITELN('STUDENT''S NAME:');
READLN; (* NEW LINE OF INPUT *)
FOR I := 1 TO 25
  DO IF NOT EOLN
        THEN READ(PTR^.NAME[I])
        ELSE PTR^.NAME[I] := ' ';
WRITELN('TEST SCORE:');
READLN; (* NEW INPUT LINE *)
READ(PTR^.SCORE)
```

The procedure LOCATE may be called by using the statement

```
LOCATE(PTR^.SCORE, ABOVE, BELOW)
```

where ABOVE and BELOW are STUDENTPTR type variables. If the value of ABOVE returned by the procedure is not NIL, the new record can be inserted into its proper position in the linked list by using the statements

```
ABOVE^.NEXTLINK := PTR;
PTR^.NEXTLINK := BELOW
```

The effects of these two statements were demonstrated in the previous example for the case in which ABOVE and BELOW (BEFORE and AFTER in the example) are both not NIL, but the proper linkage will be established by the same statements even if BELOW is NIL (the new link is to be inserted at the bottom of the list.) When ABOVE is NIL, the new link is to be inserted at the top of the list and so the FIRST pointer must be changed. Here is the proper program segment to use no matter where the new link must be inserted.

```
IF ABOVE = NIL
  THEN BEGIN (* INSERTION AT THE TOP OF THE LIST *)
       PTR^.NEXTLINK := FIRST;
       FIRST := PTR
       END (* OF INSERTION AT THE TOP OF THE LIST *)
  ELSE BEGIN (* INSERTION ELSEWHERE IN THE LIST *)
       ABOVE^.NEXTLINK := PTR;
       PTR^.NEXTLINK := BELOW
       END (* OF INSERTION ELSEWHERE IN THE LIST *)
```

Now we consider how a link can be deleted from an ordered list. Suppose that TARGETSCORE is a GRADES type variable that has been given some value. The procedure LOCATE could be used to find the topmost link whose SCORE value matches TARGETSCORE, if a match exists. The procedure call

LOCATE(TARGETSCORE, ABOVE, BELOW)

will result in the assignment to BELOW of either the value NIL or a pointer value such that BELOW↑.SCORE is the topmost SCORE that is greater than or equal to TARGETSCORE. If BELOW is NIL or BELOW↑.SCORE is greater than TARGETSCORE, there is no link whose SCORE is equal to TARGETSCORE and so no deletion is necessary. Otherwise, BELOW↑ is the record to be deleted. Two cases must be considered: ABOVE = NIL and ABOVE <> NIL. If ABOVE = NIL is TRUE, then BELOW = FIRST is also TRUE and the record to be deleted is at the top of the list. If ABOVE <> NIL is TRUE, then there is a link immediately preceding BELOW↑ (namely, ABOVE↑). The proper program segment with which to delete and DISPOSE of the topmost link whose SCORE matches TARGETSCORE is shown below.

```
IF BELOW <> NIL
  THEN IF BELOW^.SCORE = TARGETSCORE
          THEN BEGIN (* DELETION AND DISPOSAL *)
              IF ABOVE = NIL
                THEN FIRST := BELOW^.NEXTLINK
                ELSE ABOVE^.NEXTLINK := BELOW^.NEXTLINK;
              DISPOSE(BELOW)
              END (* OF DELETION AND DISPOSAL *)
```

For a linked list composed of STUDENT type records, it is more likely that a deletion will be based on matching a NAME to some TARGETNAME rather than on matching a SCORE to a TARGETSCORE. In this case, the procedure LOCATE cannot be used to determine the existence of the desired link because the search conducted by LOCATE is based on the SCOREs in the links. Furthermore, the list is ordered by SCOREs so that any search for a matching NAME will require that the entire list be scanned whenever no match exists. An appropriate procedure to use to search for a matching NAME is given below.

```
PROCEDURE LISTSEARCH (NAMEMATCH : STRING25; VAR BEFORE, AFTER : STUDENTPTR
  TYPE
        SEARCHSTATUS = (GO, STOP);
  VAR
        ACTION = SEARCHSTATUS;
  BEGIN (* PROCEDURE LISTSEARCH *)
  BEFORE := NIL;
  AFTER := FIRST;
  ACTION := GO;
  WHILE (ACTION = GO) AND (AFTER <> NIL)
    DO IF AFTER^.NAME = NAMEMATCH
        THEN ACTION := STOP
        ELSE BEGIN (* POINTER ADJUSTMENTS *)
            BEFORE := AFTER;
            AFTER := BEFORE^.NEXTLINK
            END (* OF POINTER ADJUSTMENTS *)
  END (* OF PROCEDURE LISTSEARCH *);
```

Suppose LISTSEARCH is called by using the statement

```
LISTSEARCH(TARGETNAME, ABOVE, BELOW)
```

If the search is unsuccessful (TARGETNAME does not match the NAME in any link), BELOW will have the value NIL. Otherwise, BELOW↑ . NAME will match TARGETNAME. Therefore, the deletion and disposal of the desired link can be accomplished by using the following program segment.

```
IF BELOW <> NIL
   THEN BEGIN (* DELETION AND DISPOSAL *)
        IF ABOVE = NIL
           THEN FIRST := BELOW^.NEXTLINK
           ELSE ABOVE^.NEXTLINK := BELOW^.NEXTLINK;
        DISPOSE(BELOW)
        END (* OF DELETION AND DISPOSAL *)
```

The ordering for a linked list composed of STUDENT type records could be determined by the NAME field in each record. That is, the arrangement of the links may be such that the NAMEs appear in alphabetical order either from top to bottom or bottom to top. Such an arrangement would certainly simplify the search for a matching NAME. The key field employed to order a list should be chosen in a way that will contribute most to the program that uses the list. If it is possible for the key fields in two or more links to have the same value, then those links will necessarily be consecutive in the ordered list. If a new link to be inserted into the list has a key field value that matches the values in one or more existing links, then it would be possible to insert the link at several different places in the list. In our example above, the new link is always inserted immediately in front of the first link whose key field (SCORE) value equals or exceeds the value of the key field in the new link.

DOUBLY LINKED LISTS

It is possible for a record to contain more than one pointer field so that a collection of these records can be linked in more than one way at the same time. If each record in a list contains two pointer fields and they are each used to establish a linkage for the list, the list is said to be **doubly linked.** The structure of a typical doubly linked list is depicted in the following diagram.

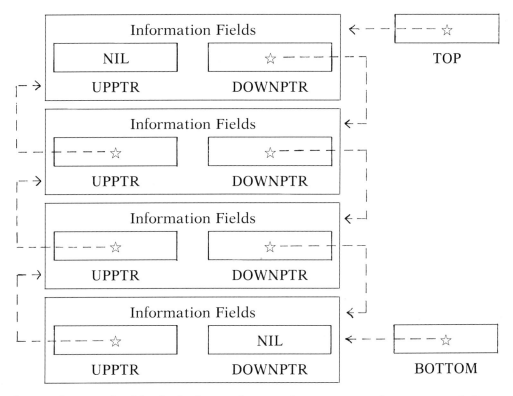

When a list is doubly linked, as shown above, it can be traversed from top to bottom or bottom to top.

Consider the following declarations.

```
TYPE
    STRING25 = PACKED ARRAY [1 .. 25] OF CHAR;
    TESTSCORES = 0 .. 100;
    LETTERGRADES = 'A' .. 'E';
    PUPILPTR = ^PUPIL;
    PUPIL = RECORD
            NAME : STRING25;
            SCORE : TESTSCORES;
            GRADE : LETTERGRADES;
            UPPTR, DOWNPTR : PUPILPTR
        END (* OF PUPIL RECORD *);
VAR
    TOP, BOTTOM : PUPILPTR;
```

PUPIL type records can form an ordered list in which they are linked both low to high and high to low by the SCOREs they contain. The following diagram shows two consecutive links in such a list.

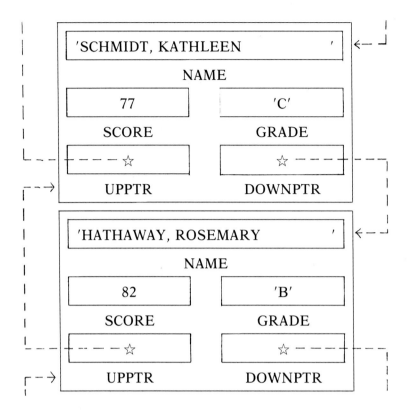

In the list described above two linkages exist but both of them are based on the SCOREs in the links. It may be advantageous to use two different key fields so that each linkage is determined by different information in each record. For instance, a list composed of PUPIL type records may be linked by SCOREs and by NAMEs. The following diagram shows linkages of these types for a linked list composed of three PUPIL type records.

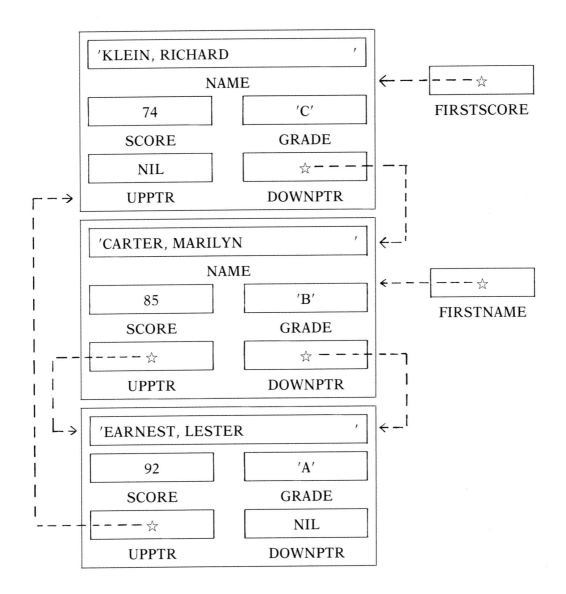

The DOWNPTR pointers in the links are used to maintain the list in SCORE order with FIRSTSCORE pointing to the link with the lowest SCORE, and the UPPTR pointers are used to maintain the list in NAME order with FIRSTNAME pointing to the link that is alphabetically first in the list.

Suppose that we want to have the contents of the records in a doubly linked list like the one shown above printed out so that the scores will appear in increasing order. Here is a program segment that will accomplish that task.

```
PTR := FIRSTSCORE;
WHILE PTR <> NIL
   DO WITH PTR^
      DO BEGIN (* OUTPUT A RECORD *)
         WRITELN(NAME, SCORE:5, GRADE:5);
         PTR := DOWNPTR
      END (* OF OUTPUT A RECORD *)
```

For the three-record list in our example the output would look like this:

```
KLEIN, RICHARD            74    C
CARTER, MARILYN           85    B
EARNEST, LESTER           92    A
```

Since the list is also linked by NAME, the contents of the records can be printed so that the names will appear alphabetically. A program segment to perform this task is given below.

```
PTR := FIRSTNAME;
WHILE PTR <> NIL
   DO WITH PTR^
      DO BEGIN (* OUTPUT A RECORD *)
         WRITELN(NAME, SCORE:5, GRADE:5);
         PTR := UPPTR
      END (* OF OUTPUT A RECORD *)
```

When this program segment is used, the output will appear in the following form.

```
CARTER, MARILYN           85    B
EARNEST, LESTER           92    A
KLEIN, RICHARD            74    C
```

A doubly linked list is the equivalent of two lists in one. However, each record is stored only once. The way that the pointers in each record are used gives the appearance that there are two lists. When a new link is created, it must be linked twice. If each linkage is based on a different key field, then two separate searches of the list will be required. To establish the linkages for a new PUPIL type record to be entered into the doubly linked list in our example, the following steps are required:

Create a NEW record PTR ↑
READ information for the record PTR ↑
Search for linkage position by SCORE
Link PTR ↑ by SCORE
Search for linkage position by NAME
Link PTR ↑ by NAME

If one key field is used to establish two separate linkages so that a list can be traversed from top to bottom and in reverse order, then only one search is required.

A list may have even more than two linkages, depending on the number of pointers available in the links. Multiply linked lists can be used to preserve several different orderings for the records. Aside from linked lists, it is possible to create a wide variety of other types of data structures by using multiple linkage such as **graphs** and **trees.** The linked structures that have been presented in this text are intended to motivate the use of pointers in Pascal. A thorough discussion of linked structures can be found in a text devoted to the development and use of data structures.

11.3
EXERCISES

1. In Section 11.3 we discussed how to insert a link in or delete a link from a sorted list by using pointers to two consecutive links in the list. Show how a link can be inserted in an ordered list of STUDENT type records by using only the pointer to the record that will immediately precede the new record in the list (the pointer returned as the value of BEFORE by the procedure LOCATE).

2. When the procedure LOCATE is used to find pointers BEFORE and AFTER that can be used to insert a new link into an ordered list of STUDENT type records, AFTER ↑ .SCORE may be the same a NEWSCORE. This means that the SCORE in the new link will be equal to the SCOREs in one or more links that already exist in the list and the new link will be inserted so that it immediately precedes all those links. Modify the procedure LOCATE so that if the SCORE in a new link is the same as one or more SCOREs in links already in the list, the new link will be inserted after those existing links.

3. Write a procedure that will delete all links from an ordered list of STUDENT type records that contain a particular SCORE. Assume that the ordering for the list is based on the SCORES as described in Section 11.3.

4. Give the definitions and declarations necessary to construct an ordered list of PART type records, where each record must contain the description of a part, the part's code number (a whole number greater than 999), and a unit price. The ordering should be based on part numbers, with the part having the smallest code number appearing at the top of the list. Write procedures that can be used to construct the list and show how they will be used.

5. Suppose that PUPIL type records (as defined in Section 11.3) are used to form a doubly linked list with both linkages based on the SCOREs in the links so that the list can be traversed from low SCORE to high SCORE or from high SCORE to low SCORE. Write procedures that can be used to construct the list and show how they will be used.

6. Write a complete program that will create a doubly linked list consisting of PUPIL type records. One linkage should be based on the SCOREs in the links so that the list can be traversed from high SCORE to low SCORE and the other linkage should be based on the NAMEs in the links so that the list can be traversed alphabetically by the NAMEs. Once a list has been constructed, the pro-

gram should print out the contents of the list in SCOREs order (high to low) as well as alphabetically by the NAMEs in the records.

11.4 PROGRAMMING PROBLEMS

1. When the binary (base 2) form of a nonnegative integer is generated by repeated DIVision by 2, the bits (binary digits) are produced in reverse order. For example, the binary form of the integer 43 is generated as shown below.

Quotients:	21	10	5	2	1	0
	2)43	2)21	2)10	2)5	2)2	2)1
Remainders: (bits)	1	1	0	1	0	1

The integer 43 is equivalent to a binary 101011, where each bit is a remainder of a division by 2 and the remainders are computed in reverse order. If the remainders are pushed onto a stack as they are produced, they can be popped off the stack in the proper order to form the binary version of a number. Write a program that uses a stack to produce the binary form of a nonnegative integer. Design the program so that it will calculate and print the binary form of a single integer or any range of consecutive integers specified as input to the program.

2. A linked list can be used to represent a polynomial in one unknown. Each term in a polynomial of this type is completely determined by its coefficient and the exponent on the unknown. Thus each link need only contain the coefficient and exponent for a term as well as a pointer to the next link (term in the polynomial). For example, the polynomial

$$3x^4 - 6x^2 + 5x - 10$$

can be represented by using a linked list as depicted below.

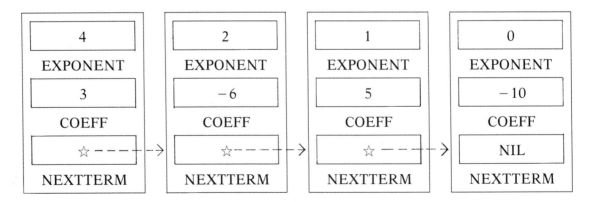

Write a program that will accept the coefficients and exponents for two polynomials and then determine the sum of those polynomials. Assume that the coefficients will be integers. The sum of two polynomials with integer coefficients will be another polynomial with integer coefficients formed by grouping like terms (terms that have the same exponent) and adding the coefficients. For instance, the sum of the polynomials $8x^3 - 3x^2 - x + 7$ and $x^2 + 6x - 15$ is the polynomial $8x^3 - 2x^2 + 5x - 8$. The program should print out all three polynomials in the form shown below for $8x^3 - 2x^2 + 5x - 8$.

$$(8)(X \uparrow 3) + (-2)(X \uparrow 2) + (5)(X \uparrow 1) + (-8)(X \uparrow 0)$$

3. The product of two polynomials can be computed by multiplying each term of one of the polynomials by the second polynomial and combining like terms. For instance, the product of $8x^3 - 3x^2 - x + 7$ and $x^2 + 6x - 15$ is computed as follows:

$$\begin{aligned}(8x^3 - 3x^2 - x + 7)(x^2 + 6x - 15) &= 8x^3(x^2 + 6x - 15) - 3x^2(x^2 + 6x - 15) \\ &\quad - x(x^2 + 6x - 15) + 7(x^2 + 6x - 15) \\ &= 8x^5 + 48x^4 - 120x^3 - 3x^4 - 18x^3 + 45x^2 \\ &\quad - x^3 - 6x^2 + 15x + 7x^2 + 42x - 105 \\ &= 8x^5 + 30x^4 - 139x^3 + 46x^2 + 57x - 105\end{aligned}$$

Using the linked list representation for a polynomial described in Problem 2, write a program that will accept the coefficients and exponents for two polynomials as input and then calculate the product of the two polynomials. All three polynomials should be printed by the program in the form shown in Problem 2.

4. One way to store a list of words alphabetically is to use an array of pointers indexed by the letters of the alphabet to point to linked lists each of which contains words beginning with the same first letter. Each list may be ordered so that the words in the list appear alphabetically, as depicted in the following diagram.

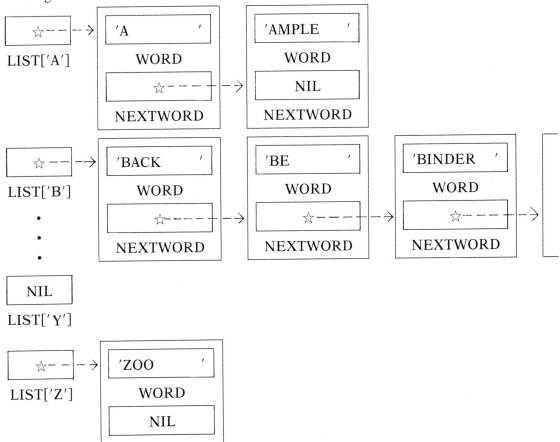

Write a program that will read lines of text, isolate words in the text, and store the words in a data structure like the one just desribed. No word should appear more than once in any of the linked lists. Once all the words have been isolated and stored, the program should print out a table of the words in alphabetical order.

5. The data structure described in Problem 4 does not allow for maintaining frequency counts for the words. Enlarge the structure by providing a frequency field in each link record. When a word is initially inserted into a list, its frequency count should be set to 1. Thereafter, each occurrence of the word should cause the frequency count for the word to be incremented by 1. Write a program that will accumulate the frequencies of words in lines of input text and then print out the words and their frequencies in a table. The words should apppear in the table categorized by the first letter of a word, but within each category the words should be ordered high to low by their frequency counts.

6. At the end of every month, a certain company must compile a report showing its sales for the month. The company has divided up its sales territory into four regions (east, west, north, and south) and each of its salespersons works in only one region. The sales report must show the total sales for all regions (in dollars), the total sales for each region, a list of all salespersons ranked according to their sales for the month (high to low), and a ranking of the salesperson by region according to their sales for the month. Write a program that accepts the names of salespersons, their respective regions, and their sales for a month and then produces the report just described.

7. Write a program that will print a student's class schedule by the day of the week and the hour of the day. Assume that each class begins on the hour and classes are held from 0800 hours to 1700 hours (5:00 P.M.) daily. Course information should be read and stored in a linked list consisting of dynamic records that have the structure depicted here.

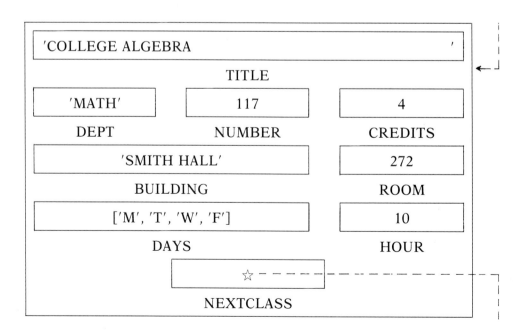

An array of pointers indexed by a user-defined data type whose constants are MONDAY, TUESDAY, WEDNESDAY, THURSDAY, and FRIDAY can be used to point to ordered lists of classes that meet on particular days. A diagram showing the typical structure for one of these lists is given below.

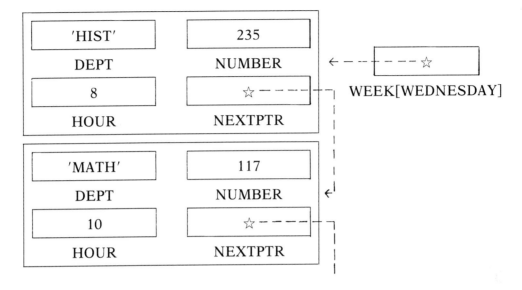

APPENDIX A/SOME COMMON CHARACTER SETS

Table A.1 The American Standard Code for Information Interchange (ASCII)[a]

Ordinal	Character	Ordinal	Character	Ordinal	Character	Ordinal	Character
32		56	8	80	P	104	h
33	!	57	9	81	Q	105	i
34	"	58	:	82	R	106	j
35	#	59	;	83	S	107	k
36	$	60	<	84	T	108	l
37	%	61	=	85	U	109	m
38	&	62	>	86	V	110	n
39	'	63	?	87	W	111	o
40	(	64	@	88	X	112	p
41	)	65	A	89	Y	113	q
42	*	66	B	90	Z	114	r
43	+	67	C	91	[	115	s
44	,	68	D	92	\	116	t
45	−	69	E	93	]	117	u
46	.	70	F	94 †	↑ or ˆ	118	v
47	/	71	G	95 ‡	_ or ←	119	w
48	0	72	H	96	`	120	x
49	1	73	I	97	a	121	y
50	2	74	J	98	b	122	z
51	3	75	K	99	c	123	{
52	4	76	L	100	d	124		
53	5	77	M	101	e	125	}
54	6	78	N	102	f	126	~
55	7	79	O	103	g		

[a] The ASCII characters whose ordinals are 0 through 31 and 127 are unprintable control characters. The ordinal for the blank space character is 32.

Table A.2   A Control Data Corporation (CDC) ASCII Subset with CDC's Ordering[a]

Ordinal	Character	Ordinal	Character	Ordinal	Character	Ordinal	Character
0	Not used	16	P	32	5	48	#
1	A	17	Q	33	6	49	[
2	B	18	R	34	7	50	]
3	C	19	S	35	8	51	:
4	D	20	T	36	9	52	"
5	E	21	U	37	+	53	_ or ←
6	F	22	V	38	−	54	!
7	G	23	W	39	*	55	&
8	H	24	X	40	/	56	'
9	I	25	Y	41	(	57	?
10	J	26	Z	42	)	58	<
11	K	27	0	43	$	59	>
12	L	28	1	44	=	60	@
13	M	29	2	45		61	\
14	N	30	3	46	,	62	↑ or ^
15	O	31	4	47	.	63	;

[a]This is actually a 63-character set, since ordinal 0 is not used. The ordinal for the blank space character is 45.

Table A.3   The Extended Binary Coded Decimal Interchange Code (EBCDIC)[a]

Ordinal	Character	Ordinal	Character	Ordinal	Character	Ordinal	Character
64		122	:	162	s	216	Q
		123	#	163	t	217	R
74	¢	124	@	164	u		
75	.	125	'	165	v	226	S
76	<	126	=	166	w	227	T
77	(	127	"	167	x	228	U
78	+			168	y	229	V
79	|	129	a	169	z	230	W
80	&	130	b			231	X
		131	c	193	A	232	Y
90	!	132	d	194	B	233	Z
91	$	133	e	195	C		
92	*	134	f	196	D	240	0
93	)	135	g	197	E	241	1
94	;	136	h	198	F	242	2
95	¬	137	i	199	G	243	3
96	−			200	H	244	4
97	/	145	j	201	I	245	5
		146	k			246	6
107	,	147	l	209	J	247	7
108	%	148	m	210	K	248	8
109	_	149	n	211	L	249	9
110	>	150	o	212	M		
111	?	151	p	213	N		
		152	q	214	O		
		153	r	215	P		

[a]EBCDIC ordinals range from 0 through 255, but many of them do not have standard character representations or they are associated with unprintable control characters. The ordinal for the blank space character is 64. (Note that the ordinals for both the uppercase and lowercase alphabetic characters are not consecutive.)

APPENDIX B/PASCAL KEYWORDS AND STANDARD IDENTIFIERS

B.1
KEYWORDS (RESERVED WORDS)

The following words have reserved meanings in Pascal that cannot be changed.

AND	DOWNTO	IF	OR	THEN
ARRAY	ELSE	IN	PACKED	TO
BEGIN	END	LABEL	PROCEDURE	TYPE
CASE	FILE	MOD	PROGRAM	UNTIL
CONST	FOR	NIL	RECORD	VAR
DIV	FUNCTION	NOT	REPEAT	WHILE
DO	GOTO	OF	SET	WITH

B.2
STANDARD IDENTIFIERS

All standard identifiers have predefined meanings in Pascal, but they may be re-defined in a program. A listing of the standard identifiers by categories according to their predefined meanings follows.

Data Types	Constants	Functions	Procedures	Files
BOOLEAN	FALSE	ABS	DISPOSE	INPUT
CHAR	MAXINT	ARCTAN	GET	OUTPUT
INTEGER	TRUE	CHR	NEW	
REAL		COS	PACK	
TEXT		EOF	PAGE	
		EOLN	PUT	
		EXP	READ	
		LN	READLN	
		ODD	RESET	
		ORD	REWRITE	
		PRED	UNPACK	
		ROUND	WRITE	
		SIN	WRITELN	
		SQR		
		SQRT		
		SUCC		
		TRUNC		

APPENDIX C/STANDARD FUNCTIONS AND PROCEDURES

C.1 FUNCTIONS

Many of the standard functions are discussed in the text. The names of these functions and where to look in the text for information regarding their use are presented here.

Function Name	Refer to	Function Name	Refer to
ABS	3.1 (Figure 3–2)	PRED	3.2 (Figure 3–5)
CHR	3.2 (Figure 3–5)	ROUND	3.1 (Figure 3–2)
EOF	4.1 (Figure 4–2) and Chapter 10	SQR	3.1 (Figure 3–2)
		SQRT	3.1 (Figure 3–2)
EOLN	4.1 (Figure 4–2) and Chapter 10	SUCC	3.2 (Figure 3–5)
ORD	3.2 (Figure 3–5)	TRUNC	3.1 (Figure 3–2)

There are six standard functions not described in the text:

Function Call	Argument Type	Type of Result	Value of the Function
ARCTAN(*argument*)	INTEGER or REAL	REAL	The trigonometric inverse tangent of the *argument*
COS (*argument*)	INTEGER or REAL	REAL	The trigonometric cosine of the *argument*
EXP(*argument*)	INTEGER or REAL	REAL	The value of e^x where x is the value of the *argument* and e is the mathematical constant that serves as the base for natural logarithms
LN(*argument*)	INTEGER or REAL	REAL	The natural logarithm of the *argument*
ODD(*argument*)	INTEGER	BOOLEAN	TRUE if the value of the *argument* is an odd integer; FALSE otherwise
SIN(*argument*)	INTEGER or REAL	REAL	The trigonometric sine of the *argument*

C.2
PROCEDURES

All but one of the standard procedures are presented in the text. The names of these procedures and where to look in the text for information regarding their use are presented here.

Procedure Name	Refer to	Procedure Name	Refer to
DISPOSE	11.1	READLN	4.1 (Figure 4–3) and 10.2
GET	Chapter 10		
NEW	11.1	RESET	Chapter 10
PACK	7.3 (Figure 7–3)	REWRITE	Chapter 10
PUT	Chapter 10	UNPACK	7.3 (Figure 7–3)
READ	4.1 (Figure 4–1) and Chapter 10	WRITE	4.3 (Figure 4–4) and Chapter 10
		WRITELN	4.3 (Figure 4–4) and 10.2

The one standard procedure not discussed in the text is PAGE, which is called by a procedure statement of the form.

$$PAGE(\textit{filename})$$

where *filename* is the name of a **text file.** This procedure causes the printer or other output device to skip to the top of a new page before printing the next line of the specified text file.

APPENDIX D/FLOWCHART SYMBOLS

Flowcharts are used as a visual aid to describe a complete algorithm or some portion of an algorithm. Each activity is symbolized by a geometric figure (node), and the nodes are connected by directed line segments (flow lines) that indicate the order of the activities. The node shapes used in the flowcharts presented in this book and the types of activities that they represent are presented below.

Node Shape	Related Activity
	Marks a point of entry to or exit from a flowchart.
	Marks points in a flowchart where two or more flow lines join together.
	Specifies input or output activities, which in an actual Pascal program are represented by READ, READLN, WRITE, or WRITELN statements.
	Specifies a condition that requires testing, as represented by a relational or BOOLEAN expression in an IF, WHILE, or REPEAT statement. The two flow lines marking exits from this type of node are marked TRUE and FALSE to signify the possible paths that may be taken as a result of the test.
	Represents selection of alternative activities as represented by a CASE statement in a Pascal program. Each flow line marking an exit from this type of node is labeled with the value of the selector that causes that path to be taken.
	Specifies any activity not signified by using one of the other types of nodes.

In addition to the nodes described in this table, a flowchart may contain open-ended annotation blocks attached by dashed lines to activity nodes. These annotation blocks supply comments that summarize the purposes of the nodes to which they are attached. They take the form shown here.

 Comment

APPENDIX E/ANSWERS TO SELECTED EXERCISES

EXERCISES 2.1 (pages 39–40)

5. a. valid   c. invalid (blank space not allowed in an identifier)
   f. invalid (minus sign not allowed in an identifier)
   h. invalid (PROGRAM is a reserved word)
   i. invalid (dollar sign not allowed in an identifier)
   k. valid

7. a. valid INTEGER constant   c. valid REAL constant
   f. valid INTEGER constant   h. invalid constant
   i. valid REAL constant   k. invalid constant

8. a. 2740.96   c. 0.00295   e. 1.90448
   g. 2695000000000000000000.0   i. −7000000000000000.0

9. a. Comma is missing between the CHAR constants 'A' and 'B'.
   b. Apostrophe marking the beginning of the character string is missing.
   c. No errors.

EXERCISES 2.2 (pages 47–49)

2. The following constant definitions are invalid.
   RATIO = 1/3; 1/3 is not a valid constant or constant identifier.
   1STCHARACTER = '$'; 1STCHARACTER is an invalid identifier.
   14.95 = CHARGE; identifier must appear to the left of the equals sign.
   VOWELS = AEIOU; AEIOU is not a valid constant or constant identifier.
   END = 7; reserved word END cannot be redefined.

8. a. The equals sign should be replaced by a colon.
   c. 100 is not a valid data type.

10. a. 924 assigned to MX7.
   c. INTEGER variable MX9 cannot be assigned a CHAR value.
   f. 235 assigned to MX9.
   h. INTEGER variable MX7 cannot be assigned a REAL value.
   i. Constant identifier GAMMA cannot appear to the left of an assignment operator.
   k. 23000.0 assigned to TARGET.

EXERCISES 2.3 (page 55)

1. a. An INTEGER expression whose value is 7716.
   c. An INTEGER expression whose value is −45.
   e. A mixed-mode expression whose value is 0.5.
   g. A mixed-mode expression whose value is 2.4.
   i. An INTEGER expression whose value is 5.

2. a. An INTEGER expression whose value is 9.
   c. A mixed-mode expression whose value is 5.5.
   e. A REAL expression whose value is −50.0.
   g. An invalid expression, DIVision requires INTEGER type operands.
   i. REAL expression whose value is 5.0.

EXERCISES 3.1 (pages 79–81)

1. The values of the expression are:

   a. 0   b. 52   c. 5   d. 8   e. 0   f. −6
   g. 40   h. 53.25   i. −27.0   j. 13.5   k. 115.0   l. −2.55

2. a. No operand specified for DIVision by 5.
   c. Valid expression whose value is 16.
   e. Operator missing between subexpressions 125 * (−3) − 42 and 19 + 432 DIV 66.
   g. Illegal division by 0 (100.0 − 1E2 = 0.0).
   i. Valid expression whose value is 33.9.

3. a. (9 − 65 DIV 7 + 60) MOD 26 + 40
   c. (4 * (−11) DIV 3 − 20) MOD (5 * 8 − 14)
   e. 4.5 * 3.0 / (0.25 − 0.75) * 6.4
   g. 11.25 / ((7.2 + 8.4) * (194.7 − 1.5 * 8.2))

4. a. (22 + 6) * (100 MOD 12) − 25 DIV 4

5. a. (16.4 − 51.0) / (4.8 * (0.6 + 74.92))

6. The function values are:

   a. 2   b. 2   c. 1.44   d. 4.0   e. 2   f. 3   g. 1

7. a. Valid expression whose value is −4.34.
   c. Invalid expression (REAL operand for MOD operation not allowed).
   e. Valid expression whose value is 90.0.
   g. Invalid expression (missing right parenthesis).

EXERCISES 3.2 (pages 91–93)

1. a. B >= A   b. C = 5   c. D < B   d. B <> C
   e. A > C   f. C <= A

2. The function values are:

   a. '+'   c. 'J'   f. 55   h. illegal (REAL argument not allowed)
   i. 'D'   k. '.'

3. a. TRUE   b. FALSE   c. FALSE

4. a. TRUE   c. FALSE   e. FALSE   g. FALSE   i. TRUE
   k. Answer depends on character set in use (FALSE for full ASCII).

5. a. CHR(45) yields a CHAR value that is not allowed in an arithmetic expression.
   b. no errors   d. no errors

EXERCISES 4.1 (pages 106–107)

1. b. Values assigned to the variables are AVAL = −75.6, KEY = 2, KOUNT = 4920, MARK1 = '■', MARK2 = '$', NUM = 8, BVAL = − 184.0, LIMIT = 10, MARK3 = '/', PART = 4, and CVAL = 1628.293.

2. a. Values assigned to the variables are LOW = 24, DIFF = − 13.46, T1 = 'T', T2 = '9', MAX = 16000.0, and HIGH = 999.
   c. Values assigned to the variables are T1 = '■', T2 = '2', LOW = 4, DIFF = − 13.46, T3 = 'T', and HIGH = 9.

4. b. Values assigned to the variables are MAX = 16000.0, T1 = '■', LOW = 999, and then an error occurs because the end of the file is encountered when an attempt is made to read a value for HIGH.
   c. Values assigned to the variables are MAX = 24.0, LOW = − 13, T1 = '.', HIGH = 16, T2 = 'E', and DIFF = 3.0.

EXERCISES 4.2 (pages 114–116)

1. a. Values assigned to the variables are BITS = 256, SEED = 42.5, SYM1 = '■', and then an error occurs when the attempt is made to read a value for DAYS.
   b. Values assigned to the variables are DAYS = 256, SYM2 = 'T', SYM3 = '1', SEED = 3.0, COST = − 194.0, WEEKS = 9, BITS = − 63, SYM1 = '*', and DIFF = 483.05.

2. a. Values assigned to the variables are SEATS = 6 and GAUGE = 22.3.
   c. Values assigned to the variables are PT1 = '■', SEATS = 22, PT2 = '.', and GAUGE = 3.0.

3. a. Values assigned to the variables are A = 1620, B = 19, and C = 485.
   c. Values assigned to the variables are A = 1620, B = 19, C = 485, D = − 80, and then more data are requested.
   f. Values assigned to the variables are A = 1620, B = 485, C = − 80, and D = 1217.

EXERCISES 4.3 (pages 125–126)

1. a.

```
■■■-135.5■■425■■■■■■■■■■■■■■■■■■ERROR:■■5.0000E-04
```

c.

```
■■■■■■■■■■■■■425■■■■-75■-1.34E+02
blank line
■ERROR■=■■0.0005■■■■■-135.48
```

2. a.
```
WRITELN(X:8:3, 'T'= :6, T:3, R:8);
WRITELN(Y:12)
```

c.
```
WRITELN('**** DATA ****':18);
WRITELN(T:9, R:9);
WRITELN(' ':4, X:14);
WRITELN(' ':4, Y:9)
```

3. a.

```
■■■■■■■■■■■■1628.290■■■■■■■■■5.02500000E+00■■■■■■■■■+■D
■■■■■■20■■■■■■■■■■■■■■■■■■■■■■8
```

4. a. valid statement
c. valid statement
e. comma not valid between P1 and the format ":12" or the item associated with this format is missing

EXERCISES 5.2 (pages 141–147)

1. a. Relational expressions A + B < C and B >= 0.0 must be enclosed in parentheses.
c. Semicolon is needed to separate the statement C := B − 2.0 * C from the statement B := 0.0.

2. When 5 and 10 are read as values for K and M, respectively, then 8 is printed as the value for K and −5 is printed as the value for M.

3. a.
```
READ(A);
IF A > 10.0
  THEN BEGIN
         WRITELN(A);
         A := 10.0 - A
         END;
READ(B);
IF B < A
  THEN B := A - B;
WRITELN(A,B)
```

c.
```
READ(A,B);
IF A > 10.0
  THEN BEGIN
         A := 10.0 - A;
         IF B < A
           THEN B := A - B
         END;
WRITELN(A,B)
```

4. If the values read for A and B are 15.5 and 24.2, respectively, the values printed are

    a. 15.5, −5.5, and 24.2   b. −5.5 and −8.7   c. −5.5 and 24.2

5. a. Semicolon after THEN clause should be deleted.
   d. No errors, although the parentheses enclosing the relational expression DI-MENSION <= 1 are unnecessary

6. When 12 and 20 are read as values for K and M, respectively, 0 is printed as the value of K and −15 is printed as the value of M. When 20 and 12 are read as values for K and M, respectively, 21 is printed as the value of K and 8 is printed as the value of M.

7. IF *BOOLEAN-expression-1*
    THEN *statement*
    ELSE IF *BOOLEAN-expression-2*
        THEN *statement*

EXERCISES 5.3 (pages 153–155)

1. a.
```
        IF A > B
           THEN WRITELN('SUCCESS')
           ELSE IF B > C
                   THEN WRITELN('SUCCESS')
                   ELSE WRITELN('FAILURE')
```

   b.
```
        IF A <= B
           THEN IF C > 0
                   THEN WRITELN('SUCCESS')
                   ELSE WRITELN('FAILURE')
           ELSE IF X = '$'
                   THEN IF C > 0
                           THEN WRITELN('SUCCESS')
                           ELSE WRITELN('FAILURE')
```

2. One possible nesting of IF statements is

```
        IF SCORE < 80
           THEN IF SCORE < 70
                   THEN IF SCORE < 60
                           THEN GRADE := 'F'
                           ELSE GRADE := 'D'
                   ELSE GRADE := 'C'
           ELSE IF SCORE < 90
                   THEN GRADE := 'B'
                   ELSE GRADE := 'A'
```

4. If RANGE = 0.0, an attempted division by zero will occur.

5. b.
```
        READ(A,B);
        IF A > 10.0
          THEN IF B < A
                  THEN B := A - B
                  ELSE (* NULL STATEMENT *)
          ELSE A := 10.0 - A;
        WRITELN(A,B)
```

EXERCISES 5.4 (pages 162–163)

1. a. no errors
   c. Strings containing more than one character are not simple data constants and are therefore not allowed as CASE labels. The proper labels to use here are the BOOLEAN values TRUE and FALSE.

4.
```
     READ(TRANS, AMOUNT);
     IF (TRANS = 'D') OR (TRANS = 'W')
       THEN CASE TRANS OF
              'W' : IF BAL >= AMOUNT
                      THEN BAL := BAL - AMOUNT
                      ELSE WRITELN('INSUFFICIENT FUNDS!');
              'D' : BAL := BAL + AMOUNT
            END (* OF TRANS CASES *)
       ELSE WRITELN('ILLEGAL TRANSACTION CODE!')
```

EXERCISES 6.1 (pages 177–179)

1. This statement will generate:

   a. six loop cycles leaving A = 192 and B = 100
   b. an infinite loop
   c. 14 loop cycles leaving A = 17 and B = 100

2. a. An infinite loop will result if the value of X is initially less than 100 because the value of X is decremented in the body of the loop.
   d. The expression after WHILE is not a BOOLEAN expression.

3. The program segment prints sequences of nonblank characters entered as input with a blank line for every blank space after the first in a sequence of two or more:

```
LOOK
TO
THE
EAST
AT
DAWN
```

A period on the input line terminates the loop.

EXERCISES 6.2 (pages 186–188)

1. This statement will generate:

    a. six loop cycles leaving A = 192 and B = 100
    d. five loop cycles leaving A = 3 and B = 56

2. a. an infinite loop (no way for P to be exactly zero)
    d. no errors, although the semicolon after REPEAT is unnecessary

EXERCISES 6.3 (pages 199–202)

1. a.
```
FOR X := 1 TO 24
  DO Y := Y + X * X
```

    b.
```
FOR I := B DOWNTO A
 DO WRITELN((B - A) MOD I)
```

    d.
```
T := 100;
K := 0;
FOR I := 0 TO 20
  DO BEGIN
      WRITELN(T - K);
      K := K + 5
     END
```

2.
```
   *
  **
 ***
****
```

3. a. A total of six lines of output are generated:

85	15	10	25
69	16	10	25
52	17	10	25
34	18	9	25
15	19	8	25
-5	20	7	25

7. a.
```
FOR LINE := 1 TO 5
  DO BEGIN
      FOR STAR := 1 TO LINE
       DO WRITE('*');
      WRITELN
     END
```

EXERCISES 6.4 (pages 207–208)

1. a.
```
READ(X);
REPEAT
   WRITE(X MOD 10:1);
   X := X DIV 10
UNTIL X <= 0;
WRITELN
```

b.
```
READ(X);
WHILE X DIV 10 >= 10
   DO BEGIN
      WRITE(X MOD 10:1);
      X := X DIV 10
      END;
WRITELN(X MOD 10:1)
```

3.
```
FOR M := 1 TO 4
  DO BEGIN
     FOR N := 1 TO 5
       DO WRITE(M * N:3);
     WRITELN
     END
```

Output produced:

```
1  2  3  4  5
2  4  6  8 10
3  6  9 12 15
4  8 12 16 20
```

EXERCISES 7.1 (pages 221–222)

1.
```
TYPE
     DAYS = (SUNDAY, MONDAY, WEDNESDAY, FRIDAY,
             TUESDAY, THURSDAY, SATURDAY);
     ONDAYS = MONDAY .. FRIDAY;
     OFFDAYS = TUESDAY .. SATURDAY;
```

2. a. Digits are not valid identifiers for user-defined constants.
   c. no errors
   d. The identifier OAK is listed twice.

3. a. TRUE   b. FALSE
   e. invalid (TIN and AUST2 are not constants of the same type.)   f. FALSE

4. a. 6   c. GOLD   e. ITALY2
   f. illegal use of function SUCC (ITALY1 has no SUCCessor.)

5. a. ATYPE = (GAMMA, DELTA, BETA, OMEGA, ALPHA);
   b. BTYPE = (DELTA, ALPHA, GAMMA, OMEGA, BETA);

EXERCISES 7.2 (pages 236–238)

1. a. In the definition of the subrange type NUMBER, the brackets surrounding 100 . . 499 must be deleted. The base type specified for the array UTILIZATION is illegal; a subrange of real numbers cannot be defined.

   b. no errors

2. a.
```
        TYPE
                INDICES = 1 .. 12;
                ATYPE = ARRAY [INDICES] OF REAL;
        VAR
                BUDGET : ATYPE;
```

   c.
```
   TYPE
        GRADE = (A, B, C, D, F);
        SUBJECTS = (ALGEBRA, ENGLISH, HISTORY, BIOLOGY,
                    FRENCH);
        CTYPE = ARRAY [SUBJECTS] OF GRADE;
   VAR
        REPORTCARD : CTYPE;
```

3. b. The values for I are not the proper index type for array MEANTEMP.

   d. Since all valid input values for TEMP must be greater than −99, the WHILE loop is infinite.

EXERCISES 7.3 (pages 246–249)

1. The values of the expressions are:

   a. TRUE (all three character sets)

   b. TRUE for the full ASCII set; FALSE for the other two sets

   e. FALSE for the full ASCII set; TRUE for the other two sets

2. a. Character string values must be read character by character:

```
        FOR I := 1 TO 25
          DO READ(X[I]);
        WRITELN(X)
```

   c. The index I will be out of range when Y[I] is referenced. This can be corrected by changing the ELSE clause in the IF statement:

```
        IF I <= 25
          THEN X[I] := Z[I]
          ELSE Y[I - 25] := Z[I]
```

3. a. ```
   THE■SKY■IS■FALLING■■
   ```

   d. ```
   THESKYISFALLING****
   ```

4. a.

```
GHIJKLMNOP
KLMNOPQRST
```

c.

```
BCDEFGHIJK
DEFGHIJKLM
FGHIJKLMNO
HIJKLMNOPQ
```

EXERCISES 7.4 (pages 261–264)

1. a. The declarations of arrays A and C are valid. Array B should be declared by

B : ARRAY [INDEX2] OF ARRAY [INDEX1]
OF INTEGER;

or, equivalently,

B : ARRAY [INDEX2, INDEX1]
OF INTEGER;

Array D should be declared by

D : ARRAY [INDEX1, INDEX2]
OF CHAR;

or, equivalently,

D : ARRAY [INDEX1] OF ARRAY [INDEX2]
OF CHAR;

2. a.

2	3	4
X[1,1]	X[1,2]	X[1,3]
3	4	5
X[2,1]	X[2,2]	X[2,3]
4	5	6
X[3,1]	X[3,2]	X[3,3]
5	6	7
X[4,1]	X[4,2]	X[4,3]
6	7	8
X[5,1]	X[5,2]	X[5,3]

c.

2	2	2
X[1,1]	X[1,2]	X[1,3]
4	4	4
X[2,1]	X[2,2]	X[2,3]
6	6	6
X[3,1]	X[3,2]	X[3,3]
8	8	8
X[4,1]	X[4,2]	X[4,3]
10	10	10
X[5,1]	X[5,2]	X[5,3]

3. a. no errors
   d. The assignment P[I,J] := R[J,I] + 1.0 is invalid because a REAL value cannot be assigned to an INTEGER variable.

4. RED is a two-dimensional array with 18 components.
   GOLD is a three-dimensional array with 90 components.

EXERCISES 8.1 (pages 281–283)

1. a. invalid (Function type is missing.)   c. valid
   d. invalid (Function type must be specified by means of a type identifier.)
   f. invalid (Procedures are not typed.)

2. a.

   | | −7 | −30 | −7 |

   c. The REPEAT loop is infinite because the function THREES always returns the value 1.
   e. Use of the procedure statement THREES (prior to WRITELN(X, R)) is illegal because THREES is a function, not a procedure.

EXERCISES 8.2 (pages 289–290)

1. a. valid statement
   c. invalid (The actual parameters are not listed in the proper order.)
   f. The relational expression PICK(SUMMARY, M, M) = '*' is invalid because the function PICK does not return a CHAR type value.

2. a. valid statement provided that the value of K + 1 is in the subrange RANGE
   c. valid statement
   e. invalid (A procedure cannot be called in a WRITELN list.)

EXERCISES 8.3 (pages 303–305)

3. a. The main program may call procedure A, function D, and procedure E, all of which are level 1 subprograms, and each function and procedure may call itself. Function D may call procedure A, and procedure E may call both procedure A and function D. Procedure A may call the level 2 subprograms function B and procedure C. Procedure E may call procedure F.

5. a.
   | | ABDG

   d.
   | | DGADG

   e.
   | | AB
   | DG

EXERCISES 8.4 (page 312)

1.
```
                    PROCEDURE STARS (N : INTEGER);
                      BEGIN (* PROCEDURE STARS *)
                      IF N > 0
                        THEN BEGIN
                               WRITE('*');
                               STARS(N - 1)
                             END
                        ELSE WRITELN
                    END (* OF PROCEDURE STARS *);
```

EXERCISES 9.1 (pages 326–327)

1. Sets of the type PEOPLE: [ ]   [MAN] [WOMAN]   [CHILD]
   [MAN,WOMAN] [MAN,CHILD] [WOMAN,CHILD]
   [MAN,WOMAN,CHILD]

   Sets of the type BITS: [ ]   [0]   [1]   [0,1]

2. a. A + B = [1..5, 7..18, 20]   c. A + B = [1..8, 11..14, 19]
   A * B = [4, 12..15]   A * B = [2, 4..6, 8, 13]
   A − B = [7..11, 20]   A − B = [1, 3, 11, 12, 14, 19]
   B − A = [1..3, 5, 16..18]   B − A = [7]

3. a. [3..8, 10, 12, 18]   c. [2..12, 15, 16, 18]
   e. [3, 6, 7, 18]   g. [6..8, 18]

4. a. TRUE   c. TRUE   e. FALSE   g. FALSE

5. a. Use of the AND operator in this expression is invalid because the operands for logical conjunction must be BOOLEAN valued.
   c. Slash (/) is not a valid set operator.
   e. E is not a set and therefore it cannot be used as an operand for a set operation. However, the expression X + Y * [E] is valid.
   f. valid expression.

EXERCISES 9.2 (pages 341–342)

1. a.

```
TYPE
     CLIENTINFO = RECORD
                    NAME : PACKED ARRAY [1 .. 30] OF CHAR;
                    ADDRESS : PACKED ARRAY [1 .. 50] OF CHAR;
                    SSN, TELEPHONE, AGE : INTEGER;
                    MARSTAT : (MARRIED, SINGLE, DIVORCED,
                               WIDOWED)
                  END (* OF CLIENTINFO RECORD *);
VAR
     CLIENT : CLIENTINFO;
```

d.
```
TYPE
     BOOKENTRY = RECORD
                    ITEMDESCRIPTION : PACKED ARRAY [1 .. 40]
                                             OF CHAR;
                    NUMBER, QUANTITY : 1 .. MAXINT;
                    WHOLESALE, RETAIL : REAL
                 END (* OF BOOKENTRY RECORD *);
VAR
     INVENTORYITEM : BOOKENTRY;
```

2. a. never valid (String characters must be read one at a time.)
   c. sometimes valid (valid when used within the range of a WITH statement that specifies one of the qualifiers NEWSPAPERS, MAGAZINE, or JOURNAL)
   e. never valid (PERIODICAL is a type identifier, not a variable identifier.)
   g. always valid

EXERCISES 10.1 (pages 369-371)

1. a. Only one parameter (the name of a file) should be specified in a call to the procedure PUT. The statements after READ(CASH) could be

   ```
   MONEY^ := CASH;
   PUT(MONEY)
   ```

   c. no errors

2. a.

1	2	8	4	5	5	7	8	2	10	●

3. b. Output: ┃ SUM = 214

   The file pointer is positioned at the component containing 47.

4. a.
   ```
   FUNCTION COUNT (CODE : CODES) : INTEGER;
   VAR
        SUM : INTEGER;
   BEGIN (* FUNCTION COUNT *)
   SUM := 0;
   WHILE NOT EOF(LIST1)
        DO BEGIN
           IF LIST1^ = CODE
              THEN SUM := SUM + 1;
           GET(LIST1)
           END;
   COUNT := SUM
   END (* OF FUNCTION COUNT *);
   ```

EXERCISES 11.1 (pages 414–416)

    1. a. invalid statement (Pointer variables cannot appear in arithmetic expressions.)

      c. valid statement

      d. invalid statement (REAL type value of RPTR1 ↑ cannot be assigned to INTEGER variable IPTR2 ↑ .)

      f. invalid statement (The value of a pointer variable cannot be printed.)

    2. a. | 13   8

      c. | 20   9   9

APPENDIX F/PROGRAMMING PROJECTS

In this appendix eight programming projects are described. These projects are open ended in the sense that the descriptions do not bind the programmer to a closed collection of tasks and data structures. The basic nature of each project is presented in a manner that does not immediately spell out all of the activities that may be involved. The programmer(s) is (are) expected to formulate the necessary algorithms and define suitable data structures to meet the needs of a project. Thus, refinements and extensions to the projects are left to programmer.

None of the projects described in this appendix should be attempted until the programmer is able to define and use structured variables such as arrays and records. The types of data structures that may be used for each project are suggested in the description of the project, but not in great detail. For many of the projects (particularly Projects F.5–F.8), it will be necessary to use external files. It is the programmer's responsibility to define the structures of these files so as to best meet the needs of the project.

F.1
TEST GRADING

OBJECTIVE

Construct a program that will grade tests when a fixed number of student responses to each question is established, such as for true/false and multiple choice questions.

GENERAL DESCRIPTION

The number of questions on the test and the correct answers to all the questions must be entered as input to the program before the grading process begins. Then the program should grade one test at a time and store the results so that a report on the test results can be printed after the grading of all the tests has been completed. The information for each student should include a name and identification number as well as the answers marked by the student. After the last test has been graded, the program should print a report showing the names of all the students who took the test and their scores. This list should be ordered alphabetically by the names or numerically by student identification numbers. The average of all the scores achieved on the test should also be computed and printed.

PROGRAMMING CONSIDERATIONS

The answer key may be an array with CHAR type components and the answers given by a student may be stored in an array of the same type. Records or arrays or both may be used to store student information and test results.

VARIATIONS

The reporting capabilities of the grading program could offer many options, such as:

1. individual reports to students showing a test score and the numbers of the questions answered incorrectly;
2. letter grades assigned to each test according to some norms fixed for the program or established by input;
3. bar graphs or tables showing the frequencies of the scores;
4. a summary of how many times each question was answered incorrectly.

Results of the grading could also be recorded in one or more data files.

F.2
A SIMULATED CALCULATOR

OBJECTIVE

Construct a program that will serve as a calculator.

GENERAL DESCRIPTION

The operation of a typical pocket calculator can be simulated by a program. In place of pushing buttons on a calculator, a user of the program would type a one-line command. A simple calculator might have two data storage locations, an ACCUMulator and a reserve MEMory location. The arithmetic operations of addition, subtraction, multiplication, and division would be implemented, as well as commands to clear the ACCUMulator and MEMory location to zero or to transfer values between these two storage locations. In order to implement such a calculator, a command language must be developed. Here, for instance, is a command language for a simple calculator:

Command Form	
OPR *operand-1 operator operand-2*	Perform the arithmetic operation indicated by the *operator* on the numbers *operand-1* and *operand-2*, leaving the result in the ACCUMulator.
AOP *operator operand*	Perform the arithmetic operation indicated by the *operator* using the value stored in the ACCUMulator and the specified *operand* with the result left in the ACCUMlator.
CLA	Set the ACCUMulator at zero.
CLM	Set the MEMory location at zero.
SUM	Add the contents of the MEMory location to the ACCUMulator.
STO	Store the contents of the ACCUMlator in MEMory
RCL	Copy the contents of MEMory into the ACCUMulator
OFF	Turn the calculator off.

The program should display the current contents of the ACCUMulator and MEMory immediately after each instruction (except OFF) is executed. It must also display appropriate error messages when illegal commands are issued. A typical use of the calculator program might produce the following results:

```
*** CALCULATOR ON ***
                            --->        0.0  (ACCUM)        0.0  (MEM)
?OPR 28.3 - 12.9
                            --->       15.4  (ACCUM)        0.0  (MEM)
?STO
                            --->       15.4  (ACCUM)       15.4  (MEM)
?CLA
                            --->        0.0  (ACCUM)       15.4  (MEM)
?ADM + 24.6
                            ---> ERROR: "ADM" INSTRUCTION INVALID
?AOP + 24.6
                            --->       24.6  (ACCUM)       15.4  (MEM)
?SUM
                            --->       24.6  (ACCUM)       40.0  (MEM)
?AOP / 0.0
                            ---> ERROR: DIVISION BY ZERO
?RCL
                            --->       40.0  (ACCUM)       40.0  (MEM)
?CLM
                            --->       40.0  (ACCUM)        0.0  (MEM)
?OFF

*** CALCULATOR OFF ***
```

PROGRAMMING CONSIDERATIONS

The calculator should be an interactive program, of course. In the sample language presented above, all the commands begin with or consist entirely of three-letter words that the program must read and validate before an operation occurs.

VARIATIONS

A more powerful calculator than the one just described can be implemented by expanding the command language to include squaring a number, finding the square root of a number, computing the values of trigonometric functions, and so on. Additional memory locations and accumulators may also be provided. In short, the calculator may be equipped with a command language as versatile as the programmer desires.

F.3
THE GAME OF LIFE

OBJECTIVE

Construct a program to simulate a game, called Life, that traces the population of a community of living organisms through generations of births and deaths.

GENERAL DESCRIPTION

The game of Life is played on an infinite grid, with each box representing a **cell** that can either be empty or contain exactly one living organism. A community of living organisms, each one represented by an asterisk, is depicted in the following diagram, which shows only the pertinent portion of the Life grid:

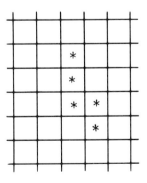

Each cell has eight neighboring cells that touch it vertically, horizontally, or diagonally. New organisms may be born and existing organisms may die, but all births and deaths occur simultaneously at the start of a new **generation.** The genetic laws that govern increases and decreases in population are

1. **Births.** Each empty cell that is adjacent to (a neighbor of) exactly three occupied cells in the current generation experiences a birth at the start of the next generation.
2. **Deaths.** Each occupied cell that has exactly one neighbor or no neighbors at all in the present generation experiences a death at the start of the next generation (the organism is said to die of loneliness and isolation). Every organism living in a cell that is adjacent to four or more occupied cells in the present generation dies at the start of the next generation as a result of overpopulation.

The status of cells not affected by births and deaths at the start of a new generation remains the same as in the preceding generation. Births and deaths are scheduled by examining the game board (grid) for the present generation, and then the board is changed all at once to give the community arrangement for the next generation. The following diagrams trace three generations in the game of Life. Each cell slated to experience a birth at the next generation is marked with a "b" on the grid for the present generation, and each organism scheduled to die at the start of the next generation is circled.

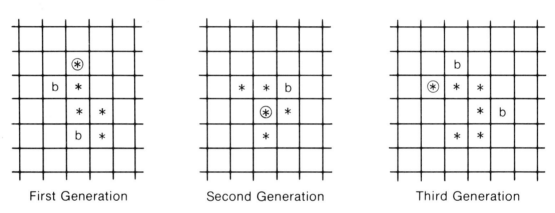

| First Generation | Second Generation | Third Generation |

There will be two births at the start of the fourth generation and one organism will die of loneliness and isolation. Notice that births and deaths slated to occur in the next generation do not influence the scheduling of births and deaths for that generation because organisms are born or die instantaneously at the start of a generation.

The game of Life is started by simply placing some community of living organisms on the game board. As the game proceeds, the population and its geographic distribution may change dramatically. It is possible for the population to die out in a finite number of generations, reach a "steady state" in which births and deaths cannot occur or occur in cycles that cause a sequence of previous generations to be duplicated over and over again, or even continue to increase and decrease to form communities that are not duplicates of previous communities.

PROGRAMMING CONSIDERATIONS

Although Life is played on an infinite grid, a modified version of the game can be played on a finite grid whose cells correspond to the components of a two-dimensional array. Cells at the corners of the game board will have at most three neighbors each, and cells on the boundaries of the game board (but not at the corners) will have at most five neighbors. This makes it impossible for an organism in a corner cell to die of overcrowding, although it can die of loneliness and isolation. For a program that uses an array to represent the game board, the initial input must include the pairs of indices for the array components that will represent occupied cells in the first generation. The program should print the game board at the start of every generation and stop the game after some fixed number of generations or when the population dies out, whichever occurs first.

VARIATIONS

It is possible to allow the game of Life to be played on a grid that is, in effect, infinite by having the program dynamically generate grid cells when they are needed. Also, each generation's geographic arrangement can be recorded in a file so that it is possible for the program to check for cycling.

F.4
A COMPUTER DATING SERVICE

OBJECTIVE

Write a program that will match partners for a date based on questionnaire responses submitted by clients.

GENERAL DESCRIPTION

Each client seeking a computer-matched date would complete a questionnaire giving personal information about himself (or herself) as well as data giving his (or her) interests and hobbies. A client should be able to designate certain personality traits, physical features, and interests that he (or she) feels a qualified partner must possess, as well as those that would make a partner more attractive. The questionnaire must be designed in a manner that facilitates the coding of the information for input to the program that will match partners. Some scoring system should be developed so that only matches at some acceptable level are made. It is conceivable that some clients will not be successfully matched because the personal traits and interests they deem most important in a partner are not to be found in the available partners. There must also be a tie-breaking procedure to use when a client can be matched equally well to two or more partners.

PROGRAMMING CONSIDERATIONS

The program may be written so that the data for every client must be input to the program via a terminal or card deck every time the program is run. However, it would be more suitable to have the data stored in a data file external to the program. Appropriate data structures can be formed by using arrays, records, and files.

VARIATIONS

If files are used to store the questionnaire information, it would also be useful to employ a file to store information about previous successful and unsuccessful computer-matched dates. These data can be checked during the matching process to avoid making a match that turned out to be unsuccessful at some previous time.

F.5
RECORD KEEPING FOR TEACHERS

OBJECTIVE

Write a program that can be used by a teacher to keep track of test and quiz scores, grades for homework assignments and projects, and other data normally recorded in a grade book.

GENERAL DESCRIPTION

Aside from creating and maintaining the file of student information, the program should compute averages for tests and quizzes and accumulate points earned by each student as requested by the user. If a fixed percentage system is used by the teacher to determine student grades, the program should be capable of reporting the current grade for each student. Output produced by the program may include:

1. a full listing the entire file;
2. listings for individual students on demand;
3. grade distributions for individual tests and quizzes;
4. frequency distributions;
5. grade reports to students;
6. sorted lists of scores and student names.

Various personal information for each student should be stored in the file, including an identification number and year in school.

PROGRAMMING CONSIDERATIONS

The file should be organized so that the information for a designated student may be easily located by using the name of the student or an identification number.

VARIATIONS

Many types of reports other than those already mentioned can be generated by the program. Also, the statistics such as averages and standard deviaitons for test scores can be generated on request, and grade distributions can be shown as graphs.

F.6
SCHEDULE PLANNING FOR COLLEGE STUDENTS

OBJECTIVE

Write one or more programs to help students plan a course of study.

GENERAL DESCRIPTION

College students are faced with the problem of earning a certain number of credits to qualify for a degree, including required credits in major and minor areas of study, general education requirements, and electives. A schedule of planned coursework developed during the first year of a four-year program of study usually requires substantial modification in succeeding years. However, it is worthwhile to have such a plan available for use when choosing appropriate courses at the start of each term. A four-year plan could be stored in a data file. Information in the file for each course would include:

1. name of the course;
2. course number and department designation (for example, MATH 235, HIST 100, ENGL 342);
3. designations indicating which requirements the course will satisfy (for example, MAJOR, MINOR, GENEDUC, ELECTIVE);
4. school term in which the course will be (or has been) taken;
5. number of credits for the course;
6. final grade (for completed courses only).

Students should be able to use the planning program(s) to:

1. create a list of planned courses;
2. change the list when necessary;
3. insert grades for completed courses;
4. get a printout of courses completed and grades organized by term or by requirement areas;
5. get a printout of the entire plan showing courses to be taken each term;
6. compute grade point averages.

PROGRAMMING CONSIDERATIONS

The data file could be a text file or file that has record type components. Course data should be ordered within the file so that the entire file need not be searched in order to discover that data for a particular course are not present.

VARIATIONS

The data stored in the master planning file need not be limited to the types of information listed above. Also, the planning program(s) may offer a student many options with respect to the printing of course information by departments and requirement areas.

F.7
A CENTRALIZED RESERVATION SYSTEM
FOR AN AIRLINE

OBJECTIVE

Write one or more programs that can be used to manage a flight reservations system for an airline as a centralized service to all cities served by the airline.

GENERAL DESCRIPTION

All the major airlines use a central computer to process flight reservations and report on the status of flights between the cities served by the airline. The airline personnel at the various airports have access to the central computer via terminals so that reservations and cancellations for flights that originate at any one of the airports will be immediately recorded in the appropriate files of flight status information. This ensures that every airport always receives up-to-date information on the status of flights when data are requested. Information stored for each flight will include:

1. a flight number;
2. arrival and departure times;
3. number of seats sold in both first class and tourist;
4. number of seats available in both classes;
5. the names of passengers who have reserved seats;
6. a waiting list (if the flight is completely booked).

The airlines reservation system should enable each local agent of the airline to:

1. get information about all flights between two specified cities on a given day;
2. inquire about the availability of seating on a particular flight;
3. make, cancel, and verify reservations;
4. correct errors in existing reservations;
5. add names to a waiting list;
6. generate a passenger list for a flight.

PROGRAMMING CONSIDERATIONS

Information regarding all flights on a given day may be stored in one or more data files. To speed up the processing, it is better to have the general data for the flights (flight numbers, arrival and departure times, numbers of seats available, etc.) stored in a file separate from the passenger lists. It is also advisable that the files be sorted in some order to facilitate the processing of data requests.

VARIATIONS

It is a common practice for airlines to overbook their flights. That is, an airline may accept more reservations for a flight than there are seats available. For instance, if a flight can handle 140 passengers, the airline may permit reservations for 105% of capacity (147 passengers) before a waiting list is started. Also, passengers usually receive seat assignments at the gate prior to boarding. Gate attendants must be able to confirm reservations and assign seats in both smoking and nonsmoking sections of the airplane. These functions can be handled by the airline reservations system if a seating arrangement for the airplane is on file.

F.8
LEAGUE STANDINGS AND TEAM RECORDS

OBJECTIVE

Construct a program that will keep track of the league standings and team records for a sports league.

GENERAL DESCRIPTION

The season schedule for a sports league (football, basketball, baseball, bowling, etc.) may be maintained in a data file and used by the program to generate schedules, compute league statistics, and print various reports. The program should be able to print the events or games scheduled for a specified day or week. When a day's results are available, the program should be used to update a results file and print a current league standings and other pertinent statistics.

PROGRAMMING CONSIDERATIONS

The quantity and structures of the data files used to store the information for a sports league depend on the sport and the manner in which league events are scheduled. One or more programs may be suitable for creating and updating the necessary files.

VARIATIONS

A program may be constructed to create a schedule of games for the league given the names of the teams and other information pertinent to designing a schedule. Rosters of players for each team and their individual performance statistics can be stored in files and updated as game results become available.

INDEX